Principles of Behavior

Fifth Edition

Richard W. Malott
Western Michigan University

Elizabeth Trojan Suárez
Riverwood Center

PEARSON
Prentice Hall

Upper Saddle River, New Jersey 07458

Library of Congress Cataloging-in-Publication Data

Malott, Richard W.
    Principles of behavior / Richard W. Malott, Elizabeth A. Trojan
Suarez. — 5th ed.
      p.   cm.
      Includes bibliographical references and index.
      ISBN 0-13-048225-0
      1. Operant behavior.   2. Psychology.   I. Trojan, Elizabeth A. II.
    Title.
    BF319.5.06M34   2003
    150—dc21   2003010823

Editor-in-Chief: *Leah Jewell*
Senior Acquisitions Editor: *Jeff Marshall*
Editorial Assistant: *Jill Leibowitz*
Managing Editor: *Joanne Riker*
Production Liaison: *Fran Russello*
Editorial/Production Supervision: *Jessica Balch, Pine Tree Composition, Inc.*
Manufacturing Buyer: *Tricia Kenny*
Marketing Director: *Beth Gillette Mejia*
Marketing Manager: *Sheryl Adams*
Art Director: *Jayne Conte*
Cover Design: *Jack Robol*
Cover Illustration: *Noma/SIS, Inc.*

This book was set in 10/11.5 Times Ten by Pine Tree Composition, Inc.,
and was printed and bound by Courier Companies, Inc.
The cover was printed by Phoenix Color Corp.

 Previously published as *Elementary Principles of Behavior*
© 2004, 2000, 1997, 1993, 1971 by Pearson Education, Inc.
Upper Saddle River, New Jersey 07458

Printed in the United States of America

10 9 8 7 6 5 4

ISBN 0-13-048225-0

Pearson Education Ltd., London
Pearson Education Australia Pty, Limited, Sydney
Pearson Education Singapore, Pte. Ltd.
Pearson Education North Asia Ltd., Hong Kong
Pearson Education Canada, Ltd., Toronto
Pearson Educación de Mexico, S.A. de C.V.
Pearson Education—Japan, Tokyo
Pearson Education Malaysia, Pte. Ltd.
Pearson Education Upper Saddle River, New Jersey

Contents

Preface to the Instructor

AUDIENCE

When we wrote the first edition of this textbook (at that time titled *Elementary Principles of Behavior* [*EPB*]), we intended it for first-year, university-level psychology courses. But an American Psychology Association committee pleasantly surprised us by also recommending it for high school psychology courses. Then we found behavior analysts using it at all levels, including graduate courses; in a variety of departments, from dentistry to social work to special education; and from community colleges to universities to in-service training programs. So we've tried to write subsequent editions with all of these audiences in mind. To assess the generality of our success, we evaluate *Principles of Behavior* (*PB*) in both graduate and undergraduate courses. Though grad students differ from undergrads, of course, the grad students evaluate the book at least as favorably as the undergrads.

We've built more flexibility into this edition to accommodate further this variety of audiences, especially with our different levels of the enrichment section. But also, we've tried to write the essential Fundamentals sections to appeal to both the jaded graduate student and the eager freshman. And, we've tried to write those Fundamentals sections so all students can easily understand them. However, though we've tried to make the Fundamentals simple, we've also tried not to make them simplistic. And though we've tried to make the Fundamentals clear, we've also tried not to make them conceptually unrigorous. (Some value a book only if it's difficult; we hope such readers will feel compelled to adopt different criteria.)

THE FUNDAMENTALS AND ENRICHMENT SECTIONS

The following material is redundant with a section in Chapter 1, but it's worth mentioning here also.

We've divided each chapter into two main sections. We call the second section the *Enrichment* section. All the subsections that come before it we call the *Fundamentals* section, the bare bones of the text. The student needs to master each Fundamentals section to understand the Fundamentals sections of following chapters. However, the student needn't master the Enrichment sections to understand the later Fundamentals sections. Also, we've usually divided the Enrichment section into three levels—Basic, Intermediate, and a few Advanced Enrichment sections. We've tried to keep the Basic sections at the same level of difficulty as the Fundamentals sections. The Intermediate and Advanced levels get progressively more difficult and esoteric; yet they assume no knowledge of behavior analysis beyond this book.

Here's the audience to whom we've aimed each level: the Basic level—beginning students who will do no further work in behavior analysis, and the Intermediate level—juniors, seniors, and others who will be doing further work in behavior analysis. We assume anyone reading the Intermediate level also will read the lower-level. The Advanced level is for true scholars. For access to other advanced enrichment sections, we invite you to visit our web site at *www.DickMalott.com*. Of course, the instructor may evaluate the levels of difficulty or appropriateness differently than we have.

IN THE SKINNER BOX

To illustrate many basic behavioral contingencies and procedures, we go to hypothetical examples in the Skinner box. We find the simplicity of the life of the rat or pigeon in the test chamber to be an excellent tool for understanding the complexity of the life of the human being in the normal environment. We also do this to emphasize the phylogenic continuity of the principles of behavior. But we put most of this in the Enrichment section, so teachers can omit it if they wish to play down that continuity. (Incidentally, we've found phylogenic continuity of behavior doesn't put off most students. Students are amazingly open to new ideas. However, their professors in the humanities and social sciences aren't always so open!)

FIRST NAMES

When we first introduce specific behavior analysts in this book, we normally do so formally, with their last name and professional title. But then we usually move into an informal first-name style. We do this for three reasons: We think this style makes for more pleasant reading about real people with real first names. We think this style may suggest that professional behavior analysts are just regular human beings and that being a professional behavior analyst is a reasonable goal to which the reader might aspire. Finally, a first-name style correctly suggests that behavior analysts form a small, close-knit, warm, and friendly family whose members know each other on a first-name basis. On the other hand, we don't intend to suggest presumptuous familiarity. Our data say that students prefer it this way.

WHERE'S THE INTRODUCTORY CHAPTER?

We omitted the traditional intro chapter because we find that general intro summaries of a discipline make great logical sense to the professional but little pedagogical sense to the novice. By being broad, summaries must be too general, too abstract, and too vague to alter effectively the repertoire of the beginning reader or to act as an effective establishing operation or discriminative stimulus that will increase the likelihood the novice will go to the next chapter. Our experience suggests it's best to start right off with case studies that will effectively reinforce reading the book. No student has said they missed having an intro chapter.

SIMPLE RIGOR

We've tried hard to make this book easy—readable, clear, interesting, and entertaining. But we've also tried hard to make it rigorous. We have tried not to compromise rigor in the name of popularization or simplification. Furthermore, we've tried to provide the basis for a solid conceptual mastery of the principles of behavior. As part of this effort, we've included compare-and-contrast sections where we help the student compare and contrast confusing

concepts and to make important distinctions—for example, escape versus punishment, reinforcer versus reinforcement, time out versus response cost, penalty versus extinction, and differential reinforcement versus reinforcement.

RESEARCH METHODS AND ETHICS

We introduce the issues of research methods in small units in the Intermediate Enrichment sections throughout this book. We do so for two reasons. First, we can introduce the issues with the research to which they are crucial. But more important, we can avoid combining all the methodology issues in one chapter too early in the book—an approach most students find deadly. When you start with the research methods first, students don't know what the heck they're researching and couldn't care less about the methodology.

In short, we think a pedagogical sequence differs from a logical sequence. Often they go in opposite directions. So we recommend an analog to backward chaining. Start with what interests most students—saving the world through behavior analysis. Spice it with small doses of methodology. Then have them review the whole area once we've got them irrevocably committed to our cause! Incidentally, we think much the same about the history of a discipline. Students appreciate it more at the end of a course than at the beginning. At the beginning, they could not care less about where the discipline came from, because they may not care all that much about the discipline itself. But if the course has succeeded in helping students appreciate our field, then they may become more interested in its history. In this book, we integrate a small amount of history as we go along. We included ethical issues in the intermediate enrichment sections throughout this book, as we've done with the research methodology issues. And for much the same reasons.

Spreading research methodology in small chunks throughout the book may cause a problem if you want your students to do research projects from the beginning of the semester and you feel they need to know some basic design concepts. So to reduce this problem, at the back of this book we've also provided a chapter on research methods. This will then give your students a more coherent view. Furthermore, Chapter 29, Research Methods, is divided into three main sections, the last two being the ones most relevant to actual research methods and the last two also being accessible after the students have read the first couple chapters of *PB*. So assigning the last two sections of Chapter 29 more or less anytime you want should work fine.

RESPONDENT CONDITIONING

We don't get to respondent conditioning until Chapter 21, for two reasons: first, respondent conditioning is not fundamental to our treatment of operant behavior, so putting it early would break the cumulative flow of the concepts and principles. Second, we think students need a good grounding in operant procedures before they can discriminate between operant procedures and respondent procedures. It ain't easy. (Most grad students and some faculty members can't discriminate between a conditioned eliciting stimulus and a discriminative stimulus, a discrimination failure exacerbated by the common practice of calling them both antecedent stimuli.) Introducing respondent conditioning before students have a firm grounding in operant conditioning puts the students at great risk of erroneously classifying every behavior they see as respondent when it's probably operant. Students have an almost genetic tendency to respondently, reflexively, immediately say *respondent conditioning* or *reflexive* whenever confronted with a novel instance of operant behavior. This latent Pavlovianism might best be prepared for by many chapters of operant analyses, before the Pavlovianism can be unleashed and extinguished. But instructors who think otherwise can assign the first nine sections of the respondent conditioning chapter right after Chapter 2 in this book with as much ease as if the chapters were physically placed early in the book. The tenth section of the respondent conditioning chapter should wait until after the extinction chapter. And the last section should wait until after the discrimination chapter. One size fits all.

FICTIONAL USE OF PUBLISHED RESEARCH

We feature fictional heroes and heroines in this book. They are Max, Sid, Dawn, Juke, the students from Sid's seminar, and some of the clients. We use this fictional approach to increase the readability of the text. Graduate students, as well as undergraduate students, prefer this approach.[1] However, our heroes and heroines refer to the original research.

[1]On an anonymous questionnaire, honors college freshmen said they strongly preferred this textbook to books by Shakespeare, Melville, and Hardy they were concurrently reading in their English class. Granted, this may say more about the tastes of college freshmen, even real bright ones, and the inability of English professors to tune in to those tastes, and the willingness of the authors of this textbook to pander to those tastes than it does about the absolute literary value of *PB*. Nonetheless, *PB* is tuned into its audience. Of course we do not choose to go head to head with *Silence of the Lambs*.

We use their referencing to illustrate that a good practitioner checks the published research before intervening. We also use this referencing and associated comments to help the reader appreciate the real people who did the real work. (All the data and graphs we present are based on the actual data from the relevant research.)

MORE FLEXIBILITY

We've included a few sections on the structure of the book, for example "How to Use the Study Questions" and "In Defense of Mickey Mouse Questions." Most reviewers said they appreciated them. That's just one more thing they wouldn't have to worry about telling their students. But some instructors might not want to use them. And probably some instructors will not want to use all the material in all the Enrichment sections. When we use the book, we vary the sections we assign depending on the level of the course.

RULE-GOVERNED BEHAVIOR

We asked a nonrandom sample of our colleagues what they thought were the most important issues to hit our field in 20 years (since the first edition of this book). Many pointed to the issues of rule-governed behavior and the control of behavior by delayed outcomes. We agree. But some think these issues are passing fads! And few seem to agree on the theoretical analysis of these issues. So we make a big deal out of it, but at the end of the book. This postponing helps: The student can approach complex rule-governed behavior, after mastering the basic concepts and principles. But this postponing also hinders: While reading the first part of the book, students risk doing simplistic analyses of complex contingencies, for example in organizational behavior management. We have tried to reduce this problem of simplistic analysis by restricting the first part of our book mainly to research based on immediate reinforcement and punishment. In theory, the students can read those later chapters on rule-governed behavior early in the course. But we've tried that, and the theory doesn't work too well; the rule-governed behavior chapters seem too difficult without reading the preceding chapters. So here's how we cope: When a student raises an example in which a delayed outcome seems to control behavior, we say, "Put it on the back burner, until we get to the advanced chapters; then we'll deal with it." If we really get our act together, as teachers, we might actually set up a back-burner section, where we store the students' examples, until the burner is hot; but that hasn't happened yet.

CHANGES FROM *EPB 4* TO *PB 5*

The changes in this edition are part of our empirical, continuous quality-improvement process as developed and implemented in Elizabeth Trojan Suárez's dissertation.[2] The evaluation process revealed sections we needed to revise and did revise to improve clarity.

Those sections are:

- Objectivity vs. Subjectivity (Chapter 2)
- The Escape Model of the Sick Social Cycle (Chapter 3)
- The Punishment Model of the Sick Social Cycle (Chapter 4)
- Penalty, Response Cost, and Time-Out (Chapter 5)
- The Law of Effect (Chapter 5)
- An Example of Functional Analysis (Chapter 6)
- Shaping vs. Behavioral Chaining (Chapter 8)
- How Learned Reinforcers are Acquired (Chapter 11)
- Noncontingent Reinforcers as a Control Procedure (Chapter 11)
- Verbal Behavior (Chapter 12)
- Prompts vs. Discriminative Stimuli (Chapter 12)
- Added vs. Built-in Contingencies for Imitation (Chapter 14)
- How Do You Know If It's Really Imitation? (Chapter 14)
- Teleology (Chapter 15)
- Discrete Trial vs. Free-Operant Procedures (Chapter 17)
- Differential Punishment of High Rate (Chapter 20) Removed it and put it in the *Advanced Enrichment* booklet.
- Respondent vs. Operant Conditioning (Chapter 21)
- Respondent vs. Operant Extinction (Chapter 21)
- Discriminative Stimulus vs. Conditioned Stimulus (Chapter 21)

- Respondent vs. Operant Conditioning (Chapter 21)
- All of Chapter 22 (converted to analogs of avoidance contingencies)
- All of Chapter 23 (converted to analogs of avoidance contingencies)
- Added Reinforceable Response Unit (Chapter 23)
- Added Why Analogs to Avoidance are not Direct-acting Contingencies (Chapter 23)
- Five Philosophies of Psychology (Chapter 26)
- Moral and Legal Control (Chapter 26)
- Sexuality (Chapter 26)
- Overall Summary of Maintenance and Transfer (Chapter 28)
- Many sections (Chapter 30)

Though much more could be done, we're happy with the way *PB* 5 has evolved. Hope you will be too.

THE *PB* USERS' GROUP ON THE WEB

If you are a teacher using *PB,* drop me an e-mail note at *DickMalott@DickMalott.com* and I'll put you on the *PB* emailing list, a nice way to stay in touch.

And if you are a teacher or a student using *PB,* check out our *PB* home page on the World Wide Web at *www.DickMalott.com.*

INSTRUCTORS MANUAL

To get our *Instructor's Manual with Tests,* contact your local Prentice Hall representative. For additional supplementary materials for *PB,* also check out www.DickMalott.com. These materials include:

Flash Cards

The term is printed on one side of the card and the definition on the other. One card for each concept, principle, and rule of thumb in the book. Ideal for memorizing the definitions so students can ace the tests. Has a big impact on quiz scores.

Advanced Enrichment Sections

This booklet contains some Advanced Enrichment sections and Conceptual Question sections that will challenge graduate students in behavior analysis but

---

[2]Suárez, E. T. (2001). *A Behavioral Systems-Analysis Approach to Textbook Quality Improvement.* Unpublished doctoral dissertation, Western Michigan University, Kalamazoo, Michigan.

might not be appropriate for any but the most masochistically inquisitive undergrads.

Advanced Study Objectives

Heavy-duty stuff. Appropriate for grad students only.

ACKNOWLEDGMENTS

We owe much to the following reviewers for their helpful suggestions based on their reviews of earlier editions of this textbook:

- For reviewing *EPB 4:* Kent Johnson, Bram Goldwater, Scott Gaynor, Philip Hineline, Thomas Waltz, and any other annonymous reviewers of whom we are unaware.
- For reviewing *EPB 3:* Centa David, Scott Gaynor, Bram Goldwater, Philip Hineline, and Dave Sidener.
- For reviewing *EPB 2:* Stanley H. Holgate, Gerald C. Mertens, David C. Palmer, and Randy Lee Williams.
- For reviewing *EPB 1* and drafts of *EPB 2:* Bill L. Hopkins, Kenneth E. Lloyd, Randy L. Williams, Robert Hoff, Janet Ellis, Max Brill, Kenneth Wildman, Jay Alperson, Robert Newman, Don E. Williams, Gerald C. Mertens, Thomas E. Billimek, Stephen Ledoux, Terry McSween, Fred R. Malott, Edward K. Morris, James T. Todd, Susan Schreider, Bryan D. Midgley, Carol Pilgrim, Janet Ellis, William Crowder, Loren Acker, Bram Goldwater, Joseph Parsons, Jack Michael, and Stephen A. Graf.

PAST AUTHORS

Donald L. Whaley

Don Whaley received his BA in psychology from Indiana University in 1961, his MA in 1963, and his PhD in clinical psychology from Florida State University in 1966. He taught at Western Michigan University (WMU) until 1969 and at the University of North Texas from 1969 to 1983.

Maria E. Malott

Maria Malott received her licenciatura in clinical psychology from Catholic University (Caracas, Venezuela) in 1980, her MA in industrial psychology in 1984 and her PhD in applied behavior analysis from WMU in 1987. She is an adjunct faculty member at WMU, the University of North Texas, the University of Nevada, Reno, the University of Veracruz, and the Veracruz Pedagogical Institute. She is executive director of the Association for Behavior Analysis and a consultant in organizational behavior analysis.

CURRENT AUTHORS

Elizabeth Trojan Suárez

Elizabeth Suárez received her BA in psychology from Michigan State University in 1993 her MA in behavior analysis in 1998 and her Ph.D. in behavior analysis in 2001 from WMU. She is progressing toward her full licensure as a psychologist in the State of Michigan and working as a Mental Health Therapist at Riverwood Center.

Richard W. Malott

Richard Malott received his BA in psychology from Indiana University in 1958 and his PhD in experimental psychology from Columbia University in 1963. He taught at Denison University from 1963 to 1969 and has been teaching at WMU since 1969.

HISTORY OF *PRINCIPLES OF BEHAVIOR*

In 1967, Roger Ulrich, Donald Whaley, and I received a contract from Appleton-Century-Crofts to write a textbook on the experimental analysis of behavior to replace the classic *Principles of Psychology* by Keller and Schoenfeld, which had gone out of print. As it turned our, Don and I ended up writing the book (*Elementary Principles of Behavior 1*), but the focus shifted from the experimental analysis to the principles of behavior, with applied , everyday, and laboratory illustrations. Prentice Hall acquired Appleton-Century-Crofts and published EPB 1 in 1971. The book was one of the first textbooks in behavior analysis and especially one of the first textbooks to emphasize applied behavior analysis, at a time when the field of applied behavior analysis was just coming into its own. Therefore, it was a great success, selling an unheard of 20,000 copies during each of its first three years.

Prentice Hall repeatedly asked Don and me to write a second edition, as the sales very slowly fell. And we repeatedly and sincerely agreed to do so. So by 1986 the sales had dwindled to a few hundred a year and the book was on its way to being history.

At that time, a friend and colleague at another university proposed to Prentice Hall that he write the second edition. They said fine but check with Malott first. Well, I felt as if they had accused me of child neglect and were going to take custody of my baby. So Maria Malott, who was just finishing her Ph.D., agreed to co-parent, I mean coauthor, EPB 2. And PH published it in 1992. Of course 21 years after EPB 1, the field had plenty of excellent behavior-analytic textbooks, so EPB 2 never approximated the stratospheric sales records of EPB 1; but I believe authoring and coauthoring successive, improved and updated editions of EPB/PB remains one of the most important contributions I can make.

I revised EPB 3 by myself and then managed to persuade a graduate student, Beth Trojan, to coauthor EPB 4. She did this as part of her PhD dissertation,[3] perhaps producing the first dissertation ever to be based on the systematic, empirical, scientific evaluation and revision of a textbook and at the same time producing perhaps the first textbook ever to have been revised with such systematic, empirical, scientific rigor.

Beth has since changed her name to Suárez and put the letters PhD after it, but she remains the coauthor on PB 5, which also formed part of her dissertation.

Oh, yes, the most conspicuous change in the fifth edition is the name change from *Elementary Principles of Behavior* to *Principles of Behavior (The Textbook Formerly Known as <u>Elementary</u> Principles of Behavior)*. Why change a good thing? A colleague who was using the book as a graduate text thought his students would be more comfortable carrying a textbook that didn't have *Elementary* in its title, and though the book is basic, it has always been far from elementary. So, with the exception of an erroneous cover for EPB 4, we've been gradually reducing the size of the word *Elementary* to the point where we hope that now we can drop it, without causing too much confusion. PB remains as warm, cuddly, and user friendly as ever.

Richard W. Malott
May 30, 2003

---

[3]See the previous footnote.

To the memory of Donald L. Whaley

I disliked Don Whaley the first time I met him. This huge, loudmouthed, glad-handing, cigar-smoking extrovert insisted on hugging me. And he hugged me with such force that he threw me off balance, physically as well as psychologically. (Real men don't hug each other in Converse, Indiana, where I grew up.)

I remember having a party for our undergraduate teaching apprentices, where we served beer with reckless, illegal abandon. Don stood with a cigar in his mouth and a beer bottle in each hand, as he convinced a cluster of undergrads that behavior analysis was the true path to the salvation of the world.

Two hours after everyone had gone home, a policeman came back with Don. He had found Don unconscious in his Volkswagen Beetle. Not only had Don passed out from the beer, but also he was having an asthma attack because he'd left his inhaler at my house. Of course, the policeman was more than willing to give Don a hand because he had been one of Don's students, and like all Don's students, he loved the man.

A few years later, Don stopped drinking and smoking. Don Whaley was a man of extremes. He fought and beat many devils. But the ice-cream parlor and other pushers of sugar, fat, cholesterol, and salt finally cut him down.

Another characteristic of Don was that you couldn't always depend on him to follow up on his day-to-day commitments. But you could always depend on him to come through like a hero when the going was really rough. Suppose you had a former student who was suicidal and who had just gotten out of the state hospital. You could depend on Don to fly from Denton, Texas (where he was then living), to Chicago to try to help him.

Or suppose a friend of a friend spent his nights as a resident of a mental hospital and his days as a student in graduate school and was going crazier and crazier. You could depend on Don to invite him down to Denton to go to school and participate in Don's therapeutic community. You could depend on Don to give more of himself and his life to that student-patient than anyone could hope for. You could depend on Don to structure, set up, and run the program that would allow the student to achieve his potential as a brilliant and behaviorally healthy scholar and to achieve his doctorate.

If Don's students were having trouble putting food on the table, you also could depend on him to come up with some task they could do, whether he needed it done or not, so he could give them some financial support by way of payment from his own pocket.

But the ice-cream parlor cut him down.

Don Whaley was a red-blooded Yankee inventor and gadgeteer. He invented a self-shocker—a series of batteries in a cartridge belt. You strapped the belt around your waist, beneath your shirt. Then you taped a pair of electrodes to your side and pushed a button to shock yourself every time you emitted an unwanted behavior.

He also invented a self-flipper—simply a big rubber band you wore loosely around your wrist. Every time you emitted that unwanted behavior, you twanged the rubber band. (A couple twangs in a row could really start that wrist a-smarting.) I used the self-flipper to suppress the high frequency of negative thoughts I was having at one point in my life.

Don also invented a variable-time beeper you could use to gain self-awareness. At an unpredictable time, the beeper would beep; and you would note, on a piece of paper, whatever you were doing or thinking. With Don's beeper, I learned more about myself than I wanted to know.

Don Whaley was a big man, 6 feet 2 inches tall, with the large barrel chest of the asthmatic. He oscillated between a gross 240 pounds and an Olympic 185 pounds. He earned whatever he got—fanatically dieting, fanatically running, day after day, week after week, month after month, getting himself in perfect shape; then gradually losing it all to the ice-cream parlor.

Once when Don was at the peak of his health—all muscle and aerobic fitness, we were doing a little 5-mile run; but he was having trouble. "Why?" I asked. "Because I ran 30 miles yesterday." he said. "In an ultra-marathon?" "No, as penance. I pigged out on ice cream the day before yesterday, so I had to pay my dues."

In 1983, Don was in bad health, eating poorly, not exercising, and feeling terrible. So, in July of that year, we set up a long-distance performance-contracting program. He limited himself to 1,200 low-fat, low-salt, low-sugar calories per day. As the pounds fell off, he gradually increased his exercise from walking a mile a day to running 10 miles a day. And he increased his writing from 0 hours per day to three hours per day. He called me more or less every day and sent a written record of his accomplishments every week. Any day he failed, he paid a small penalty.

Don Whaley made a hero's effort, and finally got his world on course—all systems go; but the lifelong combination of sugar, fat, and cholesterol (ice cream) took its toll. We didn't get his coronary arteries unclogged soon enough. The ice-cream parlor clogged his coronary arteries and killed him with a heart attack on October 27, 1983.

Don Whaley died at his peak, his fingers on the keyboard of his computer, his feet in a pair of well-worn running shoes, kicking out the heroic words and the heroic miles every day. He was the senior author of the first edition of this book.

With love and respect, this edition of *Principles of Behavior* is dedicated to Donald L. Whaley (1934–1983).

1 The Reinforcer

FUNDAMENTALS

Example
Behavioral Clinical Psychology[1]
I'M A WOMAN TRAPPED IN A MAN'S BODY—PART I[2]

"I want sex-change surgery. I want a woman's body. I'm a woman trapped in a man's body. I want the right body. I want a woman's body," the young man continued in a high-pitched, almost falsetto voice.

"Is that possible?" Sidney Fields asked, looking at this strange young man who was about five six and appeared to weigh less than 100 pounds.

"Yes, if you've got the money, and if you can find a surgeon who will do it, and if you're 21. But I don't have the $70,000 or whatever it is. I don't know the right doctor. I'm only 18. I've got 3 more years of hell to live through. Even then, I won't have the money."

"Why is it hell?"

---

[1] In these contexts, we use the term *behavioral clinical psychology* to facilitate a quick understanding of what we're talking about. But we generally prefer to use simply *behavior analysis,* because the procedures are straightforward, learning-based behavior analysis and have essentially nothing to do with medical-model–based clinical psychology. The problems are, however, those that traditional clinical psychology has grappled with in vain for nearly a century. A controversial point, no doubt.

[2] Like all cases in this book, Bobbie's is based on actual research. In this instance, David Barlow and his colleagues at the medical school of the University of Mississippi did this research. The work of these behavior analysts with a transgender client represents one of the most dramatic cases of behavior modification in the history of psychology. We will follow the progress of this case (and others introduced in this chapter) throughout the rest of the book. See: Barlow, D. H., Hayes, S. C., Nelson, R. O., Steele, D. L., Meeler, M. E., & Mills, J. R. (1979). Sex role motor behavior: A behavioral check list. *Behavioral Assessment, 1,* 119–138; and Barlow, D. H., Reynolds, E. H., & Agras, W. S. (1973). Gender identity change in transsexuals. *Archives of General Psychiatry, 28,* 569–579.

"You can't understand. No one can. Mr. Fields, suppose you woke one morning and discovered your body had changed into a woman's body."

Sidney Fields flinched.

"You'd give anything to have your man's body back. Well, that's the way it is with me. Oh, I know; it sounds like a dirty joke. But it isn't a joke. It depresses me so. That's why I came to you, Mr. Fields. I'm in your intro psych class, and I thought maybe you could help me. No one else can."

Sid put his left elbow on the arm of his desk chair, closed his eyes, and then rubbed his left eye with his index finger. He couldn't come to grips with the reality of this extremely effeminate young man and his plight. He wasn't like a woman; he was more like a caricature of a woman.

"Mr. Fields, you've got to help me. If you don't help me, I'm afraid I'll commit suicide. I tried suicide once. I overdosed on antihistamines, but it didn't work."

The young man went on to explain that when he first started high school he ran away from home and tried to commit suicide. Everyone had made fun of him in high school, and it was just too aversive; so he dropped out. When he returned to high school, he had fainting spells. A psychiatrist had seen him. His parents put him in a hospital. The psychiatrists gave him antidepressants and phenothiazines for 9 months. Nothing helped.

Sid was not a clinical psychologist; he was a psychology teacher; so he felt awkward in this role into which the young man had cast him. "I'm afraid I haven't learned all my students' names after just one class, so . . ."

"Sorry, Mr. Fields, *Bobbie*—*Bobbie* with an *ie,* not a *y.* That was my mother's idea. She wanted a girl. *Bobbie Brown* is my name."

"Tell me more about yourself, Bobbie. When did you discover you were gay?"

"I'm not *gay;* Mr. Fields; I'm not attracted to gay men, not at all. I'm a transgender person; I'm only attracted to straight heterosexual guys; I'm a woman in a man's body."

"Thanks for the clarification, Bobbie. So when did you discover you were a woman and not a man?"

"Mr. Fields, suppose I asked you, 'When did you discover you were a man and not a woman?' Oh, I don't mean to be sarcastic. It's just that no one understands. I was born a female. I started out as a little girl in a little boy's body. As long as I can remember, I always preferred girls' clothes. But they wouldn't let me wear my girls' clothes in school. I more or less stopped wearing them, even at home, when I was about 13. People were giving me too much grief. When I was in grade school, I read the encyclopedia so I could learn how to cook and knit and crochet and embroider. I made the prettiest things. I've always hated the things my brother enjoys, like basketball and hunting."

Bobbie also said he had started having sexual fantasies when he was 12. He always imagined himself as a female having intercourse with a male. He masturbated to these fantasies but had never had an orgasm or ejaculated.

"Bobbie, I can see you're hurting, but I'm not sure what you want me to do. I'm not a surgeon," Sid said, as he tried to find his way back to his more comfortable role as the college teacher.

"I know, Mr. Fields; please don't joke with me. You *are* a psychologist, and I sure need your help."

"What do you want?"

"I want to stop hurting. I want to feel good about myself. My dad hates me. My brother teases me and makes fun of me because I'm majoring in secretarial sciences. People beat on me. No one likes me but my mother. I don't fit in anywhere. I'm always on the outside looking in. There's no place in this world for a woman in a man's body."

The more Bobbie talked, the more Sid sympathized with him and the more Bobbie's plight moved Sid. Though Bobbie was different from Sid, in fact different from anyone Sid had ever known, Sid also could see that Bobbie had the same feelings, fears, and concerns as everyone else Sid knew, including Sid.

"Do you want to be a man in a man's body?"

"No! I'm not a man. I'm a woman. Besides, my psychiatrist said they've never ever been able to take a transgender person like me and change her into a man. That's what I am, you know—a transgender person. He says the treatment of choice is sex-reassignment surgery. But even if I had the money, I'm not 21; and even if I were 21, I have no idea where I could get the money. I don't know what to do."

"What are your options?"

"I saw a movie about one transgender person who became a prostitute. Oh, gross! I don't want to do that. And I don't want to be a female impersonator on the stage. I am not an impersonator; I *am* a female. I just want to marry a nice man and have children and lead a normal life, just like any other woman."

"What are your odds?"

"Terrible. That's why I'm so upset."

"If you were a woman in a woman's body, there'd be a place for you and you'd be OK."

"Of course!"

"If you were a man in a man's body, there'd be a place for you and you'd be OK."

"It wouldn't be OK!"

"Maybe not. But, like I said, I'm not a surgeon; I can't give you a woman's body. Also, I don't think I can help you become happy as a woman in a man's body, at least not in our society; and I'm afraid we aren't going to change society fast enough to be of much comfort to you. But I do have some ideas about how we might help you become a man in a man's body. Also, I have some ideas about how we might help you like it that way. Dr. David Barlow and his colleagues dealt with a problem like yours when he was at the University of Mississippi Medical Center."

"My psychiatrist said no one has ever done it."

"No one had done it before Dave Barlow. And I don't think anyone has done much since then. It's hard, stressful work, and the outcome is not certain."

"I'm used to hard work, and I'm used to stress. But I don't want to be a man any more than you want to be a woman."

"I know, Bobbie. I feel bad that I can't solve your problem any other way. I can't change your body. I can't change society, at least not fast enough. I'm afraid I can't do more. If it doesn't work out, you could still pursue the sex-reassignment surgery later."

"I'm not sure, Mr. Fields; I'm going to have to think about that."

Intervention
A MAN'S MOVES

Bobbie did think about it. He thought about it for the next week. He had to make a big decision. We often don't make big decisions unless our life is so aversive we can't bear it. Bobbie's life was so aversive that he decided to escape from that aversiveness with the help of Sid Fields. He didn't want to solve his problem this way, but he had no better way; it beat suicide, and he appreciated that.

Bobbie and Sid started on a program that would consume much of their lives for the remainder of Bobbie's freshman year at Big State University. But they didn't start this program alone. Dawn, Sid's wife, was a licensed psychologist, and she also worked on this project with them.[3] It was an experimental program that might never help or that might make Bobbie's life even worse—desperation's solution. Sid hoped only that he could repeat the heroic work that Barlow and his colleagues had done.

Sid didn't want this job. He didn't have the time. And he was happiest teaching his courses and reading journal articles about how others solved psychological problems; he'd rather read about Barlow's work than actually do it. But Bobbie's suffering had moved Sid so much that he had promised to help. It was too late to back out now. Nothing to do but go for it—go for it with more intensity than is the custom in clinical psychology—go for it 30 minutes a day, 5 days a week.

They started with the problem that caused Bobbie the most misery—the scorn and ridicule from his peers for his effeminate behavior. To change from a woman to a man, Bobbie would have to act like a man. He would have to sit like a man, walk like a man, and stand like a man.

"I don't want to be John Wayne," Bobbie said.

"I agree. I don't either," Sid said, "but there is a middle ground, the behavior style of the typical male. It's fundamentally no better nor worse than your style. But using the typical male style will greatly reduce the amount of hassles you have."

"Am I really that different?"

"I've noticed in class and I've noticed in our meetings that almost 100% of the time you handle your body more like a typical woman than a typical man."

"What do you mean?"

"For instance, the way you're sitting. You've crossed your legs with one knee on top of the other, like a woman."

"Isn't that the way everyone sits?"

"I'm not." Sid was sitting with his legs crossed, but the ankle of his left leg was on top of the knee of his right leg. "This is a more masculine way of sitting. Try it."

Bobbie slowly moved the calf of his left leg to the knee of his right leg, glanced at Sid, and then kept moving until his left ankle almost touched his right knee.

"That looks great, at least if you want a more traditional masculine image," Sid said.

"Perhaps, but it feels terrible," Bobbie replied.

"We'll keep working on it until you naturally sit in the traditional masculine way and feel comfortable doing so. I'll show you how to sit. Then you try it, and I'll tell you how you're doing. We'll use what we call a reinforcement procedure."

"I'm willing to keep trying, but I'm sure I've seen many guys sitting with their legs crossed the way I had them before, with one knee above the other," Bobbie said.

"Yeah," Sid said, "you're right, but at this point you need all the masculinity you can get, so go with this slightly exaggerated style awhile."

Sid started with a **task analysis.** He started with the seemingly simple and natural act of sitting. He divided sitting into four components, including leg crossing. Each day he and Bobbie went through a series of practice trials, component by component. Sid modeled a component of masculine sitting, and Bobbie tried to imitate him. Sid then gave Bobbie feedback and praised his successes. At the beginning of each day's session they also reviewed a videotape of Bobbie's performance from the end of the day before.

After five sessions, Bobbie comfortably, naturally, and reliably sat in the John Wayne way. Then they worked on walking and finally on standing, succeeding with each class of responses. Walking and standing also took five sessions each. It was slow, hard work for Bobbie. He often said he wanted to quit. Sid often thought he too wanted to quit. Instead they plotted Bobbie's progress on a chart at the end of each session. These signs of progress, small though they were, encouraged the behavior analyst and the client[4] to hang in.

---

[3]We point out at this point that a fictional, licensed PhD psychologist (Dawn) was involved in this fictional project because a few readers of earlier editions of this book were concerned about the ethical and legal implications of having an unlicensed fictional psychologist (Sid) take on such a serious problem. Unfortunately, the training that normally leads to becoming a licensed psychologist (e.g., a traditional clinical psychologist) in no way prepares the psychologist to help Bobbie solve his problems. We should also mention that to reduce any problems of conflict of interest between Sid's role as Bobbie's teacher and his and Dawn's role as Bobbie's behavior analysts, they did not charge him for their help.

[4]Various terms have been used to designate the recipient of the services of the psychologist and, more generally, the behavior analyst. In the classroom, the term *student* has done the trick and continues to do so. But in other settings, the appropriate designation has proven more evasive: Originally, the term *patient* dominated, but that term implies a medical cause when the problem may have been the learning of dysfunctional behavior or the failure to learn functional behavior; so *client* seemed more appropriately neutral. Now, however, *consumer* is in the ascendency; so in preparing the fourth edition of this book, I did a search-and-replace, replacing *client* with *consumer*. But it started getting too weird; so I checked with users of this book and other professionals and students, and almost everyone said to stick with *client* or some such term and to bag *consumer*. So I did a reverse search-and-replace and am pretty much hanging in with *client,* at least for a while longer.

After several weeks, Sid said, "Bobbie, you've done it. You've now got the moves of a man. Congratulations!"

"Thanks for the compliment, Mr. Fields. And thanks for your help. It feels good. People are treating me better now, not like some sideshow freak. You know, I feel like I'm an actor and you're my director, like you're teaching me to play a role—the role of a normal, red-blooded, all-American male. Yet I also feel like we're tricking them, because that's not the real me there on that stage."

"Did you ever hear of method acting?" Sid asked. Not waiting for Bobbie to reply, he went on. "That's a technique people like Marlon Brando have used. Sometimes the actors almost become the characters they're playing."

"You think I'll become your all-American male? You think I'll stop feeling like a woman in a man's body?"

"I know, Bobbie. It's hard. We're not there yet. But we're getting there. Tomorrow we'll start on the next leg of the journey."

Will Sid repeat Barlow's success? Will he succeed in changing a personality more completely than almost anyone in the history of psychology? Will Bobbie become a man? And if he does, will he be happy? Dear readers, only future chapters will tell.

Analysis

The major key to the success Sid and Bobbie had on the first leg of their journey was probably Sid's use of praise as a **reinforcer.** He praised Bobbie, each time Bobbie made the right moves. That praise probably **reinforced** (strengthened) those moves, making the male moves occur more and more frequently until they occurred as often as with any other male.

Another key to their success was the detailed **task analysis** Sid borrowed from Barlow and the University of Mississippi crew. The task analysis allows for an interesting approach to life. Behavior analysts look at life as a set of tasks. They ask: "Are you having trouble with life? What part of your life?" Then they say, "Well, that part of life is just a task—just a job to be done. Yet the task may be too large and too complex to cope with. So let's break it down into its components. And let's make sure you can do each component. Then you'll be able to do the big task, and you will have solved your problem!" For instance, if you're having trouble acting like a man instead of a woman, let's break down the task into its components and go from there. Let's break acting like a man into such small components

as sitting, standing, and walking. Then let's break those components into even smaller components, like putting your ankle over on your knee when you're sitting. That's a revolutionary way of looking at life. And it seems to work!

In doing a task analysis, you must **be concrete.** That brings us to a fundamental general rule.

Definition: General Rule
Be concrete
  ○ Always pinpoint specific behaviors
  ○ when you deal with a behavioral (psychological) problem.

Specify exactly what behavior you want to change. Sid couldn't just say Bobbie was too effeminate. He couldn't just say Bobbie acts too much like a woman. He had to specify exactly what behavior he would and wouldn't reinforce. He would reinforce Bobbie's crossing his legs with the ankle of one leg resting on the knee of the other. He wouldn't reinforce the knee of one leg resting above the knee of the other. You've got to play it that way, even if it seems ridiculous. If you don't, you won't reinforce any one behavior with enough consistency to increase its frequency. It's even more crucial to pinpoint the specific behavior if you want someone else to do some of the reinforcing. What that person thinks is effeminate may not be what you think is effeminate.

Here's another thing Sid did: When he started the reinforcement program, he also gave Bobbie specific **feedback.** After each of Bobbie's responses, Sid told him what he had done right and what he had done wrong. For sure, he was concrete. He got so concrete he'd say, "Put your ankle closer to your knee." He didn't just say, "Be more masculine and less effeminate." That would help about as much as giving the feedback in Greek. He also showed Bobbie the videotapes of his responses.

As we will see, to change behavior, you must analyze tasks, specify concrete behavior, reinforce, and give feedback. (By the way, we'll sometimes use technical terms, like *reinforcement* and *feedback,* in our analyses before we define them. Don't worry; we're just breaking you in. Their meaning should be clear from the context, and they will become familiar friends by the time we formally introduce and define them.)

Well, you've met Sid at the university. Now let's follow him home.

Example of Reinforcer
Behavioral Child and Family Counseling
FAMILY LIFE—PART I[5]

The baby's scream sounded like someone's finger-nails scraping over a chalkboard. Sid Fields pounded his fists on the battered computer, jumped up from his desk, and ran into the nursery.

Fortunately, Dawn had gotten there before him. She picked up their crying baby, hugged him, rocked him, cooed, and then said to her husband, "Sid, calm down. Rod will be asleep in a minute."

"That kid's driving me crazy," Sid said. "I'm having enough trouble getting my dissertation written without having to put up with Rod's constant crying."

"Sid, he's just a baby," Dawn said.

"He's going to be a baby with an unemployed father if I don't get this dissertation written. You know the chair of our department said he couldn't rehire me if I don't finish my dissertation and get my doctoral degree by the end of this year."

"You'll get your doctoral dissertation written, Sid. I know you will." Dawn put her right arm around Sid's waist, while she continued to cradle Rod in her left arm.

"Shhh, Rod's asleep now," Dawn said as she placed the baby back in his crib.

Dawn took Sid's hand and both smiled as they looked down on their sleeping son. Then they started to leave the room as quietly as they could. But before they'd reached the door, Rod started whimpering. So they sat on the floor of the nursery, waiting for their son to fall asleep again. Their smiles had disappeared.

Concept
REINFORCER

As Sid Fields and Dawn Baker sat on the floor of their son's nursery, they began talking in low voices. "You know, Dawn, I think you increase Rod's crying each time you pay attention and cuddle him when he cries. I think your paying attention reinforces his crying.

---

[5]Based on Williams, C. D. (1959). The elimination of tantrum behavior by extinction procedures. *Journal of Abnormal and Social Psychology, 269.*

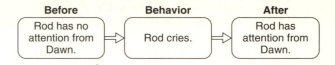

I think even our entering Rod's room is a reinforcer that reinforces his whimpering."

"What about my giving you a hug when you were so upset about your dissertation? Was that a reinforcer that reinforced your complaining?" Dawn smiled and took Sid's hand.

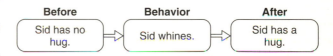

"I wasn't complaining about my dissertation; I was stating a fact."

Dawn thought, even if the shoe fits, Sid refuses to wear it. She said, "I have a PhD in behavior analysis, and you soon will have . . ."

"Let's hope!"

"I earn my living using behavior analysis to help other people," Dawn continued. "And yet, why can't I use behavior analysis to help my own family? Surely we can figure out how to use behavior analysis to help Rod stop crying and causing such a fuss. Surely we can figure out how to help him stop making life so hard for all three of us."

"What about a little help on my dissertation, too?"

"OK, we've also got to figure out how to help you get over your writer's block and finish your dissertation so you can keep your job in the psych department."

Two hours later, Rod was sleeping soundly enough that his parents could finally slip out of his nursery without his starting to cry again.

You may have sensed that Sid and Dawn use the word *reinforcer* in a technical manner. You're right. Here's what they mean by *reinforcer*.

Definition: Concept

Reinforcer (positive reinforcer)

○ Any stimulus, event, or condition

○ whose **presentation** immediately follows a response

○ and **increases** the frequency[6] of that response.

For example, Dawn and Sid's attention and comfort immediately followed Rod's crying and increased the frequency of his crying. So attention and comfort are a reinforcer for Rod's behavior.[7] And

---

[6](Warning to beginning students of behavior analysis: This technical footnote makes use of several concepts you will meet formally only in later chapters.) Starting with Skinner, behavior analysts have traditionally used the expression *probability of response* or *rate of response* rather than *frequency of response,* the term we will generally use. The problem with probability is that it applies only to discrete-trial responding, where there is an opportunity for only a single response on each trial. It does not apply to free-operant responding, where the frequency of the response is free to vary from zero to 100 or more per minute. In the case of discrete-trial training, for example, with an autistic child, we can ask a question or give an instruction and then score each discrete trial as to whether or not the child made the response. If the child responded on 7 of the 10 trials, the probability of the response is 0.7. But suppose in the free-operant Skinner box, Rudolph, the rat, pressed the lever 7 times in the first minute; what's the probability of his response? Not 7 divided by 10, nor 7 divided by 60. The concept of response probability doesn't apply in these free operant settings because there's no way you can compute it. Skinner rarely (perhaps never) tried to compute free-operant response probability; instead, his use of response probability was more like his use of response strength, a concept he later criticized as being a reification in behavior analyst's clothing.

On the other hand, as Jack Michael pointed out, response rate applies to the free-operant Skinner box, but not the discrete-trial training session. Rudolph pressed the lever 7 times in the first minute, so his response rate was 7 per minute. But it doesn't make sense to say the autistic child's response rate was 7 per minute, because, whether he had a minute or 10 minutes to make those 7 responses is, at least in part, under the control of the trainer. So a slow trainer would artificially cause the child to appear to have a slower response "rate" than would a fast trainer. Thus, rate is a poor measure of the child's behavior.

So, at Jack's suggestion, we usually use response frequency to refer to both the rate of free-operant responding and the relative frequency (probability) of discrete-trial responding.

[7]The infant's crying raises an interesting problem—the cry-wolf phenomenon. The infant's crying is a very functional escape response because it will bring a watchful parent to the rescue when the diapers are wet. Crying will also be reinforced by the watchful parent when the child is hungry. But it is very easy for crying to become dictatorially dysfunctional, when the overwatchful parent reinforces crying with attention and comfort every time it occurs. It's not always easy for the outsider to discriminate between functional and dysfunctional crying, though most parents may learn that discrimination.

Sid's praise immediately followed Bobbie's manly moves and increased the frequency of those moves. So Sid's praise is a reinforcer for Bobbie's behavior.

Here's another example: It might be a big reinforcer for you to see the crucial concepts in this book highlighted in yellow. If so, now's the time for you to pick up that yellow highlighter and go for it.

In Chapter 13, we will see that this increased frequency occurs in situations similar to those in which the response had previously produced that reinforcer.

QUESTION[8]

1. *Reinforcer*—define it and give an example of attention as a reinforcer. (When we ask for examples, we will normally be happy with examples from the text. We won't mean original examples, unless we say so. But your instructor might want original examples; better check.)

HOW IMMEDIATE IS IMMEDIATE?

If the reinforcer is to reinforce a particular response, it must immediately follow that response. But how immediate is immediate? We don't have any experimental data on this one for human beings, but the research on nonverbal animals suggests that a minute or two pushes the limit (even 30 seconds is hard). And if you talk to most behavior analysts working with nonverbal children, they'd agree. They'd quit their job if they had to wait 60 seconds before delivering each reinforcer to their children. Such a delay is a good way to ensure that no learning would occur, even with people—at least no desirable learning.

So, if you're trying to reinforce a response, don't push that 60-second limit. Push the other end—the 0-second end. The direct effect of reinforcers drops off quickly as you increase the delay, even to 3 or 4 seconds. And even a 1-second delay may reinforce the wrong behavior. If you ask a young child to look at you and then give the reinforcer 1 second after the response, you're liable to reinforce looking in the opposite direction. So one problem with delayed reinforcement is that it reinforces the wrong response—the one that occurred just before the delivery of the reinforcer. Probably a reinforcer must be delayed no longer than 1 second to be considered immediate and the closer to 0 seconds, the better.

---

[8]The "questions" in these "study questions" sections are often stated as study objectives (e.g., be able to give an example of such and such), but to keep things simple, we'll call these sections "Question" sections and not "Objective" sections.

QUESTION

1. How immediate is immediate, when reinforcing a response?

Example of Reinforcer?
WHO WAS THAT MASKED STUDENT WITH THE SILVER STAR?

Now back to the main point. You tell your friend you'll paste a silver star on her forehead as a reinforcer every time she helps you with your homework. But that may not do the trick. Just because you call the silver star a reinforcer doesn't mean it will work as one. Another way to put it is: Will she more frequently help you with future homework? Will the silver star on her forehead help you to become a star pupil in class? If it does, then you've probably got a reinforcer on your hands, or at least on her forehead.

Example of Reinforcer
Behavioral School Psychology[9]
ERIC'S CLASSROOM TANTRUM— PART I[10]

Eleven-year-old Eric sat quietly in the classroom, cute enough to be on a Norman Rockwell cover of the *Saturday Evening Post.* Middle America's stereotype of the American kid—unruly red hair, freckles, dimples, worn Nike shoes, the back of his plaid shirt pulled out of his Levis, his fly half unzipped. Then he started glancing around the room, at first on the sly, and then twisting his whole body in the process, a bit disruptive, but still cute. He wrinkled his face and began making soft noises—less cute. The soft noises quickly became sniffles, then cries, then shouts, "I hate it! I hate it! I want out! Let me out! I hate you!" The American-kid fists began pounding the desk. Eric fell out of his seat and lay on his back, now pounding the floor with his fists and kicking it with his Nikes. He was shouting and crying with more intensity than

seemed possible from his small, trembling body, "Hate it! Hate it! Hate it!" The truth behind the cover boy.

Sue sprang from her desk when Eric hit the floor. Now what? She paused an instant, unprepared. Then she ran to Eric and tried to pick him up, but his body went rigid and he started pounding on her stomach. She withdrew in pain.

"Eric, Eric, what's the matter?" she asked, with as much of a calming tone as she could achieve.

"Hate it! Hate it! Want out!"

The class fell apart immediately. None of the other kids had ever seen anything like this. They stared at Eric, ignoring their studies.

Eric stopped more than Sue's classroom; his shouts and pounding paralyzed the whole school, as all the teachers and staff ran into Sue's classroom. She stood there, her arms dangling at her sides, helpless, embarrassed, ashamed. Her first day on the job and already a failure.

She felt better when Bob went over to Eric, with all the confidence his senior status and experience justified, but he, too, had to retreat from the pounding Eric gave him. If Bob couldn't handle Eric, then who could expect her to?

The staff settled for long-distance psychotherapy, being careful to stay out of Eric's reach. "It's OK, Eric." "Do you want your mommy, Eric?" "What's the matter, Eric?" And with firm finality, "All right now, Eric; enough of this nonsense. Get back in your seat and settle down." Followed quickly by a guilty, "We love you, Eric." "That boy's throwing a regular hissy fit."

Also consultation: "What's the matter with this poor child?" "Just an extreme anxiety attack." "Fear of failure." "Probably dyslexic." "School phobia." "Frustrated." "He's expressing a deep-seated insecurity." "The kids tease him." "We do not," shouted a defender of juvenile morality.

Analysis

While Eric was throwing his tantrum in the school building, Dr. Mae Robinson was parking her Skylark in the school's parking lot. She got out, still thinking about the meeting she had just left with the principal of West James Elementary School. She felt flattered that he had referred Eric to her school, the Rosa Parks Academy. The principal thought maybe she could help Eric, after the West James school psychologist and special education teachers had given up on the boy. She smiled as she wondered if it bothered them to ask for the professional expertise of a black woman, the youngest principal in the school district. Maybe they were just dumping Eric

---

[9]We will use the terms *behavioral school psychology* and *behavioral special education* somewhat synonymously, though the traditional approaches to these two areas are quite different. Traditional school psychology concentrates on performing psychological tests of students, largely to determine whether they should go into a special education classroom, but behavioral school psychology and behavioral special education both concentrate on using behavioral techniques to improve classroom teaching, especially for students with difficulties.

[10]Based on Zimmerman, E. H., and Zimmerman, J. (1962). The alteration of behavior in a special classroom situation. *Journal of the Experimental Analysis of Behavior, 5,* 59–60.

on her, getting rid of a problem, with no hope that she could help the poor boy. Educators sometimes grow cynical after years of disillusion. She had to force herself to stop thinking that way. She had to give them a chance, like they seemed to be giving her. But still. . . .

As for Eric, well, she would just have to see. But she thought she knew what caused his problem. No internal demon expressed itself through his tantrums. No warped perception separated Eric from reality. He acquired his obnoxious, pitiful, disruptive behavior because of its consequences. And the way they described Eric's problem, it sounded like he got plenty of reinforcing consequences. He was getting more attention in 5 minutes of tantrums than most people get all day. Attention is a social reinforcer. Attention is contingent (or dependent) on Eric's tantrums. Here, attention reinforces his tantrums. He may throw a lot more tantrums than he would if no one attended to his tantrums.

The analysis seemed simple to her, though neither the principals, the school psychologists, nor the special education teachers had suggested it. She knew the cause, but what about the cure? She'd have to think about that.

Mae walked across the gravel parking lot to the 80-year-old, two-story, brick school building. She had saved it from the demolition crew to house her new special school. As she approached, Eric's shouts gradually caused her to stop thinking about Eric's conference and to start thinking about Eric's reality. She quickened her pace, hurrying to the entrance of the shabby old building. Then she bounded up the inside stairs to the second floor and into Sue's classroom.

Mae stood a minute, amazed. By this time, spectators had packed the room; not only were the teachers from the other classroom watching and giving advice, but so were their students. This was no time to speculate further about the causes of poor Eric's problems. Mae had to act. She had to solve the problem.

What will she do? Will she succeed? Or would we be so devious as to include studies that are failures? Hold tight, dear readers; only future chapters will tell.

QUESTION

1. Give a classroom example of the way tantruming might be related to social reinforcers. Notice that we say "might be" because we have not experimentally shown that social reinforcement is maintaining Eric's tantruming. So far, all we've got is Mae's educated guess.

Examples and Nonexamples
REINFORCER

Here's a list of questions with our answers. Now, would it be naive of us to ask you to think through your answer to each question before you look at ours? We know thinking is harder than just reading, but give it a shot anyway.

Question

What's your guess? Would a silver star on your friend's forehead normally act as a reinforcer?

Our Guess

Probably not, not unless your friend is about three years old, or into punk fashions, or both. Of course, we're just guessing, based on our experience. You'll only know for sure if you try it and see if she helps you more frequently in the future because of her star-spangled forehead. (Of course, whether something is a reinforcer or not depends on many things, such as the person whose behavior you are trying to reinforce and the specific response you're trying to reinforce.)

Question

What about other things on her face—like mascara on her eyelashes, eye shadow on her eyelids, rouge on her cheeks, and lipstick on her lips? Might they act as reinforcers?

Our Answer

It usually depends on what her female friends paint on their faces. But if she paints her face, then the paint on the face is probably a reinforcer for the act of putting it there. And if she pays cold cash for the stuff, then owning it must be a reinforcer for such consumerism.

Question

Mae thought that all the attention Eric got for his tantrums probably acted as a reinforcer that caused the tantrums to occur. At least that reinforcer probably kept the tantrums going once they got started. But what reinforcer maintained the giving of that attention; what was the reinforcer for staring at poor Eric?

Our Answer

The spectacle is our guess. Remember, **behavior such as attending occurs because it has been reinforced.** So if they're attending to that behavior, the spectacle is probably the crucial reinforcer.

Keep the following in mind: In the examples of this section, we're just guessing about what the reinforcers might be. You'd have to do an actual experiment to be sure.

QUESTIONS

1. Give an example of something that is probably a reinforcer for some people and not for others. Also, while you are at it, explain it.
2. Give a few examples where the sight of something probably reinforces the behavior of looking at it.

MORE CONCEPTS THAN YOU'D CARE TO KNOW

Here are a few concepts of a semitechnical, semiobvious nature. Still it may help to discuss them for a couple of minutes, so they won't cause any trouble later.

Behavior

What is behavior? Maybe more than you might think. **Behavior** is anything a dead man can't do. Like scratch his nose. Talk. Smile. Cry. Think. Dream. Behavior may even be the firing of a neuron in the nervous system. Behavior is not necessarily falling over a cliff. A dead man can do that, with a little help from his friends. If a dead man can do it, it ain't behavior.

Definition: General Rule
Dead-man test[11]
  ○ If a dead man can do it, it ain't behavior.
  ○ And if a dead man can't do it, then it is behavior.

We find the first line of the **dead-man test** one of our most helpful tools in trying to understand complex instances of human behavior. Without it, we'd often end up analyzing the wrong thing—nonbehavior.

However, apply the dead-man test only to behavior, not to reinforcers. For example, sometimes silence is the golden reinforcer, without a living soul

---

[11]Be serious. You don't really want us to say *dead-person* test do you? *Dead-man test* is in the tradition of the classic *Dead Men Don't Dance* and the more recent *Dead Men Don't Wear Plaid* flick. And, in an non-anonymous survey, 11 students said definitely keep it, 2 said maybe keep it, and only 1 said maybe bag it. By the way, Ogden Lindsley invented this concept in 1965.

---

around but you. So don't apply the dead-man test to the reinforcer of silence.

The second part of this general rule is also useful: *If a dead man can't do it, then it is behavior.* Dead men don't dance. Dead dogs don't bark. But Dead heads *do* go to rock-and-roll concerts (in other words, this is just a rough, general rule, and you shouldn't get completely bent out of shape if you find an exception now and then). This second line may come from a less flamboyant and more traditional definition of behavior: *Behavior is anything an animal (including the human animal) does.*

But here's the most common definition of behavior:

Definition: Concept
Behavior
  ○ A muscle, glandular, or electrical activity.

However, we make more use of the dead-man test than the more formal definition of behavior because we consider thinking, dreaming, and having images as part of the subject matter of behavior analysis; and we're not sure those activities involve muscle or glandular activities, though they probably do involve electrical activity. Furthermore, we suspect reinforcers can increase the frequency of those activities; so that's even more reason to want to consider them behavior.

Here's something that confuses many students: **Behavior analysts use *response* and *behavior* almost interchangeably.** So we might say *Bobbie's crossing his legs is **behavior,*** and we might say *it's a **response.*** In other words, we don't necessarily restrict *response* to mean a reaction to something, as when you react to a joke by smiling.

Behavior = Response

Here are some other words that mean more or less the same as *behavior* or *response: act, action, movement,* and *reaction.* When we speak of *behavior,* we don't restrict its meaning to "comportment" or "manners." For example, our technical use of the term wouldn't include "I want you to be on good behavior" or "she was ill-behaved." This means that *Principles of Behavior* is not about how to avoid getting a scolding from your mother for being rude or for talking with your mouth full.

Behavior Analysis

Behavior analysis is the study of the behavior of human beings and other animals. And that's what this book is about.

Now let's get more precise:

Definition: Concept
Behavior analysis
- The study of the operation of the principles of behavior with both human beings and other animals.

Behavior Analyst

If you know what behavior analysis is, the following shouldn't come as a major shock: **A *behavior analyst* is a person who studies the operation of the principles of behavior.**

Many behavior analysts are psychologists. Many are not. They might be special education teachers, social workers, nurses, or business administrators—anyone studying the effects of behavioral procedures.

Behavior analysts often work as *performance managers*. Performance managers include all sorts of people trained in the principles of behavior—teachers, parents, coaches, supervisors, clinicians, social workers, animal trainers, and those who manage their own personal performance (though managing one's own behavior is no easy trick). Of course, most teachers, parents, and so forth are not performance managers (as we use the term) because they are not knowledgeably using the principles of behavior.

We slightly prefer *performance manager* or *behavior manager* over *behavior modifier*. Why? Because a manager may have the goal of supporting an already satisfactory performance with no need to modify it. Said another way, if it isn't broke, don't fix it—don't modify it. *Behavioral engineer* is another acceptable term that means about the same thing—though for some people, it implies that we're working with machines and not people.

Whatever label we use, keep in mind that we're talking about using the principles of behavior, like the principle of reinforcement, to manage performance. We're not talking about brain surgery or drugs when we speak of managing performance or modifying behavior.

You might consider the behavior therapist to be a behavior modifier who specializes in working with abnormal behavior, traditionally the kind seen in a psychiatric hospital or mental health clinic. Behavior therapists are often clinical psychologists or social workers, though not always. Normally you wouldn't apply the term *behavior therapist* to a behavior analyst who sets up reinforcement procedures to improve productivity in a factory.

Repertoire

Your **repertoire** is your bag of tricks. If you've gotten this far in our book, then your repertoire must include reading English. Or else you're wearing out your thumb with a foreign-language dictionary. By the time you finish this book, we hope your repertoire also will contain behavior analysis. Dancing may be in your repertoire. Perhaps playing baseball, or at least talking about playing baseball, also is in your repertoire. Or if you can't throw a baseball, can you at least throw a tantrum, like Eric? Is tantruming part of your repertoire?

The reinforcement of novel behavior puts that behavior in your repertoire—you learn it. Reinforcement of established behavior maintains that behavior in your repertoire. You learn Spanish, and then you practice it or else you lose it. You learn behavior analysis, and then you practice it or lose it. "Use it or lose it" is a good folk principle of behavior.

But: Repertoire is not a thing. You don't have a repertoire that holds all your tricks. It's just a way of speaking, a risky convenience. Your repertoire is just the total collection of things you can do. It's not a warehouse from which you retrieve your stored tricks.

Definition: Concept
Repertoire
- A set of skills.
- What a person or animal can do.

If, by the end of this book, you can pronounce *repertoire* correctly and with grace, you'll be ahead of most people. *Reper* is no big problem. You don't get much credit for that part. Except you pronounce *re* as in *represent*, not as in *repeat*. So try it: *reper*. Remember, don't say it like *reaper*, as in the grim *reaper*. The hard part: *toire*. Like *twar*, as in *car*, not like as in *war*.

Behavioral Intervention

By *behavioral intervention*, we mean the use of a behavioral procedure. We don't mean a military intervention. For example, Mae plans to intervene in

Eric's classroom tantrums. But don't think a behavioral intervention means to interrupt behavior. Mae might also use a behavioral intervention to increase the amount of time Eric studies. (We don't want to make such a big deal of behavioral intervention as to require you to memorize a formal definition. We just want you to tune in.)

We prefer to stay neutral and say *the performance manager intervenes with behavioral problems or performance problems*. We tend not to talk of "treating" behavior problems, because we don't want to imply a medical model (see Chapter 2 to read our rantings on the evils of the medical model myth).

BASIC ENRICHMENT

THE FUNDAMENTALS VS. THE ENRICHMENT SECTIONS

We've divided this and the other chapters into two main sections. We call the second section the Enrichment section. We call all the subsections that come before it the Fundamentals section. You need to master all the issues, concepts, procedures, analyses, and examples in the Fundamentals section to understand the Fundamentals sections of the following chapters. The Fundamentals are the bare bones.

However, you don't need to master the material in the Enrichment sections to understand the Fundamentals in later chapters. But many professors and students thought the Enrichment sections were the best part of the first edition of this book. Your professor may agree and may wish to include parts or all of the Enrichment sections on your quizzes as well. He or she probably will let you know.

Also, we have divided the Enrichment sections of many chapters into two levels—basic and intermediate, with an occasional advanced enrichment section, as well. We've tried to keep the basic level on the same level of difficulty as the Fundamentals sections. The intermediate level is more difficult, though it assumes no knowledge of behavior analysis before you read this book.

WHY JUST A BEHAVIORAL VIEW?

Sid's Seminar

Max: I've been reading ahead, and it looks as if this book deals mainly with behavior analysis. It doesn't say much about other approaches to psychology. Why not psychoanalysis, Freud, Piaget, information processing, cognitive psychology, humanistic psychology?

Joe: What do you expect? The title of the book is *Principles of Behavior*.

Tom: That may be the title of the book, but shouldn't we be getting a broader view of the various psychological theories in this class?

Sid: An interesting point. Psychology sure isn't short on theories. We've got Freud, Jung, Piaget, cognitive psychology, humanistic psychology, gestalt psychology. . . .

Joe: The people in California produce a new pop theory almost every week.

Sid: Here's what I've found in teaching this course. I used to try to cover all the theories, but the students got shortchanged. They didn't learn enough about any one theory to really understand it, let alone make use of it. At best they learned a few clichés they could use in making small talk. They don't appreciate or understand. They gain no solid knowledge. They learn no useful skills. On the other hand, when I devote a whole course to a single approach, the students understand and appreciate that approach—both its strengths and its weaknesses.

Tom: OK, but why behavior analysis? Why not Freud?

Sid: Because I'm a professional behavior analyst. Behavior analysis is what I teach best.

Joe: Also, behavior analysis has more scientific data supporting it and can be applied to more areas than any other approach.

Sue: Professor Harper said if you want to study Freud, you have to go to the English department. He said almost no major psychology department in North America takes Freud too seriously any more.[12]

---

[12]*Official unbiased recommendation:* If you want to read more about the general field of psychology, including Freud and Piaget, though from a behavioral perspective, you might check out Malott, R. W., & Whaley, D. L. (1976), *Psychology,* New York: Harpers College Press (out of print). This book also features Mae, Dawn, Sid, and Juke when they were undergraduates at Big State University.

INTERMEDIATE ENRICHMENT

MAKE SURE YOUR ASSUMED REINFORCER REALLY REINFORCES

Remember how we define reinforcer? A stimulus, event, or condition that will increase the future frequency of a response it has immediately followed. We do things that will get us reinforcers. And we also stop doing things that cost us reinforcers. For example, we might get reinforcers, like smiles and approval, by being halfway decent to people. And we might lose those reinforcers by being halfway nasty to them; so we could stop losing those reinforcers by stopping our nastiness.

Still we don't know for sure if someone's smile is a reinforcer for us, at least not until we find ourselves doing things that produce that reinforcer or no longer doing things that cause us to lose that reinforcer.

For example, a crocodile smile might not be a reinforcer, unless you're another crocodile.

We all tend to use the term *reinforcer* to describe conditions whose reinforcer value we have not shown. We tend to assume that something will reinforce a particular response of a particular person just because it has reinforced other responses of other people in the past or just because we think it would if we were that person. It's OK to start that way, though it's risky business if you don't check out your **assumed reinforcer** before going any further. Many so-called failures to modify behavior are often just failures to use a true reinforcer.

Definition: General Rule
Check the assumed reinforcer first
- Before spending much time trying to reinforce behavior,
- make sure you have a true reinforcer.

For example, suppose you plan to use raisins to reinforce a mentally handicapped[13] girl's talking.

Make sure the girl will eat the raisins first. Does the taste of the raisins reinforce her response of picking up one and putting it in her mouth?

Will this reinforce eating raisins?

If it doesn't, you may be in for many long, tedious, so-called reinforcement sessions with no progress when you try to use raisins to reinforce talking. Failure to use this general rule may account for much wasted time of behavior analysts and their clients. Once we were working with a child with serious academic problems. So we were giving him an M&M candy every time he read a sentence correctly. After his mouth and pockets were bulging with the candies, he said, "Look, I'll keep reading the sentences, but please stop giving me those M&Ms."

Remember, we define reinforcers in terms of their effect on behavior, not in terms of what people say. The people may not know, or they may lie. For example, "Boys, would looking at dirty pictures be a reinforcer for you?" "Oh, no, Mother!"

QUESTION

1. State the "check the reinforcer first" general rule, and then give an example of where and how you should use that general rule.

---

[13]Some people have failed to acquire various functional (helpful) behavioral repertoires and have acquired other dysfunctional (harmful) behavioral repertoires. In the past, such people were often designated as *idiots*. This term became so distasteful that *retarded* came into professional use. Then *retarded* became so dis-

tasteful that *developmentally delayed* or *developmentally disabled* became the most acceptable designation. Unfortunately, *developmental* implies an erroneous cause or underlying process for these problems. *Developmental* implies that the person's repertoire was growing, just as the body grows or, just as a seed becomes a flower; but something interrupted or slowed down this automatic, biological growth process, with the result that the person's repertoire development failed to keep up with the physical development. There is little if any evidence to support the claim that repertoires develop automatically as a result of biological maturation. Now, the terminology most accepted in the education field is now *mentally impaired* and *mentally handicapped*. So we will try to use that terminology in this book.

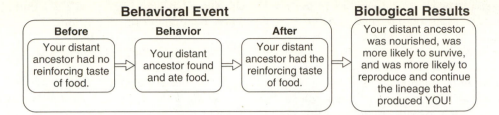

BIOLOGICAL EVOLUTION
AND REINFORCERS

Life is full of stimuli, events, and conditions that help us survive (they nourish our body's cells and/or help our population survive). Fortunately, most animals, including the human animal, have evolved so that many of those biologically helpful conditions also act behaviorally as reinforcers. For example, we tend to repeat acts that produce food, water, and sex. Food and water help us as individuals and thus as a species to survive. Sex helps us as a species to survive.

Your ancestor found and ate the food. The food and its taste reinforced that finding and eating; in other words, when your ancestor doesn't have any food, he will repeat those behaviors that had found food in the past and he will eat the found food. The biological result is that he will be better nourished and more likely to survive. And if he survives, he will be more likely to have offspring, unto your generation, with the miraculous result that you were born to carry on the cycle of repeating behaviors that have been reinforced and will, hopefully, lead to your survival.

Sex is slightly different. Sex is fun (reinforcing) for us as individuals, but it doesn't help our survival as individuals. We have evolved in such a way that food and water are reinforcers because consuming food and water has allowed individuals to survive long enough to produce and raise offspring. The reason we have evolved in such a way that sexual stimulation is a reinforcer is that the resulting sexual stimulation has caused individuals to copulate and thus produce offspring. Unfortunately, not all beneficial or helpful stimuli or conditions are sufficient reinforcers for many of us. For example, most adults in the United States fail to find the stimulation from physical exercise much of a reinforcer. So they fail to do the exercise needed to keep their bodies in good shape.

And, unfortunately, not all reinforcers are good for us. Salt, sugar, and fat are examples. "I'll have a fudge sundae after I finish these nachos." Or you can trash yourself big time by having a cup of coffee with cream and sugar as you finish off your cigarette. Harmful reinforcers have become so prominent in our modern world that I've adopted this policy:

> **If it feels too good, be careful.
> 'Cause it'll likely sneak up from behind
> and bite you on your rear end.**

QUESTION

1. Give three examples of
   ○ An example of a reinforcer that is helpful for you.
   ○ A helpful stimulus or condition that is not a reinforcer.
   ○ A reinforcer that is harmful.

HOW TO USE THE STUDY QUESTIONS

Now we're starting to roll. But before we start rolling so fast we get out of control, let's take a brief break and spend the next two sections discussing how to use this book. Then we can really get up to speed. We interrupt now because you may need this information to most effectively reread this chapter and read the remaining chapters.

Question

What are the main questions of the previous sections? What are the main points? What are the main goals? What are the main questions your professor *might* ask you on the next quiz?

Answer

The questions listed under the "Question" headings. (Your professor will probably tell you what, if any, relation there is between our questions in the book and his or her questions on quizzes and exams.)

Whenever you finish a section or so, you should be able to answer those questions placed at the end of those sections. If you can't, then give the section another shot. Whenever you finish a chapter, you should still be able to answer those questions. So review it quickly to be sure. Whenever you take a quiz or exam, you should still be able to answer the questions. So take at least a half hour or more to review the questions for each chapter before each quiz.

But there's more to life than study questions. You also should read the sections to which the study questions refer. For one thing, it may be tough trying to memorize answers that don't make sense. A quick skim won't be enough. Carefully reading the relevant sections should put more sense into the questions, the answers, and you. For another thing, if we were your professors, we'd probably ask you a few more questions that weren't in the list of questions, just to keep you sharp. Or from a more long-range view: The questions list only the main points, not all the points. We can't test you on much of what we hope you will get from reading our book—for example, an appreciation of the field of behavior analysis.

IN DEFENSE OF "MICKEY-MOUSE" QUESTIONS

My view of the level of these study questions may shock you. They require no more intellectual skills than you'll find in your average turnip. Yet memorizing their answers requires more work than we should ask of a self-respecting college student. They don't require you to think, just memorize—every concept, principle, and general rule, word for word. (It doesn't have to be word for word, just perfect—but word for word is the safest.)

Why? Because of a surprising report from our best, most thoughtful, and most creative students. Over the years, they've reported that it helped them to memorize everything first. Like memorizing the vocabulary for your Spanish course. Memorize our concepts, and you'll *use* them with greater ease—and use them you must! Then, as a result of your using the concepts and principles awhile, you will understand them. You no longer will need to worry with your memorized definitions. Memorize and you take one small but helpful step toward enlightenment.

Also, there's a good chance your instructor will be a real stickler on the quizzes. You'll define a term in a way that looks good to you, but your instructor will say, "No, you left out a word that changes the whole meaning of the definition."

"It was just one word!"

"Right, the most crucial word."

"But I was close."

"Not close enough."

"But I meant to include that word; I just forgot."

"Right. See you in class next week."

The thing is, even with years of experience in behavior analysis, we've had to spend hours defining these terms so the definitions would say exactly what they need to say. (We even had to enlist the help of many of our friends and colleagues and undergrad students, too.) The odds aren't too high that you can do it casually if this is your first tour of the land of behavior analysis.

Of course, you should check with your instructor to see the exact relation between these study objectives (questions) and the quizzes and tests in your particular course.

And when we ask for examples, you can just tell us the ones in the book; fine with us! They don't have to be original. Here's why I don't usually require original examples on my quizzes: My experience is that, by itself, a textbook such as this can't get your repertoire to the point where you can reliably discriminate between examples and nonexamples of concepts, let alone reliably generate correct, original examples, so we think just remembering our examples is a step in the right direction. When I use this book, I supplement it with a workbook, *How to Analyze Behavioral Contingencies.* That workbook trains students to creatively generate original examples and analyze novel examples of our concepts. However, whether or not your professor is using this workbook, he or she may want you to generate original examples on the quizzes. There's also a good chance he or she will tell you in advance, but you know how professors are, so you might want to check up front.

HOW TO READ TEXTBOOKS

Here are some guidelines to follow when you're reading a textbook:

○ **Know the title of the book.** That may help you better understand what the book is talking about while you're reading it. It may help you keep the big picture. We know one professor, Jerry Mertens, who's so convinced of the importance of this knowledge that he asks for the textbook titles on his exams—not a bad idea.

○ **Know the title of the chapter and section.** Remembering the chapter and section title while you're reading a section will help you understand what the examples are about. And re-membering that will help you answer quiz questions such as *What's Rod's sleep problem an example of?*

○ **Relate examples to concepts and principles.** Look at the concept and principle defined just before or just after an example and see how the example illustrates that concept or princi-ple. Doing this will also help you better under-stand what both you read and how to answer quiz questions.

Controversy
TRANSGENDER CONCERNS

We received a few questions and expressions of concern about our treatment of transgender issues in the second edition of this book. So we decided to eliminate it from the third edition. But almost all my students thought it was too important to elimi-nate, as did most of the faculty with whom I checked. So then I asked an old friend of mine I've known since I was 3 years old. He was gay. I asked him what I should do. He described the isolation, agony, and suicidal tendencies of gay men he had known and who had sought counseling from him (both he and I consider this unhappiness to result from society's oppression). Then he said these is-sues of sexuality are too important to ignore. He advised me to keep Bobbie's case but to discuss its implications more fully and to face the issues di-rectly. In these subsequent editions, we've followed his advice; and we will discuss the implications of behavior analysis for sexual orientation in the In-termediate Enrichment section of Chapter 26, after you've studied the various relevant concepts in this book.

2 Reinforcement

FUNDAMENTALS

Example of Reinforcement
Behavioral Social Work
THE GRANDFATHER[1]

John "Juke" Jackson enjoyed telling people he was the first black student to receive a master's degree in organizational behavior management at Big State University. His audience would always show how impressed they were with his success. And they would always comment on what a scandal it was that BSU was so racist. Why had BSU waited so long to allow a black student to graduate from that program? Then Juke would laugh and tell them he was the first student, either black or white, to enter that program.

But he didn't bother to tell them he had graduated with straight As and in only 16 months from a 24-month program; no one had yet come close to his record. And he didn't tell them he was the first football player to earn a graduate degree from any program in the Psych Department or that he also had a graduate minor in sports psychology.

He didn't tell them he drove a metallic-blue BMW Roadster and lived in the second-most-expensive condo in town. He didn't tell them he spent as much time coaching kids in sports for no pay as he did coaching managers in business and industry for more pay than he ever imagined he'd earn.

And he didn't tell them he cried for an hour without stopping when his mother called to tell him his grandfather had had a stroke and that his right side was paralyzed. His grandfather had taught him how to throw a football. His grandfather had come to every game he'd played from junior high through college. His grandfather had paid for his books and tuition in grad school. His grandfather always had a joke for him.

Juke's heart was broken when he saw the old man lying in the intensive-care unit. His grandfather no longer had a joke for anyone. He just lay there staring at nothing. This wasn't someone else's grandfather; this was Juke's grandfather. Juke didn't know a football star and the hottest man in organizational behavior management could cry so much. Juke, the man of many cool moves, had no moves.

Four weeks later, Juke, in an impeccable $700 suit, and his metallic-blue BMW Roadster again headed 3 hours south, to his hometown. The grandfather was in his own house now, sitting in an antique rocking chair. Just a few months ago, the old man had run out of the house to greet him, even before Juke had time to get out of his car. Now he didn't even get out of his rocking chair. He just sat there, staring at nothing.

"That's the way he is," Juke's grandmother said. "He just sits there. And when he does talk, he doesn't make any sense. He's no better than he was in the hospital. John, honey, will he always be like this? Won't he ever get any better?"

Juke didn't trust his voice to reply. He hugged his grandmother and hid his eyes.

The grandmother went into the kitchen to prepare dinner. Juke sat and watched his grandfather. Only once during the next hour did the old man say anything spontaneously—something about the snow outside, though it was May. Juke questioned his grandfather several times, trying to get him to talk.

---

[1]Based on Green, G. R., Linsk, N. L., & Pinkston, E. M. (1986). Modification of verbal behavior of the mentally impaired elderly by their spouses. *Journal of Applied Behavior Analysis, 19,* 329–336.

The old man would answer, but often his answers made no more sense than snow in May.

Like the rest of his gang from BSU, Juke was a thoroughgoing, 24-hour-a-day behavior analyst. He naively believed that, with behavior analysis and hard work, he could solve all the world's problems. At least he hadn't found any he couldn't solve. So the man of many moves began to make his moves.

"Grandma, here's what I think we should do."

"I'll do anything you say, honey, 'cause I can't stand it like this. He doesn't get any better. He just sits there."

"OK, Grandma, now we're going to start a reinforcement program. I want you to set aside an hour each day where you just concentrate on this program. Every time Grandpa makes any remark, I want you to count it. And I want you to ask him a few questions to try to get him to talk. Keep track of the number of times his answers make sense and the number of times they don't."

Juke started to tell his grandmother this would be the baseline period but instead said, "We'll just keep track of things for a few days. We have to make sure Grandpa isn't improving on his own and we're just not seeing it."

"Honey, I know your grandpa isn't getting any better."

His grandmother was right. Though Juke insisted on a few weeks of baseline, his grandfather averaged less than one spontaneous remark per hour, and only 67% of his answers made sense.

Then Juke made his next move. He set up what he hoped would be a reinforcement procedure. For one hour each day, the grandmother attempted to reinforce spontaneous remarks and sensible answers. Each time the grandfather responded properly the grandmother would smile, say a few kind words, and caress the old man. But she caressed only the left side of his head and body, where he could still feel her touch. Juke hoped the smile, kind words, and caresses would act as reinforcers for his grandfather.

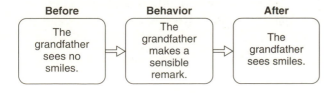

Before	Behavior	After
The grandfather sees no smiles.	The grandfather makes a sensible remark.	The grandfather sees smiles.

Juke coached his grandmother just as he coached the athletes and the managers. He told her what to do. He showed her what to do. He praised her when she did it right and suggested corrections when she didn't. It took a few sessions before she was delivering her reinforcers immediately after her husband's sensible responses. But Juke was as patient and as skilled in shaping the behavior of his grandmother as he was with everyone else he coached. Juke was the master with the praise contingency, putting that praise at just the right place at just the right time—immediately after the correct response or an approximation to the correct response.

The BMW Roadster made the 3-hour trip every weekend. Juke plotted the data his grandmother had recorded, showed her the graphs, watched her working with his grandfather, praised her appropriate efforts, and suggested concrete changes. He also ate his share of his grandmother's cooking and put on a couple of pounds over those weekends.

During the next 6 weeks, his grandfather's spontaneous remarks rose from fewer than 1 to 2.5 per hour, and his sensible replies rose from 67 to 84%. Now it was time to help his grandmother maintain the reinforcement program more independently. Juke replaced his visits with weekly phone calls and then stopped the calls, asking his grandmother to call whenever she had any questions. At Christmas time, the grandmother was still faithfully maintaining the program on her own, and the grandfather was maintaining the same reasonably high rate of spontaneous and sensible remarks as he had when Juke had been helping with the reinforcement procedure.

Christmas was bittersweet that year. The grandfather was not as he had been the Christmas before, but he was much better than in May and June. Juke's grandmother said, "John, I thank the Lord I've got such a fine grandson as you. I don't know what I'd have done without you, honey." Juke covertly wiped a tear from his eye.

QUESTION

1. Briefly describe how to use reinforcers to improve behavior in stroke victims. What were the behaviors, the reinforcers, the procedures, and the results?

Concept
REINFORCEMENT CONTINGENCY

We've been talking about the concept of reinforcer, a fundamental concept in the analysis of behavior. Now we need a principle for tying the reinforcer to the behavior. **Reinforcement principle:** *a response will occur more frequently if a reinforcer or an in-*

crease in a reinforcer has immediately[2] followed it in the past.[3] However, we'll concentrate on the definition of the relevant contingency because that's the definition you'll use most:

Definition: Concept
Reinforcement contingency
  ○ the immediate,
  ○ response-contingent
  ○ **presentation** of[4]
  ○ a reinforcer
  ○ resulting in an **increased** frequency of that response.[5]

So, what does this mean?

Response contingent means *caused by the response (the behavior)* or *produced by the response (the behavior).*[6] For example, the grandfather's re-

---

[2]Most definitions of reinforcement do not require that the reinforcer immediately follow the response. We've added this requirement to distinguish between *reinforcement* and *analogs to reinforcement,* as we will discuss in later chapters. With verbal human beings, sometimes a reinforcer will follow the response by several days, and yet, as a result, the response will occur more frequently in the future. We will later argue that this is an analog and not true reinforcement.

[3]Here's a more elegant but less obvious statement of the principle of reinforcement: A response will occur more frequently if an increase in a reinforcer has immediately followed it.

[4]Instead of just *presentation of a reinforcer,* we would be more precise to say *presentation or increase in a reinforcer.* For example, suppose you're sipping a soda through a crimped straw. Well, the presentation of that sugar-filled soda into your mouth is reinforcing the sipping response. So, *you have no soda ⇒ you sip ⇒ you have soda* is a reinforcement contingency. But also suppose your straw's got a crimp in it, so that the soda's not flowing as rapidly as it might. You straighten out your straw to get rid of the crimp, and now you've got an increase in the reinforcer, the flow of the soda into your mouth. So, *you have slow flow ⇒ you straighten straw ⇒ you have fast flow.* That's another reinforcement contingency, this time based on the increase in the amount of the reinforcer, not the mere presentation of it. Just to keep life simple, we won't put *increase* in the formal definition, but you should understand that we're always implying it.

[5]This last clause is a little redundant, because if a reinforcer is presented, the frequency will increase, by definition. But redundancy in the name of effective teaching is no vice.

[6]Incidentally, we talk about a *reinforcement contingency* wherein the response caused the reinforcer to occur; and as a result, the future frequency of that response increases. But suppose the reinforcer accidentally followed the response a time or two, but the response didn't cause the reinforcer to occur. In other words, it was just an accident that the reinforcer happened to follow the response. Would that accidental relation between the response and the reinforcer also increase the future frequency of the response? Would reinforcement have occurred? Yes. The important thing is that the reinforcer immediately follow the response. All a contingency does is guarantee that the reinforcer will immediately follow the response often enough that you will get a significant increase in the frequency of the response. The contingency is just a practical way of making sure you reinforce what you want to reinforce. In Chapter 18, *Time-Dependent Schedules,* we'll talk about *superstitious behavior* resulting from such accidental contingencies.

sponse of making a sensible remark caused the presentation of the grandmother's reinforcing smile. So this was a response-caused presentation of a reinforcing smile. It was a response-contingent presentation of a reinforcer. Her reinforcing smile was contingent on his response. Her smile was response contingent. Or we might say, *response dependent.* Whether or not she smiled depended on his response of making a sensible remark.

Also, when we use *response* we mean essentially the same thing as *behavior.* We don't necessarily mean *response* in the sense of a *response (or reaction) to something.*

RESPONSE = BEHAVIOR

Again, how immediate is immediate? Certainly less than 60 seconds; ideally, only a fraction of a second. But it's not all or nothing; as the delay between the response and the outcome increases, there is a rapid decrease in the effectiveness of the reinforcement contingency. This is described in the following principle.

Definition: Principle
Outcome Gradient
  ○ The effect of reinforcement and punishment procedures decrease
  ○ as the delay between the response and the outcome increases.
  ○ Reinforcers and aversive conditions delayed more than 60 seconds
  ○ have little or no reinforcing or punishing effect.

Generic Reinforcement Contingency

Results: Response frequency increases.

Each time the grandfather said something sensible, the grandmother said a few kind words and caressed him—reinforcement by the presentation of reinforcers. And each time his grandmother properly reinforced his grandfather's talking, Juke immediately praised her—more reinforcement by the presentation of reinforcers.

In Chapter 1, Rod cries and Dawn runs into his bedroom—unplanned reinforcement by presenting reinforcers. Dawn reinforces the crying response, increasing the frequency of Rod's crying on future nights.

In the same way, the student and staff attention reinforces Eric's throwing fits.

We hope the new concepts you learn as you read this book reinforce your reading so that you'll become a behavior analysis junkie—or at least finish this book.

By the way, we've added a phrase to the usual definition of the concept of *reinforcement.* We've added that an *increase* in a reinforcer also will reinforce behavior. In other words, behavior analysts usually recognize that reinforcement will occur if Dawn attends to Rod when no one was attending to him before. However, we want to point out that reinforcement also will occur when she increases the extent that she attends to him: Perhaps at first she was only looking at him, but now she picks him up, caresses him, and talks to him Rod is getting more reinforcers, and that increase in reinforcers should reinforce whatever he was doing at the time—perhaps smiling or perhaps still crying.

You can strengthen concrete by sticking steel rods in it. Then you have reinforced concrete. You can strengthen behavior by sticking a reinforcer after it. Then you have reinforced behavior. Of course, reinforcement for the civil engineer differs from reinforcement for the behavioral engineer. But they're similar, too.

Here's a hypothetical example: Your professor's calling on you reinforces raising your hand in class. Laughing at your professor's jokes reinforces your professor's telling jokes. Your professor's jokes reinforce your efforts to stay awake. But eventually sleep wins. Then your startle response reinforces the professor's telling a boisterous joke about the student sleeping in the back row.

More examples: We take a bite of a delicious apple—reinforcement by the presentation of a reinforcer, the taste. We take a delicious kiss—reinforcement by the presentation of a reinforcer. We watch a TV show—reinforcement. True, the reinforcers from watching the tube often hold little value—you don't get much out of it; but then you don't put much into it either, as you sit there like a spaced-out zombie, staring at some lame *Leave It to Beaver* show. Hang your head in shame! Why aren't you reading *Principles of Behavior* instead? Reinforcement by the presentation of fascinating new knowledge. (Of course, we're just interpreting everyday life. To be sure we're interpreting correctly, we would have to show that our assumed reinforcers really are reinforcers. And assuming they're reinforcers without checking them out can lead to failure when trying to modify behavior.)

Question

Rod toddles quickly across the room, falls down, and hurts himself. Is this reinforcement?

Our Answer

Is getting hurt a reinforcer? No. Will getting hurt cause the quick toddling to occur more frequently? No. So for those two reasons this is not reinforcement. As you will see in Chapter 4, it's punishment.

QUESTION

1. *Reinforcement contingency*—define it and diagram three examples.
   Warning: Each line of a definition is a separate, crucial component of the definition. Any line missing means you ain't got it. My students sometimes leave out "immediate." Unfortunately, their definition is counted wrong when they do. And "immediate" will crop up in quite a few of the definitions to come. Remember, precision is next to godliness.

2. *Reinforce*—define it and correctly use it in a sentence.

3. *The principle of the outcome-gradient effect*—state it.

Concept
BEHAVIORAL CONTINGENCY

There is a **contingency** between Rod's tantrums and Dawn's attending. Put another way, there is a **dependency** between the tantrums and the attending. The attention depends on the crying: no crying, no attention or, at least, less attention. So a **contingency** is a *dependency* or a *causal relationship.* And **to be contingent** means *to be dependent on or to be caused by.*

Now don't let "dependency" mislead you. We say Janis was *dependent* on heroin. Would we also say she was *contingent* on heroin? No. We don't mean "dependent" in that sense; we don't mean "reliant" or "addicted."

And we might say Rod is a *dependent* infant. But would we also say he is a *contingent* infant? Of course not. We don't mean "dependent" in that sense either. We don't mean "helpless" or "weak." We also wouldn't say Sally has a *contingent* personality.

What would we say? Getting good grades is *contingent* on studying. Sid's happiness is *contingent* on Dawn's saying she loves him. Your car's starting is *contingent* on your turning the key in the ignition. Mae and Juke's going to the beach is *contingent* on the weather.[7]

Thus, Dawn's attention is often *contingent* on (dependent on or caused by) Rod's crying. Of course, she sometimes attends to him when he's not crying; so on those occasions her attention is not contingent on his crying. Note that we would not normally say Rod's crying is contingent on Dawn's attention.

And we'd say the grandmother's smiles are contingent on the grandfather's sensible remarks, but we wouldn't normally say his remarks are contingent on her smiles.

Definition: Concept
Behavioral contingency
  ○ The occasion for a response (behavior),
  ○ the response (behavior), and
  ○ the outcome of the response (behavior).

Here are some other behavioral contingencies:

Your boyfriend's being with you is the **occasion** in the presence of which crying and smiling will produce their outcomes—a kiss. Your teacher's looking at you is the **occasion** in the presence of which raising your hand will produce the outcome of being called on. *The **occasion** is a stimulus, event, or condition in the presence of which a particular response (behavior) will produce a particular outcome.*

In Chapter 12, we introduce *discriminative stimulus,* the technical term for *occasion,* as behavior analysts use the word. So we will make no further use of this concept until that chapter.[8] Just note that

---

[7]Andy Lattal and Al Poling pointed out that the dictionary definition of *contingency* is almost the opposite of the customary behavior-analysis definition. The dictionary says *contingency is the condition of being dependent on chance.* But we think it will cause less confusion if we stick with the behavior-analysis definition provided in the text.

[8]Our experience has been that introducing *occasion* in a formal way causes much more trouble than it's worth. However, we will be able to deal gracefully with nondiscriminated contingencies and pussyfoot around the discriminative stimulus in discriminated contingencies until we get to Chapter 12, where we can give the concept of discriminative stimulus the rigorous treatment it needs; then the students can use it correctly. We've found that introducing discriminative stimuli prematurely is asking for trouble.

By *nondiscriminated contingencies,* we mean those contingencies for which the response will produce the reinforcing outcome on almost any occasion. For example, almost always when you breathe, you will get air. We've found that many, if not most contingencies in everyday life are nondiscriminated, and a premature introduction of the concept of discriminative stimulus causes students to try to force a discriminative stimulus on every contingency, even when it doesn't fit. But we'll deal extensively with this later.

---

the *occasion* and the *before condition*[9] are **not** the same thing.

We usually leave the before condition in the contingency diagram, even though it's not an official part of the definition of a behavioral contingency. We stress the before condition because it helps students distinguish between the various types of contingencies we'll be looking at in the remaining chapters.

So you can see the contingency between the behavior and the reinforcer is the big deal. The reinforcer is **contingent** on the behavior; in other words, the reinforcer **depends** on the behavior, or the reinforcer is **caused by** the behavior. And that behavior-reinforcer contingency results in the reinforcement of the behavior; put another way, the behavior occurs more frequently. In turn, the reinforcement makes future occurrences of the behavior more frequent.

When *behavior analysts* talk about reinforcement contingencies, they mean *the **contingent relation** between the behavior and the outcome.* And the reinforcer is always the outcome. There are a couple of other dependencies, but they aren't what the behaviorists are referring to. In a sense, the behavior is contingent on the occasion, in that the behavior occurs more frequently when the proper occasion arises. And in a sense, the occurrence of future responses is dependent or contingent on past reinforcement of that response class. But, by custom, neither of those two types of contingencies is what behavior analysts emphasize when they talk about behavioral contingencies.

So it's true that improved performance depends on reinforcement. But we wouldn't say the behavioral contingency is between the reinforcement and the improved performance. However, we would say the behavioral contingency is between the behavior and the delivery of the reinforcer.

---

[9]For those of you familiar with the concept *establishing operation,* the before condition is also not necessarily the same as the establishing operation, except in the case of reflexive establishing operations, as you will see in Chapter 9.

Now, to really understand a concept, you need to be familiar with nonexamples of the concept as well as examples. So let's take a look at a few noncontingent events. *A **noncontingent event** is an event that is not dependent on anything.* The kind of contingencies in which we are most interested are response contingencies, contingencies where the event is contingent on the response (caused by the behavior). So when we speak of noncontingent events, we mean events that aren't contingent on the response of interest.

In theory, at least, a parent's love should be noncontingent; that is, the parent should not make the love contingent on the child's behavior. On the other hand, the wise parent will provide approval only when the child is behaving well. So approval would be contingent.[10]

You might think rain is contingent on your going on picnics. But it probably is noncontingent. However, your going on picnics is contingent on its not raining. Or what about the child who sneezed right before the electricity failed and the lights went out all over New York City? The power failure was not contingent (dependent) on the sneeze. The lights would have gone out even if the child had held back the sneeze.

QUESTIONS

1. *Behavioral contingency*—define it and give an example.
2. Use some version of the verbal expression, *to be contingent,* in a nontrivial sentence. By trivial I mean like "I must use 'to be contingent' in a sentence." In other words, I want you to use "to be contingent" in a way that shows you understand how to use the term correctly. For example, "Attention is contingent on Rod's crying."

SID'S ADVANCED SEMINAR IN BEHAVIOR ANALYSIS

Sid: OK, our first seminar went well, except I did all the talking. Of course, the chance to talk nonstop for 2 hours is a big reinforcer for me. But that

---

[10]Incidentally, students sometimes raise the point that the teacher's approval isn't always a reinforcer, especially for older children when they're in front of their buddies. In that case, we would call the approval a *conditional reinforcer*—approval is a reinforcer **conditional upon** (depending on) the absence of the buddies. In other words, the conditional reinforcer is the compound stimulus consisting of approval **and** all buddies absent.

may not be the best way for you to learn behavior analysis. I want you to learn how to think and talk like a behavior analyst. But if all you do is listen to me, then all you may learn is how to watch a behavior analyst think and how to listen to a behavior analyst talk. You learn what you do, at least if what you do gets reinforced. So I want you to start thinking and talking. Meanwhile, I'll keep thinking but do less talking. So who's first? Who wants to start thinking and talking like a behavior analyst?

Suddenly six sets of eyes looked everywhere but at Sid. Silence. Sixty seconds of aversive silence. A cough. More silence.

Sid: OK, let's put it this way: You've had a chance to read the first chapter of *Principles of Behavior.* What do you think about the concepts of *reinforcer* and *reinforcement?* Do you have any questions? Any comments?

Silence for another awkward 60 seconds.

Sid: OK, let's put it this way: We just did a 2-minute baseline. Now we'll intervene. You earn a point every time you recite, at least if you say something relevant. The points will all count toward your final grade. They add in with your weekly quizzes, term paper, and midterm and final exams. Now, any questions or comments?

Ten more seconds of silence. Max raised his hand.

Sid: Yes, Max?

Max: Is this behavioral intervention a reinforcement procedure?

Sid: Why don't you tell me?

Max: I think it is.

Sid: What's the behavior?

Max: Saying something relevant?

Sid: Right. And what's the reinforcer?

Max: The points.

Sid: You get 1 point! Next?

Joe: I don't think you should be so sure you've got a reinforcer.

Max: Why not?

Joe: You don't know for sure that your points are a reinforcer. To know if they're reinforcers, you'd have to show that our talking increases because of their contingent use.

Sid: Excellent objection. I'm only assuming I've got a reinforcer. And you've just earned one assumed reinforcer.

QUESTIONS

1. Give an example of an assumed reinforcement contingency in college teaching.
2. How can you tell if the points are reinforcers?

Example
Behavioral Special Education
THE NONCONTINGENT DELIVERY OF REINFORCERS

Skip Larson was the principal of Street School, an alternative high school for street kids, dropouts who spent most of their time hanging out. He and Mae were chatting.

Mae asked, "So how are things going at Street School these days?"

Skip answered, "Not bad, except we have a hell of an attendance problem. Trying to keep those kids in school's like trying to keep water in a sieve."

"You mean they walk out in the middle of school?"

"Yeah—if they show in the first place. We have about 30% attendance. The lowest in the district."

"What do their parents say?"

"Darn little, if they say anything at all. They're as hard to get a hold of as the kids. Some kids don't seem to have parents. Any ideas?"

"I'm not sure. You've got a tough one, all right," Mae paused a moment, to give the impression that she was thinking, before she started giving the advice she had given so often before to other principals and teachers. "I'm not sure, but I think you have to make Street School the best game in town, the most reinforcing place these kids can find. It's got to beat the street."

"Yes, but they've got to work in school. It can't be all fun."

Mae thought, another yes-but guy, but she said, "You've got a good point there. Still, you might need to flood your school with reinforcers."

"Yes, but I've heard you say noncontingent reinforcers don't work."

"True," Mae said, "if the reinforcers are not contingent on specific behaviors at school you won't get much learning. But if you simply fill your school with free reinforcers, reinforcers that are not contingent on studying, they still will be contingent on one crucial behavior." Mae paused, to give Skip a chance to ask, "What's that?"

"Going to school," Mae replied. "Creating a generally reinforcing environment should reinforce entering that environment. And being a generally reinforcing person should reinforce interacting with that person." Mae smiled, an act that reinforced

Skip's interacting with her, though both were unaware of the reinforcement taking place before their eyes.

"So, we should make sure that even a poor student contacts plenty of reinforcers in school. That way, the kid will need less coercion to get him or her to come to school."

"I think you're right, Skip."

Now Skip smiled—at least for Skip, a smile indicates that he just received a reinforcer.

Mae went on, "But, of course, the more we also manage to make those reinforcers contingent on studying, the more frequently we will reinforce studying and the more the poor student will learn."

"And the more the kid will change from a loser into a winner."

This is an example of the **environmental-quality general rule**—*you can increase the frequency of entering a setting by putting more reinforcers in that setting, but you will have to make some reinforcers contingent on productive behavior if you want to increase productivity in that setting.*

We make a big deal of the fallacy of environmental quality, because we think it's a loser, not because it's a winner. Most people change the environmental quality with the false notion that it will increase productivity, not with the correct notion that all it will do is increase the frequency of entering a setting. The problem is that such people don't understand the principle of reinforcement—the need for making reinforcers **contingent** on the behavior they want to increase. This general rule is not a basic one in behavior analysis; it's mainly something you should know about so you can avoid being confused by it.

(By the way, when we critique the notion of *environmental quality,* we're using the phrase in a different way than those concerned with the protection of our environment. We, too, think a clean, healthy, well-preserved environment is crucial to the salvation of humanity.)

Example
Organizational Behavior Management[11]
THE NONCONTINGENT DELIVERY OF REINFORCERS

Dorra Dollar (President of Monster Machines, Inc.): Productivity is down 25% in the last quarter. How can we expect good Americans to buy our cars if we don't manufacture them? Before long, we'll

---

[11]We tend to use interchangeably the terminology *organizational behavior management* (OBM) and *behavioral industrial-organizational* (behavioral I/O).

all be driving foreign cars if we keep going at this rate. Now's the time for you high-priced consultants to earn your keep. Give me a hand with this one.

Harry Human (Representative from Sensitive Souls, Inc.): Well, frankly, Ms. Dollar, who could work in this icky factory? It's so gray and cold. You need to add many rich warm colors. And add music. Yes, some peppy music to make the workers want to work. And company picnics where they can get to know you better.

Dorra Dollar: Sounds good to me. Now let's hear from the new kid. What do you call yourself? A behavior analyst? Well, what do you think of Harry's proposal.

You (Representative from Behavior Analysts, Unincorporated—your first day on the job since graduating from the university last week):

(Please fill in the blank with your response to Dorra's question. Indicate what's wrong with Harry Human's suggestion—how it is a case of a misunderstanding of the environmental-quality general rule, and show how your use of contingent reinforcers would increase productivity.)

Dorra Dollar: The most brilliant, yet tactful, critique I've ever heard. Would you consider heading our Department of Human Resources? Of course, we'll double your current salary.

Harry Human: I've got to hand it to you kid, you sure know your stuff.

You: Gee, thanks. I owe it all to my diligent study of *Principles of Behavior.*

Harry Human: Where can I get a copy of that book?

QUESTION

1. *The general rule of environmental quality*—give a couple of examples.

THE DELIVERY OF REINFORCERS BEFORE THE BEHAVIOR

Remember the reinforcement principle? *A response will occur more frequently in the future if a reinforcer or an increase in a reinforcer has immediately followed it in the past.* Check out that word *followed.* Remember it, and it'll save you grief. The reinforcer must follow the response for reinforcement to occur.

Is "thanks" a reinforcer? Might be. Does thanking in advance reinforce the behavior thanked? No way. The reinforcer must follow the behavior, not precede it.

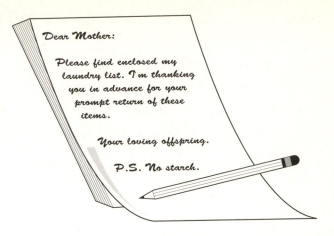

Dear Mother:

Please find enclosed my laundry list. I'm thanking you in advance for your prompt return of these items.

Your loving offspring.

P.S. No starch.

The Bribe

The sleazy, middle-aged man pulled an envelope out of his pocket and slipped it into the hand of the tall, lean, young woman. Then he spoke without looking her in the eye and without removing the cigarette from the corner of his mouth. His left eyebrow twitched as he said, "The odds are 5 to 1 in favor of your team's winning the NCAA volleyball championship. Mr. Big has bet much money on your team's losing. So here's $10,000 for you to throw the game."

Reinforcement? No. Because, the $10,000 comes before the despicable act, not right after it.

Bribery? Yes. Bribery is the use of a reinforcer, often (but not always) given in advance, for the performance of an illegal or immoral act.

But advanced payment for a good deed isn't bribery. For example, paying someone $20 before she mows your lawn isn't reinforcement, because it occurs before the act. But it isn't bribery either, because lawn mowing is neither illegal nor immoral.

And payment after an evil deed is bribery. For example, Evil Ernie could pay someone after the person helped him cheat on an exam.

We make a big deal of bribery because critics often accuse behavior analysts of using bribery. Such critics aren't thinking too clearly. True, bribery involves reinforcers. True, the behavior analysts' reinforcement uses reinforcers. But that doesn't make reinforcement the same as bribery. Along the same line, our critics get paid for their work, and, no doubt, that pay is a reinforcer. But that doesn't make their pay for their work the same as bribery. Here's the crucial moral distinction: On the one hand, bribery involves reinforcers for immoral or **illegal** deeds; on the other hand, the behavior analysts' use of reinforcement and most pay-for-work involves reinforcers for **good** deeds.

Note that we usually assume money is a reinforcer even when it's not being used in a reinforcement procedure. For example, giving money in advance of the behavior isn't reinforcement for that behavior, but the money is probably a reinforcer. That means we could use the money to reinforce behavior if we made that money contingent on some behavior.

They "Should Ought" to Want to Do It

Now here's what may be part of the confusion: In our culture, many people have a sort of simple-minded, false morality, whereby they don't want to give someone a reinforcer for doing something they think the person should do without that added reinforcer.

Parents don't want to give their kids special treats for being good because kids should ought to want to be good without the treat. Teachers don't want to give their students special privileges for doing well on quizzes because students should ought to want to do well on quizzes without the special privilege contingency. And employers don't want to give their workers time off from work for meeting production goals because the workers should ought to want to meet the goals without the time-off contingency.

This is a false morality because using reinforcers in these sorts of contingent ways can only make life better for everyone. No one gets hurt. Refusing to do it is cutting off your nose to spite your face. Nonetheless, many people object. And when they do so, they often say I don't want to **bribe** my kids, my students, my workers. But we think they're just confusing their own cultural prejudices with bribery. (By the way, we borrowed the phrase *they should ought to want to do it* from Robert Mager, one of the most prominent teachers of performance management in the field.)

QUESTION

1. Give two examples that at first glance might appear to be reinforcement but are not because the apparent reinforcer comes before the response.

Example of Reinforcement
Behavioral Child and Family Counseling
BUBBLEGUM AND BOWEL
MOVEMENTS—PART I[12]

Soon after Dawn arrived at her office in the psychology clinic, she got a phone call.

"This is Dr. Baker. Can I help you?" she said.

---
[12]Based on Tomlinson, J. R. (1970). Bowel retention. *Journal of Behavior Therapy and Experimental Psychiatry, 1,* 83–85.

"Yes, Dr. Baker, this is Dr. Mario Acosta from the children's wing of University Hospital. I've got a problem—a 3-year-old boy, Todd. For the last year he's been averaging only one bowel movement per week; sometimes he goes for 10 days without a bowel movement; he claims it hurts."

I'd think it would after a week, Dawn thought.

"We've done all the exams in the book, including a barium enema x-ray."

Dawn flinched; she had gone through that procedure herself—not something she wanted to try again.

"The exams found nothing. We've changed his diet several times; only helps for a week or so. The poor kid is hurting, and we've done all we can. Would you look at him?"

The next day Dawn talked to Todd and his mother. She thought about her little boy as the mother described the discomfort Todd suffered. Then she thought of Sid and how he would laugh at the simple-minded solution she was mulling over. If a behavior isn't occurring often enough, what can you do? Well, you can try to reinforce that behavior. Reinforce bowel movements? Sounds crazy. Let's hope it doesn't sound crazy to Todd's mother.

After talking more, Dawn said, "Here's what I'd like you to do. I'd like you to give Todd a reinforcer each time he has a bowel movement. I think that will help him. Within a few weeks, he should be having a bowel movement almost every day." She tried to sound more confident than she was.

"Are you serious, Dr. Baker? I don't see how a reward can help Toddie with his natural biological processes."

"No guarantees, but it's our best first bet. Besides, Dr. Acosta said he'd prescribe a mild laxative to reduce the pain. Also, the laxative will help Todd have some bowel movements so you will be able to use the reinforcers."

"What should I use as a reinforcer, Doctor?" While the mother asked her question, Todd pulled on her sleeve and mumbled something Dawn couldn't hear. The mother reached in her purse, pulled out a piece of bubblegum, unwrapped it, and gave it to her son—a well-practiced ritual.

Dawn said, "Bubblegum."

"Oh, I'm sorry," the mother said. "How rude I am. Would you like a piece of bubblegum, Doctor?"

"No, thank you. I meant use bubblegum as the reinforcer."

Todd's mother did use Dawn's procedure and the bubblegum reinforcer. She gave Todd a piece of gum immediately after each bowel movement, but not before.

Dawn's simple intervention worked! If you want a behavior to occur more frequently, reinforce it. During the 2nd week, Todd had six bowel movements. He was a proud young man—a young man in control. From the 4th week on, he had six or seven bowel movements each week (Figure 2.1).

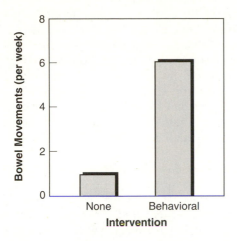

Figure 2.1   Bubblegum Reinforcement of Bowel Movements

This happened each week, except one. Todd spent the 14th week with his grandmother, but his parents had forgotten to tell her about the bubblegum intervention. So Todd fell to a humiliating and painful two bowel movements that week. Then he returned home to his bubblegum contingency, he became his old six- or seven-per-week self again.

Todd's mother confessed a side benefit of the bubblegum contingency: "Dr. Baker, I didn't tell you, but Todd and I hadn't been getting along too well. I used to nag at him about his bowel movements and force him to sit on the stool for long periods of time. All without success. And my temper got short at times. But now we're getting along just great. It's fun to be a mother again. I like giving him his reinforcer."

Todd was happy, his mother and father were happy, his grandmother was happy, Dawn was happy. Everyone was happy, except Sid. "Fine, now you've got a 3-year-old kid addicted to bubblegum? A bubblegum monkey on his back. Will his mother have to go to college with him to deliver the bubblegum after each little success?"

Sometimes Dawn wished Sid were less of a wet blanket, but, as usual, he had a good point mixed in with his sarcasm. Now what should she do? Future chapters, dear reader, will tell.

QUESTION

1. Suppose you had a child with severe problems of bowel retention. How could you use the principle of reinforcement to help the child? Describe:
    a. the behavior.
    b. the contingency.
    c. the reinforcer.
    d. the expected results.

Example of Reinforcement
Behavioral School Psychology
POVERTY'S CHILDREN—PART I[13]

Mae's father, the Reverend E. L. Robinson, had programmed a set of values deep into Mae's soul. She should always give 10%, a tithe, to the church and more to the black community. Nothing is lower than black folks who forget where they had come from. You have the blessing of a fine education. You have the blessing of a fine job. Now you've got to give some of that back to where you came from, and Mae knew he did not mean back to her parents.

Reverend Robinson had retired from the pulpit, but he hadn't stopped preaching. Every Sunday night, when Mae called home, she got a sermon. He didn't exactly ask her what she had done for the black community that week, but he might as well have.

So Mae couldn't refuse when some friends from her sorority asked her if they could use one of her classrooms as a preschool for 15 children from low-income families, especially when she found out they were black children. Not only did she find the space, but she also found some money to run the program. And she herself helped supervise.

Her friends enrolled fifteen 4- and 5-year-old children in the preschool. Then Mae's staff went through the ritual of giving the children the Peabody Picture Vocabulary Test. And they got the results Mae knew they would. The children scored an average of 79, 21 points below the national average. This meant terrible language skills, of course. Poverty almost forces you to have weak formal language skills. If you're poor and you're 4 or 5 years old, you hardly have a chance, at least not in school.

Even though Mae knew how the tests would turn out, hearing the results depressed her. She hated psychological tests. They didn't help people. They just pigeonholed victims. Then the authorities would have an excuse for failing to teach the children.

When Mae talked to Juke about the results, he reminded her that the tests were culturally biased.

---

[13]Based on Hart, B. M., & Risley, T. R. (1968). Establishing use of descriptive adjectives in the spontaneous speech of disadvantaged preschool children. *Journal of Applied Behavior Analysis, 1,* 109–120.

For example, these white-oriented tests didn't measure the rich, expressive language her black children had.

True, but the tests did predict how a poor black child would do in school. With a score of 79, they had terrible formal language skills and would most likely fail in school.

Juke also reminded her that IQ tests measure learned behavior, not some innate intelligence.

True.

Then all Mae had to do was to teach her 15 children what they would need to know so they could succeed in school. Wasn't she the best behavior analyst in the school system? So what if everyone else had failed in trying to help kids like these. Not many people who really cared about black children knew as much about behavior analysis as she did. She could do it.

Thank God for Juke. She would do it.

That night, Mae couldn't sleep. The test showed that these children have terrible language skills. And the national statistics show that if you have terrible language skills, you're likely to fail in school. (Fifty percent of the black students in Detroit never make it through high school.) If you're poor and black, you hardly have a chance. (Forty-five percent of the black children in the United States live in poverty, with family incomes of less than $10,000 per year.) If you're poor and black and you fail in school, you're likely not to find a good job, or any job. (The unemployment rate is more than twice as high for blacks as for whites.) If you don't find a job, you're more likely to die a violent death before you're 30. (Forty-eight black males and eight white males per 100,000 were homicide victims.) You're more likely to do time in prison. (Though blacks were only 12% of the population, they were 46% of the people arrested for violent crimes.) You're more likely to try heroin. Your children are more likely to die before they're old enough to enter preschool. (Eighteen out of 1,000 black infants died, in comparison with 8 out of 1,000 white infants.)[14] And your children who do survive? They're likely to end as more victims in the statistics of black poverty. Also your grandchildren after them. And your great grandchildren, too.

Mae knew these horrible statistics by heart. And she knew they didn't apply to middle-class blacks like herself. They applied to the 45% of the black children who were victims of poverty. They applied to her 15 children. She also knew this sounded melodramatic, like something out of a soap opera, but it was true. All the data on poverty and race said so, and she'd seen too much of it to deny

the statistics. She knew that poverty wasn't a direct cause of these problems, but the conditions so often associated with poverty were. She had to change some of those conditions.

Only Mae could save those 15 children and the generations that would follow them. Mae tried to tell herself that she exaggerated, but she knew these particular statistics didn't lie. And she knew that if she didn't help these particular 15 children, no one would. Only she could help these children get the skills they needed to pull themselves out of poverty and poverty's fate. These thoughts frightened her, but they also made her high. This was life with a purpose!

The next day Mae and the preschool teachers started a program to help the children. What were their language skill deficits? After a few observations, the teachers concluded that the children rarely used adjectives. They might say *car*, but not *red car*; they might say *ball*, but not *big ball*. They didn't use color names, size, shape, or numbers.

So what should the teachers do? Try reinforcement—what else! Using adjectives is behavior. If behavior doesn't occur often enough, reinforce it. Each time a teacher heard a child correctly using an adjective with a noun (*red car*), the teacher would smile at the child and offer an approving comment. The teachers used this reinforcement procedure throughout the 3-hour session every morning, during breakfast, structured time, and free play—wall-to-wall reinforcement of adjectives.

And what happened? Nothing! Twenty-eight class sessions. Nothing. A dismal three or four adjectives per hour. Nothing.

Should we conclude that the children were genetically inferior, as some racists argue? That they were too dumb to learn? Mae knew that wasn't true. Should we conclude that reinforcement didn't work with these children? Mae knew that wasn't true; reinforcement works with all God's creatures. Should we conclude that the teachers' approval wasn't a reinforcer? Perhaps, but Mae didn't think so; she'd never known anyone for whom approval wasn't a big reinforcer. Then what should we conclude? Mae wasn't sure.

She and the teachers talked it over. Maybe the children didn't have the words in their vocabulary, in their repertoire. And even if they could say the words, maybe they couldn't use them correctly. Even if they could say *car*, maybe they couldn't say *two cars, red car, small car, long car*, at least not at the right time. Hard to believe, but maybe.

For the time being, they would conclude that the children's baseline rate (preintervention rate) of using adjectives correctly was too low for reinforcement to have much effect. Maybe the frequency of using adjectives was too low to provide enough

---

[14]All these stats are from 1985.

occasions for reinforcement. The children had to respond correctly at least sometimes so the teachers could reinforce those responses frequently enough to produce an effect. So maybe they hadn't had wall-to-wall reinforcement.

Poverty had won this round, but Mae, the teachers, and her 15 children hadn't quit fighting. You'll read more about their noble battle with poverty in a later chapter.

QUESTIONS

1. How does poverty relate to language skills and IQ scores? Language skills and success in school? Success in school and employment? Employment and a halfway decent life for yourself? Employment and a halfway decent life for your children, for your grandchildren, for your great-grandchildren?

2. After an initial failure to improve behavior with a reinforcement procedure, what should we *not* conclude about the person's genetic quality, intelligence, ability to learn, ability to have behavior reinforced?

BASIC ENRICHMENT

In the Skinner Box
Experimental Analysis of Behavior
REINFORCEMENT WITH WATER

You're looking through a small window at a white laboratory rat (Rudolph) in a rat-sized room—about 1-foot square. Three inches from the floor, a small lever sticks out of the side of a wall. There is a dime-sized hole in the floor, beneath the lever. The rat presses the lever downward with its forepaws. You hear the click of a tiny water dipper as he comes to the hole. The dipper is large enough to hold only one drop of water. The rat also hears the click and is off the lever and onto the cup in a flash, licking it dry. Then he raises back up to the lever, presses it again, and the whole cycle repeats itself. You're witnessing reinforcement of the lever-press response by the presentation of a reinforcer (the drop of water).

This drama is taking place in a Skinner box. (Douglas Ellson was the first to invent this test chamber, and Burrhus Frederick Skinner made it the most famous apparatus in the history of psychology. Skinner preferred to call this apparatus an experimental space, but we'll stick with the simpler and more popular name, for two reasons: First, more people will know what we mean, and second, it's easier to say.)

If you ever get a chance to work with a rat in a Skinner box, grab it. Reading about reinforcement is like reading about sex. It's not bad, but it hardly compares to the real thing. Nowhere else can you see the process of reinforcement so clearly and so powerfully as in the Skinner box—the microscope of behavior analysis. We aren't saying you'll come to prefer the Skinner box to sex. But we are saying you'll become a true believer when you see the ef-

fects of reinforcement, as you give the rat a drop of water each time the rat presses the lever.

Professor Skinner and those who joined him did all the original research in behavior analysis, using rats and then pigeons in Skinner boxes. He started this research in the early 1930s. Even today, most of the basic research in behavior analysis takes place in the Skinner box, though the experiments have grown to a complexity and subtlety that you could hardly imagine from a simple rat in a simple box.

We introduce you to the Skinner box because it gives us a simple situation where we can look at the basic principles of behavior. We will touch bases with it throughout the book. For the time being, you've seen how reinforcement works in the Skinner box: The rat is deprived of water for a few hours. Then each time he presses the lever, he gets a drop of water. And so he presses the lever frequently (several times a minute).

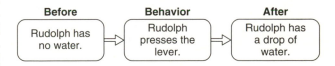

Before	Behavior	After
Rudolph has no water.	Rudolph presses the lever.	Rudolph has a drop of water.

The water is contingent on Rudolph's lever press, but we wouldn't normally say his lever press is contingent on the water.

A *Skinner box* is a test chamber with a response device and a source of reinforcers. *(Of course, some of us think the whole world is just one big Skinner box. Others find that thought very disturbing—or very disturbed.)*

QUESTION

1. *Skinner box*—give an example of its use. In the example, describe:
   a. the apparatus
   b. the procedure
   c. the results

General Rule
AVOID CIRCULAR REASONING

Here's another way to express the problem. Why does Rudolph drink the water? Because he wants it. How do you know he wants the water. Because he drinks it. Why does he drink the water? Because he wants it. How do you . . . and around and around in a circular reasoning pattern resembling Rudolph chasing his own tail.

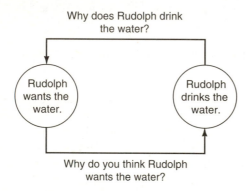

In other words, this attempt at an explanation looks like an explanation, but it ain't. It looks like we've added some new information, when we say *Rudolph wants the water.* But that only gives us a false sense of understanding. To say *Rudolph wants the water* doesn't tell us anything we don't already know; it just tells us that Rudolph is drinking the water. That's circular reasoning.

What would be a noncircular explanation? Rudolph drinks the water because the temperature in his box is 120°F. That's new information. How do you know the temperature is 120°? That's what the thermometer reads. (We don't say, *because Rudolph drinks the water;* that would be circular.)

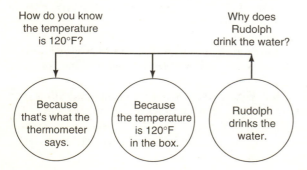

So whenever you're talkin' technical, don't use *want*, because it probably means you're caught in the horrible trap of circular reasoning.

Circular reasoning occurs when the only proof you have is the existence of the thing you're trying to prove.

> **Avoid circular reasoning!**

QUESTION

1. What's the name for the kind of reasoning involved with terms like *want*?
2. Diagram an example of circular reasoning.

CIRCULAR REASONING AND THE ERROR OF REIFICATION

I think the major problem with psychology is the high frequency with which psychologists and psychiatrists invent explanations for behavioral (psychological) problems. And they always seem to commit the **error of reification** when they invent these explanations.

> *Definition: Concept*
> **The error of reification**
> ○ To call a process or activity a thing.

For example, why does she act so strangely (**an activity**)? Easy, because she has a mental illness (**a thing**). And how do you know she has a mental illness? You've got it: because she acts so strangely.

I call this type of reification *circular reification*—inferring an internal entity which is just a label for the behavior.[15] And we'd justify our inferred per-

_____

[15]I think there is also a second type of reification, which I call *process reification*—inferring an internal entity which is just a label for a controlling process (typically contingencies). In other words, traditional psychologists infer an internal entity rather than deal directly with the behavioral contingencies that are really controlling the behavior. *Why did Johnny act so selfishly? Because his id is strong and his superego and ego are underdeveloped.* Freud perceptively identified three types of control processes, roughly those involving contingencies with unlearned reinforcers and aversive conditions, those involving moral and religious outcomes, and those involving the learned reinforcers and aversive outcomes associated with being logically correct or incorrect. Then he fell into our culture's reification trap by inferring things called *id, superego,* and *ego.* That's an example of process reification, which may be a subcategory of circular reification.

sonality disturbance by pointing to the behavior as the symptom that proves the existence of the underlying personality disorder.

Almost always when you hear professional psychologists use the term personality, they are committing the serious error of reification. Why does she act in a dysfunctional manner? Because she has a dysfunctional personality. Why does he get drunk and drive fast without his seat belt? Because he has a thrill-seeking personality.

And psychologists have invented a major industry (intellectual and personality testing) based on circular reifications. Why does he act so dumb (activity)? Because he has a low IQ (inferred thing).

QUESTIONS

1. *The error of reification*—define it and give an example.
2. Show how the error of reification is an example of circular reasoning.

OBJECTIVITY VS. SUBJECTIVITY

In The Classroom

Have you ever turned in a term paper for one of your courses and gotten it back only to receive a *C* and not known why you hadn't gotten an *A?* On the other hand, have you ever taken a math exam and known when you turned it in that you would deserve and receive a *C?*

What's the difference? The grading for the essay was **subjective;** you didn't know your teacher's grading criteria; so you didn't know how to evaluate the quality of your essay.

Definition: Concept
Subjective
- ○ The observation,
- ○ measurement,
- ○ or criteria for measurement
- ○ are **not** assessable to more than one person.

An important disadvantage of subjective measures is that independent observers **cannot** reliably agree on the measurement; so you and your professor may not agree that you earned only a *C* on your essay.

Your teacher measured the quality of your essay with criteria only the teacher had, and even if

the teacher had tried he or she would not have been able to list the grading criteria for you.

But your math teacher measured the quality of your math exam using clear-cut, **objective** criteria, and you were painfully aware of those criteria (i.e., whether you had gotten each problem correct).

Definition: Concept
Objective
- ○ The observation,
- ○ measurement,
- ○ or criteria for measurement
- ○ are accessible to any competent observer.

An important advantage of objective measures is that independent observers can reliably agree on the measurement; so you and your professor can reliably agree, though perhaps with reluctance on your part, that you earned only a *C* on your math exam.

In Science

Science is based on objective measures and observations; therefore the science of behavior analysis is based on objective measures and observations. Objective measures allow independent observers to reliably agree on their observations and measurements. This reliable agreement is called *interobserver reliability.* Objectivity and high interobserver reliability are why science in general is such a powerful tool for understanding the nature of the world and how the world works. Objectivity and high interobserver reliability are also why behavior analysis is such a powerful tool for understanding the nature of the psychological world and how that world works.

In the 19th century, psychologists broke away from the discipline of philosophy and struggled to turn psychology into a natural science. But, unfortunately, they had difficulty shedding their history of subjectivism. Though they established an experimental laboratory, they failed to abandon subjectivity. Instead, they attempted to measure the subjective experiences of their experimental subjects. These 19th-century experimental psychologists would present a stimuli to their experimental subjects and ask the subjects to report on the resulting inner, subjective feelings, sensations, and perceptions. But each subject's inner experiences could be observed only by that subject. And, because of this subjectivity, the early experimental psychologists could not achieve interobserver reliability. And because they could not achieve interobserver reliability, they could not develop the base of reliable data necessary for a science.

Fortunately, 20th-century experimental psychologists emancipated psychology from the tradition of subjectivity and concentrated on the objective measurement of psychological phenomena, thereby bringing psychology into the prestigious fraternity of the natural sciences.

In Applications

Unfortunately, applied psychology (e.g., clinical, counseling, educational, and organizational psychology) generally has failed to follow the lead of experimental psychology. Subjectivism still dominates the measurement and evaluation of real-world practice and intervention, especially in clinical/counseling practice, public schools, and business organizations, even though some university research in those areas use objective measures. Therefore, most practice by most psychologists in most applied settings is based on subjective impression rather than scientific proof.

Unfortunately, as a result, there is little reliable evidence that most psychologists in most applied settings are actually helping anyone. And usually, no benefits are found, when the benefits of the psychologists' help are objectively measured and evaluated. This may seem harsh, but the subjective practice of most 21st-century psychologists is so far behind the objective practice of most 21st-century physicians that contemporary psychological practice is more comparable to the primitive, ineffective practice of early 18th-century physicians.

Fortunately, there is a little light in the darkness. That light emanates from the experimental analysis of behavior and applied behavior analysis. The experimental analysis of behavior shares the objective measurement system of general experimental psychology—not surprising. What is surprising is that applied behavior analysis has remained firmly rooted in the objective measurement system of the experimental analysis of behavior, from which it sprang, whereas subjective, applied psychology never had a close relation with objective experimental psychology. As a result, applied behavior analysis has generated a wealth of effective interventions designed to help people lead better lives, interventions that have been objectively, scientifically proven to be effective and helpful, whereas traditional applied psychology has only generated practices that seem very plausible but usually fail to stand up to objective evaluation.

Moral: Just because a psychological intervention makes a lot of sense and sounds good, don't believe it until you see an objective evaluation.

Concept
MEDICAL MODEL MYTH

We behavior analysts are always battling the **medical model myth.** Here's how traditional psychologists apply the medical model to psychology: They say an undesirable behavior is a symptom. And they say the symptom suggests some underlying psychological disease, just as a fever might suggest an infection. So, according to the medical model, Eric's tantrums suggest a more profound underlying psychological problem, perhaps insecurity. We behavior analysts don't trust such interpretations. Instead, we suspect Eric's tantrums are learned behavior reinforced by their immediate consequences—for example, his parents' attention. Behavioral research shows that problem behavior is usually not a symptom of the big deal; it **is** the big deal.

What you see is what you get.
Or maybe what you see is what he's got.

This doesn't mean behavioral problems don't sometimes result from underlying biological problems—for example, brain injury or Down syndrome. Still, traditional psychologists misuse the medical model by guessing about or inventing underlying psychological causes for observable behavior. Then these psychologists end up caring more about their invented causes than about the actual problem—the behavior.

Definition: Concept
Medical model myth
- An erroneous view of human behavior—
- that behavior is always a mere symptom of
- an underlying psychological condition.

The medical model suggests that the behavior is of little importance in its own right. We behavior analysts disagree.

By the way, we're using *model* more or less to mean a representation. In the present context, a medical disease would be a model of a psychological problem, somewhat as a toy airplane would be a model of a real one.

Understand that traditional psychologists who use a medical model don't mean that taking medicine will cure the problem. Instead, they are just guessing that some hidden, deeper, underlying psychological problem causes the obvious behavior problem. The behavior problem is just a symptom of the underlying psychological problem. Behavior analysts think most uses of the medical model in psychology are wrong; it's generally a model to avoid.

QUESTION

1. *Medical model myth*—define it and give examples.

MEDICAL MODEL MYTH[16]

Students say the medical model is a tough concept, so let's look at other examples.

Passive Aggression

A professor once complained about a graduate assistant he was working with. He said, "That guy is passive-aggressive."

"Why do you say that?" I asked.

The professor replied, "Well, he agrees to do tasks I ask him to do. But then he doesn't do them. He's passively aggressing against me because he doesn't like me."

Here's an alternate interpretation, more behavioral: The professor's approval is a powerful reinforcer, and it certainly reinforces the assistant's agreeing to do the tasks. But without clear-cut deadlines, even that powerful reinforcer will fail to control the assistant's behavior—that old devil, procrastination, will take over. The spirit is willing, but the flesh is weak.

Now this isn't just a meaningless academic debate between two professors. The medical model would have us try to correct the hypothesized, deep, underlying problem; this particular medical model would have us try to convince the assistant that the professor is really a good guy and not someone he should try to hurt.

We've had more success with a behavioral approach: For her doctoral dissertation, Barb Fulton[17]

did an experiment, the results of which support a behavioral approach. She measured her assistants' task completion during baseline in which she used a traditional approach of assigning tasks orally and not following up when the assistants didn't complete the tasks. While intervening, she held weekly meetings. There she assigned tasks in writing, gave due dates, and checked that they'd completed the tasks assigned the previous week. Her results are shown in Figure 2.2.

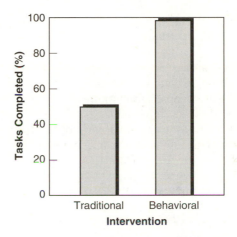

Figure 2.2   Assistants' Task Completion

We'll be using a lot of graphs like this throughout the book, so it's important that you know how to read them. Usually the measure of the results we obtain is shown on the vertical axis and our interventions on the horizontal axis. If you look at the graph of Barb's data you see there were two approaches—the traditional and the behavioral. Now what results did the traditional approach produce? Note that the bar for the traditional approach goes up to about 50% on the vertical axis. So assistants completed about 50% of their tasks when Barb used the traditional approach. In the same way, you can see that they completed almost 100% of their tasks with the behavioral approach. In other words, Barb's behavioral approach was almost twice as effective as the traditional approach.

Fear of Success

Consider the woman who often fails to get her homework done in time to hand it in. Some traditional psychologists might use the medical model to say her failure to hand in her homework is a mere symptom of the underlying cause—an unconscious fear of success. The woman fears that she will lose her feminine charm if she becomes a successful scholar. The guys won't like her. She won't get that

---

[16]The *medical model myth* is a hard concept to come to grips with. It would probably take a couple of chapters to really get it under control because there are so many gray areas and hard-to-decide areas. And we can't afford to devote two chapters just to this topic. However, it is such an important topic that we hoped this brief introduction would be better than none.

[17]Fulton, B. J., & Malott, R. W. (1981–1982). The structured meeting system: A procedure for improving the completion of nonrecurring tasks. *Journal of Organizational Behavior Management, 3(4),* 7–18.

Prince Charming her parents programmed her to pursue.

Here's an alternate view, a behavioral view, of course: Doing almost anything else is more reinforcing and less effortful than doing her homework. So she does everything but her homework.

Most people use the medical model when they explain human behavior. But usually a simpler, behavioral interpretation is more accurate and will help us intervene to better effect.

Other Examples

Why do people smoke cigarettes? Because they have an underlying death wish? Give us a break. How about because smoking has reinforcing chemical effects?

Why does Eric have temper tantrums? Because he has low self-esteem? So much time has been wasted in the futile attempt to improve people's performance by improving their self-esteem that it's a human tragedy, thanks to this misuse of the medical model. Eric has temper tantrums because they are reinforced with attention.

Why does "schizophrenic girl" act one way sometimes and another way other times? Because she has a split personality? No, because sometimes acting one way produces reinforcers and other times acting another way produces the reinforcers.

Prescience

As the science of medicine was developing, it had to battle a superstitious model: Why is that person ill? Because she has evil spirits inside her. How shall we cure her illness? Exorcise the evil spirits. Today the practice of medicine based on science has largely replaced the practice based on superstition.

Psychology has the same problem. As the science of psychology develops, it is having to do battle with a misapplied medical model: Why is the person acting inappropriately? Because she has a mental illness inside her. How shall we help her act appropriately? Cure her mental illness. Today the practice of psychology based on science is struggling to replace the practice based on the misapplied medical model.

Root Causes

Does the medical model address the root causes of psychological problems, and the behavioral model address just the superficial symptoms of the problems? No. The medical model invents fictional cause, and the behavioral model addresses actual cause. It's just that the actual causes of our behavior are often (in some senses) much simpler than a psychodynamic (type of medical model) view of psychology would lead us to think. In other words, we don't smoke cigarettes because we are fixated on our genital stage of infantile development, especially not if we are females; instead, we smoke because smoking behavior is reinforced by the outcome. Granted, figuring out just what those reinforcers are isn't always that simple.

QUESTION

1. Medical model—give examples of how it differs from the behavioral view.

   Hint: When reading examples, be sure you know what they are examples of. Know the title of the chapter you're reading and know the title of the section you're reading, and know how the examples relate to the section headings and chapter titles.

CIRCULAR REASONING AND THE MEDICAL MODEL MYTH

It turns out that what's wrong with most of the medical model applications in psychology is that they're based on circular reasoning.

Why does Eric tantrum? Because he's insecure (underlying psychological condition). How do you know he's insecure? Because he tantrums (a symptom). Circular reasoning.

Why is there this behavior problem? According to the medical model, it's because of an underlying psychological problem. How do you know there's this underlying psychological problem? Because there's the behavior problem that is a symptom of that underlying psychological problem. Circular reasoning.

Why doesn't the grad assistant do the tasks he's agreed to do? Because of his underlying psychological problem of passive aggressivity. How do you know he's passive-aggressive? Because his failure to do what he agreed to do is a symptom of his passive aggressivity. Circular reasoning.[18]

---

[18]I think all instances of the medical model myth are instances of circular reasoning, but not all instances of circular reasoning are instances of the medical model myth. For example, saying *Rudolph drinks water because he wants it* is circular but probably not an example of the medical model myth. Although we don't explicitly say so in our definition, the medical model myth probably best applies to inappropriate behavior or some sort of assumed inappropriate cause.

QUESTION

1. How is the wrong use of the medical model an example of circular reasoning? Please give an example.

HOW TO TALK ABOUT BEHAVIOR

Often people really screw things up when they use everyday language and everyday approaches in a scientific context. Here's an example of what not to say: *Rudolph the rat pressed the lever because he* **expected** *to get a drink of water.* What's wrong with that? *Expected* is what's wrong, for two reasons: First, you don't know what the rat expects; you're making an unjustified inference (guess). Furthermore, your guess is just another example of the error of circular reasoning: Rudolph pressed the lever because he expected water, and you know that he expected water because he pressed the lever, and so on—around and around.

Second, the verb *to expect* describes a pretty complex activity, when you stop to think about it. Probably expecting something involves language skill (verbal behavior). And we have no reason to think rats can talk or even think (as most thinking is probably based on language).

So what should you do? Keep it simple; talk about only what you know. *The rat pressed the lever because that response has produced a drop of water in the past.* Keep it simple.

The same with *knows*. Don't say *the rat knows it will get a drop of water.* More circular reasoning.

And the same with *thinks*. An unjustified circular inference of activity that's probably a little too much for Rudolph.

For example, why does Sid scratch himself? Because he thinks scratching will stop his itch? Really? *Hey, Sid, did you know you were scratching yourself in a private part of your body, when you were standing in front of your class lecturing? Oh, my gosh, no! Was I really? How embarrassing.* See, in this example, not only did Sid not think his scratching would relieve his itch, he didn't even think he was scratching. Of course, the relief from the itch probably reinforced Sid's scratching in the past, and that's why he's doing it now; but that happens automatically, even though Sid isn't even thinking about it. So we can't even assume Sid, let alone Rudolph the Rat knows, expects, or thinks the reinforcer will follow his response. And that's true, even though the occurrence of past reinforcers has reinforced that response and is why Sid or the rat is currently responding.

Along the same line, don't say, *Rudolph the rat* **figured out** *that he would get a drink of water if he pressed the lever.* That implies that Rudolph has language and has thought through the problem, solved it, and now can state the rule describing the contingency to himself. No way. And the same goes for the nonverbal autistic child.

Also stay away from **learned that,** as in *Mr. R. learned that his lever press would produce a drop of water.*

Also, don't say, *Rudolph pressed the lever* **in order to get** *the drop of water.* Don't even say, *Rudolph pressed the lever* **to get** *the water.* Why not? Because that implies a certain intentionality, as though Rudolph has figured out what to do and is doing it because he knows what he'll get for doing it. The same goes for nonverbal human beings. Don't say, *Rod cries* **to get** *attention.* Rod just cries because that behavior has been reinforced. Along the same lines, don't say, *Rod's* **trying** *to get attention by crying.*

And don't say, *Rudolph* **makes the connection** *between his lever press and the reinforcer.* Don't even say, *It's important to deliver the reinforcer immediately because then it's easier for Rudolph* **to make the connection** *between his lever press and the reinforcer.* Why not? Well pretty much the same as the others. It sort of implies Rudolph is a thinking, verbal organism. And, if you're serious about it, it's circular. At the very least, it adds nothing. And, as always, the same goes for nonverbal human beings.

Same goes with *associates,* as in *Rudolph* **associates** *the lever press with the water.*

As we suggested before, you can say, *Rudolph presses the lever now, because that response has been reinforced in the past.* Simple, clean, elegant, no nonsense, no unjustified inferences.

Same with **wants.** Don't say *the rat* **wants** *a drop of water.* Just say what you know: *The rat has had no water to drink for several hours, and the temperature is real hot.*

This applies not only to Rudolph the Rat but also to your pet guppy, Rover, and the 6-month-old child crying in the apartment next door. None have language. None expect, know, or think. Of course the 6-month old child will learn to speak and will learn to think and expect and will come to know. But not yet. As a matter of fact, often you can't make these inferences about any particular behavior of a verbal human being either, as Sid's scratching demonstrates.

Prohibition, prohibition, prohibition. Give us a break. What can we say? Well, we can say our set of prohibitions is more than a mere, abstract, intellectual nicety. All those taboo words get in the road of your really understanding what's going on. And correctly understanding can be important. Suppose you're working with a nonverbal mentally handi-capped child, as many of you may be doing at some point. And suppose the child has some self-destruc-tive behavior that's really dangerous, like gouging his own eyes. Or suppose he really needs to learn to do something, such as talk, for instance. You need to figure out what contingencies are controlling his be-havior or failing to control his behavior. And then you need to design contingencies that will help him acquire a healthy repertoire. Discussing his problem in terms of knows, thinks, wants, and so on will just slow you down and may prevent your helping the child at all. We're talking serious stuff here.

All these extra words represent the error of circular reasoning and reifications, the major sins of psychologists.

However, once children learn to talk, they have the tools to *expect, know,* and *think.* But the analysis of those behaviors is so complex and so con-troversial, we won't even begin to touch on them until the last few chapters of this book. In the mean-time, wash out your mouth with soap whenever you use *expect, know, think,* or any of the following simi-lar sorts of expressions like *figures out, in order to, trying to, makes the connection, imagines, associates, learns that,* or *understands,* with a nonverbal human being or nonhuman animal, and *wants* with anybody, at least when doing behavioral analyses. That leads us to our **don't say rule.**[19]

+---+
| *Definition: General Rule* |
| **The Don't Say Rule** |
| ○ With nonverbal organisms, don't say |
| ○ *expects* |
| ○ *knows* |
| ○ *think*s |
| ○ *figures out* |
| ○ *in order to* (or *so that* he, she, or it could ...) |
| ○ *trying to* |
| ○ *makes the connection* |
| ○ *associates* |
| ○ *learns that* |
| ○ *imagines* |
| ○ *understands.* |
| ○ With any organisms, don't say *want*s. |
+---+

---

[19]Old Spike Jones record (probably older than you are): Phone rings. Guy picks it up. Listens, while commenting, *You don't say. . . . You don't say! . . . . You don't say.* Hangs up. Other guy asks, *Who was it?* First guy replies, *He didn't say.*

That ought to teach you not to read footnotes.

QUESTIONS

1. What are the 12 verbs and expressions you shouldn't use with nonhuman animals and nonverbal human beings?
2. Give an example of how each can be misused.
3. Give an example of how to say the same thing without having to wash your mouth out with soap.

REINFORCE BEHAVIOR, NOT PEOPLE

Dawn doesn't reinforce Sid. Instead, she might unin-tentionally reinforce his pouting. She also might re-inforce his smiling by smiling back at him. We often lose focus when we talk about reinforcing people rather than some specific class of responses, like pouting or smiling. For example, even in behav-iorally based classrooms, teachers who talk about re-inforcing the child may end up giving noncontingent reinforcers and thus fail to reinforce appropriate be-havior. The secret to understanding how the behav-ioral world works is always to focus on the contin-gency—not the behavior by itself, not the reinforcer by itself, but the contingency. So stay sharp, don't lose focus. A deal? Using *reinforce* correctly will put you ahead of 95% of the professional behavior ana-lysts. Keep an eye on your professor and see how sharp he or she stays. Keep an eye on us, too. And don't reinforce any of us when we don't deserve it. Right?

+---+
| *Definition: General Rule* |
| **Reinforce behavior—** |
| ○ Reinforce behavior, |
| ○ not people. |
+---+

A more general version of this rule is *reinforce behavior, not organisms.* In other words, we also don't reinforce rats, pigeons, monkeys, etc., just their behavior; but *organisms* sounds so pompous.

QUESTION

1. We just snuck a tiny joke in the last couple of sentences; so tiny that only 15% of our stu-dents got it. *Hint:* We violated our own rule. OK? Now, please explain it.

Compare and Contrast
REINFORCER VS. REINFORCEMENT

What's wrong with this sentence? *The shocked look on his sister's face was the reinforcement for his telling the dirty joke.* Hint: The word *reinforcement* is wrong. So what word should you use? *Reinforcer.* The shocked look is a *reinforcer,* not a *reinforcement.* Remember: The *reinforcer* is the stimulus or event (or thing) that will increase the likelihood of responses it immediately follows. The sister's looking shocked is the event that reinforced telling the dirty joke.

Then how does *reinforcement* fit into the picture? *Reinforcement* describes the whole scene. *Reinforcement* is what took place. Remember: **Reinforcement** is the process or procedure of reinforcing a response. *Reinforcement* occurred as the boy told the dirty joke and his sister's mouth fell open, her head jerked back, her face turned red, and her whole body stiffened. Of course, we'll only know for sure that reinforcement occurred if the boy increases his frequency of shocking behavior.

In other words, we can use *reinforcement* to describe that a reinforcer followed a response and now that response occurs more frequently. *Reinforcement* refers to the whole process, and *reinforcer* refers to one component in that process.

Many people, even pros, say *reinforcement* when they should say *reinforcer.* But that's no excuse for you. Be sharp.

**Reinforcer = thing, event,
change of conditions
Reinforcement = the delivery
of the reinforcer and the resulting
change in behavior**

QUESTIONS

1. What is the difference between *reinforcer* and *reinforcement?*
2. Correctly use *reinforcer* and *reinforcement* in the same sentence.

Baseline

A couple sections back we said Barb Fulton measured her assistants' task completion during **baseline,** where she used a traditional approach. So what's baseline?

Definition: Concept
Baseline
  ○ The phase of an experiment or intervention
  ○ where the behavior is measured
  ○ in the absence of an intervention.

QUESTION

1. *Baseline*—define it and give an example.

3 Escape

FUNDAMENTALS

Example of Escape
Behavioral Medicine
DR. YEALLAND'S CHAMBER OF HORRORS[1]

During World War I, Ed B. fought with the U.S. Army in France. In one battle, several of his friends were killed. When he was finally rescued, Ed said his right leg felt weak. Within an hour, he couldn't move his leg at all; he broke out in a sweat each time he tried. His leg had become rigid and sometimes trembled.

In the spring of 1917, Ed came on crutches to see Dr. Yealland. Yealland listened thoughtfully to Ed's story as he examined Ed's leg. Then Yealland did a strange thing. He walked to the door of his office, the only exit from the room, and locked it securely. Turning to Ed he said, "Ed, I don't know the exact cause of your paralysis, but apparently the tissue is OK. It is a subtle problem of the muscles and the nerves, but one I can treat. We will stay in this room until I have cured you."

With that, Yealland walked across the room to a metal cabinet where he carefully opened several drawers. Various pieces of apparatus lay within. An electric generator was alongside. Before reaching into the drawer, he hesitated and turned to Ed.

"I can see," he said, "that your muscles have become antagonistic. By the proper stimulation, we can alleviate this condition. I'm going to apply a faradic stimulator to your leg."

He withdrew a roller-like object and, turning on a switch, applied it to Ed's paralyzed leg. Ed's muscles jerked as electric current passed throughout his leg.

Yealland withdrew the roller and applied it again. After several such applications, Yealland said, "The muscles seem joined in their antagonism; therefore, I must increase the intensity of the faradic stimulation."

With some ceremony he turned up the dial and again stimulated Ed's leg. Soon he saw a slight movement in the leg. He immediately jerked the roller away.

"Ah-ha," he said, "movement." He increased the intensity and applied the roller again. This time the movement was greater. Again he promptly withdrew the roller.

"Ah-ha," he said again, as he further increased the intensity of the electricity.

After 10 minutes of this procedure, Ed said he could move his leg without any more stimulation. Yealland quickly removed Ed's crutches and asked him to place weight on the leg. Ed did so, cautiously at first, with little trouble.

Yealland looked at Ed and smiled, "This condition should bother you no longer. Of course, if it does come back, I'm always here. I am always ready to give you further treatment. If, on the other hand, the cure remains intact, I'm sure you will be happy to leave the hospital and resume your life as a civilian."

As he prepared to leave the office, Ed grabbed the doctor's hand, and shaking it with enthusiasm, thanked him for his help. Taking one last look at his crutches lying in the corner, he strode boldly out the door and returned to his ward. A week later he left the hospital and went back to his farm in Iowa.

Yealland had used this intervention with dozens of veterans suffering from the same sort of problems. In all but a few cases, he had complete success. In his few failures, other doctors later found previously undetected tissue damage that caused some of the problems.

---

[1]This section is based on Yealland, L. R. (1918). *Hysterical disorders of warfare.* London: Macmillan.

Analysis in Terms of the Escape Contingency

In the past, people used "shell shock" to refer to these common problems among veterans. Shell shock didn't always mean shock from exploding shells. Often it referred to a process that took place as time and experience in combat lengthened. Physicians used the label "shell shock," for example, when combat soldiers suffered blindness, deafness, or paralysis without any trace of physical damage. The problem was behavioral, not physical, but it caused great suffering nonetheless.

Yealland developed a complex theory to explain the shell-shock phenomenon. But we won't focus on his theory, because it makes no sense at all to modern medicine. However, this does not detract from Yealland's great success with his clients. Without his treatment, many veterans would have spent their days in military hospitals, confined to wheelchairs or in cheerless and somber seclusion.

Yealland's procedure didn't involve basic principles of medicine; instead, it involved a basic principle of behavior—*reinforcement by the removal of an aversive condition.* The removal of the electric stimulation (aversive condition) reinforced Ed's leg movement.

Before	Behavior	After
Ed receives shock.	Ed moves his leg.	Ed receives no shock.

Put another way, the removal or reduction of an aversive condition, contingent on a response, reinforces that response; as a result, the rate of that response class increases. An *escape response* is one that removes or reduces an aversive condition. So the movement of Ed's paralyzed leg was an escape response that removed the aversive electric stimulation.

At first, you might think of escape behavior only as behavior involving your leaving the place of aversive stimulation. For example, you escape from the heat by moving out of the bright sun and into the cool shade. But as you think about it, you'll realize that escape behavior also can involve removing the aversive condition from the place where you are. For example, you escape the heat in your house by opening a couple of windows and letting a refreshing breeze blow through; you may not have to escape from your house.

QUESTIONS

1. *Escape* response (behavior)—give an example.
2. Give an example of the use of reinforcement by the removal of an aversive condition. Specify the aversive condition and the escape behavior.

Concept
AVERSIVE CONDITION

In Chapter 1, we defined *reinforcer* as any stimulus, event, or condition immediately following a response that increases the frequency of the response. Now, check out this parallel definition of **aversive condition.**

Definition: Concept

Aversive condition (negative reinforcer)
- Any stimulus, event, or condition
- whose **termination** immediately following a response
- **increases** the frequency of that response.

The only difference between the two conditions is that we're talking about the *stimulus, event, or condition* **terminating.**

Concerning the *stimulus, event,* or *condition,* we will use those three terms somewhat interchangeably, depending on the context. The traditional *stimulus* sometimes seems limiting and strained. For example, making a fool of yourself in public would be an aversive condition, but it seems awkward to call making a fool of yourself an aversive stimulus.

Note that one way you can minimize contact with an aversive condition is to make responses that have escaped that aversive condition in the past. (By the way, this is not the official definition of aversive condition—just a characteristic.)

Life is full of conditions that are harmful for us (they will damage our body's cells). Fortunately, most animals, including the human animal, have evolved so that many of those biologically harmful conditions are also psychologically aversive. For example, we tend to minimize immediate contact with high and low temperatures, loud sound (unless we call it rock and roll), bright lights, painful stimuli that can cut or bruise us, and spoiled food that has an aversive odor. It's only because of much social pressure that we overcome the aversive taste of other harmful substances and manage to become addicted to them, such as alcohol, nicotine, and coffee. Yealland's electric shock is just one more potentially harmful stimulus that, fortunately, is also aversive.

Unfortunately, not all harmful stimuli or conditions are aversive. For example, many of us fail to minimize, or at least moderate, contact with salt, processed sugar, and fat—all substances that can harm our bodies when consumed in typical American quantities. And once we become addicted, alcohol, nicotine, and caffeine lose their aversive properties. The gum- and tooth-destroying plaque that accumulates on our teeth often fails to be aversive—we don't minimize contact, contact of the most intimate sort, with it. And the thrilling stimuli resulting from driving a car faster than we should are often not as aversive as they should be. We human beings have changed our world faster than we can biologically adapt to it. We can no longer depend on our animal nature to steer us away from harmful substances.

QUESTIONS

1. *Aversive condition*—define it and give an example of how you could use an aversive stimulus to modify behavior.
2. Give an example of
   ○ an aversive condition harmful to you.
   ○ a harmful condition that is not aversive.
   ○ an aversive condition that is not harmful.

Aversive vs. Adversive

By the way, notice the term we're using is *aversive,* not *adversive. Adversive* is not a word[2]; and *aversive* is a word only because psychologists coined the term. *Aversive* is a cousin of *aversion,* which means "intense dislike." Ed has an *aversion* for Dr. Yealland's electric shock. He dislikes the shock. He finds the shock *aversive.*

But *dislike* is not a reliable criterion. For example, people may claim to dislike seeing swimmers chased by sharks and then pay $5 to see the movie *Jaws.* So, to be safe and to get more reliable results, behavior analysts don't use the commonsense *dislike* as their criterion for whether a condition is aversive. Instead, they use our formal definition: They ask if a condition will increase the future likelihood of a response if the condition is terminated immediately after the response. Put more simply, we say a condition is aversive if its termination reinforces an escape response. By that criterion, Dr. Yealland's electric shock was aversive.

Along the same lines, suppose something makes you feel bad or sad. Is that something or that feeling an aversive condition? Maybe, perhaps often—but not always. Again, many people plopped down many dollars to see *Titanic* so they could cry their eyes out. And again, the only way we can be sure is to go back to our formal definition and ask: Does termination of this particular sad feeling reinforce the response that

terminates it? If not, then we don't have an aversive condition, no matter how much we cry.

QUESTION

1. You should be so hyped up about how dumb it is to use "adversive," that you'd spot it immediately on a written quiz and get full credit for correcting it. And, of course your sly but caring professor might occasionally slip an "adversive" into her lecture, just to give you an opportunity to correct it. When that happens, feel free to blurt out, *I heard the really dumb thing you said*! She will probably be so impressed she'll offer you a full-ride assistantship on the spot.

Concept
ESCAPE CONTINGENCY

We've been discussing *aversive condition,* a fundamental concept of behavior analysis. Now let's formally introduce a principle that relates the aversive condition to behavior. ***The escape principle:*** *A response becomes more likely if it has immediately removed or reduced an aversive condition in the past.*

This is a form of reinforcement—reinforcement by the removal of an aversive condition (negative reinforcement). And the procedure involved is an **escape contingency.**

Definition: Concept
Escape contingency
   ○ the immediate,
   ○ response-contingent
   ○ removal of[3]
   ○ an aversive condition
   ○ resulting in an **increased** frequency of that response.

---

[2]*Adversive* is not a word, however, *adverse* is a word. It is an adjective meaning acting against or in a contrary position. But in any case, *aversive* is the word we want here, not *adversive* and not *adverse.*

[3]Instead of saying **removal** of an aversive condition, we would be more precise to say **removal or reduction** of an aversive condition. For example, suppose the temperature is 90° and you turn on your funky air conditioner that reduces the temperature only to 80°. Well, the reduction of that aversive condition from 90° to 80° reinforced your turning on your air conditioner, even though you were not able to completely remove the aversive heat. So, *you're suffering a 90° temperature ⇒ you turn on your air conditioner ⇒ you're suffering only an 80° temperature.* That's an escape contingency based on the reduction, not the removal of an aversive condition. As with our definition of *reinforcement contingency,* just to keep your life simpler we won't put *reduce* in the formal definition, but you should understand that we're always implying it. Also, we could attach similar footnotes to the remaining six contingencies we present in later chapters; however, just to keep your life simpler, we won't, but you should understand that we're implying them.

And remember:

RESPONSE = BEHAVIOR

So Dr. Yealland's procedure is an escape contingency; Yealland turned off the electric shock contingent on each leg movement. And, sure enough, the principle worked—Ed's leg movements became more likely.

Here's the strongest example of an escape contingency I've ever personally experienced: Years ago, in my decadent days of cigarette smoking, I was driving with a friend through rural Ohio late at night. I pulled out a pack of cigarettes, stuck one in my mouth, pulled out a pack of matches, struck one, and yeeooww! A spark from the match hit the cornea of my left eye—the most pain I've ever experienced!

We sped through the Ohio night in desperate search of a town large enough to have a physician. I was crying because of the pain and because of the certainty that I would lose my left eye. Finally, we found a hospital and rushed into the emergency ward. The physician on duty laid me down on the examination table, put a drop of dutyn sulfate in my eye, and immediately the pain disappeared and my eye was perfect. I thought that physician, with his magic drops, was God. You can bet your bottom dollar that if I ever get a spark in my eye again, I'm going to rush to Ohio in search of that physician and his magic drops. Talk about reinforcement by the removal of an aversive condition!

Yealland's shock removal reinforced leg movements. The pain removal by the physician in Ohio reinforced lying on the examining table and gamely trying to hold open my left eye. Reducing an itch reinforces scratching. Reducing bladder pressure reinforces getting up in the morning and going to the bathroom. Escape from the drip, drip, drip reinforces blowing your nose. The contingent removal of various aversive conditions reinforces many of our crucial everyday actions.

QUESTIONS

1. *Escape contingency*—define it and diagram an example.
2. To escape—use it in a sentence in a technical sense.

Compare and Contrast
REINFORCEMENT BY THE PRESENTATION OF A REINFORCER VS. REINFORCEMENT BY THE REMOVAL OF AN AVERSIVE CONDITION

The two types of reinforcement produce the same results—an increased response rate. But one procedure increases the response rate by the contingent presentation of a reinforcer and the other by the contingent removal of an aversive condition.

Suppose the radio is playing your favorite song. But the volume is so low that you can hardly hear it. You turn up the volume. The louder sound (reinforcer) reinforces turning up the volume (response).

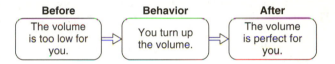

Before	Behavior	After
The volume is too low for you.	You turn up the volume.	The volume is perfect for you.

But now suppose your sister's stereo is almost blasting you out of the house. Then you turn down the volume. Here the reduction of the sound (removal of an aversive condition, relief) reinforces your turning the volume down (escape response). Each response would be more likely to occur the next time the proper occasion arose.

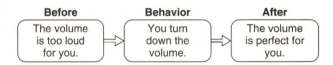

Before	Behavior	After
The volume is too loud for you.	You turn down the volume.	The volume is perfect for you.

Suppose, you're watching *Halloween XII,* and a scene comes on the screen that is too violent. You close your eyes. No longer viewing the aversive event (removal of an aversive condition, relief) reinforces closing your eyes (response). Again, in similar circumstances, you will be more likely to close your eyes in the future. So this is an escape contingency.

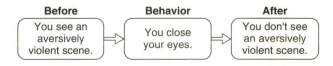

Before	Behavior	After
You see an aversively violent scene.	You close your eyes.	You don't see an aversively violent scene.

You're sitting at your desk completely engrossed in *Principles of Behavior*. You haven't eaten for a few hours. You are sharing your desk with a huge bowl of popcorn. After a few minutes, you notice all the popcorn has disappeared. But there's no one else in your room. Our guess is that the taste of the popcorn in your mouth reinforced your responses of taking an occasional bite of that nutritious food, though you may have been largely unaware that you were making those responses. Reinforcement by the presentation of a reinforcer.[4]

The following contingency table summarizes all this. Here's how you read this particular one: First, read one of the cells (boxes) from the white row across the top, then a cell from the white column along the left, and finally, the matching gray cell in the center. So you might select *Present* and *Reinforcer.* The corresponding gray cell in the center is "Reinforcement." This means: *If you **present** a **reinforcer**, you call the contingency **reinforcement**,* and the frequency of the behavior increases (⇑). *Or if you **remove** an **aversive** condition, you call the contingency **escape** and the frequency of the behavior also increases. And, instead, you can go from the inside to the outside of the table: If you want to increase the behavior (⇑), you can use either a reinforcement contingency, with which you present a reinforcer, or an escape contingency, with which you remove an aversive condition.

Contingency Table (preliminary #1)		
Stimulus, Event, or Condition	**Present**	**Remove**
Reinforcer	Reinforcement ⇑	Go to Chapter 4
Aversive condition	Go to Chapter 5	Escape ⇑

Here's another form of essentially this same table some professors prefer. You can read it this way: If you present a stimulus (a cell from the white row across the top) and the response frequency increases (a cell from the white column along the left), then you've got a reinforcement contingency (corresponding inside gray cell), which you can call reinforcement by stimulus addition or, more commonly, positive reinforcement (S^{+R}).

Similarly, if you remove a stimulus (a cell from the white row across the top), and the response frequency increases (a cell from the white column along the left), then you've got an escape contin-

gency (corresponding gray cell), which you can call *reinforcement by stimulus subtraction or, more commonly, negative reinforcement (S^{-R}).*[5]

Contingency Table (preliminary #1)		
	Present Stimulus Event or Condition	**Remove Stimulus Event or Condition**
Response frequency increases ⇑	**Reinforcement contingency** Reinforcement by stimulus addition Positive Reinforcement (S^{+R})	**Escape contingency** Reinforcement by stimulus subtraction Negative Reinforcement (S^{-R})

The tree diagram in Figure 3.1 is saying that we use *reinforcement contingency* in two ways:

○ the specific way, where we refer to the contingency involving the presentation of reinforcers, and
○ the general way, where we refer to any contingency that reinforces behavior (increases the rate of behavior), and that includes both reinforcement and escape.

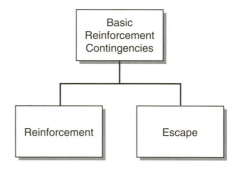

Figure 3.1   Tree Diagram of the Two Basic Reinforcement Contingencies

Review Question

Are behavior analysts concerned with *aversive* stimuli or *adversive* stimuli?

Our Answer

The correct technical adjective is aversive, not *adversive.* Impress your instructor by never saying "adversive."

---

[4]What about our classic example—Rudolph presses the lever and gets a drop of water. Reinforcement by the presentation of the water reinforcer, or escape from aversive thirst, from aversive dehydration? Traditionally, we behavior analysts have considered this as an example of reinforcement by the presentation of the water reinforcer, because the water is the thing we directly deal with, not the thirst. But students typically think of the thirsty guy crawling across the parched desert, crying water, clearly suffering, clearly the place for an escape contingency. So that's a gray area.

[5]My students strongly prefer the first version of this table, the simpler version. Me, too. But if they ever plan to leave my protective custody and mingle with other professors, they might do well to get familiar with the second table also.

QUESTIONS

1. Compare and contrast reinforcement by the presentation of a reinforcer vs. reinforcement by the removal of an aversive condition. Illustrate your points with an example.

2. Draw the contingency table (preliminary #1) and explain it.

3. Draw the tree diagram of the two basic reinforcement contingencies.

   Warning: Whenever you see a table in the text, there's a good chance you'll see a blank table in the quiz and you'll be expected to fill it in. But that's not all: the blank table might be rearranged, so you have to really understand it; rote memorization won't cut it.

Example of Escape
Behavioral Clinical
THE GOIL WITH THE DOITY MOUTH[6]

The beauty of Grace's thin, 19-year-old face was enhanced by the contrast between the pale skin she had inherited from her German-Swiss father and the dark eyes and hair she had inherited from her Mexican mother. Her mother's family was dining with them, and they all chatted and laughed gaily, chili peppers spicing the food and recorded, high-intensity mariachi trumpets spicing the talk and laughter. Everyone was having a great time. Everyone but Grace. She could feel it coming.

Grace stood abruptly. Her body became rigid. The talk and laughter stopped. Silence, except for the mariachi band. Now the whole family could feel it coming.

Grace's clenched fists flew to her collar bones. The fists stayed there, rigid, vibrating back and forth. Her face grimaced. Her lips twisted to the left. From her mouth came the sound "f-f-f-f" merging into "uck."[7]

Grace's body relaxed. She sat back down. No one said anything. No one ate. Then her father said, "That's all right, Grace. You can't help it."

Grace stood again. This time more slowly. "I hope you'll excuse me. I don't feel too well." She went to her room, lay down on her bed, and cried. Now the house was as silent as a death watch. No mariachi trumpets, no talk, no laughter—just Grace's quiet weeping.

The reason for Grace's tears was not that she had ruined the family dinner. This had happened often. The family could cope. She thought she already heard the sound of forks discretely clicking against the dinner plates, as the family began, again, to eat the enchiladas and refried beans.

Grace cried because she knew she would ruin her wedding ceremony. She knew she would break out in a full-blown display of the Gilles de la Tourette syndrome, right in the middle of the wedding ceremony, as she had at dinner. The wedding ceremony was just the kind of stressful occasion that caused the display. Then that awful word would come out of her mouth. And that would be the last she would ever see of Greg—the man she loved more than anything else in her life—the only good thing that had ever happened to her.

Grace cried, but she didn't give up. She never gave up. She had always had to work extra for what her friends took for granted. Nothing had ever been easy for Grace. Not from the day she was born. She had been a "blue baby," with a defective mitral valve, the valve that controls the flow of blood from the auricle to the ventricle chambers of her heart. In parochial school the nuns treated her as much like a normal child as they could. But her mother had to come to the playground at every recess to make sure she did not overexert herself or to take care of any emergency that might arise.

At the age of 11, Grace had successful heart surgery, but the physicians told her she should never exert herself. She largely ignored their advice, doing the best she could to live a normal life. Her classmates accepted her spasms as something beyond her control and just gave her the nickname of "the goil with the doity mouth." At the age of 17, she had gone to the famous medical school at Johns Hopkins University for further diagnosis and treatment. But nothing had changed. Nothing, except one thing. She had met Greg on the flight back from the hospital to her home.

Now Grace was 19. Her lips and nails were bluish, because of poor blood circulation. And her phalanges, the bones in her fingers and toes, were slightly enlarged and bulb like. She was going to college. She and Greg planned to get married. And she would do anything to prevent her Gilles de la Tourette syndrome from spoiling that. She would even go back to the university hospital.

Intervention

Fortunately for Grace, on her return to the hospital, psychiatric services assigned her to Dr. Israel Goldiamond. He worked on her case with Dr. Sheldon Glass, who was doing his psychiatric residency

---

[6]Based on Goldiamond, I. (1984). Training parent trainers and ethicists in nonlinear analysis of behavior. In R. Dangel & R. Polster. *Parent training foundations of research and practice.* New York: Guilford Press.

[7]We apologize for this profanity, but this is true to the actual case study, and we thought it was important for you to understand the seriousness of this problem.

in that hospital. They designed a behavior-analytic intervention.

"Doctor," Grace asked, "does my problem have anything to do with a death wish?"

"What makes you ask that?" Could there be something to this death-wish nonsense, so popular with traditional psychoanalysts?

"Every time I say something like 'this will be the death of me,' all the doctors look at each other significantly, and make notes in their notebooks."

The behavior analyst smiled. "I wouldn't worry too much about that one, Grace. Instead, why don't you tell me more about what happens before you display the syndrome and what happens afterward."

"Well, I have my attacks when things get too stressful. Like when the Mexican side of our family comes to visit. They're so much more noisy than the Swiss side of my family."

"Grace, you sound almost racist. Don't you like Mexicans?"

"I don't mean to be racist. And I love my family. It just . . . Oh, I don't know . . ."

"OK, let me see if I understand. Your reactions may result from living in a racist environment, where Mexican-Americans are discriminated against. And that may make you too sensitive to racial and cultural stereotypes. In any event, you're having trouble coping. So, at least to you, your mother's family seems noisy. And at the least, you find that aversive. And . . ."

"Yes, it's horrible. It upsets me so much that I have an attack and start twitching, and you know."

"And then what happens?"

"I guess everyone gets quiet, and I leave the room."

"Why don't you just ask them to be a little less noisy?"

"I do, but they don't listen to me."

"OK, why don't you try this. Tell them your doctors have said noise and excitement will harm your condition, and then say you sure would appreciate it if they would be a little more quiet."

"They'll never listen to me."

"But didn't you say the other day that the Mexican side of your family is especially fond of children? And didn't you say they're generally concerned about other people?"

"Well . . . yes."

"So?"

Sooooo, maybe you're right. Maybe they would quiet down if they understood that it was important for my health. Of course, they would. I know they would. You're right. I'll do that. I'll explain it to them."

"Great. And at our next meeting, we'll discuss ways you can reduce the stress in other situations."

The behavior analysts also spent two sessions helping Grace acquire a more mild form of her tic, so that when it did occur, it would be much less disruptive. The results? Grace married right on schedule. No problems. No syndrome. No embarrassing swear words disrupting the sacred ceremony. And like 50% of the normal American couples who get married, a few years later Grace and Greg divorced, right on schedule. Only rarely did the Tourette syndrome recur, and then in a much milder form. Fifteen years after the behavioral intervention, Grace was holding down a regular job as an administrative assistant.

Analysis
UNDESIRABLE BEHAVIOR MAINTAINED BY REINFORCEMENT BY THE REMOVAL OF AVERSIVE CONDITIONS

Sid's Seminar

Sue: Is that it? Is that all Goldiamond and Glass did to help Grace?

Sid: That's it. That's all they needed to do. And now, because I'm the teacher, I get to ask a few questions, too. First, how does Grace's problem relate to the topic of this section—reinforcement by the removal of aversive conditions?

Tom: I know the answer you want, but I doubt if it's true. You think Grace is having her attacks so she can escape from aversive situations, like the relatives she thought were too noisy. That seems far-fetched to me.

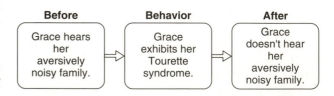

Joe: Doubting Thomas, I wouldn't put it like that. When you say, "So she can escape," it sounds like she's doing it on purpose. I doubt if she meant to exhibit the Gilles de la Tourette syndrome. **I doubt if she was even aware of the contingency between those episodes and her escape from the aversive condition.** It's like the reinforcement contingency snuck up and grabbed her, without her even knowing it. And before long she was having these attacks and couldn't do anything about it. And it was all because those attacks took her out of the aversive condition. Escape responses without awareness.

Tom: Well, then, if her attacks were so helpful for her, why did she want to get rid of them?

Joe: First, she wasn't aware of how helpful they were. And even if she had been, the price was too high. So a big part of the behavioral intervention was helping her acquire more appropriate escape responses—responses that wouldn't disrupt her life so much, that wouldn't humiliate her so much.

Tom: So you're saying the attacks occurred because relief from an aversive situation reinforced them. Then why was she so concerned about having an attack in the middle of her wedding ceremony? That doesn't make sense to me. She wanted to get married.

Sue: Let me answer that one. I'm a married woman. And I went through a big wedding ceremony. And it was the most frightening thing I ever did. It was really aversive. But I wanted to get married, and I also wanted the big ceremony. But when I was in the middle of it, I was shaking so badly I could hardly walk down the aisle. *Aversive* is the word all right. It's . . .

Joe: Yes, what's going on here is . . .

Sue: Now, Joe, let me finish. If Grace were deciding rationally, she would decide to put up with the aversiveness of the ceremony to marry Greg. But she's not deciding rationally. She's not even deciding irrationally. She's not deciding. The escape contingency just gets hold of her behavior and produces the attack. So the immediate reinforcement of escape from an aversive condition might win out over the long-range reinforcer of a marriage with Greg.

Sid: Let me summarize your behavior analysis like this: Immediate escape from an aversive condition (family commotion) reinforced an inappropriate response (attacks). This unfortunate reinforcement could occur without the person's being aware of the contingencies of reinforcement. This reinforcement might maintain that escape response (attacks), though that response would have undesirable long-range outcomes (a less reinforcing and more humiliating life). And this reinforcement might maintain that escape response, though the person is aware of those undesirable long-range outcomes. Excellent analyses. Excellent class discussion. One point for Sue, 1 for Joe, and 1 for Tom.

Tom: Why me? I didn't agree with the party line.

Sid: No, but you knew what the party line was, and you presented a thoughtful, well-reasoned critique. I want to reinforce careful analysis, no matter what you conclude.

Tom: Then, Mr. Fields, you probably should present your points immediately after the analysis rather than at the end of the seminar. Or, you should say you want to give reinforcers for careful analyses and omit the misuse of *to reinforce* for the delayed delivery of reinforcers.

Sid: OK, then, Tom, let me give you 1 more point because you corrected my use of a technical term. Class dismissed.

QUESTION

1. Give an example of an unacceptable behavior maintained by an escape contingency and show how you might get rid of the bad behavior by substituting a more acceptable alternative escape response.
   - What is the unacceptable behavior?
   - What is the aversive condition?
   - What do you think would be the undesirable outcome of that behavior?
   - What is the acceptable alternative response?
   - What is the role of awareness in all this?

*Example of Differential
Reinforcement of Alternative Behavior
Behavioral Special Education*
JIMMY, THE AUTISTIC CHILD[8]—PART I

Mae Robinson stood up as her secretary showed Herman Lewis into her office. Forty years old, gray temples, a little overweight, a dark blue, pinstriped suit, a beige camel's hair coat, a refined and confident style. Completely out of place in her ramshackle school building.

Yet he seemed at ease.

Once they sat, Herman Lewis wasted little time in social formalities. Instead, he began, "As I said on the telephone, Dr. Robinson, my son, Jimmy, is autistic. He's 6 years old and has the IQ of a 2½-year-old. He can't speak in sentences, can't dress himself, and isn't toilet-trained. He often has tantrums. Sometimes he pulls his hair out and bangs his ear with his fists. He shows no love or affection. He seems happiest when we just leave him alone to

---

[8]Based on Carr, E. G., & Durand, V. M. (1985). Reducing behavior problems through functional communication training. *Journal of Applied Behavior Analysis, 18,* 111–126.

sit all day spinning his toy top. As I understand it, that pretty much defines what an autistic child is.

"We've flown him all over the country to five different specialists and two different residential treatment programs. Nothing works. He just gets worse. And so we've brought him back home. We'd rather have him with us, though he's a burden, especially for my wife. He's a full-time job for her.

"One doctor who belongs to our club, Dr. Taylor, recommended you. He said that if anyone in this town could help, it was you. Dr. Robinson, we'll do anything to help Jimmy. We know he will never be normal. But if his life could be just a little more human, it would be such a relief to us. We'll do anything. And money's no problem. We just want to enroll him in a special program in your school."

Mae sat silently for a few seconds, looking at the man. Then she said, "Mr. Lewis, I'm terribly sorry about the distress you and your wife are experiencing and about the tremendous difficulties your son is having. If I could do anything of value for you, I would. The problem is the intermediate school district is in such bad financial shape that they're closing down our school after this semester. And they're transferring me to a regular elementary school. In the few months left, we couldn't make any lasting progress with your son. And our staff is already working overtime. I'm really sorry."

"Dr. Robinson, I heard from Dr. Taylor about the future of your school, and I expected an answer something like that. But as I said, money is not a problem. Jimmy is our only child."

Lewis continued, "I'm a businessman, Dr. Robinson. And I'll make you a business deal. If you take Jimmy on, and if he shows signs of progress this semester, I'll guarantee you that your school will not close down, at least not until the end of the school year. And if by that time Jimmy has made substantial progress, I'll guarantee you that you'll have a permanent school. I have the connections, I have the friends with money, and I have the money myself."

Jimmy Lewis enrolled the next day.

During the following week, Mae saw that Jimmy's problems were at least as bad as his father had said. Mae wanted to get more baseline data on Jimmy's behavior. But there wasn't time, not if she was going to make enough progress with Jimmy in the next few months to be of any value to him. And not if she was going to convince Herman Lewis to do what it would take to keep her school open.

But she was working right at the edge of human knowledge. The only interventions that had helped any autistic child were behavioral interventions. She would have to search through her behavioral journals to get all the knowledge she could to work with Jimmy.

Jimmy sat across a small table from Sue. Sue held up a card divided into four quadrants. Each quadrant contained a different picture. "Jimmy, point to the ball." Nothing.

"Jimmy, look at the card. Now point to the ball." Nothing.

"Jimmy, look at the . . ." Jimmy hit the card with his fist, knocking it out of Sue's hand.

Sue picked up the card. "Now, Jimmy, don't do that. You're a good boy." Sue patted him on the shoulder. "Now, Jimmy, point to the ball." Jimmy tried to hit the card, but Sue pulled it out of his reach. Then he started pounding his fists on the table and screaming.

Sue got up from her chair, walked around to Jimmy, and gave him a soothing hug. "Just be calm, Jimmy. Everything will be OK."

The Label "Autistic"

Children vary greatly in terms of the frequency of adaptive and maladaptive behaviors they exhibit. Some children may exhibit a high frequency of adaptive behaviors and a low frequency of maladaptive, dysfunctional, inappropriate behaviors. This varies from child to child so much that some children may exhibit almost no adaptive behaviors and almost all maladaptive, dysfunctional, inappropriate behaviors. Children who exhibit a high frequency of maladaptive behaviors and a low frequency of adaptive behaviors, especially verbal behavior, are often labeled "autistic."[9]

Examples of Appropriate Behaviors: eye contact, social interaction with others, and age-appropriate talking.

Examples of Inappropriate Behaviors: excessive crying, tantruming, aggression, hand-flapping, teeth-grinding, nonsensical talking, and toe walking.

Children whose repertoires are sufficiently dysfunctional for them to be labeled "autistic" rarely show improvement unless they undergo training in an intensive behavior-analysis training program.

---

[9]Many people, including me, are uncomfortable with applying labels to people, such as saying, *Jimmy is autistic.* It would be more accurate to say, *Jimmy has an autistic repertoire.* Recently some people have started using the expressions, *with autism* and *with retardation.* And while I think the desire to stop labeling people is a noble one, I'm afraid such expressions as **with** *autism* cause even more problems. It suggests that autism is a thing, like a disease, like a cold, that a person has caught. But inferring a causal entity from a person's behavior is an illogical form of analysis called *reification.* It's an illogical form of reasoning called *circular reasoning:* Why does Jimmy act strangely? Because he has autism. How do you know he has autism? Because he acts strangely. Why does he act strangely? Because he has. . . . And around in the circular argument you go. Better just to say he has *autistic behaviors* and then to look independently for the causes—for example, in the child's past and present reinforcement and escape contingencies.

Intervention and Analysis

Mae knew she would need to find the contingencies maintaining Jimmy's disruptive behavior before she could help him. So she sat quietly in a corner of the room, behind Jimmy, so she could observe all the details of the teaching session without disturbing it. She wore an earphone connected to a small cassette tape recorder fastened to her belt. She held a pencil and a clipboard that contained a ruled form.

The tape recorder beeped in her ear and said, "Interval 15." Mae recorded on the form that Jimmy pounded and screamed during that interval. Ten seconds later the recorder beeped again and said, "Interval 16." This time Mae recorded that Sue comforted Jimmy during that 10-second interval. Mae continued observing and recording in 10-second intervals throughout the teaching session. As she continued to observe Jimmy's disruptive behavior, she began to see the contingencies maintaining that behavior.

Right after the session, Mae and Sue evaluated their intervention. Sue began: "I know what you're going to say, Dr. Robinson. You're going to say I reinforced Jimmy's disruptive behaviors by attending to him and by comforting him. And I suppose you're right."

Inappropriate Natural Contingency

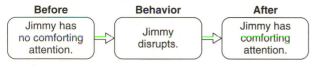

But it's so hard to sit there while the poor little guy feels so bad."

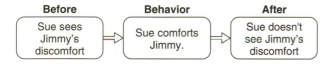

"It sure is," Mae replied. I sympathize with your plight, and I may have some good news. I've been reading about an interesting technique—**differential reinforcement of alternative behavior.** It might help us deal with this problem, and we sure have to deal with it right away.

"We both suspect your approval and affection are reinforcers for Jimmy. Nothing wrong with that; that's good. What's wrong is the response that gets that reinforcer. So far, your approval and affection have reinforced his disrupting. As a result, no matter what tasks he works on, Jimmy screams, or pulls his hair, or hits. And we can't get any teaching done while he's disrupting."

"Yes, but what's differential reinforcement of alternative behavior, Dr. Robinson? I've never

heard of it." Sue smiled for the first time since the start of the evaluation session.

"In the future, you should **differentially reinforce a more appropriate alternative response.** Only when Jimmy makes a more appropriate alternative response will you provide the reinforcers of your approval and affection."

"What alternative response will I reinforce, Dr. Robinson?"

"*Am I doing good work?*"

"Oh, yes, Dr. Robinson, you're doing great work. I just wanted to know . . ."

"Thank you, Sue, but I want you to teach him that. I want you to teach him to ask, '*Am I doing good work?*' " Sue blushed. Mae ignored her embarrassment and went on, "And then, whenever he asks, you tell him if he is doing good work. Also, if he is doing good work, shower him with love."

Performance-Management Contingency

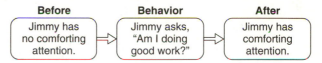

"I still don't understand."

"OK, what will happen when you differentially reinforce the appropriate alternative response, 'Am I doing good work?' Is that you will do two things: You will decrease the frequency of his disrupting, and you will increase the frequency of his asking 'Am I doing good work?' You will replace a horrible class of responses that's preventing your teaching with an undisruptive question."

"Sounds good in theory, but his language skills are so poor that it won't be easy. I'll do my best," Sue said.

"Yes, it won't be easy."

We can best show Sue's new procedure like this:

Differential Reinforcement of Alternative Behavior

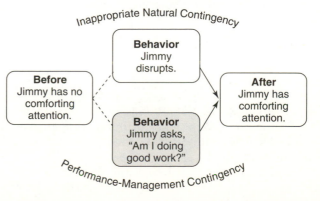

This is a combination of the two previous diagrams of the contingencies on Jimmy's behavior. This combined diagram makes it clear that the before and after conditions are the same for both the inappropriate natural contingency and the performance-management contingency. The only difference between the two is the appropriateness of the behavior.

Recycling

The next time she started training Jimmy, Sue laid out a row of three picture cards, one with the infamous ball, one with a cat, and one with a shoe. (These were the sample cards.) Then she gave Jimmy a stack of similar cards, pointed to the top card on the stack, an identical cat picture, and said, "Match them, Jimmy. Put them on top of the cards that look like them."

After a couple of false starts, Jimmy picked the picture of the cat from the stack and placed it on top of the sample card with the picture of the cat. Then he took the next card from the stack, a picture of the shoe, and placed it on the correct sample card.

Now Sue was wearing the "bug in the ear," the earphone connected to the cassette recorder. It said, "Beep." And Sue asked, "Do you have any questions?" She paused, and then prompted, "Say, 'Am I doing good work?' "

Jimmy stared past Sue for 5 seconds and then said, "Good work," without looking at her.

Sue grinned, nodded her head, tickled Jimmy briefly, and said, "Oh, Jimmy, you're doing great work. You're putting the pictures where they belong."

By the middle of the session, she was asking, "Do you have any questions?" But now she had faded her prompt to such a low whisper that Jimmy could barely hear her say, "Say, 'Am I doing good work?' " And Jimmy was responding quickly and loudly, "Am I doing good work?" Her enthusiastic praise immediately followed.

By the end of the session Jimmy no longer needed any prompt when Sue posed her twice-a-minute query, "Do you have any questions?"

Differential Reinforcement of Alternative Behavior

A week later, Sue again came into Mae's office to evaluate her work. "Dr. Robinson, I'm so discouraged," she said. "Working with Jimmy is like riding a roller-coaster, with all its ups and downs. In one session, he's great—almost no problems. Then, in the next session, he's back to disrupting."

"How often?" Mae asked.

"About 30 to 40% of the 10-second intervals the staff are recording. I don't know about him, but I'm not sure how much more of this *I* can take."

"Yes, our slow progress can discourage us," Mae said. "It's often harder to intervene than you would think, from reading a book or a few journal articles. Often you have to recycle and recycle on your procedures until you close all the loopholes."

"I guess so," Sue said, with little enthusiasm.

"Now we need to look at another part of this new alternative response intervention. There's a clear pattern to the way Jimmy disrupts. Before you started giving him an alternative response that would produce the reinforcer of attention, he ruined every session we had. But now he's out of control in only half of them, and they're the same half every day. He never causes problems in the picture-matching sessions. And if you look at the functional analysis data the staff recorded, he always causes problems in the receptive-labeling sessions where he has to point to the picture that matches the word you've spoken."

"Why is that?" Sue asked.

"I think those sessions he's still disrupting are too hard for him."

"Could be," Sue said.

"I think working on those hard tasks is aversive for Jimmy. And what happens when he disrupts? We immediately stop insisting he work on those aversive tasks. Instead, we start trying to cope with his disrupting. We start assuring him and calming him. So, without meaning to, we're reinforcing his disrupting by allowing him to escape briefly from the aversive academic tasks."

Inappropriate Natural Contingency

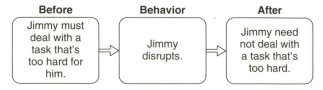

"But I don't know what else to do. I can't just sit there and let him pull his hair out."

"Right, I'm not blaming you, Sue," Mae answered. "We'd all do the same thing, in your place."

"What should I do?" Sue asked.

"Remember, you've been using **differential reinforcement of alternative behavior.** You used your attention to reinforce Jim's asking, 'Am I doing good work?' and you stopped attending to his disruptions. You broke the inappropriate contingency between disrupting and attention, and you established an appropriate contingency between 'Am I doing good work?' and attention. Now I think you should use differential reinforcement of alternative behavior to break another inappropriate contingency."

"I'm getting confused, Dr. Robinson." Sue frowned. "What other inappropriate contingency?"

"It's complex. When life gets confusing, I always take a look at *Principles of Behavior*."

Sue wasn't sure whether Mae was serious or joking.

Mae said, "Take a look at this definition," as she opened the book to a marked page.

Definition: Concept

Differential reinforcement of alternative behavior (DRA)

- The replacement of an inappropriate response
- with a specific appropriate response
- that produces the same reinforcing outcome.

Note that that *same reinforcing outcome* could be either the presentation of a reinforcing condition or the removal or reduction of an aversive condition.

Mae said, "So far, you've used the presentation of a reinforcing condition—your approval and affection. Now let's add the removal of an aversive condition—tasks that are too hard for him. Help him acquire a normal, nondisruptive alternative response that will allow him to escape the aversiveness of tasks that are too hard."

"How could I do that?" Sue asked.

"Just like you established the healthy alternative response of asking for attention—a response that produced the reinforcer of attention. Now you should establish the healthy alternative response of asking for help. And the alternative response will remove the aversive condition of struggling with a task that's too hard for him."

"It's beginning to make sense," Sue said, returning to her former smiling self. "Just as before, every 30 seconds I'll ask, 'Do you have any questions?' Except now I'll prompt with something like, 'Say, will you help me?' And instead of praising him when he asks that question, I'll help him."

Performance-Management Contingency

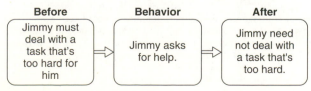

"I think you've got it. What kind of help would you give him if he asked for help on a receptive-labeling task?" Mae asked.

"If he were having trouble with the word-picture pair for horse, I'd answer his request for help by pointing to the picture of the horse and saying, 'This is a horse.' Then I'd say to him, 'Point to the horse.'"

"Go for it, Susan."

Here's a way of showing the relation between those two previous contingencies that may help you better understand differential reinforcement of al-

Differential Reinforcement of Alternative Behavior

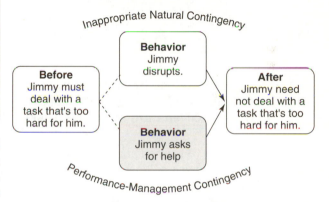

ternative behavior.

Check out this diagram and note that when you do differential reinforcement of alternative behavior.

- the before and after conditions are the same for the new performance-management contingency as they are for the inappropriate natural contingency, and
- you've just substituted an appropriate behavior in the performance-management contingency for an inappropriate one in the natural contingency.

The results? The new use of differential reinforcement of alternative escape behavior got rid of the inappropriate responses that escape from the aversive tasks had reinforced. This new procedure worked as well as the first when it got rid of the inappropriate responses that approval had reinforced. In other words, the two approaches to the use of differential reinforcement of alternative behaviors got rid of most of Jimmy Lewis's inappropriate behavior during the teaching sessions (Figure 3.2).

And Herman Lewis? He was so pleased with Jimmy's progress in Mae's program he promised her that her school would stay open for at least one more semester. Now, her school had a chance.

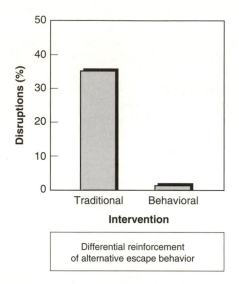

Figure 3.2   An Autistic Boy's Disruptive Escape Responses (Tantrums, Self-Injury, Opposition) When Given Hard Academic Tasks

And you? You've learned about *differential reinforcement of alternative behavior.* This case illustrates the two uses of differential reinforcement of alternative behavior—it can be used to get rid of inappropriate behavior reinforced by the presentation of a reinforcer and to get rid of inappropriate behavior reinforced by escape from an aversive condition. And note, in neither case did they use a punishment procedure to get rid of the inappropriate behavior.[10]

FUNCTIONAL ASSESSMENT, NOT JUST A QUICK FIX

"You amaze me, Dr. Robinson," Sue said.

"Why is that?" Mae asked.

"Well, to tell you a secret, I used to dread coming to work with Jimmy because he was such a monster. But now I can hardly wait to get here so I can be with him. You seemed to know just what we should do to turn him into a lovable kid. Sometimes I think you're psychic!"

Mae laughed. "Right. I'm psychic enough to realize we couldn't figure out how to help Jimmy without knowing what is reinforcing his behavior. In the old days, it was thought that behavior analysts would just move in with the giant M&M to fix problems and that they could ignore the cause of the problem—the contingencies maintaining the problem behavior. But in recent years, it has become clear that it helps to understand the problem contingencies. That allows us, for example, to then make the same reinforcer contingent on more appropriate behavior, as we do in the case of differential reinforcement of alternative behavior. Finding the problem contingencies is called a **functional assessment.**

Definition: Concept
Functional assessment
- An assessment
- of the contingencies responsible for
- behavioral problems.

In order to discover the contingencies maintaining a problem behavior, behavior analysts often complete a functional assessment of contingencies maintaining a problem behavior before designing an intervention to eliminate that behavior. In other words, they look for the contingencies that support the problem behavior. There are three ways to do a functional assessment:

Three Functional-Assessment Strategies:
- **Interview.** Talk to the person with the behavior problem and those who interact with and have direct contact with that person.
- **Observe.** Observe the person in his or her daily routines for an extended period of time.
- **Intervene.** Present, remove, or modify the contingencies that may be reinforcing the problem behavior.[11]

Of course, behavior analysts also use variations on these three strategies of functional assessment when the problem is that the person fails to do the right behavior, though most often they use func-

---

[10]Some research suggests that the necessary component in procedures such as these is not that we differentially reinforce alternative behaviors but that we stop reinforcing the undesirable behaviors and that, without reinforcement, those undesirable behaviors decrease in frequency regardless of whether we differentially reinforce alternative behaviors. In any case, it seems the humane thing to do—helping our clients acquire appropriate alternative responses to get their reinforcers and to escape aversive conditions. (Incidentally, the procedure of withholding reinforcers is called *extinction,* as you will see in the next chapter.)

[11]This last strategy is also called a functional analysis. Functional analysis is a specialized form of functional assessment in which contingencies are experimentally manipulated. Some behavior analyst erroneously call *all* functional assessment strategies, functional analysis, but that's like calling all dogs poodles. All poodles are dogs, but not all dogs are poodles. All functional analyses are functional assessments, but not all functional assessments are functional analyses.

tional assessment when the person is doing something he or she shouldn't do rather than not doing something he or she should do.)

Sue looked up from her favorite principles of behavior text (heh, heh) and smiled. "Oh, I get it. You used the second functional assessment strategy, *observation,* to discover the contingencies reinforcing Jimmy's problem behaviors. First, attention reinforced his disruptions. And then, after we stopped attending to his disruptions, escape from the adversively difficult task reinforced those disruptions. In both cases, differential reinforcement of a more appropriate behavior eliminated the inappropriate problem behavior."

Mae laid a hand on her shoulder. "Sue, you've got it. Now just one thing—remember, it's aversive, not adversive!"

QUESTIONS

1. *Differential reinforcement of alternative behavior*—define it.
2. Draw the contingency diagrams for the use of the two procedures for differential reinforcement of alternative behaviors with the same person to get rid of
   ○ problem behavior reinforced by the removal of an aversive condition,
   ○ problem behavior reinforced by the presentation of a reinforcer.

   In each case, draw the diagram combining the contingency supporting the problem behavior with the diagram showing the differential reinforcement of the alternative, appropriate behavior.
3. Does differential reinforcement of alternative behavior involve the use of punishment to suppress the inappropriate behavior?
   Warning: Students who can't answer this one will probably screw up the test.
4. *Functional assessment*—define it.
5. What are the three functional assessment strategies?

Example of a Functional Assessment
School Psychology
ATTENTION DEFICIT
HYPERACTIVITY DISORDER[12]

Bob Ball stood tall and relaxed. The band blared the Lincoln Junior High fight song. And the crowd

chanted, "Sink it, Bob! Sink it, Bob!" They knew he would. He knew he would. And he did: Whoosh—the basketball slipped through the net without touching the rim. Bob, the state's junior-high free-throw king had just raised his free-throw percentage from 82 to 84. The ball barely got back in play before the whistle blew and the game was over, 42 to 41. Lincoln Junior High had won again.

Bob Ball stood tall; Bob Ball walked tall though the halls of Lincoln Junior High. But all was not well at Lincoln J. H. All was not well with Bob Ball. The day after his big victory, Bob Ball had just been suspended from the team; his grades were so lousy that he was ineligible to play. And as things stood, Bob Ball would have to repeat the 7th grade.

When all else fails, including Big Bob, it's time to call in a behavior analyst. The coach, who was understandably concerned about Big Bob, called his old football-playing college buddy, Juke; and in this old-boy network, the buck eventually stopped with Mae.

Functional Assessment

With the permission of Mr. and Mrs. Ball, Mae did a functional assessment, using the interview strategy first.

Teacher Terry: Bob's work is great—when he does his work. He understands the material. He just can't stay on task long enough to complete his work. He continually disrupts class with his smart-aleck remarks and behavior. When I reprimand him, he insults and threatens me. Then I send him to the principal's office.

Mae thought: Bob isn't learning much in the principal's office.

Teacher Terry: According to our regular school psychologist, Bob has attention deficit hyperactivity disorder (ADHD) and oppositional defiant disorder (ODD). He can't concentrate.

Mae thought: We could solve student problems so much more easily if other school psychologists would stop putting labels on the kids and start doing functional analyses of the problem behaviors.

Mae asked: When does Bob make his smart-aleck remarks and disrupt?

Teacher Terry (after a thoughtful pause): When he has to do a written assignment. Every day in my writing class, I require the students to write in their journal for about 6 minutes and to write a story for about 20. Bob hates writing.

---

[12]Based on Ervin, R. A., DuPaul, G. J., Kern, L. & Friman, P. C. (1998). Classroom-based functional and adjunctive assessments: Proactive approaches to intervention selection for adolescents with attention deficit hyperactivity disorder. *Journal of Applied Behavior Analysis, 31,* 65–78.

Mae continued her functional assessment, moving on to the observation strategy. She observed Bob Ball and Teacher Terry in the writing class for a week. During that week, Bob started to disrupt the class every time he was told to begin writing. And Teacher Terry sent him to the principal's office.

Mae thought: Looks like this is the contingency:

1. What kind of contingency is this?
    a. reinforcement by the presentation of a reinforcer
    b. escape—reinforcement by the removal of an aversive condition

Then Mae talked to Bob: What could we do to help you?

Bob Ball: I need more time to think about what I have to write. I can't stand the pressure.

Later, Teacher Terry said: Yes, Bob is more likely to get down to work and less likely to disrupt when we have a discussion about the topic before he has to start writing.

Intervention

There are various procedures Mae might have used to help Bob, including differential reinforcement of alternative behavior, such as allowing him to escape the writing tasks if he politely asked to do so; but then he might never learn to write. Instead, she and Teacher Terry wanted to decrease the aversiveness of the task, thus giving Bob less reason to escape. (As you will see in Chapter 9, that involves changing the *establishing* operation.) Giving Bob less reason to escape would result in his learning to write better and would also make life more pleasant for everyone, including Bob Ball and Teacher Terry. As Bob had indicated, maybe he needed more time to think about his writing before he started. So, before each journal-writing session, Bob was allowed to brainstorm with a peer for a few minutes.

Mae recorded the percentage of time Bob was on task (e.g., actually writing) during the writing sessions as opposed to being off task (e.g., calling out, gesturing, talking to peers, playing with objects, making funny faces). As you can see in the following graph, the brainstorming worked. Bob Ball was right; he just needed a little more time to think be-

fore he wrote. His on-task behavior increased 26.6% when Mae and Teacher Terry allowed the brainstorming (Figure 3.3).

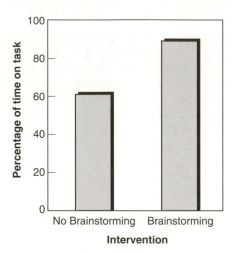

Figure 3.3   Brainstorming Intervention to Increase Bob's On-Task Behavior

Mae and Teacher Terry tried a different intervention for the story-writing assignments; they allowed Bob (and the rest of the students) to write the stories with a computer rather than by hand. And that worked, too. Bob's on-task behavior increased 32% when he could write with the computer (Figure 3.4).

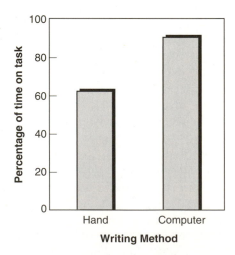

Figure 3.4   Computer Intervention to Increase Bob's On-Task Behavior

Now it's not clear how writing with the computer changed the effect of the escape contingency that reinforced Bob's disruptions. Maybe writing with the computer was less aversive than writing with a pencil, and thus Bob was less likely to escape the task by being disruptive. Or maybe writing with the computer was actually fun, because it was novel and because computers are just fun. And so, even though writing was still aversive, hard work, maybe Bob was less likely to escape that work by disrupting because that would mean he would also lose the opportunity to type on the computer (as you will see in Chapter 5, such a contingent loss is a *penalty contingency*).

Oh, yes, Bob Ball's grades went up enough that the school lifted his suspension, and he was able to lead Lincoln Junior High's 7th-grade basketball team through the season undefeated.

Example of the Sick Social Cycle (Victim's Escape Model) Behavioral Family Counseling **FAMILY LIFE—PART II**

Dawn puts Rod in his bed and tiptoes out of the room. But Rod starts crying as soon as she crosses the threshold. So Dawn returns and picks him up in a soothing way. His crying turns to a whimper, and his whimper turns to sleep.

Now what are the behavioral contingencies operating here? In analyzing a behavioral episode, the first step is to specify whose behavior you're considering and what that particular behavior is. If you don't, you'll botch it four out of five times. We've already looked at Rod's crying, and we've said Dawn's comforting attention may have reinforced it.

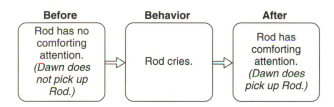

So now let's look at Dawn's behavior—her response of picking up Rod. What reinforced that response? Relief from Rod's crying. Then what kind of reinforcement contingency is this? Hint: Nothing is more aversive than the sound of a crying baby, especially yours. Of course, this is an instance of escape—reinforcement by the removal of an aversive condition (Rod's crying).

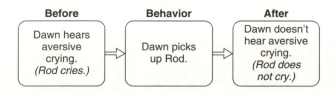

This is all obvious to us as we sit here safely looking at life from behind a one-way mirror. But it's not always so obvious if you're on the other side of the one-way mirror trying to deal with a crying baby, especially yours.[13]

Dawn's problem is a good example of the **sick social cycle (victim's escape model).** Someone behaves in an aversive way (your baby cries whenever you leave him). You make an escape response (pick up your baby) that causes the person (your baby) to stop acting aversively. Escape from that aversive stimulus reinforces your escape response, so you will be more likely to make the same escape response the next time. But your escape response (picking up your baby) reinforces the aversive behavior (your baby's crying). So the aversive behavior also will be more likely to occur in the future. And the sick social cycle goes around and around.[14]

In the next set of diagrams, we show how the sick social cycle is constructed out of its two component contingencies—the contingency reinforcing the aversive behavior and the contingency reinforcing the escape response. We've rewritten those contingencies slightly to make their interaction clearer, and in so doing, we repeat the name of the person behaving in the before and after conditions.

The first contingency is Rod's reinforcement contingency that we just looked at:

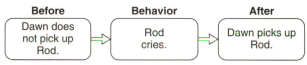

And the second contingency is Dawn's escape contingency that we just looked at:

We then combine Rod and Dawn's diagrams to show the interaction between them, the sick social cycle:

---

[13]My guess is that crying and sounds of distress are *unlearned* aversive stimuli. This may often promote the survival of the infant, when Ma and Pa make an appropriately nurturing escape response. On the other hand, there are also nonnurturing responses that escape (or terminate) the sound of a crying, stressed-out infant.

[14]I've designated the person creating the inappropriate aversive condition *the perpetrator* (Rod) and the person escaping that aversive condition *the victim* (Dawn). In truth, of course, they are both victims of the sick social cycle, but later, it helps to distinguish between the two roles. As you read this and the next chapter, maybe you can suggest a better terminology. If so, please e-mail it to me for some pseudo bonus points.

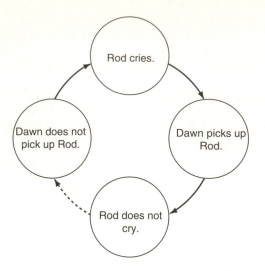

We start with Dawn's not picking up Rod. In a sense, that causes Rod to cry (the solid arrow between the two). And in a sense, Rod's crying causes Dawn to pick him up (the next solid arrow) And in a sense, Dawn's picking up Rod causes him to stop crying (the third solid arrow). For the final connection, we've drawn a dashed arrow, indicating that it might be better here just to say Rod's not crying is **followed** *by* Dawn's putting him down, rather than that Rod's stopping the crying causes her to put him down. But these arrows are starting to get pretty metaphysical, and you or your teacher may want you to say *followed by* for all four arrows.

Finally we unite all three diagrams to show how the two component diagrams make up the sick social cycle (see below).

The tints and the vertical and curved dashed arrows are to help you see how the components in the top two contingency diagrams combine to form the sick social cycle beneath them.

Unfortunately, the sick social cycle is typical of many of our efforts to correct behavioral problems. The parent or teacher (victim) attempts (victim's escape behavior) to quiet a child or get the child to start studying. And that attempt produces momentary success. But, in the process, the adult also reinforces the (perpetrator's) undesirable (aversive) behavior when he or she attends to that behavior. Picking up the child reinforces crying, and the child's stopping crying reinforces picking it up. And the sick social cycle goes around and around.

The generic diagram for the sick social cycle (victim's escape model) and its components is shown on p. 53.

Look at the first two component contingencies. Note that the first one is for the aversive behavior of the perpetrator. Also note that the before and after conditions for that contingency refer to the behavior of the victim. Similarly, note that the second contingency is for the escape behavior of the victim. And the before and after conditions for that contingency refer to the behavior of the perpetrator. Usually it will help to diagram those two contingencies that way.

Rod and Dawn's Sick Social Cycle
(Victim's Escape Model)

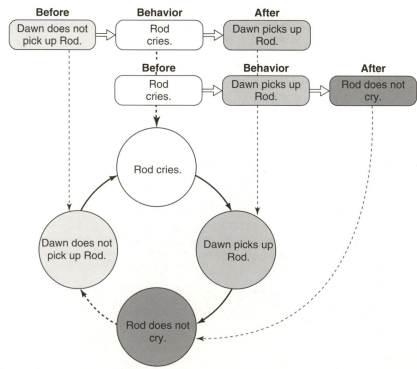

The Generic Sick Social Cycle
(Victim's Escape Model)

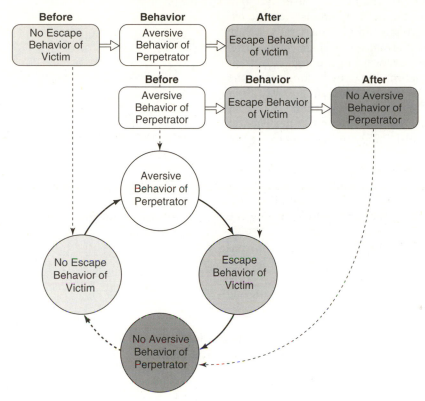

Note that the first contingency is always some sort of reinforcement contingency, either reinforcement by the presentation of a reinforcer or reinforcement by the removal of an aversive condition, but, in either case, the perpetrator's inappropriate behavior is reinforced.

Note that the second contingency is always an escape contingency, in which the victim's inappropriate escape behavior is reinforced.

Also note the arrangement of the names the diagram of Rod and Dawn's sick social cycle. In these cycle diagrams, we do it differently from previous diagrams; here it works better to have the name of the person whose behavior we are analyzing in the behavior condition, of course, but to have the name of the other person in the before and after condition. So for Rod's diagram, Dawn is in the before and after conditions; and for Dawn's, Rod is in the before and after conditions. If you look at the generic diagram, you'll see that same arrangement applies.

Note that the dead-man test does *not* apply to the before and after conditions of a contingency. So it's OK that the victim is not behaving in the before condition of the first contingency, because that's really a stimulus condition for the perpetrator. And similarly, it's OK, if there's no aversive behavior by

the perpetrator in the after condition of the second contingency diagram.

Definition: General Rule

The sick social cycle (victim's escape model)
- In escaping
- the perpetrator's aversive behavior,
- the victim unintentionally reinforces
- that aversive behavior.

Here's our original version of this shortened definition: *Often, aversive behavior occurs because such behavior is reinforced by the attention, approval, or compliance of another person. In turn, the temporary relief from that aversive behavior reinforces the giving of that attention, approval, or compliance by the other person.* But this longer definition was too long to memorize. So read both a couple of times, and the longer definition will help you understand the shorter definition. Then memorize the *Reader's Digest* version.

Most of the time, most of the victims seem unaware that the ways they reduce aversive behavior often increase the future frequency of that behavior.

For example, Spot jumps up on Katie; and Katie throws Spot's rawhide chewy bone to get him off. And Katie's escaping the pathetically aversive sight of Spot's begging at the dinner table is a classic example. As is Dad's giving Junior some candy to stop his crying at the supermarket. I think most often perpetrators are also unaware of the impact of their behavior on the victim. Of course sometimes the perpetrators may be quite aware of the way their aversive behavior is manipulating their victim, as when Susie Creamcheese says to one of her friends, "Watch me whine until Daddy buys me an ice-cream cone."[15]

And many times these social cycles are not sick but quite healthy, as when the baby with the wet diaper cries, thereby creating an aversive condition for the parent who escapes that crying by changing the diaper.

Always, the behavior of the victim is controlled by an escape contingency, though the behavior of the perpetrator might be controlled by either escape (e.g., escape from a tough task) or reinforcement (sympathy and comfort).

QUESTION

1. *Sick social cycle*—define it and give an example.
   - Draw the two contingency diagrams for your example.
   - Draw the circular diagram of the sick social cycle.
2. Now please fill in the diagram for your whole sick social cycle. (The contingency for the perpetrator goes in the top row; the contingency for the victim goes in the second row.)

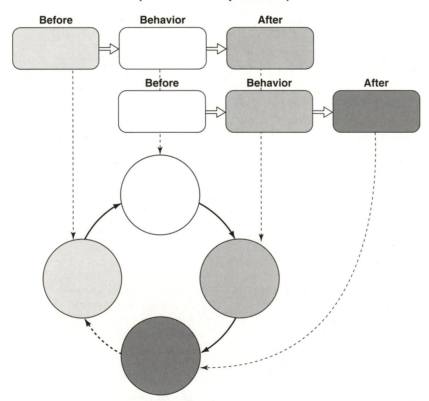

Your Sick Social Cycle
(Victim's Escape Model)

---
[15]Thanks to Michelle Seymour for this true story.

BASIC ENRICHMENT

In the Skinner Box
Experimental Analysis
ESCAPE FROM ELECTRIC SHOCK

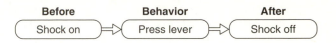

Before	Behavior	After
Shock on	Press lever	Shock off

The next time you look through the window of the Skinner box, you notice that now the floor is a series of parallel, quarter-inch stainless steel rods, spaced half an inch apart. There's no hole for the water cup. But the familiar response lever still protrudes from the wall. The rat is standing with its paws right above the lever. Suddenly it pushes the lever down and then releases it slowly. A little later, the same thing happens again.

What's going on here? Every now and then, a small electric current passes through the grid of steel rods that make up the floor—an aversive condition. The electric shock stays on, until the rat presses the lever; then it goes off. This is reinforcement of the lever press response by the removal of the aversive electric shock.

After some exposure to this contingency, the rat responds so quickly that it experiences practically no aversive electric shock; still, this is a gruesome procedure—one that reflects more of our everyday life than we might care to admit. This is an escape contingency—reinforcement by the removal of an aversive condition.

QUESTION

1. Diagram an escape contingency in a Skinner box.[16]

INTERMEDIATE ENRICHMENT

FEAR, PARSIMONY, AND ELEGANCE

Scientists are cautious about littering their sciences with unnecessary terms and concepts. They call this caution **parsimony.** To be parsimonious is to be economical. Another way to put it is to say we want to develop *elegant* theories. An *elegant* theory is one that explains as many facts as possible with as few concepts, principles, and assumptions as possible. So we look at each concept, principle, and assumption cautiously, admitting it into our theoretical framework only if we must to understand our world. We think you should be cautious about the following quote, though we found it in an excellent behavioral text.

"At 1 year, a child becomes particularly fearful of strangers." What does that tell us about aversive stimuli for the 1-year-old? It suggests that strangers are aversive; put another way, the removal of strangers will probably reinforce escape responses, such as hiding. Maybe we should restate the quotation as follows: "Strangers become particularly aversive for a 1-year-old child." That restatement makes *fear* and *fearfulness* unneeded concepts. If we can

understand the behavior of the child in terms of a concept we already have, the concept *aversive,* then why add the others?

> *Definition: Principle*
> **Parsimony**
> ○ The use of no unnecessary concepts, principles, or assumptions.

---

[16]*Didactic diddling:* The professor who encounters our simple little contingency diagrams for the first time may find the *before condition* unnecessarily redundant with the *after condition.* And logically, that's a good criticism; but we think it's not a good criticism pedagogically or didactically. Redundancy is the foundation of clear exposition. Students have a hard time understanding the nature of contingencies, understanding that the response produces a change from one condition to another, from the before to the after. They have a hard time seeing the relation between the before and after condition. And laying it all out in this super-explicit manner greatly helps. In support of our argument, we invite the skeptical professor to observe the students' initial difficulty in applying these little diagrams to novel examples. And we also invite the skeptical professor to do a social validity check with the students at the end of the semester: Ask them if they found the diagrams helpful (by the way, we're talking about grad students, as well as undergrads).

QUESTION

1. *Parsimony*—define it and give an example of how to convert an unparsimonious analysis to a parsimonious analysis.

QUESTIONS

1. Compare and contrast psychiatry and psychology.
2. Who is the most famous real psychologist in the world?

Compare and Contrast
PSYCHIATRY VS. PSYCHOLOGY

Who's the most famous psychologist in the world? Freud. Right, Freud (1856–1939). What's his first name? Ah, Sigmund? You've got it. Except Freud wasn't a psychologist. He was a physician whose specialty was neurology. Today we would call him a psychiatrist, not a psychologist. What's the difference? Psychiatry is a specialty in medicine, just like surgery. A psychiatrist must have an MD degree. A psychologist must have a PhD, an MA, or a BA (BS) degree, depending on the licensing requirements in the state where the psychologist works. Even psychologists who specialize in behavioral medicine are PhDs, not MDs. So psychiatry is a medical specialty, and psychology is a branch of the arts and sciences.

We've seen how psychiatry and psychology contrast. How are they comparable? Both deal with the understanding and improvement of behavior or the mind, depending on whether you're a behaviorist or a mentalist.

OK, if Freud isn't the most famous psychologist in the world, then who is? Gets tougher, doesn't it. Pavlov? Yes, probably Pavlov (1849–1936), for the average person, the layperson, the nonpsychologist. He did the famous conditioning experiments with salivating dogs. But Ivan Pavlov also wasn't a psychologist; he was a physiologist.

Then, who's the most famous **real** psychologist according to other psychologists (determined by a poll of the chairs of U.S. psychology departments), not necessarily according to *People* magazine? The answer: B. F. Skinner (1904–1990). Incidentally, Skinner even beat out Freud in a count of the number of times his name was recently cited in scholarly journals—again, not necessarily in *People* magazine.

Skinner started out working with animals as Pavlov had, except Skinner worked with lever-pressing rats and disk-pecking pigeons. But the influence of his work has spread a long way from the simple behavior of the rats and pigeons. He started what we now call *behavior analysis,* an approach to psychology that forms a basis for understanding all human behavior, the approach we present in this book.

Compare and Contrast
PSYCHOANALYSIS VS. BEHAVIOR ANALYSIS

Behavior analysis is a behavioristic approach to the study and improvement of behavior. One of its central notions is: Past consequences cause current behavior.

Psychoanalysis is a mentalistic approach to the study and improvement of behavior and the mind. One of its central notions is: Past experiences cause current behavior by channeling unconscious mental forces.

Behavior analysis and psychoanalysis are similar in that both argue that experience causes current behavior. They differ in that behavior analysis points to the past consequences of behavior as the crucial cause, and psychoanalysis points to unconscious mental forces (influenced by experience) as the crucial cause.

Freud is the father of psychoanalysis. Skinner is the father of behavior analysis.

**A basic principle of behavior analysis:
The consequences of past behavior
cause current behavior.**

**A basic principle of psychoanalysis:
Past experience causes current behavior
by channeling unconscious mental forces.**

QUESTION

1. In simple terms, compare and contrast behavior analysis and psychoanalysis.

THE TOOTHPASTE THEORY OF ABNORMAL BEHAVIOR

Remember Tom's concern about the escape behavior interpretation of Grace's Tourette syndrome? He probably was making a common mistaken assumption—that her abnormal behavior reflected some inner mental force that had gone haywire and forced this abnormal behavior out of her. Most people in our culture, including most psychologists, seem to look at abnormal behavior as something that issues forth from a person like toothpaste squeezed from a tube. They know, somehow, that an inner pressure builds inside the person, forcing out the behavior.

A mass murderer kills 13 people. Why? The common view is that internal pressure built up (perhaps the result of a bad chromosome). And that pressure forced the violence to erupt from within the murderer like psychic boils.

People tend to overlook the complex nature of this violence. It involves a complex set of responses. And each of those responses is precisely controlled by its behavioral consequences. To understand these episodes, we must look at the direct-acting contingencies (the stimulus conditions, the response, and the behavioral consequences). We also must look at the behavioral history that may have established those consequences as reinforcers or as aversive events. And we must look at the behavioral history that may have provided the contingencies for the acquisition of those responses. To do less is to cop out.

Definition: False General Rule
The toothpaste theory of abnormal behavior
- Abnormal behavior flows out of sick people
- like toothpaste squeezed from a tube.
- The abnormal behavior results from inner pressure.

People often fall back on the toothpaste theory to account for bizarre behaviors of autistic children, like Jimmy's disruptive and aggressive behavior. They say, "He's expressing an inner hostility that needs to come out." Watch out whenever anyone talks about "expressing" anything, like expressing anger or even expressing love. This toothpaste view always distracts us from looking for the contingent presentation of reinforcers and termination of aversive conditions that actually control the behavior.

QUESTION

1. *The toothpaste theory of abnormal behavior*—state and give an example of this false general rule.

POSITIVE AND NEGATIVE REINFORCERS AND REINFORCEMENT

Now it's time to mention some traditional but unpopular terminology we've hinted at earlier.

Fundamental Terms	
Traditional	*Ours*
Positive reinforcer	Reinforcer
Positive reinforcement	Reinforcement by the presentation of a reinforcer
Negative reinforcer	Aversive condition
Negative reinforcement	Reinforcement by the removal of an aversive condition

Behavior analysts often use the term *negative reinforcer* rather than *aversive condition*. As the table suggests, the two expressions mean about the same thing, but we prefer aversive condition because it's less confusing. Here's a refresher: **Aversive condition** (**negative** *reinforcer*): any stimulus, event, or condition whose termination immediately following a response increases the frequency of the response.

For both nonhuman animals and people, stimuli and events exist that will function as aversive conditions or negative reinforcers. In other words, both animals and people will be more likely to do things that have previously removed those stimuli, events, or conditions—those negative reinforcers. For example, Ed's leg movement seemed to become more likely because each movement immediately stopped the electric shock.

Warning: *Negative reinforcer* refers to the aversive condition (the shock)—not the condition of relief (no shock). This distinction will completely confuse you at least 10 times during your studies of behavior analysis. That's one reason we prefer aversive stimulus, condition, or event.[17]

But if you're going to deal with other behavior analysts or their writings, you may need to work hard on the use of negative reinforcer because it's so difficult to use correctly. To keep it simple, let's take another peek inside the Skinner box. Let's look at the rat in the escape experiment. What's the negative reinforcer?

---

[17]Such confusion has been our experience and the experience of most students and teachers we've talked to, though some teachers seem to have had few problems presenting the terminology *negative* and *positive* reinforcers.

"It's when the shock goes off. It's the absence of shock."

Close; you're only 100% wrong. The negative reinforcer is the shock. We know it doesn't make sense, but look at the definition again and maybe it will: **Negative reinforcer:** any stimulus, event, or condition whose **termination** immediately following a response increases the frequency of that response. *Termination* is the key word here.

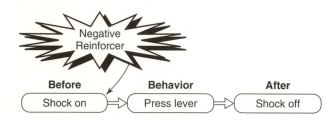

You said the absence of shock was the negative reinforcer. Does the termination of the *absence* of shock reinforce the lever press response—the escape response? Put another way, does the presentation of the shock reinforce the lever-press response? Of course not. It's the termination of the shock itself that reinforces the lever press, not the termination of the *absence* of the shock. So the shock is the negative reinforcer.[18]

We tend to think of the reinforcer as something good. But it ain't necessarily so—not if *negative* precedes it. The negative reinforcer is the condition you escape from, not the condition that provides relief. In this context, *negative* means "subtraction" or "removal." So the negative reinforcer is something you remove.

Still confused? Then remember this: The negative reinforcer is the *aversive* condition.

Just as we have *negative reinforcer,* we also have *negative reinforcement. Negative reinforcement* is the same as *reinforcement by the removal of an aversive condition.* Here, *negative* means *removal.*

QUESTIONS

1. Be able to construct the table contrasting our fundamental terms and traditional fundamental terms. Then be able to use that table in answering the following questions.
   Warning: To pass the quiz, mere memorizing won't cut it; you must understand it; and you must be able to construct the table with the rows and columns in a different order than in the book, at least if your pro-

fessor is as tough as I am. If you're not sure, ask your professor if he or she is as tough as Malott.

2. Which of the following is the negative reinforcer in a Skinner box escape experiment?
   Warning: Please be sure you've got this one cold because too many students are blowing it on the quiz, and we find the sight of a poor quiz score a negative reinforcer.
   a. the shock
   b. the food
   c. the termination of the shock
   d. the termination of the food

3. Please explain your answer to the previous question by the logic of the definitions and the table.

PRONUNCIATION

Does your professor love you?
   a. yes.
   b. no.

If you answered *yes,* that means your professor cares about your education and your well-being, which means your professor will give you an oral quiz to make sure you can pronounce the following words properly:

- *aversive,* not *adversive*
- *aversive* with the *a* sounding soft like the *a* in *a**ttention*
- not hard like the *a* in *ape*
- and not supersoft like *a* in *father;*

also

- *escape* not *exscape*

And for good measure,

- *et cetera* for *etc.,* not *ex cetera*
- *especially,* not *exspecially*

If your professor really loves you and cares for your well-being, he or she will provide corrective feedback any time you mispronounce one of these words in class. If your professor makes a condescending smirk while giving this feedback, however, his or her motivation might be questioned.

---

[18]We'll worry about the exceptions some other time. For the moment, give us a break. This concept is hard enough to deal with without the exceptions.

4 Punishment

FUNDAMENTALS

Example
Behavioral Medicine
BRUXISM[1]

Thirty-two-year-old Velma was born deaf and with both eyes closed. In addition, she would now be classified as having a profound mental impairment. She also ground her teeth—a behavior called *bruxism*. She had been grinding her teeth for at least 14 years. She had lost all but five of her upper teeth (a dental consultant said this probably resulted from her bruxism). She still had a full set of lower teeth.

Sixteen-year-old Gerri couldn't walk and would now also be classified as having a profound mental impairment. She had been grinding her teeth since she had had them. She had not yet lost any of her teeth, but their biting surfaces were severely worn.

Their teeth grinding had many bad effects: It was destroying their teeth. It probably produced headaches. They more frequently cried and had tantrums during high periods of teeth grinding (possibly because of the resulting headaches). They were less responsive to training programs while grinding their teeth. And the sound of their teeth grinding and their unresponsiveness were so aversive that the teachers and direct-care staff preferred not to work with them.

The behavior analysts who worked either directly or indirectly with Velma and Gerri were Ronald Blount, Ronald Drabman, Norma Wilson, and Dewanda Stewart. They considered using various complex reinforcement techniques to reduce the teeth grinding, but none seemed likely to work. So they selected a mild punishment. It consisted of touching the client's face with an ice cube for a few seconds each time she audibly ground her teeth. To protect the rights of clients, most institutions have review panels that must approve interventions that are experimental or use aversive control. So the behavior analysts obtained both the approval of the review panel and the informed consent of the parents before starting their intervention.

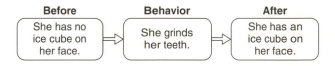

Before	Behavior	After
She has no ice cube on her face.	She grinds her teeth.	She has an ice cube on her face.

Both Velma and Gerri decreased their teeth grinding within the first few days of the ice-cube contingency. After two months of that contingency, they had stopped grinding their teeth almost completely (Figure 4.1).

For both women, several good things happened because of their reduced teeth grinding. For example, Gerri laughed and played more. Her mother was happier to have her home on weekends because Gerri was more sociable and not constantly making the irritating sound of her teeth grinding. Teachers and direct-care staff said the same thing. Also, the teachers said she was more cooperative

---

[1]Based on Blount, R. L., Drabman, R. S., Wilson, N., & Stewart, D. (1982). Reducing severe diurnal bruxism in two profoundly retarded females. *Journal of Applied Behavior Analysis, 15,* 565–571. These behavior analysts were from West Virginia University, University of Mississippi Medical Center, and Millsaps College. (Both West Virginia University and the University of Mississippi Medical Center are major centers of behavior analysis, and Ronald Drabman has played a crucial role in the research and supervision of doctoral interns in behavioral clinical psychology at Ole Miss, which is considered a choice spot to do behavioral clinical internships.)

and, therefore, learned more rapidly. And everyone was willing to spend more time with her than before.

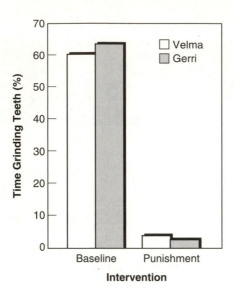

Figure 4.1   Ice-Cube Punishment of Teeth Grinding

QUESTION

1. Diagram the punishment contingency to get rid of bruxism (teeth grinding). What was the intervention and what were the results?

   Remember: To do well on the quizzes, you must be able to diagram all interventions described in the chapters.

Concept
PUNISHMENT CONTINGENCY

In the first chapters, we talked about increasing behavior with the reinforcement contingency. Now we need to look at the dark side of life—decreasing behavior with the **punishment contingency.**

Definition: Concept
Punishment contingency
- the immediate,
- response-contingent
- **presentation** of
- an aversive condition
- resulting in a *decreased* frequency of that response.

We'll concentrate on the definition of the contingency, but of course there is a corresponding prin-

ciple behind the contingency. ***Punishment principle:*** *A response becomes less frequent if an aversive condition or an increase in an aversive condition has immediately followed it in the past.*[2]

Like the principle of reinforcement, the principle of punishment is a fundamental principle of behavior, constantly governing our daily lives. And, on second thought, punishment isn't the dark side of life. It's our friend. Punishment protects us from the dark side of life. Suppose you're a middle-aged college professor. And suppose your favorite library is your bathroom. Suppose that for the last 40 years you've attained most of your book learning sitting on a toilet. Now suppose your toilet seat is cracked so that every time you get up from the toilet, the treacherous seat pinches your rear end.

What's the contingency? Only the most cautious or most kinky would question that the pinch is an aversive event. But it wasn't until we replaced the seat with a less vicious one that the college professor realized how effectively the pinch-punishment contingency controlled his incautious rising from the seat. Without thinking, he slowly shifted his weight, cautiously raising his rear end off the seat. On seeing how foolish his caution was with the new seat in place, he realized how effectively the friendly punishment contingency had protected his back side from the dark side of life.

Not only do you appreciate the value of aversive stimuli and punishment when you no longer need it, but you also appreciate it when you do need it but don't have it. Because of a damaged nerve, people sometimes lose the sense of pain from part of their body, such as from a finger. So the principle of punishment doesn't apply to that finger. That means they have a hard time keeping their finger from getting burned, cut, pinched, or further damaged. This loss of sensation occurs in certain forms of leprosy, where the main damage to the limbs doesn't result from gangrene. Instead, the limbs lack pain reception, so the principle of punishment can't protect them.

Remember this:

An aversive condition is one we tend to minimize contact with.

This is consistent with the principle of punishment—a response occurs less frequently if an aver-

---

[2]Here's a more elegant but less obvious statement of the *principle of punishment:* A response becomes less frequent if an increase in aversiveness has immediately followed it.

sive condition or an increase in an aversive condition has immediately followed it.

If the response that produces that aversive condition occurs less frequently, we'll minimize contact with that aversive condition.

Without the principle of punishment, we'd constantly trash our bodies. The principle of punishment does a good job of preventing us from scalding ourselves in the shower or when we drink a hot drink, from freezing ourselves in the winter, or even from walking into door frames instead of through them.

QUESTION

1. *Punishment contingency*—define it and diagram an everyday example.

Example
Behavioral Medicine
LEMON JUICE AND LIFE-THREATENING REGURGITATION[3]

Sandra was born with a cleft palate (split in the roof of her mouth) and a cleft lip, so for her first few days of life she had to be tube fed. She was from a poor family and was raised by her aunt. Actually, many different people, including neighborhood children, took care of her. There were indications of neglect.

When Sandra was 6 months old, her aunt had her admitted to the University of Mississippi Hospital. She was severely underweight, weighing less than she had when she was born. She regurgitated (threw up her food) and lay passively without smiling, babbling, grasping, moving, or hardly even crying. Sandra was seriously malnourished and dehydrated and in danger of dying. However, in spite of exhaustive examinations, the university physicians could find no medical cause for her problems.

The behavior analysts who worked with Sandra were Thomas Sajwaj, Julian Libet, and Stewart Agras. They observed that as soon as she had been fed, Sandra "would open her mouth, elevate and fold her tongue, and vigorously thrust her tongue forward and backward." Soon she would be bringing up the milk and causing it to flow out of her mouth. She didn't cry or show sign of pain during this regurgitation.

[3]Based on Sajwaj, T., Libet, J., & Agras, S. (1974). Lemon juice therapy: The control of life-threatening rumination in a six-month-old infant. *Journal of Applied Behavior Analysis, 7,* 557–563. These behavior analysts were at the University of Mississippi Medical Center at the time of this work. Stewart Agras is a prominent researcher in our field and held the prestigious position of editor of the *Journal of Applied Behavior Analysis.*

They started a mild punishment procedure. They squirted some unsweetened lemon juice into Sandra's mouth as soon as she started the vigorous tongue movements.

Before	Behavior	After
Sandra receives no squirt of sour lemon juice.	Sandra starts vigorous tongue movements.	Sandra receives a squirt of sour juice.

Sandra decreased her regurgitation by half during the first 20-minute punishment session, following her feeding. By the 12th day, she stopped throwing up her milk (Figure 4.2). And what about instances of her vigorous tongue movements that had been part of her regurgitation? From that time on, they dropped out. So the important part of this punishment procedure lasted only 12 days.

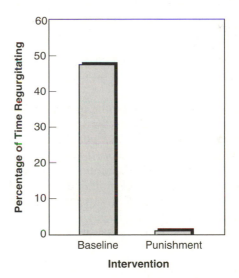

Figure 4.2   Using Lemon-Juice Punishment to Reduce Reurgitation

Further, 2 months after the start of the punishment procedure, Sandra's weight increased from 8 to 12 pounds, and a year later to 24 pounds. Also, Sandra became more attentive and started smiling, babbling, and grasping objects. When she was 19 months old, tests showed that she had almost acquired the behavioral repertoire typical for her age.

QUESTION

1. Describe the use of a punishment contingency to get rid of regurgitation. What was the intervention, and what were the results?

Example
Behavioral Medicine
SELF-INJURIOUS BEHAVIOR[4]

Nine-year-old Jack pounded his head on the concrete floor. He pounded his head so hard he had a serious concussion. When his parents brought him to the hospital ward of an institution for mentally handicapped human beings, bruises and cuts covered Jack's face and head. (One out of five mentally handicapped people do self-injurious behavior.[5])

Jack had started his self-injurious behavior early in life. By now, it had become a threat to his welfare. The staff had to supervise him constantly. Often they had no choice but to restrain him or keep him in a crib. But this restraint and confinement prevented him from acquiring normal skills.

We would expect that the pain of the head banging would serve to punish Jack's self-injurious behavior and thus cause him to stop banging his head. It didn't. Why not? Jack may have acquired his dangerous head banging over a long period, gradually increasing the force of the banging. And, as he did so, his body adjusted to the stress. In that way, he drifted into the pathetic state where the severe blows to his head were not aversive enough to punish his head banging.

In spite of Jack's seeming indifference to aversiveness and pain, we hoped we could get rid of his self-injury by presenting a mild aversive stimulus each time he banged his head. The difference would be that this new aversive stimulus would be novel to Jack. In spite of Jack's seeming indifference to punishment, we were betting on our intervention—punishment by the presentation of an aversive event.

To collect baseline data, we brought Jack to a special room fitted with a floor mat to protect him from hurting himself. We allowed him safely to bang his head as often as he wished for an hour. During this time he banged his head 1,440 times.

Then we taped a pair of small electrodes to his leg and delivered a mild electric shock each time he banged his head. The first time he banged his head and got a shock, Jack stopped and looked about the room in a puzzled way. He didn't bang his head for a full 3 minutes, and then he hit the padded floor three times in quick succession, receiving a mild shock after each time. Again he stopped banging his head for 3 minutes. He banged his head one more time and got the mild electric shock. After that, he didn't bang his head for the remainder of the 1-hour session.

During the next session, we had to shock Jack only once. And within a few sessions, he had completely stopped his head banging. Then we could remove the mat from the room. Later, we also got rid of Jack's head banging in other areas of the ward.

The staff no longer needed to restrain or confine Jack, and no one again saw him bang his head. We thought it was ethical to use punishment with this child because it was so effective in getting rid of the extremely dangerous behavior and involved only a few mild shocks, in comparison with the severe damage the self-injury was causing.

Analysis

We have trouble understanding self-injury because it persists though the consequences are painful and harmful to the individual. You might ask, what reinforces and maintains such harmful behavior? Different contingencies could maintain self-injurious behavior, depending on the behavioral history of each individual. Sometimes it is escape from an aversive event; other times it is an automatic, built-in reinforcement contingencies (e.g., sensory stimulation). But often the contingent presentation of attention reinforces and maintains self-injury.

For example, other things had preoccupied Jack's parents; they had little time to spend with him. But if he had accidentally fallen down, his parents might have rushed over and picked him up, thus giving Jack more attention than he would otherwise get. Because his parents would have unintentionally reinforced falling down, Jack might fall down again. But after a few more falls, his parents might again ignore him, until he fell and hit his head. Again his parents might have rushed to shower him with love and attention. Then the gradual shift to ignoring him might begin again. After awhile Jack could be banging his head with such force that his parents could no longer ignore him. And he might continue hurting himself as long as his self-injury produced the immediate reward of attention.

Processes like this may occur with most children, but they have little lasting effect and don't lead to the learning of serious self-injurious behavior. When self-injurious behavior is learned, the parents must often place the child under physical restraint in a hospital.

QUESTION

1. Describe the use of a punishment contingency to prevent self-injurious behavior. What was the intervention and what were the results?
2. Explain how a child might gradually acquire self-injurious behavior reinforced by attention.

---

[4]Based on Cowart, J., & Whaley, D. (1968). Punishment of self-mutilation behavior. Unpublished manuscript.

[5]Bakke, B. L. (1990). *Self-injury: Answers to questions for parents, teachers, & caregivers.* Minneapolis: Institute for Disabilities Studies, University of Minnesota.

Example
Behavioral Medicine
THE SNEEZE[6]

You sneeze. A friend says, "God bless you." Or if your friend is supersophisticated, he or she says, "Gesundheit." You both find this mildly amusing. Not as amusing, or as embarrassing, as flatulence, but mildly amusing and ever so slightly embarrassing. Then you sneeze again, and again, and again. After a few minutes of constant sneezing, you start to realize what a violent activity it is, how it stresses your whole body. You realize how tiring and uncomfortable it can be. And after a few hours of sneezing once a minute, you start to develop this nightmare, this fantasy of torture—maybe you'll never stop sneezing. Maybe you'll sneeze every minute for the rest of your life!

But this was no joke for 17-year-old Ange. This was no neurotic fantasy. This was reality. She had been sneezing about once every 40 seconds for the last 6 months—ever since she had accidentally breathed some paint fumes.

Allergists and other medical specialists couldn't help. They tried hypnosis, drug therapy, minor operations involving packings in her nostrils and mouth cavities, psychiatry, and prolonged uses of sprays and antihistamine preparations. One physician administered a sleep-inducing drug that made her sleep for several days. During her big sleep she didn't sneeze; but she started again as soon as she woke up.

Then Dr. Kushner, a behavior analyst from a nearby Veterans Administration hospital, took on Ange's case. Kushner thought that, although sneezing had caused Ange 6 months of discomfort, something must have been reinforcing it. Besides providing some momentary relief from the irritation, the sneezing provided Ange with more attention than she had ever gotten in her life. Possibly the attention reinforced and maintained her sneezing.

So Kushner hung a special microphone from Ange's neck. Though she could talk and laugh normally, when she sneezed the microphone responded and caused a mild shock to sting her forearm. The shock began as soon as she sneezed and lasted for half a second after she stopped sneezing. The results? Within a few hours, Ange sneezed less often; and within 6 hours she had completely stopped sneezing. For the first time in 6 months, other than during her big sleep, Ange spent a full night and day without a single sneeze. Two days later she left the hospital. And her sneezing remained under control

with the help of a follow-up punishment intervention once in a while.

A few brief, mild electric shocks applied at precisely the right moments allowed Ange to escape the months of extreme discomfort, the heavy medication, and the hours of painful and inconvenient treatment she had received. How much total electric shock did Ange receive during the entire intervention? Three minutes!

QUESTION

1. Describe the use of punishment to help a person stop chronic sneezing.

Compare and Contrast
ESCAPE VS. PUNISHMENT

Escape—Reinforcement by the Removal of an Aversive Condition

You've just completed a major pig-out. Your jeans are so tight around your stomach you can't slip your palm between your waistband and you! As you've done so often in the past when in this condition, you secretly lower the zipper to half mast. The tight jeans were an aversive condition you removed by making the escape response of lowering your zipper. We suspect that the tight jeans were aversive, and removal of that aversive condition reinforced the escape response because you often unzip after a pig-out.

Punishment—Punishment by the Presentation of an Aversive Condition

You've just completed a major pig-out. Now it's time to dress for your evening on the town. You put on your favorite jeans—right, the tight ones. But because of the pig-out, you have to take a deep breath before you can zip them all the way. After you've repeated this fiasco on a few evenings, you find yourself preferring your old jeans, for some strange reason. We suspect that the tight jeans were an aversive condition, and we suspect that their tightness punished your putting them on after a big meal.

People often have a hard time distinguishing between reinforcement by the removal of an aversive condition and punishment by the presentation of an aversive condition. One problem is that both contingencies involve aversive conditions. And it may seem like aversive conditions always decrease performance, but it ain't necessarily so.

Remember that reinforcement makes a response occur more frequently, but punishment makes a response occur less frequently. Reinforce-

[6]Based on Kushner, M. (1968). Faradic aversive controls in clinical practice, in C. Neuringer & J. L. Michael (Eds.), *Behavior modification in clinical psychology* (pp. 26–51). New York: Appleton-Century-Crofts.

ment by the removal of an aversive condition and punishment by the presentation of an aversive condition both involve aversive conditions. But for reinforcement to occur, we should remove that aversive condition; for punishment to occur, we should present the aversive condition.

This contingency table summarizes the relations between the contingencies. We've added one new one since the last chapter. First select "present" from the white row and "aversive condition" from the white column. Then select the corresponding cell from the gray area—"punishment" (rate decreases). This means that *if you **present an aversive condition,** you have a **punishment** contingency that will **decrease the rate** of the response.* (By the way, the empty cell in the table may give you some hint about the contingency we'll cover in the next chapter.)

Contingency Table (preliminary #2)		
Stimulus, Event, or Condition	*Present*	*Remove*
Reinforcer	Reinforcement ⇑	Go to Ch. 5
Aversive condition	Punishment ⇓	Escape ⇑

Remember: This ⇑ means the response becomes more frequent. So you don't need to be a rocket scientist to know what this means.

Here's the other form of essentially this same table. If you present a stimulus (a cell from the white row across the top) and the response frequency decreases (a cell from the white column along the left), then you've got a punishment contingency (corresponding inside gray cell), which you can call *punishment by stimulus addition* or, more commonly, *positive punishment* (S^{+P}).

Contingency Table (preliminary #2)		
	Present Stimulus Event or Condition	*Remove Stimulus Event or Condition*
Response Frequency Increases ⇑	**Reinforcement Contingency** Reinforcement by Stimulus Addition Positive Reinforcement (S^{+R})	**Escape Contingency** Reinforcement by Stimulus Subtraction Negative Reinforcement (S^{-R})
Response Frequency Decreases ⇓	**Punishment Contingency** Punishment by stimulus addition Positive Punishment (S^{+P})	

QUESTION

1. Use an example or two to compare and contrast the following (also construct and use a contingency table in doing your comparing and contrasting):
   a. reinforcement by the removal of an aversive condition,
   b. punishment by the presentation of an aversive condition.

Remember: To do well on the quizzes you must be able to construct or fill in any tables you see. And memorizing without understanding won't get it, because the tables may be arranged differently on the quizzes.

Example
The Mentally Handicapped
VISUAL SCREENING VS. GENTLE TEACHING[7]

David had lived in an institution for the mentally handicapped for the last 9 years. Although 21 years old, he scored as a 21-month-old infant on an appropriate behavior test. He frequently did stereotyped behavior such as weaving his head, staring at his hands, sniffing his hands, and repeatedly manipulating an object. This high rate of inappropriate behavior prevented him from taking part in vocational placement and embarrassed his family during their regular weekend trips to the community.

Jennifer Jordan, Nirbhay Singh, and Alan Repp tried several procedures to help David get rid of his problem behavior. They did this while providing special vocational training—sanding breadboards and assembling cardboard divisions for packing materials. The trainers who worked directly with David were experienced graduate and advanced undergraduate psychology majors from Northern Illinois University.

During baseline, the trainers would tell David what to do and then leave him alone, unless he left his seat. He spent almost all his time performing stereotyped self-stimulating behaviors and almost none doing his vocational training tasks.

Then they started an intervention combining several standard behavioral training procedures, including physical guidance and reinforcement with praise and touching. They continued to ignore his stereotyped behaviors. These behavioral procedures immediately reduced David's stereotyped behaviors

---

[7]Based on Jordan, J., Singh, N. N., & Repp, A. C. (1989). An evaluation of gentle teaching and visual screening in the reduction of stereotypy. *Journal of Applied Behavior Analysis, 22,* 9–22. These behavior analysts were from the Templeton Hospital and Training Center, Educational Research and Services Center, Inc., and Northern Illinois University.

by more than 50%, so that he was on task 68% of the time.

During the next phase they kept using the standard behavioral training procedures, but they alternated two added approaches. These approaches were *teaching quietly* and punishment with visual screening.

While *teaching quietly,* they used almost no vocal instructions, only gestures and signals. Why didn't they use vocal instructions? Because the advocates of teaching quietly assume that vocal praise would be more reinforcing if it were the only speech David heard during these training sessions. (The mere sound of the vocal praise might be more reinforcing because David had been recently deprived of hearing sounds. So he might be more "hungry" for sounds. Or the meaning of the vocal praise might be clearer and thus more reinforcing if the praise were not part of a confusing mishmash of instructions and chatter.)

John McGee, from the Nebraska Psychiatric Institute, uses the quiet-teaching procedure as part of a general intervention package he calls *gentle teaching.* McGee's gentle-teaching program is a combination of standard behavioral training techniques with the teaching quietly technique. His standard behavioral techniques include the techniques mentioned—physical guidance, reinforcement of desirable behavior, and extinction of undesirable behavior. What they definitely do not include is punishment. McGee's main point is that you can prevent extreme forms of inappropriate behavior in the mentally handicapped without using punishment.[8]

The addition of quiet teaching gradually reduced David's stereotyped behavior more, and it increased his time on task to 81%. Not bad, but Jennifer and her colleagues wanted more than not bad. They wanted the best they could get. That's why they compared McGee's gentle teaching with a punishment contingency—to see which was more effective.

The alternating comparison sessions using the punishment contingency went like this: Each time David did a stereotyped behavior, such as sniffing his hands, the trainer would cover David's eyes with one hand and hold the back of his head with the other hand. Each use of this *visual screening* would last about 5 seconds. They assumed this visual screening would be a mildly aversive condition for David.

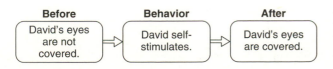

Before	Behavior	After
David's eyes are not covered.	David self-stimulates.	David's eyes are covered.

This visual screening immediately reduced David's stereotyped self-stimulation behaviors to 14% of the time, and his time on task increased to 88%. With a few more punishment sessions, David's stereotyped behaviors further reduced to 7% (Figure 4.3).[9]

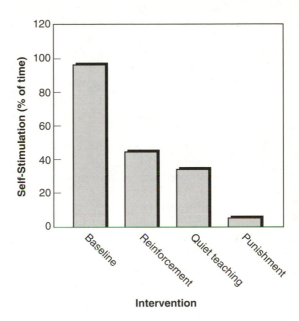

Figure 4.3   Reducing a Developmentally Disabled Man's Self-Stimulation

QUESTION

1. Describe the use of a punishment contingency to prevent self-stimulation. What was the intervention and what were the results?

Example
Behavioral Clinical Psychology
UNDESIRABLE HABITUAL BEHAVIOR[10]

Sid had been staring at his writing on the computer screen for the last 10 minutes. Sitting, staring, his left elbow propped on the left arm of his swivel desk

[8]McGee, J. J. (1985). Gentle teaching. *Mental Handicap in New Zealand, 9,* 13–24.

[9]Note that in the text we've reported the percentage of time David was on task, and in the graph we've reported the percentage of time he was doing his inappropriate stereotyped behavior. The two sets of data are not perfectly correlated with each other, because David could do some of his stereotyped behavior and still be on task. Those two response classes weren't completely incompatible.

[10]Based on Miltenberger, R. G., & Fuqua, R. W. (1985). A comparison of contingent vs. non-contingent competing response practice in the treatment of nervous habits. *Journal of Behavior Therapy and Experimental Psychiatry, 16,* 195–200.

chair, his head propped by his left hand, his index finger rubbing his left eye. Pause . . . more rubbing, and rubbing, and rubbing.

Dawn stood in the doorway, observing but unobserved. "Sid, quit it!" Sid jumped and immediately pulled his finger from his eye and started typing. Then he stopped and laughed.

"You caught me that time. I know rubbing my eye bugs you. What's wrong with a little eye rub now and then?"

"Sid, it looks awful, and you do it all the time." She sat in the chair next to his desk, put her right elbow on the desk, and began chewing her right thumbnail. "Besides it can't be that good for your eye. Your eyelid even looks red from all the rubbing."

"Come on, Dawn, that's from lack of sleep."

"Just your left eyelid?"

"Can't I rub my eye in the privacy of my study?"

"No. And you can't rub your eye when you lecture to your classes; they think it's a joke. And last year when you presented your paper at the Association for Behavior Analysis, you stood there rubbing your eye the whole time. It was embarrassing."

"I'll stop rubbing my eye when you stop biting your nails."

Now it was Dawn's turn to jump. She jerked her hand from her mouth and sat on it. Then she grinned, gave her head a nod that set her long, blond hair billowing, and rolled her eyes to the heavens in a show of innocence. This had been an effective escape response, always getting her off the hook with her father, but it was less effective with her husband.

"You're a PhD, not a 5-year-old girl, and I'm not going to let you cutesy your way out of it this time. You're right, I don't want to rub my eye. But you don't want to bite your nails either. So here's what I'll do."

Dawn stopped grinning.

"You come up with a behavioral intervention to help you grow those long, sensuous, elegant, sophisticated nails you want. And if you can apply that same intervention to my minor eye rubbing, I'll let you, 'cause I'll admit I don't want to be the weirdo of the Psych Department."

The next evening at dinner, Dawn said, "I spent the afternoon in the library, and I found an article by Miltenberger and Fuqua. It looks to me like they've got the intervention. But before I tell you what it is, let's collect baseline data for 6 days. Always carry this 3 × 5 card with you, and each time you rub your eye, record it. I'll do the same with my nail biting. This way we can get a better idea of how effective the Miltenberger-Fuqua intervention is."

"Dawn, I'll carry that card every place but in the shower."

At dinner 6 days later, Dawn asked, "Are you ready to hear about Miltenberger and Fuqua's procedure?" But she didn't wait for Sid to reply before she started to explain. "I interpret it as a simple self-punishment procedure."

"What kind of apparatus will we need? Will we have to strap electric shock electrodes to my arm?"

"All you'll need is your eye-rubbing hand. Each time you catch yourself rubbing your eye, you should stop immediately, make a fist, and hold it for three minutes."

"How do you figure that's a punishment procedure?" Sid asked.

"Having to clench your fist is effortful, it's a nuisance, and sometimes it might be embarrassing. I don't mean it's real aversive, but it seems aversive enough," she answered. "So each eye-rubbing response will immediately produce a slightly aversive condition, the clenched fist. That should be a punishment procedure."

"I'm not 100% sure you've got a punishment procedure there, but we can talk about that later. Are you going to use the same punishment contingency for your nail biting?"

"You bet," Dawn replied.

"Then let's go for it."

What were the results? Sid kept intervention data on himself for 24 more days—and the data looked good. Sid's eye rubbing dropped from a mean of 11 per day to 3. Dawn collected baseline data for 4 days more than Sid and intervention data for 20 days. And Dawn's nail biting dropped from 20 episodes per day to 5 (Figure 4.4).

Sid became a little less the departmental weirdo with the raw red eye. And Dawn became a little more the sophisticated lady with the long red nails. Each was happier to be seen in public with the other.

QUESTION

1. Diagram the punishment contingency for getting rid of a habitual behavior.

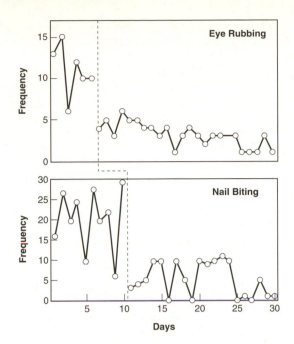

Figure 4.4   Multiple-Baseline Design Across Subjects and Behaviors

Example
Child and Family Counseling
THREE'S A CROWD[11]

Oh-oh, another sleeping problem. Not Rod this time, but 5-year-old Byron. He can't sleep alone; he hops out of his bed and climbs into bed with Mom and Dad. They say "no"; they reason with him; they take him back to his own room, but soon they hear the irritating pitter-patter of the little intruder's feet as he barges into their bedroom again.

They tried reasoning with him. And they tried direct action: Mom was more permissive, but Dad would often return him to his own bed, only to wake up in the morning finding Byron had snuck back in. Often, they would reluctantly relent, move over, and make room for Byron, though they found his presence disrupting of their relationship as well as their sleep.

In the meantime, they went from psychotherapist to psychotherapist in search of help, eventually discovering a team of behavior analysts—Ayllon,

Garber, and Allison. And this is the behavioral intervention they used: They would no longer scoot over to make room for Byron when he forced his way into their bed. If anything, while pretending to be asleep, they spread out a bit. If Byron was between them, they would both roll toward the center of the bed. If he climbed to one side, they would move in that direction. Initially, this tactic resulted in his accidentally falling off the bed without the parents' giving signs of having been awakened.

The inappropriate natural contingency is a reinforcement contingency. Byron's inappropriate entrance to his parents' bed is reinforced by their presence. But what's the performance-management contingency? Punishment by the presentation of an uncomfortable sleeping arrangement.[12]

Inappropriate Natural Reinforcement Contingency

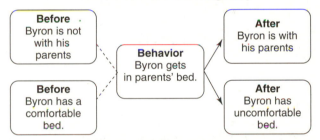

Performance-Management Punishment Contingency

And it worked. After just 1 week of this mild punishment contingency, Byron's nighttime visits dropped from 13 per week to 0 per week (Figure 4.5). Now all three sleep more comfortably.

Question: How many professional behavior analysts does it take to outfox a professional 5-year-old boy?

Answer: Three.

Question: How many traditional psychotherapists does it take to out fox a nontraditional 5-year-old boy?

---

[11]Based on Ayllon, T., Garber, S. W., & Allison, M. G. (1977). Behavioral treatment of childhood neurosis. *Psychiatry, 40,* 315–322. Here we are presenting only one component of their intervention package. Incidentally, Ted Ayllon is one of the most creative researchers in the field of applied behavior analysis; you will see a number of examples of his imaginative solutions to perplexing problems throughout this book.

[12]I've reviewed the other examples of punishment in the fundamentals section of this chapter to see if I could add to their contingency diagrams the inappropriate, natural reinforcement contingency that was maintaining their undesired behavior. But none of those examples had involved a functional assessment to discover the reinforcement contingency; and, in those cases, I was reluctant to speculate about what that reinforcement contingency might be.

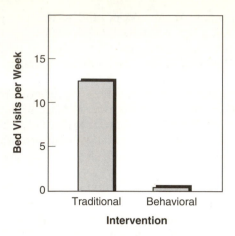

Figure 4.5   Using Mild Punishment To Decrease Poor Bedtime Behavior

Answer: More than two because two tried and failed.

And, of course, the combined efforts of Byron's two college-educated parents had been no match for him.

QUESTION

1. Diagram the punishment contingency used by Ayllon, Garber, and Allison for getting rid of a child's inappropriate nighttime visits.

Example
The Mentally Handicapped
CONTINGENT EXERCISE[13]

Ten-year-old Peter choked, kicked, hit, pulled, and pushed people an average of 63 times each 6-hour school day. His teachers had transferred him from a classroom for mentally handicapped children to a classroom for severely disturbed children.

---

[13]Based on Luce, S. C., Delquadri, J., & Hall, R. V. (1980). Contingent exercise: A mild but powerful procedure for suppressing inappropriate verbal behavior and aggressive behavior. *Journal of Applied Behavior Analysis, 13,* 583–594. These behavior analysts were from the Shawnee Mission Public Schools, where Peter was a student, and the Juniper Gardens Children's Project, which is part of the Bureau of Child Research of the University of Kansas. (Incidentally, the bureau and Juniper Gardens have been responsible for some of the most important applied work in behavior analysis, and Vance Hall has played a major role in the Juniper Gardens work.)

The behavior analysts who worked with Peter in the new classroom were Stephen Luce, Joseph Delquadri, and Vance Hall. They knew that much of the work in punishing aggressive behavior has used painful stimuli, like electric shock. But they also knew that such procedures are usually not allowed in public school classrooms. So they sought and found a more acceptable aversive outcome—exercise. Each time Peter assaulted someone the teacher required him to alternately stand and sit on the floor 10 times. They selected this task because Peter did it frequently during playtime; and yet if the task were required and repeated 10 times, it might be effortful enough to be aversive. Another reason for selecting this effortful task was that the physical education consultants said it would benefit Peter's physical fitness.

Peter's physical attacks decreased from an average of 63 per day, during baseline, to 10, during the first day of the punishment procedure. After 10 days of the punishment procedure, the attacks dropped to an average of 2.3 per day (Figure 4.6).

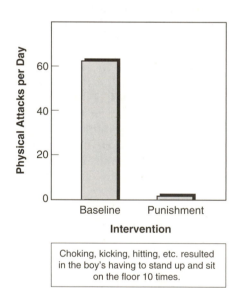

Choking, kicking, hitting, etc. resulted in the boy's having to stand up and sit on the floor 10 times.

Figure 4.6   Punishing Aggression with Contingent Physical Exercise

The punishment procedure was so successful in suppressing Peter's aggression that it actually provided little opportunity for physical exercise.

QUESTION

1. Describe the use of a punishment contingency to reduce aggression. What was the intervention and what were the results?

Example from the Mentally Handicapped
OVERCORRECTION[14]

Ann was a violent, 50-year-old woman with an IQ score of 16 (100 is average). She had been in an institution since she was 4 years old and had been violent since she was 13. About 13 times per day she completely trashed her ward, overturning beds, chairs, tables, anything not nailed down. Life for residents in a ward for people classified as mentally handicapped is never that great, but it was unbearable with Ann there.

Drs. Richard Foxx and Nathan Azrin used a procedure they had developed and made famous—*overcorrection.* With this procedure the person overcorrects for any problem behavior. Not only do people who overcorrect make things right with the environments or the people they've disturbed, but they make things better than they were before their disruptions. And they must do so with effort, and with no opportunity to rest until they've overcorrected. (When needed, the staff use physical guidance to ensure that the client overcorrects.)

In Ann's case, she had to set the furniture right and then, for example, remake the bed neatly and fluff the pillows on all the other beds in her ward. Or she had to clean the entire dining room after sweeping and mopping the food from the table she had upset. After that she had to apologize to the people whose furniture she had overturned. Because she couldn't talk, she nodded "yes" when the attendant asked if she were sorry.

Some students have said they didn't understand why having to straighten and clean the ward

was aversive. Because it's hard work! People who don't understand that hard work is aversive probably have never done any.

The results? After 37 years of violence, the overcorrection procedure reduced Ann's rate of overturning furniture from 13 times per day during baseline to less than 4 per day, within 1 week (Figure 4.7). After 11 weeks of overcorrection, Ann stopped her violence completely! Imagine that: Foxx and Azrin got rid of a 37-year problem in 11 weeks—no small trick!

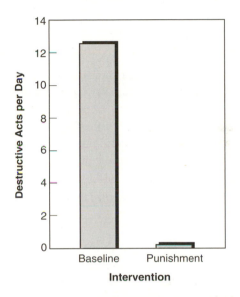

Figure 4.7 Punishing Destructive Acts with Overcorrection

This type of overcorrection is called *restitutional overcorrection,* in which the person repairs his or her damage and then some. Overcorrection sometimes has additional features. It may involve *positive practice,* where the person practices doing correctly what he or she had done wrong. Overcorrection always involves corrective behavior relevant to the inappropriate behavior and may have an educational value. But many behavior analysts think the main virtue of overcorrection is that it involves an effective punishment procedure that is usually socially acceptable (it has social validity). In other words, overcorrection is really a punishment procedure, but it is one that can often be used when other punishment procedures are prohibited. It is also true that contingent exercise may be more acceptable than traditional forms of punishment.

---

[14]Foxx, R. M., & Azrin, N. H. (1972). Restitution: A method of eliminating aggressive-disruptive behavior in retarded and brain-damaged patients. *Behavior Research & Therapy, 10,* 15–27. Richard Foxx and Nate Azrin are prominent behavioral researchers who did this work at Anna State Hospital, a hotbed of behavioral research. Both Richard and Nate have been president of the Association for Behavior Analysis. In addition Nate was president of the American Association for the Advancement of Behavior Therapy, as well as the Midwestern Psychology Association, and an editor of the *Journal of the Experimental Analysis of Behavior.* Nate is a very unusual researcher in that he is one of our field's most productive researchers in both the experimental analysis of behavior (basic animal research) and applied behavior analysis. Professional and intellectual reinforcement contingencies are such that few researchers can be strong in both areas. Nate's creative productivity is reflected in the large number of studies we cite in which he is one of the co-authors.

QUESTION

1. *Overcorrection*—define it and give an example.

Definition: Concept
Overcorrection
  ○ A contingency
  ○ on inappropriate behavior
  ○ requiring the person
  ○ to engage in an effortful response
  ○ that more than corrects
  ○ the effects of the inappropriate behavior.

CONCLUSIONS

These experiments suggest several conclusions:

1. In many cases, you don't need to use electric shock. You can get rid of inappropriate behavior using more acceptable aversive outcomes, such as
    a. the effort of squeezing your fist
    b. the effort of correcting for past disruptions
    c. the effort of physical exercise
    d. the brief touching of an ice cube to the face
    e. a squirt of sour lemon juice
    f. a reprimand
    g. visual screening.
2. These aversive outcomes can quickly and effectively suppress behavior, even if the person has been doing that behavior for many years—for example, in the cases of
    a. habitual behavior
    b. self-injurious behavior
    c. aggressing
    d. teeth grinding
    e. goofing off
    f. self-stimulating.
3. Even with excellent reinforcement programs, added punishment sometimes greatly improves performance, as in the cases of
    a. a remedial grade-school classroom, and
    b. vocational training for people classified as profoundly mentally handicapped.
4. Because the punishment contingency usually suppresses behavior so quickly and effectively, the client usually makes little contact with the aversive outcomes, as in the cases of
    a. lemon-juice punishment of regurgitation
    b. shock punishment of self-injurious behavior
    c. shock punishment for harmful sneezing
    d. visual screening for disruptive self-stimulation
    e. contingent exercise for aggression against people

f. overcorrection for aggression against property.

*Example of the Sick Social Cycle
(Victim's Punishment Model)
Behavioral Special Education*
JIMMY, THE AUTISTIC CHILD[15]—PART II

Remember, from Chapter 3, how Jimmy escaped difficult tasks by disrupting the training sessions. Well, he and Sue had a type of **sick social cycle** going, because she reinforced his aversive, violent disruptions by allowing him to escape the difficult training task. On the other hand, Jimmy's violent disruptions punished Sue's insisting that he stay on task. In this case, Sue (the victim) stopped her appropriate insistence that Jimmy stay on task because her insistence was being punished by Jimmy's (the perpetrator's) aversive disruptions (see the top diagram on p. 71).

We start with Sue's asking Jimmy to do a tough task. In a sense, that causes Jimmy to disrupt (the solid arrow between the two). And in a sense, Jimmy's disruption causes Sue to stop insisting that he do the tough task (the next solid arrow). And in a sense, Sue's no longer insisting causes Jimmy to stop disrupting (the third solid arrow). For the final connection, we've continued with our dashed-arrow tradition; here it indicates that it might be better here just to say Jimmy's not disrupting is **followed by** Sue's asking him to do a tough task. But once again, these arrows are becoming metaphysical, and you or your teacher may want you to say *followed by* for all four arrows.

We should not read more into Jimmy's violent disruptions than is there. He is simply making a response that has been reinforced in the past. We should not say that he is trying to escape, or trying to control Sue, or trying to communicate his needs, or on a power trip. He is not necessarily even aware of what he's doing and most likely not aware of the contingencies controlling what he's doing. And the same might be said of Sue; she might not have realized that she was letting Jimmy off the hook when he disrupted, let alone that her failure to hang in was reinforcing his disruptions. Such lack of awareness is almost certainly the case for many classroom teachers, even special ed teachers.

In Chapter 3, we saw an example of the sick social cycle based on an escape contingency for the victim; Dawn's inappropriately timed behavior was

---
[15]Based on Carr, E. G., & Durand, V. M. (1985). Reducing behavior problems through functional communication training. *Journal of Applied Behavior Analysis, 18,* 111–126.

Jimmy & Sue's Sick Social Cycle
(Victim's Punishment Model)

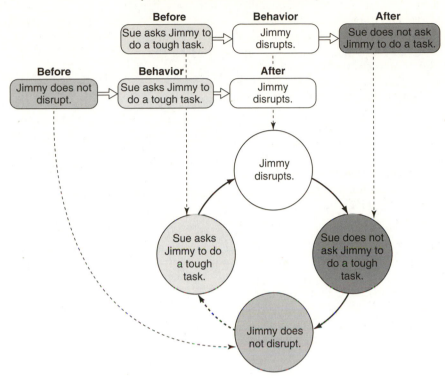

The Generic Sick Social Cycle
(Victim's Punishment Model)

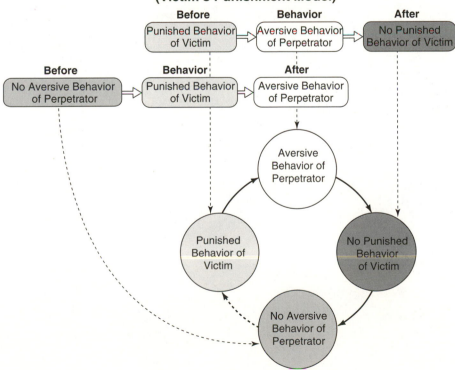

reinforced by escape from Rod's crying. In the case of Jimmy and Sue, we have a different type of sick social cycle, one based on punishment of the victim's appropriate behavior. The diagram at the bottom of p. 71 is a generic diagram of this sort of social interaction.

Note that the first contingency is always an escape contingency, whereby inappropriate behavior is reinforced by escape from an aversive condition.

Note that the second contingency is always a punishment contingency, whereby appropriate behavior is punished.

Remember that the dead-man test does *not* apply to the before and after conditions of a contingency diagram. So it's OK that the victim is not behaving in the after condition of the first condition, because that's really a stimulus condition for the perpetrator. And similarly, it's OK, if there's no aversive behavior by the perpetrator in the before condition of the second contingency diagram.

QUESTION

1. *Sick social cycle (victim's punishment model)*— define it and give an example
   ○ Draw the two contingency diagrams for your example.
   ○ Draw the circular diagram of the sick social cycle.
2. Now please fill in the diagram below for your whole sick social cycle. (The contingency for the perpetrator goes in the top row; and the contingency for the victim goes in the second row.)
   ○ Make sure the first contingency is an escape contingency, where the inappropriate behavior of the perpetrator is reinforced by escape from an aversive condition.
   ○ Make sure the second contingency is a punishment contingency where the appropriate behavior of the victim is punished.

Definition: General Rule

The sick social cycle (victim's punishment model)

○ The perpetrator's aversive behavior punishes
○ the victim's appropriate behavior.
○ And the victim's stopping the appropriate behavior
○ unintentionally reinforces that aversive behavior.

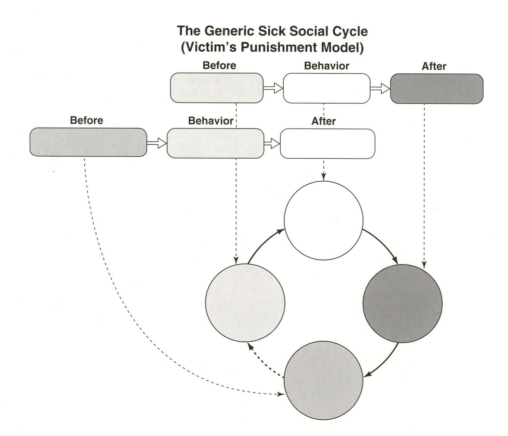

**The Generic Sick Social Cycle
(Victim's Punishment Model)**

BASIC ENRICHMENT

In the Skinner Box
Experimental Analysis
PUNISHMENT OF THE LEVER PRESS

This time, when you peep through the window of the Skinner box, you see the water dipper is there again, but the notorious metal rods that make up the floor are still there, too. And of course it wouldn't be a Skinner box without a device with which the animal can respond. For the rat, it's usually the lever, as it is again this time.

On this occasion, the rat acts weird. It keeps approaching the lever and then backing away. It raises its paws above the lever and then pulls quickly away. It touches the lever, ever so leery, and then jerks away. Finally, the rat presses the lever all the way down and jerks slightly; the water dipper raises, and the rat's on that dipper in a flash, licking it clean. Then, slowly, the rat approaches the lever again, as leery as before.

What's going on here? Of course, you only have to look at the title of this chapter to tell. The presentation of an aversive condition (a brief and mild electric shock) punishes the lever-press response. The rat is in a bind—the same bind you and I are often in: The same response produces both a reward (the drop of water) and an aversive stimulus (the shock). Just like the spoonful of hot soup can produce a good taste *and* a burned mouth. And just like the rat approaches the lever, we approach the hot soup, ever so leery.

Once again, how does this punishment contingency compare with the escape contingency?

For escape, the **removal** of the shock reinforces the lever press.

Escape Contingency

For punishment, the **presentation** of the shock punishes the lever press.

Punishment Contingency

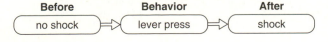

But wherever you see a punishment procedure suppressing a response, you know it must be working against a reinforcement procedure maintaining that response. Either a reinforcement contingency must be operating at the same time as the punishment history, or, at least, the reinforcement contingency must have been operating prior to the punishment contingency. If there is no reinforcement contingency and never has been one, then there would be no response for the punishment contingency to punish. Here, the presentation of the water reinforces the lever press while at the same time the presentation of the shock suppresses the lever press.

Reinforcement Contingency

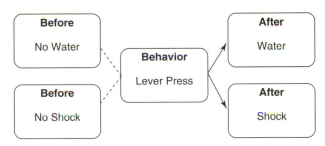

Punishment Contingency

QUESTION

1. Using the Skinner box, compare and contrast punishment and escape.

FOR EVERY PUNISHMENT CONTINGENCY, THERE'S A REINFORCEMENT CONTINGENCY IN THE BACKGROUND

Here's an important point:

> **Whenever you have a punishment contingency, you must also have a reinforcement contingency.**

Why is that true? Suppose you wanted to demonstrate punishment of the lever press in the Skinner box. You'd need the rat to press the lever before you could punish that response. But how would you get the lever-press response? You'd have to reinforce it—for example, with water.

In other words, for punishment to occur, you need behavior; and for behavior to occur reliably, it must be reinforced. Now it's easy to miss this important point if you just look at the case studies we presented in the Fundamentals section. In most of those cases, we knew the strange behaviors occurred at high rates. We didn't ask why they occurred. But if they occurred, you can be sure they were producing reinforcers. In these cases we don't know what the reinforcers were. But we assume there must have been reinforcers.

What do you think reinforced Velma's and Gerri's grinding their teeth, Sandra's regurgitating, Jack's banging his head, the grade school kids' disrupting, Ange's sneezing, David's self-stimulating, Sid's rubbing his eye, Dawn's biting her nails, Peter's aggressing, and Ann's trashing the ward? Whew, what a list! Now, most of these studies were done before the common use of functional analysis—an analysis of the contingencies responsible for behavioral problems (nowadays, functional analyses would normally have been done before intervention, to see if it would be possible to decrease the behavior without using a punishment procedure). But in these examples, we don't really know what the relevant reinforcement contingencies were that maintained the undesirable behaviors. But here are a couple wild guesses, just to show you what the contingency diagrams look like:

Inappropriate Natural Reinforcement Contingency

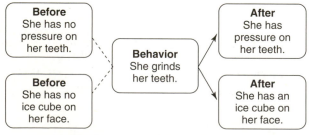

Performance-Management Punishment Contingency

As you will see in Chapter 10, under some conditions pressure on the teeth seems to be a reinforcer. We call this reinforcement contingency *inappropriate* only because it is exerting more control over the behavior of the two women than it should.

Inappropriate Natural Reinforcement Contingency

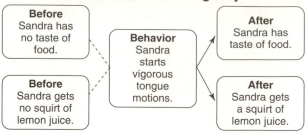

Performance-Management Punishment Contingency

Sandra's vigorous tongue motions caused her to throw up her food, which in turn produced the taste of the food. And, strange as it seems, research suggests that the taste of regurgitated food may sometimes be a reinforcer.

In any case, whenever you use a punishment contingency, you should keep your eye on the reinforcement contingency as well. One of the values of the Skinner box is that it highlights the need for a reinforcement contingency. And concern for the reinforcement contingency's maintaining the undesirable behavior is even more important now that the use of punishment has decreased considerably in popularity. In many instances, we are almost forced to do a functional analysis in order to find the undesirable reinforcement contingency. Then we can counteract that undesirable contingency in one way or another—for example, by extinction of inappropriate behavior combined with differential reinforcement of alternative behavior.

In The Skinner Box
From the Experimental Analysis of Behavior
BASIC RESEARCH[16]

With Jack's self-mutilation, we saw how the process of reinforcement and punishment may work in opposite directions. We guessed that Jack's head banging occurred because attention reinforced it. We also guessed that the severe physical stress from his head banging wasn't very aversive for Jack. Perhaps his head banging had gradually increased in intensity, causing it to lose its aversiveness.

This may seem like wild speculation, so we need to test the notion with an experiment in the

---

[16]Based on Azrin, N. H. (1959). Punishment and recovery during fixed-ratio performance. *Journal of the Experimental Analysis of Behavior, 2,* 301–305.

lab. The first question is: Are there circumstances under which a small reinforcer will maintain a response, in spite of an intense physical stressor contingent on each response? If yes, then the second question is, why? What are those circumstances? Research lab-based answers to these two questions will help us understand Jack's case.

Dr. Nathan Azrin used pigeons rather than human beings in a relevant study at Anna State Hospital. Past experiments have shown that most results of this sort of animal research are as true of human beings as they are of other animals.

If we had walked into Nate Azrin's lab then, we might have seen a pigeon inside a Skinner box pecking a small disk that served as a response key (instead of a rat pressing a lever).

Immediately after each key peck, the pigeon flutters its wings, lurches violently, and almost falls down. Looking closer, we notice a pair of wires connected to the pigeon. Through these wires the bird receives a brief but intense shock each time it pecks the key. The shock is so powerful it almost knocks down the pigeon. Yet the bird keeps pecking the key and getting shocks. Why? Jack kept banging his head, in spite of the physical stress. In the same way, the bird keeps pecking the key, in spite of the electric shock.

In fact, why does the pigeon peck the key in the first place? As we keep looking at this peculiarly persistent pigeon, we notice that some key pecks cause a feeder full of grain to come up to a trough in the wall of the Skinner box. Of course, the bird is quick to start eating the food for the few seconds the feeder remains in the trough. Put another way, reinforcement by the presentation of a food reinforcer maintains the key-peck response. Just as Jack's head banging produced the potential reinforcer of attention, the pigeon's key pecking produces the occasional reinforcer of grain.

So the answer to our first experimental question is this: Yes, sometimes an animal, and we assume a human being, will tolerate much physical stress contingent on each response, though that response produces only a small reinforcer, even when that small reinforcer occurs only occasionally.

Then what about our second question: Why? What are the circumstances? The answer: We will tolerate much physical stress when the intensity of the physical stress increases gradually.

As we *imagined*, day by day, Jack gradually increased the intensity of his head banging; we *know*, day by day, Nate gradually increased the intensity of the electric shock.

Other work had shown that if Nate had started out with a high-intensity shock, the bird would have greatly decreased its rate of pecking and might have

stopped altogether. So Nate Azrin's careful laboratory work supports our speculations about the processes underlying this bizarre behavior from the everyday world.

QUESTION

1. Compare and contrast Jack's case with Azrin's Skinner box experiment.

Ethics
SHOULD YOU USE ELECTRIC SHOCK IN A PUNISHMENT CONTINGENCY?[17]

Sid's Seminar

Tom: I hate this punishment contingency, especially with electric shock. Shock is awful just to read about, let alone to experience. There's no way I'd ever use electric shock in a punishment procedure.

Sue: I feel the same way, especially with children who have it forced on them. But then I ask myself if their lives were better after the punishment procedure. And in the cases we read about, I have to answer yes.

Tom: Were they enough better to justify the electric shock?

---

[17]Based on: Goldiamond, I. (1984). Training parent trainers and ethicists in nonlinear analysis of behavior. In R. Dangel & R. Polster (Eds.), *Parent training foundations of research and practice* (pp. 504–546). New York: Guilford Press; Griffith, R. G. (1983). The administrative issues: An ethical and legal perspective. In S. Axelrod & J. Apshe (Eds.), *The effects of punishment on human behavior* (pp. 317–338). New York: Academic Press; Iwata, B. A. (1988). The development and adoption of controversial default technologies. *The Behavior Analyst, 11,* 149–157; McGee, J. J. (1987). Ethical issues of aversive techniques: A response to Thompson, Gardner, & Baumeister. In J. A. Stark, F. J. Menolascino, M. H. Albarelli, & V. C. Gray (Eds.), *Mental retardation and mental health: Classification, diagnosis, treatment, services* (pp. 218–228). New York: Springer-Verlag; Martin, G., & Pear, J. (1988). *Behavior modification: What it is and how to do it* (pp. 195–197). Englewood Cliffs, NJ: Prentice Hall; Thompson, T., Gardner, W. I., & Baumeister, A. A. (1987). Ethical issues in interventions for persons with retardation, autism and related developmental disorders. In J. A. Stark, F. J. Menolascino, M. H. Albarelli, & V. C. Gray (Eds.), *Mental retardation and mental health: Classification, diagnosis, treatment, services* (pp. 213–217). New York: Springer-Verlag; Van Houten, R., Axelrod, S., Bailey, J. S., Favell, J. E., Foxx, R. M., Iwata, B. A., & Lovaas, O. I. (1988). The right to effective behavioral treatment. *The Behavior Analyst, 11,* 111–114; We've cited many references here because this is an important and controversial issue. In addition, some references present views that directly oppose ours, but they are views with which the serious behavior analyst should be familiar.

Sid: Good question. We must always ask whether the benefit was worth the cost.

Sue: Let's look at the cases: For Jack the cost was perhaps a couple dozen brief, mild shocks. The benefits were that he stopped injuring his head and he no longer had to be tied or imprisoned in a crib. That also meant he might have a better chance of acquiring some normal behavior. As for Ange, the cost was 3 minutes of mild shocks. And the benefits were relief from a life of constant sneezes. Also, she no longer had to suffer difficult medical treatments.

Joe: In both cases, the physical stress of the punishment procedures seems a lot less than the physical stress of the horrible conditions the children suffered. I think the benefits much more than justify the costs.

Eve: In spite of Mr. Field's point contingencies, I haven't talked much in this seminar. But I've got to say something now. The lives of those children seemed almost inhuman, in both of those cases, and especially in the cases of Jack and Ange, I can't even imagine it. I sure wouldn't volunteer to give those electric shocks. I don't even like to watch a physician stick a needle in someone. But I'd force myself to overcome my squeamishness to help those poor kids live a slightly more human life.

Tom: Maybe so, but is that what it takes? Aren't there other ways of helping those kids?

Sid: That's a good point, too. We should always make sure we're using the least aversive and the least drastic, the least restrictive, and the least intrusive intervention.

Sue: Yes, in my work with Jimmy, an autistic child, we decided our attention was reinforcing some of his disruptive behavior. So we used contingent attention to reinforce a more acceptable alternative response. That helped us get rid of part of his disruptions. Maybe in Jack's case, they could have used attention to reinforce an alternative to head banging.

Sid: An excellent idea.

Joe: Maybe. But maybe not. Suppose they had wasted several weeks messing around with differential reinforcement of alternative behavior and perhaps some other less drastic procedures. And suppose you finally found one that worked. If I were Jack's father, I'd say this to the professionals: "Why in the heck did you subject my kid to several extra, needless weeks of head banging, while you wasted time searching for some wimp procedure? Why didn't you use a few brief, mild shocks right away, so he could stop destroying himself? My kid has a right

to the most effective and prompt intervention you've got."

Sid: You're saying not only should we (1) weigh the costs of the punishment procedure and the benefits of getting rid of the inappropriate behavior, but we also should (2) weigh the costs of searching for a less drastic procedure. We should consider both factors when doing a cost-benefit analysis of punishment.

Joe: Yes, and I'll say this, too: I think the physical stress these punishment interventions cause is much less than the physical stress physicians often cause with their treatments involving drugs, injections, and surgery. Yet most people don't get bent out of shape about that.

Max: I read an article by Dr. Brian Iwata where he describes recent work similar to that done with Jack. He writes about the development of a device that automatically shocks self-injurious behavior. They call it *SIBIS, the Self-Injurious Behavior Inhibiting System.* Here's what he has to say about the need for punishment contingencies: "Our treatment program on self-injury had an overall staff-to-client ratio of about 5:1 (five staff for each client), with BAs, MAs, and PhDs outnumbering clients by better than 2:1. Despite all this expertise, our reinforcement-based approaches to treatment were not always successful. We clearly needed to have available a treatment option based on aversive stimulation." He then adds that his reading of the literature suggests that electric stimulation is often the best way to go, for the client's sake.

Sid: Regarding that, let me read a message from Dr. Peter Holmes that I downloaded last night from the Behavioral Bulletin Board: "A court case in Flint, MI, may have broad implications for the 'use-of-aversives' controversy. Yesterday it was reported that a U.S. district court awarded a grandmother $42,500 in damages because a school system had refused to permit her granddaughter to wear a SIBIS device in her special ed. classroom. (The granddaughter has blinded herself from self-hitting.)

Eve: That poor child. That's so sad.

Joe: It sure is sad, but I'm happy to hear that the courts are beginning to rule that people have a right to effective behavioral interventions, even if they go against a simplistic set of values of some school policy makers.

Tom: Maybe, but one problem with punishment is that the punishers may end up being role models. And the clients themselves may imitate that use of punishment. And another problem is that caregivers can easily abuse the use of punishment.

Sid: Yes. Children, clients in centers for the mentally handicapped, and clients in psychiatric hospitals are easy to abuse because they often don't have much power to defend themselves.

Max: That's why at least half the states now have laws designed to protect the rights of defenseless clients in the use of punishment. And most institutions have guidelines for punishment, for example:

- The person's behavior must be dangerous to himself or herself or to others.
- The person probably will benefit from the intervention.
- Solid data suggest that less drastic or less intrusive interventions will not work.
- Generally, use reinforcement to establish appropriate behavior, with any uses of punishment to get rid of inappropriate behavior.
- A well-trained, professional behavior analyst must design and supervise the procedure.
- A clients' rights committee must approve the procedure.

Sid: So we use punishment as a last resort and with guidelines to protect the client.

Max: Let me just add that in future chapters the authors describe procedures that may sometimes be good alternatives to punishment.

QUESTIONS

1. What are two factors you should consider in doing a cost-benefit analysis of using punishment?
2. What are six considerations you should include in guidelines for punishment?

CONFUSION BETWEEN PUNISHMENT AND AGGRESSION

In our view, we should not be allowed to use punishment as a performance management or training technique without considerable supervision and accountability for our actions. Here's the problem: Suppose, for example, our child or an autistic child or a mentally handicapped adult acts inappropriately. Suppose they spit at us. That will be aversive for us. So what do we do? We "implement a punishment contingency." We slap the offender. Why? Because that was a well-thought out behavioral intervention? No, because when we're aversively stimulated (like when we're spit at), it's reinforcing to strike back, to aggress. And whether we're a parent, a teacher, or a direct-care staff member in a training center for the mentally handicapped, we will tend to hit first and ask questions later. We will tend to go for the aggression reinforcer of striking our tormentor and *then* try to justify our actions in terms of a punishment procedure designed for the best interests of the person whom we're supposed to be helping, the child or client. So it's good that we're restrained in our use of punishment; it's good that we have to have special training and special approval before we even squirt a kid with a little mist in the face. (Some students have misread this to mean that punishment doesn't work, but the point of this whole chapter is that carefully used punishment works very well. The following summarizes the point of this paragraph.)

> **Don't use punishment in wrath.**
>
> **Don't confuse the behavioral use of punishment with divine retribution.**
>
> **Forget the eye-for-an-eye notion. Divine retribution is God's job; your job is to make that punishment as short as possible; all you want to do is modify behavior, not make people atone for their sins.**

INTERMEDIATE ENRICHMENT

Research Methods
DEPENDENT VARIABLE AND INDEPENDENT VARIABLE

The concepts of *cause* and *effect* are complex, and not all philosophers of science consider them of value. But at least they're a place to start. You turn on your kitchen stove, and the water starts to boil. Roughly speaking, the heat from the stove caused the water to boil. The heat was the cause. The boiling was the effect.

Each time the rat presses the lever, you give it a drop of water—you reinforce the lever presses. In the future, the rat presses the lever more frequently. Your reinforcement caused the rat's increased frequency of lever pressing. Past reinforcement is the cause; the increased frequency of pressing is the effect. Cause and effect.

And that's what scientists study—cause and effect. The scientist asks, Why does something happen? What causes it? I wonder what would be the effect of doing this or that. Cause and effect.

But scientists don't often use the words *cause* and *effect*. Instead, they use the expressions **independent variable** and **dependent variable.** *Independent variable* means "cause" and *dependent variable* means "effect," more or less. You might say a particular value of the independent variable causes a particular value of the dependent variable.

You might say a particular temperature of the water causes it to boil at a particular rate. The temperature is the independent variable and the boiling is the dependent variable. And you might say a particular amount of reinforcement causes the rat to press the lever at a particular frequency. The amount of reinforcement is the independent variable and the frequency of pressing is the dependent variable.

So two basic concepts of science are dependent and independent variables. In behavior analysis, the *dependent variable* is a measure of the client's or subject's behavior. The *independent variable* is the variable the behavior analyst or experimenter systematically manipulates to influence the dependent variable. In the case of Sandra's regurgitation, the behavior analysts selected as the *independent variable* a small amount of unsweetened lemon juice squirted into Sandra's mouth contingent on her throwing up; and they observed its effects on the *dependent variable,* her frequency of regurgitation. Sandra eventually stopped throwing up her milk.

The frequency of future regurgitation was *dependent* on the punishment contingency of the sour lemon juice in her mouth whenever she had regurgitated in the past. But the experimenters could implement the contingency or not, whenever they wished. So the implementation of that contingency was independent; it was the *independent variable.* Another way to put it is the *independent variable* is the *intervention* and the *dependent variable* is the *target behavior.*

Definition: Concepts
Dependent variable
  ○ A measure of the subject's behavior.
Independent variable
  ○ The variable the experimenter systematically manipulates
  ○ to influence the dependent variable.

QUESTIONS

1. Define each of the following concepts:
   a. dependent variable
   b. independent variable
2. Describe an experiment that illustrates these two concepts.

Research Methods
GRAPHS

When collecting data on the behavior of interest, you might find that the data don't make much sense at first glance; you need to organize and study them. Let's look at the case of Sandra's regurgitation. The behavior analysts organized the data as shown in Figure 4.8.

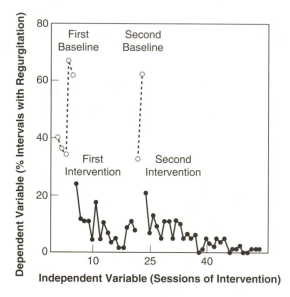

Figure 4.8   Effects of a Lemon Juice Contingency on Reurgitation

Figure 4.8 shows details of the results of the lemon-juice intervention. The vertical axis (*y-axis* or *ordinate*) represents percentage intervals of Sandra's regurgitation. The horizontal axis (*x-axis* or *abscissa*) represents the days when the data were collected. This axis is divided into four separate segments, the first 5 days of baseline, 4 days of the lemon contingency, 2 days of baseline again, and 27 more days of the lemon contingency. Usually we indicate the dependent variable on the vertical axis and the independent variable on the horizontal axis. But it's not simply days of the independent variable here; it's days of exposure to the intervention versus days of exposure to the baseline conditions.

The data points show that the values of the dependent variable (percentage of intervals of regurgitation) decreased when we presented the intervention value of the independent variable (the contingent sour lemon juice in Sandra's mouth).[18]

This more detailed look at the data shows that Sandra's regurgitation decreased as soon as the behavior analysts started using the lemon-juice contingency. So this suggests it was the lemon-juice contingency that controlled Sandra's regurgitation.

We use bar graphs in the main part of this book because they show the results in a quick and dramatic way; but behavior analysts usually make daily use of more detailed graphs that show the change in performance over time, that show trends in the data, like the preceding graph. This way, they can do more detailed analyses of the effects of the independent variable on the dependent variable. A bar graph of the data would look like the lemon-juice graph in the first part of this chapter. That bar graph is based on the mean percentage intervals of regurgitation by phase. The bar graph also shows the effect of the independent variable on the dependent variable. (The experimental design the behavior analysts used to study Sandra's regurgitation is called a **reversal design**—an experimental design in which we reverse between intervention and baseline conditions to assess the effects of the intervention. We will study the reversal design in Chapter 5.)

QUESTIONS

1. What information can be obtained from a line or bar graph?
2. What information is represented in the *x*-axis, or abscissa?
3. What information is represented in the *y*-axis, or ordinate?

Research Methods
MULTIPLE-BASELINE DESIGNS

Earlier, we omitted this part of the discussion between Sid and Dawn:

Sid, the professional skeptic, said, "Before I agree to spend my time and energy on your intervention, I want to know more about Miltenberger and Fuqua's evidence that it works."

"First," Dawn said, "their clients recorded their undesirable habitual behavior, during at least 6 days of baseline before the intervention, just like we did. The undesirable habitual behavior occurred at a lower rate after the intervention."

"Coincidence?"

"The more times you repeat or replicate an intervention, and the more times you get the same results, the more confident you are those results came from your intervention and not just chance variation. So they replicated the experiment five times. They collected the baseline of five different clients and then intervened. They used a **multiple-baseline design.** More specifically, they used a **multiple-baseline-across-subjects design.** Five different clients each showed a decrease in the frequency of their undesirable habitual behavior from the baseline to the intervention." [The other types of baselines are multiple-baseline-across-behaviors and multiple-baseline-across-settings designs.]

Definition: Concept
Multiple-baseline design
- An experimental design
- in which the replications involve
- baselines of differing durations
- and interventions of differing starting times.

"Yes, but maybe they were getting better anyway. Maybe if Miltenberger and Fuqua hadn't intervened at all, the frequency of undesirable habitual behaviors would still have decreased."

"Maybe, except when you look at the data for each day, there's no decreasing trend during baseline. In other words, the baseline shows no evidence that the undesirable habitual behaviors were becoming less frequent."

"But a week might not be enough time to see a slow decrease."

"Whether that's a problem depends on how abrupt the change is from baseline to the first days of the intervention. In all cases, there was an abrupt and fairly large decrease from the baseline to the intervention—much larger than could result from a slow trend in the baseline," Dawn replied.

"OK, I'll go for it, but is their intervention self-punishment, as you interpret it, or is it just increased self-awareness?" Sid asked. "Maybe recording and clenching their fists just made them more aware that they were doing the undesirable habitual behaviors. And once they were aware of their behavior; they could control it; they could eliminate it."

"I doubt if increased self-awareness caused the decreased frequency of undesirable habitual behaviors during the intervention, but it might have during baseline. During baseline, maybe their recording of their own behavior did increase their awareness of their undesirable habitual behaviors. So maybe that

---

[18]Note that we might say there are two values of the independent variable in this study, 0% contingent sour lemon juice (baseline) and 100% contingent sour lemon juice (intervention).

self-recording caused them to make the undesirable response less frequently during baseline than before they started recording. Still, the contingent fist clenching during the intervention decreased the frequency of the undesirable habitual behaviors, even below the baseline. So I guess the fist clenching must have been aversive and the contingent clenching must have been a punishment procedure."

"Yes," Sid said, "that's a pretty good example of the value of a baseline. You can't do the research without having the clients self-record. So if you include their self-recording during the baseline, then you can rule that out as the sole cause of the changed frequency during intervention."

In experimental research, you should clearly show that changes in your independent variable caused changes in your dependent variable. For instance, look at the reduction of Sid's eye rubbing and Dawn's nail biting between baseline and the intervention. With that goal, let's make explicit the four criteria of good research Dawn and Sid implied:

1. You must have something to compare. You must record the dependent variable under at least two different values of the independent variable. In behavior analysis, we often compare the intervention with a baseline condition (self-recording plus contingent fist clenching during the intervention versus self-recording only during the baseline).
2. You need to replicate the change in your independent variable enough times to rule out coincidence (for example, do the same intervention with five different people). You could replicate the experiment across subjects, settings, or behavior.
3. With a baseline comparison, you need to record data long enough to rule out the chance that your dependent variable would have changed even if you hadn't changed the independent variable (for example, record for several days).
4. You need fewer days of baseline if the change in your independent variable will produce abrupt changes in your dependent variable.

QUESTIONS

1. *Multiple-baseline design*—describe it and give an example.
2. List three types of multiple-baseline designs.
3. Explain and illustrate four of the criteria for good research using a simple baseline design.

Ethics and Research Methods[19]
THE IMPORTANCE OF GOOD RESEARCH DESIGNS

As you just saw, the use of aversive contingencies generates hot debate among students. But the debate gets even hotter among professionals: John McGee, the main advocate of gentle teaching, has little doubt about the immorality of using the punishment contingency to prevent inappropriate behavior. In spite of the sort of research we've presented in this chapter, he would say we have "two decades of failed punishment-based research." He goes on to say:

> I hold that the use of punishment is . . . the use of ill-conceived, poorly tested, and counterproductive methods. . . . Chains have been replaced by forced relaxation. Lobotomies are replaced by grotesque practices such as squirting noxious substances in people's faces, eyes, and nostrils. Hydrotherapy is now water mist sprayed into the face. Punishment and neglect are now termed aversive therapy. . . .
>
> At best, punishment results in submissive, obedient persons. More typically, after severe forms of punishment fail, the individuals are restrained or encased in helmets for the balance of their lives.
>
> The fact of the matter is that in those places where punishment is used correctly and systematically, it is still repugnant and unnecessary.

McGee cites his work at the Nebraska Psychiatric Institute with 82 people classified as mentally handicapped or mentally ill. These 82 people all did severe self-injurious behaviors. He claims that for all 82 clients he and his colleagues prevented or reduced the self-injurious behavior to a manageable level. And they did it without the use of punishment.

If McGee is right in his critique of the use of the punishment contingency, and if he's right about the effectiveness of gentle teaching, then behavior analysts face a serious moral problem. But, of course, most behavior analysts don't accept his criticism. They would argue that he uses superficial, erroneous analogies in comparing the behavior analyst's use of the punishment contingency with failed

---

[19]Based on: Jordan, J., Singh, N. N., & Repp, A. C. (1989). An evaluation of gentle teaching and visual screening in the reduction of stereotypy. *Journal of Applied Behavior Analysis, 22,* 9–22. And based on McGee, J. J. (1987). Ethical issues of aversive techniques: A response to Thompson, Gardner, & Baumeister. In J. A. Stark, F. J. Menolascino, M. H. Albarelli, & V. C. Gray (Eds.), *Mental retardation and mental health: Classification, diagnosis, treatment, services* (pp. 218–228). New York: Springer-Verlag.

psychiatric techniques of the past, and that his assessment of the punishment research and its results is wide of the mark. They also might suggest that he selected the label *gentle teaching* as a misleading emotional appeal akin to the language manipulation of Madison Avenue. And they might suggest that a more descriptive, though perhaps less salable, label would be *behavioral training based on reinforcement and quiet teaching.*

In addition, they would question the data he has offered in support of gentle teaching, on two grounds: First, the data are not consistent with the published scientific data and their direct experience in working with self-injurious behavior. But such objections are open to many interpretations and can be challenged. More to the point, they question the validity of the data he offers because of their informal nature.

The history of the practice of science is the history of men and women seeking truth and instead discovering what supports their biases, their prejudices. And the history of scientific method is the history of the development of procedures to protect us scientists from our own biases. (We have placed these sections on scientific research methods throughout this book. In a sense, these sections are about that—methods scientists have developed to protect themselves from their biases.)

Scientists have learned to distrust informal evidence. It's too easy to fool ourselves (even though we are honorable people with noble intentions). To protect ourselves from our own biases we must follow the following scientific practices:

○ We must use good experimental designs that provide for clear comparisons between various experimental conditions. And when one experiment leaves room for more than one interpretation of the results, then we must do another experiment, and another.

○ We must describe our experimental procedures and measurements so completely and objectively that other scientists can repeat (replicate) our experiments to see if they get the same results.

○ We must take **reliability measurements** on both our independent variables and our dependent variables. Put another way, we must have two or more different people—**independent observers**—measure our behavior as scientists to ensure that we and our staff do the procedures as we have described them. We must be sure we reliably intervened as we said we did. And we must be sure we are recording the behavior we say we're recording. To do this, independent observers must record the same dependent variables and then compare their results. If they are not in high agreement about what the subject was doing, then the results are not reliable and we can't trust them.

Definition: Concept
Reliability measurement
○ The comparison of measurements
○ of dependent variables and
○ independent variables
○ obtained by independent observers.

Informal data provide a good place to start in our quest for knowledge. But eventually the advocates of gentle teaching must meet the strict requirements of scientific method in their use of research designs, description of procedures, and reliability measurements.

The ethical question is: Are the clients of behavior analysts being treated with inhumane callousness, as the gentle-teaching advocates seem to suggest? Or are the clients of the gentle teachers deprived of their rights to effective treatment, as the behavior analysts may suspect? This is not an empty debate. And the requirement that the answers must come from high-quality scientific research is no ivory-tower, intellectual requirement. Answers to these ethical questions must meet this requirement if those answers are to rise above the biases of the participating scientists.

QUESTIONS

1. *Reliability measurement*—define it.
2. What scientific practices must we follow to protect ourselves from our biases?

Ethics and Research Methods
INFORMED CONSENT
AND SOCIAL VALIDITY

Before Stephen Luce and his colleagues began using contingent exercise to reduce Peter's aggression, they talked it over with Peter's parents. They described the aggression. Of course this wasn't news to Peter's parents, and they desperately wanted help to get rid of this aggression. The behavior analysts also described various possible interventions, with their risks and benefits. Then they explained that the parents could ask the behavior analysts to stop the intervention anytime they wished. Only after all these issues had been discussed, did the behavior analysts ask the parents for their **informed consent** to intervene. This informed consent process is ethically and legally crucial whenever we use an experimental intervention or aversive control, even one with an aversive outcome as mild as this set of exercises.

Definition: Concept
Informed consent
- ◦ Consent to intervene in a way
- ◦ that is experimental or
- ◦ risky.
- ◦ The participant or guardian
- ◦ is informed of the risks and benefits
- ◦ and of the right to stop the intervention.

Even if an intervention works, the participants might not like it. For example, they might not think it was worth the effort, or they might think it had negative side effects. An intervention can be behaviorally valid (it works) but not **socially valid** (people don't like it). So the behavior analysts individually asked the participating teacher and teacher's aides about it. Each said it was effective, and some mentioned that such a procedure would generally not raise objections (a problem with using electric shock). Also, later, the teacher independently used contingent exercise as an effective punishment procedure in reducing other problem behaviors and in working with other children. All this suggests that the procedure is socially valid.

Definition: Concept
Social validity[20]
- ◦ The goals,
- ◦ procedures, and
- ◦ results of an intervention
- ◦ are socially acceptable to
- ◦ the client,
- ◦ the behavior analyst, and
- ◦ society.

QUESTIONS

1. *Informed consent*—define it and give an example.
2. *Social validity*—define it and give an example.

---

[20]Based on: Bernstein, G. S. (1989). In response: Social validity and the report of the ABA task force on right to effective treatment. *The Behavior Analyst, 12, 97.*

Compare and Contrast
NEGATIVE REINFORCEMENT VS. PUNISHMENT

In Chapter 3, we warned you that the concept *negative reinforcer* confused most students. We said you could escape the confusion by substituting *aversive condition* for *negative reinforcer,* at least until the proper use of *negative reinforcer* becomes a strong part of your repertoire. We also said *negative reinforcement* means the same thing as *reinforcement by the removal of an aversive condition.*

Now for the big problem: discriminating between negative reinforcement and punishment. *Negative reinforcement* is the contingent *removal* of an aversive condition. It *increases* the rate of behavior. *Punishment* is the contingent *presentation* of an aversive condition. It *decreases* the rate of behavior.

Fighting the Confusion		
Positive Reinforcement	*Negative Reinforcement*	*Punishment*
Presentation of a reinforcer	Removal of an aversive condition	Presentation of an aversive condition
Increases response rate	Increases response rate	Decreases response rate

Think you've got it? Let's see. Suppose you burn your mouth with a spoonful of hot soup. Then, with no hesitation, you gulp down a glass of cold water.

Let's analyze that one. You've got two responses here. First, let's look at the response of putting the spoonful of hot soup in your mouth. The outcome? The soup burns your mouth (probably an aversive condition). What's the contingency? *Negative reinforcement?* Not even close. Remember, just because it's bad doesn't mean it's *negative,* at least not as behavior analysts use the term. For behavior analysts, *negative* means *removal* and *positive* means *presentation.* So, instead, we've got punishment—punishment by the presentation of an aversive condition.

Punishment

Before	Behavior	After
You have a cool mouth.	You eat hot soup.	You have a burning mouth.

The second response is gulping down the water. But what's the negative reinforcer? The water? Sorry. The negative reinforcer is the burning mouth (the aversive condition)! And what kind of a reinforcer is it? A negative reinforcer. It's negative because it would reinforce by its removal. And the contingency? *Negative reinforcement—reinforcement by the removal of an aversive condition.*

Negative Reinforcement (Escape)

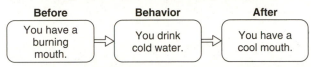

Remember: Don't confuse *negative reinforcement* with *punishment.* In everyday English, negative and punishment mean something unpleasant. But negative reinforcement and punishment differ, though both involve aversive conditions. In the negative reinforcement contingency, the response removes or reduces the aversive condition; but in the punishment contingency, the aversive condition follows the response. Also, negative reinforcement increases the frequency of the response, but punishment decreases the frequency. Here is another example:

You get a splinter while grabbing a stick of wood. The pain in your finger (aversive condition) probably will decrease the frequency with which you repeat such a careless act in the future: Punishment by the presentation of an aversive condition.

Punishment

Before	Behavior	After
You have no splinter in your finger.	You grab a stick of wood.	You have a splinter in your finger.

You pull out the splinter. The reduction in pain (aversive condition) probably will increase the frequency that you pull out splinters in the future: negative reinforcement or reinforcement by the removal of an aversive condition.

We've tried to write this book so that you won't often have to grapple with the "positive" and "negative" terminology. But once you sail out of the safe haven of *Principles of Behavior,* you should be ready to deal with any confusion.

QUESTION

1. Compare and contrast negative reinforcement and punishment. Use an example and a contingency table in doing so.

5 Penalty

FUNDAMENTALS

Example
Behavioral Juvenile Corrections
FEAR AND LOATHING IN THE SCHOOL SHOP[1]

"Mark, I'm gonna kick your rear end!" Herb said. Mark had bumped Herb's elbow (maybe accidentally, maybe not). Herb was having enough trouble following the pattern using the jigsaw, without hassles from Mark.

Mark picked up his hammer. "No you ain't. You try it, and I'll kill ya!"

"Boys, that's no way to talk," Bruce Black, the fifth-grade shop teacher, said.

Herb looked at Mark. "Yeah, and I'm goin' to smash your woodworking project too."

"Boys, stop that kind of talk."

"Mr. Black, I ain't gonna stop it, and you can get outta my face, or I'll smash you, too."

After several weeks of problems of this sort, Bruce went to see the principal. "Dr. Robinson, I don't think it was a good idea to let those juvenile delinquents into our school. They're completely out of control. I can see why the court sent them to that Achievement Place home. They steal, they fight,

they disrupt—when they come to school at all. They're the hardest 13-year-olds I've ever seen! They almost scare me."

"What are they doing?" Mae Robinson asked.

"They have so much aggression inside them that they keep exploding."

The toothpaste theory of abnormal behavior, Mae thought. She asked, "Can you tell me more specifically what they do?"

"Well, they're very aggressive, with each other and even with me."

It sure is hard to get people to talk about specific behaviors and not talk in the vague terms that prevent intervention, Mae thought. "Bruce, what specific things do they do that are aggressive? Do they hit each other?"

"Sometimes, but it's not so much that it's more that they're constantly threatening violence and destruction."

"That's our boys, all right. That repertoire of threats is a big part of what got them classified as predelinquents in the first place. I have an idea about what we should do that may help those kids."

Mae explained to Bruce that the group home for juvenile offenders, where the boys lived, used the Achievement Place approach, an approach developed by Drs. Montrose Wolf and Elery Phillips and their team at the University of Kansas. In the group home, the boys earned points for good behavior and for productive behavior. They lost points for bad behavior. The points were reinforcers because the boys could use them like money at the group home. They could buy things with them, like permission to use the bikes, watch TV, eat a snack, go downtown, stay up past bedtime, and come home late after school.

Phillips had published his master's thesis on the use of this point system. In one of his studies, he

---

[1]Based on Phillips, E. L. (1968). Achievement Place: Token reinforcement procedures in a home-style rehabilitation setting for "predelinquent" boys. *Journal of Applied Behavior Analysis, 1*, 213–223. The late Elery Phillips, Montrose Wolf, and their colleagues at the University of Kansas developed Achievement Place, a behavioral program for "predelinquent" children. Because of the research they did to develop an extremely high-quality program and because of their efforts at helping others start such programs, now Achievement Place style programs function all over the United States. And because of Mont's crucial role in the development of the Achievement Place model, he received the 1998 Distinguished Service to Behavior Analysis award from SABA.

had used a penalty procedure involving the loss of points to get rid of the threats the boys were always making.

Bruce agreed to try Phillips's procedure in his shop.

Back in the shop:

"This school stinks. I'm going to blow up the whole damned thing!" Mark said.

"Mark, that threat cost you 50 points," Bruce Black said, in as calm a voice as he could manage with his heart pounding as fast as it was.

"Fifty what?"

"We're working with your group home. They've given us permission to dock any of you boys 50 points whenever you threaten violence or destruction." I hope it works, Bruce thought.

"Fifty points! I'm gonna blow up the home, too!"

"That's another 50 points." Gosh, I hope it works.

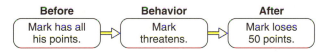

Before	Behavior	After
Mark has all his points.	Mark threatens.	Mark loses 50 points.

It did work. Mark went from over eight threats an hour down to none after Bruce Black used the penalty procedure for a few classes. The others improved much the same way. Within a few classes, the penalty procedure had completely gotten rid of the threats of violence and destruction that had filled the air (Figure 5.1).

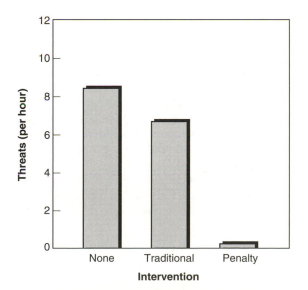

Figure 5.1 Using a Penalty to Reduce a Pre-delinquent Boy's Threats

And the boys were one small step closer to acting in a way that would keep them out of trouble

with the world and give them a chance to lead a normal, decent life, not the sad life of the petty crook.

QUESTION

1. Describe the use of a penalty procedure to reduce inappropriate social interactions. Describe
   ○ the person whose behavior was modified
   ○ the undesirable behavior
   ○ the reinforcer used
   ○ the contingency
   ○ the results.

Concept
PENALTY CONTINGENCY

In Chapter 4, we talked about decreasing behavior with punishment by the presentation of an aversive condition. Now we need to look at punishment by the loss of reinforcers—**the penalty contingency.**

Definition: Concept
Penalty contingency
○ the immediate,
○ response-contingent
○ **removal** of
○ a reinforcer
○ resulting in a **decreased** frequency of that response.

Behind the penalty contingency is the **penalty principle:** *A response becomes less frequent if loss of a reinforcer or a decrease in a reinforcer has immediately followed it in the past.* Note that this is a form of punishment—punishment by the loss of reinforcers. The other form is punishment by the presentation of an aversive condition.

The last game of the state finals. Third quarter. Your senior year. The high point of your life. You steal the ball from that obnoxious guard who has been bugging you since the start. You make a break for the other end of the court, dribbling with the speed that makes Forrest Gump look like a turtle. The crowd roars like a jet plane. The bass drummer pounds his drum so hard, he busts the drum head. And the referee's whistle says you fouled that obnoxious guard. That's your fifth foul. You're out. And the obnoxious guard comes to give you a condescending, sportsmanlike handshake. The loss of a reinforcer—the opportunity to play in the state finals. Penalty? Let's see how often you foul obnoxious guards once you start playing college ball.

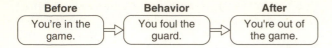

Before	Behavior	After
You're in the game.	You foul the guard.	You're out of the game.

What would sports be without penalties? You lose the ball, you lose the puck, you lose the yardage. This loss of reinforcers may penalize your sloppy playing enough that you become a halfway decent player.

Though the light's yellow, you can make it. But the cop sees you, and you lose $40. Pushing the yellow may become a less frequent response in your repertoire, suggesting punishment by the loss of a reinforcer.

We thought this was a good example of a penalty contingency, until a student pointed out that the loss of the $40 is delayed by more than 60 seconds. So the delay is too great for it to penalize pushing the yellow. Instead we've got an analog to a penalty contingency, as we will see in a later chapter. This would work only for people who knew the rule describing the penalty.

This next one's a little better: Though the light's yellow, you can make . . . almost. The eager beaver in the crossroad smashes your car's tail end, and you lose the beauty of your car. Punishment of pushing? Could be.

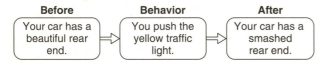

Before	Behavior	After
Your car has a beautiful rear end.	You push the yellow traffic light.	Your car has a smashed rear end.

All this is bad news. But it would be worse if punishment by the loss of reinforcers didn't occur. It would be worse if you kept making the same clumsy, dumb, costly mistakes all your life. It would be worse if the loss of reinforcers didn't suppress carelessness.

Yes, boys and girls, let's all thank our friend Mr. Punishment for making our lives livable. "Thank you, Mr. Punishment."

By the way, the reinforcer lost in a penalty contingency cannot be the one that's maintaining the penalized response. Look at this pair of contingencies that are working concurrently (at the same time).

Inappropriate Natural Reinforcement Contingency

Before	Behavior	After
Mark has no attention.		Mark has attention.
	Mark threatens.	
Mark has all his points.		Mark loses 50 points.

Performance-Management Punishment Contingency

1. Look at the reinforcer maintaining Mark's threats. Is it the one that's removed in the penalty contingency?
   a. yes.
   b. no.

The penalty contingency involves a different reinforcer from the one maintaining the penalized behavior. (In the next chapter, we will introduce the extinction procedure, with that procedure, we simply withhold the reinforcer that previously maintained the response; but that's not the same as a penalty contingency.)

QUESTIONS

1. The principle of punishment by the loss of reinforcers—state it and give a couple of everyday examples.
2. Must the reinforcer removed by the penalty be the same as the one maintaining the penalized behavior?

Example
Developmental Disabilities
USING PENALTY
TO DECREASE SELF-INJURING[2]

Jim was in trouble from the beginning of his life. His parents put him in a hospital shortly after his birth. During the next 4 years, he got individual and group psychotherapy and dozens of drug treatments to reduce his hyperactivity, screaming, and self-injuring. Nothing worked.

His self-injuring started at age 4. By the time he was 9, he was a real threat. Besides slapping his face, he often banged his head against the floors and walls, punched his face and head with his fist, hit his shoulder with his chin, and kicked himself. Also, his self-injury had partially detached the retinas of both of his eyes.

Jim was all but blind when he was transferred to the Murdock Center in North Carolina where Dr. Tate and Dr. Baroff worked with him. Jim was 9 then, and aside from the scars on his face, he was a good-looking boy. He didn't speak, though he often uttered a few words—high-pitched, whining words, mostly gibberish.

But Jim did respond to people. He would always try to touch those who approached him, wrapping his arms about them, climbing into their laps, or clinging to them. Then he would be more tranquil.

---

[2]Based on Tate, B. G., & Baroff, G. S. (1966). Aversive control of self-injurious behavior. *Behavior Research and Therapy, 4*, 281–287.

But when he was alone and free, he would cry, scream, hit himself, and bang his head. There seemed no choice but to keep him tied in bed for the rest of his life. When they untied Jim, he hit himself several times per minute. He would destroy himself, if he were alone with his arms and legs untied.

Typically, Jim would lie, tied to his bed, except for his morning baths and daily walks. During these walks, two assistants walked beside him, each holding one of his hands. But even with this physical contact, Jim continued hitting his chin on his shoulder. During five daily 20-minute baseline sessions, when the assistants did not intervene, Jim banged his chin on his shoulder at the rate of 396 times per hour! After they had measured the size of the problem, the behavior analysts decided it was time to intervene. But how?

Remember that Jim quickly grabbed on to any nearby human being. This suggests that such contact was a strong reinforcer for Jim. Why? Perhaps because Jim was almost blind, and other people had to serve as his eyes. Also, contact with people looking out for his welfare produced food, candy, comforting words, and warmth.

Tate and Baroff reasoned that the contingent loss of this potential reinforcer might punish Jim's self-abuse. So during the daily walks, whenever Jim banged his chin on his shoulder, the two assistants immediately let go of his hands until he'd stopped banging for 3 seconds—a loss of the reinforcer of human contact.

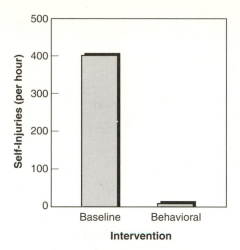

Figure 5.2 Using a Penalty to Reduce a 9-year-old's Self-injury

○ the reinforcer used
○ the contingency
○ the results.

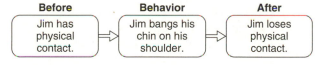

Before	Behavior	After
Jim has physical contact.	Jim bangs his chin on his shoulder.	Jim loses physical contact.

The results? By the second walk, Jim's self-injury had dropped from a rate of 396 to 6 per hour—a fast and effective intervention (Figure 5.2)! Jim still had many problems (which Tate and Baroff worked on with other techniques), but at least he could now go for walks with a minimum of self-injury. A major achievement in his barren life.

By the way, during baseline, Jim whined, cried, walked hesitantly, and ignored his environment. But as soon as he stopped banging his chin, he also stopped whining and crying and started walking without hesitation, attending to his environment, and even smiling.

QUESTION

1. Describe the use of a penalty contingency to reduce self-injury. Include
   ○ the person whose behavior was modified
   ○ the undesirable behavior

Example
Behavioral Juvenile Corrections
IT AIN'T GOOD TO SAY "AIN'T"[3]

Bruce Black was back in Mae Robinson's office. "Dr. Robinson, remember the intervention we did to get rid of the verbal threats those two boys were always making in my shop?" Mae nodded. "We used a penalty procedure, and it worked real well," Bruce continued, "so I wonder if we couldn't use the same procedure to deal with another problem."

"What's the problem?" Mae asked.

"One of those boys, Mark, doesn't talk well," Bruce answered.

"Can you be more specific?"

"Well, his grammar's terrible."

"Can you be even more specific? Can you give me an example?"

"Well, he says *ain't* all the time," Bruce said. "Now I know a person's grammar isn't as important as what the person says. And I know this may just be my middle-class prejudice. It may be more my problem than his. But it bugs me."

"It may be your prejudice, but it's also the prejudice of many other people, especially people who are likely to be employers or who can otherwise help Mark. It's OK to use street talk on the street, but if he ever wants to escape from street life to get a

[3]Phillips, E. L. (1968). Achievement Place: Token reinforcement procedures in a home-style rehabilitation setting for "pre-delinquent" boys. *Journal of Applied Behavior Analysis, 1,* 213–223.

job, for instance, it will be much easier if he can speak standard English," Mae said.

Bruce said he'd tried correcting Mark every time he said *ain't*—a reasonable intervention to try.

Traditional Intervention

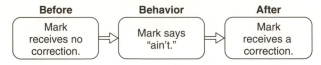

Unfortunately, this was worse than doing nothing. Mark's frequency of saying *ain't* rose from 55 per day, when Bruce had ignored it (baseline), to 74 per day with the correction procedure. This suggests that the corrections were actually reinforcing Mark's saying *ain't.* Mae explained to Bruce that Elery Phillips also had used the response-cost penalty contingency to reduce poor grammar at Achievement Place. So they decided to try to replicate Elery's intervention.

Behavioral Intervention

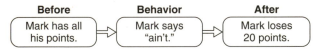

After 15 days, during which Bruce fined Mark 20 points each time he said *ain't,* the boy had completely stopped saying the word (Figure 5.3).

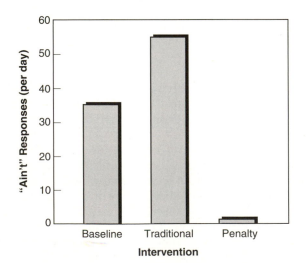

Figure 5.3   Using a Penalty to Reduce a Predelinquent Boy's "Ain'ts"

The Achievement Place houseparents used the same penalty procedure and got Mark's rate of saying "ain't" down from 37 to 0 per day. A month after

they had stopped the intervention, Mark was still free of the taint of "ain't."

QUESTION

1. Describe the use of a penalty contingency to reduce poor English. Include
   ○ the person whose behavior was modified
   ○ the undesirable behavior
   ○ the reinforcer used
   ○ the contingency
   ○ the results.

Concept
RESPONSE COST

Response cost is the name for the particular penalty procedure Mae and Bruce used when they reduced the verbal threats and "ain't." It's the price you must pay for bad behavior; but, it's like fly now and pay later: You pay the price after the bad behavior rather than before.

Definition: Concept
Response-cost contingency
   ○ the immediate,
   ○ response-contingent
   ○ removal of
   ○ a **tangible** reinforcer
   ○ resulting in a decreased frequency of that response.

By tangible reinforcers we mean food, money, points, tokens, and the like.

Question

To get praise from the coach, the athletes must do 100 push-ups. Is the requirement of 100 push-ups an example of *response cost?*

Our Answer

No, that's a *response requirement,* not *response cost.* That's effort of the response class, not removal of reinforcers. Doing 100 push-ups may be aversive, but it's not a penalty procedure like response cost. Effort isn't response cost, as behavior analysts use the concept.

Question

The coach hears one of the players using foul language in the middle of the game and immediately sends her to the showers. She never swears again, at least not within earshot of the coach. Is that *response cost?*

Our Answer

No. The coach removed an **activity** reinforcer (playing the game), not a **tangible** reinforcer such as money. The swearing did become much less frequent, so it was a penalty procedure. But not the kind called *response cost;* we'll see shortly that it's called *time-out.* We will look at another example of response cost in the next section.

QUESTION

1. *Response cost contingency*—define it and show how the intervention to reduce threats meets the three criteria needed for that procedure to be response cost. Also, diagram the contingency for that example.

Example
Behavioral Child and Family Counseling
THE JOYS OF MOTHERHOOD[4]

"Dr. Baker, I try to love Sam, like every mother should. I try, but I can't. I hate my son. He makes our lives miserable. How can a 4-year-old boy destroy a family?"

Even if she didn't have a PhD with a specialty in behavior analysis, Dawn Baker would have had no trouble answering Mrs. Spade. In the first 15 minutes of their interview, Sam had answered the question himself. Not only was he making his parents' lives miserable and destroying their family, he was also making this interview miserable and destroying Dawn's newly decorated office. Though Sam's mother often told him to quit his destructive disruptions, Sam had managed to smash one flowerpot, knock over a chair, rip the cover off the latest issue of the *Journal of Applied Behavior Analysis,* lick the window, spit at his mother, scream, and conspicuously wet his pants.

"Mrs. Spade, why don't we all go into the play-therapy room, next door," Dawn said. She locked the door of the childproof playroom as soon as the

three of them entered. Dawn and Mrs. Spade sat at the plain table, doing their best to continue their interview, while Sam did his best to destroy the indestructible toys he quickly scattered about the floor.

"Mrs. Spade, I think we should try a time-out procedure with Sam. If it's OK with you, I'd like to start it now."

"Would you please!"

Dawn stood up, took a child's chair and placed it in the corner, facing the wall. At that moment, Sam was standing in the middle of the room, screaming and stamping his foot on the floor. Dawn calmly said, "No, Sam. Go to the time-out chair." Then she took the child by the hand and led him to the chair. She moved all the toys away and stood directly behind him. Every time he turned his head or started to get up, she guided him back onto the chair and turned his head back to the wall. After 2 minutes had elapsed, she said, "OK, Sam, you can go play quietly now."

Sam played quietly for 15 seconds before he started bouncing a child's basketball off his mother's head. So he and Dawn recycled through the time-out again. And they went on in this way for the rest of the interview. Dawn explained to Mrs. Spade the time-out procedure for Sam's disruptions, and she showed the use of time-out every time Sam disrupted.

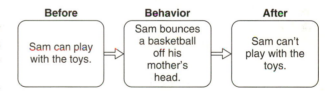

Before	Behavior	After
Sam can play with the toys.	Sam bounces a basketball off his mother's head.	Sam can't play with the toys.

In nontechnical terms, Dawn explained that *time-out* is a procedure for getting rid of bad behavior—a punishment procedure based on the loss of reinforcers. So *time-out* means time out from the reinforcers that are normally available, like the toys in the playroom.

The results: As soon as Sam had started tearing the heck out of Dawn's office, she automatically started recording baseline. So she had something with which to compare her intervention. During the first 15-minute intervention session in Dawn's playroom, time-out produced an amazing drop in disruption. With time-out contingent on disruption, Sam immediately went from disrupting 60% of the time to disrupting only 3% of the time (Figure 5.4)!

And he maintained that low level of disruption during the remaining sessions of Dawn's intervention. Mrs. Spade was ready to nominate Dawn for president of the United States.

---

[4]Based on Mace, F. C., Page, T. J., Ivancic, M. T., & O'Brien, S. (1986). Effectiveness of brief time-out with and without contingent delay: A comparative analysis. *Journal of Applied Behavior Analysis, 19,* 79–86.

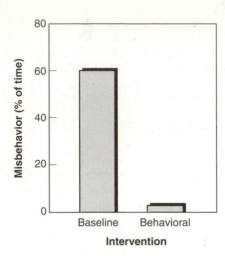

Figure 5.4   Using Time-out to Reduce a Child's Disruption and Destruction

QUESTION

1. Describe the use of time-out to reduce disruptive and destructive behavior. Include
   - the person whose behavior was modified
   - the undesirable behavior
   - the reinforcer used
   - the contingency
   - the results

Concept
TIME-OUT

Both at home and at school, many behavior analysts find time-out to be an excellent procedure for getting rid of bad behavior in young children. Generally, they combine time-out contingent on bad behavior with reinforcement contingent on good behavior. For example, Dr. Lynn Clark recommends time-out to get rid of biting, screaming, swearing, back talk, fighting for control over the TV, refusal to eat, hurting pets, playing in the street, throwing food, name-calling, and persistent pestering.[5]

Lynn suggests that time-out is effective, fast, easy to use properly, helps parents and teachers get rid of bad behavior without themselves becoming too angry and upset, improves the relations between the child and the adults, and clears the air for the child to acquire good behavior. He advocates it as a

fast, clean way of getting rid of problems without many hassles between the child and the adult. Everyone feels better than in the more traditional nagging and bickering ways in which so many parents and children interact.[6]

Of course, something like **time-out** is nothing new. For years, a variation on this theme has been used in sports. The best example is hockey: Violate a rule and it's time out of the match and into the penalty box. Without straining too much we can see other examples: Three strikes and you're out at bat. Five fouls and you're out of the basketball game. One swear word at the referee and you're out of any game.

But don't confuse the behavioral use of time-out with solitary confinement in prison or the usual penalties in sports. In behavior management, we don't put the kid in time-out and throw away the key. We don't even kick the kid out of the game. **Usually, a brief time-out of just a couple of minutes or so will do the trick;** as soon as we can, we let the kid get back into the normal, richer environment where he or she can have a chance to acquire a good, healthy repertoire.

Is this *time-out?* "Johnny, you're making too much noise here in the classroom. Go out to the playground, and stay there until I tell you to come back in." Time-out? Maybe not. It might be reinforcement. There's a good chance Johnny will find more reinforcing activities on the playground than in the classroom. So the teacher may be reinforcing disruptive behavior by making access to a more reinforcing environment contingent on that behavior. It may be naive and even egotistical for the teacher to assume the playground is less reinforcing than his or her classroom. Often a danger when you try time-out.

---

[5]Clark, L. (1985). *SOS! Help for parents.* Bowling Green, KY: Parents Press (P.O. Box 2180). This is an excellent book for parents and teachers, full of many useful suggestions and guidelines, especially on the effective and humane use of time-out.

[6]How long should time-out be? It is often recommended that the length of the time-out should be determined by the child's age—optimally, 1 minute per year of age; but that doesn't impress me. When working with a 4-year-old autistic child, 15 seconds will often do the trick; and 4 minutes would unnecessarily take to much time away from the valuable discrete-trial training. And my guess is, a 15-second time nonexclusionary time-out would work pretty well with me, too, if you pinched the straw on my fruit smoothie for 15 seconds, every time I made a rude slurping noise, for example.

Here's a reply from the experienced and wise Bobby Newman: I don't use any kind of formula for figuring out how long time-out should be. I generally use 30 seconds, two minutes, or five minutes, usually depending on how "out of control" the person is when the they're coming to time-out, and also how reinforcing the activity they left is. More important to me is the termination of time-out. If they don't "have it together" when the timer rings, I say "I'm sorry, you need to get it together. I'll set it for one more minute and then we'll see." I rarely have to reset more than once.

Here's a formal definition of time-out:

> *Definition: Concept*
> **Time-out contingency**
> - the immediate
> - response-contingent
> - removal of
> - **access to** a reinforcer
> - resulting in a decreased frequency of that response.

Behavior analysts sometimes distinguish between two types of time-out: *exclusionary* time-out and *nonexclusionary* time-out. *Exclusionary time-out* means the person is excluded from the immediate setting—for example, by having to go to a separate room for a couple of minutes. *Nonexclusionary time-out* means the person remains in the immediate setting during time-out, for example, by sitting, in a chair away from the regular activities. Sam's case involved nonexclusionary time-out.

QUESTIONS

1. *Time-out contingency*—define it and diagram a couple of examples where parents might want to use it.
2. Show how the previously described intervention to reduce Sam's disruptive behavior meets the three criteria in our definition of time-out.
3. How does time-out differ from solitary confinement and penalties in sports?
4. Describe the Br'er Rabbit problem in trying to use time-out.
5. Compare and contrast exclusionary and nonexclusionary time-out.

Example from
Behavioral Special Education
THE TIME-OUT RIBBON[7]

Mike was 8 years old, and he had an IQ of 27; he lived in a state institution structured around cottage living. He and four other low-functioning boys attended a special-ed classroom in a room of their cot-

tage. They met an hour and a half each day—an hour and a half of bedlam. Mike was so hyperactive (i.e., overly active) he was completely off the wall, running around the classroom yelling and throwing everything he could grab. For the 7 months of the class, the teacher, with all her reprimands, could do nothing.

Foxx and Shapiro, who were at the University of Maryland, Baltimore County, during this time, came to the teacher's aid. Punishment seemed a reasonable intervention, but neither shock nor traditional time-out was too popular in the institution. Traditional time-out, also called *seclusionary* or *exclusionary* time-out, involves putting someone in an isolated room. Many people, including some behavior analysts, find shock too aversive even to think about, let alone to use. And, for some people, isolating a helpless client in a time-out room hints of medieval brutality and neglect, though behavior analysts use time-out rooms in a careful way, keeping the duration of the time-out as short as possible (and, for safety reasons, keeping the door to the room unlocked). What Foxx and Shapiro needed was a punishment procedure that didn't turn people off. Maybe *nonexclusionary time-out* (time-out without being excluded) would be more socially acceptable.[8] In nonexclusionary time-out, the student is no longer able to participate in the activity and is removed to a location, where he or she can still see and hear the activity.

So they collected baseline data for 7 days. Then they started a reinforcement phase for 10 days. During this phase they asked the teacher to give each child a smile, praise, a touch, or a small snack about every 2½ minutes. They were going to use time-out in the next phase, so they had to make sure they had a reinforcing environment to time the boys out of. The frequency of reinforcement had to be high enough so that it was aversive not to be allowed to participate in it. The reinforcement-plus-time-out phase lasted 12 days.

During both reinforcement phases, each boy, including Mike, wore a colored ribbon around his

---

[7]Based on Foxx, R. M., & Shapiro, S. T. (1978). The time-out ribbon: A nonexclusionary time-out procedure. *Journal of Applied Behavior Analysis, 11,* 125–136.

[8]Incidentally, some people call nonexclusionary time-out *contingent observation.* We prefer *nonexclusionary time-out* because *contingent observation* implies that the procedure is contingently adding something rather than contingently removing. In other words it implies that the opportunity to observe the activity is contingent on misbehaving. This is not true because the student could also observe the activity he was participating in, before his inappropriate behavior.

But terminology anarchy doesn't end there. Some use *seclusionary time-out* rather than our *exclusionary time-out* and, even more confusing, *exclusionary time-out* for our *nonexclusionary time-out!* I guess the bottom line is, that you will need to be careful to make sure you and whoever you're talking to or reading understand each other.

neck, in the style of a bolo tie. But when a boy started acting up, the teacher would take the ribbon away from that boy for 3 minutes. During that time, the boy got no reinforcers.

Before	Behavior	After
Mike has his ribbon.	Mike runs, yells, grabs, or throws.	Mike loses his ribbon.

This was nonexclusionary time-out because the boy stayed in the classroom; he wasn't excluded from it. If, instead, the teacher had put the boy in the hallway for 3 minutes, that would have been exclusionary.

How'd it work? Like a charm. The boys were noisy and unruly when they first entered the classroom each day. They quieted down as soon as they put on their ribbon ties (Figure 5.5). A behavioral charm. (Incidentally, you should probably not take seriously the slight increase from the baseline to the reinforcement condition, because that increase is probably just random fluctuation in the data and not a reliable, significant change in frequency.)

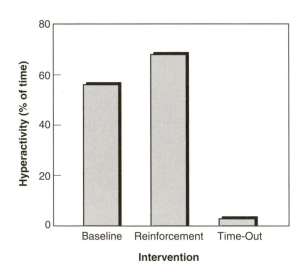

**Figure 5.5   Using Time-out
to Reduce Hyperactivity**

Keep in mind that for any time-out procedure to be effective, the activity or environment the student is removed from must be reinforcing.

QUESTION

1. Describe a behavioral intervention using nonexclusionary time-out to reduce hyperactivity. Specify
   ○ the response classes
   ○ the punishment contingency
   ○ the presumed reinforcers
   ○ the contingency diagram
   ○ the results
   ○ any other interesting features of the intervention.

Compare and Contrast
PENALTY VS.
THE THREE OTHER
BASIC BEHAVIORAL CONTINGENCIES

This contingency table summarizes the relations among the four basic contingencies. For example, select "remove" from the white row, "reinforcer" from the white column, and "penalty (frequency decreases)" from the corresponding cell in the gray area. This means: *The contingent removal of a reinforcer is a penalty contingency and it causes a decrease in frequency.*

Contingency Table (final)		
Stimulus, Event, or Condition	***Present***	***Remove***
Reinforcer	Reinforcement ⇑	Penalty ⇓
Aversive	Punishment ⇓	Escape ⇑

1. What do ⇑ and ⇓ mean?

Here's the other form of essentially this same table. If you remove a stimulus (a cell from the white row across the top) and the response frequency decreases (a cell from the white column along the left), then you've got a penalty contingency (corresponding inside gray cell), which you can call *punishment by stimulus* subtraction or, more commonly, negative punishment (S^{-P}).

Contingency Table (final)		
	Present Stimulus Event or Condition	***Remove Stimulus Event or Condition***
Response Frequency Increases ⇑	**Reinforcement contingency** Reinforcement by stimulus addition Positive reinforcement (S^{+R})	**Escape contingency** Reinforcement by stimulus subtraction Negative reinforcement (S^{-R})
Response Frequency Decreases ⇓	**Punishment Contingency** Punishment by stimulus addition Punishment (S^{+P})	**Penalty Contingency** Punishment by stimulus subtraction Punishment (S^{-P})

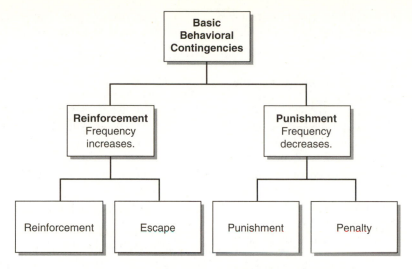

**Figure 5.6   Tree Diagram of the Four Basic
Behavioral Contingencies**

We have two punishment contingencies: One, involving the presentation of an aversive condition, we call *punishment*; the other, involving the removal or loss of a reinforcer, we call a *penalty contingency* (we do this to reduce confusion, though we also can call the penalty contingency *punishment*). We can decrease behavior either by presenting aversive conditions or by removing reinforcers contingent on that behavior.[9]

We also have two reinforcement contingencies: One, involving the presentation of a reinforcer, we call *reinforcement;* the other, involving the removal of an aversive condition, we call an *escape contingency* (we also can call the escape contingency *reinforcement.*) We can increase behavior either by presenting a reinforcer or removing an aversive condition contingent on that behavior.

So we can use a reinforcer either to increase or decrease behavior, depending on whether we present or remove the reinforcer. And we can use an aversive condition either to increase or decrease behavior, depending on whether we remove or present the aversive condition.

We also have two contingencies involving the removal of something: One, involving the removal of an aversive condition, we call *escape;* the other,

involving the removal of a reinforcer, we still call a *penalty contingency*. (No big surprise here.) We can use removal contingencies either to increase or decrease behavior, depending on whether we remove an aversive condition or a reinforcer (see Figure 5.6).

QUESTIONS

1. Draw or fill in the complete contingency table of the four basic contingencies, all properly labeled. You must understand it; memorizing won't get it.
2. Compare and contrast the penalty contingency with the other three.
3. In the same way, compare and contrast the punishment contingency with the two reinforcement contingencies.
4. Be able to draw, fill in, and explain the tree diagram of the four basic behavioral contingencies.

Example of Time-out
Behavioral Medicine
**HELPING A BABY WITH
COLICKY BEHAVIOR**[10]

Jenny: Since she was 2 weeks old, April's been crying day and night. Her constant crying, her pierc-

---

[9]Although suggesting a different solution, Stephen Ledoux concurs with our analysis of the confusion traditional terminology causes: "In everyday usage *positive* connotes good or pleasant while *negative* connotes bad or unpleasant. As a result people have some difficulty with the concept of a *negative* reinforcer strengthening behavior. They have even greater difficulty with the concept of *positive* punishment; they have trouble imagining much that is positive about punishment." From S. F. Ledoux (in press). Increasing tact control and student comprehension through such new postcedent terms as added and subtracted selectors and consequences. *The International Behaviorologist*.

[10]Based on Larson, K., & Ayllon, T. (1990). The effects of contingent music and differential reinforcement on infantile colic. *Behavior Research and Therapy. 28,* 119–125. The graphed data are from Ayllon, T. & Freed, M. (1989) *Stopping Baby's Colic.* New York: Perigee. This outstanding book is a must for all parents whose babies have crying, eating, or sleeping problems.

ing shrieks, are driving me crazy. I get so angry, I want to beat her. I feel like abusing her.

Dawn: I know how you feel. Constant crying often causes child abuse.

Jenny: My husband, Jim, and I haven't been able to get any sleep. Jim goes to work so sleepy he almost fell off the scaffolding at his construction site. And now he's started sleeping over at his mother's so he can get a decent night's rest. And I'm about ready to divorce him. When he comes for supper all we do is listen to April cry and fight with each other. He says April's crying is my fault—I'm too nervous and uptight.

Dawn: Well, that's one popular theory—it's Mom's fault. But the scientific research doesn't support that theory.

Jenny: I don't know. I feel so guilty, like a bad mother. I told my pediatrician she had to give April something or give me something. So we tried all sorts of drugs with April, like Mylanta, belladonna, and paregoric. Nothing helped, at least not much. Now April's 5 weeks old and she just keeps shrieking. It's horrible. It breaks my heart.

Dawn: Yes, I know, you're all having a rough time. That's not an easy thing, what you're going through. This may be the hardest time in your life.

Jenny: I don't know what to do; my pediatrician says no medical condition is involved, no severe constipation, no gastroesophageal reflux, no intussuception, I think she called it—nothing to cause April to scrunch up and act like she's got severe abdominal pain. My pediatrician says it's colic. Do you think my baby has colic, Dr. Baker?

Dawn: Well, as the pediatrician Dr. William Sears put it, *Colic is something a baby **does**, not something it has.* He's got a point. We should talk about the colicky behavior, not the colicky baby. It's a behavior problem; not a medical problem. A baby who is said to *have colic* is just one who cries and is irritable much of the time.

Jenny: I guess that's why my pediatrician referred me to you. She said you were a behavior analyst.

Dawn: There is no known physiological, anatomical, or medical cause of colicky crying. In fact it seems so unlikely that one will be found that medical researchers have pretty much stopped looking.

Jenny: Everyone's told me it's because poor little April has too much gas in her stomach, and that was hurting her and making her cry. I will say Jim did his best, too. He put warm towels on her stomach, held her under warm showers, even

took her for midnight car rides. Nothing helped much. I did things like put her on top of a running clothes dryer, swing with her, and just hold her and try to love her with all my heart. Still nothing helped.

Dawn: An English researcher, Dr. Ilingsworth, has shown that babies who act colicky have no more gas than those who don't. Again, it looks like colic is neither a disease nor an illness. It's just a way of behaving; it's just excessive crying.

Jenny: Doctor, we'll do anything you say. Just help us, please.

Dawn: Well, here's what I'd like you to try:

- Get a CD player and a CD of your favorite singer. Then, keep the music on as long as April is awake and quiet for at least 30 seconds. You should also interact with her at those times—look at her, talk softly to her, rock her, play with her, be loving and affectionate.
- But as soon as she starts to cry, turn off the tape player and take care of any needs she might have, like feeding her or changing her diaper.
- If she keeps crying, put her in your portable infant carrier. She should stay there for 3 to 5 minutes—longer if she keeps crying. We call this **time-out.** Withdraw both music and attention during time-out.

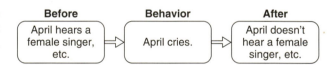

And it worked the very first day Jenny began the time-out procedure (sometimes it takes a few days, but rarely as long as a week). Even 2 months later, when Dawn did a follow-up to evaluate the maintenance of the behavior change, April was fine, crying no more than is typical for a baby her age (Figure 5.7).

Jenny: I sure do thank you, Dr. Baker. Now, April, Jim, and I are happy being together. Now I love my baby and feel like a normal mother. I feel as if we have a normal family again.

Here's an interesting point: **No one in the history of medicine or in the history of psychology had been able to solve the problem of colic—not until Larson and Ayllon applied behavior analysis to its solution.** Imagine that. Impressive. Just a simple, little timeout intervention—though a very creative

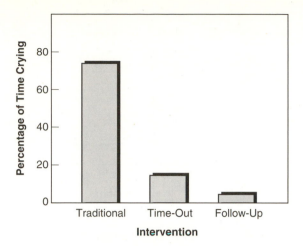

Figure 5.7   Using Time-out To Reduce Colicky Crying

time-out intervention. Most of us may not be as clever and creative as Larson and Ayllon, but looking at the world from a behavior-analysis perspective can help us understand and solve many problems that traditional approaches have failed to solve.

QUESTIONS

1. Be able to diagram the contingency Dawn used to help April stop her crying (Larson and Ayllon).
2. What kind of contingency is it?
   a. reinforcement
   b. escape
   c. punishment
   d. penalty

(Yes, you're on your own in terms of answering this one. We've taken off the training wheels. No hints.)

Example of Time-out
Behavioral Medicine
HELPING A FAILURE-TO-THRIVE BABY[11]

About one out of seven failure-to-thrive infants die. This is serious business. They don't eat properly; and as a result, they lose weight, they don't grow, they become dehydrated, their electrolytes become imbalanced, and they die. For one-third of the failure-to-thrive infants, there is no known physiological,

[11]This case is based on Larson, L. L., Ayllon, T. & Barrett, D. H. (1987). A behavioral feeding program for failure-to-thrive infants. *Behavior Research and Therapy, 25,* 39–47. This article was part of Karen Larson's MA thesis; now that's one heck of an MA thesis!

anatomical, or medical cause. These cases are called *nonorganic.* And **behavior analysis seems to hold the only solution for nonorganic failure-to-thrive babies;** nothing else works.

Consider Claude's case: He was 21 months old "with nephrogenic diabetes insipidus, a congenital hereditary disorder in which the kidneys do not respond" properly.

Claude was in the hospital for the fourth time because of his failure to thrive. He wouldn't eat much, and he would vomit or spit out most solid food he did eat. For the last 16 months he had been put on nasogastric (nose to stomach) tube feeding, to keep him alive. In the hospital, they tube fed him 15 hours a day and kept him on four different drugs. In spite of Claude's kidney problem, his failure to thrive seemed to be nonorganic. He needed to eat normally in order to gain the weight he had to have to survive the surgery for his kidney problem.

1. Suppose you are now a professional behavior analyst and you're called in to help Claude. First, you would ask if Claude needs to increase appropriate behavior, or decrease inappropriate behavior. Claude needs to do both. He needs to increase his acceptance and eating of food that is given to him. So please fill in the following reinforcement diagram.

Reinforcement Contingency for Eating

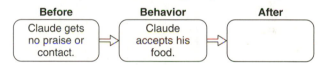

Every time Claude accepted and ate a bite of food, his mother would praise him and run her fingers up and down his arm, tickle his stomach, or rub his knees. Of course, he would get none of that if he didn't accept his food.

2. But you might also use a time-out contingency to decrease Claude's refusal of his food. You might dig out your old copy of *POB (Principles of Behavior)* and review the contingency Dawn used with April; so diagram the following performance-management contingency, using exactly the same contingency as April's (except make allowance for Claude's mother's preference for Elvis Presley).

Time-out Contingency for Refusing to Eat

Not only did Claude's mother turn off the music immediately, she also said *"No"* firmly, removed Claude from his chair, put him in his crib, turned her chair away, and refused to look at him. After 3 minutes without crying, she would put him back in his chair and continue with his meal.

    3. And she used the same contingency every time Claude vomited. Please diagram it:

Time-out Contingency for Vomiting

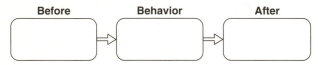

How long do you think it took for these three simple contingencies to get Claude eating more or less normally? About 3 days for him to accept 89% of the bites his mother offered him. Ten days out of the hospital and Claude was eating everything he got (Figure 5.8).

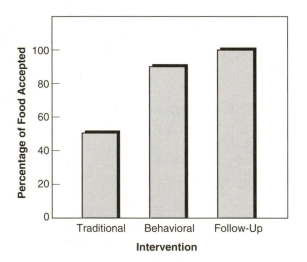

Figure 5.8   Using Reinforcement and Time-out to Increase Food Acceptance

And what about Claude's vomiting? Another success story; within 4 days he'd decreased from a baseline of six vomits a day to less than one a day (Figure 5.9).

During baseline (the traditional intervention), Claude "emitted deep, loud, coughing and gagging noises, and demonstrated repeated voluntary contractions of his stomach muscles that would induce vomiting. However, after 5 behavioral feeding sessions, he no longer emitted vomit-inducing behavior. Additionally, he appeared happier and more pleasant at mealtime and no longer kicked and screamed during feeding sessions. . . . Thirteen months after

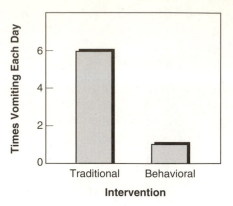

Figure 5.9   Using Time-out to Decrease Vomiting

Claude's hospitalization, he had shown significant and constant improvement and had undergone a successful kidney transplant."

Imagine how powerful a little reinforcement contingency and a couple of time-out contingencies can be. They can solve a problem that has baffled the medical profession from the beginning.

How would you feel if you were able to make such a significant positive impact on the life of another human being and his family, perhaps even saving that life? Well, here's the deal: The world is full of little Claudes and darn few behavior analysts. What are your plans for the next few years?

QUESTIONS/OBJECTIVES

1. Be able to diagram the three contingencies Larson, Ayllon, and Barrett used to help Claude become a thriving baby.
2. Be able to label each contingency.

Principle
THE LAW OF EFFECT

Edward Thorndike (1874–1949) did the classic experiment that involved his puzzle boxes. A puzzle box is a cage containing dangling ropes, levers, and latches that a cat (or other organism) can manipulate. If the cat makes the proper responses with those manipulanda, the cage door could would unlock and the cat could exit. Thorndike locked the cat in the puzzle box and placed food outside the box, just out of the cat's reach. At first, the cat would spend a lot of time approaching the food but, of course, could not get it. However, soon the cat would happen to bump into the lever that unlocked the door; then the cat would get the food. After about three minutes of trials, it would quickly press the lever, exit the cage, and get the food reinforcer. So the cat decreased its unreinforced behavior and increased its speed of pressing the lever, exiting the cage, and getting the food reinforcer. Thorndike called this *trial-and-error behavior*. He concluded that cats do not learn by developing insight into a problem, instead they learn through trial and error. In contemporary terms, if they happen to make a response that happens to produce a reinforcer, they will make that response more quickly the next time. He also believed this is how human beings learn.

Thorndike's **law of effect** simply states that *responses made just prior to "pleasant" events are more likely to be repeated, while responses made just prior to "unpleasant" events are more likely to diminish*. He called these "pleasant" events *satisfiers* and the "unpleasant" events *annoyers*.

We think the law of effect is the most important law in psychology. And, in our view, the law of effect forms the basis of behavior analysis, and behavior analysis forms the basis of most worthwhile psychology. The law of effect is the most powerful tool available for understanding human behavior. However, psychologists criticized the original law of effect for being either circular or involving subjective terms (*pleasant* and *unpleasant*). So here's a modern version that eliminates both circularity and subjectivity:

> *Definition: Principle*
> **The law of effect**
> ○ The effects of our actions
> ○ determine whether we will repeat them.

Here *effect* means *results* or *outcomes*. So we could say *the law of results says the results of our actions determine whether we will repeat them*. (For a discussion of the circularity of the law of effect, see *www.DickMalott.com*.)

It's so simple! Right? It's just a summary of our four basic contingencies of reinforcement and punishment. If our actions produce reinforcers or reduce aversive conditions, we tend to repeat those actions. And if our actions produce aversive conditions or remove reinforcers, we tend to stop repeating those actions. So simple—and yet so powerful. It summarizes everything you've read so far, and everything you will read in the rest of this book. It summarizes life! That means that if you understand how the law of effect works, you understand the

prime mover of our lives. And you'll have a fighting chance to do something about it.

Question

She winks at him as he enters the classroom. He smiles. The next time he enters the classroom, he smiles, before she has a chance to wink. Is this an example of the *law of effect?*

Our Answer

The action we're analyzing is his smiling. The effect or result of his action is not her wink, because the wink occurs before the smile. So even if he does repeat the smile, it's not because of the effect of that action. The example says nothing about its effect or results, so the law of effect doesn't apply.

Question

He normally ignores her, but this time she winks at him as he enters the classroom. He sits down next to her and begins to chat. Now she will more frequently wink at him when he enters, and he usually sits next to her on those occasions. *Law of effect?*

Our Answer

Without a doubt. The effect, or result, of her wink was the reinforcer of attention. So her winking eye is becoming muscle-bound because of its frequent use.

QUESTION

1. State the Law of Effect and comment on its value.

Sid's Seminar
ROLLING OVER THE DEADMAN

Sid: Who's got a good example of reinforcement in everyday life?

Tom: My girlfriend kisses me as long as I'm not chewing tobacco.

Sid: What behavior are you analyzing?

Tom: My not chewing tobacco.

Joe: No, that fails the dead-man test; dead men don't chew tobacco either. And if a dead man can do it, it ain't behavior.

Tom: So, how do I fix it?

Sid: You roll over the dead man. First, you roll over the behavior. You make the behavior the opposite of what you have. What's the opposite of not chewing tobacco?

Tom: Chewing tobacco. But that doesn't work: I chew tobacco and my girlfriend kisses me?

Sid: Right, you've got behavior because dead men don't chew tobacco. And you're right, that contingency's not what you want. So now you roll over the contingency; what's the opposite of "my girlfriend kisses me"?

Eve: My girlfriend stops kissing me.

Sid: Right, and that's what goes in the after condition. Of course the opposite goes in the before condition—my girlfriend is kissing me. So let's diagram the whole contingency.

Before	Behavior	After
My girlfriend is kissing me.	I put some chewing tobacco in my mouth.	My girlfriend stops kissing me.

Joe: So when we roll over the dead man, we find he's lying on a penalty contingency—punishment by the loss of kisses.

Tom: Women are so unreasonable.

Sid: We roll over the dead man by first rolling over the nonbehavior (making it the opposite of what we thought we had and, thus, making it real behavior). And then we roll over the after condition (making it the opposite of what we thought we had). And we find that our correct contingency is also the opposite of what we thought we had; for example, the opposite of reinforcement is penalty. Let's try one more.

Tom: OK, how about this one: After I eat dinner at my girlfriend's, I'm lying on the couch, and I don't move; so she doesn't ask me to do the dishes. That's like, ahh, avoiding doing the dishes.

Sid: What's the behavior you're analyzing?

Tom: Not moving; it allows me to avoid the aversiveness of doing the dishes.

Joe: That one fails the dead man test, too; dead men are experts at not moving, at least not without a little help from their friends.

Tom: So, how do I fix this one?

Max: Let me say it, this time: You roll over the dead man. And you roll over the dead man by first rolling over the nonbehavior (making it the opposite of what you thought you had, thus, making it real behavior). Then you roll over the after condition (making it the opposite of what you thought you had).

Sid: Our readers have been sitting there patiently; why don't we give them a turn?

1. Dear reader, would you mind filling in this diagram for the pseudo sleeping beauty?

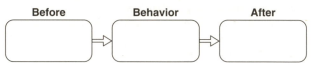

Before	Behavior	After

2. And we find that our correct contingency is also the opposite of what we thought we had; for example, the opposite of escape by the removal of an aversive condition is
    a. reinforcement by the presentation of a reinforce.
    b. punishment by the presentation of an aversive condition.
    c. penalization by the removal of a reinforcer.

Sid: **And what do we do when we find the dead man, boys and girls?**

Boys and Girls: **We roll him over,** Mr. Fields.

Sid: And how do we roll him over?

Eve: We roll over the behavior, and we also roll over the before and after conditions by reversing them.

BASIC ENRICHMENT

FOR EVERY PENALTY CONTINGENCY, THERE'S A REINFORCEMENT CONTINGENCY IN THE BACKGROUND

Remember, we made a parallel point in the punishment chapter:

> **Whenever you have a penalty contingency, you must also have a reinforcement contingency.**

For punishment to occur, you need behavior; and for behavior to occur reliably, it must be reinforced. Now it's easy to miss this important point if you look at only the case studies we presented in the Fundamentals section. In most of those cases, we knew the strange behaviors occurred at high rates. We didn't ask why they occurred. But if they occurred, you can be fairly sure they were producing reinforcers. In these cases, we don't know what the reinforcers were. But we assume there must have been reinforcers. Here is a guess at one, just to give you another example of what the contingency diagram looks like:

Inappropriate Natural Reinforcement Contingency

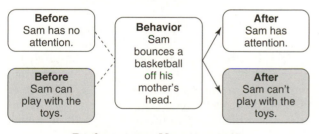

Performance-Management Punishment Contingency

In any case, whenever you use a penalty contingency, you should keep your eye on the reinforcement contingency as well. Nowadays, behavior analysts often do a functional analysis to find the undesirable reinforcement contingency. Then they can counteract that undesirable reinforcement contingency one way or another; for example, they might terminate the reinforcement contingency and thus extinguish the inappropriate behavior; and at the same time, they might use differential reinforcement of alternative behavior.

Ethics
THE BENEFITS OF BASIC RESEARCH

Let's take a moment to discuss the concepts of *basic research* and *applied research*. Scientists do basic research when they want to find out how the world works. They do applied research when they want to find out how they can make the world work better. Practitioners are not necessarily doing research, but hopefully they are applying well-researched practices in their efforts to make the world work better.

Most scientists doing basic research like to see the results of their work used to **help humanity;** and such uses sure help scientists justify their work to their friends and neighbors. But many scientists don't need these applications to justify their work to themselves. They consider basic research of value just because it **adds to human knowledge,** regardless of its use in human affairs.

For years, behavior analysts doing basic research insisted on working with rats and pigeons in the lab, with little concern for human applications. Before these basic researchers realized they could contribute to the immediate well-being of humanity, they spoke out on the virtues of pure science and sometimes scorned those concerned with the everyday world. Still, in spite of their lack of concern, their work laid the foundations for the development of a psychology of effective application to human affairs. You've seen that, in this book. On the other hand, traditional psychologists who concerned themselves exclusively with the problems of humanity had little success. So the scientists who seemed to care the least about the welfare of humanity have contributed the most to it.

Now that experimental behavior analysts see they have something to contribute to the outside world, they are as eager to make such contributions as anyone else would be. At this point, our greatest danger may be that these basic researchers have trouble resisting the social reinforcement involved in applied behavior analysis. And if too many leave their "ivory towers," we may soon run out of new scientific developments to apply to human affairs.

Incidentally, if you ever have the chance to work on a basic research project, grab it! You'll soon see that these scientific problems are every bit as reinforcing to study and solve as are the problems outside the lab.

1. What are the two main values of basic scientific research?

INTERMEDIATE ENRICHMENT

Compare and Contrast
PENALTY, RESPONSE COST, AND TIME-OUT

We're using *penalty* as a briefer and slightly more informal way of saying the same thing as *punishment by the loss of reinforcers*. The *penalty* contingency is the general or generic term, and response cost and time-out are the two subcategories.

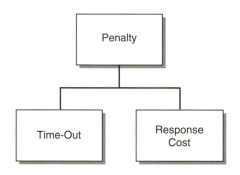

We've seen the two types of penalty contingencies—response cost and time-out. The difference in the definitions of *response cost* and *time-out* is darn slight—only two words. Let's look again at the general form of the two definitions.[12]

Definition: Concept

_____

○ response-contingent
○ removal of
○ _____ reinforcer
○ resulting in a decreased frequency of that response.

---

[12]Not only is the difference between the two concepts subtle in the structure of their definitions, it's also subtle in application. Many penalty contingencies fall in a gray area, where they may, more or less, be both response cost and time-out. Nonetheless, the two concepts are in common use by behavior analysts; so we should use them as consistently as we can.

If you fill the first blank with *response cost,* then you should leave the second blank empty or write in a *tangible*. This means response cost involves the removal of reinforcers. But if you fill the first blank with *time-out,* then you should fill the second blank with *access to*. This means that time-out involves the removal of **access** to reinforcers. Mark lost the points he already had every time he threatened someone, so that's *response cost.* Sam lost access to all the toys on the floor for 2 minutes every time he became a royal pain, so that's time-out. Of course Dawn also had to remove any toys Sam had in his hands at the time, so the distinction gets fuzzy around the edges.

Here's another way to put it: Time-out is usually the removal of the opportunity to make reinforced responses. When hockey players go to the penalty box, they lose the opportunity to make reinforced responses for a period of time; that's time-out. They don't lose points they've already earned; that would be response cost.

I visited a junior high school classroom for emotionally disturbed children where Dr. Robert Hawkins had set up a behavioral incentive system called a *token economy.* The students earned tokens for constructive work and academic behavior. They lost points for inappropriate behavior. The teacher and one of the boys were playing chess. The boy made a dumb move and the teacher captured his pawn. The boy swore. The teacher held out her hand and said, "That'll be one token." The so-called emotionally disturbed boy pulled a token out of his pocket and handed it to the teacher, without saying a word and without taking his eyes off the chess board. That was a loss of a reinforcer; so it was a response-cost contingency. If she had said they would have to stop playing for 2 minutes because he'd sworn, it would have been a time-out contingency.

By the way, in the face of the loss of a token reinforcer, why was the so-called emotionally disturbed boy able to control himself with such cool maturity? Because if he'd argued, or thrown a tantrum, or sworn at the teacher, the behavior would not have been reinforced; it would have cost him even more tokens! Professionals pin the label of *emotionally disturbed* on these kids, but instead, maybe they should pin the label of *emotionally disturbing* on the environments that reinforce such behavior.

Sometimes there also may be another difference: With response cost, you normally lose the reinforcers forever. For example, when the boys in Achievement Place lost points, they could never get those **specific** points back, though they could earn future points. But in some time-out procedures, the loss of a reinforcer need not be permanent. Consider this example of time-out: The parents send their daughter away from the dinner table for a couple of minutes when she pesters her little brother. But after those couple of minutes, she can return to finish the meal with no permanent loss of reinforcers. Contrast that use of time-out with the following response-cost contingency: For the same offense, the parents might send the daughter to bed with no supper. She's lost it forever.

On the other hand, at least one of the two actual case studies we looked at involved permanent loss of reinforcers. Every 2 minutes of Sam's time-out from play represented an opportunity lost and gone forever, because Dawn had limited the length of each session to 15 minutes. So sometimes even time-out produces a permanent loss. But response cost is almost always a permanent loss. For example, when you get a traffic ticket and must pay a fine, the violations bureau doesn't just keep your $50 for a few days and then return it to you. That response-cost-like procedure is a permanent loss of that $50, even though you may earn other $50 bills in the future.

Here's another cue: Response cost **often** involves tangible reinforcers, like tokens or money (we say *often,* because response cost might involve the loss of nontangible reinforcers such as approval or it might involve an increase in effort). Time-out **usually** involves activity reinforcers, like playing hockey. But, again, there are exceptions.

Response Cost vs. Time-out	
Response cost	*Time-out*
Removal of the reinforcers themselves	Removal of **access** to reinforcers
Loss of earned reinforcers	Loss of **opportunity to earn** reinforcer
Lost forever	Lost temporarily
Tangibles	Activities

Keep in mind that these criteria are just guidelines. Sometimes a penalty contingency will have some of the features of response cost combined with some of the features of time-out. That's life. That's the twilight zone; and when a contingency falls in the twilight zone, we don't waste too much time trying to decide if it's response cost or time-out; we just call it by its more generic and useful name—*penalty.*

Most of these distinctions are not hard and fast—and we don't mean to make a big deal of the overall distinction between response cost and time-out. **The big deal is that both response cost and time-out are types of penalty contingencies.**

Before	Behavior	After
Mark has all his points.	Mark threatens.	Mark loses 50 points.

So what is it?
a. Time-out?
b. Response cost?
c. Neither—it falls in the twilight zone?

It meets all the criteria in the preceding table for response cost. So that's easy.

Now, remember this one?

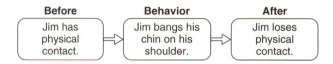

Before	Behavior	After
Jim has physical contact.	Jim bangs his chin on his shoulder.	Jim loses physical contact.

So Jim is losing the reinforcer itself and it is tangible, but the loss is only temporary. So what is it?
a. Time-out?
b. Response cost?
c. Neither—it falls in the twilight zone?

QUESTION

1. Compare and contrast punishment by the loss of reinforcers, penalty, response cost, and time-out.
    ○ Construct a table comparing and contrasting time-out and response cost. Remember that it's hard to get a good grade on the quizzes if you don't understand the tables and can't reproduce them.
    ○ Recognize examples of each.

Research Methods
REVERSAL DESIGNS (EXAMPLE 1)

The scientist needs to know if the changes in the independent variable are responsible for the changes in the dependent variable. And the performance manager needs to know if the intervention is responsible for the changes in the client's behavior. But to know this, the scientist must look at the dependent variable when the independent variable hasn't been changed and when it has and then compare the two values of the dependent variable. And the performance manager must look at the client's behavior when the intervention is in effect and when it isn't and then compare the two performances.

That's why the baseline is so important. Remember the use of time-out from physical contact to reduce Jim's self-injury. We showed the data for the baseline followed by the intervention and compared the two. The data looked good; Jim's frequency of self-injury dropped, from the baseline days to the intervention days.

But maybe it was just a coincidence. Maybe something else important just happened in Jim's life at the same time. And maybe that something else was the real cause of the decrease in his self-injury. For instance, maybe the weather became more comfortable, and that caused him to decrease his self-injury. Or maybe his parents had visited him. Or maybe the dietitian had changed his diet. Or maybe any one of a thousand coincidences.

In their original research, Tate and Baroff were aware of those possible coincidences. So to rule them out, these behavior analysts used a **reversal design.** That is, they reversed their procedure: They withdrew their time-out contingency and returned to baseline conditions. Then they waited to see if Jim would start his self-injury again. He did. So now they were more confident that their time-out contingency was responsible for the decrease in his self-injury. But, of course, they didn't want to leave Jim in this unhealthy condition, so they intervened again with their time-out contingency. And again Jim's self-injury reduced to a low level. This second reversal had two benefits: It improved the quality of Jim's life, and it made Tate and Baroff even more confident that they were not dealing with a coincidence, that the time-out contingency was responsible for Jim's improvement.

How did the second reversal make them more confident? Maybe the changes in Jim's behavior resulted from two coincidences. For instance, maybe the original decrease in Jim's self-injury resulted from an improvement in the weather. And maybe the increase in his self-injury resulted from a worsening in the weather. And their first intervention and reversal just happened to occur at those times. It's possible. Not likely, but possible. So the second reversal, where they started the time-out contingency again, increased their confidence in the importance of the time-out. The odds of three coincidences in a row seemed too low to worry about.

Now Tate and Baroff could continue their use of time-out with confidence. They also could recommend that the staff at Murdock Center consider it for similar problems. And they could publish the results of their intervention with considerable confidence, so that other behavior analysts also could consider using it to help other unfortunate people like Jim.

Definition: Concept
Reversal design
- An experimental design
- in which we reverse
- between intervention and baseline conditions
- to assess the effects of those conditions.

By the way, *research design* means the way you arrange the various conditions of your experiment or intervention; and the *reversal design* is one type of research design. We sometimes call the *reversal design* an *ABA design,* where the first *A* refers to the first baseline condition, *B* to the experimental intervention, and the final *A* to the reversal back to the baseline condition. The *simple baseline design* with no reversals is another type of research design. Intervention, without measuring performance during baseline, might be an example of a *case study*—a weak research design.

Question

I check my addition twice. First I add from the top of the column of numbers down to the bottom. Then I reverse the direction and add from the bottom up. I get the same results both times. So now I'm more confident of my answer. Is this a *reversal design?*

Our Answer

No way. A *reversal design* is an *experimental design* where you compare an experimental *intervention* with a *baseline.* Adding numbers has none of those features.

QUESTION

1. *Reversal design*—define it and show how Tate and Baroff's original research on the use of time-out to reduce self-injury meets the three components of the definition.

Research Methods
REVERSAL DESIGN

Here are more details on the actual experimental evaluation Larson and Ayllon used.

The experimental evaluation of the time-out intervention actually involved six different phases, with each phase usually lasting a few days (Figure 5.10).

1. For the moment, look at baseline 1, time-out 1, baseline 2, and time-out 2. Do those four phases represent a reversal design?
   a. yes
   b. no
2. Please explain your answer.
3. Does that reversal design you discovered in answering question 1 increase your confidence that the time-out intervention is what actually reduced the colicky crying?
   a. yes
   b. no
4. Please explain your answer.

To make their experimental design even better, their second phase involved the noncontingent presentation of the music. The mother turned on the music sometimes, regardless of whether or not the baby was crying.

5. Does the noncontingent presentation of the music reduce the crying?
   a. yes
   b. no
6. Please explain your answer.

7. In the noncontingent music phase, they presented and removed the music independently of whether the child was crying. Does this phase increase your confidence that the time-out intervention reduced the colicky crying? In other words, what reduced the crying?
   a. the soothing effects of the noncontingent music
   b. the music actually being **contingent** on crying
8. Please explain your answer.
9. The last phase is the follow-up phase. It occurred 2 months later. Here, all they did was measure the amount of crying. Does the follow-up phase increase your confidence that the time-out intervention was worth doing?
   a. yes
   b. no
10. Please explain your answer.

QUESTION/OBJECTIVE

1. Be able to explain the function of each phase in the Larson and Ayllon experiment on the use of time-out to reduce colicky crying.

Research Methods
THE IMPORTANCE OF BASELINES

Let's imagine what might happen if you don't use a proper research design. Sometimes you need a good design, even when you're not doing research—when you're working as a practitioner. Consider the case

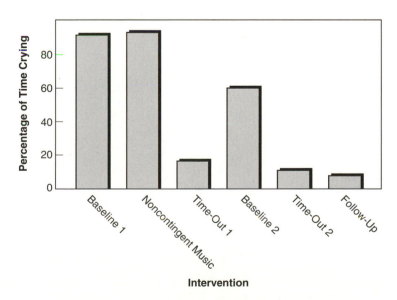

Figure 5.10   Experimental Evaluation Time-out and Colicky Crying

of Frank, a young man who was referred to the Psychology Service. He spent so many hours slapping his face, the staff had to restrain him. Before we started a behavioral intervention, we collected baseline data on his unrestrained frequency of self-injurious slapping. It was a good thing we did.

During eleven 30-minute observation periods, his frequency of face slapping rapidly dropped from over 600 an hour to nearly 0. But we hadn't done anything! This was just baseline.

Imagine this hypothetical situation: Imagine we had used a pharmacological intervention in which Frank took a tranquilizer every day in the hopes that this would get rid of his face slapping. And suppose we had used the drug without getting baseline data first. It would have looked as if the drug had caused the decrease in slapping. Then Frank might have unnecessarily been on that drug the rest of his life!

Moral: We often need to collect baseline data to make sure our intervention, our independent variable, is causing any changes we see in the dependent variable. It's important to be sure of what's causing what, both for scientific and practical reasons. So as scientific researchers we need to collect baselines, and even as practitioners, we sometimes need to collect baselines (for example, physicians often withhold the prescription of antibiotics for a few days to be sure the antibiotics are needed to cure your sore throat). Practitioners may need to collect baseline data when they're not sure whether an elaborate, expensive, or potentially hazardous intervention is needed.

QUESTION

1. Give an example of the importance of collecting baseline data and what might happen if you didn't.

6 Extinction and Recovery

FUNDAMENTALS

Example of Extinction
Behavioral Clinical
LUCILLE, THE RESTLESS RESIDENT[1]

Lucille was a psychiatric resident in a hospital in Canada. She wandered from the ward for the psychiatric residents into the nurses' office. A nurse took her by the hand and led her back onto the ward. Lucille and the nurses repeated this ritual several times a day, day after day. Sometimes the nurses took her by the hand; other times, they just pushed her out of their office. But she kept returning.

Teodoro Ayllon was doing his doctoral internship there. He asked a nurse, "What's going on?"

"That Lucille drives us crazy. She keeps coming into our office and pestering us. She's a real nuisance. We have to keep taking her back onto the ward," the nurse replied.

"Can't you just ask her to stop coming into your office and interfering with your work?"

"We've tried that, we've tried scolding, we've tried everything; but she's too dumb to understand. She's mentally defective," the nurse said.

"Well, how long has this been going on?" Ted asked.

"At least for two years, that I know of," the nurse said.

Ted and his dissertation adviser, Dr. Jack Michael, thought the consequences of Lucille's entering the nurses' office might be controlling that response, like any other response. Put another way,

some reinforcer must be maintaining it. In a problem of this sort, the first thing you should do is look at the events that follow the undesirable behavior. These events probably reinforce the behavior. Here, the undesirable behavior was Lucille's entering the nurses' office. And the event normally following involved removing her from the office, one way or another. But how could that be a reinforcer? In an abrupt way, the nurses were paying attention to Lucille.

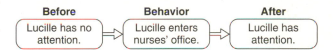

Before	Behavior	After
Lucille has no attention.	Lucille enters nurses' office.	Lucille has attention.

Now, it might seem that this sort of attention could not act as a reinforcer, but it might be a powerful reinforcer because residents on the back wards of most psychiatric hospitals don't get that much attention from the nurses. Usually the best way to get attention in a psychiatric hospital is to act crazy. So this aspect of life in a psychiatric hospital may help maintain the crazy behaviors. Suppose the attention involved in removing Lucille from the office reinforced her entering. Then they might get rid of this undesirable behavior by no longer giving her attention—by no longer removing her from the office when she entered. This could be true, though it seems strange that the best way to stop Lucille from coming into the office might be to no longer try to stop her. We call this stopping of reinforcement the **extinction procedure**.

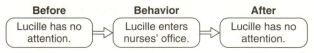

Before	Behavior	After
Lucille has no attention.	Lucille enters nurses' office.	Lucille has no attention.

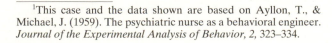

---

[1]This case and the data shown are based on Ayllon, T., & Michael, J. (1959). The psychiatric nurse as a behavioral engineer. *Journal of the Experimental Analysis of Behavior, 2,* 323–334.

You can imagine how reluctant the nurses were to try this extinction procedure, but they finally agreed. Each time Lucille entered the office during extinction, the nurses continued their activity as if she were not there. After a few minutes, Lucille would leave and the nurses would relax. Over the 8 weeks of extinction, the frequency of Lucille's entering the nurses' office gradually dropped from 16 times a day to only twice a day (Figure 6.1). Extinction worked!

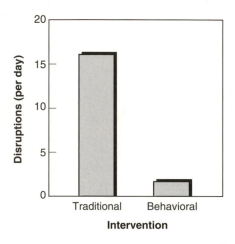

Figure 6.1   Using Extinction to Reduce a Psychiatric Resident's Disruptive Behavior

The traditional approaches failed to solve a problem for 2 years; yet the simple procedure of extinction solved the behavior problem in 16 weeks.

QUESTION

1. Describe the use of extinction to reduce disruptive behavior. Include the
   ○ client.
   ○ reinforcer withheld.
   ○ results.

Principle
EXTINCTION FOLLOWING REINFORCEMENT

In previous chapters, you saw that reinforcement increases the frequency of a response. And in this chapter, you saw that contingent attention increased the frequency of Lucille's entering the office. But now we want to decrease the frequency of reinforced behavior. Also, as you've seen, we could do this by using a punishment or a penalty procedure. Still, we can do it another way. We can break the reinforcement or escape contingencies. We can stop

the contingent presentation of reinforcers or stop the contingent removal of aversive conditions. With Lucille, the nurses stopped a reinforcement; they no longer paid attention to her when she entered their office. As a result, they got rid of, or *extinguished,* her uninvited visits.

Definition: Principle
Extinction
   ○ Stopping the reinforcement or escape contingency
   ○ for a previously reinforced response
   ○ causes the response frequency to decrease.

You run into extinction every day. For instance, you stop putting coins in a pop machine when it's empty. You stop writing with a pen once it runs out of ink. You stop dialing your friend who never answers. You eventually stop trying to push down the clutch in your new car with the automatic transmission. Extinction. Extinc. . . . Ext. . . . E . . .

QUESTION

1. The *principle of extinction*—define it and give an everyday example.

Example of Extinction
Child and Family Counseling
FAMILY LIFE—PART III: CRYING[2]

Remember Rod's bedtime crying in Chapter 1? Such episodes occurred so often that Dawn and Sid's life became miserable at bedtime.

"I'm beginning to think having a child was a mistake," Sid said. Sid and Dawn had just spent 30 minutes waiting for Rod to fall asleep to prevent the aversive crying. "Rod's crying really bugs me."

"Come on! Don't blame Rod, he's just an innocent 21-month-old baby," Dawn said.

"Maybe, but whatever happened to your idea of using your skills as a professional behavior modi-

---

[2]This section and the graph are based on Williams, C. D. (1959). The elimination of tantrum behavior by extinction procedures. *Journal of Abnormal and Social Psychology, 59,* 269. This study by Dr. Carl Williams is a classic in our field. Carl Williams was a pioneer in the application of the science of behavior to significant human concerns. And like many such pioneers, he had to go way out on a limb. And he had to go against common sense. He had to take the big risk. Fortunately, his confidence in the principles of behavior paid off.

fier to help the three of us out of this mess?" Sid asked.

"OK, a while back you said our attention (and especially mine) might be reinforcing Rod's crying," Dawn said.

"To be more precise, our attention is *contingent* on his crying," Sid corrected.

"Yes, of course. Well, I remember the classic article by Williams. He described a procedure to get rid of an infant's temper tantrums—an extinction procedure. It was simple: The parents stopped paying attention to their child's crying at night. And it worked!"

"You mean, we should leave Rod awake in the bedroom by himself in spite of his crying?" Sid asked.

"Yes, that's exactly what I mean," Dawn replied.

After a long conversation, Dawn and Sid agreed to try Williams's extinction procedure. On the first day, Rod screamed and raged for 45 minutes before going to sleep! He cried even more intensely than before. But Dawn and Sid persevered. Most of us wouldn't tolerate a crying baby for even a few minutes before we returned to comfort the baby—and in doing so, we'd reinforce crying. Dawn and Sid did resist that temptation, and Rod's crying gradually decreased. By the 10th bedtime, Rod didn't even whimper (Figure 6.2). He simply smiled as Dawn and Sid left the room. They could hear him making happy sounds as he fell asleep.

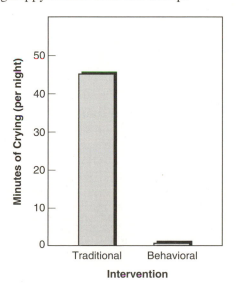

Figure 6.2   Using Extinction to Reduce an Infant's Nighttime Crying

A week later, Sid put Rod to bed and left the room as usual. Rod immediately began screaming and fussing. Sid gave in. He returned to the room and remained there while Rod went to sleep. Rod's

crying needed no more reinforcement. After that one instance of backsliding, Dawn and Sid had to go through the whole extinction process again; the next time they put Rod to bed, he cried for 50 minutes before going to sleep. But everything was in good order by the ninth time, when this crying stopped for good. In less than 2 weeks, they had gotten rid of a problem that had been making their lives miserable. And Rod's crying never became a problem again.

QUESTIONS

1. Describe the traditional way parents attempt to reduce bedtime crying. What's wrong with this technique?
2. What reinforcers may maintain excessive bedtime crying?
3. Describe the use of extinction to reduce bedtime crying. Include
   ○ the reinforcer withheld.
   ○ the results.
4. After a week of the extinction procedure, the infant began to cry again at night. Why?

Example of Extinction
Developmental Disabilities
EXTINCTION TO REDUCE A MULTIPLY MAINTAINED BEHAVIOR[3]

The halls of the Rosa Parks Academy rang with confusion and chaos.

"Get him!"

"He ran into the cafeteria."

Shouts echoed through the school. A teacher and two classroom aides chased a grinning boy. He was an 11-year-old, severely mentally handicapped child with autism, named Josh, who rarely stayed in one place. Dr. Mae Robinson walked toward the chaos just in time to see Josh bolt into a classroom. Jaci Jacobs, Josh's teacher, and two classroom aides ran after him. Jaci stopped when she saw Mae.

"Dr. Robinson! Thanks goodness, you got my message. Help!" Jaci pleaded.

"Let's sit down," Mae suggested, "and you can tell me about the problem."

Jaci saw one of the aides leading Josh back to the classroom. Though the aide was winded and sweaty, Josh appeared relaxed and content, happily munching potato chips. Jaci took a deep breath and told Mae about the problem.

---

[3]This study and its graphs are based on Piazza, C. C., Hanley, G. P., Bowman, L. G., Ruyter, J. M., Lindauer, S. E. and Saiontz, D. M. (1997). Functional analysis and treatment of elopement. *Journal of Applied Behavior Analysis, 30,* 653–672.

The Problem

Josh had been running away from people more than 20 times an hour. This behavior had started a month ago. Jaci and her teacher's aides were baffled. They didn't know why he was running away or how to handle the problem.[4]

Jaci began, "At first, I thought he was running away because the tasks we were asking him to do were too hard. But he never runs away when he's in an instructional session."

May asked, "What usually happens after Josh runs out of the room?"

"Well, we run after him, catch him and bring him back." Jaci said

"It sounds as if he gets a lot of attention by running away," Mae said.

"Yeah, I guess he does," Jaci said "but he doesn't seem to be pleased by the attention. Sometimes we even have to give him whatever he has picked during these episodes just to calm him down and get him back in the classroom."

As Jaci talked and Mae took notes, Mae began to see several contingencies that could be reinforcing Josh's running away:

1. Josh got attention for running away.

2. Josh got things (like the potato chips) when he ran away that he was allowed to bring back to his classroom.

Functional Analysis

Mae did a functional analysis to find out if attention and tangible items were reinforcing Josh's running away. She arranged a special environment so she could focus on the different contingencies separately. Using two small adjoining rooms in the school basement, she set up four contingencies for running away. One room she called the "before" room, which corresponded to Josh's classroom and is shown in the before condition in the following contingency diagram. The other room she called the "after" room, which corresponded to where ever Josh ran away to, and is shown in the after condition. Then she looked at Josh's behavior in each condition (with each of the contingencies in effect).

Generic Contingency for Running Away

Results of the Functional Analysis

During the condition where Josh got a tangible reinforcer (such as potato chips or a toy) after running away, he ran out of the room at least once a minute even when he didn't receive attention from Jaci. Josh also ran out of the room at least once a minute when he received attention from Jaci but no tangible reinforcers after running away (Figure 6.3).

Mae studied the data carefully. "Thank goodness for functional analysis!" she thought. "Now I can easily see that Josh's running away was reinforced by both attention and tangible reinforcers. I'll use two extinction procedures to decrease Josh's running away."[5]

Intervention

First, Mae told Jaci and the classroom aides to ignore Josh's running away (in other words, not to reinforce his running away with attention).

---

[4]Running away, also known as elopement in many applied settings, can be hazardous because children who run away may encounter dangerous situations (traffic, for example).

[5]Functional analyses have gained much recognition, over the years. A well-planned functional analysis can produce much information about a problem behavior; however, we must always make sure the benefits are worth the costs. Functional analyses can take time and cost money. Therefore, it often may be more practical to take an educated guess at the contingencies maintaining a problem behavior and develop an intervention based on that guess. For instance, in the present example, Mae guessed that attention and tangible reinforcers were maintaining Josh's running away. Had she used these educated guesses to design an intervention, it would have been similar to the one produced by the functional analysis, and the problem would have been solved more quickly. Even if Josh hadn't stopped running away, the trial-and-error intervention would have provided information about the problem behavior. Mae could have made a new educated guess based on the information from the first intervention. But for purposes of generating a publishable and clear demonstration of these underlying behavioral processes, the exact, experimental, scientific approach of the functional analysis is more convincing.

Condition	The Before Room (Classroom)	Consequences for Josh's Running into the After Room
Attention in the After Room	Josh was given toys and asked to play quietly.	Jaci followed him, reprimanded him (a form of attention), and brought him back. No tangibles
Tangibles in the After Room	Josh was given toys and asked to play quietly.	Josh was allowed to eat the potato chips and play with the toys that were in the after room. No attention
Ignore Josh's Behavior in the Before and After Room	Jaci and Josh sat in the Before Room. No other materials were present.	No attention and no tangibles
Play in the Before Room	Jaci and Josh sat in the classroom playing with toys. Every minute that Josh sat playing and did not run away, Jaci gave him praise and chips.	No attention and no tangibles

Second, she told them not to allow Josh to keep any tangible reinforcers he grabbed when he ran away.

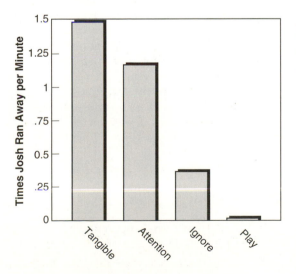

Figure 6.3 Functional Analysis of Running Away

In other words, they were extinguishing his running away, at least with regard to the attention and tangible reinforcers; that's why the before and after conditions in the preceding two diagrams are the same.

Also, because Josh hadn't run away at all when playing with Jaci, Mae guessed that the attention and praise during toy play reinforced playing in the room. So, Mae asked Jaci to give Josh more positive attention when he was in the classroom, regardless of what he was doing. (We'll analyze this contingency in Chapter 16.)

Results

It worked. The number of times Josh ran away dropped from more than once per minute to none (Figure 6.4). The classroom staff continued to give Josh noncontingent attention in the classroom and

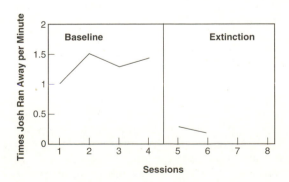

Figure 6.4 Extinction of Josh's Running Away

no attention when he left the classroom. Now Josh hardly ever ran away. However, these results were for the experimental rooms in the basement. But when Jaci and her aides used the same procedures in the real, upstairs classroom, again Josh hardly ever ran away.

In addition to running away from his classroom, Josh had also been running away from his home. So Mae did a similar functional analysis there and then helped Josh's mother implement a similar set of procedures that essentially eliminated his running away from there also.

Josh's running away had been a big problem, not only because of the potential physical danger, but because it was driving the school staff and his mother crazy, because it took teacher time away from the other children, and because it caused Josh himself to waste so much time that he lost many chances for learning valuable skills in the classroom. Therefore, solving this problem with functional analysis, extinction, and other procedures was a big deal in everybody's life.

QUESTIONS

1. Describe a functional analysis that led to an intervention to stop an autistic child's running away.

Principle
EXTINCTION BURSTS AND SPONTANEOUS RECOVERY

The extinction process may involve **extinction bursts**—initial increases in the response frequency, magnitude, or intensity, especially if that response has an "emotional" or aggressive component. For instance, when Dawn and Sid stopped paying attention to Rod's crying, that crying increased at first before it began to extinguish. Such initial increases often seem emotional—temper tantrums resulting from the failure of the previous temper tantrum to produce reinforcers.

Such an extinction burst raises an interesting problem. Suppose your little brother interrupts frequently when you are talking with other adults. And suppose you try to extinguish his interruptions by no longer paying attention to him. The first time you use this procedure, you might get an emotional extinction burst—your little brother might be even more disruptive than usual. He might talk more loudly, and he might even cling to your arm, wave

his hand in front of your face, or stand between you and the other adults. But if you can put up with such an aversive condition, his disruptions will extinguish. Have faith!

But aside from this brief emotional extinction burst, extinction has another interesting feature. Rod stopped crying after 45 minutes of extinction, during the first bedtime. But though they had won the battle, Dawn and Sid knew they had not yet won the war. They had more battles ahead. And sure enough, the third time they put him to bed, Rod's crying recovered spontaneously. Rod's crying recovered, though his parents had not reinforced it. He cried for only 9 minutes this time, though. And during the fourth bedtime, his crying **spontaneously recovered** for an initial 5 minutes of crying.

> *Definition: Principle*
> **Spontaneous recovery**
> ○ A temporary recovery of the extinguished behavior
> ○ during the first part of each of the extinction sessions
> ○ that follow the first session.

Read that definition over carefully and think about it. Spontaneous recovery occurs only during the first **part** of each of the first few sessions that follow the first extinction session. Also, note that spontaneous recovery can't occur during the first session of extinction. Why not? Because there's nothing to recover from. The frequency of responding during the first part of the first session of extinction is as high as the responding during the reinforcement sessions. But then, during that first session, the frequency of responding gradually reduces. However, during the first part of the second extinction session, the response frequency recovers somewhat, so that it is much higher than it was during the end of the previous extinction session. That's spontaneous recovery.

QUESTIONS

1. What's liable to happen at the beginning of your first extinction session?
2. *Spontaneous recovery*—state the principle and give an example.

Example of Extinction
Behavioral Special Education
ERIC'S CLASSROOM TANTRUMS— PART II[6]

Because of Eric's classroom tantrums (see Chapter 1), the principal of West James Elementary School had given Mae Robinson the task of helping Eric. His frequent temper tantrums completely disrupted the whole school and interfered with his learning anything worthwhile; the attendants often had to drag Eric down the hall to his classes, kicking and screaming all the way. Mae didn't buy into the popular belief that Eric's tantrums resulted from his inner frustrations. She knew that crying might occur initially without reinforcement, but attention also could reinforce it and cause great difficulty. Now she had to act.

Mae had read a study by a schoolteacher, Elaine Zimmerman, and her husband, Dr. Joseph Zimmerman. They used an extinction procedure to get rid of a child's temper tantrums in the classroom. She thought extinction also might work with Eric. So she explained her plan to Sue, who was in charge of Eric's classroom.

The next time a tantrum occurred in the hallway outside the classroom, Sue asked the attendants to bring Eric into the room. The attendants placed him at his desk and left. Then Sue closed the door and waited. "When you finish crying, we can start working," she said. Eric cried for 8 minutes and then said he was ready to work. Sue went to his desk to help him with his English exercises. Eric cooperated for the remainder of that class. After several weeks of extinction, Eric completely stopped his tantrums in Sue's class.

QUESTION

1. Describe the use of extinction to reduce temper tantrums. Include
   ○ the client.
   ○ the reinforcer withheld.
   ○ the results.

---

[6]Based on Zimmerman, Elaine H., & Zimmerman, J. (1962). The alteration of behavior in a special classroom situation. *Journal of the Experimental Analysis of Behavior, 5,* 59–60. This is another early example of classic research requiring extraordinary bravery, pioneering spirit, and confidence in the principles of behavior. When you read this, think about how much courage it took to implement an extinction procedure for such violent behavior, especially in a setting where two dozen other teachers were dying to say, "I knew it wouldn't work!"

Compare and Contrast
EXTINCTION FOLLOWING REINFORCEMENT VS. PENALTY CONTINGENCIES (RESPONSE COST AND TIME-OUT)

Sid and Dawn were visiting Sid's sister and her family last summer. Sid's sister worried because her two children had the foulest mouths of any children in their school district. They used words that would have made a fraternity man blush. So Sid offered his professional services.

The next morning at breakfast, the little boy said, "Pass the #$%! lox and a bagel, please."

Sid intervened with the lightning-like speed of a true professional. "Young man, you are in time-out. Go sit in the living room for 2 minutes. I'll tell you when the time's up."

The whole family sat in shocked silence as the little boy trudged off to fulfill his penalty. "And now, young lady," Sid said, addressing his niece, "did you learn anything from this?"

"You can bet your #%@&! I don't want any of those #$%! lox and bagels!" she replied.

Sid was using a punishment procedure, more specifically a penalty procedure, and even more specifically a time-out procedure.

Time-Out

The goal was to reduce the swearing. How might he have used extinction to reduce the swearing? Instead of taking away an existing reinforcer, as in the penalty procedure, he would simply have withheld a reinforcer from his nephew. He would have ignored the foul-mouthed request for the lox and bagel.

Extinction

Both extinction and the penalty contingency involve a decrease in the frequency of the response because of the lack of the reinforcer. But the penalty contingency involves the contingent *removal* of reinforcers. And extinction involves stopping the reinforcement contingency. In extinction, you don't remove something; you just stop presenting it.

In the extinction procedure, the reinforcer you stop giving is the one that had maintained the behavior. In penalty contingencies, the reinforcer you remove differs from the one reinforcing the behavior.

This might be clearer if Sid had used a response-cost procedure. For example, he might have said, "That cost you your dessert." The dessert is not the reinforcer maintaining the swearing.[7]

Time-Out
Punishment by the Withholding of a Reinforcer

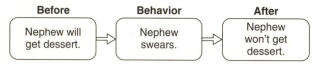

Before	Behavior	After
Nephew will get dessert.	Nephew swears.	Nephew won't get dessert.

But we may have already pushed the fable of the lox and bagels further than we should have, because the reinforcer for the swearing is not too clear in that example. It might be some sort of automatic reinforcer (Do you ever swear to yourself?), it might have been a social reinforcer (the reaction of the adults or other children), or it might have been the receipt of the bagel and lox. So let's modify it slightly and assume the shocked reaction of the adults is a major reinforcer for the nephew's swearing (that's true in my case).

And now, as Uncle Sid sits reading the *New York Times,* he hears his niece say, "'Sesame Street' is the most educational -#$! TV show I've ever seen." Now, Uncle Sid could ignore the remark—he could ignore the swearing. That would be extinction. He could say, "That cost you a quarter from your piggy bank." That would have been response cost. Or he could say, "Turn the TV off for 2 minutes." That would have been time-out.

In extinction, the frequency of her swearing would have no effect on the availability of the reinforcer, Uncle Sid's attention. But with the penalty contingencies, the niece's swearing would have the immediate effect of removing a reinforcer, either the quarter or the TV. Her behavior controls the removal of the reinforcer.

Another difference between extinction and penalty contingencies lies in the process of the behavior change. In extinction, the frequency of the response may initially increase and then decrease slowly. In penalty procedures, the frequency of the response often decreases immediately and rapidly.

To read the following table, select one of the cells from the white column, one from the white row, and the corresponding cell from the gray area—for example, *"extinction," "procedure,"* and *"stop giving the reinforcer."* Then it reads like this: *The **extinction procedure** consists of **no longer giving the reinforcer.***

Differences Between Extinction Following Reinforcement, Response Cost, and Time-out		
	Procedure	*Process or Results*
Extinction	Stop giving the reinforcer maintaining the behavior	Response frequency decreases.
Response Cost	Contingent loss of a reinforcer currently possessed	Rate may decrease rapidly.
Time-Out	Contingent removal of access to a reinforcer	Rate may decrease rapidly.

QUESTION

1. Compare and contrast extinction with response cost and with time-out.
   - Show the similarities and the differences.
   - Use examples to make your points.
   - Be able to fill in the relevant compare-and-contrast table.

Example of Extinction
Behavioral Special Education
SELF-STIMULATION[8]

"Jimmy, put your toy on the shelf," Sue repeated for the third time. But Jimmy was too busy flapping his hands. He would continuously flap his hands during much of the training sessions. This high frequency of self-stimulation interfered with Sue's helping Jimmy.

Self-stimulation dominates the lives of many unfortunate children, as Jimmy's hand flapping dominated his. This self-stimulation prevents them from learning much else. High rates of inappropriate

---

[7]This is a more complex form of response cost than we've seen before. What is lost is a future reinforcer (the dessert the nephew *will* get, not one he now has). In a later chapter, we'll study this *punishment by the prevention of the presentation of a reinforcer.*

[8]This case and the graphed data are based on Rincover, A., Cook, R., Peoples, A., & Packard, D. (1979). Sensory extinction and sensory reinforcement principles for programming multiple adaptive behavior change. *Journal of Applied Behavior Analysis, 12,* 221–234.

behaviors like self-stimulation, echolalia, tantruming, and aggression cause psychologists to classify these children as mentally handicapped, developmentally delayed, retarded, or autistic.

Jimmy's hand flapping was independent of Sue's reinforcers. Mae had read a *JABA* article by Dr. Rincover and his colleagues; these experts in the treatment of self-stimulation thought the automatic, built-in reinforcement contingencies of sensory stimulation might be maintaining such hand flapping. We call this type of stimulation *proprioception*—stimulation arising from muscle movement.

Dysfunctional Natural Contingency

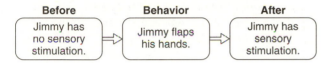

With more imagination and creativity than we have any right to expect, Rincover and colleagues designed the following extinction procedure: They taped small vibrators to the back of the hands of a child with autistic behavior. The vibrator generated a low-intensity, high-frequency pulsation. Such a device didn't physically restrict hand flapping. Instead the researchers hoped the vibration would mask the proprioceptive stimulus and thereby remove its reinforcing value. In other words, the child could flap his hands without feeling them flap. And this is the procedure Sue tried with Jimmy.

Performance-Management Contingency

Their extinction procedure worked for Rincover's child, and it also worked for Jimmy. After they strapped on the vibrator, Jimmy's hand flapping decreased to zero (Figure 6.5).

Rincover and his colleagues designed equally successful extinction procedures for other children who had little or no intelligible speech, Reggie and Karen among them. Reggie twirled objects such as plates on a hard table and then listened as they spun. Auditory stimulation seemed to reinforce his plate spinning. So they carpeted the table and prevented the sound. This procedure completely extinguished his plate spinning.

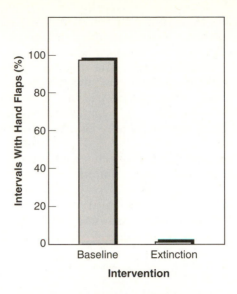

Figure 6.5   Sensory Extinction of Self-Stimulation

Karen picked feathers, lint, or a small string from her clothes and threw it in the air, trying to keep it afloat by waving her hands vigorously below it. Perhaps the visual reinforcers of the sight of the floating objects were maintaining this strange behavior. They turned the overhead lights off because they found this made it impossible for her to see the floating material, though the room was well-lit from the sunlight. This extinction procedure completely got rid of Karen's self-stimulation.

QUESTION

1. Describe the use of extinction to reduce hand flapping self-stimulation.
   - Diagram the dysfunctional natural contingency.
   - Diagram the performance-management contingency.

Example of Extinction
of Escape Behavioral Special Education
AGGRESSION[9]

"Bob, sit in your chair. I said, sit down . . . Don't you hear me? *Sit down*!" Fourteen-year-old Bob jumped at the teacher, hitting him, scratching him, biting him, and kicking him—drawing blood and bruising the teacher's arms and legs. After his assault, Bob

[9]Based on Carr, E., Newsom, C. D., & Binkoff, J. (1980). Escape as a factor in the aggressive behavior of two retarded children. *Journal of Applied Behavior Analysis, 13,* 101–118.

sat on the floor in his favorite corner of the class-room for mentally-handicapped children. For the last 9 years, Bob had attacked adults and sometimes a child. Nothing helped. The medical doctors had failed, with their heavy-duty drugs like the major tranquilizers Thorazine, Stelazine, and Mellaril. Nothing cooled out Bob's aggression. So behavior analyst Dr. Edward Carr and his associates came on the scene.

We know behavior results from reinforcement contingencies. But what reinforced Bob's aggressive attacks? The behavior analysts tried to answer that question first. They guessed that stopping the teacher's instructions reinforced Bob's aggression. In other words, reinforcement by the removal of an aversive condition—escape.

Inappropriate Escape Contingency

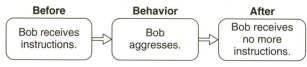

Now they needed to test their guess—to find out if Bob's aggression really was an escape response from adult instructions. They would use extinction of the escape response; they would no longer allow Bob to escape instructions by aggressing.

Performance-Management Extinction

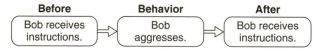

A dangerous task! The behavior analyst working directly with Bob needed to protect himself. So he wore a thick corduroy coat and rubber gloves during the 5-minute observation sessions. He sat facing Bob's chair; the other two behavior analysts sat safely on the opposite side of the room, recording the frequency of Bob's aggression.

They required that Bob sit in the chair. When-ever he raised himself 3 inches off the chair, the be-havior analyst facing Bob would say, "Sit down," and physically would prompt this response, if needed. That was enough to cause Bob to kick, hit, bite, and scratch more than 120 times in each 5-minute session. But in conditions where the be-havior analyst made no requests, Bob did not aggress at all; instead, he spontaneously sat on the floor in one corner of the room. It looked more and

more as if Bob's aggression was an escape response from instructions.

The behavior analysts used the extinction pro-cedure to get rid of Bob's aggression so he could function well in a regular class. The behavior ana-lysts working directly with Bob still wore protective clothing during each 1-hour extinction session, though they fastened Bob to his chair with a seat belt across his thighs in order to keep him in place.

"Sit down," the behavior analyst said. *(These instructions were aversive for Bob.)* And Bob, as usual, hit, kicked, bit, and scratched as much as the seat belt allowed. *(He made his escape response.)* "Sit down, sit down, sit down," the behavior analyst kept repeating while Bob aggressed. *(They were no longer reinforcing the escape response; they were no longer stopping the instructions; they were extinguish-ing the escape response.)* He aggressed over 500 times in each of the first 3 sessions; but after 5 gruel-ing hours of this procedure, Bob emitted only one or two aggressive acts per session (Figure 6.6). *(His ag-gressive behavior had extinguished.)*

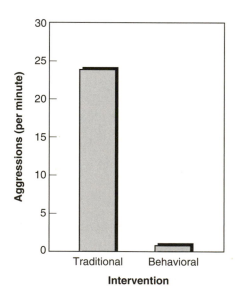

Figure 6.6   Using Extinction to Reduce the Aggressive Behavior of a 14-Year-Old

But a seat belt and protective gloves are not appropriate for a regular class. So the behavior ana-lysts slowly made the intervention conditions more like a regular class. They removed the seat belt first, the coat second, and the gloves third. They also rein-forced compliance to instructions; eventually, they would say, "Do this." Then, for example, a behavior analyst would clap his hands, and they would praise Bob's compliance or prompt the correct response when he didn't comply. By the end of this interven-tion, Bob responded correctly to instructions 97% of the time, and his aggression dropped to nearly 0.

This was extinction of a response that escape from an aversive condition had reinforced.

QUESTIONS

1. As always, when you see contingency diagrams in the text, be able to reproduce and explain them—in this case, it's the inappropriate contingency and the performance-management contingency.
2. How did the behavior analysts make the conditions of their intervention more similar to the conditions of the regular class?

Example of Two Types of Extinction
Behavioral Medicine
A MENTALLY-HANDICAPPED CHILD'S VOMITING[10]

Nine-year-old Laura could not speak. Physicians diagnosed her as "suffering from mental retardation, cerebral palsy, aphasia, hyperirritability, and brain damage." She entered the Rainier School, an institution for the retarded in the state of Washington. When Laura arrived, she had a strange tendency to vomit frequently, but within a few weeks her vomiting decreased to once or twice a month. Soon everybody forgot the vomiting. After 6 months at the school, Laura started a class that met every day. A month later, she began vomiting occasionally in class, and within 3 months, she vomited nearly every day. Laura became a markswoman with her vomiting. Her favorite targets included the teacher's desk and the table where other members of the class sat.

Each time she vomited, Laura also screamed, tore her clothes, and destroyed nearly everything she could. She often vomited on her dress; whenever this happened the teacher took her back to the residence hall. Physicians used drug therapy, but it didn't help. After 3 months, the teacher permanently excused Laura from class because of her vomiting.

Two months later, a brave teacher volunteered to take Laura into her class with the idea that Dr. Montrose Wolf and his colleagues would help her, because a physician said Laura's vomiting was not caused by medical factors.

People often assume that reinforcement cannot control vomiting; but Dr. Wolf decided to see if it could. He guessed that the consequences of vomit-

ing reinforced Laura's vomiting. As you can well imagine, her vomiting attracted attention even in an institution for the mentally handicapped, where bizarre behavior is the rule.

Dysfunctional Reinforcement Contingency

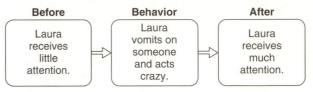

Dr. Wolf and his colleagues decided to stop the special attention everybody paid her and to stop taking her from the classroom, because that might be reinforcing the vomiting. The only attention following her vomiting was the removal of her mess as soon as possible.

Performance-Management Extinction

At the beginning of the extinction procedure, Laura vomited many times in each daily, 1½ hour class. The frequency of vomiting was so great that, in one class, she vomited 21 times (behavior may at first increase in frequency during extinction, especially aggressive behavior). The teacher who put up with this to help Laura deserved the humanitarian-of-the-year award. By the end of 30 days, the frequency of vomiting had gradually decreased to zero. Surely, that teacher felt relieved when the vomiting had finally extinguished.

Notice that Dr. Wolf's intervention involved the combination of two extinction procedures. One extinction procedure involved breaking a reinforcement contingency. Attention produced by Laura's vomiting might have reinforced such undesirable behavior. So, in extinction, Laura's vomiting no longer resulted in the presentation of the reinforcer—attention.

The other extinction procedure involved breaking an escape contingency. Being in class might have been an aversive condition for Laura. And vomiting ended this aversive condition when the staff removed her from the class—an escape contingency.

[10]Based on Wolf, M., Burnbrauer, J., Williams, T., & Lawler, M. (1965). A note on apparent extinction of the vomiting behavior of a retarded child. In L. P. Ullmann & L. Krasner (Eds.), *Case studies in behavior modification* (pp. 364–366). New York: Holt, Rinehart & Winston.

Dysfunctional Escape Contingency

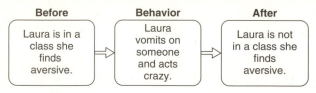

But during extinction, vomiting no longer resulted in removal from class. In the next section, we'll look more at extinction following escape reinforcement.

Performance-Management Extinction

QUESTIONS

1. Diagram a dysfunctional reinforcement contingency and a dysfunctional escape contingency that might maintain vomiting.
2. Also diagram the relevant performance-management escape contingencies.

Example of Recovery from Punishment
Behavioral Clinical Psychology
SELF-INJURING[11]

Five-year-old Judy put her hand in her mouth beyond her first knuckles. She did this so much that she had damaged her hands and face, producing sores, calluses, and displaced teeth. This multiply handicapped child had been in the hospital for 3½ years, confined to a wheelchair she could not control. She had impaired vision and hearing, and she had major seizures.

Several psychologists had tried different interventions to get rid of Judy's self-injurious behavior—her putting her hand in her mouth—but all had failed. There seemed no hope for Judy. Then Mike

---

[11]Based on Dorsey, M. F., Iwata, B. A., Ong, P., & McSween, T. (1980). Treatment of self-injurious behavior using a water mist: Initial response suppression and generalization. *Journal of Applied Behavior Analysis, 13,* 343–353.

Dorsey (with the help of Dr. Brian Iwata and some fellow students from Western Michigan University) agreed to work with her. Mike was doing this as part of the research for his master's thesis.

Mike wasn't sure what was reinforcing Judy's self-injurious behavior, so he couldn't extinguish that behavior by no longer giving the maintaining reinforcer. Instead, he tried to decrease the frequency by using a punishment procedure. Because he wanted to use as mild an aversive stimulus as possible, he used a fine mist of water sprayed in Judy's face. Now if he had asked us, we'd have told him he was a dreamer. We'd have thought that no way could such a mild irritant effectively suppress such a well-established response. But he didn't ask us.

Performance-Management Punishment

Before their intervention, Judy had her hand in her mouth 80% of the time. But the mild mist punishment was so effective that within the first 20-minute session, she decreased this long-standing self-injurious behavior to only 20% of the time. And after ten sessions she had almost completely stopped putting her hand in her mouth. It was a good thing Mike had not asked us.

To show that the punishment contingency had caused Judy's decrease in self-injury, Mike and his colleagues stopped the punishment contingency for a few sessions.

Recovery from Punishment

And during the recovery procedure, Judy had her hand in her mouth 90% of the time. In other words, Judy's self-injurious behavior recovered after the punishment contingency was stopped. When they started the punishment contingency again, her self-injury immediately dropped to nearly 0% (Figure 6.7).

Incidentally, this mist punishment didn't work just with Judy. As part of his master's thesis, Mike used it with six other clients with self-injurious behaviors, such as hand biting, skin tearing, and head

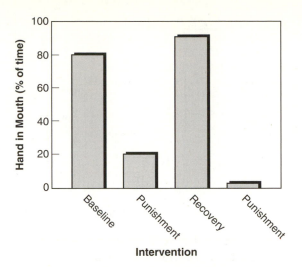

Figure 6.7   Using Mild Mist to Punish a Multiply Handicapped Child's Self-Injurious Behavior

banging. Always, this mild punishment was fast and effective.

QUESTIONS

1. What was the punishment contingency used to get rid of self-injury?
2. Describe the use of punishment to reduce self-injury. Include
   ○ the client.
   ○ the behavior.
   ○ the aversive stimulus.
   ○ the results.
3. What happened when the punishment contingency was stopped?
4. What happened when the punishment contingency was resumed?

Principle
RECOVERY FROM PUNISHMENT

We have seen that the frequency of the response decreases when we stop reinforcement and escape contingencies. In other words, extinction takes place. But we get the opposite results when we stop punishment or penalty contingencies. Then the frequency of the behavior increases. That's why we looked at Judy's case. The behavior analysts punished self-injury with the immediate presentation of mist. But when they stopped this punishment contin-

gency and self-injury no longer produced the mildly aversive mist, the frequency of self-injury increased. We call this **recovery from punishment**—the increase in response frequency resulting from the stopping of punishment or penalty contingencies.

Definition: Principle
Recovery from punishment
○ Stopping the punishment or penalty contingency
○ for a previously punished response
○ causes the response frequency to increase
○ to its frequency before the punishment or penalty contingency.

Here's another example. Suppose you often talk with your friends in the library, in spite of the "be quiet" signs. Then a new librarian intervenes with a punishment procedure. Every time you talk out loud, she rushes to your table to ask you to be quiet. She does so with the aversive, condescending style of the Church Lady from *Saturday Night Live*. She makes you feel as if you're a naughty grade-school student rather than a sophisticated college student. Of course your frequency of talking decreases. But after a few weeks, Church Lady is canned. And her replacement no longer punishes your boisterousness. So you, again, become your inconsiderate loud-mouth self. Thank heavens for the recovery process!

You might think that if stopping punishment contingencies results in the recovery of previous undesirable behavior, then punishment procedures are not effective in the long run. But it's not only with punishment that we get a return to the previous behavior after stopping a behavioral contingency. The frequency of behavior also decreases when we stop reinforcement contingencies; in other words, extinction occurs. Of course, behavior recovers when you stop a punishment contingency if a reinforcement contingency is still there to maintain that behavior.

QUESTIONS

1. *Recovery* from punishment—state the principle.
2. After you stop a punishment contingency, the original frequency of behavior recovers. Is this unique to punishment? If not, then what's another example where the original frequency of

behavior returns, after the contingency is stopped?

Example of Recovery from a Penalty Contingency Behavioral Clinical Psychology
SELF-STIMULATION AND DESTRUCTIVE BEHAVIOR[12]

Lynn Larson, a 6-year-old with autistic behavior and an IQ of 20 was referred to the hospital because of extreme self-stimulation and extreme destructive behavior.

Two behavior analysts sat behind a one-way mirror, watching Lynn play. Every 10 seconds they marked their recording sheets. In the experimental room, another behavior analyst sat on a sofa in front of Lynn. A box containing a variety of toys was on the floor. Often Lynn stopped her playing and self-stimulated: She walked on her toes, arched her body, flapped her hands, or flapped toys in front of her eyes. She also threw the toys, scraped the wall and a table with a toy car, and knocked over a chair. In the baseline sessions, Lynn self-stimulated or destroyed property during 86% of the 10-second recording intervals.

Later, Marjorie Charlop and her colleagues started a time-out contingency. Whenever Lynn acted inappropriately, the behavior analyst in the room faced her toward the wall and held her there for 5 seconds. We can't imagine that a mere 5-second time-out could reduce Lynn's self-stimulation and destructive behavior. But it did. In the four sessions of this time-out procedure, Lynn acted inappropriately during only 27% of the intervals.

Then, to show that the time-out caused the decrease of problem behavior, the behavior analysts stopped the time-out contingency. And Lynn's problem behaviors recovered to occupy 55% of the intervals (Figure 6.8).

This recovery procedure showed the importance of time-out. (After that, the behavior analysts started another punishment contingency to reduce futher Lynn's self-stimulation and destructive behavior.)

Analysis

Lynn's problem behaviors decreased when the behavior analysts used the time-out procedure. This is what we expect from contingent removal of the op-

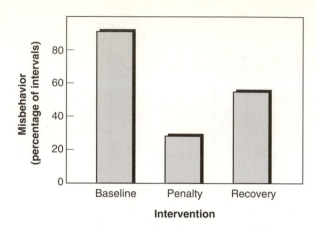

Figure 6.8   Using Time-Out to Reduce Self-Stimulation and Destruction

portunity to play; penalty contingencies cause the response frequency to decrease. Stopping the time-out contingency resulted in recovery; the frequency of self-stimulation and disruptive behavior increased nearly to the frequency before the penalty contingency. With more time, the frequency probably would have returned all the way to baseline.

We should get a similar recovery after stopping a response-cost contingency. Suppose a teacher had reduced disruptions with a response-cost procedure. Let's say he set up what we call a *token economy*, where the students could use their tokens, as if they were money, to buy other reinforcers at the end of the day. He gave tokens to each child at the beginning of the class and removed one immediately after a child was disruptive. If the teacher stopped using the response-cost contingency, the frequency of these response-cost suppressed disruptions probably would recover to their original high baseline frequency. So we expect recovery to baseline after stopping either type of penalty contingency, either the time-out contingency or the response-cost contingency.

QUESTIONS

1. Describe the use of time-out to reduce self-stimulation and destructive behavior. Specify
   ○ the client.
   ○ the reinforcer involved in the time-out.
   ○ the results.
   ○ what happened when that time-out contingency was stopped.
2. Give an example of recovery from a response-cost contingency.

[12]Based on Charlop, M. H., Burgio, L. D., Iwata, B. A., & Ivancic, M. T. (1988). Stimulus variation as a means of enhancing punishment effects. *Journal of Applied Behavior Analysis, 21,* 89–95.

BASIC ENRICHMENT

In the Skinner Box
Experimental Analysis of Behavior
EXTINCTION AND RECOVERY

Extinction after Reinforcement

It's time to glance inside the Skinner box again, to make sure you've got the concept of extinction wired. This time, you're in charge. You walk into the animal colony. Go to the rack with the rat cages. Open the one with your name on it—cage #27. You reach in and pick up your buddy, Rudolph. Yes, Rudolph has a red nose—would you believe pink? And white fur. You place him on your left arm and pet him as you go to the lab. You open the door of the Skinner box and place Rudolph inside.

You're going to show extinction following reinforcement. How do you do it?

You've already reinforced the bar-press response with water reinforcers. So you let Rudolph get clicking with a few reinforced responses, and then you take your hand away from your end of the water dipper. Sit back, put your feet on the table, pick up your stopwatch, pen, and notepad, and watch the *process* of extinction unfold. By doing nothing, you've set up the extinction *procedure*. At first, Rudolph presses the bar furiously for a few minutes. (Remember that burst of responses you often get at the beginning of extinction?) Rudolph responds more and more slowly, and before the hour session is over he has curled up in the corner for a snooze.

The next day, you put him in the Skinner box again and sit back to watch and record; you don't reinforce nothin'. But Rudolph starts responding again anyway, even without the reinforcers (Figure 6.9). However, he peters out pretty soon. (*Spontaneous recovery* is short-lived, and it gets shorter with each session until it stops altogether.)

Extinction after Escape Training

This one's tough, both conceptually and physically—physically because it involves electric shock. So let's look into the Skinner box of a professional experimental analyst this time. You see that the rat is pressing the bar every 20 seconds. You also see that, between responses, it stands with its paws just a fraction of an inch from the bar. You know that every

20 seconds a mild electric shock turns on through the steel rods in the floor and stays on until the rat presses the bar, which it does in a split-second. Escape from the shock reinforces the bar press (this escape contingency is often called *negative reinforcement*).

Now comes the tricky part: extinction following escape. Your job is to tell the experimenter how to do it. No problem, right? Just turn the shock off and watch the bar press extinguish. Gotcha! Oh, that life were so simple and so gentle. No, turning the shock off and then expecting this rat to press the escape bar would be like filling Rudolph with water and then expecting him to make the water-reinforced bar press. Water would have lost its value as a reinforcer for Rudolph because he had just drunk his fill. So you wouldn't call it extinction. And if the shock is not on, there's nothing to reinforce the rat's bar press; there's nothing to escape from. And you wouldn't call this extinction either.[13]

Once again, how do you extinguish the escape response? You turn the shock on, and you leave it on, no matter what the rat does! We have the shock on, and the bar press is ineffective in

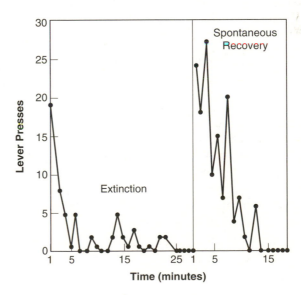

Figure 6.9   Extinction and Spontaneous Recovery of a Rat's Lever Presses in an Introductory Psychology Lab

---

[13]This part is a little gruesome. We don't know that anyone has actually done this extinction experiment with shock.

turning it off; that's like having Rudolph deprived of water and having the bar press ineffective in getting the water, in reducing the deprivation.

> **In extinction following either reinforcement or escape training, everything stays the same, except the response no longer has any effect.**

We would expect the same sort of results in extinction following escape training as we get following reinforcement. We would expect that the frequency of responding might be high at first and then gradually fall off to zero, *though the shock was still on.* We also would expect decreasing amounts of spontaneous recovery in the following sessions (we don't know of anyone who's done that part of the experiment).

Recovery from Punishment

Now we look inside another of the experimenter's Skinner boxes. Here, contingent drops of water reinforce the rat's bar press, and contingent electric shock punishes that response. The result is that the rat spends much time oscillating back and forth between bar presses. So it presses the bar at a much lower frequency than if there were no punishment contingency.

How are you going to show recovery from punishment? This one's easy. Disconnect the wire going from the response lever to the shock generator. Then the response will stop producing shocks. So the frequency of bar presses will gradually increase until it recovers to where it was before, with just food reinforcement and no shock punishment.

QUESTION

1. Describe Skinner box experiments that would show the following and also describe the results:
   - extinction following reinforcement by the presentation of a reinforcer
   - extinction following escape training
   - recovery from punishment

Ethics
EXTINCTION VS. PUNISHMENT

Sid's Seminar

Sid: One of the hottest, most emotional controversies in our field is whether and when you should use punishment to reduce problem behavior.

Tom: It looks to me as if this chapter argues well that you don't ever have to use punishment. You can always use extinction instead.

Eve: I agree that sometimes extinction would be better. But in some cases of self-injury, it might take too long and clients might injure themselves too much before the response is extinguished.

Sue: And in some cases of self-stimulation, it might not be possible to stop the reinforcement contingency and get extinction.

Max: That's the whole point of a study by Rincover and his buddies. If you're clever enough, you can even use extinction with self-stimulation. (You'll read about this in Chapter 9. You know me, I'm always reading further ahead than I should.)

Sue: Maybe, but I'm not sure. I'd like to see more examples where behavior analysts have done that with a variety of forms of self-stimulation before I'd agree 100%.

Sid: Those are all good issues, each worth 1 point. In summary, maybe we can at least agree that we should use extinction rather than punishment when we can figure out how to do it and when the behavior is not so harmful that the extinction procedure might be dangerously slow.

Joe: I want to file a minority report: I think punishment using a mild aversive stimulus is no big deal. It's no big ethical issue whether a physician gives a drug through a slightly painful hypodermic needle or through painless pills. It may be a practical issue, though. If you use the needle, you know the patient got the drug; but often patients forget to take the pills.

Tom: So?

Joe: So, just as with the physician, I think it's no big ethical issue whether the behavior analyst uses extinction or mild punishment. It may be a practical issue, though. If you use punishment, the behavior may stop more quickly.

Sue: I think it's strange that we don't talk about extinction as an aversive procedure. We've basically implied that extinction is gentle and nonaversive, but I think that being in extinction is very aversive. Nothing irritates me more than putting my dollar into a pop machine only to have it spit back at me without a pop. If I think that's aversive, maybe people with problem behaviors find extinction to be aversive too.

Sid: Another good point, Sue. Extinction can be aversive, though it isn't usually talked about that way.

QUESTION

1. What are the ethical issues involved in using extinction rather than punishment?

INTERMEDIATE ENRICHMENT

Compare and Contrast
EXTINCTION VS. FORGETTING

Students often confuse the everyday concept *forgetting* with the technical concept *extinction*. So let's do a little comparing and contrasting: To understand forgetting, it helps to distinguish between the procedure that is traditionally expected to cause what we call *forgetting* and the traditionally expected results of that **forgetting procedure.** We say we have forgotten something or can't remember something if we can't make the right response when needed. But there's more to it than that. *Forgetting* involves a decrease in the frequency of a response because that response has not been made for a long period.

Definition: Concept
Forgetting procedure
  ○ preventing the opportunity (or occasion) for a response.

And the ***traditionally expected results of the forgetting procedure***—*a decreased frequency of a response following a period when that response could not occur.*

Recall that the extinction procedure involves allowing the previously reinforced response to occur without reinforcement. If the extinction procedure gets rid of a response, then the extinction results have occurred.

The **forgetting procedure** and the extinction procedure differ as follows: The forgetting procedure prevents the response from occurring for some time. The extinction procedure allows the response to occur while stopping reinforcement. **Forgetting results** look like extinction results in that both **"should"** consist of a decrease in the frequency of the response. They differ in that forgetting is caused

by the lack of an opportunity to respond and extinction is caused by responding without reinforcement. The following table shows the difference between forgetting and extinction.

Extinction vs. Forgetting		
	Procedure	**Results**
Extinction	Withhold (stop giving) the reinforcer	Response frequency decreases.
Forgetting	Remove the opportunity for a response	Response frequency **"should"** decrease.

Forgetting is a common, everyday term, whereas ***extinction*** is not. So you might think forgetting is more important and that we should emphasize it more than extinction. Perhaps a pigeon experiment by Dr. B. F. Skinner will show otherwise.[14]

Using the occasional presentation of some bird seed as a reinforcer, Skinner reinforced the pigeons' pecking a particular spot on a target. After he had established precise pecking, Skinner retired his birds to their coop. Six years later, he gave them another shot at the target. Each bird immediately pecked the precise spot on the target that had produced reinforcement 6 years before! They didn't forget.

You can take the pigeon out of the Skinner box, but you can't take the Skinner box out of the pigeon.

---

[14]Based on Skinner, B. F. (1960). Pigeons in a pelican. *American Psychologist, 15,* 28–37.

You may know you forget things nearly every day. Does this mean you'd be better off if you had a bird brain like Skinner's pigeons? Perhaps not. For example, once you learn to bike, skate, water ski, or dance, you never forget, even if you haven't used your skills for years. Score one for the human brain! On the other hand, suppose you switch from a car with a manual transmission to one with an automatic transmission, and then switch back. Big trouble! It seems as if you forgot how to drive with a clutch. Score one for automotive engineering! But let's check it out more closely.

What happens when you switch over to the automatic transmission? You come to a stop sign. You put your foot on the clutch. But there's no clutch! Extinction city. After a while, the stop sign stops acting as a cue for pushing down on the clutch. Fine. Fine, except what happens when you switch back to the manual transmission? You come to a stop sign. You put your foot on the brake. And you kill the engine! You failed to use the clutch. Punishment city. In everyday terms, we'd say you forgot to use the clutch because you hadn't used it. But here's what we think really happened. Using the clutch extinguished, and you acquired the response of going directly for the brake instead: extinction of one response and reinforcement of another.

Then what about biking, skating, and dancing? Those sequences or chains of responses don't have a chance to extinguish. If they did, then competing chains of responses could replace them.

We think the same thing occurs with verbal responses as well. Remember the phone number of your ex-lover? You don't? But you used it five times a day for a year! Of course, that was a while back. Here's the number, if you're interested: *345–1623*. Why isn't that number still in your repertoire? Because of reinforcement of competing chains of responses. You no longer dial 345–1623, but you do dial a similar number—*345–1729;* and that chain of responses gets reinforced. This new number gets the garage that repairs your car. And that's just one of dozens of other numbers that replace the old lover's number. Reinforcement of competing behavior. By the way, for 25 years I had said dialing the former lover's phone number was also extinguished. Then one of my students pointed out that extinction couldn't occur if you had broken off relations and had stopped calling. Good point! So we explain this one just in terms of learning competing phone numbers.

What about when you "forget" to turn in your homework for a class? You may argue that you really forgot. We would argue that there were other competing contingencies supporting competing behaviors. For example, at the end of class, when you were supposed to turn in the paper, Jim walked up and asked if you were going to happy-hour and whether he could bum a ride with you. The social contingencies reinforcing planning your evening competed with the contingency for turning in the paper and you walked out of the class without turning it in. Remember, you don't have to be aware of these contingencies. We are not suggesting that you decide to chat with Jim rather than turn in your paper. Talking with Jim disrupts the sequence of behaviors that would have resulted in your turning in your paper.

Definition: General Rule
Forget forgetting
  ○ There's no such thing.

We think the forgetting procedure does not produce the forgetting results. In other words, you can use the forgetting procedure, as Skinner did with his pigeons, but that doesn't mean the forgetting results occur. That doesn't mean pigeons or the people forget. If we think there's no such thing as forgetting, why are we making such a big deal out of it? Because most people (including you before you read this section) think forgetting is a big deal. **We're trying to show that behavior analysis can reduce forgetting to two more basic behavioral processes—extinction and reinforcement.**

Here's another way to put it: We have two competing theories to explain what people call forgetting. The popular theory is the forgetting theory—that people simply forget. The theory most psychologists think is correct, however, is the behavioral theory of extinction and competing responses. The popular forgetting theory is a superficial analysis. The behavioral theory digs deeper.

QUESTIONS

1. *Forgetting procedure*—define it.
2. Compare and contrast forgetting and extinction. Be able to construct the extinction vs. forgetting table.
3. Describe Skinner's forgetting experiment and the results.
4. Do a behavior analysis of switching from a manual to an automatic transmission and back.
5. Do a behavior analysis of forgetting your former lover's phone number.
6. *Forgetting general rule*—define it.

THE MORAL NECESSITY TO EVALUATE INTERVENTIONS

Though it was important to help Laura with her particular vomiting problem, the study has an even greater value: Vomiting of this sort is more common among young children than you might think. The high frequency of this problem demands a solution. The present study shows not only that we can accidentally reinforce such vomiting, but it also shows that we can use behavioral technology to get rid of the problem. This study points out the importance of the extinction procedure as a tool for the behavior analyst.

When using a new behavioral intervention, we have a moral obligation to collect data and carefully evaluate the effectiveness of our intervention. Then we have a moral obligation to publish the results as a scientific experiment that shows the effectiveness of the intervention. In this way, behavior analysts not only directly help the person they're working with but they also indirectly help hundreds or even thousands of other people. Such long-range concerns mark behavior analysts who are also scientists. When we treat behavior modification as an experiment, we show concern not only for the individual but also for all humanity.

QUESTION

1. Why is it morally necessary to evaluate novel interventions?

Research Methods
THE REVERSAL DESIGN (EXAMPLE 2)[15]

Dr. Montrose Wolf and his colleagues needed to evaluate their intervention with Laura to provide effective behavioral technology that would help other children. But also, for Laura's sake, they needed to be certain that the teacher's attention and Laura's removal from the classroom reinforced vomiting. They needed to be certain so they could advise the residence hall personnel and future teachers how to manage Laura's behavior if she ever started vomiting again. Because this intervention was so new and radical, they especially needed to convince the skeptics. You can imagine how hard it would be to convince a teacher who didn't know the principles of reinforcement that the way to stop Laura from vomiting would be to let her vomit as much as she "wanted."

It is possible that the extinction procedure had nothing to do with the decrease in Laura's vomiting. The decrease might have been mere coincidence and not the result of her teacher's no longer unintentionally reinforcing her vomiting. (Presumably, the teacher had unintentionally reinforced the vomiting by paying attention to it and also by removing her from the classroom when she vomited.) They were going to use a reversal design—a research design in which they reverse the experimental conditions to assess the effects of those conditions. How would they do it? They'd try to reinforce the response again, and they might even try to extinguish it a second time. The frequency should go up when they again reinforce the response and down when they again reextinguish it. If this happened, they would have much more confidence that the attention and the removal from the classroom acted as a reinforcer for her vomiting; they would know they were not dealing with a coincidence.

But to reinforce the vomiting, they had to wait until Laura vomited. The extinction procedure had been so effective that they had to wait for more than 50 class periods before she vomited. At that point, the teacher began reinforcing vomiting. The teacher reinforced vomiting for 51 more class periods. As soon as Laura vomited once, the teacher took her out of the class for the rest of the day. This meant she could vomit no more than once per day during the reinforcement phase. Laura vomited on 23 days of the reinforcement phase; and toward the end, she vomited nearly every day.

Of course, Mont, his colleagues, and for sure the teacher were unwilling to let things stand at that. They had made their point—attention and escape from class were the culprits. Now they insisted on doing one more reversal; they insisted on extinguishing the response again. If they succeeded with this final extinction phase, they would have achieved two goals. They would have even more clearly shown that the attention and Laura's removal from the classroom reinforced vomiting, and they would, again, have gotten rid of Laura's serious problem, a problem that prevented her education.

During this final extinction phase, the teacher kept Laura in the class for the entire 1½-hour period. This meant Laura could vomit more than once per class, and she took frequent advantage of that opportunity. During the first part of this extinction phase, she vomited as many as 29 times in a single class period. It may seem strange that the frequency was higher during the first part of extinction than it was during the previous reinforcement phase, but

---

[15]Based on Wolf, M., Burnbrauer, J., Lawler, M., & Williams, T. (1967). The operant extinction, reinstatement, and reextinction of vomiting behavior in the retarded child. Unpublished manuscript.

Recovery from Punishment vs. Spontaneous Recovery			
	Procedure	*Results*	*To eliminate recovery*
Recovery from Punishment	Stop the punishment contingency.	Response rate recovers to level before punishment.	Start the punishment contingency again.
Spontaneous Recovery	Continue the extinction sessions.	Response rate recovers briefly at the beginning of each extinction session.	Continue the extinction sessions.

remember that Laura could vomit only once per day during the reinforcement phase. Mont and his colleagues could not show the effectiveness of this procedure until she could vomit an unlimited number of times. Eventually, however, the extinction procedure took effect and the frequency of vomiting decreased to zero; by the end of 34 more class periods in extinction, vomiting had stopped completely. The presumed reinforcers for vomiting were removal from the classroom and attention. As Mont and his colleagues withheld, presented, and again withheld the presumed reinforcers, the frequency of vomiting decreased, increased, and finally decreased again. This evidence should convince the most skeptical that Mont Wolf and his crew were not presumptuous in their presumption.

QUESTION

1. Explain how to use a reversal design to show that attention and removal from the classroom can reinforce vomiting.

Compare and Contrast
RECOVERY FROM PUNISHMENT VS. SPONTANEOUS RECOVERY FROM EXTINCTION

Two of the major ways we can reduce the frequency of behavior are punishment and extinction. So *recovery from punishment* and *spontaneous recovery* from extinction both involve recovery (an increase in frequency of behavior whose frequency had previously been reduced). Recovery from punishment occurs when we stop punishment contingencies involving either the presentation of aversive conditions or the removal of reinforcers. But spontaneous recovery occurs when we use the extinction procedure in several consecutive sessions; in other words, we don't stop the extinction procedure (Figure 6.10).

In recovery from punishment, the response frequency recovers to the frequency occurring before the punishment contingency. And recovery main-

tains unless we start the punishment contingency again. But in spontaneous recovery, the response frequency is lower than when the reinforcement contingency was in effect. And recovery is only temporary.

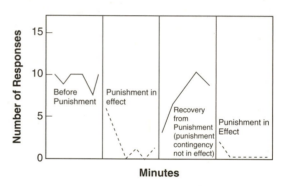

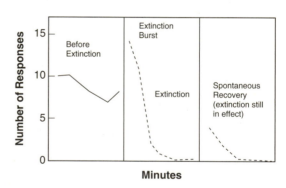

Figure 6.10   Recovery from Punishment (top); Spontaneous Recovery (bottom)

QUESTIONS

1. Compare and contrast recovery from punishment and spontaneous recovery from extinction. In other words, what are their similarities and differences?
   (Hint: some students find it helpful to memorize which kind of recovery goes with each procedure.)
2. And, as always, whenever you see a table in the text, learn it. Be able to fill it out even if

the rows and columns are switched around on you.

Research Methods
CONFOUNDED VARIABLES

Tobacco-Breath Tobbie Hanna was testing a punishment procedure to get rid of thumb sucking in her 16-year-old son. Every time he stuck his thumb in his mouth, she put her face right next to his and shouted, "No!" Soon his thumb stopped looking like a prune and started looking like a thumb.

Tobbie concluded that "no" was an aversive stimulus whose contingent presentation had punished her son's thumb sucking. Her dentist might tell her there was a **confounding** between "*no*" and a whiff of her horrible breath. In other words, each time she shouted, "No!" she also breathed directly into her unfortunate son's face. She may have confounded, or confused, the aversiveness of her breath with the aversiveness of her "no."

So we can interpret her intervention in at least three ways: The punishment might have resulted from the aversiveness of "no," the bad breath, or a combination of the two. Those three possibilities are confounded.

A major job of the scientist is to rule out confounded variables—to show what independent variables caused the results and what didn't. Was it the "no," the breath, or what?

Definition: Concept

To confound variables

- To change or allow to change two or more independent variables at the same time
- so you cannot determine what variables are responsible for the change in the dependent variable.

If Tobbie were a scientist, she might separate the confounding variables and present them one at a time. She might try contingent breaths for a week and then contingent "no's." That way she can see which outcomes were aversive enough to punish the thumb sucking.

If she hopes to publish her results in the *Journal of Applied Behavior Analysis*, she might even use a reversal design—a week of contingent breaths, a week of contingent "no's," a week of contingent breaths, and so forth. (Of course, even if she designs her experiment well, Tobbie still runs the risk that the journal would reject her article. We never said the life of a scientist was easy.)

QUESTIONS

1. To *confound variables*—define the term and give an example.
2. Using your example, show how you would get rid of the confounding.

Research Methods
CONTROL CONDITION

The major use of recovery from punishment is to control for possible confounding between the presumed punishment procedure and other changes in the person's life. You compare the intervention condition with the baseline condition. We call this comparison condition the ***control condition*** because it helps us rule out or control for a possible confounding.

Mike Dorsey and his colleagues wanted to know if their water mist punishment contingency had caused the decrease in the frequency of Judy's sticking her hand in her mouth. They wanted to control for the possibility that some other change in Judy's life had actually caused the change. So they compared the punishment condition with a control condition in which they stopped the punishment. If Judy's self-injury recovered during the control condition, then they'd be more confident that the punishment condition was the cause of her decreased self-injury. They'd also be more confident that their success was not the result of coincidence.

Marjorie Charlop and her colleagues also wanted to know if their time-out contingency had caused the decrease in the rate of Lynn's self-stimulation and destruction. They also wanted to control for the possibility that some other change in Lynn's life had been the cause (that is, they wanted to rule out that possibility). So they compared the time-out condition with a control condition in which they stopped using time-out. If Lynn's self-injury recovered during the control condition, then they'd be more confident that time-out was the cause of her decreased self-injury. They, too, would be more confident that their success was not the result of coincidence.

Definition: Concept

Control condition

- A condition not containing the presumed crucial value of the independent variable.

The control condition is important because a comparison between the intervention condition and the control condition shows whether the value of the independent variable really was crucial to the results obtained.

Incidentally, behavior analysts also often make temporary use of extinction as a control condition. They use extinction in reversal designs to show that their presumed reinforcer really is a reinforcer. For example, suppose you want to find out if your smile really is the fantastic reinforcer you think it is for the preschooler you're teaching to read. Suppose you've been reinforcing sentence reading with your warm smiles. During the control condition, stop smiling awhile and see what happens to the frequency of reading. Does it remain unchanged? Hmmm.

Behavior analysts often do research with single clients or subjects. So baseline is the most common form of the control condition in such single-subject research. However, we sometimes do research with two or more groups of subjects. For group research, we might implement a positive value of our independent variable with one group (we would intervene with that group). For another group, we might implement a zero value of the independent variable (we wouldn't intervene with that group). This second group would be a *control group. Control condition* is a more general concept that includes both *baseline* and *control group*.

QUESTION

1. *Control condition*—define it, give an example, and explain its importance by referring to your example.

7

Differential Reinforcement and Differential Punishment

FUNDAMENTALS

Example
Behavioral Sports Psychology
TERRIBLE TENNIS[1]

Principal: I want to get rid of it; IT DOES NOT WORK! [He paused for a few seconds embarrassed, cleared his throat, and gave it another try with a softer tone.] You know, every year, the girls' tennis team plays so poorly they disgrace our entire junior high school.

Juke: I don't blame you for wanting to get rid of your tennis team. I'd feel the same way, if I were you. The team did have a bad season last year.

Principal: And the year before that! And the year before that! Since we've had a team. I never was too sure about competitive sports for girls.

Juke: But, still, isn't tennis the most popular girls' sport in your school? What would happen if you disbanded the team?

Principal: I'd have heck to pay. But our team never makes it past the first match in the league playoffs anyway. And we're the laughingstock of the school district. We were even the butt of half the jokes at the last principals' meeting!

Juke: I see. (Complete silence for a few seconds.) Well, here's what I've found in coaching. You get out of it what you put into it. The best teams get

---

[1]Based on Buzas, H. P., & Ayllon, T. (1981). Differential reinforcement in coaching tennis skills. *Behavior Modification, 5,* 372–385. The data presented are from the same article; however, the issue of team standing is fiction.

the best training. They don't play well just by accident; they . . . .

Principal: Darn it, Juke, you gave me the same rigmarole last year when I wanted to disband the team. Remember, I followed your advice and hired a new tennis coach. It still didn't work.

Juke: You've got me there, Albert. Maybe the coach needs coaching. Tell you what: If you keep the team one more season, I'll work with the coach and see if we can't turn things around.

Principal: More than generous of you, Juke; but frankly, why do you think you can do any better than our regular tennis coach? I've known you for a long time, and I've never seen you with a tennis racket in your hand.

Juke: Hilary Buzas and Ted Ayllon at Georgia State have worked it out. I think if we just apply the technology they've developed, we'll make big progress. I've used Ayllon's approach in other sports; it always works.

Principal: You're a slick-talking son-of-a-gun, Juke. Here's what I'll do: You've got five weeks before the regular training season starts. You and Coach Craigflower take the three worst klutzes and see what you can do. If you impress me with them, then I'll keep the team for one more season; and you can use your fancy Buzas-Ayllon behavior mod techniques on the whole bunch of 'em.

Coach Craigflower was happy to work with Juke. They selected three basic skills to improve: the forehand, the backhand, and the serve. Then they did a task analysis of the skills, breaking each skill into five to nine components. For instance, among other behaviors, the forehand return of a right-handed player includes the following:

- When stroking the ball, pivot and step toward the net with your left foot forward.
- Transfer your weight from your right foot to your left foot.

(Of course, behavior analysts usually can't do this sort of task analysis and intervention by themselves. They need an expert in the field to help with the component analysis. And they also may need an expert to recognize when the component responses are correctly performed during baseline and intervention.)

Craigflower chose the three worst beginners, and Juke collected baseline data. During baseline, Coach Craigflower instructed her players as usual. She started each session with a five- or ten-minute lecture and demonstration of all the components of the three targeted skills. Then she corrected them as they practiced those skills. She mainly criticized their errors, and she mainly ignored correct or nearly correct components of each skill. For example, for Sherry, on the average, Coach Craigflower criticized her performance 23 times and praised it 5 times per practice session.

Yes, they had picked three lousy players; all three were terrible at all three skills. Sherry was typical. Juke computed the percentage of serves and returns where Sherry got all the components correct. What do you think it was? Twelve percent! And that was for 16 practice sessions. In other words, she wasn't going anywhere.

After Juke, the careful scientist, got his baseline data, he was ready to make his move—the behavioral intervention. He asked Coach Craigflower to stop all criticisms and just use praise. But instead

of waiting for a player to do all the components of an entire skill correctly, he asked her to praise any nearly correct component.

And Coach did a good job implementing the procedure. In working with Sherry, her criticisms went down from 23 times a session to 2 times a session. And her praises went from 5 per session to 21 per session. You can imagine life was a lot more pleasant for Sherry and the other players during the behavioral intervention.

But what about the players' performance? Our typical player, Sherry, went from 12% correct to 49% correct in 15 practice sessions (Figure 7.1). With a traditional approach, she'd gone nowhere for 16 sessions; with reinforcement, she quadrupled her performance in 15 sessions.

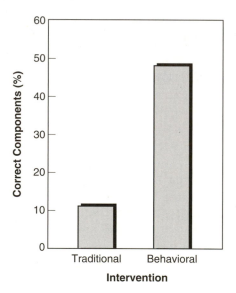

Figure 7.1   Task Analysis and Differential Reinforcement of Components of Tennis Skills

Oh, yes, these results so impressed the principal that he let the team play for that season. And with their new behavioral coaching procedure they placed third in their league.

Differential Reinforcement

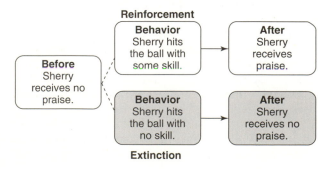

QUESTION

1. Describe a behavioral intervention to improve tennis skills. Specify:
   a. the response classes
   b. the reinforcement contingencies
   c. the presumed reinforcers
   d. the results
   e. any other interesting features of the intervention.

Concept
TASK ANALYSIS

Before he intervened with the players, Juke did a **task analysis.** He and the coach broke each task or skill into its detailed component skills. Then the coach could evaluate a player's skills according to each component and reinforce and give feedback more precisely. Instead of just saying, "Good," Coach Craigflower could say, "Good follow-through," or "Good grip."

It often helps to do task analyses when training complex behaviors: sports, dance, sitting like a man, table manners, writing poetry, doing a behavior analysis. And it also often helps to do component analyses when managing already established performance: sportsmanship, working industriously, interacting pleasantly.

Definition: Concept
Task analysis
- An analysis of complex behavior
- and sequences of behavior
- into their component responses.

When you do a task analysis, you're looking at the *process* and not just the final *product:* the sequence of motions in the serve or return and not just where the ball lands on the opponent's side of the net; lateness, time on task, time at the water cooler, and not just number of pages typed per day.

Sometimes you need only reinforce or give feedback on acceptable final performance—on product. That makes life simpler for the behavior modifier or performance manager. But if that isn't working, then you need to address the details of the process.

Definition: General Rule
Process vs. product
- Sometimes you need to
- make reinforcers and feedback contingent on
- the component responses of the process,
- not just the product (outcome).

Make reinforcers and feedback contingent on the component responses of the process, when you can't get quality products of sufficient quantity, even though you've made reinforcers and feedback con-

tingent on the ultimate production of those products.

For example, suppose you praise a child's performance each time she completes a long-division problem. But suppose she rarely completes the problems, and when she does, her answers are wrong. You may need to do a task analysis and make reinforcers and feedback contingent on each component in the task of doing long division. In fact, the first component you might have to reinforce is the child's sitting in her seat.

QUESTIONS

1. *Task analysis*—define it and give an example.
2. *Process versus product*—state this general rule, and explain how you can apply it in sports.

Concept
RESPONSE DIMENSIONS

The forehand tennis swing differs from the swing of a baseball bat and the swing of a golf club. The bat moves on a horizontal plane and then arcs to the left, for the right-hander. The club moves on a vertical plane, going from the tee to high above, then pausing and changing direction. The movements in a swimming stroke differ greatly from those of dancing or running track. We call these differences of movement *differences in response topography.* If you extend your little finger when you daintily drink tea, you're using a response topography different from the one I use.

Definition: Concept
Response topography
- The sequence (path of movement)
- form
- or location
- of components of a response
- relative to the rest of the body.

Here's what we mean by two responses that differ in topography because they differ in the *sequence* or path of movement: Suppose you and I both write the word *slob.* Our resulting handwriting will be much different—yours precise, sensitive, pleasant, artistic, legible; mine sloppy, illegible, smudged, torn, scarred by broken pencil leads, eraser-marred—work of a true slob. The handwriting is the result of our making the same response but with slightly different sequences of movement—in other words, with slightly different topographies.

Here's what we mean by *location relative to the rest of the body:* If you wave your hands above your head, that's a different location than if you wave them below your head. So waving your hands in the two locations represents two different topographies. Location in space is with reference to the body of the person making the response.

Here's what we mean by *form:* There are many ways to do push-ups. If you're using the correct form, your back should be straight. If, like me, you tend toward butt-in-the-air push-ups, you are using incorrect form. As another example, two divers competing in the Olympic Games may use different forms when executing the same dive (e.g., one points his toes while the other doesn't).

As far as topography goes, "It ain't what 'cha do; it's the way what 'cha do it." If Rudolph the rat presses the lever with its right paw, that's a different topography than if it presses it with his left paw or his nose; Rudolph does press the lever, but there are topographically different ways he can do it. So responding with different parts of your body also illustrate differences in topography.

Different cultural groups have different ways of walking, as do men and women and people of different ages. It's all the same response class but different topographies. You'll get to your reinforcing goal whether you walk gracefully or awkwardly; the only difference is your style, your response topography.

Now here's a common confusion: Students often confuse *response topography* in terms of *response location* relative to your body with response location relative to the external environment. Suppose you have two levers in your Skinner box. Rudolph can press either the right or the left lever. So now the responses can differ according to their location relative to the Skinner box (e.g., the right or left lever); and they can also differ according to their location relative to Rudolph's body (e.g., pressing with its front leg extended directly in front of him or pressing with his front leg extended from his side.) Pressing the right versus the left lever is an example of stimulus discrimination, not response differentiation. Rudolph is "discriminating" between two elements of his environment, the right and left levers. We'll study stimulus discrimination in Chapter 12.

But responses can differ in more than topography. These potential differences are the ***dimensions of the response.*** Besides topography, other dimensions include **force**[2] (the loudness of your voice when you speak in public), **duration** (the duration of each key press when you use your pocket calculator), and **latency** (the time it takes you on an oral quiz to name the concept when your professor gives you the definition).

Definition: Concept
Latency
○ The time between
○ the signal or opportunity for a response
○ and the beginning of that response.

You put Rudolph in the Skinner box (opportunity for a response), and he wanders around for a few seconds (latency of the response) before he presses the lever. Then he holds the lever down for a couple seconds (duration of the response).

Definition: Concept
Duration
○ The time from
○ the beginning
○ to the end
○ of a response.

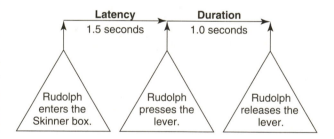

The difference between duration and latency often confuses students. So let's check it out again: When I say "go," I want you to take a deep breath and hold it as long as you can. Now think about the time between when I say "go" and when you start to take your deep breath. Which is it—the *latency* of the response or the *duration?* And think about the time between when you start to take your deep breath and when you pass out. Which is it—*latency* or *duration?* Right; we measure the *latency* from *"go"* to the start of your deep breath, and we measure the *duration* of the time you hold that breath.

---

[2]Often we use the term *intensity* rather than *force* when speaking of loudness. But the two terms mean about the same thing. We often speak of the *force* of a response and the *intensity* of a stimulus.

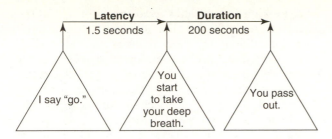

We also could measure the latency between when father finishes saying grace at the dinner table and when you have your fork loaded with peas. And we could measure the latency between when you load your fork and when you deliver those peas to your mouth; but this is a slightly unusual use of the term *latency* because it's the time between one of your responses (loading your fork) and another of your responses (dumping the peas in your mouth.) Most often we measure the latency between some external event (like the end of the prayer) and your response.

1. What is the time between the light turning green and your slamming your foot down on the accelerator?
   a. response duration
   b. response latency
2. What is the length of time you blow your horn at the driver in front of you who doesn't notice the light has turned green?
   a. response duration
   b. response latency

Definition: Concept
Response dimensions
- The physical properties of a response.

Topography, latency, and duration are examples of **response dimensions.** They're physical properties of a response. Here are some other physical properties or dimensions of a response: **force** (how hard the batter hits the ball, how loudly you cheer when the ball soars over the outfield wall) and **pitch** (how high you have to sing when you struggle through our national anthem). The skill with which Sherry served the tennis ball was a dimension composed of several components such as pivoting, moving forward, and transferring her weight.[3]

---

[3]If you needed to be more precise, you might say that each component of the serving skill was a separate dimension.

By the way, you sometimes have to watch out for metaphorical or poetic uses of these terms. For example, Dawn might say, "Sid is studying intensely." But that differs from shouting intensely; studying intensely is not a response dimension. What Dawn really means is that Sid is studying continuously without interrupting his studying by making other responses, such as looking around or chatting.

We can classify responses according to their dimensions, but also we can classify them according to their *function*—their effects on the environment: depressing a lever, getting a laugh, totaling a car, or ringing a doorbell. Now most of us would ring the doorbell with our index finger. But we might make the bell ring by pressing the button with our little finger, big toe, elbow, forehead, nose, chin, or rear end (just stand tall). Though each response differs in topography, force, duration, and latency, they all have the same effect on the environment—they all ring that bell.

(Note that response function is **not** an example of response dimension. For example, the function of the response ringing the bell might be to bring someone to the door. And that functional response has various dimensions, such as force and duration.)

It often helps to do task analyses to define responses according to their dimensions. But it is usually more convenient to define them according to their function—their product. For example, you might define children's lunchroom behavior as too noisy if it makes a sound meter go past a certain limit. Then you need not deal with the details of the response dimensions; and you can arrange for computer-like equipment that automatically punishes noisy behavior, possibly using a penalty contingency.

QUESTIONS

1. Define and give an example of the following concepts:
   a. response dimension
   b. response duration
   c. response latency
   d. response topography.
2. Give an example of responses that vary across the following dimensions:
   a. topography
   b. force
   c. duration
   d. latency.
3. Give an example of responses that differ along various dimensions but have the same function.

Example Urban Myth[4]
THE PECULIAR PROFESSOR

According to popular legend, a professor used to stand on the right side of the classroom while he lectured, rarely moving to the left side. Students on the left side had to strain to hear. And students on the right side grew tired of the professor's breathing down their necks for the whole class period.

One student recorded the prof's bias. He spent 46 minutes lecturing from the right side of the classroom, 3 minutes from the podium in the middle of the room, and only 1 minute from the left side, while he wrote on the left section of the blackboard.

The students got together one evening before class and agreed on the following: They would reinforce lecturing only from the left side of the room. They wouldn't reinforce lecturing from any other place. They had no trouble selecting a potential reinforcer. As with all professors throughout the universe of universities, nothing was more reinforcing than the smiling face of a student hanging on his every word. So whenever he lectured from the left side of the room, 35 faces would smile and look at him. But when he moved from that spot to the right side of the room, all students would suddenly look down at their desks.

Differential Reinforcement

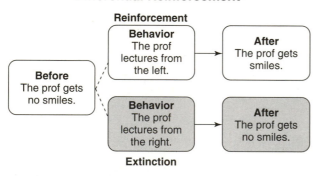

At the next class, the students started percolating their pernicious plot. The professor began to lecture from his favorite right corner; and all eyes looked away. As soon as he filled the right-hand half of the blackboard with definitions and diagrams, he started on the left-hand half. And when he turned from the blackboard to the class, 35 smiling faces

were looking at him. He stayed there for 5 minutes. When he moved to the other side, his attentive audience immediately fell away. During the next several minutes, he moved from one side of the room to the other. Then he stopped at the far left spot and lectured from there for the last 20 minutes of the class. After class, the students checked their records. The professor had spent a total of 28 minutes on the "smiley" side of the room, not his measly 1 minute of the day before.

QUESTION

1. Describe a behavioral intervention to increase your teacher's lecturing from a specific location in the classroom. Then convince your teacher why you'd never dream of doing such a dastardly deed.

Concept
RESPONSE CLASSES

Notice that the stealthy students allowed their professor/victim a little freedom. He didn't have to stand in one specific place before they would deliver their smiling attention. He could stand any place, if it were somewhere on the left-hand side of the room. They defined the reinforced "response class" as being on the left side—anywhere on the left. We've included three different ways of defining ***response class*** (three different criteria):

Definition: Concept
Response class
  ○ A set of responses that either
   a. are similar on at least one response **dimension,** or
   b. share the **effects** of reinforcement and punishment, or
   c. serve the same **function** (produce the same outcome).

So we can define a response class either in terms of

   a. **dimension,** or
   b. **effects,** or
   c. **function.**

The students defined their innocent professor's response class in terms of the physical **dimension** of location; reinforcement occurred when the professor stood on the left.

---

[4]An *urban myth* or *urban legend* is a myth that spreads throughout society and that everyone takes to be true—but it isn't. The most famous example is that evil people put poison, pins and razor blades in Halloween trick-or-treat candy. No such case has been documented. *Urban myth* will *not* be on your final exam, but the concept might enrich your life a little bit.

But all instances of standing on the left also served a similar **function** (produced the same reinforcing outcome—attention from the students). So those responses form a response class according to that criterion, as well.

What about the criterion of sharing the **effects** of reinforcement and punishment? That's trickier. Consider two spots: the first, 1 foot to the left of center; the second, 2 feet to the left of center. Now each time the poor professor stands on the 1-foot spot, the students reinforce that response with attention. And that reinforcement will make standing on the 1-foot spot more likely. But the effect of that reinforcement also spreads over to the 2-foot spot. That means the professor also will be more likely to stand there, as well. In other words, the effects of reinforcement are not precise. In sum, the professor's standing to the left met all three ways of defining a response class—dimension, effects, and function.

When reinforcing one response also reinforces another, the two responses are sharing the effects of that reinforcement. And because they meet the criterion of sharing reinforcement, they are members of the same response class. This analysis applies to punishment and extinction as well.

So a set of responses can meet the standards required to be a response class in three slightly different ways: They can be physically similar along some dimension; or they can share the effects of reinforcement and punishment and extinction; or they can serve similar functions (produce similar outcomes). A set of responses need meet only one of those three standards for us to call them a response class. They need not meet all three standards, though often they do. For example, the various responses of standing on the left are similar along at least the dimension of location though they may differ from each other slightly. Those responses all produce the reinforcing outcome of student attention. And probably reinforcing one instance of the response class also will make other similar but slightly different instances more likely.

But this concept of *response class* is hard enough to get a handle on that we may need to look at a few more examples.

We've already seen several examples of **dimension:** topography, latency, duration, location. Other examples would be the force of Rudolph's pressing the response lever, the distance he presses it down, and the speed with which he presses it. The side of the room where the lecture stands.

For **effects,** we're **not** talking about the effects of the response on the environment; instead, we're talking about the effects of the response outcome on the frequency of occurrence of members of the set of responses. We are talking about the effects of the reinforcer or aversive condition on the set of responses. If people laugh when you tell one funny story, you're likely to tell other stories that are similar, that are funny. If people give you sympathy when you whine, you're liable to talk about other problems in a whiny way. On the other hand, if people ignore you when you whine about one problem, that particular whine is being extinguished; but that extinction will probably reduce other similar, but different, whines. In other words, reinforcement and punishment of one specific response may affect other similar responses. And when that happens those responses are said to be part of the same **response class.**

Now, for **function,** we're **not** talking about the effects of the response outcome on the frequency of occurrence of members of the set of responses; instead, we're talking about the effects of the response on the environment. For example, Rudolph might press the lever with his right paw, his left paw, both paws, his nose, or even his butt. All those actions serve the same function of depressing the lever. So in terms of function, they form a single response class. And, yes, we've had accidentally, differentially reinforced nose presses and butt presses in our undergrad Skinner-box lab. But we think later experiments work better, if Rudolph only press with both paws; so now we require our students to reinforce only those lever presses that involve both paws. In this case, the other variants of the lever press don't meet our response-class criterion of *effect,* even though they do meet the criterion of *function.*

QUESTION

1. *Response class*—define it and give one or more examples of each of the three criteria in the definition.

Concept
THE DIFFERENTIAL-
REINFORCEMENT PROCEDURE

The students treated that class of responses differently from other classes of responses—standing on the right, for instance. Thus, they used a **differential-reinforcement procedure;** they reinforced the left class of responses and didn't reinforce the other classes of responses. Of course, differential reinforcement could involve either the presentation of reinforcers or the removal of aversive conditions (escape).

Definition: Procedure

The differential-reinforcement procedure
- Reinforcing one set of responses
- and withholding reinforcement for another set of responses.[5]

What would have happened if the students had kept on using their differential-reinforcement procedure, day after day, without mercy? Probably the prodigal professor would have ended spending most of his time on the left-hand side. Standing on the left would have come to differ in frequency from standing on the right; he might have ended there nearly 100% of the time. We call this **response differentiation**—*the reinforced response class occurs more frequently than the response class that is not reinforced, usually as a result of differential reinforcement.* (As we will see, differential punishment also can produce response differentiation.)

Becoming a skilled golfer results from a long exposure to the procedure or differential reinforcement of proper swings. The new golfer hits the ball with a variety of swings. But only a particular class of swings produces reinforcers—the golf ball soaring straight toward the green and a low score. With enough differential reinforcement, this successful swing will occur a high percentage of the time; response differentiation will have occurred.

You might have observed the differential-reinforcement procedure in conversations between two people. Participants differentially reinforce verbal responses of each other. This is why we talk about one topic with Jack or Bill and about a different topic with our Aunt Hattie. A good conversationalist says things that others reinforce with reactions of interest or amusement.

Notice that differential reinforcement also implies differential extinction: If you're differentially reinforcing one response class, you must be differentially extinguishing the other. The stealthy students reinforced standing on the left and extinguished standing on the right.

---

[5]Terminology note: Prior to the 5th edition, we defined **the differential-reinforcement procedure** as reinforcing one set of responses and extinguishing another set of responses. But one of our students pointed out that often the other set of responses has never been reinforced. Instead, what often happens is that the reinforcement of the first set of responses is also increasing the frequency of the second set of responses, even though that second set of responses has never been reinforced. But if we allow that second set of responses to continue occurring without reinforcement, the frequency of that second set will eventually decrease to near its original zero level.

QUESTIONS

1. *Differential-reinforcement procedure*—define it and give an example.

*Example Behavior Analysis
of Clinical Psychology*
THE UNINTENDED USE OF DIFFERENTIAL REINFORCEMENT BY A PSYCHOTHERAPIST

A group of traditional psychotherapists, *nondirective therapists,* argue that the therapist shouldn't be active in the changes that come about in the therapy sessions. They say the psychotherapist should provide a sympathetic and permissive ear to the clients. And because of this gentle, kindly influence, the clients begin to understand their problems and thereby (presumably) heal themselves.

But we, behavior analysts, don't believe that clients spontaneously begin talking in a positive way. Rather, the therapist differentially reinforces the clients' statements. The therapist's comments of appreciation, agreement, and understanding reinforce the clients' clear and optimistic statements. Extinction consists of silence and cool indifference following the clients' confused and pessimistic comments. The following dialogue shows the use of differential reinforcement in a therapy session.

Differential Reinforcement

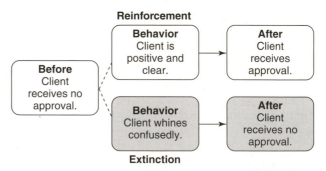

Client: I just don't know how I feel about my parents. . . . Surely they love me. . . . Yes! I know they love me! Why, just yesterday, they bought me a new swing, sliding board, and monkey bars.

Therapist (Sits up abruptly, leans toward the client with interest, smiles at the client slightly.): Uh-huh, I guess you're saying, "My parents must love me or else they wouldn't worry about providing me with recreation."

Client: Yes . . . that's it. One thing puzzles me, Doctor. Why should my parents give the workmen orders to have the recreation equipment placed in the middle of the freeway?

Therapist (Looks out the window, and after a few seconds of silence changes the subject.): You didn't happen to see the "David Letterman Show" last night, did you? There was this great dog act. . . .

Dr. Carl Rogers was the leading proponent for the nondirective view of psychotherapy. Rogers thought of the therapy session as a set of conditions that "helped" personal growth and integration. One behavior analyst, Dr. Charles Truax, decided to see if what Rogers said was true, or if he did differentially reinforce positive, constructive comments of his clients without being aware of it himself.[6]

Truax listened to several recordings of Rogers's therapy sessions involving a long-term client, and he analyzed Rogers's response to each statement. He found that Rogers responded with warmth and affirmation to the client's positive comments, but he didn't reinforce confused, self-deprecating, pessimistic, or generally negative comments. He also reinforced clear comments but not unclear ones. So the positive and clear comments increased in frequency, but the negative and ambiguous ones didn't.

Truax showed that differential reinforcement determined the results of Rogers's therapy, although Rogers didn't intend to use the principles of reinforcement. At the same time, Truax confirmed that basic principles of behavior also apply in the therapy session.

QUESTION

1. Describe and diagram the use of differential reinforcement in traditional, nondirective psychotherapy.

Example
Behavioral Clinical Psychology
I'M A WOMAN TRAPPED
IN A MAN'S BODY—PART II[7]

In Chapter 1, Bobbie Brown asked Sid for help. Though Bobbie was born a biological man, his behavioral history had caused him to act and feel like a

woman. Sid thought Bobbie's safest bet would be to learn to act like a typical man, think like a typical man, and value what a typical man values. That way, Bobbie would stop being an object of scorn and ridicule. He would stop being excluded.

Sid had started with modeling, feedback, and differential reinforcement to help Bobbie acquire classes of responses most people would label as masculine. They worked with three masculine response classes: sitting, walking, and standing. Sid had defined each response class according to its topography—movement in space—and he used differential reinforcement, praising instances of the masculine response classes and withholding praise for instances of feminine response classes. So Bobbie acquired the male topography—the male moves, of sitting, walking, and standing.

Not enough. Bobbie still acted like a woman in other ways.

Sid: Bobbie's getting the right moves, at least in the Psych Department. But everywhere else he's having as much trouble as before. Any ideas?

Dawn: Well, you've begun with the general basics, like sitting and standing. Now, maybe you need to get more specific.

Sid: Like what?

Dawn: Like talking to a woman. I met him at your office last week, and I couldn't ignore his awkwardness around me. He never looked me in the eye. He answered my questions only with a short "yes" or a curt "no." He never said anything unless I said something first. Except once: He asked me about my nails and my haircut!

Sid: You've listed the next target behaviors. But I need a woman for the training. Could you help?

Again, Sid defined the appropriate response classes, the ones he would differentially reinforce; and Sid and Dawn modeled typical conversations, demonstrating the appropriate response classes—eye contact, extended answers, initiation of conversation, and typical masculine content (most men would not ask women about the brand of nail polish they preferred). He asked Bobbie to try these appropriate response classes while talking to Dawn. They videotaped Bobbie, gave him feedback, and differentially reinforced with praise each correct instance of a response from a masculine response class. Bobbie's frequency of acting in masculine ways increased for each response class.

But Bobbie was still in trouble. He talked like a woman, or like a caricature of a woman, in a clipped, precise way, with a high pitch and feminine

[6]Based on Truax, C. B. (1966). Reinforcement and non-reinforcement in Rogerian psychotherapy. *Journal of Abnormal and Social Psychology, 17,* 1–9.

[7]Based on Barlow, D. H., Reynolds, E. J., Agras, W. S., & Miss, J. (1973). Gender identity change in a transsexual. *Archives of General Psychiatry, 28,* 569–576.

inflections. The masculine response class included a more relaxed way of speech, even some slurring. It was time for more modeling, feedback, and differential reinforcement: Sid read sentences and asked Bobbie to repeat them. He differentially reinforced with praise instances of the masculine response class. He also taped each session and played the tape back, to give Bobbie precise feedback—and it worked. After three weeks of daily training, Bobbie said even family and friends didn't recognize his voice over the phone.

Differential Reinforcement

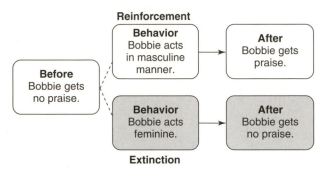

Sid and Dawn had differentially reinforced masculine behavior across different response classes: sitting, standing, walking, conversing, and voice control. They succeeded; Bobbie was acting like a man. But Bobbie still fantasized about having a woman's body, and he still played the role of the woman in his sexual fantasies. Sid and Dawn intervene on these problems in the next chapter.

Keep in mind that it was at Bobbie's request that Sid and Dawn were helping him change to a masculine style. Only with Bobbie's informed consent is such an intervention ethical.

QUESTION

1. Using the concepts of differential reinforcement, response class, and topography, describe an intervention to help a male transsexual acquire masculine behavior. Specify:
   a. the response classes.
   b. the reinforcement contingencies.
   c. the presumed reinforcers.
   d. the results.
   e. other features of the intervention, such as modeling and feedback.

Example
Behavioral School Psychology
CREATIVE BEHAVIOR[8]

People often think of creativity as a trait or personality style. They talk of creativity as if it were an entity or a thing. But behavior analysts talk in terms of creative *behavior*—behavior controlled by the principles of reinforcement, just like any other behavior. This means you can differentially reinforce creative behavior and thus increase the frequency of that response class.

In fact, Karen Pryor and her team went so far as to use food to reinforce the response class of creative water gymnastics with two porpoises! The frequency of novel topographies increased over common ones. In other words, they differentially reinforced novel behavior. So the porpoises exhibited a high frequency of original movements. Karen also taught creative responses to two dolphins at Sea Life Park in Hawaii. She reinforced anything the dolphins did different from what they had done before. The dolphins showed amusing behaviors. Karen said, "They became real nuisances, opening gates, stealing props, and inventing mischief."

If you can increase the frequency of creative responses in porpoises and dolphins, imagine what you can do with human beings. Elizabeth Goetz and Donald Baer reinforced creative block building with four-year-old girls. These behavior analysts defined 20 possible block-building forms. Then they asked the teacher to praise only novel forms of block building.

Differential Reinforcement

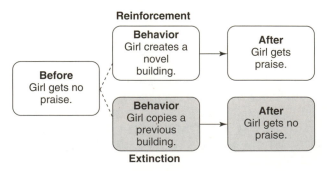

[8]Based on: Pryor, K. W., Haag, R., & O'Reilly, J. (1969). The creative porpoise: Training for novel behavior. *Journal of the Experimental Analysis of Behavior, 12,* 653–661; Pryor, K. (1985). *Don't shoot the dog!* New York: Bantam: Goetz, E. M., & Baer, D. M. (1973). Social control of form diversity and the emergence of new forms in children's block building. *Journal of Applied Behavior Analysis, 6,* 209–217. The data presented are from this article.

The results? During baseline, the children built an average of 0.33 new forms in each session of playing with the blocks. And during differential reinforcement for creativity, they built 1.5 new forms per session (Figure 7.2). They were more than four times as creative during differential reinforcement.

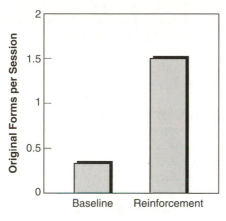

Four-year-old girls received praise when they created original building-block forms.

Figure 7.2   Differential Reinforcement of Creative Block Building

In both examples we've stressed only the novel or original side of creative behavior. But usually behavior must be correct or appropriate before we consider it *creative*. Otherwise, it may just be crazy. For instance, our conceptual questions ask for creative answers, but those answers must be correct as well as novel. Suppose a question asks for an example of reinforcement, and you give an example of extinction. That's novel; but it's not creative, because it's wrong.

Sometimes people withhold reinforcement for novel work they think is wrong and others later reverse that judgment, saying the novel work was correct. History then says the creator was ahead of the times. This is common in religion, the arts, humanities, and sciences. For instance, only after years of work did many psychologists acknowledge the correctness of Skinner's intellectual creativity, and even now behaviorism still causes controversy.

Though we've emphasized differential reinforcement of creative behavior, we also should mention differential punishment of noncreative behavior. Suppose that in every meeting of his seminar Sid required each of his students to make one creative response—to answer one conceptual objective in a creative, original, correct way. And suppose every time a student gave an unoriginal answer Sid took away a point or made a sarcastic remark. That probably would decrease the frequency of the students' noncreative answers and might increase the frequency of creative answers. Of course, such punishment also might decrease the frequency of attending the seminar!

But let's end this section on a more positive note: Our main point is that there's nothing mysterious about creative behavior. The principles of behavior control creative behavior just like they control all other types of behavior. That's good news, because it suggests that college students can acquire creative behavior, through differential reinforcement. If porpoises, dolphins, and 4-year-olds can do it, why not you? Of course, it will be trickier for your professors to devise the contingencies of differential reinforcement for creative thinking, talking, writing, and analyzing. In other words, you want to do more than aquatic gymnastics and block building. But the prospects are exciting.

QUESTION

1. Give two examples of the use of differential reinforcement to increase creative behavior. In each case describe:
   a. the subjects.
   b. the behavior.
   c. the reinforcer.
   d. the results.

Example
Everyday Life
**DIFFERENTIAL REINFORCEMENT
BY ESCAPE FROM
AN AVERSIVE CONDITION**

Sid sits in his one-room combination office and vacation apartment, overlooking Paw Paw Lake, editing what he hopes will be the world's greatest doctoral dissertation on behavior analysis. Dawn has also been writing all day, and now she's fallen asleep, stretched out on the mattress they're using as a bed. Sid tries try to be as quiet as he can. But his finger lies too heavily on the escape key, causing the computer to scream out in alarm, "Beep! Beep! Beep!" The feeble 1,000-cycles-per-second beep sounds like the screech of a wild animal, as it intrudes into the silent night. He glances at Dawn; she's starting to stir. The sound is now doubly aversive: first, because it just sounds horrible; and second, because it may wake Dawn. Desperately he starts pounding keys, trying to slay the beastly dragon and save the sleeping beauty. As he slashes out randomly at the keyboard, the dragon's cries seem to increase. He retreats and then moves back in with greater care. He hits ESC; "Beep! Beep!" He follows with a jab at ENTER: "Beep! Beep!" His little finger flashes out to CTRL, while his index finger prods C: "Beep! Be. . . ." Silence. The beauty stirs slightly, smiles, but never opens her eyes. The dragon rolls over on its back, its four legs pointing rigidly in the air, *X*s forming where its eyes once were, a wisp of smoke gently drifting upward from its nostrils. This is an example of differential reinforcement of a small response class (holding down the CTRL key while pressing the C key) by the removal of an aversive condition (that blasted beep).[9]

Differential Reinforcement

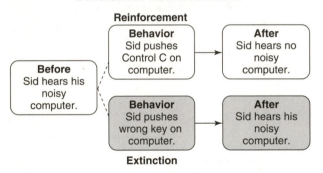

Note that we've described a procedure of differential reinforcement by escape, but we don't know for sure that differential reinforcement has actually happened; in other words, we don't know for sure if Sid will more quickly and more directly press CTRL C the next time that aversive tone comes on. How would we find out? Watch what happens the next few times the tone comes on. If he more frequently presses CTRL C and less frequently presses other keys, then differential reinforcement has actually occurred.

---

[9]Recall that we had previously defined *extinction* in terms of withholding reinforcement for a previously reinforced **response.** But that definition is a little too narrow. We really need to think of extinction in terms of a previously reinforced **response class,** because pushing the wrong key had never been reinforced by termination of the computer noise. But pushing the wrong key was originally in the same **response class** as pushing the right key—*CTRL C.* It was in the same response class because they were physically similar along the location dimension. And for that reason, they also shared the same response class because they shared the effects of reinforcement; in other words, reinforcing *CTRL C* would also increase the frequency of physically similar responses such as *CTRL V.* But the differential reinforcement procedure the computer is imposing on Sid is creating two separate response classes—*CTRL C* versus all other key combinations. This is response differentiation.

QUESTIONS

1. Diagram an example of differential reinforcement involving the end or reduction of an aversive condition.

Compare and Contrast
DIFFERENTIAL REINFORCEMENT VS. REINFORCEMENT

How does the differential reinforcement discussed in this chapter differ from the regular, friendly, old, plain-vanilla reinforcement you've read about in the earlier chapters? A tough question. And the answer is that reinforcement and differential reinforcement are almost the same—almost, but not quite.

When do we use plain reinforcement? When we just want to increase the frequency of a response and don't care too much about its details. (In his seminar, Sid started out giving points for almost any off-the-wall comments his students made, just to increase the frequency of talking.)

Plain Reinforcement

But we may explicitly use differential reinforcement, when a large response class is occurring at a high frequency and we wish to increase the frequency of one subset of those responses and decrease the frequency of another subset. For example, after the overall frequency of commenting was high, Sid required that the comments be well thought-out and that they show that the student had read the day's assignment; off-the-wall comments no longer produced points. He was trying to get response differentiation between two similar response classes: on-target comments and off-the-wall comments.

Differential Reinforcement

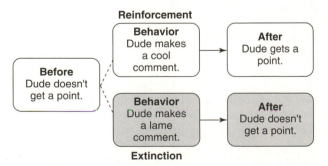

Of course, plain reinforcement always involves differential reinforcement, in some small way. (If

Max doesn't speak loudly enough, Sid won't hear him and won't be able to reinforce his comments.) Differential reinforcement is always implicitly involved in reinforcement, because some responses will be reinforced and others will not. In plain reinforcement, however, the unreinforced class is defined by exclusion—any behavior that is not eligible for reinforcement. We normally analyze the contingencies only in terms of differential reinforcement, when we're explicitly concerned with increasing the frequency of one response class and decreasing the frequency of another, similar response class. (If Max frequently spoke too softly to be understood, then Sid might want to differentially reinforce the class of comments that were loud and clear.)

So plain reinforcement and differential reinforcement are comparable: Both involve a reinforcement contingency that produces a high frequency of one response class. But they also contrast: We analyze the contingencies in terms of plain reinforcement when we're concerned only with increasing the frequency of one response class. And we analyze in terms of differential reinforcement when we want to increase or maintain one response class and decrease a similar response class—*differential extinction* might be a better label.

And what about reinforcement versus differential reinforcement when both involve the removal of aversive conditions? The baby wets its diapers, cries, and the parent changes the diapers. This is *simple reinforcement* by escape from an aversive condition, because almost any crying response will be reinforced.

Plain Escape Reinforcement

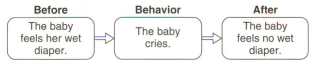

On the other hand, what do we have when the baby wets its diapers, cries at the top of its lungs, and the parent, listening to heavy metal on his Walkman, changes the diapers? This is *differential reinforcement of* the class of forceful crying by escape from an aversive condition, because only loud cries get reinforced.

Differential Escape Reinforcement

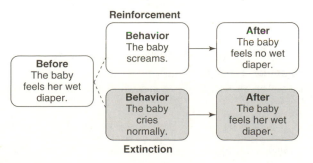

QUESTIONS

1. Compare and contrast reinforcement vs. differential reinforcement.
   a. Give two pairs of examples to illustrate the difference (one pair should involve presentation of reinforcers and the other removal of aversive conditions).

Example
Everyday Life
ON BECOMING A LADY

This was the most important day in the life of 8-year-old Carmen Rodriguez. Today her parents were enrolling her in El Colegio Maria Inmaculada—the girls' finishing school where Carmen would live for the next 10 years.

El Colegio sat atop a mountain overlooking the remote Mexican town of Poco Seco. Carmen caught glimpses of the school as their car climbed through the mist of the subtropical rain forest. At first it appeared smaller than the dollhouse she had to leave in her Mexico City bedroom. But the school grew and grew, as they approached, until they found themselves standing outside the 10-foot-high adobe walls that surrounded it. Carmen could just barely see the sharp tips of broken glass embedded in the mortar that crowned this masonry chastity belt.

Inside the courtyard, Carmen looked up at the gray, four-story Spanish colonial building. A pair of 20-foot-tall wooden doors barred their entrance. Carmen's father lifted the metal door knocker to announce their arrival. Two minutes later, 60-year-old Sister Sabina opened the door a few inches and peered out.

When Mr. Rodriguez explained who they were, the nun opened the door just far enough to allow them to enter. She did not smile, she did not speak, she just stood there in her long, black dress, with the black hood, the full-length black sleeves, her black hose, and black shoes. She just stood there, while Mr. Rodriguez got Carmen's luggage.

The grand salon, with its cathedral-like ceiling, dwarfed the three waiting figures. Each time Carmen shuffled her feet on the dark-red tile floor, the sound echoed from wall to wall.

Then Carmen saw it—the handrail on the stairs leading down from the second floor. A bannister, just like the one in her grandparents' home. Her favorite toy.

She let go of her mother's hand and raced up the stairs, two steps at a time. The sound of her feet striking the granite stairs echoed throughout the grand salon. When she reached the top, she hoisted up her long skirt, hopped on the polished mahogany banister and began her toboggan ride to the bottom, screaming and giggling all the way.

Then Sister Sabina spoke: "Young lady, never do that again! Always ascend and descend the stairs one step at a time. Keep your chin parallel to the stairs, and raise your dress to your knee with your right hand." Sister Sabina showed how and then asked Carmen to go up and down the stairs lady-like. Carmen did, humiliated, almost in tears. She counted 30 steps round trip. Then Sister Sabina said, "Now go up and down five more times." One hundred and fifty steps!

A few days later, Carmen walked down the stairs, her head bent and her eyes downcast, looking as if she had lost her last friend and might find a trace of that friend on one of the granite stair steps. When she reached the ground floor, she looked up to see Sister Sabina. "Young lady, please go up and down the stairs five times; but remember: keep your chin parallel to the stairs, and raise your dress to your knee with your right hand." One hundred and fifty steps.

From then on, Carmen made no more errors.

At the age of 23, Carmen ascended the stairs to the Cathedral del Sagrado Corazon, her left hand on her father's arm, her right hand, raising her flowing white dress to her knee, her chin parallel to the stairs. As they walked down the aisle to the waiting bridegroom, the audience of 400 admired this elegant, graceful, natural-born lady.

From the last row, a 75-year-old nun in a long, black dress sat watching. A faint smile was on her lips, and a single tear on her cheek.

QUESTION

1. Describe the punishment procedure used to educate a natural-born lady. Include:
   a. the behavior.
   b. the consequences.
   c. the contingency.

Concept
DIFFERENTIAL PUNISHMENT

Nature divides her pupils' actions into two response classes—those that slip by and those that are **differentially punished.** Sid looks at the nail, brings his hammer down, swift, powerful, true, and the nail slides into the wooden planter with a soul-satisfying "swaaap"—a built-in reinforcement contingency. Sid looks at his hammer, brings it down, swift, powerful, false—Sid, stop! Stop! Don't do it! Look at the nail, not the hammer! Too late. "Thump." "Yeoooow!" Built-in aversive stimulation. Differen-

tial punishment of uncraftsmanlike behavior—looking at the hammer instead of the nail. Sid's response class of looking at the hammer instead of the nail will be less likely in the future.

Differential Punishment

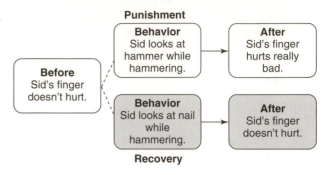

Definition: Concept
The differential-punishment procedure
- Punishing one set of responses
- and withholding punishment of another set of responses.

Sister Sabina divides her pupils' actions into two response classes: those she lets slip by and those she punishes. She differentially punishes unladylike behavior—looking down at the stairs, instead of straight ahead. Carmen's response class of looking at the stairs will be less likely in the future.[10]

Differential Punishment

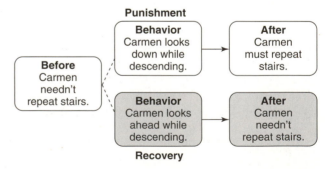

Sister Sabina differentially punished unladylike behavior. Response differentiation resulted: less unladylike behavior and more ladylike behavior. But Sister Sabina might have tried differential rein-

---

[10]This might best be interpreted as avoidance of an aversive condition (Chapter 15), rather than recovery. But in any case, it's an example of a procedure for achieving response differentiation.

forcement; she might have praised Carmen for each instance of ladylike behavior. And if the sister's praise were a reinforcer, the same response differentiation also would result.

Differential punishment differs only slightly from plain punishment, as differential reinforcement differs only slightly from plain reinforcement: Plain punishment and differential punishment are comparable. Both involve a punishment contingency that reduces the frequency of a response class. But they also contrast: We analyze contingencies in terms of plain punishment when we're concerned only with decreasing the frequency of one response class. And we analyze in terms of differential punishment when we want to decrease one response class and increase or maintain a similar response class.

In Chapter 4, we introduced *overcorrection*: Ann, a violent woman, had to overcorrect her destructive acts on the ward; she had to make the ward neater than it was before she trashed it. We call this *restitutional overcorrection*—correcting the consequences of inappropriate behavior. Sister Sabina's differential punishment also is a form of overcorrection. We call her form of punishment *positive practice*—repeating the correct response after making an incorrect response: five times up and down the stairs, but properly.

QUESTIONS

1. The *principle* of differential punishment—define it and give an example.
2. What is the difference between differential punishment and plain punishment?

Example
DIFFERENTIAL REINFORCEMENT AND DIFFERENTIAL PUNISHMENT IN TEACHING CLASSICAL BALLET[11]

Madam Cupet: Ballet dancers are born, not made. They have a God-given talent.

Juke: But don't your "born" ballet dancers also get the best training? Doesn't training count, too?

Madam Cupet: In a sense, I think training does not count. If the dancer does not show signs of outstanding talent by the age of seven, she or he will never succeed, despite the amount or quality of the training.

Juke: I'm a true believer in training, Madam Cupet; but I'm just an old football player, so I've got to

respect your judgment about ballet. Mae told me you yourself trained with the best teachers and danced with some of the best ballet companies in the United States, and you have an outstanding reputation as a choreographer and teacher.

Madam Cupet: Dr. Robinson was kind. She told me you have an outstanding reputation as a trainer; and that is precisely why I am asking for your help, Mr. Jackson. I told Dr. Robinson I was going to ask Bunny Lee to withdraw from my ballet school. But this is terribly embarrassing. Her mother is my best friend. Years ago, we were in the corps de ballet together. She gave up dance, when Bunny was born. And now she wants Bunny to have the career she never had. But God has not blessed the child with an ounce of talent. She is the worst student I have ever had.

After more discussion, Juke and Madam Cupet agreed to work together. Juke was a strong advocate of the training techniques Dr. Teodoro Ayllon had pioneered in sports; so he was eager to try out a procedure Ayllon and James Fitterling developed for ballet, when Fitterling was working on his master's thesis.

Madam Cupet and Juke helped Bunny with three basic ballet exercises: the dégagé, frappé, and developpé. They used the amazingly detailed task analyses Ayllon and Fitterling had done to define the correct response classes, mainly in terms of topography: weight of body on balls of feet, pelvis neither tucked in nor sticking out, hips and shoulders horizontal, heel of the front foot between first and second joint of big toe of the back foot, little toe is first part of foot to come off floor, side of big toe being the only point of contact with floor, and so on—nothing left to chance.

During baseline, Madam Cupet used her traditional style of instruction: lecturing and modeling the skills without music, modeling with music while counting the beats of the exercise, performance by the students, a rare praise, an occasional correction of errors, an occasional loss of temper when Bunny repeated an error, sometimes physically placing Bunny in the right position. Using videotapes, the behavior analysts later recorded the percentage of exercises Bunny performed correctly, during baseline: dégagé—33%, frappé—46%, and developpé—11%. Bunny was as terrible as Madam Cupet had said.

For the intervention, Juke instructed Madam Cupet to teach her class using behavioral coaching procedures. As in baseline, she started with instructions (a description of the relevant response class): "When the music begins, I want you to prepare in first position and then do the dégagé by moving your

[11]Based on Fitterling, J. M., & Ayllon, T. (1983). Behavioral coaching in classical ballet. *Behavior Modification, 7,* 345–368. The data presented are from the same article.

Dégagé

Frappé

Developpé

right foot straight back while keeping your leg straight and your body facing the front. . . ."

If Bunny did an exercise correctly, Madam Cupet praised her performance and commented on the correct components.

Differential Reinforcement

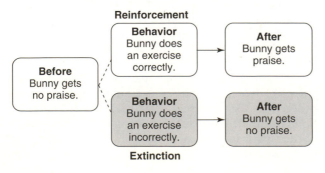

But each time Bunny made an error, Madam Cupet moved in with *differential punishment*, besides feedback, modeling, instructions, physical guidance, and more practice: The instant Bunny made an error, Madam Cupet said, "Freeze! Don't move." While Bunny stayed in an awkward, uncomfortable, presumably aversive, frozen position, Madam Cupet pointed out her error. "You allowed your hip to follow on back with your leg; this caused you to lose much of your turn-out." Bunny remained frozen. Madam Cupet modeled the correct topography. Bunny remained frozen. Madam Cupet described the correct components missing in Bunny's performance. Bunny remained frozen. Madam Cupet physically guided Bunny from the frozen position into the correct position, in which Bunny remained frozen. Madam Cupet described those features of the response class Bunny needed to change to make the performance correct. Bunny remained frozen. "Now, you try it once." Bunny thawed out and gave it another shot. This way, Bunny always ended doing it correctly. Then Madam Cupet started the exercise sequence with music. Each correction took at least one long, painful, aversive, frozen minute—differential punishment.

Differential Punishment

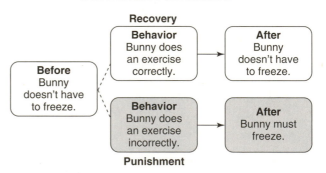

The results: Behavior technology won again—did you ever doubt it? Bunny's percentage correct improved from 33 to 92% for the dégagé (Figure 7.3), from 46 to 100% for the frappé, and from 11 to 88% for the developpé.

Bunny became nearly perfect. Never again was there any question about her withdrawing from Madam Cupet's class.

This is another example of the use of differential punishment to decrease the frequency of one set of response classes and thus increase the frequency of another. The punished response classes were incorrect performance of the three ballet exercises; the unpunished classes were the correct performances. Madam Cupet and Juke defined the response classes topographically (in terms of the movements of the dancers).

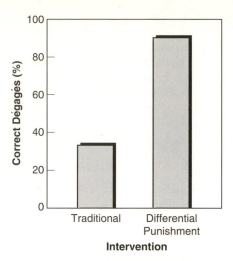

Figure 7.3   Using Differential Punishment to Improve Ballet Exercises

QUESTIONS

1. Describe the use of differential punishment to improve ballet skills. Include response classes, response dimension, freeze contingency, and results.
2. Explain how this is an example of response differentiation.

Differential Penalizing

Your term paper is due today. So, of course, you've been up all night writing it. It's the best thing you've ever written. This paper will allow you to hold on to the A you're getting in the course. You have to be at class in 30 minutes, just time enough for your computer to print your masterpiece. You push the print key, and . . . oh my gosh! It wasn't the print key. You just erased the computer memory and lost your paper and your *A*! Computers differentially penalize sloppy typing: They penalize by the removal of reinforcers.

In everyday life, the loss of reinforcers differentially penalizes much of our behavior—that old penalty contingency. Even without meaning to, our family and friends differentially penalized our vocal skills when we were learning to talk. We'd pronounce a crucial word so poorly they couldn't understand it, and they'd ask us to say it again, thus disrupting the normal flow of our conversation. Probably the loss of that normal flow would act as a punishing loss of a reinforcer—a loss that would decrease the likelihood of our poor pronunciation in the future. (Note that this is different from extinction. In extinction, the parents simply wouldn't respond to our poorly pronounced words.)

Please complete the diagram for this differential penalizing.

Differential Penalizing

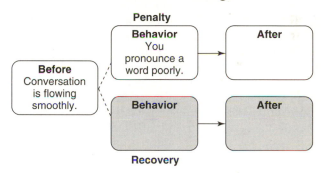

When we talk about a topic others find boring (for example, our dreams), we may lose the attention of our audience. This might be a penalty that will cause us to spend less time talking about our dreams in the future.

And how often did the ice cream have to topple off your ice-cream cones before the losses of that reinforcer suppressed your excitedly waving the arm that held the hand that held the cone that held the reinforcer. Such differential penalty contingencies caused you to acquire the skill of holding onto your precious treasures with the greatest care.

Please complete the diagram for differential penalizing poor ice-cream-cone holding:

Differential Penalizing

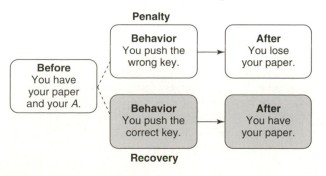

Differential Penalizing

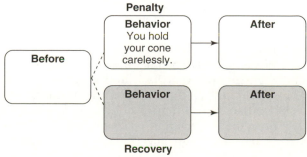

Thank you, Mr. Differential Penalty, for helping us acquire our skilled repertoires. If the loss of reinforcers didn't punish the offending acts, we'd be in a heck of a mess—no ice cream, no friends, no term papers written, not much of anything.

QUESTION

1. Give an example of differential punishment involving a penalty contingency. Include the response, the presumed reinforcer, the contingency, and the expected results.

BASIC ENRICHMENT

In the Skinner Box
Experimental Analysis
DIFFERENTIAL REINFORCEMENT

Back to Rudolph Rat in the Skinner box—this time, to check out differential reinforcement. We'll work with the response dimension of topography and measure it in terms of the distance Rudolph presses the lever. We'll reinforce with a drop of water the class of responses that presses the lever 1 inch or more, and we'll extinguish the class of responses that presses the lever less than that 1 inch.

Differential Reinforcement

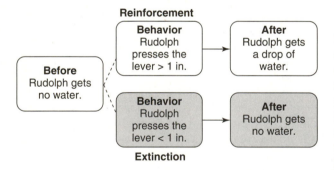

Here's what happens: At first most of the bar presses go less than 1 inch; we extinguish them. But now and then, one meets our 1-inch criterion, and we reinforce it. Gradually, the substandard presses decrease in frequency, and the acceptable ones increase in frequency. After a while, Rudolph usually presses the bar 1 inch or more and only occasionally slips in a substandard press. That's response differentiation.

What would happen if we stopped differential reinforcement and went back to a lower criterion? What would happen if we reinforced any bar press, even one that moved the bar only a hair's breadth? Over time, the frequency of 1-inch presses would decrease, and the frequency of very slight presses would increase. After a while, most of the presses would be way short of 1 inch.

QUESTIONS

1. Please describe and diagram an animal experiment using differential reinforcement to increase the percentage of bar presses that are greater than 1 inch.

In the Skinner Box
Experimental Analysis
DIFFERENTIAL PUNISHMENT

Now how would we show differential punishment of short presses? To avoid confounding our example with differential reinforcement, we could continue to reinforce all presses, no matter how slight. But, in addition, we'd punish presses that were less than 1 inch. We might use electric shock; however, the shock would have to be mild, not only for humanitarian reasons, but also so we wouldn't suppress all lever presses. So short presses would produce water plus a mild shock, and 1-inch presses would produce water with no shock.

Differential Punishment

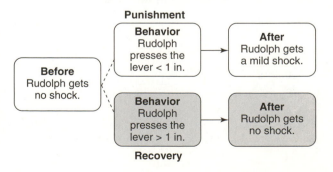

We don't know anyone who's done this experiment, but probably the results would be much the same as with differential reinforcement: a gradual decrease in substandard presses and an increase in acceptable ones. (Incidentally, this might make a good honors project or master's thesis. Let us know how it works out.)

QUESTION

1. Please describe and diagram and describe the use of differential punishment to increase the percentage of a rat's lever presses that are greater than 1 inch? Please explain your answer.

INTERMEDIATE ENRICHMENT

Research Methods
FREQUENCY GRAPHS

Let's go back to the experiment on differential reinforcement with Rudolph. Suppose you measured the distance of each bar press and then plotted some graphs. You might do it like this: Say you start recording the distances before you begin differential reinforcement. Perhaps the first press is 0.1 inch. You'd write 0.1 in your data log. The next is 0.6. The next 1.1. Then another 0.6. The first part of your data log would look like this:

Data Log for Differential Reinforcement	
Response	Distance
1	0.1
2	0.6
3	1.1
4	0.6
5	0.8
6	1.1
7	0.6
etc.	etc.

Now suppose you made a table showing the number of times Rudolph pressed each distance. *The number of times* means the same thing as *the frequency of times* so we call it a *frequency table*. It would look like this for the first several responses.

A frequency graph based on this frequency table would look like Figure 7.4. All the lever presses represented in this graph would be reinforced whether they were longer or shorter than 1 inch. But after you start reinforcing the 1-inch lever presses, only those to the right of the dashed vertical line will be reinforced.

Frequency Table Before Differential Reinforcement	
Distance	Frequency
0.1	1
0.2	0
0.3	0
0.4	0
0.5	0
0.6	3
0.7	0
0.8	1
0.9	0
1	0
1.1	2
1.2	0

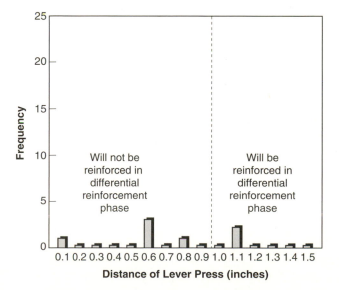

Figure 7.4   Frequency Graph Before Differential Reinforcement (a few responses)

Figure 7.5 is what the frequency graph might look like if you recorded a few more lever presses *before* you started differentially reinforcing 1-inch lever presses.

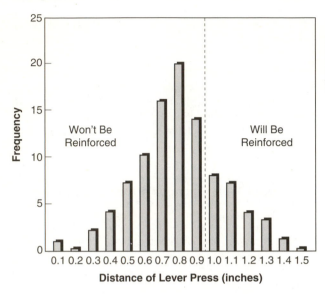

Figure 7.5　Frequency Graph Before Differential Reinforcement (many responses)

Notice that most of the distances are less than 1 inch. Why should Rudolph press the lever any further than he has to? But also notice that Rudolph isn't perfect; the distance he presses varies quite a bit from response to response. In fact, many times he does press the lever more than 1 inch. And that's good news for you. That means you'll have something to reinforce, when you start trying to differentially reinforce lever presses of a distance of 1 inch or more.

If Rudolph were a precision lever-pressing machine and always pressed the lever exactly 1 inch, you'd be in big trouble. You'd have nothing to reinforce when you started your differential-reinforcement procedure.

Figure 7.6 shows how the frequencies might look after you've differentially reinforced the 1-inch bar press for a few sessions.

Notice that you've managed to shift the majority of Rudolph's lever presses to the right of the vertical dashed line. Now the majority are presses of at least 1 inch. You can also see that the frequency of presses at each distance increases until it hits a maximum of 24 presses at the 1-inch distance. Then the frequency of presses decreases as the distance of the press gets greater and greater.

QUESTION

1. Prepare a frequency table and then draw a frequency graph for the following data (the grams

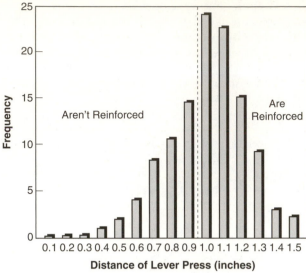

Figure 7.6　Frequency Graph After Differential Reinforcement

of force with which Rudolph pressed the lever): 1, 5, 2, 5, 4, 2, 5, 2, 3, 2, 4, 3. Be sure to include the label for the *x*-axis and the *y*-axis; and be sure to include the values along each axis, just like in the preceding graphs.

Ethics
USING AVERSIVE CONTROL TO SHAPE GRACEFUL MOVEMENTS

Madam Cupet: I'm concerned about this "freeze" technique. Maybe it's too aversive. Maybe it's made learning ballet too unpleasant an experience for Bunny.

Juke: True, it probably involves a mildly aversive condition.

Madam Cupet: But ballet is pure beauty, an art of perfection. It seems contradictory to teach beautiful movements with what you call "aversive control."

Juke: Maybe, but I think traditional techniques of teaching ballet may have used even more aversive techniques: When Bunny made the same error over and over, you might have said things like, "Are you deaf? What have I just said?" Now isn't that aversive control?

Madam Cupet: You make sense. My first ballet professor made me walk 10 minutes with a book on my head each time she saw me with my back bent. No other procedure worked.

Juke: But education also involves praise and other nonaversive procedures. In spite of the use of mild punishment, learning also can be fun.

QUESTION

1. What is the role of aversive control in the freeze technique and traditional approaches to teaching ballet?

Research Methods
VARIABLE-TIME STIMULUS PRESENTATION

In Chapter 6, we saw that extinction was a good way to find out if your presumed reinforcer was a real reinforcer—to see if the presumed reinforcer was really what was maintaining the behavior. For example, you can stop presenting your response-contingent smile for a while, and see if the frequency of the response of interest (your pupil's reading sentences) decreases. If the frequency does decrease when you withhold the smile, that suggests your smile was the reinforcer maintaining the behavior.

But what it really shows is that your smile was important in maintaining the behavior, but maybe not because it was functioning as a reinforcer. Maybe your smile wasn't a reinforcer, but, instead, your pupil just liked to work hard for a smiling teacher, regardless of whether those smiles immediately followed her responses of reading sentences or whether you were simply smiling all the time.

But we have another procedure we can use to see if reinforcement itself was involved. This procedure is even better than extinction at determining if two independent variables are confounded—are occurring at the same time so you cannot determine what variables are responsible for the change in your dependent variable. This procedure is an improved control condition that does not contain the presumed crucial value of your independent variable.

As an example of what might have been done, let's look at a classic experiment in behavior analysis. Dr. Paul Fuller published this research back in 1949.[12] Paul worked with an 18-year-old boy. What is remarkable is that this boy was classified, in the old-fashioned terminology of that day, as a *vegetative idiot.* In other words, psychologists and psychiatrists considered him a human vegetable, incapable of learning anything. They considered him incapable of even moving his trunk or his legs.

Paul challenged this notion. He wanted to see if the boy could at least learn some simple response—the response of raising his arm. Paul used a warm sugar-milk solution as a presumed reinforcer to reinforce the boy's arm raising. After two reinforcement sessions, the boy's arm raising increased

from a baseline frequency of 1 per minute to a frequency of 3 per minute. The so-called vegetative idiot could learn.

Paul showed that the frequency of arm raising was much higher when he was using the milk than when he wasn't—that is, during baseline. And at first glance, that suggests the milk was a reinforcer, but that ain't necessarily so.

Usually pioneering research such as this can be improved as research methods improve. Nowadays, we might require better evidence the presumed reinforcer was really functioning as a reinforcer. For example, maybe Paul Fuller was so happy during the intervention that his constant singing and smiling caused the boy to wiggle more and thereby raise his arm more frequently. This would suggest that the increased frequency of arm raising had nothing to do with the milk.

We need a **control condition**—*a condition that does* not *contain the presumed crucial value of the independent variable.* We could then contrast the control condition with the **experimental condition**—*a condition that* does *contain the presumed crucial value of the independent variable.* That way we can find out if the changes in the dependent variable are caused by the presumed crucial value of the independent variable or if those changes are caused by something else.

We could use extinction as a control condition. We could stop the reinforcement and see if the boy's arm raising dropped back to the baseline frequency of 1 per minute. And we could even use a **reversal design** where we alternated sessions of reinforcement and extinction.

Suppose we got our high frequency of arm raising during reinforcement and the low baseline frequency during the control condition. What would that show? It would show that presenting the warm, sweet milk increased the arm raising. But it wouldn't prove reinforcement.

Why not? Maybe squirting the warm, sweet milk in the boy's mouth simply made the boy more active. And, as part of that increased activity, the frequency of the boy's arm raising increased. Perhaps, when Dr. Fuller withheld the milk, the boy became less active and the frequency of his arm raising decreased.

In other words, the presentation of milk may have increased the arm raising. But reinforcement might not have caused that increase. Reinforcement means the increase resulted from the milk's immediately following the response, not just its mere presentation. Reinforcement means the *contingent* presentation of the presumed reinforcer immediately after the response.

So you see extinction isn't a good enough control condition, because it changes two things at the

---

[12]Fuller, P. R. (1949). Operant conditioning of a vegetative human organism. *American Journal of Psychology, 62,* 587–590.

same time: not only does extinction remove the contingency, but it also removes the milk itself. We need a way to keep presenting the milk without making it contingent on the response, without its reliably following immediately after the response. We need to just squirt the milk into the boy's mouth every now and then, regardless of whether he's just raised his arm. And that procedure is called **variable-time stimulus presentation.**[13]

Definition: Concept
Variable-time stimulus presentation
- The presentation of a stimulus,
- with variable periods of time between presentations,
- independent of the occurrence of a response.

Suppose this variable-time stimulus presentation doesn't increase the boy's frequency of arm raising. Then we can conclude that it wasn't just the milk, it was that the milk was contingent on the arm raising that caused the increase in arm raising. Then we can be much more confident that we've shown reinforcement with this boy and not just some sort of excitation. To be sure we have reinforcement, we must be sure the contingency is crucial.

In summary,

- we can use variable-time stimulus presentation during the control condition,
- and we can use that same stimulus or stimulus change as part of a presumed reinforcement or punishment contingency during the experimental condition.

This comparison shows

- whether the mere noncontingent presentation of the stimulus or stimulus change caused the change in the dependent variable,
- or whether the contingency of the presumed reinforcement or punishment procedure caused that change in the dependent variable.

The comparison shows this because the only difference between the control and the experimental conditions is the contingency—both have the same stimulus presentation.

---

[13]Behavior analysts also refer to this as noncontingent reinforcement or noncontingent delivery of a reinforcer. We prefer not to use the term noncontingent reinforcement as it technically incorrect.

QUESTION

1. *Variable-time stimulus presentation*—define it and use an example to show its importance as a control condition.
   a. When do you use variable-time presentation—during the experimental or control condition?
   b. Which is the better control condition, extinction or variable-time presentation; and why?
2. For such evaluation purposes, when would you use variable-time stimulus presentation, during the
   a. experimental condition?
   b. control condition?

Research Methods
CONTROL GROUP

Dr. Fuller showed that a so-called vegetative idiot could acquire a simple response. What about normal, 4-month-old babies? Dr. Siqueland showed that they could, too.[14] This is important because it says that the principles of reinforcement may be crucial to the early acquisition of effective repertoires in infants. And that causes us to question the traditional notion that infants simply develop, lying in their cribs or playpens, just like potted plants develop, rooted in their pots.

Siqueland worked with a group of 4-month-old infants. In the experimental sessions, he gave them some milk as the presumed reinforcer each time they turned their heads. Here's what he got: an increase in the frequency of their head turning.

Reinforcement? It looks like it, but could it be that old devil coincidence? Probably not, because he got these results with several babies, not just one. Good, but could it be an excitatory effect from the stimulation of the milk? Again, maybe they're just moving around more, and head turning is one thing they're doing.

Well, Siqueland asked that same question. Except Siqueland controlled for that possibility in a slightly different way from any of the previous studies we've read. In all those studies, we dealt with single clients, called *single subjects* when we're talking about research. Sometimes we replicated an intervention with other subjects, but it was still one subject at a time. Those research designs are called *single-subject research designs*.

---

[14]Based on Siqueland, E. R. (1964). Operant conditioning of head turning in four month old infants. *Psychological Science, 1,* 233–224.

Definition: Concept

Single-subject research design

- The entire experiment is conducted with a single subject,
- though it may be replicated with several other subjects.

But traditional psychologists experiment with groups, using **group research designs**.

Definition: Concept

Group research design

- The experiment is conducted with at least two groups of subjects.
- And the data are usually presented in terms of the mean (average)
- of the performance of all subjects
- combined for each group.

And their control conditions are in a separate group of subjects called the **control group**.

Definition: Concept

Control group

- A group of subjects
- not exposed to the presumed crucial value of the independent variable.

The **experimental group** is the group that gets the special intervention (for example, reinforcement).

Definition: Concept

Experimental group

- A group of subjects
- exposed to the presumed crucial value of the independent variable.

The control group is important, because a comparison between the experimental group and the control group shows whether the value of the independent variable really was crucial to the results obtained.

In Siqueland's research, the experimental group got the presumed reinforcer of the milk, contingent on head turning. And the control group got the milk on a variable-time schedule, independent of head turning. The results were that the experimental group increased their head turning and the control group did not. The only difference was the contingency. So the contingency was crucial to the results. Siqueland had controlled for any excitatory effect and had obtained reinforcement.

Science depends on the general procedure of controlling for the effects of unknown factors. Control procedures help make the scientific method the most reliable way of finding out about the world.

QUESTIONS

1. Define and give an example of each of the following:
   - experimental group
   - control group
   - single-subject research design
   - group research design.
2. What is the function of a control group, and how does it differ from a control condition?

Compare and Contrast
DIFFERENTIAL PUNISHMENT VS. DIFFERENTIAL AVOIDANCE

We've looked at a few examples of differential punishment: punishing the response classes of incorrect ballet moves and unladylike behavior. In each case, the punished response classes decreased in frequency, but also the unpunished response classes increased in frequency—correct ballet moves and ladylike behavior. In both cases, there were no other options, you either made the incorrect moves or you made the correct moves; you either didn't act like a lady or you did.

Because there were no options, we also can consider the differential contingencies to be avoidance contingencies: The correct moves and acting like a lady avoided aversive conditions—the deep freeze and the forced march up and down the stairs. So when there are no options, the contingencies of differential punishment and differential avoidance are identical. (You'll learn more about avoidance contingencies in Chapter 15.)

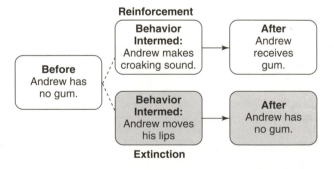

8 Shaping

FUNDAMENTALS

Example
Behavioral Clinical
HELPING A MENTAL HOSPITAL RESIDENT SPEAK AGAIN[1]

Andrew entered Big State Hospital when he was 21 years old; from the day he entered, he hadn't said a word. Nineteen years of silence in the hospital.

Andrew attended Dawn's group therapy session with patients who did speak. They talked about their feelings and problems. In one session, Dawn accidentally dropped a stick of chewing gum on the floor when she was taking a pen from her pocket. Andrew looked at the stick of gum. This was an unusual reaction, because Andrew always seemed to be in his own private world. The external world didn't exert much control over his behavior. So Dawn thought the gum might be a reinforcer for Andrew.

In the next group session, Dawn held a stick of gum in front of Andrew's face and waited until Andrew looked at it. Then Dawn immediately gave him the gum. Andrew opened his mouth and chewed it. After two weeks, Andrew looked at the stick of gum any time Dawn placed it in front of him. The sight of the gum reinforced looking at it.[2]

Dawn wanted Andrew to speak. But before reinforcing a behavior, it must first occur, and Andrew had not spoken for more than 19 years. Early in the third week, Dawn saw Andrew move his lips slightly. So she reinforced Andrew's lip movement with gum.

---

[1]Based on Isaacs, W., Thomas, J., & Goldiamond, I. (1960). Application of operant conditioning to reinstate verbal behavior in psychotics. *Journal of Speech and Hearing Disorders, 25*, 8–15.

[2]The sight of the gum had become what we call a *learned reinforcer*, because it had been paired with the sweet taste of the gum (an unlearned reinforcer). We study learned reinforcers in Chapter 11.

Simple Reinforcement

Before	Behavior	After
Andrew has no gum.	Initial: Andrew moves his lips	Andrew receives gum.

By the end of that week, Andrew was often looking at the gum and moving his lips.

At the beginning of the fourth week, Dawn held a stick of gum before Andrew's face. Andrew looked at the gum and moved his lips. But she didn't give Andrew the gum as she had always done before. Then Andrew emitted a sound, and Dawn immediately gave him the gum.

Differential Reinforcement

Reinforcement

Behavior Intermed: Andrew makes croaking sound. → After Andrew receives gum.

Before Andrew has no gum.

Behavior Intermed: Andrew moves his lips → After Andrew has no gum.

Extinction

By the end of the fourth week, Andrew was frequently making a croaking sound.

One day, after Andrew made a croaking sound, Dawn said, "Say, 'gum, gum.'" Andrew began to make his croaking sound after her prompt. At first, the croak was like those heard before. Dawn hesitated until the croaking sound faintly resembled *gum* and then reinforced the response. The next time, she waited until Andrew's sound more closely approximated *gum*. Then she reinforced that response.

Differential Reinforcement

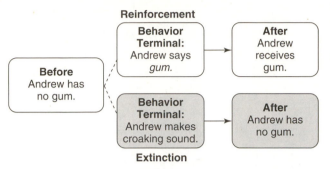

In the sixth week, Dawn had just asked Andrew to say *gum,* when Andrew clearly said, "Gum, please." Before the session had finished, Andrew was answering questions about his name and his age! After that day, he would answer any question Dawn asked. Also, he began to chat with her at times and places other than at the therapy sessions.

A nurse came to Andrew's room one day. Andrew smiled at her. So Dawn asked the nurse to visit Andrew daily. After a month, he began to answer her questions. That was the first time Andrew talked to anyone other than Dawn.

One sunny day, Andrew brought his coat and hat, gesturing that he wanted to leave. Without a word from Andrew, a new volunteer worker unfamiliar with Andrew's case took him outside. Dawn saw that Andrew didn't speak to the volunteer worker because he didn't have to; Andrew's gestures did the trick. Because he didn't talk, everybody assumed he couldn't, so they interpreted his gestures and signs. When two responses produce the same reinforcers, we tend to do the one needing the least effort. We may not intend to take the easy route; it just works that way.

Perhaps that's what had happened with Andrew. The contingencies of reinforcement had caused Andrew to drift down the stream of least resistance. Without anyone planning it, the contingencies reinforced responses less effortful than speaking, by producing those reinforcers most of us have to ask for verbally.

But the contingencies changed when Dawn entered Andrew's life. Dawn's contingencies required more and more effortful vocal and verbal behavior before she delivered the reinforcer.

Dawn asked the staff not to give their service and attention to Andrew unless Andrew asked for it. But not all the staff required Andrew to talk. So

Andrew continued to speak to those who required it, and he was silent with those who interpreted his gestures.

By the way, notice that Andrew's complex talk came about in only six weeks of intervention. This is because he could speak 19 years ago. In other words, speech had been part of his repertoire.

QUESTION

1. Describe and diagram the procedure used to help a hospital resident speak again.

Concept
THE PROCEDURE
OF SHAPING
WITH REINFORCEMENT

Clear, fluent speech was the terminal behavior[3] Dawn chose for Andrew. (The **terminal behavior** is the final goal of the intervention.) The terminal behavior didn't occur at all before shaping; its operant level was zero. (The **operant level** is the frequency of responding before reinforcement.[4])

If the operant level is lower than we want but still **significantly** above zero, we can use simple reinforcement. But if the operant level is at or near zero, there's nothing to reinforce differentially. So, when the response doesn't occur at all, we need to get trickier.

---

[3]A terminology note of interest to only the most inquisitive: Usually we can use *response* and *behavior* interchangeably. But not always. I found I was writing *terminal behavior* and *initial response*. So to be consistent, I started to change to *terminal response*. But it didn't fit this sentence. I think this is why: Response tends to refer to a fairly narrow response class, like lever pressing, but behavior tends to include broader response classes, like fluent speech.

[4]The concept of *operant level* comes from work in the Skinner box. The operant level is the frequency with which the rat presses the response lever before the experimenter introduces a reinforcement contingency for lever pressing. Normally the rat will have a low but measurable operant level of lever pressing. Now that doesn't mean there was no reinforcer for pressing the lever; it might have been the sound of the lever clicking when it hit the bottom, or it might have been the feel of the lever on the rat's paws. Or the lever press might have been incidental to the rat's raising it's body above the lever and putting it's nose and whiskers along the top edge of the box. To be most precise, we might say *operant level* is the frequency of responding before the **experimenter, or teacher, or parent added** a reinforcement contingency; but we'll keep the formal definition a little simpler, as shown in the definition box. The *operant level* is the same as the baseline for the reinforcement intervention. But, normally, we wouldn't not speak of the operant level before adding a punishment intervention contingency, at least not if someone had previously added a reinforcement contingency; normally, *operant level* applies only to reinforcement.

Definition: Concepts

Operant level

- The frequency of responding before reinforcement.

Terminal behavior

- Behavior not in the repertoire or not occurring at the desired frequency; the goal of the intervention.

With Andrew, Dawn needed to get trickier. Using chewing gum as a reinforcer, first she reinforced lip movements, the **initial behavior.** Unlike the terminal behavior, the initial behavior must occur at least with a minimal frequency. Dawn reinforced lip movements until their frequency increased. Often the first phase of shaping involves only simple reinforcement to get the initial behavior occurring at a high frequency.

Then she chose a new behavior, emitting vocal sounds of any nature. She differentially reinforced this behavior until it occurred frequently, while extinguishing lip movements without any vocal-sound production.

Next, she differentially reinforced vocal sounds that more and more resembled the word *gum*, while extinguishing croaks and other sounds not resembling *gum.* Finally, she reinforced the terminal behavior, speech.

The initial and **intermediate behaviors** were prerequisites for the next behavior in the successive approximations. For instance, lip movement was a prerequisite for speech sound; and speech sound was a prerequisite for saying a word. (Unless you're a ventriloquist, you can't speak without moving your lips.) Dawn reinforced **successive approximations** to speech. She **shaped** the terminal behavior.[5]

Definition: Concepts

Initial behavior

- Behavior that resembles the terminal behavior along some meaningful dimension and occurs at least with a minimal frequency.

Intermediate behaviors

- Behavior that more closely approximates the terminal behavior.

The procedure of shaping with reinforcement

- The differential reinforcement of only that behavior which more and more closely resembles the terminal behavior.

Shaping Reinforcement

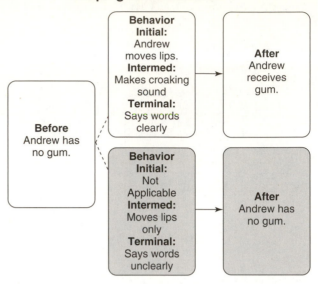

Summing up: Use the procedure of shaping with reinforcement when you want to bring about new responses. To shape with reinforcers, identify an initial behavior that resembles the terminal behavior along some meaningful dimension. The initial behavior must occur at least with a minimal frequency. Reinforce the initial behavior until it occurs frequently. Then abandon that response. Select and differentially reinforce another response that more closely approximates the terminal behavior. Continue this procedure until the terminal behavior occurs, and reinforce it until it occurs frequently.

QUESTION

1. Define and give an example of the following concepts:
   - terminal behavior
   - operant level
   - initial behavior
   - intermediate behaviors

2. *Shaping with reinforcers*—state this principle and give an example. In your example, include:
   - the terminal behavior
   - the initial behavior
   - the intermediate behaviors

---

[5]The *method of successive approximation* and the *procedure of shaping with reinforcement* mean the same; you can use either. However, *shaping* has a more active connotation for us. *Shaping* makes us think of a keen-eyed behavior analyst reinforcing first one behavior and then another slightly different, shaping the behavior as a sculptor shapes a piece of clay. But *successive approximation* refers to the logical aspects of the procedure; it plays down Dawn's role.

○ the response dimensions
○ the reinforcer
○ the results.

Example
Behavioral Medicine
HELPING AN AUTISTIC CHILD WEAR GLASSES[6]

Three-year-old Dicky was in danger of losing his eyesight. At 9 months of age, cataracts in both of Dicky's eyes clouded the lenses and blocked the passage of light. Dicky had a series of eye operations ending in the removal of both lenses. He was only 2 at the time. If Dicky were to see, he would have to wear corrective glasses the rest of his life. For almost a year, his parents pressured him to wear glasses, but Dicky refused. They consulted several specialists. Each gave a new diagnosis, but none helped Dicky wear his glasses.

Dicky entered Western State Hospital in Washington when he was 3½ years old. Dr. Montrose Wolf's team studied his case. Normally at this age, children develop rapidly and learn to interact with their world. But without good vision, they are at a great disadvantage.

The glasses on his head might have been aversive for Dicky, too uncomfortable. If so, tossing the glasses off removed the discomfort—an escape contingency. In other words, removal of physical discomfort might have reinforced taking the glasses off. And Dicky never left his glasses on long enough for the natural reinforcement contingency of seeing better to reinforce his putting on the glasses or for the loss of the better vision to punish his taking them off.

Mont Wolf's team started with frames without lenses, to prevent breaking expensive prescription lenses. That way, later, they could switch to prescription lenses more easily. Each day, a member of Wolf's team spent two or three 20-minute sessions with Dicky in his room. The behavior analyst reinforced Dicky's carrying the glasses, bringing them closer and closer toward his face and actually putting them on—a gradual shaping process. Bites of candy and fruit were the presumed reinforcers. (Topography is the response dimension along which they were shaping Dicky's putting on his glasses.)

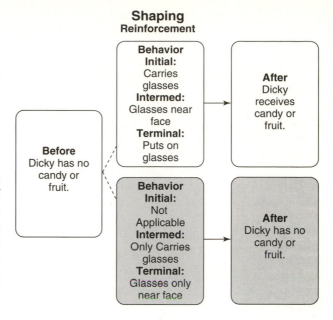

Shaping
Reinforcement

| Before Dicky has no candy or fruit. | **Behavior** **Initial:** Carries glasses **Intermed:** Glasses near face **Terminal:** Puts on glasses | **After** Dicky receives candy or fruit. |
| **Behavior** **Initial:** Not Applicable **Intermed:** Only Carries glasses **Terminal:** Glasses only near face | **After** Dicky has no candy or fruit. |

However, Dicky always failed to put the glasses on in the right position. He put them cocked to one side, with the ear pieces below his ears rather than on top of them. To correct these errors of placement, the behavior analyst put larger ear pieces on Dicky's glasses and fitted a bar from one ear piece across his head to the other ear piece. But nothing changed. Then the behavior analyst added a second bar to the back of the glasses, making them fit like a cap.

Now the glasses were easier to put on properly. But Dicky was progressing too slowly. Candy and fruit were not acting as reinforcers, maybe because Dicky wasn't hungry at the time of the sessions. So the behavior analyst withheld breakfast and continued using candy and fruit. Still nothing changed.

One day the behavior analyst tried ice cream. That hit the spot! It was the third session that day, and Dicky had eaten only a few pieces of cereal. The behavior analyst gave ice cream to Dicky each time he complied with requests. Progress was so fast during the first few minutes that the behavior analyst replaced lensless frames with Dicky's prescription glasses. After 30 minutes of shaping, Dicky put the glasses on properly and looked through the lenses at various toys the behavior analyst displayed. After this session, Dicky improved rapidly. Soon he put on his glasses at mealtimes in his room.

At this point, Mont's team used other reinforcers that didn't rely on food deprivation. For instance, an attendant said to Dicky, "Put on your glasses and we'll go for a walk." Dicky complied. Favors, treats, excursions, and outings were available to him if he put on his glasses and didn't take them

[6]Based on Wolf, M., Risley, T., & Mees, H. (1964). Application of operant conditioning procedures to the behavior problems of an autistic child. *Behavior Research and Therapy, 1,* 305–312. Is this really desensitization?

off. Soon Dicky was wearing his glasses 12 hours a day on the average. Excellent for any child his age.

Here's a problem we found interesting:

1. Is *wearing glasses* behavior?
   a. Yes.
   b. No.

No, it fails the dead man test; you could bury someone who was wearing their glasses. We hadn't realized this when we wrote earlier editions of *EPB*; at that time, we still weren't fluent enough with our new friend, the dead man.

2. In terms of behaviors, what should we normally be talking about?
   a. Putting on the glasses.
   b. Taking off the glasses.
   c. Both.

Yes, Mont's team had to both shape putting on the glasses and punish taking off the glasses. In terms of doing a proper task analysis of what is meant by *wearing glasses* we must look carefully at both those component responses. Sometimes we still find it too convenient to use the term *wear*, but we should always make it clear that we really mean *putting on* occurs and *taking off* does not occur; and that the crucial behaviors of *putting on* and *taking off* are two separate behaviors under the control of two separate contingencies.

QUESTION

1. How would you shape putting on glasses? Include:
   ○ the terminal behavior
   ○ the initial behavior
   ○ the intermediate behaviors
   ○ the response dimensions
   ○ the reinforcer
   ○ the results.
2. Is wearing glasses behavior? Please explain.

Compare and Contrast
THE DIFFERENTIAL-REINFORCEMENT PROCEDURE VS. THE PROCEDURE OF SHAPING WITH REINFORCEMENT

Differential reinforcement involves reinforcing a single set of responses within a response class and withholding reinforcement from another set of re-

sponses within that response class.[7] So the frequency of the reinforced set of responses increases compared with the frequency of that nonreinforced set. The reinforced set of responses becomes differentiated from the other set.

It may occur to you that shaping and differential reinforcement are similar. They are. Both involve differential reinforcement; we reinforce a single set of responses, within a response class, and not another set of responses. Both procedures increase the frequency of one set of response and decrease the frequency of the other.

The **procedure of shaping with reinforcement** consists of a series of successive differential reinforcements. After one set of responses has become differentiated from the other, we raise our standards; now we must reinforce another set of responses even closer to the terminal behavior. We use this shaping procedure when we want people to exhibit a new behavior or one that almost never occurs. Simple differential reinforcement won't work in this case. To use simple differential reinforcement, the behavior we want to differentiate must occur often enough for reinforcement to have a reasonable effect. Simple differential reinforcement is not too effective at producing new or almost new responses. So, if the response rarely occurs, we may need to use the shaping.

To distinguish between differential-reinforcement procedure and the shaping procedure, you should ask two questions. First, **does the terminal behavior occur at all now?** If it doesn't, **probably** we are talking about shaping; if it does, **probably** we are talking about differential reinforcement. For Dicky, the terminal behavior was to wear the glasses all the time. Dicky didn't do it before the intervention. (Note: Sometimes we may use the shaping procedure when the response occurs, but at such a low frequency that it might take too long if we used simple differential reinforcement.)

Second, **does the procedure involve successive approximations to the terminal behavior?** If it does, we are talking about shaping; if it doesn't, we are

---

[7]Grad-level issues: Grad student O-Song Kim raised the following point in my behavior analysis seminar: In Chapter 7, we define *response class* as a set of responses that either (a) are similar on at least one response **dimension,** or (b) share the **effects** of reinforcement and punishment, or (c) serve the same **function** (produce the same outcome). But when we shape behavior, we do successive approximations within a response class defined in terms of response dimension, not defined in terms of effects or function. If we didn't have a response dimension along which to successively approximate, it wouldn't work. For example, consider the response class consisting of both pointing to something you want and verbally asking for it. With an autistic child, we might differentially reinforce asking as opposed to pointing; but there is no response dimension along which we could successively approximate from pointing to asking.

talking about differential reinforcement. In Dicky's case, the behavior analyst reinforced different topographies. The topography of approaching the glasses differed from the topography of picking them up and from putting them on. The topography of correct placement differed from incorrect placement, although the difference was of a lesser degree. Each topography successively approximated the terminal behavior.

Differential Reinforcement vs. Shaping		
	Differential reinforcement	**Shaping**
Number of response classes	One	A series
Successive approximations to the terminal behavior	No	Yes
Some terminal behavior at the start	Yes	No

QUESTIONS

1. Construct a table comparing differential reinforcement with shaping.
2. Give a pair of related examples showing these differences.

Example
Behavioral Speech Pathology
RAISING THE VOICE INTENSITY OF AN APHONIC CHILD[8]

Thirteen-year-old Melanie had been aphonic for several years. This means her voice sounded like a low, raspy whisper. Although articulate, her speech was of such a low intensity that people couldn't understand what she was saying. Melanie's parents took her to one doctor after another; the only result was that she came to dislike doctors. At last, she visited Drs. Bangs and Friedinger—professional behavior analysts who took great pains to win Melanie's affection and respect.

Of course, approval is a reinforcer. But noncontingent kindness, friendship, and approval will

_____
[8]Based on Bangs, J. L., & Friedinger, A. (1949). Diagnosis and treatment of a case of hysterical aphonia in a thirteen-year-old girl. *Journal of Speech and Hearing Disorders, 14*, 312–317.

not be enough. To be most effective, they must immediately follow the response you want to reinforce. That's what the behavior analysts did. They immediately praised and approved Melanie's attempts to comply with their requests.

They started by reinforcing her compliance with breathing exercises, similar to those exercises singers and public speakers practice. These exercises make the voice stronger and might develop greater speaking force.

Next, they asked Melanie to hum. But her humming was as faint as her speaking. So they praised successive approximations to normal humming intensity until it reached normal. They reinforced approximations to saying consonants and then reading aloud. However, Melanie read softly, like a whisper. They asked her to try harder, and if she succeeded even by a barely noticeable amount, they praised her efforts. Reading intensity increased until it reached normal intensity. Finally, in conversation, they reinforced intensities of her speech that were higher than previously. Soon Melanie talked at a normal intensity.

Helping Melanie involved a series of successive approximations; first they shaped breathing, then humming, then saying consonants, then reading, and finally conversing. It's not clear if they really needed to go through the whole series; it may be that if they had simply started with the last topography, conversing, they would have gotten the same excellent results.

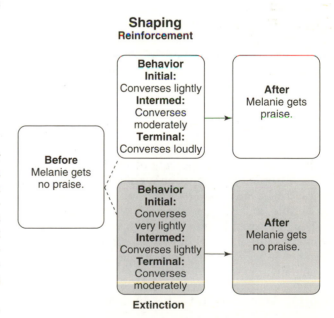

Shaping
Reinforcement

Before Melanie gets no praise.

Behavior
Initial: Converses lightly
Intermed: Converses moderately
Terminal: Converses loudly

→ **After** Melanie gets praise.

Behavior
Initial: Converses very lightly
Intermed: Converses lightly
Terminal: Converses moderately

→ **After** Melanie gets no praise.

Extinction

Note that the reinforced behavior or intensity of behavior in the initial phase was extinguished in the intermediate phase; and the reinforced behavior or intensity in the intermediate phase was extinguished in the terminal phase.

With these shaping procedures, the behavior analysts got rid of a problem Melanie had suffered for many years. And it took them only ten sessions! But even more important is that Melanie's change was permanent, as the behavior analysts verified two years later. Melanie spoke loud and clear in a routine follow-up.

QUESTION

1. Describe a shaping procedure to raise voice intensity. Include:
   ○ the terminal behavior
   ○ the initial behavior
   ○ the intermediate behaviors
   ○ the response dimension for each behavior
   ○ the reinforcer
   ○ the contingency
   ○ the results.

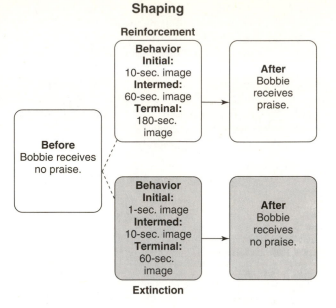

Example
Behavioral Clinical Psychology
I'M A WOMAN TRAPPED IN A MAN'S BODY—PART III[9]

Even though Bobbie behaved like a typical man, he thought like a woman. He fantasized having a female body and having sex with males. But the goal Bobbie had selected was to become completely like a typical male in all ways. So Sid helped Bobbie change his fantasies; their goal was for Bobbie to fantasize himself as a man having sex with a woman.

Bobbie chose four pictures of *Playboy* models that were least aversive to him. Then Sid asked Bobbie to fantasize sexual acts with the female in the picture. Often, Sid gave him ideas of acts that could enrich his fantasies. When his image was clear, Bobbie raised his index finger. If Bobbie kept the fantasy for 10 seconds, Sid showed him another photo that Bobbie had chosen before as a potential reinforcer (for instance, pictures of food and animals). When Bobbie had no trouble holding the image for 10 seconds, Sid raised the criterion by 5 seconds. He was able to raise the criterion about once a day. Then Sid asked Bobbie to fantasize having sex with any woman he saw daily. Sid praised increased length of appropriate fantasies, until Bobbie could maintain the fantasy for 3 minutes. After 34 sessions, Bobbie not only behaved like a typical man but also fantasized like one, at least most of the time.

Then, using an automatic measuring device, Sid measured the circumference of Bobbie's penis during these sessions. The results showed that pictures of males still turned Bobbie on; and pictures of females still didn't, even though he could tolerate extended fantasizes about sexual relations with them.

In addition, Bobbie was still reporting that about five times a day he found himself sexually attracted to a male. Sid asked Bobbie if he wanted to leave it at that, if he really wanted to be turned on by women. Bobbie said, "Yes, if I'm going to go for it, I'm going to go all the way."

"Well, you have come a long way."

"Yes, but I have a long way to go, if I'm going to achieve my goal of becoming completely like a typical male," Bobbie replied. "I'm not saying there's anything wrong with same-sex fantasies. And I'm not saying every man has to be turned on to women. But I'm so sick and tired of being on the outside that I want to go all the way."

In later chapters, we'll see further steps along the path to Bobbie's goal.

QUESTION

1. Describe a procedure to increase male fantasies. Include:
   ○ the target behavior
   ○ the response dimensions
   ○ the successive approximations
   ○ reinforcer contingency
   ○ the results.

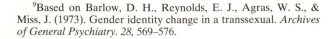
[9]Based on Barlow, D. H., Reynolds, E. J., Agras, W. S., & Miss, J. (1973). Gender identity change in a transsexual. *Archives of General Psychiatry. 28,* 569–576.

Example
Everyday Life
THE PROCEDURE OF SHAPING WITH PUNISHMENT

Sid's Seminar

Sid: I've bet Juke Jackson 20 bucks. If he loses, we'll have a party this weekend. And he isn't here, so looks like we won.

Juke: (Enters the room, out of breath . . .): Wait a minute, we didn't bet I'd be on time.

Sid: Excuuuse me! My man, you are on.

Juke put his briefcase on a desk, hung his coat on the back of a chair, emptied his pockets, unbuttoned his cuffs, and rolled up his sleeves. Then he moved Sid's desk against the blackboard to clear space in front of the class. And without another word, he crouched down, leaned forward, and soon, he was standing on his head, his hands balancing him, his legs straight in the air, a vertical rod, not a muscle twitch. And he stayed perfectly still, one minute, two minutes, three minutes, four minutes, five minutes, until the class started applauding and cheering wildly; then he gracefully flipped over and stood up and bowed with solemn dignity.

Sid: Gang, we lost the party; and I lost 20 bucks. Juke tried to stand on his hands a month ago but almost ended in the hospital. And I said he'd never be able to do it, even with the football team's help. That's when we came up with the bet.

Juke: Simple, I know the principles of behavior work, don't you? (Immediately all the students looked at Sid, and smiled silently.)

Sid: (Clearing his throat) Well, why don't you tell us how you did it?

Juke: It took time, practice and a little behavior analysis. To begin, I started with my legs over my head, leaning against the wall. It was hard. Gravity worked against me. I'd fall, and almost fall. Behavior analysis versus physics. But I kept practicing until I could hold my feet against the wall for a minute. Then I raised the criterion; I tried to stand on my head without touching the wall. Again, I fell and almost fell. But I got better and better; I stopped falling, and stopped almost falling, and after a lot of practice, I got to the place where I don't even wobble, my legs straight above my head. What a feeling of accomplishment.

Sid: Was that an example of the shaping procedure?

Joe: Yes, Mr. Jackson's standing on his head with straight-up topography and long durations was at a zero operant level before training; and he acquired responses that successively approximated the outstanding performance he just demonstrated.

Sid: Excellent. You get a point. Now, a hard one: What was the contingency?

Sue: Punishment. Wrong moves immediately caused Mr. Jackson to fall or almost fall or wobble.

Tom: Wrong! Reinforcement. Right moves caused Juke to feel good about himself. Isn't that true, Juke?

Juke: It sure did. But hurting and almost hurting and looking clumsy because of dumb moves also had a lot to do with it.

Tom: But the target behavior was to do it right, not to do it wrong.

Sue: It depends on how you look at it.

Tom: But shaping brings about new responses. And you can't bring about new responses with punishment, can you?

Sid: Look at it this way: Shaping with reinforcement is like the sculptor who starts to work with a handful of clay and adds to it, molding it with her hands. **Shaping with punishment** is like the sculptor who starts with a piece of solid granite and chisels pieces out until she has her sculpture. In shaping with reinforcement, she adds; and in shaping with punishment, she takes away. But in both cases she gets her sculpture. I think shaping with punishment and reinforcement both played a role in my losing 20 bucks.

Definition: Concept
The procedure of shaping with punishment
- The differential punishment of all behavior **except** that which more and more closely resembles the terminal behavior.

As with all punishment procedures, the general response class needs some history of reinforcement. In the case of shaping with punishment, at least the nonpunished terminal behavior and its approximations need to be reinforced. Otherwise, the punishment would suppress the entire response class. If some reinforcement contingency were not maintaining Juke's attempts to stand on his head, the punishment of falling would soon suppress all such efforts.

QUESTION

1. *The procedure of shaping with punishment*—
define it and give an example. Include:
   - the terminal behavior
   - the initial behavior
   - the response dimension
   - the shaping procedure
   - the punishment contingency
   - the reinforcement contingency
   - the results.

Example
Everyday Life
LEARNING TO WALK AND RUN: VARIABLE-OUTCOME SHAPING

Little Rod's sitting in one corner of his crib, bored. Nothing's shaking. Ah, but his favorite toy, his rattle, is in the opposite corner. He leans toward it; too far. He squirms toward it; and finally scores the rattle. Now it's shake, rattle, and roll. And what can be more reinforcing than noise you, yourself, produce?

But it was a long, slow haul from one corner of the crib to the other for little Rod the squirmer. And over the next few weeks Rod got better and better at squirming, to the point that his squirm evolved into a crawl. And over the next few months, his crawl evolved into a toddle. Then the toddler became a walker and finally a runner.

But how'd that happen? It's natural; it just happens. Yes, but what's the behavioral process underlying this natural happening? Differential reinforcement and shaping.

Differential Reinforcement Along the Force Dimension

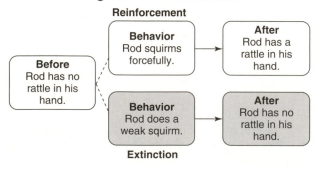

The natural environment differentially reinforced squirming. Force was the response dimension. Rod got the reinforcing rattle, only if he squirmed with sufficient force.

At first, it took a long time for Rod to squirm from one corner of the crib to the other. But, after a while, he became such a forceful little squirmer that he was onto the rattle in a jiffy. In other words, the natural environment shaped more and more forceful squirming. But how did that happen? After Rod had become a forceful squirmer, did Father Nature stop giving the rattle until Rod did a very forceful squirm? And then after Rod became a very forceful squirmer, did Father Nature stop giving the rattle until Rod did a super-forceful squirm?

No, nature doesn't shape like that. It's just that the more forcefully Rod squirmed, the more quickly he got to the rattle. And getting to the rattle quickly is more reinforcing than getting to the rattle slowly. So the more forcefully Rod squirmed, the more quickly he got the rattle; and thus the bigger the reinforcer; getting the rattle in 6 seconds is more reinforcing than getting it in 10 seconds, and getting it in 4 seconds is more reinforcing than getting it in 6 seconds.

Variable-Outcome Shaping Along the Force Dimension

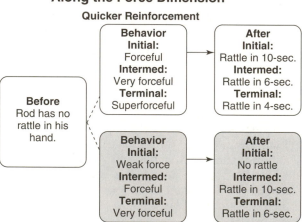

Father Nature differentially reinforced the initial behavior of forceful squirming by presenting the rattle in 10 seconds vs. not getting it at all. Then Father Nature differentially reinforced Rod's intermediate behavior of very forceful squirming by presenting the rattle in 6 seconds instead of 10. And finally he differentially reinforced Rod's terminal behavior of super-forceful squirming by presenting the rattle in 4 seconds in stead of 6. And how did Rod move from the squirmer class to the crawler, toddler, walker, and finally runner class? Again, through variable-outcome shaping, the natural environment shaped the different topographies of movement. And again, each improvement in topography from squirming to running produced a more immediate rattle, and thus a more powerful reinforcer.

For example, when Rod performed at the intermediate level, toddling was reinforced with the rattle in only 2 seconds (as seen in the top two white boxes); but if he slipped back, squirming would be reinforced with the rattle with a delay of 4 seconds (as seen in the bottom two gray boxes).

Variable-Outcome Shaping Along the Topography Dimension

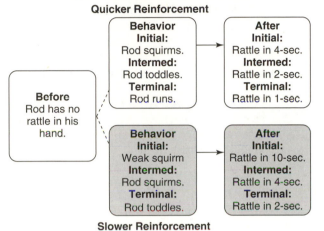

The world is a skills factory for little Rod; every day, it helps him learn new skills and improve his existing ones, often through variable-outcome shaping.[10]

Why does Rod complete his Barney puzzle more and more quickly as time goes by? Because he gets the reinforcer (sight of a completed puzzle) more quickly when he puts the pieces together in the right order more quickly. So probably this is also variable-outcome shaping. In general, variable-outcome shaping will produce improved skills if they result in getting the reinforcer more quickly.

QUESTION

1. Diagram a variable-outcome shaping procedure to improve squirming as a means of locomotion.
2. Diagram a variable-outcome shaping procedure to improve locomotion from squirming up through running.

---

[10]Of course I've simplified quite a bit, to keep this example from getting out of control. Nature's training occurred with more reinforcers than the rattle and in more settings than Rod's crib. Also the crib might not be the ideal place to learn to run. I don't think anyone's done an analysis of the natural shaping of a general skill such as locomotion simultaneously in many different settings with many different reinforcers.

Compare and Contrast
FIXED-OUTCOME SHAPING VS. VARIABLE-OUTCOME SHAPING

Usually, nature shapes behavior using **variable-outcome** shaping. The more skilled the behavior, the bigger the reinforcer. Let's contrast Father Nature's variable-outcome shaping with Father Sid's **fixed-outcome shaping.** As part of his efforts to produce Rod the Superkid, Sid added a fixed-outcome shaping procedure to nature's variable-outcome shaping. At first, each time Rod squirmed forcefully enough to get to the rattle, Sid jumped up and down with enthusiastic joy and rained praise on Rod. Then, after Rod was reliably, though slowly, squirming to the rattle, Rod raised the criterion for his praise; now Rod had to squirm with sufficient force that he got there in 6 seconds, before Sid would get excited and praise him. And then he raised the criterion again to 4 seconds. But each time, the outcome Sid used as the reinforcer remained the same, his excited praise.

Fixed-Outcome Shaping Along the Force Dimension

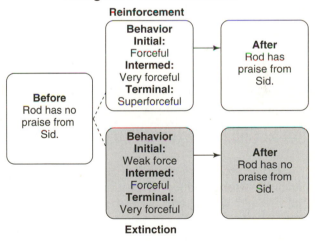

Please look at the earlier diagram of Rod's being shaped by nature to squirm with more force and contrast it with this one. What's the difference?

Nature's variable-outcome shaping is just like the human trainer's fixed-outcome shaping except for three things:

1. As the names implies, with variable-outcome shaping, the outcomes varies (improves) as the performance improves (moves from the initial behavior to the terminal behavior), while with fixed-outcome shaping, the outcome remains the same, as the performance improves.

2. With variable-outcome shaping, it is always possible to get a reinforcer, if the performance slips back to a lower level (for example from the intermediate behavior to the initial behavior); it's just that the reinforcer will be less. But with fixed-outcome shaping, if the performance slips back to a lower level, that performance will receive no reinforcer.

3. Variable-outcome shaping is usually an unplanned interaction with the natural environment, and fixed-outcome shaping is usually a planned interaction with a trainer (behavior modifier).

Fixed-Outcome vs. Variable-Outcome Shaping		
	Fixed outcome	*Variable outcome*
Number of outcome sizes	One	Many
Regression to earlier levels	No reinforcers	Weaker reinforcers
Usual source of shaping	Behavior modifier (planned)	Nature (unplanned)

Now let's look at some other examples: Remember Melanie? The behavior analysts used a classic shaping procedure with her. They gradually required better and better speech before they'd reinforce her efforts with praise. They gradually raised their standards for reinforcement. But they kept the amount of reinforcement the same, all the way along. The reinforcing outcome remained the same, but the standards increased—fixed-outcome shaping.

Here are a couple other examples of the planned, or programmed shaping used by behavior modifiers—fixed-outcome shaping. Dawn used the same size of a reinforcer (a single stick of gum) but kept raising the criterion for reinforcement (closer approximations to language). Also Bangs and Friedinger seemed to use the same size of a reinforcer (praise) but kept raising the criterion for reinforcement (Melanie's closer approximations to normal speech intensity).

The unplanned, or nonprogrammed, automatic shaping of Father Nature is usually variable-outcome shaping. Learning most skills involves this sort of nonprogrammed, automatic, variable-outcome shaping: Your tune on the guitar sounds better and better, as your skill in playing it improves. The tennis ball skims over the top of the net with greater and greater speed, as your serve improves. The golf ball stops closer and closer to the hole, as your stroke improves.

Definition: Concept

The procedure of variable-outcome shaping
○ Shaping that involves
○ an increase in the magnitude of a reinforcer or
○ a decrease in the magnitude of an
○ aversive outcome as performance more and more
○ closely resembles the terminal behavior.

The procedure of fixed-outcome shaping
○ Shaping that involves
○ the delivery of a fixed magnitude of a reinforcer,
○ when performance meets the changing criterion,
○ or the delivery of a fixed magnitude of an aversive outcome,
○ when performance fails to meet the changing criterion.

But it's not just artistic and athletic skills; Father Nature also uses variable outcomes in shaping our skills of everyday life: As we learn to speak, the more clearly and loudly we ask for a cookie, the more quickly we get it. The more accurately we aim our spoon of mashed potatoes, the more we get in our mouth and the less we get on our face.

While most instances of variable outcomes may involve natural, unplanned shaping, sometimes people do intentionally use variable-outcome shaping when teaching skills. For instance, in shaping an autistic child's articulate speech, a behavioral technician may intentionally be more enthusiastic in praising more articulate speech. However, I know of no data showing that this variable-outcome shaping works any better than fixed-outcome shaping. (In fact, I suspect the child will acquire articulate speech more quickly, if the tech praises with wild enthusiasm, each time the child meets the current articulation criterion.)

QUESTIONS

1. *The procedures of fixed- and variable-outcome shaping*—define them.
2. *The procedures of fixed-outcome shaping and variable-outcome shaping*—diagram two similar examples showing the difference and give an example to show the difference.
3. Fill in a table contrasting fixed- and variable-outcome shaping. Be able to explain it.

BASIC ENRICHMENT

In the Skinner Box[11]
Experimental Analysis
SHAPING WITH REINFORCEMENT

In Chapter 7, you differentially reinforced Rudolph's lever presses of 1 inch or more. This time you'll work with the force dimension rather than distance. (You'll use something like a tiny set of scales to measure the force of his lever presses.) Before you start the differential-reinforcement procedure, the frequency graph of the forces of Rudolph's lever presses might look like Figure 8.1.

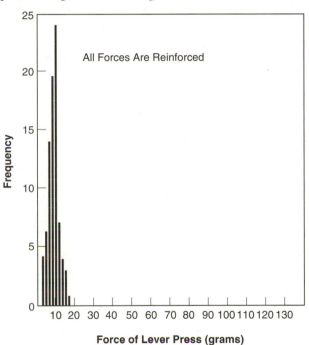

Figure 8.1   Frequency Graph Before Differential Reinforcement

No big deal. But now, you want Rudolph to press the lever with a force of 100 grams. This is a big deal. It's so big that, if you wait until he does it once so that you can reinforce it, you'll wait forever. He'll never press the bar with that force unless you reinforce lever presses of successively increasing forces.

If you've got a sharp eye or a magnifying glass, you can see in this graph that several of Rudolph's

[11]Based on Skinner, B. F. (1938). *The behavior of organisms* (pp. 310–311). Acton, MA: Copley Publishing Group.

lever presses were greater than 11 grams, though the peak was around 8 grams. So you should succeed if you try to differentially reinforce presses of 11 grams or more. That means you'll reinforce all presses of at least 11 grams and extinguish those of lesser force. Soon most of his presses tip the scales at least 11 grams (Figure 8.2).

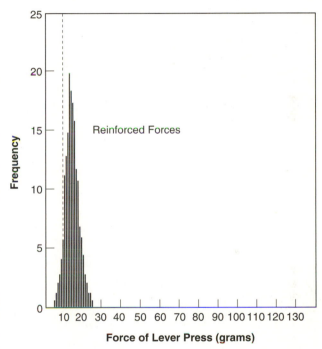

Figure 8.2   Frequency Graph After Differential Reinforcement of 11-Gram Presses

You're doing well, but you've sure got a long way to go to get Rudolph up to 100 grams.

This time, notice that some of his lever-press forces are at or above 20 grams, though the peak is at 11 grams. So why don't you raise your criterion to the 20-gram value? It's time to differentially reinforce all forces at or above 20 grams and extinguish the others (Figure 8.3).

Not bad. And now you're getting quite a few 35-gram responses. So you can jump your criterion up to that level now. You know what you'll get; the most frequent forces will be around 35 grams, but sometimes Rudolph will put a few over the 55-gram limit. This means you can raise your criterion to that value; and then on and on, until you and Rudolph

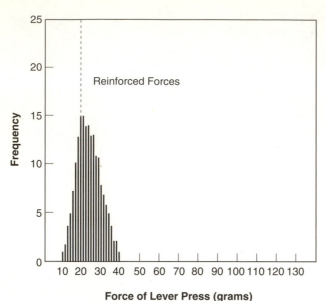

Figure 8.3   Frequency Graph After Differential Reinforcement of 20-Gram Presses

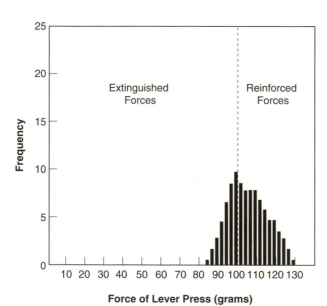

Figure 8.4   Frequency Graph After Differential Reinforcement of 100-Gram Presses

have hit the 100-gram goal. Your final results should look something like Figure 8.4.

Now you've got it. Now you've got an amazing 100 grams of force that resulted from your using the procedure of shaping with reinforcement—a series of differential-reinforcement procedures where you raised the force criterion in successive approximations. (In reality, you probably would have moved

through the successive approximations much more rapidly than the graphs show. You might have increased your force requirement in smaller steps and stayed at each level only long enough to get a few responses at a slightly greater force.)

QUESTION

1. How would you shape lever presses of 100 grams' force using a reinforcement contingency?

In the Skinner Box
Experimental Analysis
THE PROCEDURE OF SHAPING
WITH PUNISHMENT

Suppose you want to shape the 100-gram lever press using differential punishment and *no* differential reinforcement. You need to use a reinforcement procedure to get the bar press occurring, in the first place; so you might use food pellets as the reinforcer. And you need to keep the food reinforcement going throughout the entire differential punishment procedure; otherwise, the bar press will extinguish.

Then you differentially punish lever presses of less than 20 grams of force. When Rudolph presses the lever with a force of less than 20 grams, he gets food and a shock as soon as he releases the lever. When he presses the lever with a force of at least 20 grams, he gets only food, no shock. After Rudolph reliably presses the lever with a force of 20 grams, you raise the criterion to 40 grams. Now any response with a force of less than 40 grams gets food and shock. As Rudolph matches each new criterion, you raise it until he presses the lever with a force of 100 grams.

QUESTION

1. How would you shape lever presses of 100 grams' force using a punishment contingency?
2. To shape 100-gram lever presses with punishment, do you need to keep a reinforcement contingency going throughout the entire shaping procedure? Please explain.

Compare and Contrast
SHAPING VS. GETTING IN SHAPE

When Sue came to Big State U, she moved into the dorms and acquired the freshman spread—the 20 pounds all freshmen gain when they live on dorm food. As a sophomore, she left the dorms, but she didn't leave those 20 extra pounds.

But Sue was not one to take her fat fanny sitting down. She stood up, and she started shaping up. She found an old aerobics videotape by Denise Austin. At first, she could get through only half the tape before, exhausted, she plopped back onto her couch and became a spud.

Yet she kept at it, day after day, increasing both the duration and the vigor of her exercise. After a few months, she could go through the whole tape without pushing the pause button or even glancing at the couch. The vigor of her exercise increased almost to Denise's level. Oh, yes, with a little extra help from a 1,200-calorie diet, she could now get back into her high school jeans.

Question

Is this an example of *shaping*?

Our Answer

No. Getting in physical shape is not the same as shaping behavior. In Sue's case, it was physically more or less impossible for her to last much more than half the tape before she was exhausted. She didn't have strong enough muscles in her arms and legs or the aerobic capacity in her heart and lungs. But Andrew had the muscle development he needed for speaking, as did Dicky for wearing his glasses, Melanie for speaking with a normal intensity, and Juke for walking on his hands.

Melanie's aphonia is a nice example of the distinction. Didn't she have strong enough muscles to speak above a whisper? If not, Bangs and Fredinger were shaping up her body. Or didn't she have the skill or perhaps the need to speak above a whisper? If not, they were shaping her behavior. (We suspect it was her behavior and not her body, because she needed only ten shaping sessions to acquire a normal speech intensity. That seems too brief to shape up the body.)

Let's look at it another way: Differential reinforcement is the building block of shaping. True, differential reinforcement shapes Sue's athletic skills, but it doesn't shape up her muscles. Reinforcement, differential reinforcement, and thus shaping increase the likelihood of a response class for which the organism already has the physical prerequisites. Getting in shape might shape up the physical prerequisites for a response class. Yes, we use *shape* in almost the same ways. And, yes, the two processes are analogous. But one is psychological and the other biological; so if your professor asks for an example of shaping, do not use getting in physical shape.

QUESTIONS

1. Is shaping the same as getting in shape?
2. Please explain.

Compare and Contrast
In the Skinner Box
SHAPING VS. BEHAVIORAL CHAINING

In Chapter 20, we'll formally introduce and formally define **behavioral chains**—a sequence of responses linked together with connecting stimuli. For example, in the Skinner box, Rudolph's lever pressing consists of a behavioral chain: Rudolph raises his head and sees the lever; he walks over to the lever and sees it up close; he raises his paws above the lever and sees the lever from a different view and feels the proprioceptive stimuli resulting from his standing on his hind feet; he presses down on the lever and hears the click of the water dipper; he walks over to the water dipper and sees it up close; he bends down and licks and gets that delicious, soul-satisfying, immensely reinforcing drop of water. So, when you train Rudolph to press the lever, you're setting up an elaborate behavioral chain, much more than a mere lever press.

Now, people often make the mistake of calling this lever-press training procedure *shaping*, but it isn't; it's *chaining* or *training a behavioral chain* because it involves a series of different responses (that is, *response classes*) behaviorally chained together. (e.g., looking toward the lever, approaching the lever, pressing the lever, approaching the dipper, and licking the dipper.)

Of course, you might also do shaping, as part of this lever-press training. For example, like the rest of us, Rudolph will do no more work than the absolute minimum; and if you let him, he'll just make a wimpy little lever press, barely brushing it with one paw, if that's all it takes to produce the reinforcing drop of water. But we've found that our later experiments don't work too well with such anemic responding; we've found it works much better to require a truly awesome lever press, a two-pawed job that comes down with such force the whole Skinner box shakes and people in neighboring counties complain about the noise. Of course, to get such righteous performance, we must shape the response, gradually increasing the force requirement, until he's rattling his cage.

So we should reserve the term *shaping* for procedures where we use a series of differential reinforcement procedures for the same response class (like pressing down the lever), one where we gradually change the requirements along some response dimension (like force of the lever press). We should use the terminology *chaining* or *training a behavioral chain* when we are working with a sequence of distinctly different responses (like approaching and then pressing the lever).

Therefore, when you give original examples of shaping,

- make sure you're dealing with only a single response class (not a chain of distinctly different responses)
- and gradually changing the requirements along some response dimension.

QUESTION

1. Be able to explain why it's often wrong to talk about *shaping* the lever press; and explain how *shaping* can be involved in lever press training.

Compare and Contrast Shaping vs. Behavioral Response Chaining		
	Shaping	**Chaining**
Several distinctly different responses (response classes)	No	Yes
Behavior changes along a single response dimension (e.g. force)	Yes	No
Skinner Box Example	Increasing the force of the lever press	Walking toward the lever, pressing the lever, approaching the dipper

Sid's Seminar

Tom: I don't understand how shaping is different from behavioral chaining. I mean, the Skinner Box example is clear, but I don't think you can make that distinction with human beings.

Sid: Tom, I'm glad you raised that issue. I've got a good demonstration that we can do with human beings. Tom, you be the subject, and who would like to shape his behavior?

Eve: Oh, I can't pass up an opportunity like this. I'll do it.

Sid: Ok. Here's what we'll do. Tom will leave the room and the class will think of a response we want to shape. When Tom comes back in, Sue will reinforce each of his successive approximations to that response by tapping on her desk. We will assume that the sound of her tapping on her desk is a reinforcer for the purpose of this exercise. OK?

Tom and Eve: OK.
(Tom leaves the room.)

Sid: OK, now what response would we like to shape?

Joe: I think we should make it complex. Like having him walk to a desk and sit down.

Eve: But Joe, that is a behavioral chain. Walking to the desk and sitting down involves two different response classes.

Joe: Oh, yeah; well, what behavior do you want to shape?

Eve: How about raising his left arm? The successive approximations will be part of the same response class.

Sid: Sounds good to me. I'll get Tom.

Tom reenters and walks to the center of the room. As he walks, he swings his arms slightly and Eve taps her desk. Tom repeats his movements in an exaggerated way lifting his left arm and his right arm higher. Sue taps again. Tom stands in one place and swings his right leg as high as he can. Nothing. Then he lifts his arm higher. Eve taps. He raises his left arm all the way up, and Eve taps again as the class claps and cheers.

Eve: Very good, Tom. We were shaping a left-arm raise.

Tom: You shaped my successive approximations to a left-arm raise. I see that now. But what would behavioral chaining have looked like?

Joe: I can answer that; I made that mistake myself. When we shaped successive approximations to exaggerated arm swings, each approximation was a subtle variation of the previous one, just a little more exaggerated. But, we would have reinforced a behavioral chain if, instead, we had reinforced several responses from completely different response classe—like walking to a chair would be one response; turning around would be a completely different response; and then sitting down would be completely different from the first two responses. Like sitting down is not just a subtle variant of turning around; it's completely different. But we could chain those three separate responses into one sequence of behaviors, which we call a *behavioral chain*.

Tom: Cool, I see the difference now. I guess the distinction between shaping and behavioral chaining does apply to human beings as well.

QUESTION

1. Be able to show the difference between shaping and behavioral chaining with a human student example.

9

Unlearned Reinforcers and Aversive Conditions

Concept
UNLEARNED REINFORCERS AND AVERSIVE CONDITIONS

Sid's Seminar

Sid: These next two chapters deal with what psychologists often call *motivation*. This chapter concerns **unlearned reinforcers** and **unlearned aversive conditions.** And let me warn you, this may be the toughest chapter in the book; so allow plenty of time to study it.

Joe: Does that mean one of the next chapters will deal with *learned reinforcers* and *learned aversive conditions?*

Max: You, bet; in Chapter 11. I've been . . .

Joe: We know, Max. So an unlearned reinforcer must be one people don't need to learn. People are born with the capacity for that stimulus or event to reinforce their behavior.

Eve: Like food and water. We inherit the capacity for those substances to reinforce our *behavior.*

Max: And, of course, we don't inherit the capacity for $5 bills to reinforce our behavior. Five-dollar bills must be learned reinforcers. I suppose they become reinforcers because you can buy other re-

inforcers with them. They've been paired with other reinforcers.

Sid: Yes, we'll read about learned reinforcers in later chapters. But now, take a look at this definition of unlearned reinforcer:

Definition: Concept
Unlearned reinforcer
- A stimulus, event, or condition that is a reinforcer,
- though not as a result of pairing with another reinforcer.

Sid: And while we're at it:

Definition: Concept
Unlearned aversive condition
- A stimulus, event, or condition that is aversive,
- though not as a result of pairing with other aversive conditions.

Sid: This chapter deals with topics that are tradi-tionally considered under the heading of motiva-tion—what motivates people and other animals to do things, what affects the extent to which they are motivated. However, the concept of motiva-tion itself is too vague. We'll need to introduce more specific terms.

QUESTIONS

1. *Unlearned reinforcer*—define it and give an ex-ample.
2. *Unlearned aversive conditon*—define it.

Concepts
DEPRIVATION
AND SATIATION

When Mae and her staff at the Rosa Parks Academy first started working with Jimmy, they needed to use hard-core, unlearned reinforcers—mainly food. And with food reinforcers, Jimmy worked and learned better just before breakfast or lunch, rather than just after. In other words, it helped if Jimmy were a little hungry, rather than a little full. It helped if Jimmy were a little deprived of food, rather than a little sa-tiated with it. Being a little hungry (a little food de-prived) helped in two ways, when using food rein-forcers:

- Food **deprivation** improved Jimmy's **per-formance** of behavior he had previously learned with food reinforcers.
- And food **deprivation** improved Jimmy's **learning** of new behaviors with food rein-forcers.

Let's illustrate this with a typical teaching ses-sion: Because it was so important to use powerful, unlearned food reinforcers, many of Jimmy's teach-ing sessions occurred during extended breakfasts and extended lunch periods.

Eve: Jimmy, touch your nose.
Jimmy did.
Eve: GOOD BOY, JIMMY! (And she gave him a quarter spoonful of cereal and skimmed milk.)
Eve: Jimmy, touch your nose. (And so on . . .)

But near the end of breakfast, Jimmy was fill-ing up with cereal and skimmed milk, becoming a little satiated.[1]

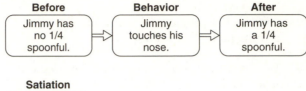

So his latency increased, and he needed more repetitions of the request and even some physical prompts. In other words, **satiation** involved a de-crease in Jimmy's **performance.**

And that's not all. If Eve had started teaching a new response, *touch your ear,* at the end of break-fast, those food reinforcers wouldn't have been very effective—satiation would have taken its toll once again. In other words, the next day, Jimmy would have shown little learning of ear touching; the fre-quency of that response would have been low. But suppose Eve had taught ear touching early in the meal when Jimmy was clearly food deprived.

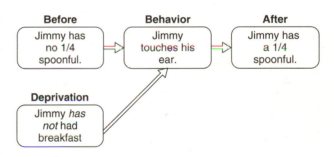

Then the next day, he probably would have re-sponded to all or most of Eve's requests that he touch his ear. Satiation while learning would hurt Jimmy's **learning** and deprivation would help it. Thus we have:

Definition: Principle
Deprivation
- withholding a reinforcer
- increases relevant learning and perfor-mance.

---

[1]We've removed the arrow connecting the satiation box from the behavior box because we don't want to give the impression that satiation causes the behavior. Really, satiation tends to pre-vent the behavior. It might be we'd be better off removing the arrow between the deprivation box and behavior also, but we haven't done that, at least not yet.

○ By *relevant* *learning* *and* *performance,* we mean

○ the learning of a response reinforced by **that reinforcer**

○ and the performance of a response previously reinforced by **that reinforcer.**[2]

We say *the reinforcer has caused* ***learning*** if the contingent delivery of that reinforcer in the past causes the response to occur more frequently now. (Note that the real test of the past reinforcement is to stop reinforcing present responding and see if the response occurs frequently anyway—at least until extinction wipes it out. If the response does occur frequently without present reinforcement, then that high frequency must be due to the past reinforcement, as there is no present reinforcement.)

So when we say *deprivation* ***increases*** *learning and performance,* we mean

○ deprivation at the time of reinforcement increases the impact the delivery of a single reinforcer has on the subsequent frequency of the reinforced response—**learning,**

○ and deprivation at the time to perform that response increases the frequency of that previously reinforced and thus previously learned response—**performance.**

Note that when we say *performance,* we mean performance of the previously reinforced response, prior to reinforcement of the present instance of that response.

You may need to read over those paragraphs a few times, because it's really hard stuff.

Of course, there's always the corollary to the principle of deprivation: it's the principle of satiation that states that the results of satiation are the opposite of the results of deprivation.

Definition: Principle
Satiation
○ Consuming a substantial amount of a reinforcer
○ temporarily decreases relevant learning and performance.

---

[2]It is not clear exactly what is the impact of deprivation on relevant learning (learning the response reinforced by the deprived reinforcer). It may be that the organism must be sufficiently deprived that it will consume the reinforcer but that further deprivation has no increase on the impact of that reinforcer; at least we know of no data to suggest otherwise. However, deprivation has a clear impact on the frequency of performance of a previously reinforced and thus previously learned response.

(We pronounce **satiation** *say-she-ay-shun.* The verb form is *satiate,* and we pronounce it *say-she-ate,* as in *Say, she ate a monstrous meal.*)

The issue of satiation is tricky too. If Rudolph consumes a large number of food reinforcers, in a brief time, he'll be "too full" to consume many more at that time. So, for a while, food won't act as an effective reinforcer to produce more **learning;** and also, for a while, Rudolph will less frequently **perform** the lever-press response that has previously produced that food. Note that the satiating effect of food is temporary; the next day (assuming Rudolph hasn't eaten in the mean time), food will again be an effective reinforcer that will produce more **learning;** and Rudolph will again **perform** the food-producing lever-press response. And, even though Rudolph will learn less when he is satiated, whatever he does learn is probably more, or less, permanent. In other words, what has been learned doesn't just "wear off" depending on satiation level.

1. By the way, why do you think Eve used such tiny reinforcers (¼ teaspoon of cereal and milk); why didn't she give Jimmy a man-sized teaspoonful? Because
   a. of the satiation principle.
   b. she doesn't want Jimmy's learning to get too dependent on cereal.
   c. Jimmy doesn't deserve more.
   d. of the principle of shaping.

You can get about four times as much learning out of a bowl of puffed wheat and milk if you use ¼-teaspoon-sized reinforcers rather than full-teaspoon-sized ones. Eve wanted to have as many learning trials as possible, before the deadening effect of satiation set in.

QUESTIONS

1. The *principle of deprivation*—define it and give an example.
2. The *principle of satiation*—define it and give an example.

Example of Satiation
Experimental Analysis of Behavior
SEX[3]

If you put a male and female rabbit together, what's the first thing they'll do? Have sexual intercourse. Haven't you heard the expression *to copulate like a*

---

[3]Based on Rubin, H. B. (1967). Rabbit families and how they grow. *Psychology Today,* December, 50–55; and Bermant, G. (1967). Copulation in rats. *Psychology Today,* July, 53–61.

pair of rabbits? And what's the second thing they'll do? Have sexual intercourse. And the third? And the fourth? What a life. Within the first hour, the rabbits may mate 15 times.

How long can they keep it up? Sometimes for over 17 hours. Does that make you feel inadequate? (Of course, we address this question only to those for whom it is appropriate because of marital status.) Well, don't feel too bad; the first hour was their hour of glory. It'll take them another 5 or 10 hours before they accumulate 15 more matings. In other words, they wait longer and longer between each mating, until they finally get down to a more human pace.[4]

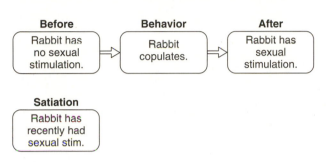

1. What is this decrease in the frequency of the copulation an example of?
   a. deprivation
   b. satiation
   c. neither
2. This satiation effect shows itself in a decrease in what area?
   a. learning
   b. performance
   c. none

More Examples
SATIATION AND DEPRIVATION

For a principle like the principle of satiation to be basic, it usually must apply to a wide variety of situations and often a wide variety of species. No problem with satiation. The more water a rat has recently drunk, the less effective water will be as a reinforcer in learning a new response. And also, the more water a rat has recently drunk, the lower the frequency of the rat's performing that previously learned response; for example, during performance, longer and longer periods of time pass between lever presses that are reinforced with water, as the rat gets more and more water to drink.

---

[4]Note that we don't connect the satiation box to the response box, because the arrow might imply that satiation cause the response to occur. What we want to imply is that satiation affects the frequency of the performance of that response in a negative way; it decreases the frequency of that performance.

Please complete the following diagram:

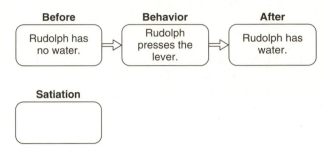

The same thing happens with the pigeon's food-reinforced key-peck response. And check out your rate of shoveling it in, as you approach the end of a pig-out. You'll find your food-reinforced shoveling response gets slower and slower as you eat your fill.

Satiation doesn't last forever—fortunately—for rabbits, rats, pigeons, and people. Sexual stimulation, food, and water eventually regain their original effectiveness as reinforcers. In other words, if we stop giving the reinforcer for a while (deprivation) we reestablish the effectiveness of that reinforcer.

Up to a limit, the greater the deprivation (time without the reinforcer), the more effective the reinforcer. Several days after complete satiation, sexual stimulation for a rat will again be an effective reinforcer to support learning a new response; and the rat will again perform previously learned responses that have resulted in sexual stimulation in the past. It takes much less deprivation for the rat to recover from the effects of satiation with food and water.

Please complete the following diagram:

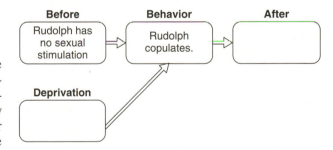

THE ESTABLISHING OPERATION[5]

Notice that the procedures of deprivation and satiation both affect learning and performance with respect to a particular reinforcer. This raises a more general concept that includes both deprivation and

---

[5]Note: The establishing operation and the before condition are not the same thing in reinforcement contingencies, though they are in escape contingencies, as we shall see.

satiation, as well as some other procedures we will discuss in the next chapter:

Definition: Procedure
Establishing operation
  ○ a procedure or condition that affects learning and performance
  ○ with respect to a particular reinforcer or aversive condition.

Deprivation and satiation are the most common examples of **establishing operations.** Other examples of establishing operations include heavy exercise, high temperature, and consumption of salt, all of which act as establishing operations for water as a reinforcer.[6]

Don't Say Knows

Don't say Rudolph will immediately start pressing the lever on Tuesday because the rat *knows* it'll get water for pressing the lever. And don't say Rudolph will immediately start pressing the lever on Tuesday because, on Monday, Rudolph *learned that* it would get water for lever pressing.

So what should you say? You should simply say Rudolph will immediately start pressing the lever on Tuesday, because lever pressing was reinforced on Monday. And you could add that he was deprived of water on both Monday and Tuesday, if you want to tie in with the theme of this chapter.

But you should also be careful about saying that Tom makes smart-ass remarks because he *knows* he'll get attention for making smart-ass remarks. Similarly you shouldn't say it's because he's *learned that* he'll get attention for smart assing.

And what should you say? Again, you should keep it simple. Tom will smart-ass frequently because a few dumb-asses have reinforced that behavior in the past.

True, Tom might know what the contingency is that's causing him to make smart-ass remarks, but the odds are he doesn't; in fact, the odds are he doesn't even know most people consider him a

---

[6]Michael defines *establishing operation* as *an environmental event, operation, or stimulus condition that affects an organism by momentarily altering (a) the reinforcing effectiveness of other events and (b) the frequency of occurrence of the type of behavior that had been consequated by those other events.* We mean for our definition to say the same thing, just in a more intuitive way. Our *learning* and *performance* correspond to his *function altering* and *evocative* terms. For a more detailed treatment of establishing operation, see: Michael, J. (1993) Establishing operations. *The Behavior Analyst, 16,* 191–206.

smart ass and that's why he has so much trouble getting dates. We usually stumble through life oblivious of the contingencies controlling our behavior (our personality) or even what our behavior or personality is. Amazing isn't it.

QUESTIONS

1. *Establishing operation*—define it.
2. Give two examples of deprivation as an establishing operation, showing how it affects both learning and performance.
3. Do the same for satiation.

Concept
THE NATURE
OF THE REINFORCER
OR AVERSIVE CONDITION

We've seen how an establishing operation such as deprivation can affect learning and performance with respect to a **particular** reinforcer or aversive condition. But, of course, changing the **particular** reinforcer or aversive condition itself can also affect learning and performance.

For example, in the work with Jimmy, generally, the greater the amount of the reinforcer, the more effective its contingent delivery is in producing learning. But you soon reach the point of diminishing returns; further increases in the amount of the reinforcer don't produce much of an increase in the amount of learning, but increasing the size of the reinforcer does increase the amount of satiation and thus decreases the number of learning trials Mae and her staff can conduct with Jimmy. That's why the best general strategy seems to be to keep those reinforcers fairly small, but not too small.

Similarly, the quality of the reinforcer can be an important feature in determining the extent to which that reinforcer will affect learning and performance. For example, not all foods are created equal. Which do you think would be a more effective reinforcer for you, a fudge sundae or boiled cabbage?

Satiation and deprivation don't really apply to aversive conditions such as electric shock, for example, in an escape condition? The relevant establishing operation for aversive conditions, like shock is simply turning on the shock (presenting the aversive condition), not deprivation or satiation. And, in those cases, it makes sense to treat the establishing operation and the before condition as the same thing. So you wouldn't diagram a separate establishing operation, but would simply indicate the shock is on in the before condition, and that would also serve as the establishing operation. Jack Michael calls this sort of establishing operation a *reflexive establishing operation.*

Reflexive Establishing Operation

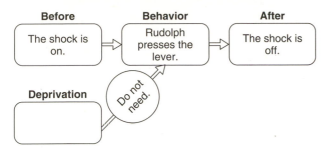

Before	Behavior	After
The shock is on.	Rudolph presses the lever.	The shock is off.

Deprivation

Do not need.

QUESTIONS

1. Suppose you were using food as a reinforcer in teaching an autistic child to identify parts of his body.
    a. What size of the reinforcer should you use?
    b. Why?
2. Be able to diagram a simple escape contingency, indicating the relation between the establishing operation and the before condition.
3. What's the establishing operation for an unlearned aversive condition in an escape contingency? (Trick question.)
4. And while we're at it: *Unlearned aversive condition*—give an example.

BASIC ENRICHMENT

IN THE SKINNER BOX

Experimental Analysis
SATIATION

OK, you've made sure Rudolph the Rat has been deprived of water for 23 hours before each session in the Skinner box, and all has gone well: he rapidly learned lever pressing; and, now, when you put him in the box he presses the lever at a good clip—several times a minute, getting a drop of water immediately after each press. But when you come in to the animal colony room one Monday morning you find . . . *Hey, who forgot to take the water bottles off the rats' home cages?!* Rudolph's been drinking his fill for the last few days; so now when you put him in the Skinner box, he barely contacts the lever, pressing it only five times in the whole session, not even bothering to lick the water dipper two of those times.

1. This is an example of
    a. deprivation
    b. satiation
2. In this case, what did satiation hurt?
    a. learning
    b. performance

Or consider this teaching tragedy: Suppose your lab instructor had failed to remove the water bottle from the rats' home cages for the first few lab sessions of the semester, when you were just starting to work with Rudolph. (Hey, it happens.) How effective do you think would be those few reinforcers Rudolph did bother to drink?

3. In this second case, what did satiation hurt?
    a. learning
    b. performance

Let's put it this way: you'd probably learn all there is to know about behavior analysis and earn your PhD degree before satiated Rudolph learned the lever press.

If you are fortunate enough to have a rat to work with, you have probably seen the effects of satiation toward the end of your experimental sessions. As Rudolph is nearing its limit of satiation, its frequency of lever pressing will go way down.

QUESTION

1. Give two examples from the Skinner box—
    a. one, the effects of satiation on performance
    b. the other, the effects of satiation on learning.

INTERMEDIATE ENRICHMENT

THE THEORY OF DIRECT AND INDIRECT BIOLOGICAL RELEVANCE

Unlearned Reinforcers

Sid: Notice that food and water both provide us with direct biological benefits. For example, they are essential to the well-being of the cells of our bodies. Can you think of any unlearned reinforcers that don't provide direct biological benefits?

Joe: What about visual stimulation? I've noticed Dr. Harper's pigeons in their home cages in the animal colony. He's got 50 of them in there. And each one stands facing out through the open grill of the cage door where there's more light. I've never seen a single one stand facing the inside of their cage, where it's dark.

Eve: My cat sits for hours staring out the window into the front yard.

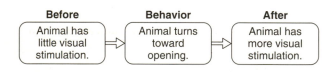

Sue: And as a baby, my daughter always oriented toward the TV, especially during the commercials and cartoons.

Sid: Yes, during the commercials and introductions to the cartoons is when the TV produces its highest rate of audiovisual reinforcers—a new sight and sound every second; we've actually measured it.

Tom: But that doesn't have anything to do with reinforcers.

Joe: Doubting Thomas. For both the pigeons and the cats, the visual stimulation reinforces the orienting response—looking out the cage door or out the window.

Max: I read an experiment Dr. Butler did with a monkey.[7] A monkey's lever press opened a window; then the monkey could see a toy train running around a track. And sure enough, the monkey often pressed the lever. That experiment also shows visual stimulation can be a reinforcer. And I suppose it was an unlearned reinforcer, because the monkey had no previous experience with the train.

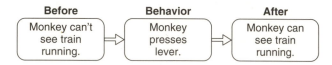

Sid: You're right, visual change does seem to be an unlearned reinforcer with no direct biological value. And so does sound. Sound will act as a mild reinforcer for rats—it will maintain a low frequency of lever press responses. Not as well as food, but better than nothing. Any others?

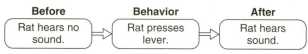

Sue: What about no-calorie sweeteners? They seem to be unlearned reinforcers. People dump nonnutritive sweeteners in their coffee by the tons.

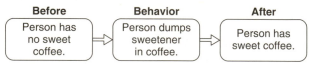

Sid: Yes, and food-deprived rats will make a response that produces a saccharine solution 100% of the time in preference to plain water.[8] But saccharine is just a taste. It has no other nutritional value.

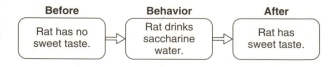

[7]Butler, R. A. (1953). Discrimination learning by rhesus monkeys to visual-exploration motivation. *Journal of Comparative and Physiological Psychology, 46,* 95–98.

[8]Sheffield, F. D., & Roby, T. B. (1950). Reward value of a nonnutritive sweet taste. *Journal of Comparative and Physiological Psychology, 43,* 471–481.

Tom: Your experiment may show the sweet taste of saccharine is a reinforcer, but how do you know it wasn't a learned reinforcer rather than an unlearned one? How do you know the sweet taste hadn't been paired with reinforcers like food?

Sid: The rats were born and raised in the lab where the experimenters controlled their diet and withheld all sweet tastes. Maybe you can't be 100% sure, but close to it.

Joe: It makes sense to me. Stimuli that help our body's cells should be unlearned reinforcers, but I can't see why sight, sound, and taste would be.

Sid: Here's one theory: More or less all animal species (including the human species) evolved in such a manner that stimuli naturally associated with food are unlearned reinforcers. These stimuli include sight, sound, taste, and smell. For example, suppose two animals see a slight movement, or hear a slight sound, a stimulus that is naturally associated with food, like the movement of prey. Which animal would be most likely to get the food and survive: the one that orients its eyes and ears toward the sight or sound and thus can better see or hear it and thus can better pounce on it, or one that ignores the stimulus?

Max: The one that looks up, of course.

Tom: But what does that have to do with sights and sounds as reinforcers?

Max: I think I've got it: The visual or auditory stimuli reinforce the response of orienting in the direction of sights and sounds. And that orientation response makes it more likely the animal will be able to attack the prey and eat it. And, also, that orientation makes it more likely the animal will survive. And surviving makes it more likely the animal will pass on to its offspring the capacity for its behavior to be reinforced by those sights and sounds.

Sid: Also, some stimuli naturally associated with harm are often unlearned aversive stimuli. For example, inexperienced baby chicks run to sheltered areas, when they see a large hawk-like shadow on the ground. My interpretation is that the sight of that shadow is an unlearned aversive stimulus; and when the chicks run under the shelter, they escape that sight; thus running under the shelter is reinforced.

Joe: I bet that if a chick could cause the shadow to disappear by pecking a key, that escape response would also be learned.

Sid: Here's an interesting way to look at these indirect reinforcers and aversive stimuli: The biologically important reason for orienting toward sights and sounds is that it helps animals (including us) to avoid injury and death (to survive). But that

natural contingency is ineffective in controlling behavior; you're liable to be dead before you can learn orienting response based on survival as the reinforcer.

Ineffective Natural Contingency

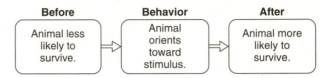

Sid: So through evolution, nature has added what we might consider a performance-management contingency, one that is not important by itself, but one that has evolved because it does control behavior effectively and does help the organism avoid injury and death (to survive)—the original outcome of the natural but ineffective survival contingency.[9]

Performance-management Contingency

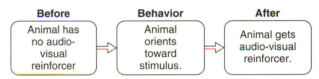

Sid: So we have two types of unlearned reinforcers—those that directly cause biological benefits and those that indirectly cause biological benefits.

Joe: And by biological benefits, you mean benefits to your body, to your body's cells.

Eve: Like food and water directly benefit your body's cells. And sights, sounds, smells, and tastes only indirectly benefit your body by making it more likely you'll get the food and water that provide the direct benefits.

Sid: And we have two types of unlearned aversive stimuli—those that directly cause biological harm and those that indirectly cause biological harm.

Eve: Like a predator bite or spoiled food directly harm your body's cells. And the shadow of the hawk or a loud noise or the taste and odor of

---

[9]Actually, this analysis should be much more complex. If visual stimuli were not unlearned reinforcers, they would have to become learned reinforcers (Chapter 11). And for that to happen they would have to function as discriminative stimuli (Chapter 12) in the presence of which "searching" for prey would be reinforced. Similarly, if visual stimuli were not unlearned the avoidance response (Chapter 15) would avoid the pain of an attack. I said it was complex; that's why this analysis is buried in a footnote.

spoiled food are only indirectly "harmful" in that when you experience those stimuli, your body is likely to be harmed.

Joe: In a weird way, you can think of those indirectly harmful stimuli as really being helpful, because you escape the unlearned aversive stimuli or they punish your approach behavior; so they help keep your body healthy.

Max: Yeah, like you escape the bad smell and bad taste of spoiled food. So you don't eat it. So the spoiled food doesn't harm you. Cool.

Eve: Remember the hand-flapping self-stimulation, of Jimmy, our boy with the autistic behavior? [Chapter 6.] Is that the same sort of unlearned reinforcer?

Sid: Yes, it's an unlearned sensory reinforcer, just like light and sound.

Tom: But his hand flapping doesn't seem to support his survival, not even indirectly.

Sid: No, sensory reinforcers like those coming from hand-flapping might have some survival value sometimes, but clearly not in Jimmy's case.

Sid: So far, Max, Joe, and Eve have each earned a point.

QUESTIONS

1. Give an example of an unlearned reinforcer with a direct biological benefit.
2. Give an example of one with an indirect biological benefit.
3. What is that indirect benefit?
4. Give an example of an unlearned aversive condition that causes direct biological harm.
5. Give an example of one that causes indirect biological harm.
6. What is that indirect biological harm?

Example of the Premack Principle
Educational Psychology
THE NURSERY SCHOOL[10]

The bell rang and the teacher shouted, "Run and scream." The 3-year-old students jumped from their chairs and ran and screamed. After 2 minutes of intense activity, the bell rang again. This time the teacher asked the students to sit quietly at their desks and look at the blackboard. The students watched the teacher as she continued her instruction at the blackboard. After a few minutes, the bell rang and the teacher sat down in her desk chair. Then she said, "Okay, now it's push-the-teacher time." The students did just that. Laughing and shouting, they wheeled her in her desk chair all over the classroom. Two minutes later the bell rang again; she instructed them to return to their seats and continued with her instruction. The next time the bell rang, the teacher allowed the students to kick the wastebaskets; and the time after that, they threw a plastic cup across the room. This process went on for nearly 3 hours. The teacher managed to get the students to concentrate on their academic task for unusually long times. She achieved this small miracle by allowing a variety of free-for-all activities and then instructing them to return to their academic tasks.

The nursery school had not always been like this. When it began, the teacher's directions had little effect on the children's actions. When the teacher asked them to sit in their chairs, the children would often continue what they were doing—running around the room, screaming, pushing chairs, and so on. But after a few days of this procedure, the children's behavior was perfect. For example, when the teacher asked the children to sit and look at the blackboard, they did so better than older children.

Premack Principle[11]

Undoubtedly, the children behaved so well because the teacher reinforced appropriate schoolwork. The unique feature of her procedure was the bizarre reinforcers she used, for instance, throwing plastic cups, shouting, and screaming. Who would have thought that these activities would serve as reinforcers?

The selection of the reinforcers was interesting. The teacher used disruptive behavior to reinforce proper work. When the students first came to the classroom, they disrupted more often than they studied, even when the teacher asked them to sit still and be quiet. This shows that disrupting was more reinforcing than sitting and listening to the teacher.

The teacher used those activities that occurred at a high frequency as reinforcers for activities that occurred at a low rate—and it worked. The low-frequency activities occurred more often. This illustrates the Premack principle. Remember? If one activity normally occurs more often than another, the opportunity to engage in the more frequent activity will reinforce the less frequent activity.

---

[10]Based on Homme, L. E., Debacha, P. C., Devine, J. V., Steinhorst, R., & Rickert, E. J. (1963). The use of the Premack principle in controlling the behavior of nursery school children. *Journal of Experimental Analysis of Behavior, 6,* 544.

[11]Premack, D. (1965). Reinforcement theory. In D. Levin (Ed.), *Nebraska Symposium of Motivation* (pp. 123–128). Lincoln: University of Nebraska Press.

Incidentally, here's why we included this example of the Premack principle in the chapter on learned reinforcers rather than in the chapter on unlearned reinforcers: We suspected much learned social reinforcement with all that running, shoving, screaming activity. So we thought we'd play it safe and put it in this chapter. But we're not sure.

QUESTION

1. *Premack principle*—give a human example.

Principle
PREMACK PRINCIPLE[12]

Why are some things reinforcing and others aren't? Over the years, psychologists have done many experiments trying to answer that question. And they've come up with many theories, but none fits all the data.

Dr. David Premack uses a different approach. Instead of talking about reinforcing events or stimuli, he talks about reinforcing behavior. Instead of calling food a reinforcer, he says eating food is a reinforcing behavior. He goes on to say that a more frequent activity will reinforce a less frequent activity.

Suppose a water-deprived rat normally spends more time drinking water than pressing a lever in a test chamber. Then we could use the opportunity to drink water to reinforce and maintain lever pressing. Suppose a food-deprived pigeon spends more time eating food than pecking a plastic response key. Then we could use the opportunity to eat food to reinforce and maintain key pecking.

Notice that Premack doesn't talk about universal reinforcers—activities that will reinforce all other activities. Instead, he talks about one specific activity reinforcing another. In specifying whether an activity is reinforcing, we must consider the response we want to reinforce. Reading this book may occur with a higher frequency than reading other textbooks. But going out with the gang might occur with a higher frequency than reading this book. Then we would predict going out would reinforce reading this book, and reading this book would reinforce reading other books.

In an experiment with monkeys, Premack showed the relative nature of the reinforcing effect of various activities: He used four activities: pushing a lever, pulling a plunger, flapping a hinge, and opening and closing a door. He found the activity that occurred most frequently could reinforce an activity that occurred with an intermediate frequency. In other words, the intermediate activity occurred more often when Premack immediately followed it with the opportunity to do the most frequent activity. He also showed that the opportunity to do the intermediate activity would reinforce an activity that occurred even less often.

Here's Premack's answer to the theoretical question, why is something reinforcing? An activity is reinforcing because it occurs more often than another activity. But then we might ask; Why do activities that occur more often reinforce other activities? We don't have a good answer to this question. For the time being, we're happy to be able to answer the first question.

We can see the importance of Premack's solution when we attempt to answer the following question: How can I tell if something will act as a reinforcer before I use it to reinforce a response? Here's Premack's answer (just a restatement of the principle):

- Measure the frequency of occurrence of the potentially reinforcing activity.
- Measure the frequency of the response you want to reinforce.
- If the potentially reinforcing activity occurs more often than the response you want to reinforce,
- then that potentially reinforcing activity will be an effective reinforcer
- for that response.

QUESTIONS

1. *The Premack principle*—state it and give an example.
2. Describe an experiment showing the relativity of reinforcement. Describe the subjects
   a. responses.
   b. reinforcers.

> Definition: Principle
> **Premack principle**
> - If one activity occurs more often than another,
> - the opportunity to do the most frequent activity
> - will reinforce the less frequent activity.

---

[12]Based on Premack, D. (1965). Reinforcement theory. In D. Levin (Ed.), *Nebraska Symposium of Motivation* (123–128). Lincoln: University of Nebraska Press.

10 Special Establishing Operations

Example
AGGRESSION[1]

Pain-Established Aggression

Human Being

Sid, the model man about the house, stood at the workbench in their basement, whistling a tune as he nailed together a wooden planter for Dawn. He was getting good—only three blows of the hammer to drive in each nail. And then, thud—one of his powerful blows hit his thumb instead of the nail. "#$%!," Sid shouted, throwing the hammer against the wall.

"What's the matter, honey?" Dawn asked through the basement door.

"What the @#$! do you think's the matter? It's your %$#! planter. That was the dumbest %#! idea you ever had!"

Rats

Two rats sit in a single box, a box much like a Skinner box but without a response lever, and those ominous metal rods make up a grid floor. By now you've come to anticipate research involving aversive electric shock when you see that grid floor. Sure enough, a mild shock occurs. But this is no punishment experiment. And there's no escape lever for the rats to press. Instead, the rats immediately stand up on their hind legs and face each other like a pair of boxers. But, as they start to attack, the electric shock

---

[1]Based on Azrin, N. H., Hutchinson, R. R., & Hake, D. F. (1966). Extinction-produced aggression. *Journal of Experimental Analysis of Behavior, 9,* 191–204. For years, traditional psychologists have talked about frustration-producing aggression. This may be the world's first animal experiment on frustration-produced aggression.

goes off. They fight briefly and then settle back down on all fours. The same sequence repeats itself every time the shock turns on. (Note: this is not an escape contingency; the shock is turned off immediately, to minimize the amount of harmful fighting the rats do.)

Research of this sort came from the laboratories of Dr. Nathan Azrin, when he was at Anna State Hospital. He and his colleagues showed that every species of animal they tested would aggress against other animals or even objects when they received painful stimuli such as electric shock.

When they received the aversive shock, the rats aggressed against each other. When he received the aversive thumb smash, Sid aggressed against the wall with his hammer, or against his hammer with the wall (whichever), and he aggressed against Dawn and the world with his swearing.

Extinction-Established Aggression

Human Being

Some of Sid's most reinforcing moments come when he purchases new software, loads it into his computer, and starts testing it, glancing only briefly at the new manual as he does so. (He's always broke because he buys so much software. Such is the life of a computer junkie.) And today is one of those days. He's been in his study with his new software for 3 hours. Suddenly, Dawn hears pounding fists, as Sid shouts his ever-familiar "#$%!"

Against her better judgment, Dawn sticks her head inside his study. "What's the matter, honey? Having trouble with your new program?"

"'What's the matter, honey!' You know #$%#! well what's the matter. How come I have to be the one who does all the work getting our new software running? How come you don't do your share? That's what I'd like to know. This is the stupidest #$% program I've ever seen. And they might as well not have bothered translating the documentation from the original Japanese. #$%! this is frustrating!"

Extinction city!

Pigeons

Another Skinner box, also contains two animals—pigeons—but there's no sign of electric shock, just a response key and a grain feeder. What's strange is that one pigeon sits restrained in a small box in the corner of the larger Skinner box. Only its head sticks out from the restraining box. The free pigeon ignores its restrained friend. Instead, it pecks the key and then eats the grain that is available for 3 seconds after each response. (What kind of schedule of reinforcement is that? Continuous reinforcement.) The bird works peacefully awhile, and then the food stops coming. No matter how hard or fast it pecks the key, nothing happens.

Extinction city!

What does the bird do? It does what Sid did. It turns on its friend and viciously attacks it. The free bird pecks the innocent friend with its beak and hits it with its wings.

Analysis

We've looked at two cases of human aggression and two of animal aggression. Now let's tie it all together; let's put it in a broader behavior-analytic framework.

Warning: What follows is a theoretical analysis, an interpretation of the data; so not everyone will agree with it.

Sid's aggression follows a smashed thumb, and the rats' aggression occurs during electric shock—in both cases, aggression during painful stimulation. Also, Sid's aggression occurs during the failure of key presses on the computer to produce its customary reinforcers; and the pigeon's aggression occurs during the failure of key pecks in the Skinner box to produce its customary reinforcers—in both cases, aggression during extinction.

No doubt, painful stimulation is an aversive condition. And maybe extinction is, too. Now the traditional analysis would say an aversive condition (either painful stimulation or extinction) automatically produces the aggressive response (throwing, swearing, attacking). But let's look at it from the point of view of establishing operations. We might say an aversive condition is an establishing operation that affects learning and performance with respect to the **aggression reinforcers**. Normally, Sid doesn't throw things or swear, and normally animals don't attack

members of their own species. This aggressive behavior usually occurs only when an aversive condition establishes the results of aggression (what we will call *aggression reinforcers*) as reinforcing.

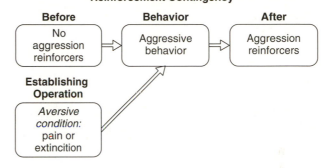

General Case
Aversive-Condition-Established Reinforcement Contingency

1. So how would we apply this analysis to our earlier examples of Sid's pain-established aggression? Please complete these diagrams.

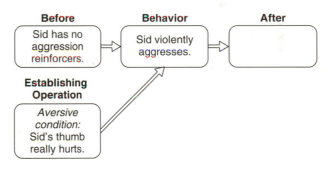

Human Being
Pain-Established Reinforcement Contingency

We think the aggression reinforcers in this case are the feel of throwing the hammer (proprioceptive[2] stimuli), the sound of its hitting the wall, and the feel and sound of shouting. Plus, for some reason it seems to be most reinforcing when those shouts are swear words!

---

[2]pro·pri·o·cep·tor (pro′prê-o-sèp′ter) *noun.* A sensory receptor, found chiefly in muscles, tendons, joints, and the inner ear, that detects the motion or position of the body or a limb by responding to stimuli arising within the organism. [Latin *proprius,* one's own + (re)ceptor.]—pro′pri·o·cep′tive *adjective.* (The American Heritage® Dictionary of the English Language, Third Edition. Copyright © 1992 by Houghton Mifflin Company. Electronic version licensed from INSO Corporation. All rights reserved.)

2. Now please apply our analysis to the earlier example of the rat's pain-established aggression by completing this contingency diagram.

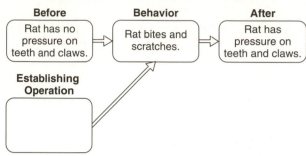

Rat
Pain-Established Reinforcement Contingency

Note that pressure on teeth and claws are examples of what we mean by *aggression reinforcers*.

3. And please apply our analysis to the earlier example of Sid's extinction-established aggression by completing this contingency diagram.

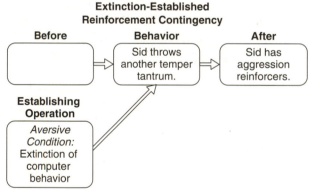

Human Being
Extinction-Established
Reinforcement Contingency

4. And also please apply our analysis to the earlier example of the pigeon's extinction-established aggression by completing this contingency diagram.

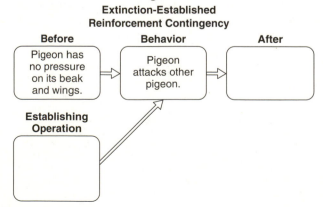

Pigeon
Extinction-Established
Reinforcement Contingency

Of course, you're skeptical. The aggression response seems so natural it's hard to imagine reinforcement playing a role. Fortunately, Drs. Azrin, Hutchinson, and Hake tested this out.

In a follow-up experiment, they put a second key in the Skinner box and temporarily removed the restrained pigeon. As before, a schedule of continuous food reinforcement maintained the pecks on the food key during the first phase. Then, in the second phase, the frustration phase, the experimenters extinguished pecks on the food key. But now there was no restrained victim bird to aggress against. However, each time the aggressor bird pecked the new key (victim-access key), the restrained victim bird was put back in the Skinner box for a brief period. What happened? The aggressor pigeon pecked the victim-access key during extinction, got the restrained victim bird, and attacked it! And during continuous food reinforcement, it ignored the victim-access key.

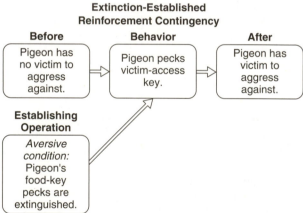

Pigeon
Extinction-Established
Reinforcement Contingency

So this shows that access to the victim bird was a reinforcer for the aggressor bird during its time of frustrating extinction. And it doesn't require much of a leap of faith to assume that the reason access to the victim bird was a reinforcer was that the aggressor bird could then aggress against it. And, in turn, this suggests that the stimuli arising from pecking on the victim bird were effective aggression reinforcers that were reinforcing that aggressive pecking. In other words, the reason the aggressor aggressed was because that aggressive behavior produced reinforcers, the aggression stimuli.

But the experimenters didn't stop there. A schedule of continuous reinforcement had maintained pecking the access key; in other words, each peck brought the restrained bird back to be the victim of more aggression. But, in the third phase of their experiment, the experimenters used a fixed ratio of 70; in other words, the aggressor bird had to peck the victim-access key 70 times before the experimenters would put the restrained victim bird back in the Skinner box. The results? During food extinction (frustration), the aggressor bird reliably pecked away at the victim-access key until it had knocked off the 70 responses and got its victim. Indeed, the opportunity to aggress was a powerful reinforcer! We think that's just another way of saying the stimuli resulting from aggression are powerful reinforcers—for example, the proprioceptive and tactile stimuli (touch stimuli) the bird gets when it pecks and hits.

In summary, aversive conditions (either pain or extinction) are establishing operations. These establishing operations affect learning and performance with respect to the reinforcing stimuli produced by aggression. Such aversive conditions increase the speed of learning aggressive behavior and increase the frequency of the performance of such behavior. (Aggression-produced stimuli would include the pressure on the pigeon's beak when it aggressively pecks another bird, the pressure on a rat's teeth when it attacks another rat, and the pressure on a man's fist when he smashes it into the wall in a fit of rage.) Let's further summarize, with a couple of definitions:

Definition: Concept
Aggression reinforcer
  ○ Stimuli resulting from acts of aggression.
Definition: Principle
The aggression principle
  ○ Aversive stimuli and extinction are establishing operations
  ○ for aggression reinforcers.[3]

What are the stimuli resulting from acts of aggression? They are fairly clear in the case of physical aggression: pressure on the rat's teeth and gums as it bites the other rat; pressure on the beak of the dove of love and peace as she pecks violently at her friend; pressure on Sid's fist as he pounds violently

on the workbench. These are strange reinforcers, but we suggest they are the reinforcers that maintain the aggressive behavior. The rat doesn't bite thin air, nor does the dove peck thin air, nor does Sid smash thin air. In other words, stimulation resulting from violent physical acts tend to be aggression reinforcers.

If this physical stimulation is so reinforcing, why don't we aggress all the time? Because the establishing operation is often missing. Like all reinforcers, the aggression reinforcers need an establishing operation. In the case of these reinforcers, the establishing operation is the presentation of aversive stimulation or extinction.

What about verbal aggression; what are the aggressive reinforcers there? That's a good question. Unfortunately, we know of no research on this topic. People swear aggressively even when there's no one to hear them. And they swear in their own language, not a language they don't know. So this form of aggression requires an elaborate learning history. However, it's not clear what that history is. But it sure seems universal.

Is letting off steam or letting out the energy generated by frustration (extinction) an aggression reinforcer? Letting off steam and letting out energy are just metaphors. We're not steam engines. And we don't build up energy as a result of extinction. There is no such *thing* as frustration; it's not a substance inside us that builds up and must be released. It's a poetic metaphor for extinction making aggression reinforcers more effective. The problem with these poetic metaphors is that people act as if they were real. So that sort of metaphorical analysis tends to encourage aggression in a way that may harm the individual and his or her friends and family. In other words, it's not OK to allow Jimmy to aggress against people and objects so he can "let off steam, or let out energy, or express his inner hostility." There's no evidence that aggression has a "mental-health" benefit for the aggressor, in spite of the common assumption that it does. And, on the other hand, it is clear that aggression is usually harmful and dysfunctional, whether it's Jimmy or Sid throwing a temper tantrum. Our advice: Don't aggress and don't tolerate aggression; it's bad business in a civilized society, even if it is reinforcing.

---

[3]Response blocking might be another establishing operation for aggression reinforcers. For example, suppose that each time a rat runs down a runway, it gets a food pellet. Then suppose that one time you put a barrier near the end of the runway that prevents the rat from continuing toward the food. That's called *response blocking* and will act as an establishing operation for aggression reinforcers. But that may be only a special case of extinction of the running response, so we haven't added response blocking to our definition. We might similarly interpret physical restraint, or physical restraint may simply be aversive in its own right, though it is also a form of response blocking.

QUESTIONS

1. Diagram an experiment that shows pain-established aggression.
2. Diagram an experiment that shows extinction-established aggression.
3. Diagram an experiment that shows that the opportunity to aggress is a powerful reinforcer.

4. *Aggression reinforcer*—define it.

5. *Aggression principle*—define it.

Example
PASSIVE AGGRESSION WITHOUT AWARENESS

Dawn slept in that Sunday morning, not feeling too well because of a sore throat. But Sid got up and went for a 1-hour, 6:00 A.M. jog, long and slow—relaxing. When he got back she was up, so he gave her a sweaty kiss, he was so happy to see her; but he worried his perspiration may have made the kiss more of an aversive stimulus than a reinforcing stimulus for her.

Sid started to describe the pleasure of his jog, the beauty of the rising sun, the freshness of the early morning air. Sharing these delights with Dawn was a reinforcer. But then he thought, "No, she finds it aversive when I manage to do more running than she does."

Discretely wiping the sweaty kiss from her lips, Dawn asked, "What do you plan to do today?"

Sid said, "I think I'll go to the library and check out a few more references for my dissertation."

She asked, "Don't you have enough references? Aren't you just procrastinating? Aren't you just avoiding the aversiveness of doing the hard part—the writing?"

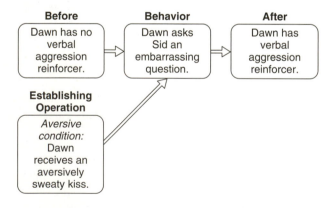

He said, "Yes, you're right." But his tone suggested he didn't enjoy her accurate behavioral analysis.

"Honey, are you angry with me for saying that?" she asked.

"No, you're right," he replied.

"But I'd rather be married to a man without a PhD than divorced from one who has a PhD."

"No, no, I appreciate your pointing out that I was avoiding the hard stuff. By the way, I had a great run today; the rising sun always turns me on, and the crisp morning air makes me feel so good. I got in a solid 6 miles."

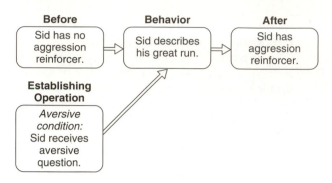

Whoops. Sid allowed a little aggression to fall on his wife, knowing, as he did, that his describing the run she hadn't participated in made her feel inadequate.

Aversive stimulation establishes aggression as a reinforcer almost too sweet to resist, especially when you can make the aggression so subtle the victim barely detects that it's happening. The victim can't put a label on it, can't point an accusing finger. And better yet, even the perpetrator of the aggression can't self-criticize because the aggression is too subtle even for him or her to detect it. In other words, often we're not only unaware of why we aggress, but we're even unaware that we are aggressing.

A mother goose and her young goslings were strolling across the road, at peace with the world, until a battered green Honda Civic sped around the curve. Sid hit the brakes and the horn at the same time.

"#$%! those birds," he said. "They crap up the sidewalks, they wake me up with their honking, and now they're going to make me late for my lecture."

1. Diagram this example of *non*passive aggression.

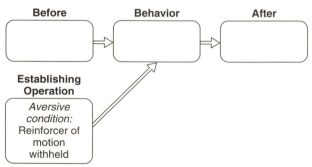

Dawn thought, Poor Sid, the tiniest interruption in the flow of his normal reinforcers, and he loses his cool. The reinforcers of aggression get hold of him. But she said, "Sid, honey, they're so cute"— a form of mild aggression on her part. She aggressed because it was aversive for her to listen to Sid's blast of the horn and his blast of anti-Audubon sentiment. (Dawn's statement was aggressive in that it caused Sid some mild discomfort by suggesting that he wasn't completely justified in his anger at the *cute little birds*.)

2. Diagram this example of passive aggression.

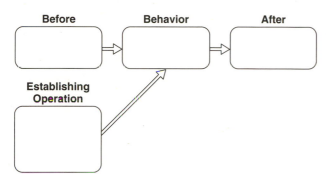

Pigeons peck at other pigeons until it hurts, and people verbally zap other people until it hurts.

QUESTION

1. Diagram three cases of passive aggression without awareness.

Example
DRUG ADDICTION[4]

Much mysticism and moral indignation surrounds drug addiction and the drug addict. Many people consider drug addicts to be morally flawed; either they have some mysterious spiritual weakness or some mysterious genetic weakness—the infamous type-x genetic pattern. But let's consider a more behavioral approach.

Q: What's the first question you ask when you begin a behavior analysis?

A: What's the response?

Q: Good. What's the main response of interest in drug addiction?

A: The self-administration of a drug.

---

[4]Based on Poling, A. (1986). *A primer of human behavioral pharmacology*. New York: Plenum Press; and Thompson, T., & Schuster, R. (1964). Morphine self-administration, food reinforcement and avoidance behaviors in rhesus monkeys. *Psychopharmacologia, 5*, 89–94.

Q: Good. Your second question?

A: What's maintaining the behavior? What's the reinforcement or escape contingency?

Q: Good. Give me a relevant example of an escape contingency.

Escape from Pain

A patient in a hospital suffers terrible pain. If she pushes a button, morphine automatically starts dripping into her blood stream through an intravenous tube. The morphine reduces the pain.[5]

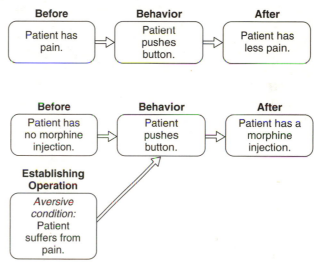

How about another example?

Escape from Poverty

The person living in the poverty of the ghetto finds life psychologically unbearable and takes heroin because it reduces that aversiveness.

No doubt, a popular analysis; and it may even be part of the story.

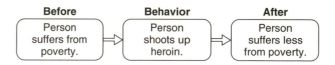

---

[5]One of my students pointed out that no matter how fast the nurse ran to the patient's bedside, my example fails the 60-second test. And I'm not going to sleaze it up by saying that the nurse just happened to be standing next to the patient with a hypodermic syringe loaded with morphine. But this example makes my point so well, I don't want to abandon it. (Instead of being an escape contingency, this is a rule-governed analog to an escape contingency.)

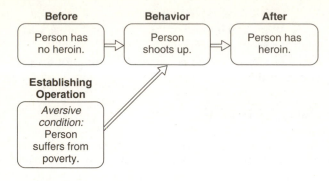

Before	Behavior	After
Person has no heroin.	Person shoots up.	Person has heroin.

Establishing Operation

Aversive condition: Person suffers from poverty.

Escape from Withdrawal

We've talked about the consumption of morphine and heroin as an escape response. What does that have to do with addiction?

One feature of addiction can be physical dependency. The patient is permanently cured of his pain and stops calling for the morphine. But then he starts having aversive physical withdrawal symptoms. A shot of morphine comes to the rescue, wiping out the withdrawal symptoms—at least for awhile.

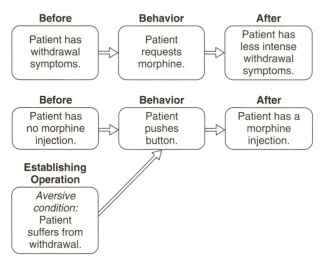

Before	Behavior	After
Patient has withdrawal symptoms.	Patient requests morphine.	Patient has less intense withdrawal symptoms.

Before	Behavior	After
Patient has no morphine injection.	Patient pushes button.	Patient has a morphine injection.

Establishing Operation

Aversive condition: Patient suffers from withdrawal.

The withdrawal-escape contingency is just like the previous pain-escape contingency, except for one thing—the establishing operation. The past consumption of the morphine is part of the establishing operation that produces the aversive withdrawal symptoms.

The Pure Pleasure of Drugs

People are more sympathetic to drug addicts if they think addicts take the drug because it reduces pain or because it reduces the harshness of poverty. But they tend to get morally indignant if they think addicts take drugs for the fun of it—in other words, because it's a reinforcer. So in behavioral terms, here's one of the big drug debates: What maintains drug abuse, the presentation of a reinforcer or the reduction of an aversive condition?

Put another way, is suffering an aversive condition an essential establishing operation for the learning and performance of drug-reinforced behavior? And, as we'll see, the answer is *no*.

Dr. Travis Thompson, Dr. Robert Schuster, and their students and colleagues have done much animal research on drug addiction. They've found that addictive drugs are unlearned reinforcers prior to addiction. This includes morphine, heroin, codeine, and cocaine. In other words, a monkey will press a lever if the lever press produces a shot of morphine. And the monkey need not be suffering any physical stress or be physically addicted to the drug. All these drugs are unlearned reinforcers. In other words, the monkeys are joy popping.

So an aversive condition and escape contingency are not essential for morphine or heroine to act as a reinforcer controlling learning and performance.

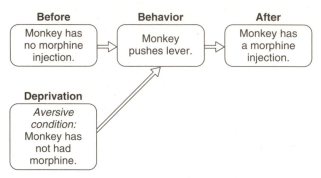

Before	Behavior	After
Monkey has no morphine injection.	Monkey pushes lever.	Monkey has a morphine injection.

Deprivation

Aversive condition: Monkey has not had morphine.

But that's not the whole story. As we said, if the monkeys keep taking morphine over a prolonged period of time, they will become tolerant to the drug; in other words, they will need increasingly larger amounts of the drug to produce the same physical effects. And withdrawal of the drug for a day or so can produce physical distress. Complete withdrawal sometimes leads to death.

Thompson and Schuster presented two establishing operations that were effective for morphine. First, they showed that deprivation of morphine acted as an establishing operation. In most of their research, the monkeys were deprived of morphine for only 6 hours. But, even so, they'd press the response lever at a moderate rate, as long as an occasional lever press produced an immediate shot of morphine. But when they were deprived of morphine for 24 hours, they'd press the lever at a tremendous rate. In other words, morphine works like most reinforcers: The more deprivation of the reinforcer up to a point, the higher the frequency of performance of the response that has been previously reinforced with that reinforcer.

They also checked out nalorphine. This drug is sometimes used to find out if a person is addicted to morphine. Morphine addicts will show withdrawal symptoms if they receive a shot of nalorphine.

Thompson and Schuster's monkeys were addicted. (If given the opportunity, monkeys will consume enough morphine to become physically dependent.) When they received a shot of nalorphine, the monkeys acted as if they had been deprived of morphine for some time. In other words, their rate of lever pressing greatly increased. This means an injection of nalorphine is another establishing operation; it increases the frequency of performance of the response previously reinforced with morphine.

> **Let he who is without sin cast the first stone.**
> **—Jesus Christ**

> **DANGEROUS DRUGS CHECKLIST**
> **Check here. I use:**
>
> ❑ Heroin   ❑ Rock and Roll
> ❑ Morphine   ❑ Nicotine
> ❑ Cocaine   ❑ Caffeine
> ❑ Speed   ❑ Processed sugar
> ❑ Barbiturates   ❑ Table salt
> ❑ Alcohol   ❑ Animal fat
> ❑ Marijuana   ❑ TV

> **Let he who is not stoned cast the first criticism at addicts.**
> **—Richard Malott**

QUESTIONS

1. Fill out the contingency diagrams for three escape contingencies involving addictive drugs. They differ mainly in their establishing operations.
2. Describe an experiment demonstrating that drugs can maintain self-administration through reinforcement other than escape from an aversive condition.
3. Describe the research on nalorphine as an establishing operation.

Concept
ADDICTIVE REINFORCERS

> **Religion is the opiate of the masses.**
> **—Karl Marx**

As behavior analysts, we generally don't label people. Here's one reason: When you label people as drug addicts or alcoholics, you tend to fall back on the so-called spiritual and genetic causes of behavior. And this almost always means you end blaming the victim—the addicts. You end up saying they just don't have the right stuff, either spiritual or genetic. Instead, we behavior analysts work hard to find the causes in the behavioral contingencies rather than in the person. This behavior analytic approach may be superior, both morally and practically.

As a behavior analyst I'm less inclined to talk about addicts and more inclined to talk about *addictive behavior* or, better yet, **addictive reinforcers**. The behavior tends to be arbitrary. It can involve pushing the nurses' call button, pressing the response lever, tying a belt around your arm and sticking a hypodermic needle in a vein, or stealing a stereo—whatever works. It's the outcome that calls the shots. So we emphasize addictive reinforcers rather than addictive behaviors.

> *Definition: Concept*
> **Addictive reinforcer**
> ○ A reinforcer for which
> ○ repeated exposure
> ○ is an establishing operation.

In considering addictive reinforcers, keep in mind that addictive drugs are unlearned reinforcers even before they become addictive reinforcers—even before their repeated use has acted as an establishing operation to increase their value as reinforcers. But addictive reinforcers differ from most unlearned reinforcers, like food; the repeated eating of food doesn't increase food's value as a reinforcer (food was a very strong reinforcer from day one).

> **Opiates are the religion of the masses.**
> **—Richard Malott**

Can you think of any other addictive reinforcers?
What about nicotine and caffeine?
All our wonderful, modern drugs?

QUESTION

1. *Addictive reinforcer*—define it and give an example.

INTERMEDIATE ENRICHMENT

A BEHAVIOR-ANALYTIC THEORY OF AGGRESSION

Is Aggression Behavior Learned?

Our position is controversial, but we argue that aggressive **behavior** is learned. Suppose an animal is being aversively stimulated or its behavior is being extinguished. Then it will learn more or less any arbitrary response, if that response produces an aggression reinforcer. When a monkey's tail is shocked, it bites a rubber tube because that biting response is reinforced with aggression reinforcers—pressure on its teeth, gums, and jaws. But if the apparatus were so rigged that gently pulling a string would produce those aggression reinforcers, we think the monkey would learn to gently pull the string as its aggressive behavior. That's just like human beings learning to be gentle and quiet in their sarcastic aggression. What **is** unlearned, innate, or inherited is the reinforcing value of pressure on the monkey's teeth, gums, and jaws, when being aversively stimulated (e.g., tail shocked). Great reinforcers for you and me, too, when someone's shocking our tail. You've heard about biting the bullet?

So what we're saying is that all of us learn aggression **behavior** because that behavior produces aggression **reinforcers**. But the aggression reinforcer, itself, is an unlearned, innate reinforcer. It's just like Rudolph learns to press the lever because that behavior produces a drop of water. And the water reinforcer, itself, is an unlearned, innate reinforcer. Lever pressing is a learned response, and water is an unlearned reinforcer. Also, aggression is a learned response; and the aggression reinforcer is an unlearned reinforcer.

What's the Value of Aggression?

In the environment where our species and most others evolved, aggressive behavior kept other animals from taking food away from our ancestors (aggression reinforcers kick in to action when reinforcers are interfered with—extinction [a.k.a. frustration]). You've heard the expression, *never take a bone away from a hungry human being.*

Also, our ancestors evolved in an eat-or-be-eaten world. If another animal attacked one of our ancestors, the painful attack produced aversive stimulation, and great, great, great . . . grandmother would be more likely to survive if that stimulation acted as an establishing operation to support her aggressive behavior. And those aggression reinforcers are still kicking in for us, even though now they may do more harm than good—most of the lions and tigers are in zoos now. Our ancestors are long gone, but not their susceptibility to aggression reinforcers.

I'm saying, that we don't come factory wired with the tendency to aggress, but we do come factory wired with aggression reinforcers easily established by aversive conditions. And those aversive conditions are occasions where aggression might have aided survival, at least for our ancestors.

Why Isn't Success in Battle Enough of a Reinforcer?

Wouldn't we learn aggressive behavior simply because such behavior allowed us to escape the painful stimuli of an attack? Maybe, but the learning might be too slow. We might have been someone else's meal before we had the opportunity to learn to fight well enough to survive. But if every time we happened to hit or bite or swing actively, such aggressive behaviors produced an aggression reinforcer, then those effective fighting responses would probably be learned more quickly than if we had to execute a successful battle plan and escape the pain of the attack before that sequence of behaviors would be reinforced and thus learned.

By the way, we're not saying that escape contingencies aren't also operating. No doubt, escape from the aversive stimulation of a predator's bite will add more reinforcement for the aggression behavior. And, it may be that, the skills of fighting aggressively will be shaped by quicker and quicker escapes—variable outcome shaping. But we are saying that we think such an escape contingency wouldn't do the trick by itself; there needs to be an initial level of aggression behavior automatically reinforced by the aggression reinforcers.

QUESTIONS

1. Is aggression **behavior** learned?
   a. learned
   b. unlearned (innate)
2. Please explain your answer.
3. Are the aggression reinforcers learned or unlearned?
   a. learned (by the way, we'll be talking a lot more about learned reinforcers in the next chapter)
   b. unlearned (innate)
4. Please explain your answer.
5. What is the value of aggression?
6. Why isn't success in battle enough of a reinforcer?

11

Learned Reinforcers and Learned Aversive Conditions

FUNDAMENTALS

Example of a Learned Reinforcer
Behavioral Clinical Psychology
PSYCHOTIC TALK

"Dr. Baker, the superintendent is still tryin' to get into my bed every night, but I always fight him off. I can't afford another illegitiate child," Helen said.[1]

As she talked, Helen jerked her head from side to side, throwing her uncombed brown hair over the shoulders of her faded pink print dress—her favorite dress. She had brought that old dress with her when she entered the State Psychiatric Hospital 15 years ago. It no longer properly contained her 210 pounds; but she wore it anyway, though her sister often brought new clothes on her monthly visits.

Sixty-three-year-old Helen kept talking, as she sat on the patient's side of the ancient oak desk in the psychology consulting room of Big State Hospital. Dawn sat on the other side. Helen fidgeted about in her chair, while talking. Dawn remained quiet, staring out the window.

When Helen paused for a few seconds, Dawn asked, "So, what activities did you take part in yesterday?" As Helen rambled on, Dawn devised an intervention she hoped would help Helen reduce her psychotic talk.

The next day at the staff meeting, Dawn said, "Let me propose a program for Helen."

---

[1]Based on Ayllon, T., & Michael, J. (1959). The psychiatric nurse as a behavioral engineer. *Journal of the Experimental Analysis of Behavior, 2*, 323–334; and Ayllon, T., & Haughton, E. (1964). Modification of symptomatic verbal behavior of mental patients. *Behavior Research and Therapy, 2*, 87–97. The data in the accompanying figure are based on the first article.

One of the psychiatric nurses replied, "I hope you've got something powerful, because Helen's getting into serious trouble. She's constantly under the delusion that men are chasing her and that she has an illegitimate child. She bothers the other residents with her constant talk about the men and her child; they've even started beating her up to stop her talking. We try to protect her, but we don't always get there in time."

The head nurse said, "I doubt if you can do much. She's suffered from these delusions for the last 3 years, and we've done everything imaginable to help her. I'm afraid she has nothing else to talk about."

The psychiatrist said, "Helen is delusional. She has a distorted perception of reality based on her inner conflicts. She feels she must express her troubles to someone else to get free. Her problems are symptoms of deep-rooted psychic disorders."

As her colleagues talked, Dawn thought: No, her problems are not symptoms of deep-rooted psychic disorders; they're the result of an unfortunate behavioral history. Her problems are not psychic excrement squeezed out of her mental toothpaste tube by the firm grip of irresistible psychic forces. Your mentalistic diagnoses sound impressive, yet they haven't helped Helen much. Out loud, she said, "I'd like you to consider an alternate view, one that may not be easy to understand; but bear with me. Suppose Helen's psychotic, delusional talk is just like any other class of complex, learned responses. Suppose she has learned the response class of delusional speech because it has produced reinforcers. Then perhaps we can use the principles of reinforcement to deal with the problem."

"That doesn't make much sense to me, Dr. Baker," the psychiatrist said. "What could possibly be reinforcing her delusional speech? I don't think anyone's going around putting M&M's in her mouth every time she experiences one of her delusions."

"Yes, Dr. Jones," Dawn replied, "I'm sure no one is giving her M&M's. But many of the reinforcers that control our behavior are not unlearned, innate biological reinforcers; they're not like the sweet taste of candy. So when we look for obvious unlearned reinforcers, we often miss the more subtle **learned** *reinforcers*—the ones really maintaining the behavior."

"Like what?" Jones asked.

"Well, some of the most powerful learned reinforcers are social reinforcers—reinforcers provided by other people—reinforcers such as approval and sometimes simply attention," Dawn answered.

"But surely no one approves of her delusional speech," the psychiatrist said. "Instead, we criticize her for it."

"I know it sounds strange, but sometimes even negative attention is more reinforcing than no attention. This is common in large institutions, where there's not enough staff to interact adequately with the residents. One of the best ways to get attention in such a place is to act bizarre. Then the staff, or other residents, or visitors will pay attention to you. Even when our attention is in the form of criticism, we often unintentionally reinforce that bizarre behavior."

"That makes some sense to me," a psychiatric nurse said. "But we need to talk to her when she's having her delusions. We need to reassure her and bring her back to reality."

"I know what you mean," Dawn said. "But that puts us in a bind, because warm, gentle reassuring talk is most likely a powerful reinforcer. So in our efforts to get Helen out of her delusions, we may unintentionally reinforce those same delusional behaviors—we may make future delusions more frequent."

"I often don't have time to talk to her in detail," another psychiatric nurse said, "but I at least nod and say something like 'Yes, I understand.' It seems so rude to ignore her."

"Yes, it seems awkward to ignore people, but often, when they're behaving inappropriately, that would be best for them," Dawn said.

"Do you mean we should ignore her for the rest of the day, whenever she has a delusion? That seems too cruel."

"I agree," Dawn said. "We should ignore her only while she's talking in a delusional way. We should go out of our way to pay attention to her when she's talking in a normal way. That way we're

extinguishing inappropriate behavior and reinforcing appropriate behavior."

"I'm skeptical that such a superficial approach is going to achieve anything, but I'm willing to try it," Jones said.

"I don't blame you for being skeptical, Dr. Jones," Dawn said. "One of the reasons I have some confidence in this intervention is that it's the same one Ayllon and Michael used with a similar case way back in 1959. It worked then, so it should work now. I appreciate your willingness to try it, so we can find out."

The Intervention

During the intervention, the nurses would check Helen every half hour. They would ignore her if she was talking in a psychotic manner but would pay attention to her if she was talking normally. For the week before the intervention, 91% of Helen's talk was psychotic. By the end of the first 9 weeks of intervention, her psychotic talk dropped to less than 25% (Figure 11.1). This was a dramatic change, especially considering the complex nature of the response class and its high frequency of occurrence for at least 3 years.

During the last 3 weeks of the intervention, some unforeseen bootleg ("illegal") reinforcement interfered with Helen's progress. In the 10th week, Helen talked to a traditional social worker who reinforced the psychotic talk. As Helen told a nurse, "Well, you're not listening to me. I'll have to see Miss Johnson again because she told me she could help me if I talked about my past."

It looks like attention was a strong reinforcer. It increased the psychotic talk in the presence of the social worker, and it also increased such talk on the ward when the social worker was absent. The psy-

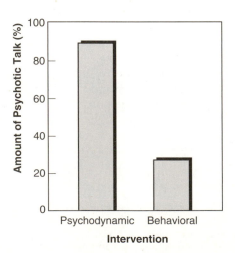

Figure 11.1   Differential Reinforcement of Normal Talk for a Woman in a Psychiatric Ward

chotic talk doubled to become about 50% of her total talk. Other sources of unauthorized reinforcement occurred when a volunteer ladies' organization came to entertain the residents and also when an institution employee came to visit the ward. In both cases, the visitors reinforced the psychotic talk by paying attention to Helen when she talked that way. After this bootleg reinforcement, it took several weeks before the staff was able to get Helen's frequency of psychotic talk back down to its lower level. To maintain their extinction program, they had to exert extreme care in getting the cooperation of everyone who interacted with Helen.

When Ted Ayllon and Jack Michael did the real study on which we based our story, most of the work you read in this book had not been done. It took intellectually independent people with much imagination to think of psychotic talk as reinforced behavior. It also took courage to test a technique for extinguishing this psychotic talk, especially because no one had tried it before.

QUESTIONS

1. What are some mentalistic interpretations of the causes of psychotic talk?
2. What are some objections to a behavioral analysis and intervention for psychotic talk?
3. Diagram the use of differential reinforcement to reduce psychotic talk.
4. What happened when Helen's psychotic talk received bootleg reinforcement after a few weeks of the extinction procedure?

Concept
HOW ARE LEARNED REINFORCERS ACQUIRED?

Remember the definition of *unlearned reinforcer: a stimulus, event, or condition that is a reinforcer, though not as a result of pairing with another reinforcer.* So it won't take too much imagination to guess the definition of a *learned reinforcer:*

Definition: Concept

Learned reinforcer (secondary or conditioned reinforcer)

- A stimulus, event, or condition that is a reinforcer
- because it **has** been paired with another reinforcer.

Attention may be a good example. We've suggested that attention was a powerful learned reinforcer for Helen. If attention was a learned reinforcer, that means it hadn't always been a reinforcer for Helen. Helen was not born with attention acting as a reinforcer for her behavior. Instead, only through learning did attention become a reinforcer for Helen's behavior. Attention became a learned reinforcer because it was often paired with other reinforcers when she was a baby. What are some other reinforcers normally available to Helen the baby, only if she had someone's attention? Water. Cuddling. Baby talk.

Pairing Procedure

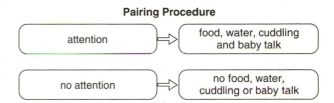

Again, Helen was not born with attention functioning as a reinforcer. It took many pairings of attention with other reinforcers for attention to become a reinforcer. Once attention becomes a learned reinforcer, it functions just like an unlearned reinforcer. It increases the frequency of any behavior it immediately follows. The following reinforcement contingency shows how smiling can be reinforced by attention. If the behavior did not increase in future frequency, attention would not have been functioning as a reinforcer.

Reinforcement

Before we go on, please take another look at the pairing—procedure diagram. Note that the pairing procedure actually involves two pairings: The top pairing is the pairing of attention with food, etc. But for that to be meaningful, we must also have the bottom paring—the pairing of no attention with no food, etc. (or at least the food, etc. is not as probable, when there is no attention). In other words, if we pair a neutral stimulus with an original reinforcer, logically that means that the absence of that stimulus is paired with the absence of that reinforcer. Please keep this in mind when you generate your own examples of the pairing procedure or deal with them on quizzes. But now back to Helen

What about Helen the adult? Even an adult must have someone's attention before getting food in a restaurant, gasoline at a full-service pump, or conversation at home.

Pairing Procedure

attention	⇒ food, gasoline, or conversation
no attention	⇒ no food, gasoline, or conversation

We are all such social animals that attention is paired with many of our most important reinforcers from the day we're born until the day we die.

Attention is a powerful but sneaky reinforcer; it often controls our behavior without our knowing it. What do you think is a hidden reinforcer that controls your professor's lecturing? If you're not sure, try falling asleep. What reinforces telling a joke? Try walking away in the middle of someone's joke to find out.

Often social approval goes hand in hand with attention, but not always, as in Helen's case, in which attention maintained inappropriate behavior in spite of the disapproval. In some circles, belching and flatulence produce reinforcing attention, though not approval. (If you don't know what flatulence means, grab your dictionary.) Do you know people, other than your professors, who run in such circles?

Incidentally, it's not clear how immediate the pairing should be between the neutral stimulus and the reinforcer. We would assume within a few seconds. Maybe no more than a fraction of a second should elapse between the presentation of the neutral stimulus and the reinforcer. It also may be that the onset of the neutral stimulus should slightly precede the onset of the reinforcer. But the main point is that probably no professional behavior analyst would expect to establish a learned reinforcer if, say, an hour, or even several minutes, elapsed between the neutral stimulus and the reinforcer. We'll call this pairing of a neutral stimulus and a reinforcer or aversive condition the *pairing procedure,* and we'll describe the results in terms of the *value-altering principle.*[2]

Definition: Procedure

Pairing procedure

- The immediate pairing of a neutral stimulus with
- a reinforcer or aversive condition.

Definition: Principle

Value-altering principle[3]

- The pairing procedure
- converts a neutral stimulus into
- a learned reinforcer or learned aversive condition.

Note that we include *immediate* in the definition of *pairing procedure;* probably the two stimuli or conditions being paired must be paired within a few seconds. For example, suppose you were working with an autistic girl, and you were trying to create a learned reinforcer out of the statement *good girl* by pairing *good girl* with other reinforcers such as little bites of favorite foods. You sure as heck wouldn't want to say *good girl* and then give her the bite of food an hour later; you'd be doomed to failure. A delay of no more than a fraction of a second would come much nearer to doing the trick.

In summary, a neutral stimulus, event or condition becomes a learned reinforcer when it has been paired with an original reinforcer. This original reinforcer could be an unlearned reinforcer. But the original reinforcer might also, itself, be a learned reinforcer that had previously acquired its reinforcing value through pairing with some third reinforcer.[4]

QUESTIONS

1. *Learned reinforcer*—define it and give a couple of examples and show how they might have acquired their reinforcing value.
2. *Pairing procedure*—define it.
3. *Value-altering principle*—define it.

---

[2]In Chapter 21, you will learn about respondent conditioning. In that chapter we will explain the difference between respondent and operant conditioning.

[3]We introduced these two concepts in the third edition of *Elementary Principles of Behavior (EPB 3.0),* because we found that students were not focusing adequately on how learned reinforcers and learned aversive conditions are acquired.

[4]In Chapter 12, you will learn about discriminative stimuli. It may be that to become a learned reinforcer, the neutral stimulus must serve as a discriminative stimulus (sort of a "cue") for the contingency involving the unlearned reinforcer. For example, it may be that the reason the dipper click becomes a learned reinforcer because it also functions as a stimulus in the presence of which approaching the water dipper will be reinforced with a drop of water. In other words, it may take more than the mere pairing of the click and the water for the click to become a learned reinforcer.

*Example of the Pairing Procedure
and Learned Reinforcers
Behavioral Special Education*
SOCIALIZING JIMMY

Jimmy has had a hard time learning the functional behaviors and the functional values kids normally have—behavior and values kids normally learn without our hardly noticing that they're learning them. But Jimmy all too easily learned and got hooked on the dysfunctional behaviors and dysfunctional values most kids normally don't learn or pass through only briefly. As we've said, Jimmy's learning history was so dysfunctional that traditional psychologists have labeled him autistic.

Often children with serious deficits in learned behaviors have not learned to value attention and approval; in other words, neither attention nor approval are social reinforcers. Somehow the normal pairing of attention and approval with other reinforcers (food, comfort, play) does not work nearly as well with a few kids as it does with most kids. And Jimmy was one of those few kids whom the normal pairing had failed.

So what's the consequence of Jimmy's failure to learn to value attention and approval? Catastrophic. We human beings are such socialized animals that we hardly notice how dependent we are on the finely tuned interactions among us. For example, our children's behavior is constantly being shaped by our attention and approval.

"Oh, look what Rod did. Isn't that cute?"

"Rod, Daddy's so proud of you!"

Or much more subtle—a glance of approval, a smile, eye contact, or even a slight turn of Dawn's head in Rod's direction—all ways of approving or paying attention. All big reinforcers for Rod and most other kids, but not for Jimmy.

Here's why we think this is so important. We think that most of what we all consider normal human behavior we learn from other human beings. And one of the crucial ways we learn normal human behavior is through social reinforcement in the form of approval and attention.

So if attention and approval aren't learned reinforcers for Jimmy, he won't learn to act like a normal human being. That's how catastrophic it is. He will be so different from a normal human being that he will be considered autistic—a psychotic child.

So what was one of Mae's first steps in teaching Jimmy how to function like human beings normally do? She and her staff did a lot of pairing of attention and approval with powerful reinforcers. Remember:

Eve: Jimmy, touch your nose.

Jimmy did.

Eve: GOOD BOY, JIMMY! (And she gave the slightly hungry Jimmy a quarter spoonful of cereal and skimmed milk.)

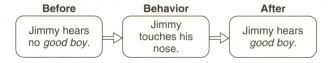

A lot of learning occurred in that single, discrete learning trial.

Not only would Jimmy's nose touching be more frequent when he was requested to do so, but for our present concern, *Good boy, Jimmy* was being paired with the powerful unlearned reinforcer of food.

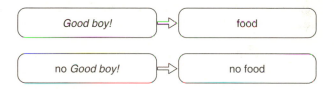

With enough pairings of a variety of forms of attention and approval with a variety of powerful reinforcers, Jimmy will continue to value attention and approval just as much as the rest of us do.

Then Mae's staff will be able to use these learned social reinforcers as the main tool in teaching Jimmy, and eventually they will be able to largely do away with the unlearned reinforcers such as food. That's important for two reasons: First, it will prepare Jimmy for a regular-education classroom where social reinforcers are a major tool. And second, it will prepare Jimmy for the incidental teaching that normally takes place during a child's interaction with others, especially his parents.

*The Generalized Reinforcer
Behavioral Clinical*
A TOKEN ECONOMY
FOR PSYCHOTICS

After Ted Ayllon did the pioneering work on which we based Helen's case history of psychotic talk, he got his PhD and moved to Anna State Hospital, in Carbondale, Illinois. There he worked with Dr. Nathan Azrin doing the first research with token economies in teaching and maintaining normal behavior of psychotic residents in a psychiatric institution. As with Ayllon's earlier work, this research involved psychiatric residents who had been on the back wards for many years. These people were women suffering from severe problems with verbal and social behavior.[5]

The structure of the token economy on this ward is so interesting it deserves special comment. The residents earned little metal tokens by making responses useful to the residents as a group, such as serving meals, cleaning floors, sorting laundry, selling items in the commissary, projecting movies, leading guided tours, and helping the nurse. The residents also earned tokens for other behaviors such as self-grooming.

They could exchange the tokens for backup reinforcers (the reinforcers with which the learned reinforcers had been paired). For example, residents with sufficient tokens (4 to 30) could pay for a particular bedroom and thus indirectly select their roommates. Residents who didn't rent a special bedroom slept in the free room. They could get a choice of eating groups (1 token) and secure locked cabinets to store their belongings (1 token). They could rent a personal chair that they didn't have to share with other residents (1 token). They also could use 1 token to rent a room divider to shield their bed. With 2 tokens, they could obtain escorted or unescorted leaves from the ward. They could exchange 100 tokens for a 1-hour, escorted visit to a neighboring town. A 10-minute private meeting with a member of the staff cost from 20 to 100 tokens, and they could extend it by using additional tokens. (They didn't need tokens for the first 5 minutes of social interaction with the ward physician, nurse, and institution chaplain.) They could exchange from 1 to 10 tokens for participation in religious services of the resident's choice.

Other backup reinforcers consisted of movies, a live dance band, exclusive use of a radio or television set, and attendance at institution activities such as dances (all from 1 to 3 tokens). In addition, with tokens they could get such consumable items such as extra clothing, grooming accessories, reading and writing materials, and a choice of items by special request such as potted plants and parakeets (1 to 400 tokens).

How do we establish learned reinforcers? We pair them with existing reinforcers. Attention probably became and continued to be a learned reinforcer for Helen (and for the rest of us) because it had been and continues to be paired with the receipt of many other reinforcers—food, conversation, service. But in the case of Ayllon and Azrin's token economy, the participants were verbal adults, so the pairing could be a verbal analog to pairing rather than direct pairing itself; the staff could establish the to-

kens as a sort of learned reinforcer simply by telling the participants they could exchange them for various backup reinforcers. Ayllon and Azrin didn't have to do direct pairing.[6]

The tokens Ted and Nate used in this study had a wide utility because the residents could exchange their tokens for a variety of reinforcers. We call this type of reinforcer a **generalized learned reinforcer**.

Definition: Concept

Generalized learned reinforcer (generalized secondary reinforcer or generalized conditioned reinforcer)[7]
- A learned reinforcer that is a reinforcer
- because it was paired with a **variety** of other reinforcers
- when the organism has been deprived of those other reinforcers.

In other words, a generalized learned reinforcer is a special type of learned reinforcer. A stimulus, event, or condition can become a learned reinforcer solely from pairing with a **single type** of backup reinforcer. But a **generalized** learned reinforcer must be paired with a **variety of other types** of reinforcers, like the many privileges the psychiatric residents could buy with their tokens. Normally those different backup reinforcers should be associated with different deprivations.

A learned reinforcer is effective only if the organism is deprived of the other reinforcers with

---

[5]Based on Ayllon, T., & Azrin, N. H. (1965). The measurement and reinforcement of behavior of psychotics. *Journal of the Experimental Analysis of Behavior, 8*, 357–383.

[6]Ted and Nate also took advantage of the residents' verbal skills in another crucial way. As you will see in the final chapters of this book, the behavioral contingencies are actually indirect-acting, rule-governed analogs to reinforcement, rather than direct-acting reinforcement contingencies. The staff told the residents what the contingencies were; in other words, the staff gave the residents rules describing those contingencies (for example, *If you make your bed, you will get some tokens*). It was the statement of the rules describing the contingencies rather than the contingencies themselves that controlled the residents' behavior, at least initially. This is especially true to the extent that the staff gave the residents the tokens at the end of each day rather than immediately. But don't worry too much about this now, as we'll get into rule-governed behavior in more detail starting with Chapter 22.

[7]To the instructor: As you know, we don't introduce the distinction between operant and respondent conditioning until Chapter 21. And, in the mean time, we studiously avoid *condition* in conjunction with any operant phenomenon, because we think using *conditioned* in both the operant and respondent contexts makes a hard discrimination even harder. Thus, we use *learned* with regard to operant phenomena and *conditioned* with regard to respondent phenomena. But we also introduce the *conditioned* terminology as we go along for those instructors who are less fastidious—or less superstitious.

which it acquired its reinforcing properties. Because generalized learned reinforcers acquired their value through pairing with a variety of other reinforcers, the organism need not be deprived of any specific reinforcer. But it's likely the organism would be deprived of at least some relevant type of reinforcer. For that reason, generalized learned reinforcers will be effective most of the time.

In a token economy, a resident would not normally have just consumed all her potential backup reinforcers during the previous day or even the previous week. So, in that sense, she would have been deprived of at least some backup reinforcers. For example, even if they had just gone for a walk, she probably hadn't just talked to the chaplain, or just seen the movie of the week, or just had acccss to a valuable grooming accessory. So generalized learned reinforcers, such as tokens, are useful in behavioral interventions because the odds are high that at least one backup reinforcer will be enough of a reinforcer that the generalized learned reinforcer will act as a reinforcer.

Definition: Concept
Token Economy
- A system of generalized learned reinforcers
- in which the organism that receives those generalized reinforcers can save them
- and exchange them for a variety of backup reinforcers
- later.

Incidentally, some token economies may have deadlines. For example, if you don't redeem your coupon before the end of the year, it won't be valid. Also, notice that this definition somewhat stretches the meaning of "token." *Tokens* normally imply a distinct set of items you can hold in your hand: subway tokens, casino tokens, poker chips, money. We think that's too restricting; it would rule out too many token economies where the "tokens" are marks on a sheet of paper rather than a set of distinct objects the participants can handle.

The Ayllon and Azrin study gives us some insight even into our own economic system. In their study, tokens functioned like money functions for you and me. Tokens are generalized learned reinforcers, and so is money. Both tokens and money have acquired their reinforcer value either through direct pairing or verbal pairing with other reinforcers.

But the main practical purpose of Ted and Nate's experiment was to show how a small staff can administer a token economy for 44 psychiatric residents, 24 hours a day, 7 days a week. (The staff consisted of a behavior analyst, a nurse, and five attendants—by the way, this is the typical staff-resident ratio.) Such a token economy allows us to work with a large number of residents at a single time. These procedures also have been valuable in applications at other institutions; and they have brought hope to normally hopeless situations.

Oh, yes, we got so excited describing the procedure, we almost forgot about the results. Success city: The frequency of various appropriate behaviors went way up. Each of the participating residents worked productively for the 6 hours available each day (Figure 11.2).

We should mention that you don't get great results like this by accident, especially when you're breaking new turf like Ted and Nate were; they spent a year and a half doing preliminary research before starting this experiment. Nothing that good comes easily, at least not in science.

QUESTIONS

1. *Generalized learned reinforcer*—define it and give an example.
2. Describe research on a token economy in a psychiatric hospital:
   - Who were the participants?
   - What were some responses?
   - What were some backup reinforcers?
   - How did the behavior analysts establish the tokens as generalized learned reinforcers?
   - What were some results?

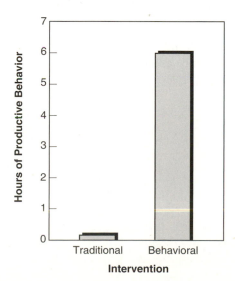

Figure 11.2   Using a Token Economy to Increase Average Daily Productive Behavior per Resident on a Psychiatric Ward

Concept
Behavioral School Psychology
THE TOKEN ECONOMY
AND REMEDIAL EDUCATION

Dr. Montrose Wolf and his colleagues at the University of Kansas headed a project to help culturally deprived children hurdle the barriers to a sound education. They helped 16 fifth-grade and sixth-grade students, who were all at least 2 years below their grade level on a reading achievement test. The children were from a low-income neighborhood in Kansas City. Most were from families of more than five children. The families got welfare support, and often no father was present. The parent or parents voluntarily enrolled the children in Mont's remedial class.[8]

Mont and his colleagues set up the classroom in the basement of a church. During the school year, the students attended the special classroom each weekday after school and on Saturday mornings for 2½ years. During summer, they attended school every morning, except Sunday.

They used a token economy that resembled a trading-stamp plan. The learned generalized reinforcers consisted of checkmarks the teacher placed in the students' folders after they had finished an assignment correctly. When the children first joined the program, the teacher gave them this learned generalized reinforcer after the satisfactory completion of each problem. As the students achieved a higher frequency of work and a more accurate output, the work needed to obtain the learned generalized reinforcers gradually increased in amount and difficulty. Sometimes students negotiated with the teacher the number of checkmarks a particular amount of work would earn.

The students could exchange these learned generalized reinforcers for various backup reinforcers:

- weekly field trips involving circuses, swimming, zoos, picnics, sporting events, and movies
- daily snacks, sandwiches, fruit, milk, and cookies, for exchange of the checkmarked pages
- money and items available in the school store, such as candy, toiletries and novelties; more expensive reinforcers, with the exchange of large numbers of tokens, such as clothing, watches, and secondhand bicycles

---

[8]Based on Wolf, M., Gives, D. K., & Hall, R V. (1967). Experiments with token reinforcements in a remedial classroom. Unpublished manuscript.

- a shopping trip to a local department store for any child who accumulated two dollars' worth of checkmarks

The children earned these tokens for three general types of activities:

- completed work from the regular classroom
- completed homework assignments and remedial work in the remedial classroom
- good 6-week report card grades (an A paid off maximally and an F paid off not at all)

The teachers also used other reinforcer-based procedures with the students:

- They made participation in favorite subjects or academic activities contingent on the completion of less favored academic work. (Thus the opportunity to do popular academic work was a reinforcer for doing less popular academic work. Tricky, eh?)
- They often reinforced academic productivity by letting the productive students instruct other students in their deficient areas.
- They allowed the productive students to grade the assignments of the other students. Even trickier, eh?
- They also gave a large bonus each month to every student who had perfect attendance for that period. The bonus was cumulative: For 2 months' perfect attendance, the bonus was twice as large; for 3 months' perfect attendance, the bonus was three times as large; and so forth.
- They held a party every 6 weeks for the students whose grade average improved. The parties involved such activities as dining in a restaurant, camping, and going on plane rides.
- On Saturdays, the students formed group games similar to TV college quiz contests with two students on each team. They competed against one another for the bonus checkmarks the teacher gave to the team with the most correct responses. The students could choose their partners; and, of course, everyone wanted a teammate who could answer the most questions—the academically skilled. The regular students sought the good scholars as heroes, much as they sought the good athletes on the playground.
- As if this were not enough, the behavior analysts developed an additional method for the presentation of social reinforcers for good academic behavior. Each group of students, who

worked with one instructor, competed with the other groups in accumulating public school tests with grades of A. Whenever a student brought in an A paper, the teacher announced it in class and tacked the paper above the student's desk. Each Saturday, the team with the most papers received reinforcers; the members of the team got the candy bars of their choice. The notion of *Saturday's hero* now has a new meaning. The mere idea of such an environment should warm the hearts of the scholars among you.

In addition, the behavior analysts used a few punishment contingencies to decrease inappropriate behavior:

○ An alarm clock rang at three random times during each 2½-hour session. Students got a negative mark after their names on the blackboard if they were out of their seats when the alarm rang.
○ They also got negative marks for any other disruptive behavior, such as hitting another student.
○ Also, the teachers in the public school classrooms could give points and remove store privileges from students who attended their classes. They did this by sending reports to the remedial classroom teacher.[9]

At the end of the day, the student with the fewest negative marks earned a large number of extra positive checkmarks in his or her folder. To put it another way, the other students lost the opportunity to earn those extra reinforcers. That wasn't all: Any student who got more than four negative marks lost a privilege, such as the use of the store at the end of the day.[10]

The behavior analysts also used reinforcers to encourage the parents to support the academic behavior of their children. Wolf and his crew included in the store items of interest to the students' families. The students could purchase those items with the checkmarks they had earned for good work.

The program also involved the use of learned generalized reinforcers for the instructors. So, in that way, Mont Wolf and his colleagues also supported effective instruction. They gave a bonus of 10 dollars to the assistant instructors whenever a student brought in a 6-week report card with a grade average higher than that of the previous 6 weeks.

This is a great arrangement, probably something only a person skilled in the use of learned generalized reinforcers could dream up. But was it effective? Yes. Students often asked to continue their academic work after the remedial session. Also, the students attended about 85% of the remedial classes, though the program regularly met on Saturdays and most holidays. (The students voted to work on school holidays. However, the instructors drew the line at working on Thanksgiving and Christmas day.)

The students worked hard, but did they learn? Yes; the results were impressive. During each of the preceding 2 years, the students had advanced 0.6 year on a scholastic aptitude test. During the year of the token economy, the typical gain was 1.5 years on the SAT. A similar group of students (the control group) who had not been in the learned generalized reinforcer program showed a gain of only 0.8 year in that same period of time. During that year, the report card grade average improved from a *D* to a *C*, while the comparison group showed practically no improvement.[11] (See Figure 11.3.)

Was it cost-effective? Was it worth it? Each student earned $250 during the school year—a small amount of learned generalized reinforcers for the large reinforcer going to the society that makes valuable citizens out of people who might otherwise be lost.

QUESTIONS

1. Describe the use of learned generalized reinforcers to help remedial grade school students:
   a. What were the learned generalized reinforcers?
   b. What were some backup reinforcers?
   c. What were three different reinforcement procedures used?
   d. What was a punishment contingency?
   e. How did the behavior analysts encourage social reinforcement in the classroom?

[9]Probably, the teachers in the public school classrooms would tell the students immediately after the relevant response that they were going to give or remove points, though the actual giving or removing would be done much later by the remedial classroom teacher. And probably a teacher's immediate statement would be a learned reinforcer or a learned aversive condition, depending on whether it involved the promise of giving or removing the points. But the delay between giving and removing and the actual giving and removing are undoubtedly too great for the statements to have acquired their reinforcing and aversive values through the simple pairing procedure defined earlier in this chapter. Instead, those values must have been acquired through some sort of verbal, rule-governed analog to a pairing procedure, a pairing procedure that would not work with animals and nonverbal human beings.

[10]Again, the extra reinforcing and aversive properties these contingencies added to the positive and negative marks must also have been the result of some sort of complex, verbal, rule-governed analog to a pairing procedure.

[11]Of the 16 students, unfortunately, one of the older 6th graders dropped out during the spring term. She married and dropped out of school. So these results don't apply to her.

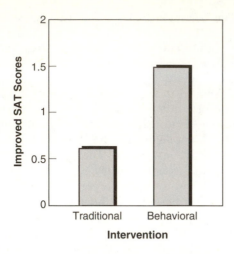

Figure 11.3   Tokens Improve Remedial Education

f. How did they encourage the parent's support of the student's academic performance?
g. What were the academic results?
h. *Token economy*—define it.

Concept
LEARNED AVERSIVE CONDITION

One-year old Rod sat stirring his applesauce with his baby spoon, *making a general mess of things. This irritated Sid.* "**No**, don't do that! **No** I said." Whack! A mild, little smack on Rod's hand.

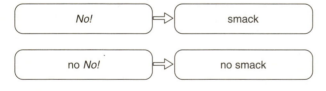

Pairing with Aversive Stimuli

Dawn looked at Sid, wishing he were a little gentler with their baby. On his part, Rod sat there whimpering. But a little later, he started making a mess with his applesauce again. Dawn was quick to intervene before Sid had a chance. All she said was "No." Rod kept messing. "No," again; but this time she immediately took his applesauce and spoon away from him.

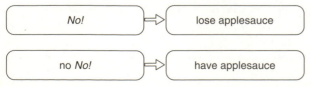

Pairing with Loss of Reinforcers

In this way, *no* was reliably paired with aversive stimuli (like the slap) and with the loss of reinforcers (like the loss of the applesauce). This also was a **value-altering procedure** that caused *no* to become a **learned aversive condition**.

Definition: Concept
Learned aversive condition (secondary or conditioned aversive condition)
  ○ A stimulus, event, or condition that is an aversive condition
  ○ because it has been paired with another aversive condition.

Remember the **value-altering principle?** *The pairing procedure converts a neutral stimulus into a learned reinforcer or learned aversive condition.* Earlier we saw how the value-altering principle describes the creation of learned reinforcers. Now Rod's story shows how the value-altering principle describes the creation of learned aversive conditions. The pairing of *no* with various aversive events and losses of reinforcers is how *no* becomes such a powerful learned aversive condition for all of us. But how do we know *no* was aversive for Rod? Because it punished behavior that preceded it. Of course the combination of *no*'s, slaps, and losses of the applesauce soon formed an effective punishment contingency that suppressed Rod's messing. But eventually all it took was a few *no*'s contingent on some undesirable behavior and that undesirable behavior would stop. That's fairly good proof that *no* had become a learned aversive stimulus. For example, every time Rod started picking at a scab on his knee, Dawn said, "No."

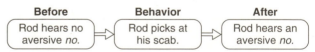

And all it took was a few contingent *no*'s from Dawn for his picking to be sufficiently punished that Rod stopped doing it, and his scrape was allowed to heal.

For most of us, the word *no* has been paired with a variety of aversive stimuli and the loss of a variety of different reinforcers. So, for example, even though we might not be deprived of applesauce, *no* is still aversive. So, just as we have generalized learned reinforcers, we also have generalized learned aversive stimuli. And they probably play a very important role in our lives, though I know of no research done on this topic. (**Generalized learned aversive stimulus**—a learned aversive stimulus or condition that is aversive because it was paired with a variety of other aversive stimuli or conditions and/or the loss of a variety of other reinforcers.)

In summary, a neutral stimulus, event or condition becomes a learned aversive condition when it has been paired with an original aversive condition. And this original aversive condition could be either an unlearned or a learned aversive condition.

QUESTIONS

1. *Learned aversive condition*—define it and diagram an example of creating a learned aversive stimulus by
   ○ pairing with an aversive condition
   ○ pairing with the loss of a reinforcer.
2. Show how we could know that *no* is a learned aversive condition.

Example of the Pairing Procedure and Learned Aversive Conditions
Behavioral Special Education
CONTINUING SOCIALIZATION OF JIMMY

We said that often attention and approval have not become powerful learned reinforcers for children who have not learned many functional behaviors and who have learned many dysfunctional behaviors. But that may be only half the story. We think that often disapproval has not become a powerful learned aversive condition. That means it will be more difficult to use a mild punishment procedure to suppress dysfunctional behavior.

Imagine how difficult it would be to raise a kid for whom *no*, frowns, head shakes, and other forms of disapproval were not powerful learned aversive conditions. In fact, think of all the normal human behaviors you do and the inhuman behaviors you don't do because of the aversiveness of social disapproval. You are polite, you wait your turn, you don't disrupt, you don't shout in the library, you answer questions when asked, you lend a helping hand, and on and on. It may be that social disapproval plays an even more important role than does social approval and attention in helping us learn and interact with one another in a normal, civilized manner.

So you can well imagine that the staff at Mae's school worked hard to establish disapproval as a powerful aversive condition for Jimmy.

Eve: **NO**, Jimmy! Stop flapping your hands! **NO**!

Then Eve used physical restraint; she forcefully held Jimmy's hands in his laps until he stopped trying to flap them. Physical restraint is usually aversive for most people, as it seemed to be for Jimmy.

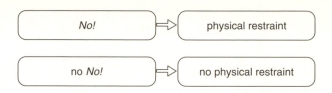

The aversive physical restraint is paired with *no*. So *no* is becoming an aversive stimulus, as are Eve's frown and her disapproving tone of voice. After enough pairings, generally, the staff and teachers will be able to stop using unlearned physical aversive stimuli such as physical restraint and will be able to rely on learned aversive disapproval. This will also prepare Jimmy to continue learning and performing appropriately when he enters the regular-education classroom and when he interacts with others, such as his parents, in a variety of locations.

Concept
HOW ARE LEARNED REINFORCERS AND AVERSIVE CONDITIONS UNLEARNED?

What happens if we stop pairing the learned reinforcer with some other reinforcer? What happens, if we stop pairing *Good boy*! with food?

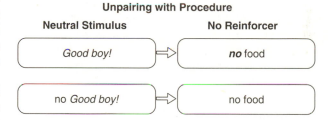

Then *Good boy*! will lose it's reinforcing value for Jimmy.

And what happens if we stop pairing the learned aversive stimulus or condition with some other aversive stimulus or condition? What happens, if we stop pairing *No*! With physical restraint?

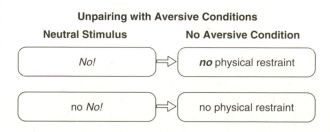

You guessed it; *No*! will lose it's aversive value.

Unpairing happens most often as a result of failing to immediately present the original reinforcer (or original aversive condition) after the learned reinforcer or aversive condition, but there's another way we can do the unpairing. We could have food continuously available. Then the food would be no more paired with "Good boy!" than with anything else.

Extinction vs. the Unlearning of Learned Reinforcers and Aversive Conditions

The unlearning of a learned reinforcer consists of no longer pairing the learned reinforcer with the original reinforcer. This is not extinction. Extinction consists of no longer making a reinforcer *contingent* on a response. You just saw a diagram of the unpairing procedure. Here's a diagram of the extinction procedure.

Extinction Procedure

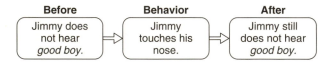

Before	Behavior	After
Jimmy does not hear *good boy*.	Jimmy touches his nose.	Jimmy still does not hear *good boy*.

The results of unpairing and extinction differ as well. As a result of umpairing, a reinforcer (or aversive condition) loses its reinforcing (or aversive) value. As a result of extinction, response frequency of a previously reinforced response decreases.

QUESTIONS

1. Give an example of how learned reinforcers and learned aversive conditions are unlearned.
2. Show how this differs from extinction.

Concept
CONDITIONAL STIMULUS

You've got a quiz over this book, and you haven't opened it since the last quiz. No big deal. But as you get closer and closer to quiz time with your book still collecting dust, the deal gets bigger and bigger. You start getting more and more anxious. The situation is getting more and more aversive. You're not quite breaking out into a cold sweat, but almost. Finally, it's so aversive that you make the escape response, you pick up your book and start studying. And the

aversiveness starts to decrease. After you've read, underlined, reread, reviewed the section questions, and memorized the definitions, you're ready to ace the quiz. You're confident. The situation has lost almost all of its aversivness, even though it's almost time for the quiz.

So what was the aversive situation? Not having studied the book? No, you've spent most of your life without studying this book; and though you may have been ignorant of behavior analysis, that was not necessarily an aversive condition. And as we just saw, being close to quiz time was not, in itself, aversive. It's a combination of being close to quiz time without having studied, without being prepared; that's what's aversive. We call such combination situations, *conditional stimuli*. Here, *conditional* means *dependent*. Not having studied is aversive, only as quiz time approaches; not having studied is aversive conditional on (dependent on) being near time for the quiz. Or, to put it the other way, being quiz time is aversive, conditional on not having studied.

Here's another one: As you are about to leave for the big Saturday-night party, Mom says, "You look very nice, dear." You immediately check yourself out in the mirror to see what's wrong, because you know, if mother likes it, you certainly won't. Her intended compliment functioned as an insult, not a reinforcer but an aversive stimulus. On the other hand, when your date says, "Hey, like, you look terrific," the compliment is a compliment, a powerhouse reinforcer. Whether the intended compliment is a reinforcer or aversive condition is conditional on its source.

Some stimuli may be learned reinforcers or aversive stimuli **only** when they occur in the presence of some other stimulus conditions.

> *Definition: Concept*
> **Conditional stimulus**
> ○ Elements of a stimulus
> ○ have their value or function
> ○ only when they are combined;
> ○ otherwise, the individual elements are relatively neutral.

QUESTIONS

1. Define *conditional stimulus*.
2. Give an example of a conditional aversive stimulus
3. Diagram a contingency illustrating that one of the elements is aversive.

LEARNED REINFORCERS AND LEARNING LANGUAGE

Babies begin to babble long before they begin to talk. Ever notice that babies tend to "babble" in their own language? Listen to a Japanese baby babble, and it will sound like Japanese. Why?

We've seen how neutral stimuli paired with unlearned reinforcers become learned reinforcers. When these pairings first take place for an infant, many neutral stimuli can acquire reinforcing properties. The parents talk when feeding, diapering, and taking care of their baby. And the sounds of the parent's talking is paired with those reinforcers (food, comfort, etc.); so the parents' vocal sounds become learned reinforcers.

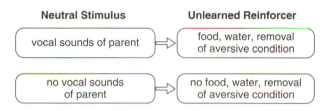

When the baby begins to produce vocal sounds, those sounds are learned reinforcers that automatically reinforce the behavior of emitting them.

But it doesn't stop there. Sounds that are more like the parent's speech are more reinforcing than sounds that aren't. Therefore, these sounds are differentially reinforced and we get variable-outcome shaping.

Differential Reinforcement

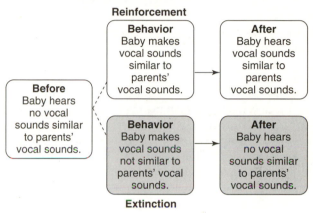

Gradually, the nonverbal vocal sounds that the baby makes will begin to sound more and more like language in general and the parents' language in particular, even though the baby's babbles don't yet have any verbal function.

QUESTIONS

1. Why do Japanese babies babble in Japanese and American babies babble in English?

BASIC ENRICHMENT

*In the Skinner Box
Experimental Analysis*
LEARNED REINFORCERS

How do you establish a learned reinforcer for Rudolph? By pairing water with the click of the brass water dipper as it comes up from the water reservoir and strikes the aluminum floor through which it protrudes.

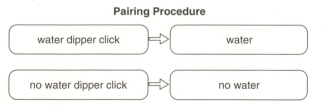

Now according to our value-altering principle, the dipper click should become a learned reinforcer, at least after it's been paired often enough with the water.

This is part of what we call *dipper training.* And it's critical that the dipper click becomes a powerful learned reinforcer, if you're going to succeed in shaping Rudolph's lever pressing. Here's how it works: Rudolph is in the other side of the cage. He turns slightly toward the lever, and you click the dipper. Because the click of the dipper has become a learned reinforcer, that sound reinforced Rudolph's turning toward the lever. Next, you require Rudolph to turn more directly toward the lever before you present the magic dipper click.[12]

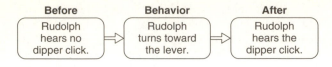

Of course *you* would make sure the time between the click and the water is very brief. So now you've got Rudolph gingerly touching the lever. You've clearly trained a response—touching the lever.

Danger: Here's something that often confuses students. We call a reinforcer a *learned reinforcer* because the value of the stimulus as a reinforcer was learned (a result of the pairing procedure). We don't call a reinforcer a *learned reinforcer* because it causes learning. All reinforcers both learned and unlearned cause learning when they follow a response. For example, water is also a reinforcer that causes learning, but water is an unlearned reinforcer, not a learned one. So all reinforcers can cause learning, but not all reinforcers are learned reinforcers.

Here's another confusion. Rudolph needn't make the response that produces the click in order for the click to become a learned reinforcer. We could completely remove the lever from the Skinner box during the pairing procedure that causes the click to become a learned reinforcer. All we need is the pairing. But, he must make the response that produces the click in order to **demonstrate** that the click has become a learned reinforcer.

And here's a final confusion. Rudolph needn't be deprived of the click for it to be an effective reinforcer. Instead, he must be deprived of the water for the water-based click reinforcer to be effective.

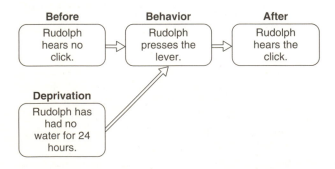

---

[12]But suppose you often clicked the dipper while Rudolph was in the other side of the cage scratching himself. And 5 minutes later he moseyed over to the dipper and got the water. Now that's not exactly what we'd call pairing the click and the water; the delay's way too great. So if you squandered most of your water reinforcers in that unconscionable manner, you'd get what you deserved—a rough time shaping Rudolph's successive approximations to lever pressing.

The same thing applies to Jimmy. Jimmy needn't be deprived of the praise for it to be an effective reinforcer. Instead, he must be deprived of at least one of the unlearned backup reinforcers that have been paired with praise, if praise is to be an effective reinforcer.

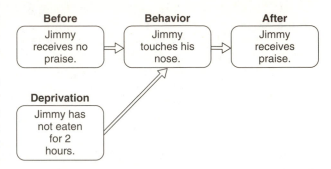

Although not all behavior analysts seem to agree, we think the crucial establishing operation is deprivation of the unlearned backup reinforcer, not deprivation of the learned reinforcer, if that learned reinforcer is to be effective. Furthermore, we think more behavior analysts would agree if they would carefully take the analysis from applied human research back to the Skinner box, where life is a little simpler and much clearer.

Finally, as long as the learned reinforcer is occasionally paired with the unlearned reinforcer, it will continue to reinforce a response, even though that response never produces the unlearned reinforcer. However, as we mentioned earlier, stopping the pairing procedure will cause the learned reinforcer to lose it's reinforcing value (this is not to be confused with operant extinction where the reinforcer is no longer contingent on the response). So the contingent sound of the click would reinforce an arbitrary response such as Rudolph's pulling a chain that dangled from the ceiling of the Skinner box. And the click would maintain the chain pull indefinitely, as long as the click were sometimes paired with water, though that pairing need not follow the chain pulls.

QUESTIONS

1. Diagram the creation of a **learned** reinforcer in the Skinner box.
2. The reason we know water is a learned reinforcer is because it helped Rudolph learn to press the lever.
   (Careful now!)
   a. true
   b. false

3. Must Rudolph make the response that produces the click, in order for the click to **become** a learned reinforcer?
   a. yes
   b. no
4. Must Rudolph make the response that produces the click in order to **demonstrate** that the click has become a learned reinforcer?
   a. yes
   b. no
5. What is the crucial establishing operation for a learned reinforcer to be effective?
   a. deprivation of the learned reinforcer
   b. deprivation of the backup reinforcer (e.g., food that had been paired with praise).

PSYCHOTIC TALK—THE SEEDS OF THE BEHAVIORAL REVOLUTION

In 1959, Ted Ayllon and Jack Michael published the first research showing a behavioral approach to what people call *mental illness* or *psychiatric disorders*. Their research included Helen's case and the case of Lucille the restless resident in Chapter 6. Their article was based on Ted Ayllon's doctoral dissertation; few dissertations have had such an impact on our field.

At that time, I was a doctoral student doing Skinner-box research in the experimental analysis of behavior at Columbia University. The article excited us grad students. We saw it as the forerunner of the application of scientifically established principles to helping psychiatric clients.

Scientists had developed these principles in the laboratory doing experiments with animals. We ourselves were doing this type of basic research, and we loved seeing the results applied to important human problems. At last, we might be able to convince our critics who couldn't see how our research was relevant to human affairs. Ted and Jack showed the relevance. But we thought the article had even greater importance than just convincing the skeptics that we weren't frivolous fops wasting time and money on effete, intellectual games.

The article also showed that it is possible to develop strong ties between the experimental analysis of behavior and applied behavior analysis. The sciences of biology and chemistry support the practice of clinical medicine; and the sciences of physics and chemistry support the practice of engineering. But, unfortunately, the science of experimental psychology did not support the practice of clinical psychology—and, to a large part, it still doesn't. Much, and

perhaps most, of clinical psychology is without scientifically proven practices. Unfortunately, there is little scientific evidence to support traditional clinical psychology. And without that scientific backbone, clinical psychology will never achieve the helpfulness and respect of clinical medicine.

Then came along Ayllon and Michael. They didn't salvage traditional clinical psychology. Instead, their experiment created a whole new field—applied behavior analysis. At last, we had an applied field (applied behavior analysis) with a solid scientific backbone (the experimental analysis of behavior); and, over the last 30-some years, applied behavior analysis has been moving up the steep hill toward achieving the same level of helpfulness and the same level of respect that clinical medicine has earned. In the mean time, traditional clinical psychology has made little progress in that direction.

Behavior analysis has revolutionized the approach to solving human problems, whether those problems be in the traditional areas of clinical psychology, educational and school psychology, special education, social work, or industrial and organizational psychology. We now have a scientifically proven base and scientifically proven practices to help us improve the well-being of humanity. No longer need we rely only on intuition, tradition, and superstition. We have much yet to learn; but now that our science and practice are one, we are systematically understanding more and more of how the human world works and how to help it work better. By whatever name, the experimental analysis of behavior and applied behavior analysis have proven an unbeatable combination.

QUESTION

1. Why was the Ayllon-Michael research so important?

PSYCHOTIC TALK— SEXUAL DISORDERS ARE IN THE EAR OF THE BEHOLDER

Remember Helen's talk about her illegitimate children and the men who were pursuing her? Such talk is typical of the sexual emphasis in the bizarre talk of residents with behavioral problems. Traditional clinical psychologists think this reveals the residents' sexual disorders. However, an analysis of psychotic talk in terms of reinforcement suggests a different picture. Residents with behavioral problems, like anyone else, will make any reinforced response in their repertoire. If the traditional clinicians pay special attention to talk with sexual overtones, this attention will reinforce that type of talk; and the sexual talk will occur more often.

Unintentional Reinforcement Contingency

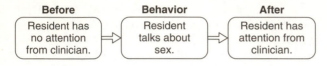

Before	Behavior	After
Resident has no attention from clinician.	Resident talks about sex.	Resident has attention from clinician.

If "deep-seated" sexual disorders exist, they may not be in the resident with the behavioral problems but rather in. . . .

QUESTION

1. Residents of psychiatric institutions often have a high frequency of bizarre talk with a sexual emphasis. Diagram a behavioral interpretation of this phenomenon.

THE MORALITY OF REMEDIAL EDUCATION

In recent years, our society has shown much concern for the culturally disadvantaged. In earlier times, society thought that impoverished people deserved their poverty. Those who were poor were poor by choice. They lacked the moral fiber, the get-up-and-go of the successful. They were lazy and shiftless, deserving nothing better than their lowly status. It was never clear what caused the faulty makeup of the poor. Was it a result of an unfortunate heredity or an impoverished environment? In either case, the rich thought the poor deserved every misfortune that befell them. The successful had no reason to pity the less fortunate. Many years ago, people held similar attitudes about men and women in insane asylums. The notion was that people have behavioral flaws, and they should suffer for them.

Today, most of us strive for a more rational, humanitarian attitude. Now most enlightened people believe we should make every effort to help others overcome the limitations of impoverished backgrounds. We should judge a society not by how it treats its successful, strong, powerful members; but, rather, we should judge a society by how it treats its weak and defenseless members. Many contemporary societies treat their weak and defenseless well—better than any time in history.

Many societies have invested much time, money, and human resources to help the less fortunate. Unfortunately, without an appropriate understanding of the laws of the behavior, the benefits

may not be great. Because of the large contribution behavior analysis is making in helping the less fortunate, we feel good to be part of the behavioral movement. We feel especially proud to be behaviorists when we read about the work of Mont Wolf and his colleagues. Their creative use of learned generalized reinforcers in helping a group of culturally deprived students impresses us.

VALUES AND TASTES

What follows is a set of quotes by famous authors. The quotes are about values and taste. I've inserted in bold, rephrasing in terms of *reinforcers* and *aversive conditions* to illustrate this point (what I replaced are the italicized, parenthetical words): **By *values* and *tastes* we mean reinforcers and aversive conditions, both unlearned and learned.** In this way we can see the relevance of behavior analysis to a major human concern—our values. Of courses these famous authors might roll over in their graves (or her bed, in Sontag's case), if they knew I had behavioralized their works. But we hope you enjoy it.

Values

The least pain in our little finger **is more aversive to us** (*gives us more concern and uneasiness*) than the destruction of millions of our fellow-beings—William Hazlitt (1778–1830).

Home is not a reinforcer (*You can't appreciate home*) till you've left it, money till it's spent, your wife till she's joined a woman's club, nor Old Glory till you see it hanging on a broomstick on the shanty of a consul in a foreign town—O. Henry (1862–1910).

The three **biggest reinforcers** (*most important things*) a man has are, briefly, his private parts, his money, and his religious opinions—Samuel Butler (1835–1902).

Taste

One of the surest evidences of an elevated taste is the **reinforcing power of** (*power of enjoying*) works of impassioned terrorism, in poetry, and painting. The man who can look at impassioned subjects of terror with a feeling of exultation may be certain he has an elevated taste—Benjamin Haydon (1786–1846).

The discovery of the **reinforcing value** (*good taste*) of bad taste can be very liberating. The man who insists on high and serious **reinforcers** (*pleasures*) is depriving himself of **reinforcers** (*pleasure*); he continually restricts what he can enjoy; in the constant exercise of his good taste he will eventually price himself out of the market, so to speak. Here camp taste supervenes upon good taste as a daring and witty hedonism. It makes the man of good taste cheerful, where before he ran the risk of being chronically frustrated. It is good for the digestion— Susan Sontag (b. 1933).

Taste is nothing but an enlarged capacity for **being reinforced by** (*receiving pleasure from*) works of imagination—William Hazlitt (1778–1830).

I cannot cure myself of that most woeful of youth's follies—thinking that those who care about us will **find reinforcing** (*care for*) the things that **we find reinforcing** (*mean much to us*)—D. H. Lawrence (1885–1930).

So when we say *we value honor, truth, justice, and beauty*, we mean *honor, truth, justice, and beauty are powerful reinforcers for us, and their violation is a powerful aversive condition*. And when people repeat the old hackneyed cop-out, *there's no accounting for taste*, they are not taking into account the science of behavior analysis as illustrated in this chapter. The concepts of the value-altering pairing procedure and learned reinforcers does allow us to account for taste. So we might say, *There's no accounting for taste, unless you're a student of behavior analysis*.

And here's the point of this section: Behavior analysis provides a powerful set of concepts and tools with which we can think about, analyze, and even improve our world. It allows us to address age-old concerns of humankind in new, exciting, productive ways. It provides us with a behavior-analytic world view. And viewing the world of values and taste in terms of learned and unlearned reinforcers and aversive conditions is just one humble instance of this behavior-analytic world view.

INTERMEDIATE ENRICHMENT

Research Methods
PROOF OF A LEARNED REINFORCER

Here's the big question:

1. Is Rudolph's reliable lever touching good evidence that the dipper click is a learned reinforcer?
   a. yes
   b. no

Not bad evidence, but not the best evidence either. His reliable touching isn't bad evidence because it would be so hard to shape successive approximations to the lever touching without the dipper click as a learned reinforcer, especially if you had a fairly large Skinner box. A large box would allow Rudolph to stray far away from the lever and make it real hard to get him moving toward it without the dipper click as a learned reinforcer.

Why isn't reliable touching the best evidence? Because it's always possible, though not probable, that Rudolph could have learned lever touching

without the click, just the water. Maybe you'd have just as good results if Rudolph were deaf and couldn't even hear that click. Not likely, but maybe.

Then what would be better evidence? Empty the water out of the water reservoir and train a new response with just the click, like maybe pushing the lever all the way down. Suppose you managed to move Rudolph from just touching the lever to actually pressing it all the way down, and all you used was the response-contingent dipper click. Then even skeptics would believe you've got a learned reinforcer in that click.

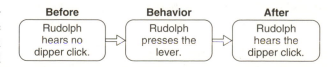

Before	Behavior	After
Rudolph hears no dipper click.	Rudolph presses the lever.	Rudolph hears the dipper click.

But if you wanted to completely freak us out, you might use only the dipper click to train a brand new response, like pulling that chain—the one dangling from the Skinner-box ceiling.

2. Suppose Rudolph were deaf and he still learned to press the lever. Does that mean the water was a learned reinforcer?
   a. yes
   b. no.

Remember that learned reinforcers were originally neutral stimuli that became reinforcers because they had been paired with other reinforcers. Water was a reinforcer, even without such pairing. Just because the water reinforcer helped Rudolph learn lever pressing doesn't make it a learned reinforcer.

QUESTION

1. How would you provide good evidence that the dipper click really was the reinforcer?

Research Methods
DETERMINING THE EFFECTIVENESS OF TOKENS AS REINFORCERS

Ruling out the Environmental Enrichment View

Recall the token economy Ted Ayllon and Nate Azrin used in the psychiatric institution. They asked whether the tokens were acting effectively as reinforcers. Perhaps the residents found the tasks themselves reinforcing enough. Or the use of the tokens might have been an example of superstitious behavior on the part of Ted and Nate. In trying to determine the effectiveness of the tokens as reinforcers, our first suggestion might be to stop giving the tokens altogether. But we have seen in an earlier chapter that such a procedure is not scientifically sound. Why not? When we know something acts as a reinforcer, we are saying that it will increase the frequency of the response that it immediately follows. Perhaps the psychiatric residents' good performance simply resulted from the mere presence of the tokens and the attention the residents received when they got the tokens. Perhaps the attention and the tokens made the residents so happy that they behaved as desired. In other words, perhaps the tokens didn't have to follow the response; it was only necessary to receive the tokens—sort of an environmental enrichment view.

To rule out the environmental enrichment view, we need to make sure the residents still get the tokens but that the tokens don't immediately follow the responses of interest. So Ayllon and Azrin gave the tokens to the residents at the beginning of each day, whether or not they did any work. In that way, the tokens were present but they didn't immediately follow the response.

Over a period of 20 days with noncontingent tokens, the group's work output decreased from 44 hours to only 1 hour per day. We may consider this to be a form of extinction: The individual residents got the potential reinforcers before having an opportunity to make any responses, and later responding didn't produce additional reinforcers. The decrease in the behavior is what we would expect of the extinction procedure. These data suggest that during the contingency phase the tokens were acting as effective reinforcers in maintaining the desired behavior.

Summary: Noncontingent Reinforcers as a Control Procedure

These concepts of research methods are hard to understand; so let's summarize them:

○ Simply withholding the potential reinforcers (extinction) is not a good enough control procedure to demonstrate the operation of a reinforcement contingency. Why? Because withholding the potential reinforcer removes two possible causal variables:
   1. the contingency involving the presentation of those potential reinforcers, and
   2. the potential reinforcers themselves.
○ But, you can **noncontingently** present the potential reinforcers. That way you've removed the contingency (one of the two possible causes), but you haven't gotten rid of the reinforcers themselves. That breaks the confounding. If the potential reinforcers no longer maintain performance when presented noncontingently, we can be sure those potential reinforcers are **real** reinforcers and their **contingent** presentation was crucial.

Ruling out Chance

A skeptic might claim that Ayllon and Azrin were just lucky. Perhaps when they stopped the contingent-reinforcer procedure, the temperature just happened to change, or something else accidentally happened that lowered the response frequency. So this decrease in the work of the residents might not have been due to the noncontingent-reinforcer procedure but rather to some uncontrolled feature. One way to convince the skeptic would be to stop the extinction procedure and reinstate the reinforcement procedure. In other words, use a *reversal design*. When Ayllon and Azrin did this, the total work of the

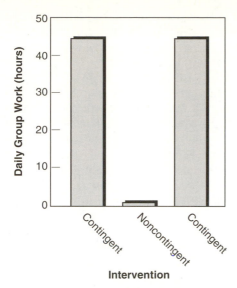

Figure 11.4   Reversal Design Showing the Value of Contingencies

group immediately rose to the preceding average of 44 hours per day, leaving little doubt that the tokens were effectively reinforcing the work (Figure 11.4).

The Flesh Is Willing, But It Needs a Few Reinforcers

Note the relation between what the residents said and what they did. During the first part of the noncontingent-reinforcer phase, several residents continued working for a few days. They said things like this: "I think I'll work even if it is a vacation." "I want to help out here; there aren't enough people to do the work." Yet, eventually, nearly all the residents stopped working. Then the residents said things like this: "I'm not going to do any work if I don't get anything for it." It's probably as true for the rest of us as it is of psychiatric residents: The frequency of our statements about working without reinforcers decrease as the opportunities to do such unreinforced work increase.

Noncontingent Reinforcers as a Control Procedure—Part II

To determine the importance of the contingency, it is better to use noncontingent reinforcers, rather than simply to stop giving the reinforcers (extinction). Why?

To answer this, let's look at another example: The students in my classes work hard and learn a lot. Why? I think it's because I assign a chapter from this book for each class and give them a quiz over that chapter; and the grade they get on each quiz contributes significantly toward their final course grade. In other words, I think the quiz grade is a learned reinforcer. And I think making those quiz grades **contingent** on their quiz performance is crucial. The contingency does the trick.

But I have colleagues who would argue that the contingency is not important. So I might keep making the assignments and keep giving the quizzes, but stop giving any quiz grades. If I did, most of the students would stop studying so hard, would do poorer on the quizzes, and wouldn't learn as much.

I say to my colleagues, "See the grade contingency was important."

But they just laugh at me and say withholding the quiz grades (extinction) doesn't prove a thing. They say I have to keep giving them the good quiz grades, but I should make them independent of their quiz performance—I should remove the contingency but keep the grades. Giving the free grades would show my students how much I respect them and they would study just as hard, and do just as well on the quizzes, and would learn just as much.

I say, "OK, but now, if my students blow off my quizzes, that proves that it was not just the grades that were crucial; it was crucial that the grades actually be contingent on their quiz performance." If my students do well when the grades are contingent and poorly when they're not contingent, that shows the contingency was crucial, not just the presence of the grades themselves.

Leaving the noncontingent grades, but removing the contingency, is a much better control procedure for demonstrating that it is the contingent grades and not just the grades that are the real cause of the studying and excellent quiz performance.

(By the way, the delivery of the quiz grade follows the studying and taking the quiz by more than 60 seconds; so the quiz-grade contingency is not really a reinforcement contingency. As we shall see in Chapter 22, it's an analog to an avoidance contingency.)

QUESTIONS

1. How can you use noncontingent reinforcers to determine the importance of the contingency?
2. To determine the importance of the contingency, it is better to use noncontingent reinforcers, rather than simply to stop giving the reinforcers (extinction). Why?
3. How can you use a reversal design to determine the importance of the contingency?

Concept
IMPRINTED REINFORCERS

The Chick and the Beer Bottle

I learned about the process of **imprinting** in my first term of teaching at Denison University. Several of us were teaching sections of introductory psychology. All the other faculty wanted to have a live classroom demonstration of the principles of behavior. I was reluctant, because the first principle of science education is "Never do an experimental demonstration in class." No matter how many times you have done it in private, as soon as you get in front of a group of students the experiment fails. It's much safer to do the demonstration on the blackboard.

My colleagues decided we should show imprinting. I opposed this because none of us had ever seen such a demonstration. Imprinting may be real, but we had no idea of the problems involved in such a demonstration. Nonetheless, my colleagues, eagerly, and I, reluctantly, began preparing the demonstration.

We needed newly hatched chicks, just a few hours old. We should have deprived the chicks of most visual stimulation from the time they hatched. Such creatures are not common around psych labs, but it happened we had them. By coincidence, some scientists in our department were doing research that involved hatching and rearing chicks in the dark. They were generous enough to take care of our needs.

I remember well the demonstration of imprinting with the chick in my class. I removed the animal from the light-proof transportation box and placed it in the center of a large 4-by-10-foot table with a 1-foot-high cardboard wall around the perimeter. The 30 students in the class immediately crowded around the table to watch. In spite of my insistence that they maintain absolute silence, the students were unable to do so. Their noise and their eager faces peering at the chick over the cardboard wall would ruin the experiment. But I went on with the futile demonstration. I took an empty beer bottle, tied it to one end of a string, and attached the string to a pole. Then I dangled the beer bottle in front of the chick, and after a few seconds it began to approach the bottle. As the bottle moved around in the enclosed space, the chick followed close behind; no matter where the bottle moved, the chick was right there. The demonstration amazed the students, but not nearly so much as it amazed me. This is a demonstration of the ***imprinted reinforcer*—a reinforcer that acquires its unlearned reinforcing properties as a result of being the first stimulus the organism contacts during a brief period shortly after birth.**

The first object the chick saw was the beer bottle. From that time on, the presence of the beer bottle was a strong reinforcer. The presence of the bottle reinforced the chick's response of following it. Normally, the first thing a chick sees is the mother hen; and the presence of the hen becomes reinforcing. So the chick spends most of its time in the presence of that reinforcer. That is the most common course of events; but when we intervened, the chick followed the beer bottle. Researchers have shown imprinting with a variety of birds and a variety of imprinted reinforcers. For example, in some situations a person has become the imprinted reinforcer for the bird; then the bird may constantly follow the person.

Bateson and Reese showed that the imprinted stimulus is truly a reinforcer; they used an imprinted reinforcer to reinforce a key-peck response. The sight of the imprinted mother is a reinforcer, and the bird will do almost anything that keeps the reinforcing sight in view. It will even peck a special response key, if that'll keep the mother in view. But no one other than a behavior analyst would require the bird to peck a key; nature required only that a bird follow its mother to keep her in sight.[13]

By the way, we've appended this section on imprinting to this learned reinforcer chapter, because we think it's a useful concept to have. Not because it's an example of a learned reinforcer. It's not; we might call it an *acquired reinforcer* though; but, in any case, we don't have a better place to put it.

And by the by way, why isn't imprinting a learned reinforcer? Because the procedure for creating an imprinted reinforcer doesn't fit the definition of the procedure for creating a learned reinforcer. Remember, a *learned reinforcer is a* stimulus, event, or condition that is a reinforcer because it has been paired with another reinforcer. But an imprinted reinforcer isn't paired with anything. A stimulus simply becomes an imprinted reinforcer by being the first stimulus the organism contacts during a brief period shortly after birth. And that's not the way a learned reinforcer acquires its reinforcing properties.

Why do we say the imprinted reinforcer is an acquired reinforcer, but not a learned reinforcer? The imprinted reinforcer is not an unlearned rein-

---

[13]Bateson, T. G., & Reese, E. P. (1969). The reinforcing properties of conspicuous stimuli in the imprinting situation. *Animal Behaviour, 17*, 692–699.

forcer, because it's not a reinforcer when the chick is born. And yet, it's not a learned reinforcer, because it doesn't need to be paired with another reinforcer to get its reinforcing value, as is the case with learned reinforcers. So we use the term *imprinted* reinforcer to describe those reinforcer that become reinforcing just as a result of early exposure. And we use the term *acquired reinforcer* to indicate that it is not unlearned but it is also not what we'd call a *learned* reinforcer.

QUESTIONS

1. *Imprinted reinforcer*—describe a demonstration of it.

12 Discrimination

FUNDAMENTALS

Concepts
Behavioral Animal Training
STIMULUS CONTROL, DISCRIMINATION TRAINING, BASED ON REINFORCEMENT, S^D AND S^Δ

The pistol pointed directly at Keller Breland's head. He breathed deeply and stood his ground. The gun sat there, mounted in a frame with one end of a string attached to the trigger. The beak of a live chicken held the other end of the string. If the chicken pulled the string, the gun would fire and the bullet would pierce Breland's head. After standing motionless for several seconds, Breland stepped aside. The chicken immediately pulled the string. The bullet entered the bull's eye of the target placed behind the spot where Keller Breland had been standing. Breland pulled a few kernels of corn from his pocket and fed them to the chicken. Only then did he wipe the perspiration from his forehead.[1]

The man who trained the chicken was Keller Breland, a behavior analyst. Breland was one of Professor Skinner's first graduate students. Breland became famous as an animal trainer, using reinforcement to do such things as train chickens to roller-skate and play baseball and train pigs to do four-brassiered strip-tease acts. For purposes of demonstration, Breland wanted the chicken to fire the gun only when he was not in sight. Breland

didn't want to become behavior analysis's first martyr.

Ah, thoughtful reader, we can see the gleam in your eye as you recognize the principles of reinforcement at work. You suspect that the kernels of corn reinforced the chicken's response of pulling the trigger. And you're right. "But," you may ask, "why didn't the bird shoot the gun when Breland was in its line of fire?" Your first reaction might be that the chicken was chicken, but we trust you wouldn't think of anything that corny. Your second reaction might be that if the chicken had done so, Breland wouldn't have been able to feed it. However, it would be an error of mentalism to imagine that the chicken restrained itself for fear of "killing the behavior analyst who laid the golden kernels."

In previous chapters, we talked about reinforcement and extinction. We used reinforcement to increase the frequency of a behavior and extinction to get rid of a behavior. Now we want to add stimuli to the procedures of reinforcement and extinction. So, if in the presence of a Brelandless target (stimulus), firing the gun (response) results in kernels of corn (reinforcer), the firing response will more frequently occur in the presence of the Brelandless target in the future. In the same way, if in the presence of Breland (stimulus), firing the gun (response) does **not** produce kernels of corn, Breland's presence will make firing **less** frequently in the future. We call the Brelandless target the ***discriminative stimulus*** (S^D) and Breland the ***S-delta*** (S^Δ). A *discriminative stimulus,* or S^D, causes a response because when that stimulus was present in the past, the response produced a reinforcer. The S^Δ makes a response less frequent because when that stimulus was present in the

---

[1]When Marian Breland confirmed the truth of this section, we found that Keller Breland had used a toy pop gun instead of a real one, but the principles we illustrate are the same.

past, the response didn't produce a reinforcer. (You pronounce S^D "ess dee," and you pronounce S$^\Delta$ "ess delta.")

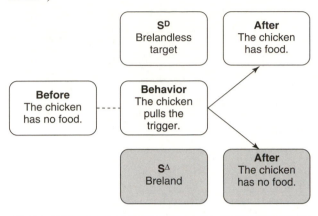

> *Definition: Concept*
> **Discriminative stimulus (S^D)**
> - A stimulus in the presence of which
> - a particular response will be reinforced or punished.

It's crucial to understand that this definition of *S^D* implies there is an S$^\Delta$ in the presence of which that response will less frequently be reinforced or punished.[2]

> *Definition: Concept*
> **S-delta (S$^\Delta$)**
> - A stimulus in the presence of which
> - a particular response will not be reinforced or punished.

Notice the following properties of our diagrams of discriminative contingencies.

- They are really two contingencies, an S^D and an S$^\Delta$ contingency.

- The before condition is the same for both contingencies.
- The response is the same for both contingencies.
- The S$^\Delta$ contingency is always extinction or recovery.

Breland used a ***discrimination training procedure.*** This procedure involves reinforcing one behavior in the presence of one stimulus, S^D (the Brelandless target), and extinguishing the behavior in the presence of another stimulus, S$^\Delta$ (Breland). When the response finally occurs more frequently in the presence of the S^D than in the presence of the S$^\Delta$, we say ***stimulus control*** or ***stimulus discrimination*** has occurred. This is what happened with Breland's **discrimination training procedure.** Stimulus control began to develop until it was perfect. At the end of training, the feathered sharpshooter never fired the gun when Breland was in its sight and always fired it when he wasn't.

> *Definition: Procedure*
> **Discrimination training procedure**
> - Reinforcing or punishing a response
> - in the presence of one stimulus
> - and extinguishing it
> - or allowing it to recover
> - in the presence of another stimulus.

> *Definition: Concept*
> **Stimulus discrimination (stimulus control)**
> - the occurrence of a response more frequently in the presence of one stimulus
> - than in the presence of another,
> - usually as a result of a discrimination training procedure.

---

[2]By the way, notice that in this book our definitions of *S^D* and *S$^\Delta$* are procedural definitions. That means we define them in terms of the procedures used—in this case, in terms of the presence or absence of a reinforcement contingency. In our definition, we don't say anything about whether the organism makes the specific response in the presence of S^D. In other words, whether or not the S^D and S$^\Delta$ exert effective control over the behavior of the organism is not relevant to our procedural definition. Your professor may choose to add the following tag line to our definition of S^D: *and in the presence of which that response will be more likely or less likely to occur.* Whether the response will be more or less likely to occur depending on whether the stimulus is an S^D for reinforcement or punishment.

Here's a more general, though less common, way to define these two concepts: Reinforcement or punishment is more likely in the presence of the S^D and less likely in the presence of the S$^\Delta$. In other words, reinforcement need not always occur in the S^D, and it need not always be withheld in the presence of the S$^\Delta$.

When we say *stimulus* we mean *stimulus condition* or *particular value of the stimulus.* For example, an S^D could be darkness (the light intensity would be at zero); we do **not** apply a dead-stimulus test, or burnt-out lightbulb test.

Finally, what do we mean by ***in the presence of,*** when we define S^D as *a stimulus **in the presence of** which a particular response will be reinforced or punished?* We apply something like the 60-second test we use in our definition of *reinforcer.* In other words, we'd hate to do discrimination training with Rudolph if the light went off more than 60 seconds before Rudy had a chance to press the lever. It would probably be a fruitless exercise. In fact, we're saying 60 seconds exceeds our meaning of *in the presence of,* so we'd have to call that proposed S^D an analog S^D rather than a true S^D. Now, such analog *S^D*s can control the behavior of verbal human beings such as you and me, probably because we have rule-governed behavior, as we shall see in the later chapters of this book; but forget it for poor Rudolph.

Remember: *Stimulus* is singular, *stimuli* is plural, and *stimuluses* is what people say who haven't had the excellent education you're paying a small fortune to get.

QUESTIONS

1. Define the following concepts and diagram an example:
   a. discrimination training procedure
   b. S^D
   c. S^Δ
2. What was the reinforcer for the chicken pulling the trigger in the Breland demonstration?
   a. Breland not shot
   b. Food
3. Why didn't the chicken pull the trigger when Breland was in the line of fire?
   a. Because it might have killed Breland.
   b. Because that response was not reinforced with food.
4. *Stimulus discrimination*—state this principle and give an example, showing how it illustrates the principle.

DISCRIMINATION TRAINING BASED ON ESCAPE

Five P.M. You're in the chaos of the big city: Everybody's going home from work, traffic flowing in all directions, horns sounding everywhere, people swarming through the streets. You're tired, hungry, cold, 30 miles from home, with no car; and if that weren't enough, it's raining. Oh, did I mention the wind is blowing like mad? How aversive! You see a taxi without a passenger. Desperately, you signal the driver to stop, but someone else signals in front of you. You miss it. Then you see a taxi with two passengers. This time you don't even bother to move. Why? Because a taxi with passengers is an S^Δ, a stimulus in the presence of which signaling to stop has not been reinforced in the past. You signal only in the presence of an S^D, a taxi with no passengers, because in its presence signaling sometimes has caused the taxi driver to pick you up, though not always.

We have just described a discrimination training procedure involving an escape contingency. The response? Signaling the taxi driver to stop. The aversive condition? Few things could be worse than being tired, hungry, cold, and wet. The escape contingency? Signaling the taxi driver to stop results in escape from a cold, wet, exhausting city street to the warm, dry comfort of a cozy cab. Finally, signaling the taxi driver to stop is under perfect stimulus con-

trol: You signal only when the taxi has no passengers and never signal when it has passengers.

Discrimination Training Using Escape

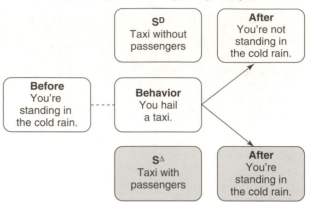

Notice that we are defining and using S^D and S^Δ not only with reinforcement by the presentation of reinforcers but also for reinforcement by the removal of aversive conditions (escape).

QUESTION

1. Diagram discrimination training based on escape.

Example
Behavioral School Psychology
MULTIPLE S^Ds AND S^Δs
TEACHING A JUVENILE DELINQUENT TO READ[3]

Jose Delgado had been in the juvenile correction department nine times by the time he was 14 years old. Like many juvenile delinquents, his prime target was school buildings. One time he shot out lightbulbs and windows in a school with a BB gun. Of course, he smoked, drank, and even got drunk occasionally. He stole, habitually lied, and used language that would make even a fraternity man blush. Jose came from a long line of juvenile delinquents. He was the fifth of eleven children, and each of his four older brothers had been to the juvenile court for misbehavior.

Home life was far from ideal. His father had completed only the 5th grade of school. Without success, the father and mother tried to control Jose's behavior by physical and verbal abuse.

---
[3]Based on Staats, A. W., & Butterfield, W. H. (1965). Treatment of nonreading in a culturally deprived juvenile delinquent: An application of reinforcement principles. *Child Development, 36,* 925–942.

Though Jose had been in school 8½ years, his reading was still at the 2nd-grade level. Teachers had promoted him from one class to another so they could get him out of their sight. They wanted nothing to do with him. Although no one had been able to help Jose, two people thought they could. One was William Butterfield, a probation officer from the juvenile correction department. The other was Dr. Arthur Staats, a behavior analyst. For several years, Staats had been working in the experimental analysis of reading and had been developing remedial reading programs based on the principles of behavior. Many people believe we can't help juvenile delinquents because they are fundamentally uncorrectable. But Staats and Butterfield didn't believe so. They thought Jose could learn to read if the instructor used appropriate teaching procedures. They thought reading was a series of discriminated responses that could be learned with reinforcement. (By *discriminated response,* we mean *a response under the control of a discriminative stimulus.*)

They prepared special stories for Jose. Each story had a new set of words. The written words were to act as discriminative stimuli for saying those words. Before starting a new story, Butterfield showed each discriminative stimulus word to Jose and asked him to make the correct reading response. If Jose answered correctly, he got a token. Each word served not only as an S^D for the proper spoken response but also as an S^Δ for improper spoken responses. For example, the written word *shoe* was the S^D for the spoken response *shoe* and the S^Δ for *hat* and all other incorrect responses.

When Jose failed to respond to a word correctly, Butterfield told him the correct response; then Jose repeated it, looking at the word. Butterfield presented each discriminative stimulus word over and over until Jose was able to make the correct response to each of them without prompting.

During the 4½ months Jose worked with Butterfield, they ran across 761 words that Jose couldn't read. After, Jose was able to read correctly 585 of them the first time he saw them in the context of a story.

Jose got a token when he responded correctly to each discriminative stimulus word in the paragraph. At that point Butterfield advanced to a new paragraph in the story. When Jose made a wrong response, Butterfield corrected it and put the paragraph aside to return to later. He did this until Jose had mastered each paragraph in the story; at that point, the words were exerting proper stimulus control over Jose's responding.

Butterfield gave Jose poker chips as tokens. Were the poker chips unlearned reinforcers or learned reinforcers? The poker chips had acquired their learned reinforcing value because they allowed Jose to purchase a variety of things. Jose exchanged the tokens for such items as shoes, hair pomade, a phonograph record, an ice-cream sundae, a ticket to a school function, and money for his brother who was going to attend a reform school.

Jose worked hard. During the total 40 sessions of reading, he made over 64,000 single-word reading responses. And he got reinforcers worth a total of only $20.31. In addition, with this reinforcement contingency, Jose was cooperative and attentive—unusual for juvenile delinquents in more traditional instructional programs. A few dollars can go a long way, when properly contingent.

This suggests that juvenile delinquents are not fundamentally bad. They behave properly when they are in an environment that reinforces desirable and cooperative behavior. But if they are not capable of making the desirable responses that produce authorized reinforcers, they make undesirable responses that produce unauthorized or bootleg reinforcers.

While Staats and Butterfield taught Jose to read out loud, they also taught him silent reading. So let's discuss the problem of teaching silent reading. To reinforce the correct reading response to a particular discriminative stimulus word, it is necessary for the teacher to know what word the student is reading and hear the reading response. This creates no problem in teaching oral reading, but how can the instructor use this method to teach silent reading?

After Jose had mastered a story at the oral level, Butterfield asked him to read it silently. Butterfield also warned him that it was important to understand the story, because he would be asked questions afterwards.

One of the first things Butterfield and Staats did was to make it likely that Jose was paying attention to the story. If he were looking at the page, he might be reading it. So looking at the page was at least a step in the right direction. Therefore, they differentially reinforced the observing response of looking at the page. They did so about every 15 seconds. If Jose was looking at the page when reinforcement became available, he received a token. It worked. Jose spent most of his time oriented toward the printed page.

Jose initially had some trouble with silent reading; he often emitted small vocal sounds and moved his lips. So he got a token whenever he read a story without making any sound or moving his lips. As a result, lip movements decreased.

But it became harder to know whether Jose was reading each discriminative stimulus word. So, to ensure he was in fact reading, he had to write out the answer to a set of questions after reading each story. He got a token for each question he answered correctly. Whenever he made a spelling error, he had to correct it before getting the token. And each time he gave an incorrect answer, he had to reread the same paragraph and correct the answer before getting a token.

When Jose completed 20 stories, he answered a review test on the words he had learned. Again, he got a token for each correct response. And when he responded incorrectly to a discriminative stimulus word, he had to respond to that stimulus word repeatedly until he responded to it correctly. Jose was able to respond correctly to 430 of the 761 discriminative stimulus words the first time he took a review test.

We can see most readily the effect of training word discriminations by looking at Jose's reading achievement test scores. In his 8½ years of school, he had progressed only to the 2nd grade (2.0) reading achievement. But in 4½ months of this special training, he progressed from the 2.0 to the 4.3 grade level—more in those 4½ months than he had in the preceding 8½ years of school.

Jose's general performance in school improved almost as much as did his performance on the reading achievement test. Jose got passing grades in all his courses: C in physical education, D in general shop, D in English, and D in mathematics. This may not strike you as anything to be excited about until you look at Jose's past academic record. In the 8½ years he had been in school, he had failed every course he had taken.

Jose also began to behave better while in school. During the 1st month of training, he committed ten misbehaviors that warranted demerits: disturbance in class, two times; disobedience in class, two times; loitering, two times; and tardiness, four times. In the 2nd month, he got only two demerits, one for scuffling on the school grounds and one for creating a disturbance. In the 3rd month, he also got two demerits; one for cutting a math class and one for swearing in class. He didn't misbehave in the 4th month or in the half month after when the school term ended.

When writing this present section, I wished I could conclude Jose's case history at this point. We'd all feel so much better if it had a happy ending. But, unfortunately, the story went on. The training Jose received improved his grades and his behavior in the school, but not enough. No one did anything to improve his behavior at the juvenile detention home where he was staying. Jose often baited the attendants at the detention home and created many minor but aversive disturbances. So he was sent to an industrial school for juvenile delinquent boys. Probably Jose had not yet reached the point where he could continue his progress without special reinforcement procedures. But Staats and Butterfield were no longer able to work with him. This most likely means that he will make little if any academic progress during the remainder of his school years. Probably Jose will be a misfit the rest of his unhappy life. Probably he'll do more harm than good both to himself and to society. It's too bad he hadn't had the chance to participate in an Achievement-Place group home rather than the traditional detention home. That might have saved him.

QUESTION

1. Using a discrimination training procedure, diagram how Butterfield and Staats taught a juvenile delinquent to read.

STIMULUS CONTROL BASED ON PUNISHMENT CONTINGENCIES

Through an underground network of outlaw health enthusiasts, Juke has learned of an internationally infamous recipe for old-fashioned rolled oats, a recipe said to have originated somewhere in the backwoods surrounding Kalamazoo, Michigan. He's brought to a boil the rich, aromatic mixture of water, apple juice, raisins, bananas, apples, pure vanilla extract, and cinnamon. Now all he has to do is pick up the pan, carry it over to the sink, and dump in 1½ cups of coarse-ground, old-fashioned, noninstant, rolled oats. He grabs the cast aluminum pan handle and "# - %$!," burns his hand.[4]

Eventually, Juke will become a seasoned rolled-oats cook. By then, the sight of the fluid boiling in his aluminum pan will be an effective punishment-based discriminative stimulus. In the presence of that discriminative stimulus, Juke's grabbing the aluminum handle with his naked hand will always produce a painful outcome. So stimulus control will develop. He'll stop grabbing the hot handle.

The wiser Juke will now make a testing response. He'll gingerly touch the handle with his index finger. If it's not too hot, he'll pick it up. In other words, a mild temperature on his index finger is a *punishment-based* S$^\Delta$ in the presence of which the burning punishment contingency is not in effect. Of course, a hot temperature on Juke's index finger is another punishment-based discriminative stimulus.

---

[4]What happened next is not crucial for this section; but if you're interested, Juke finally stopped cursing, took a kitchen knife, went into his solar greenhouse, cut off a piece of an aloe vera plant (one that had grown so big it was about to take his beloved greenhouse from him), sliced it open, and smeared its slimy, green innards over his burning palm. Instant relief. A perfect escape contingency: terrible pain, rub a little slimy aloe vera on the painful palm, no pain. So if you'd like to experience a powerful escape contingency, go burn or cut yourself and then slop on some aloe vera. Go ahead . . . give it a shot.

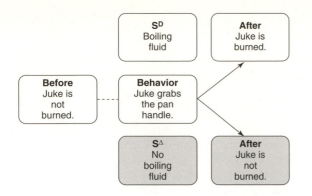

We know of no other behavioral textbook that discusses the grim issue of stimulus control based on a punishment contingency. But because such stimulus control contributes greatly to keeping our bodies intact, we thought the only honorable option was to call it to your attention.

QUESTION

1. *Punishment-based discriminative stimulus* and *punishment-based* S^{Δ}—diagram an example of each.

Compare and Contrast
REINFORCEMENT-BASED DISCRIMINATIVE STIMULI VS. PUNISHMENT-BASED DISCRIMINATIVE STIMULI

A stimulus that always precedes a reinforcement or an escape contingency acquires causal functions. This means that in the future, the mere presentation of that stimulus will cause the response. For instance, Jose said the word *shoe* (response) when he saw a card with the letters S H O E (S^D) because in the past, when Jose did so, he got tokens and praise (reinforcers). As a result of the discrimination training procedure, the mere presentation of the card caused Jose to make the correct response. The letters were an S^D based on a reinforcement contingency.

Reinforcement-Based Discrimination

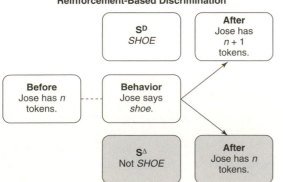

On the other hand, a stimulus that always precedes a punishment or penalty contingency acquires suppressive functions. This means that in the future the response in that contingency will occur less frequently in the presence of that stimulus. In the presence of Butterfield (S^D), lip movements during silent reading (response) occurred less frequently. Why? Because when Butterfield was around and lip movements occurred, Jose lost the opportunity to get a token. Losing the opportunity to get a token contingent on lip movements is a special type of punishment contingency (we'll read about later), so Butterfield's presence was a punishment-based S^D. **A *punishment-based* S^D is a stimulus in the presence of which a response will be punished.**

Punishment-Based Discrimination

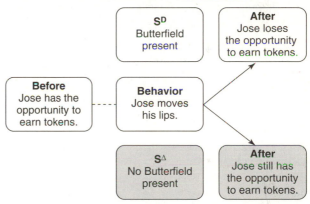

But punishment can take place in either of two ways—not only by the removal (or prevention) of a reinforcer but also by the presentation of an aversive condition. So Butterfield's presence also could have acted as an S^D based on the presentation of an aversive condition. Instead of taking away a reinforcer, he could have made an aversive comment each time Jose moved his lips during silent reading. If so, the frequency of lip movements also would have decreased in Butterfield's presence.

In the same way, you use swear words (response) less frequently when your mother is present (punishment-based S^D), because in the past, her presence always resulted in a sermon (aversive stimulus) about her degenerate kids. And what about when your mother isn't there? A *punishment-based* S^{Δ}—no punishment contingency.

The punishment-based S^D plays the same role with punishment as the reinforcement-based S^D plays with reinforcement. In both cases, these stimuli are associated with the contingency. And the punishment-based S^{Δ} plays the same role with punishment as the reinforcement-based S^{Δ} does with reinforcement. In both cases, these stimuli are associated with the absence of the contingency.[5]

Our behavior is often under the control of combinations of reinforcement-based S^Ds and S^Δs and punishment-based S^Ds and S^Δs. Getting your mail is usually a big reinforcer. So the clock on the wall pointing to the time for mail delivery is an S^D for going to the mailbox. The clock pointing to an earlier time is an S^Δ.

1. Please complete the following diagram.

Reinforcement-Based Discrimination

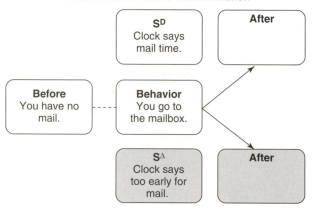

If you live in the country, as I do, the sight and sound of rain are punishment-based S^Ds for going to the mailbox. And a silent, dry lane is a punishment-based S^Δ.

So you can see how those four stimulus conditions might combine to exert stimulus control over your behavior.

QUESTIONS

1. What are the similarities between a reinforcement-based discriminative stimulus and a punishment-based discriminative stimulus?
2. Diagram an example of reinforcement-based discrimination.

3. Diagram an example of punishment-based discrimination.

Punishment-Based Discrimination

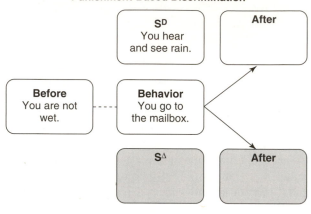

In the Skinner Box
Compare and Contrast
THE DIFFERENTIAL-REINFORCEMENT PROCEDURE VS. THE STIMULUS-DISCRIMINATION PROCEDURE

Before we compare the differential-reinforcement and stimulus-discrimination procedures, let's look at simple, nondiscriminated, nondifferential reinforcement.

The Nondiscriminated, Nondifferential Reinforcement Procedure

With Rudolph the Rat, we reinforce any lever press, more or less regardless of the force with which he presses the lever. In other words, we're defining the response class in terms of its function (its effect on the environment)—moving the lever down.

Simple Reinforcement

Now we're ready to compare the differential reinforcement and stimulus discrimination procedures.

[5]Another way we might define S^D and S^Δ that would be consistent with our approach is as follows: S^D—*a stimulus in the presence of which a contingency is operative. S^Δ—a stimulus in the presence of which a contingency is not operative.* I don't know of any other published source that addresses the terminological problem of S^D and S^Δ for punishment (if you do, please let me know). Some prefer to define S^Δ as *a stimulus in the presence of which behavior occurs at a low rate frequency or not at all.* In other words, they would say both extinction and punishment occur in the presence of the S^Δ. I think we should generally define our procedural terms in terms of procedure and not in terms of the effects of the procedure, and I think people have a hard enough time distinguishing between punishment and extinction without lumping them together under S^Δ; but your professor may disagree, and your professor is always right.

tial response class into two smaller classes (subclasses). So we've defined the larger response class in terms of a response function—the depression of the lever. And we've defined the two smaller classes in terms of a response dimension—force.

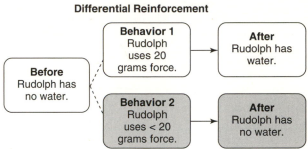

The Differential-Reinforcement Procedure

In differential reinforcement, we combine reinforcement and extinction. We reinforce one response class and extinguish other response classes. So the frequency of the reinforced response class increases relative to the frequency of the unreinforced response classes.

For example, in the rat lab, we start by reinforcing any lever press, more or less regardless of the force with which the rat presses the lever.[6] In other words, we're defining this initial response class in terms of its function (its effects on the environment—the downward movement of the lever.

After initial nondifferential reinforcement, we start our differential-reinforcement procedure. Now we reinforce only those lever presses that occur with at least 20 grams of force. We extinguish less forceful presses. In other words, we divide the larger, ini-

Stimulus-Discrimination Procedure

In the simple stimulus-discrimination procedure, we also combine reinforcement and extinction. But, usually, we deal only with one response class, not two or more response classes, as we do in the differential-reinforcement procedure. For example, in the simple stimulus-discrimination procedure, we deal only with the response class functionally defined in terms of the depression of the lever.

What we vary in stimulus discrimination is the S^D; the response remains constant. In stimulus discrimination, we reinforce a response class in the

---

[6]Notice that in saying *more or less,* we're copping out slightly to avoid making a complex topic even more complex. The problem is that whenever we reinforce lever pressing, we are differentially reinforcing along the dimension of force, whether we mean to or not. Here's why: If the rat doesn't use at least enough minimal force, the response won't even budge the lever. So it's impossible to reinforce a response without involving this most basic form of the differential-reinforcement procedure. But usually we analyze the contingencies in terms of the differential-reinforcement procedure only when we explicitly want to shift the frequency of the response along some response dimension.

presence of one stimulus and extinguish **the same response class** in the presence of another stimulus. So, for example, we reinforce the lever press when the light is on (S^D), and we extinguish the press when the light is off (S^Δ).

Stimulus Discrimination

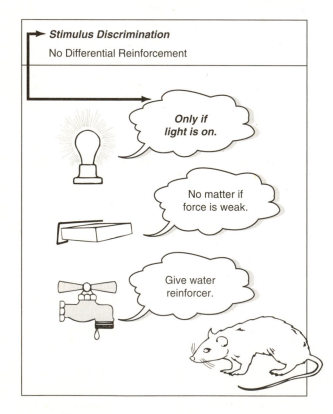

(Now we don't care about the force of the response, as long as it's great enough to cause the lever to move down.)

In sum, in our differential reinforcement example, we use **two response classes** (responses with a force of 20 grams or more and responses with a force less than 20 grams) and only **one stimulus** (the light). However, in the stimulus discrimination example, we use only **one response class** (lever presses) and **two stimuli** (light on and light off).

The Differential-Reinforcement Procedure vs. the Stimulus-Discrimination Procedure		
	One Stimulus	*Two Stimuli*
One Response Class	No differentiation or discrimination	Stimulus discrimination
Two Response Classes	Response differentiation	Combined differentiation and discrimination

Differential-Reinforcement and Stimulus-Discrimination Procedures Using Punishment

Of course, the same differences apply to differential punishment procedures and stimulus-discrimination procedures using punishment contingencies. For example, in differential punishment the lever press produces shock as well as food if its force is less than 20 grams. But it produces only food if its force is 20 grams or more. (Of course, the light is on all the time.) So the frequency of the lower-force lever presses decreases relative to the frequency of the higher-force lever presses. As with our example of the differential-reinforcement procedure, this example of the differential punishment procedure involves two response classes and one stimulus.

Now consider an example of a stimulus-discrimination procedure based on punishment. The lever-press produces shock as well as food if it occurs when the light is off (punishment-based discriminative stimulus). But the press produces only food if it occurs when the light is on. So the light's being off suppresses responding, and the light's being on causes responding. As with our example of a stimulus-discrimination procedure based on reinforcement, we use one response (the lever press) and two stimuli (light on and light off).

Many instances of everyday life involve stimulus-discrimination procedures, in addition to differential reinforcement and punishment procedures. We drive more carefully when our parents are riding with us. We talk more quietly in church. We practice harder when the coach is around. We speak more slowly when talking to someone learning English. We eat more politely in the presence of guests. All because of differential reinforcement or differential punishment procedures associated with particular S^Ds or S^Δs.

QUESTIONS

1. Compare and contrast the differential-reinforcement procedure and stimulus discrimination. Be able to:

a. fill out each of the three balloons in each of the three drawings

b. do each of the three contingency diagrams

c. understand and fill out the table.

2. Give an example of the differential-reinforcement procedure and stimulus discrimination involving a reinforcement contingency. Now do the same using a punishment contingency.

Example
Educational Psychology

MULTIPLE S^{D}S AND S$^\Delta$S: POVERTY'S CHILDREN—PART II[7]

Remember when some of Mae's friends asked her if they could use one of her classrooms as a preschool for 15 black children who came from poor families? These children scored an average of 21 points below the national average IQ score. Much of their problem was poor verbal skills. For example, these children didn't use adjectives, like color, size, or number names. Mae's goal was to improve their use of descriptive adjectives. Her solution to problems was always the same: If a behavior doesn't occur often enough, we should reinforce it. So the teachers did, at Mae's request.

They began by providing wall-to-wall reinforcement of the use of color-noun combinations during the 3-hour session in the morning that included breakfast, structured time, and free play. Each time a teacher heard a child correctly use a color-noun combination, he or she smiled at the child and made an approving comment. The teachers used this procedure for 102 days, but the frequency of color-noun combos didn't increase! So they began to lose faith. They concluded that the children didn't have the words in their repertoire, or if they had, they couldn't use them correctly. But Mae didn't doubt for a second that reinforcement works; this was just the beginning of the battle.

But where did they go wrong? Only one child used an average of one color-noun combination per hour; ten of the children didn't use any. The teachers couldn't reinforce behavior that wasn't occurring.

So Mae asked the teachers to use another procedure—a discrimination training procedure. She wanted to establish the various colors as S^{D}s for the proper color-naming responses and as S$^\Delta$s for the wrong color-naming responses. For example, a red car should be an S^D for the response *red car* and a green car would be an S$^\Delta$ for the response *red car*. A teacher would show various objects of various colors to the children and then point to one—for instance, the red car—and ask a child what it was. The teacher would then praise the child and give the child a small snack if he or she correctly named the object and the color by saying, for instance, *red car*. (If the child named the correct color without naming the object, the teachers praised her or him and then asked for the complete phrase before giving the snack.)

1. Please complete the following diagram.

Tact (Naming) Contingency

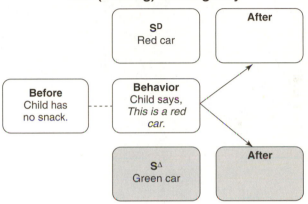

The results of the discrimination training were good, in terms of the stimulus control they established in the training sessions. At the end of 50 days of training, six different colors were exerting proper stimulus control over the naming responses of eight of the children, as were nine colors for the seven other children. These results hadn't come easily, but they were satisfying to both the teachers and the children.

Now the proper stimulus control by these colors was in the children's object-naming repertoires. But that turned out not to be enough. Mae and her team were in for another disappointment, right after their triumph: Outside of the training session, in their normal, day-to-day interactions, the children made almost no use of the color names they had learned. The group average of proper color-adjective use increased from 0.5 to 1.8 an hour; color-noun combinations increased from 0.2 to 0.4 per hour. Not much for 50 days of hard work!

Mae couldn't stop asking herself, *What's going to happen to these kids, if they don't improve their language skills now? What am I going to tell the teachers who are discouraged with my interventions? What am I going to tell my father, who is so proud of the help I'm supposed to be giving the black community? Some help!*

Mae decided to stop fretting and start solving. So she went into one of the classrooms, took a seat

---

[7]Based on Hart B. M., & Risley, T. R. (1968). Establishing use of descriptive adjectives in the spontaneous speech of disadvantaged preschool children. *Journal of Applied Behavior Analysis, 1,* 109–120.

in one corner, and watched the children as they interacted with the teacher. Mae noticed the children in that group used color-name combinations more often than usual. Why? The teacher always required the children to use proper color names to get the toys they wanted. For instance, a child asked the teacher for the pegboard materials by pointing at a piece. The teacher took that piece in her hand and waited until the child asked for it using the right color adjective. Then she gave it to the child.

2. Please complete the following diagram.

Mand (Requesting) Contingency

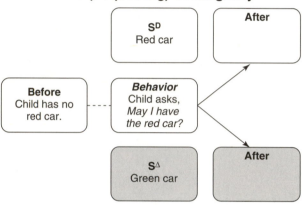

Of course, Mae said to herself, why didn't I think of this before? Why would the children use color-noun combinations if they can get their toys without going to that effort? But getting the toy would be a reinforcer and would reinforce their use of color adjectives in more natural settings. The teachers should do **incidental teaching.** They should differentially reinforce using color-noun combinations, and they should reinforce only correct color-noun combinations. In other words, they should combine differential discrimination training, so the colors of the objects would come to exert accurate stimulus control over the children's use of those color-noun combinations.

Definition: Concept
Incidental teaching
  ◦ The planned use of
  ◦ behavioral contingencies,
  ◦ differential reinforcement, and
  ◦ discrimination training,
  ◦ in the student's everyday environment.

So Mae asked all the teachers in her preschool project to use incidental teaching. The teachers would give the children the toys they asked for only

when they asked for them using color-noun combinations. The teachers did this incidental teaching for the next 19 days. The teachers also used this incidental teaching with requests for snacks. Asking for a cookie or some fruit was no longer enough. Now the children had to request the brown cookie, the yellow banana, or the red apple; the red car, the doll with blue eyes, the white bear, the orange airplane, or the pink Barbie dress. It worked! The average frequency of each child's using correct color-noun combinations increased from 0.4 to 14.2 an hour. Another way to put it is: When only praise followed the correct color-name combinations, the children used adjectives only 22% of the times they named objects; but when the teacher gave the object to the child contingent on correct color-noun combinations, the children used adjectives 75% of the times they named objects.

Mae had made her case. The teachers were convinced that they could help these children improve their verbal skills. It wasn't a question of inherited inferiority but of environmental contingencies. Where traditional methods of teaching language failed, behavior analysis once again made a difference.

TRANSFER OF TRAINING

At this point in your study of behavior analysis, you're not surprised that reinforcement works. You're not surprised that the teachers could increase the frequency of little kids saying, *this is a red car,* rather than just, *this is a car,*[8] when the teacher holds up a red car and asks, *What is this*? But, like Mae and her teachers and most of the rest of the world, you might be surprised that this color-adjective training didn't transfer outside the training setting to the rest of the classroom, the play area, and the snack area.

Why is everyone so surprised? We think it's because they think of the problem like this: *The kids clearly did **know** the color of the car; so why didn't they use the color names in other settings?*

And those surprised people fail to follow the don't-say rule; they say *know. The kids did **know** the color of the car.* It may make sense to use *know* in the context of some complex uses of language by sophisticated users of language; but this was certainly not one of those contexts. These children were by no

---

[8]Author's formatting note: throughout most of the book, we have put dialogue in quotation marks. In this section, we chose to use italics to represent those statements that might in some contexts be dialogues, but more importantly are defined as verbal operants.

means sophisticated users of language and color adjectives are far from complex language.

The closer we can keep our analyses to those we'd do of nonverbal Rudolph, the rat in the Skinner box, the less frequently we'll screw up things. Similarly, the more we avoid circular reasoning and reifications like *know,* the less frequently we'll screw up things.

What's the S^D for saying, *red car?* To elaborate slightly on the previous diagrams, the S^D is the teacher's holding up a red car and asking, "What is this?"

And, what's the S^Δ for saying, *red car?* And this time, to elaborate greatly on the previous diagrams, the S^Δ is much more than the teacher's holding up a green car and asking, *what is this?* It's everything in the kids' lives that doesn't involve the S^D. The S^Δ is all those occasions when the teacher doesn't hold up a red car and ask, *what is this?*

1. Please complete the following diagram.

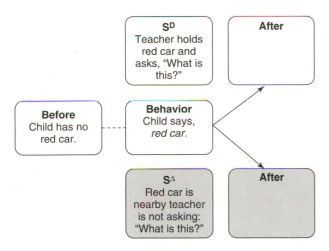

So, what have we got when the red car is nearby, but the teacher doesn't ask, "What is this?" That's also an S^Δ for the kid saying, *red car.* Why? Because *red car* has never been reinforced with a snack on such occasions.

So, we shouldn't be surprised that the children didn't request the red car in other settings. In fact, we should have been surprised if they had requested the red car. Why? First, *red car* had never been reinforced in any circumstance except when the teacher was holding the car and asking "What is this?" So the other settings were S^Δs for saying *red car.*

Second, when the response *red car* had been reinforced in the training sessions, it had been reinforced with praise and snacks. So when the children's establishing operation was not-having the red car, of course the children did not say *red car,* be-

cause in the past, *red car* had been reinforced with praise and snacks, not receipt of the red car itself.

Finally, we should have been shocked if the children had actually said *may I have the red car,* because that response had never been reinforced in any circumstance.

(We'll elaborate on transfer of training in Chapter 28.)

VERBAL BEHAVIOR (A.K.A.[9] LANGUAGE)

While we're drilling down into research on teaching kids to use adjectives, let's drill a little deeper, until we hit the verbal vein.

When the teachers held the red car and asked the students "What is this?" the students would name (tact) the red car; the behavioral term for *naming* is **tacting.** When they correctly tacted the red car, they received a snack and praise from the teachers. Tacting is one form of language. **Verbal behavior**[10] is the behavioral term for *language.* In the case of the tact, the form of the response (for instance, *red car* vs. *green car*) is determined by an S^D (the teacher holding the red car and asking *What is this*?). The reinforcer for tacting is usually approval from an observer. Because, in this case, the teachers were teaching a new form of tacting to the children, they added a snack to the praise as the reinforcer for proper tacting.

The behavioral term for *requesting* is **manding.** Manding and tacting are two different forms of verbal behavior The mand is usually reinforced by the receipt of the object or event requested rather than by praise. So people make mands, when having the object or participating in the event would be a reinforcer. In other words, an establishing operation (no red car) usually causes the person to state the request (mand).

In training verbal skills to non-verbal clients, such as mentally-handicapped and autistic children, behavior analysts explicitly train manding in addition to tacting, rather than doing what traditional teachers do, which is to teach tacting and naively assume that such teaching will transfer to manding. Furthermore, behavior analysts often start with

---

[9]*A.K.A.* stands for *also known as,* a term commonly found on FBI wanted posters. I'm sort of sticking it to my behavior-analytic buddies for using pompous jargon, when everyday English would do the trick (e.g., *verbal behavior, mand,* and *tact*). But we all use it; so you have to learn.

[10]Skinner, B. F. (1992). *Verbal Behavior.* Acton, MA: Copley Publishing Group.

mand training, because it lends itself so readily to incidental teaching. As a result of this emphasis on the mand, behavior analysts' clients acquire much more verbal behavior much more rapidly.

A *mand* is verbal behavior that specifies its own reinforcer. For example the mand, *please pass the hot sauce,* specifies the reinforcer for that mand, namely the hot sauce. **Mand**—*a verbal relation where the form of the response is determined by an establishing operation.* The form of the verbal response *please pass the hot sauce* is determined by the establishing operation, not having the hot sauce.

A *tact* is verbal behavior where the form of the response is controlled by an S^D, not by the reinforcer. For example, for the tact, *that's a bottle of hot sauce,* the reinforcer might be the listener's approval, not the receipt of the hot sauce. The actual bottle of hot sauce is the S^D that causes the person to say *That's a bottle of hot sauce.* **Tact**—*a verbal relation where the form of the response is determined by a nonverbal S^D.*[11]

Compare and Contrast Mand vs. Tact		
	Mand	*Tact*
Also called	Requesting	Naming
Caused by	Establishing operation	S^D
Reinforced by	Receipt of object requested	Praise

By the way, be sure to avoid the common and reasonable mistake of thinking that when behavior analysts use the expression *verbal behavior,* they just mean *vocal behavior* or *vocal verbal behavior* (*talking*). No, for behavior analysts, *verbal behavior* also includes listening, reading, writing, sign language, etc. *Verbal* means *language,* not *vocal;* of course some dictionary definitions and everyday use tend to treat *verbal* as meaning *spoken.*[12]

QUESTION

1. Diagram the two stimulus-discrimination procedures used to increase the frequency of the children's descriptive adjectives:

---

[11]These formal definitions are based on Michael, J. (1993). *Concepts and Principles of Behavior Analysis.* Kalamazoo, MI: Association for Behavior Analysis (pp. 95–96).

[12]For a more sophisticated treatment of verbal behavior, see Catania, A. C. (1998). *Learning.* Upper Saddle River, NJ: Prentice Hall.

a. Discrimination training procedure: tact (naming) contingency
b. Discrimination training procedure: mand (requesting) contingency

Prompts

Sid's Seminar

Tom: When we use reinforcement, the behavior has to occur before we can reinforce. But the operant level was too low for reinforcement to work with most of Dr. Mae Robinson's children. So I don't understand what was going on there.

Sid: Excellent point. What did the teachers do to get the children to use color-noun combinations in the first place?

Joe: The teachers gave the children verbal directions, like "Tell me, what color is the car?"

Sid: Right. That's a *verbal prompt.* At first, the teachers helped the children use color-noun combinations by prompting the response—by presenting a supplemental stimulus before the response. The teachers used various prompts adjusted to each child's needs. The most obvious prompt was to say the correct response just before the question, "The car is red. What color is the car?" The less obvious prompts were to name a color, give its initial sound, or ask the color of an object that another child had named correctly right before.

Joe: I see now that Butterfield and Staats also used prompts to teach Jose to read. Remember? When Jose failed to respond to a word, Butterfield told him the correct response and Jose repeated it, looking at the word. Butterfield presented the discriminative stimulus words over and over until Jose was able to make the correct response to each of them without prompting.

Sid: Yes. There's no question that verbal directions can serve as prompts. Can anyone think of other ways to prompt behavior?

Sue: Yes! Remember in Chapter 7, the story of Madame Cupet, the ballet teacher? Besides giving verbal instructions to Bunny, she did two things. She modeled each exercise so Bunny could see how to do it correctly. She also physically guided Bunny's leg throughout each exercise. So, I guess that, besides prompting behavior before it occurs, we also can prompt behavior during performance, like when we guide a behavior physically.

Joe: She provided a **physical prompt.**

Sid: You're right. Tom gets a point for raising an important issue. Joe and Sue each get a point for discussing it. To summarize our seminar for today, remember we can *prompt behavior with verbal instructions, modeling, and physical guidance.*

Definition: Concept
Prompt
- ○ A supplemental stimulus
- ○ that raises the probability of a correct response.

Sue: It helps me to think of a prompt as a supplement to the S^D or S^Δ.

Eve: Then how does a prompt differ from a regular S^D or S^Δ?

Sue: A prompt doesn't stand by itself. *The car is red* is a prompt that supplements the S^D *What color is the car?* But the prompt doesn't stand by itself. Suppose the teacher just says, "The car is red." That by itself would usually not be an S^D for the child's saying, "The car is red." But it will supplement the S^D *What color is the car?* And it will prompt the correct response.

Joe: I think of a prompt as a hint. It's often a hint as to the correct response, like the teacher might say *rrrr*. That would prompt red. This sort of prompt or hint is a partial response. And, as you say, it wouldn't function as an S^D by itself.

Compare and Contrast
PROMPTS VS. DISCRIMINATIVE STIMULI

The S^{prompt} is **not** a type of S^D. Here's how they differ: Reinforcement or punishment of the relevant response is more likely to occur in the presence of an S^D than in the presence of a corresponding S^Δ.

Consider Dicky's response, *I was swinging.* It will produce the reinforcer of praise and a bite of food in the presence of the conditional S^D (having swung AND having been asked, *what did you do outside*). *I was swinging* won't be reinforced in the presence of the S^Δ (not having swung OR not having been asked).

But the S^{prompt} has nothing corresponding to the S^Δ. For example, Dicky's proper answer to the question *what did you do outside* will also be reinforced in the absence of the trainer's prompt *I was swinging,* not just in its presence.

Whew! Complex. You may want to read this section over a couple more times to make sure you've got it; I had to.

	S^D	S^{prompt}
A stimulus	yes	yes
in the presence of which a particular response will be more likely to be reinforced or punished	yes	no

QUESTIONS

1. *Prompt*—define it and give an example.
2. Name and give an example of each of the three types of prompts.
3. Please describe and explain the crucial difference between an S^D and an S^{prompt}.

Behavioral Special Education
PREPARING JIMMY TO BE A STUDENT

When Mae first started working with Jimmy, he was all over the place, and she found it impossible to teach him. Jimmy was not functioning like a proper student.

1. So the first thing Mae did was decide what would a child do to be considered a proper student; in other words, Mae performed
   a. differential reinforcement
   b. a shaping procedure
   c. a task analysis
   d. an establishing operation

Her analysis suggested that first the tasks of a good student were to sit down, look at the teacher, and not indulge in competing behavior such as self-stimulation. So Mae started with sitting down. She would give Jimmy a food reinforcer every time he sat down upon request.

2. Please complete the diagram for Jimmy's discrimination-training procedure:

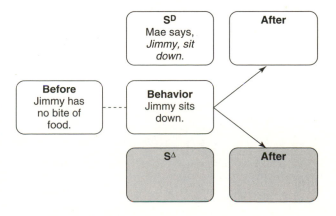

3. At first, Jimmy never sat down in the presence of the S^D, *Jimmy, sit down*. So Mae would take hold of him and sit him down. This is an example of what?
   a. an S^Δ
   b. a prompt
   c. an establishing operation
   d. a task analysis

As the training procedure progressed, Mae gradually faded out this physical prompt, reducing the pressure she used to sit him down, until she merely had to place her hand lightly on his shoulder. Eventually, she could fade out the prompt completely.

QUESTIONS

1. Diagram the procedure for bringing sitting down under stimulus control.
2. Describe the relevant physical prompt procedure.

BASIC ENRICHMENT

In the Skinner Box[13]
THE DISCRIMINATING PIGEON

Now, back to the Skinner box. How would you show stimulus discrimination? Skinner showed it with a pigeon pecking a single response key. Sometimes the key was lighted and sometimes it was dark (when it was lit, it was lit from behind, so that the light showed through the key—transilluminated). The pigeon got food when it pecked the key in the presence of the lighted key, the S^D; but it didn't get food when it pecked the key in the presence of the dark key, the S^Δ. Stimulus control was so great that the bird's head moved back and forth as if it were on the end of a rubber band; when the key light was off in the middle of a key peck, the bird jerked its head back just before hitting the key. If the bird was still in the process of withdrawing its head when the light came on again, the bird immediately returned to work.

   Incidentally, much of the basic research on stimulus control with animals involves situations such as this. The experimenter presents the S^D for a period of time and then presents the S^Δ for a period of time, and he or she records the frequency of responding in the presence of each stimulus.

1. Please complete this diagram describing the preceding pigeon demonstration:

Discriminated Reinforcement

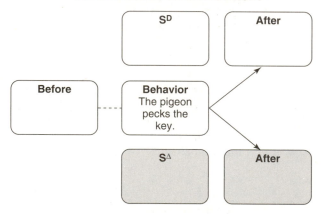

QUESTION

1. Diagram an experiment that would show stimulus discrimination with pigeons.

REQUIREMENTS
FOR STIMULUS CONTROL

Preattending Skills

Remember how Butterfield and Staats taught Jose to read? They began by making sure Jose looked at the words (S^Ds); orienting himself toward it was a prerequisite for the written word to control Jose's response. If you don't believe us, try to read without looking at the page. Orienting yourself toward the discriminative stimulus is what some behavior analysts call *preattending skills*.

---

[13]Based on *Learning and Behavior* (a motion picture). Columbia Broadcasting System, "Conquest" series.

Sensory Capability

Of course, to develop preattending skills you need *sensory capabilities*. You need vision, hearing, touch, taste, and smell for stimuli to control your behavior. For instance, oral requests won't control your behavior if you're not able to hear. (Though, sometimes, your little brother's calls don't control your behavior although you are able to hear, and you indeed have heard it. Any ideas why?)

Conspicuous Stimulus

But even if you have sensory capabilities and preattending skills, some stimuli don't control your behavior. Why do only some stimuli from the environment control your behavior and others don't? The effectiveness of stimulus control depends in part on how the stimulus is presented. Some stimuli are more conspicuous than others. A conspicuous stimulus is one that contrasts with its background because of its large size, its brightness, its loudness, its uniqueness, or the like. Have you ever gotten a traffic ticket for not having money in the meter? If you look carefully, you might find tiny letters perpendicular to the major text saying that if you hurry on and get to the nearest violations bureau in less than an hour from the time of the ticket, you'll pay only half the penalty. Most often those tiny letters don't control reading behavior. On the other hand, have you ever seen one of those *WARNING—MAD DOG* signs? When those signs are well displayed, probably you'll see the dog before the dog sees you. The more conspicuous the stimulus is, the higher the probability that that stimulus would control behavior.

Discrimination-Training Procedure

Another requirement for stimulus control is the history of behavioral contingencies in the presence of that stimulus. For instance, let's think of a stimulus paired with a reinforcement contingency. Only if a behavior has repeatedly produced a reinforcer in the presence of that stimulus, will that behavior occur more frequently in the presence of that stimulus in the future. Why do you always tell dirty jokes to your roommate? Because she loves it; when you do so, she laughs like crazy. **Naughty** roommate. Naughty you.

QUESTION

1. List four prerequisites for stimulus control and give an example of each.

INTERMEDIATE ENRICHMENT

Compare and Contrast
DISCRIMINATIVE STIMULUS VS. BEFORE CONDITION

Students and professionals alike often confuse before conditions with S^Ds. So let's try to clear up this confusion. Suppose a child's mother has normal hearing, but the father has impaired hearing. Then the sight of the mother probably acts as an S^D, a stimulus in the presence of which asking for food is reinforced. The sight of the father acts as an S^Δ for food asking.

   Now further suppose the child hasn't eaten for a couple hours. Then, of course, the child will request food more frequently when he has no food than when he does. And the request for food will

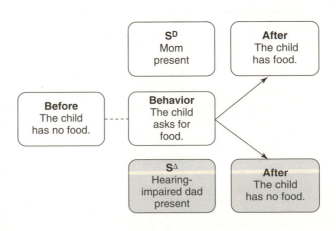

also occur more frequently in the sight of the mother than in the sight of the father. The before condition and the S^D share some common characteristics. Both occur before the behavior.[14] And both increase the frequency of the behavior.

However, you should distinguish the before condition from the discriminative stimulus. A before condition is needed before an after condition can be reinforcing, but it doesn't guarantee the presentation of that reinforcer. However, an S^D does guarantee that a reinforcer will more likely follow the response. For instance, that the child has no food (before condition) doesn't mean he'll get food when he requests it; the request won't produce food, if no one's there. However, in Mom's presence the child's request will produce food, though Mom's presence doesn't guarantee the child will give a damn (it doesn't guarantee there's no food in the before condition or that he had been food deprived earlier).

For reinforcement to occur, you often need both the before condition and the discriminative stimulus. If the before condition is absent, a particular event doesn't act as a reinforcer. If stimulus control has been established and the discriminative stimulus is absent, the behavior that produces the reinforcer might not occur, so it can't be reinforced.

Discriminative Stimulus vs. Before Condition		
	Before	*S^D*
Occurs	Before behavior	Before behavior
Effect	Increases behavior	Increases behavior
Will make the after condition reinforcing	Yes	No
Is associated with increased likelihood of reinforcers	No	Yes

1. Most people fail to discriminate between the before condition and the S^D in the case of the escape contingency. Here's your chance to show you're not one of the confused:

2. This time, Rudolph has Dr. Richard Malott in the Skinner box. When the shock is on, Malott can press the lever and escape the shock. What is the shock?
   a. before condition
   b. S^D

(Most people make the mistake of saying the shock is the S^D. It might be easier to see why the shock is not the S^D if we look at a good example of an S^D: The shock comes on, but his lever presses will turn it off only when the light comes on. When the light's off, he can pound his little fists raw, and the lever still won't turn off the shock. Poor Dr. Malott.)

3. What's the light?
   a. before condition
   b. S^D
4. What's the shock?
   a. before condition
   b. S^D
5. Please diagram Dr. Malott's plight.

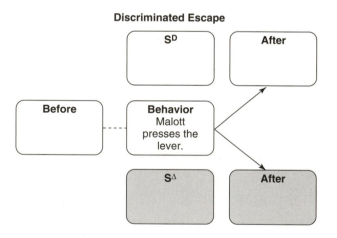

Discriminated Escape

QUESTION

1. Fill out the table that compares and contrasts the before condition and the reinforcement-based discriminative stimulus.

2. Diagram an example of discriminated escape.

---

[14]Dear Professor: Here are three expressions we've dropped: We've stopped using the expression *antecedent stimuli* as the generic term to encompass both the *before condition* and the S^D because we think it causes professionals, as well as students, to confuse the before condition with the S^D. We have stopped using *evoke, evocation,* and *evocative* because we think students have too much trouble understanding the words. Instead, we simply word the sentences differently, or use some variant of *cause,* at the risk of offending those who think *cause* means *ultimate* or *sole cause.* And, as mentioned earlier, we've stopped using *response likelihood,* as well as *response probability* because Jack Michael said we should. We've long objected to the almost metaphorical or hypothetical-construct use of *response probability* (what's the probability of a response that occurs 100 times per minute?). And Jack convinced us that *response likelihood* ain't much better. We've found that *response frequency* is a perfect and easy replacement, applying to both relative and absolute frequency; in other words, it also applies to those discrete trial occasions where *response probability* is an appropriate term, as well as to those free-operant occasions where *response probability* is metaphorical. However, in all three cases, these textbook changes are compatible with your continuing to use the more traditional terminology if you prefer; they don't contradict and can comfortably coexist.

Compare and Contrast
DISCRIMINATIVE STIMULUS VS. OPERANDUM

Students and even professionals often confuse the operandum with the discriminative stimulus. So let's work on that distinction.

Definition: Review Concept
Discriminative stimulus (S^D)
- A stimulus in the presence of which
- a particular response will be reinforced or punished.

Definition: Concept
Operandum (manipulandum)
- that part of the environment
- the organism operates (manipulates).

Tricky plurals: *Stimulus* is singular. *Stimuli* is plural, not *stimuluses. Operandum* is singular. *Operanda* is plural. *Manipulandum* is singular. _____ is plural.

These are Latin words. They're what them smart folks use. But we'll use them, too; and if we don't screw up the plurals, no one will never know whether we're also smart folks.

IN THE SKINNER BOX

1. When the light is on, Rudolph presses the lever and receives a drop of water. When the light is off, Rudolph will receive no water, even if he presses the lever. Is the light something Rudolph operates or manipulates?
   a. yes
   b. no
   (Hint: The light's in the ceiling; Rudolph can't even touch it.)
2. Will Rudolph's response be reinforced when the light is on?
   a. yes
   b. no
3. So what's the light?
   a. S^D
   b. operandum

What's the lever? Well, it's something Rudolph operates. Lever pressing can't occur without it. So lever pressing can't be reinforced without it. Can the lever be both an S^D and an operandum for the same response? That's where the confusion enters. So check this.

**The S^D is associated with the opportunity for reinforcement.
The operandum provides the opportunity to respond.**

We're distinguishing between the opportunity to respond and the opportunity for reinforcement, **given that you have the opportunity to respond.** The S^D is associated with the opportunity for reinforcement when a response is possible. If the lever is in the box, then Rudolph can press it; the lever provides him the opportunity to respond.

But that's not the same as the opportunity for reinforcement. When the light is off, lever pressing won't produce water, even though the lever's in the box and Rudolph is pressing like mad. But when the light comes on, Rudolph now has the opportunity for reinforcement; he presses the lever and gets a drop of water. **The light is the S^D. The lever is the operandum.** The lever **cannot** be both operandum and S^D for the same response.

1. Please diagram Rudolph's contingencies in the previous example. In the behavior component, mention the operandum. But first, review this definition: **S-Delta (S^Δ)**—*a stimulus in the presence of which a particular response will not be reinforced or punished.*

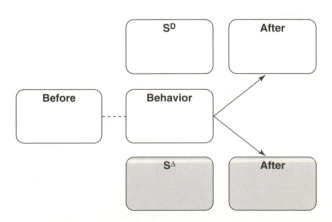

Just as the lever is not an S^D for lever pressing, so too the Skinner box itself is not an S^D for lever pressing. The lever and the box are just part of the environment associated with the opportunity to respond; the Skinner box is not especially associated with the opportunity for reinforcement, given that a response has occurred.

Here's another way to distinguish between the S^D and the operandum:

2. What's an S^D?
   a. an opportunity for the response to be reinforced
   b. an opportunity for the response to be made
3. What's the response lever?
   a. an opportunity for the response to be reinforced
   b. an opportunity for the response to be made
4. What's being in the Skinner box?
   a. an opportunity for the response to be reinforced
   b. an opportunity for the response to be made

So you want to avoid confusing the opportunity for reinforcement (the S^D) with the opportunity to make the response (the operandum or the environment containing the operandum).

Compare and Contrast
DISCRIMINATIVE STIMULUS VS. UNDISCRIMINATED REINFORCEMENT CONTINGENCY

> **Note**
> **Sometimes there is no S^D,**
> **especially if there's no S^Δ.**
> **Instead there's an**
> ***undiscriminated reinforcement***
> ***contingency.***

Sometimes you will have trouble finding the S^D. Then look for the S^Δ. If you don't have an S^Δ, then you don't have an S^D. Ask if the response can be reinforced any time it has an **opportunity** to occur. If the answer is *yes,* that also means you have no S^D. Instead, you have an ***undiscriminated reinforcement contingency***—there is no S^D associated with the reinforcement contingency. In other words, maybe the reinforcement contingency isn't always in operation; but when it is, there is no special stimulus (S^D) present. However, in most examples of the undiscriminated reinforcement contingency, the reinforcement contingency actually is in operation at all times, 24 hours a day, 7 days a week, at least at all times when the response can occur. In other words, there is no S^Δ condition; instead, if the operandum is present, the response can be reinforced.

On the other hand, if you do have an S^Δ, then you must also have an S^D, and then you have a ***discriminated reinforcement contingency***—*the reinforcement contingency is in operation only when the S^D is present, not when the S^Δ is present.* If a response never being reinforced, then we'd just call that plain old *extinction.* Of course we can also have discriminated and undiscriminated escape and punishment.

The Skinner Box

You put experimentally naive Son of Rudolph in a modified Skinner box for the first time. There is no special light in the box, just the ambient light of your laboratory. But the major modification of the box is that you can remove and insert the response lever at will. You shape up lever pressing and then begin inserting and removing the lever.

1. Does this experiment involve an S^D?
   a. yes
   b. no

Remember: A ***discriminative stimulus*** *is a stimulus in the presence of which a particular response will be reinforced or punished.* Sounds like the response lever might be the S^D. But the lever is the operandum; and the operandum can't be its own S^D. You might think inserting it into the Skinner box makes it the S^D and its absence would be the S^Δ. But think. Will the lever press be reinforced anytime it has an opportunity to occur? Yes. An S^D deals with opportunity for reinforcement, not the opportunity for the responding.

2. So which does this Skinner box experiment involve?
   a. an S^D
   b. an undiscriminated reinforcement contingency

Just to get yourself centered on more familiar turf, you stick a light in the Skinner box and turn it on when you will reinforce lever pressing and turn it off when you won't.

3. Now what does this experiment involve?
   a. an S^D
   b. an undiscriminated reinforcement contingency

Remember: **If you can't find the S^Δ then there's no S^D.** But not to worry, much and maybe most of life consists of undiscriminated reinforcement, escape, and punishment contingencies. When you itch, you scratch and you get some relief from that aversive condition; and the scratch always works, more or less, not just when the green light is on.

Behavior Mod: Undiscriminated Punishment Contingencies

Remember Velma and Gerri's problem with teeth grinding (Chapter 4, Punishment)? The use of the ice cube on the cheek following teeth grinding was an undiscriminated punishment contingency. Although the contingency wasn't always operating, there was no functional S^D associated with the occasions when the experimenters were present, because both Velma and Gerri were deaf and blind.

Summary

By way of summary, you'd do well to master the following criteria:

Definition: Criteria for Diagramming Discriminated Contingencies

S^Δ contingency test
- Is there also an S^Δ? (If not, then you also don't have an S^D.)

Same before condition test
- Is the before condition the same for both the S^D and the S^Δ?

Response test
- Is the response the same for both the S^D and the S^Δ?

Extinction/Recovery test
- Is the S^Δ contingency always extinction or recovery?

Operandum test
- Does the S^D differ from the operandum?

Different before condition test
- Does the S^D differ from the before condition?

QUESTIONS

1. Know the criteria for diagramming discriminated contingencies and be able to recognize when there is and is not an S^D.

13 Complex Stimulus Control

FUNDAMENTALS

Example of Concept Training
Experimental Analysis
THE PECKING PIGEON
PEOPLE PEEPER[1]

What is a person? Plato defined a person as a two-legged animal without feathers. Sly Diogenes then plucked the feathers from a chicken and brought it into the academy. Academicians then realized they would have to change their definition. They thought awhile. "A person is a two-legged animal without feathers but with broad, flat nails," they finally claimed.

In only a few moments you can think of exceptions to this rule. You can think of a creature that fits the rule but is not a person. You also can think of a creature that doesn't fit the rule but is a person. A chimpanzee fits the rule but isn't a person. A human being without arms or legs doesn't fit the rule but is a person.

It may well be an impossible task to give a set of rules that describes and defines the concept person. Interestingly enough, we correctly use the concept of *person,* though we can't give a good explicit definition. It seems that almost intuitively we know what a person is. This shows what we mean when we say we are doing something according to **intuition.** When we behave intuitively, our behavior is being controlled by a concept we can't define.

We won't make this a formal definition, but here's the way we see it: **Intuition (intuitive control)**—control by a concept or set of contingencies the person or organism does not define or describe.

Note that the person may or may not be able to define the concept, but at the time of interest, a statement of that definition is not exerting stimulus control over the person's behavior. For example, "I may not be an artist, but I know what good art is." Even an artist probably would have a hard time giving a set of rules that allows you to select good art from bad art; yet what the artist selects might be under reliable control of stimulus characteristics of good artwork. Intuitive concepts of good and bad art are exerting stimulus control over the behavior of the artist.

An intellectual woman once asked the jazz musician Fats Waller, "How do you define jazz?" Fats replied, "Honey, if you don't know what jazz is, I can't tell you." In other words, jazz was exerting intuitive stimulus control over Fats' behavior. When he lit a cigar and sat down at the piano to play, Viennese waltzes didn't roll forth from his fingertips.

And what about you? You may be able to tell the difference between generic rock, heavy metal, punk, new wave, and new age; but can you define them, or are these concepts exerting intuitive control over your behavior?

How do such intuitive concepts come to have stimulus control over our behavior if no one knows the rules defining the concepts? Consider the concept of *person.* Intuitive stimulus control might evolve something like this: A young girl correctly points to a person or a picture of a person. The child says, "Person," and her parents' approval reinforces this behavior. When the child points to a picture of a chimpanzee and says, "Person," the parents tell the

---

[1]Based on Herrnstein, R. J., & Loveland, D. H. (1964). Complex visual concepts in the pigeon. *Science, 146,* 549–551. For a simple procedure with which students can replicate the original Herrnstein and Loveland results, using simple apparatus that should cost no more than about 10 bucks and is easily done in an undergraduate lab, you might check out the following: Malott, R. W., & Siddall, J. W. (1972). Acquisition of the people concept in pigeons. *Psychological Record, 31,* 3–13. Please send us a note if you tried this experiment and let us know if it worked out.

child, "No." This might mildly punish the incorrect response. After many such trials, an intuitive concept of *person* may come to exert stimulus control over the child's behavior.

Dr. Herrnstein and Dr. Loveland studied this process of intuitive concept learning in an interesting experiment at Harvard University. These scientists showed that even the behavior of pigeons could come under the control of the concept of *person*—to be more exact, under the control of the concept of *picture of person*. Of course, at the same time, their behavior also came under the control of the concept of *nonperson*.

Training

Herrnstein and Loveland used a straightforward concept-training procedure. They projected a variety of pictures (one at a time) on a viewing screen in the pigeon's Skinner box. The experimenters reinforced pecking the response key when the pictures contained people. But they withheld reinforcement when the pictures didn't contain people. So pictures with people served as the S^D (discriminative stimulus) for the key peck, and pictures without people served as the SΔ.

The photographs came from various settings, such as countrysides, cities, expanses of water, lawns, and meadows. As Herrnstein and Loveland said, many of the human beings were

> . . . partly obscured by objects such as trees, automobiles, window frames and so on. The people were distributed throughout the pictures: in the center or to one side or the other, near the top or the bottom, close up or distant. Some [pictures] contained a single person; others contained groups of various sizes. The people themselves varied in appearance: They were clothed, seminude, or nude; adults or children; men or women; sitting, standing, or lying; black, white, or yellow. Lighting and coloration varied: Some [pictures] were dark, others light; some had either reddish or bluish tints, and so on.

As you can see, they used a tremendous variety of stimuli. The S^Ds contained many different specific examples of persons, and the S^Δs contained many different pictures of nonpersons.

The concept of *person* is complex, and to our knowledge, this was the first attempt to teach such a complex concept to a nonverbal animal. But the birds' behavior came under proper stimulus control rapidly. In fact, sometimes when the birds appeared to make mistakes, the experimenters looked more

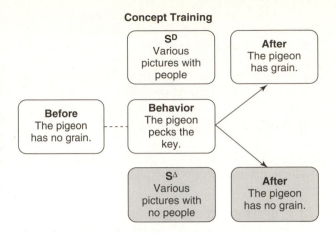

Concept Training

closely and would find a person hidden in some corner of the picture. The pigeons were about as good as the experimenters at responding to the presence of human beings in the pictures.

Testing

We have seen that the pigeon's key peck was under the control of the concepts of *person* and *nonperson*. This concept didn't hold just for the specific stimuli in training. After much concept training, they tested for stimulus generalization to novel pictures to the birds.

Results

When the experimenters showed a novel picture of a person or a nonperson, the birds responded correctly to it. This is a most important aspect of conceptual control. It results in responding correctly in novel situations.

Discussion

So the point of this classic experiment is that conceptual stimuli such as the pictures of people can exert stimulus control over the behavior of a pigeon, just as conceptual stimuli such as new wave can exert stimulus control over your behavior, causing you to properly label the music as *new wave*.

1. In spite of the title of this section and the example being analyzed, many students still seem to think that only human beings can be under conceptual stimulus control. What do you think?
   a. Conceptual control works only for human beings.
   b. It works with other animals as well.
2. Please justify your answer.

Notice that we don't say that people and pigeons *have concepts*. Instead, we say that their *behavior is under the stimulus control of concepts*. A little longer, but it may help us focus on what concepts are really about; they're a set of stimuli, and they either exert stimulus control or they don't.

QUESTIONS

Danger: Study this section extra carefully, because students often mess up their answers to this one on the quiz.

1. Concerning the experiment to teach the concepts of *picture of person* and *picture of non-person to* pigeons:
   ○ Diagram the training contingencies.
   ○ What was the testing procedure?
   ○ What were the results?

Concept
STIMULUS CLASS, STIMULUS GENERALIZATION, AND CONCEPT TRAINING

Herrnstein and Loveland used a **conceptual discrimination training procedure** to establish conceptual control over the pigeons' key-peck response by the concept of *person*. Such a procedure is more complex than the simpler discrimination-training procedure. The simpler procedure uses only a single S^D and a single S^Δ (for example, a green light versus a red light). However, instead of two individual stimuli, Herrnstein and Loveland used two stimulus classes (people versus nonpeople). So let's take a brief look at stimulus class.

The notion of **stimulus class** parallels that of response class. A stimulus class consists of a set of stimuli that all have some common property. In the Herrnstein-Loveland experiment, one set of stimuli, pictures of persons, had the common property of containing at least one person. This stimulus class also had another common behavioral property: All pictures of persons served as S^Ds for pecking the key. Nonhuman pictures served as S^Δs for pecking. Another name for stimulus class is *concept.*

We know that conceptual stimulus control (or just conceptual control) is occurring when two conditions are met:

1. The observer responds in a similar way to all stimuli in a stimulus class (including novel stimuli not previously experienced).
2. But the observer does not respond that way to stimuli outside that class (including novel stimuli).

When the observer responds in a similar way to different stimuli, we say **stimulus generalization** is occurring. Herrnstein and Loveland reinforced key pecks in the presence of specific human pictures. Then the effects of the reinforcement generalized to novel pictures of other persons. So **conceptual stimulus control** consists of generalization within a concept or stimulus class and discrimination between concepts or stimulus classes. To establish conceptual stimulus control, we must reinforce one response in the presence of one stimulus class or concept and extinguish that response in the presence of all other stimulus classes or concepts.

Often, critics of behavior analysis argue that our approach is too limited. But such critics don't understand how concept training can explain the occurrence of appropriate responses in new situations, situations the organism has never experienced before. And, as you can see, the notion of conceptual stimulus control allows us to understand and even predict the occurrence of appropriate responding in novel situations.

Notice that the definition of concept training is identical to that of stimulus discrimination training, except for one word: *Concept training* deals with stimulus classes, whereas discrimination training deals with individual stimuli. But what a difference a single word can make. It's the difference between being able to recognize your best friend from many different angles and distances and in many different clothes (the stimulus class of your friend) versus being able to recognize your friend from only one specific view, for example (individual stimulus).

Imagine that our behavior was so limited we could respond correctly only in situations where we had received specific training. This would severely handicap us because, day to day, even moment to moment, we find ourselves in situations slightly different from any we have experienced before. But those situations also are slightly similar. And they generally fall within some concept. It might be the concept of dining room, food, classroom, teacher, or classmate. Our training in the presence of earlier examples of the concept generalizes to the new instance, and we respond accordingly. As we have seen, this valuable ability to generalize within stimulus classes is available not only to human beings but to pigeons. The pigeons respond accurately when we show them novel pictures.

So a pigeon's behavior can be under the control of complex concepts, such as person and nonperson. We don't know the exact limitations of the pigeon's concept of person. For example, what would happen if we showed a pigeon a picture of a scarecrow or a chimpanzee? Would the bird classify it as person or nonperson? It may well be that if the pigeon didn't have specific training using such examples, its behavior might not be under perfect control of the concept. But that's true of human behavior, too: Without specific discrimination training, we might overgeneralize from person to chimpanzee and scarecrow, just as the young child overgeneralizes from father to all men.

Definition: Concepts

Stimulus class (concept)
- A set of stimuli,
- all of which have some common physical property.

Stimulus generalization
- The behavioral contingencies
- in the presence of one stimulus
- affect the frequency of the response
- in the presence of another stimulus.

Concept training
- Reinforcing or punishing a response
- in the presence of one stimulus class
- and extinguishing it
- or allowing it to recover
- in the presence of another stimulus class.

Conceptual stimulus control
- Responding occurs more often in the presence of one stimulus class
- and less often in the presence of another stimulus class
- because of concept training.

QUESTIONS

1. *Stimulus class (concept)*—define it and give an example.
2. *Stimulus generalization*—define it and give an example.
3. *Conceptual stimulus control (conceptual control)*—define it and give an example.
4. *Conceptual discrimination training procedure*—define it.

Example of Concept Training
Experimental Analysis
ART APPRECIATION 101 FOR PIGEONS[2]

Here's a brand-new and even more exciting extension of the classic Herrnstein and Loveland experiment. This experiment was conducted by Dr.

---

[2]Editors. (1995). Animals–Everyone's a Critic. Breakthroughs in science, technology, and medicine. *Discover, 16,* (Number 5, May), p. 14. (Thanks to John Eshleman for abstracting this article and sharing it on the Behavioral Bulletin Board of Compuserve.)

Shigeru Watanabe and his colleagues at Keio University, the behavior analysis center of Japan.

Training

The first group of pigeons was shown slides of paintings by the impressionist Monet and by the cubist Picasso (the slides were projected from behind onto the pigeon's response key). When the Monet paintings were projected, key pecks were reinforced with food. And when the Picasso paintings were projected, key pecks were extinguished. The reverse was done for the second group—when the Picasso paintings were projected, key pecks were reinforced; and when the Monet paintings were projected, key pecks were extinguished.. After 20 or so sessions, the discriminations were clear. Pigeons reliably pecked at the Monets in the first group and the Picassos in the second, rarely making mistakes.

Please diagram the training contingencies for the Picasso group:

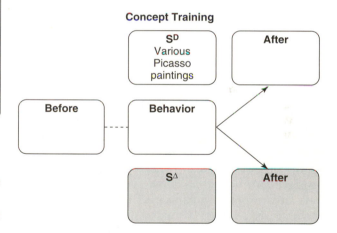

Testing and Results

Shigeru and his fellow art lovers then did generalization tests with novel paintings by Monet and Picasso. The Monet-pecking pigeons readily pecked at the new Monets but not at the new Picassos, while the Picasso-pecking birds reliably did the opposite.

Then the researchers went even further and presented the birds with impressionist paintings by Renoir and cubist paintings by Braque. The impressionist Monet-trained birds pecked the impressionist Renoirs, not the cubist Braques. The Picasso-trained birds, on the other hand, pecked the Braques but not the impressionistic Renoirs. At this point, apparently, the Monet pigeons were clearly aficionados of the impressionistic school of art, while the Picasso birds had become aficionados of cubism!

Going even further out on a limb, where few pigeons would dare to roost, the scientists removed color and projected only black-and-white renditions of the artwork. Excellent stimulus control was maintained.

Then they projected the paintings out of focus to reduce the sharp edges and make the paintings equally blurry. But excellent stimulus control still maintained.

I don't know how it is in Japan, but those pigeons would pass any U.S. art appreciation course with flying colors. Now, if someone will do the same experiment with jazz versus polka, Fats Waller will be able to rest in his grave.

QUESTIONS

1. Concerning the experiment to teach the concepts of *Picasso paintings* to pigeons:
   ○ Diagram the training contingencies.
   ○ What was the testing procedure?
2. What were the results?

Examples and Nonexamples
CONCEPTUAL CONTROL AND OTHER CONCEPTS

Let's take a brief glance at a few examples of these and other relevant and potentially confusing concepts. This way, we can make sure they're exerting proper conceptual control over your behavior. First, look at the possible concepts. Then look at each example and select the possible concept or concepts that example best illustrates. Use a card or piece of paper or your hand to cover up our answers as you read. That will help you give it your best shot.

The Concepts

1. S^D
2. S^Δ
3. Punishment-based discriminative stimulus
4. Simple discrimination training procedure
5. Stimulus discrimination (stimulus control)
6. Stimulus class (concept)
7. Stimulus generalization
8. Conceptual stimulus control
9. *Conceptual discrimination training procedure*

The Examples

Question

A set of pictures of people. Did you select your answer? Yes. Good, it's a pleasure to work with a noncheater. Now look at our answer.

Our Answer

Of course, this was our original example of a stimulus class. And any stimulus class also is a concept. We just put this one in to see if you're alive.

Question

Sid puts a red apple and a yellow banana in front of Rod. Sometimes he asks Rod to point to the red apple and sometimes to point to the yellow banana. What are the red apple and the yellow banana?

Our Answer

Tricky. The apple is both an S^D and an S^Δ. It's an S^D for pointing to it when Sid says, "Point to the red apple." It's an S^Δ for pointing to it when Sid says, "Point to the yellow banana." We'll let you work out the details regarding the yellow banana.

Question

The sweet taste of the red apples reinforces Rod's eating them. The tart taste of the green apples does not. Over a period of a few weeks, last fall, Rod eventually stopped eating the green apples but continued eating the red ones. What are the red apples?

Our Answer

A stimulus class or concept (the same thing). You might have said an S^D, and that's right, but not specific enough. The reason is that we're talking about a large number of different red apples. So they are part of the stimulus class we call "red apples."

Question

What kind of control are those red and green apples exerting over Rod's eating?

Our Answer

Conceptual stimulus control. Again, saying "stimulus control" is not specific enough.

Question

Is this also an example of stimulus generalization? Why or why not?

Our Answer

Yes, it is stimulus generalization—stimulus generalization among the various examples of the concept of red apple and stimulus generalization among the various examples of the concept of green apple.

Question

What kind of training procedure caused Rod to become a discriminating apple eater?

Our Answer

A conceptual discrimination-training procedure, because the eating response is reinforced in the presence of a number of different specific red apples, and it is extinguished (maybe even punished) in the presence of a number of different green apples.

Question

Whenever Rod sees his Uncle Ben, he looks at the man, smiles, and says, "Candy, please." This always gets the uncle, and Ben always reaches into his pocket, pulls out a Lifesaver, and gives it to the young panhandler. However, Uncle Jim, the dentist, is unwilling to sacrifice the child's dental health just to gain immediate approval. So, eventually, Rod hits only on Ben. Technically, what is Ben and what is Jim?

Our Answer

Ben is an S^D for requesting candy. Jim is an S^Δ. We've got only one Ben and one Jim, so we don't have stimulus classes (at least not from a simple point of view).

Question (for Advanced Students Only)

Suppose, by the end of this chapter, you can discriminate between novel examples of simple stimulus control and conceptual stimulus control. What would this be an example of?

Our Answer

Conceptual stimulus control. One concept or stimulus class is the examples of stimulus control and the other is the examples of conceptual stimulus control.

Question (for Advanced Students Only)

Now suppose instead we gave you only one example of simple stimulus control and one of conceptual stimulus control. And in this case, you could not discriminate between novel examples of simple stimulus control and conceptual stimulus control. However, you were a killer when it came to the two examples we had given you. What would this be an example of?

Our Answer

Simple stimulus control, because there's only one example in each set of stimuli.

Compare and Contrast
DISCRIMINATION VS. GENERALIZATION

Generalization is the opposite of discrimination. If an observer responds in nearly the same way to two different stimuli, then the observer is showing much generalization and little discrimination. On the other hand, an observer may respond differently in the presence of two different stimuli. Then the observer is showing ample discrimination and little generalization. The greater the discrimination, the less the generalization, and vice versa.

Usually when two stimuli are physically similar, considerable generalization will occur between such stimuli, and good discrimination (stimulus control) will be hard to establish. If two stimuli are completely different, there may be little stimulus generalization between them, and a good discrimination (stimulus control) will be established easily.

For example, suppose you know two sisters, Sally and Sarah, who are only a year apart in age. You may sometimes tend to confuse the two. In other words, you may respond to Sally with responses that have been reinforced by Sarah; for instance, you might call Sally "Sarah." Your reinforcement history with Sarah generalized to Sally. But they aren't that much alike, so the two sisters probably exert some stimulus control over your use of their names. Most of the time, you discriminate accurately between the two.

Now suppose, instead, that the two sisters are actually fraternal twins—probably more physically similar than ordinary sisters. That might generate more generalization and less discrimination between the two. Or suppose Sally and Sarah are identical twins who have the perversity of always dressing alike. They find it amusing to confuse their innocent and well-meaning friends. Now we're talking generalization city, not much discrimination, not much stimulus control anymore.

QUESTION

1. What is the difference between discrimination and generalization?

Concept
STIMULUS DIMENSIONS AND FADING[3]

To understand the fading procedure, we first need to understand the concept of *stimulus dimensions*—the characteristics of stimuli. Often, we mean physical characteristics, such as roundness, smoothness, size, height, weight, luster, color, or shade.

Definition: Concept
Stimulus dimensions
  ○ The physical properties of a stimulus.

We also can think of stimulus dimensions in terms of the ways stimuli can differ from each other. For example, a house differs from an automobile along many obvious dimensions—size, shape, weight, material, and so on. The more dimensions along which objects differ, the easier it is to establish discriminative stimulus control. So it's easy to establish a discrimination between a house and an automobile. Rarely do you hop into your house and try to drive to school (probably you'd have trouble getting it into first gear because you couldn't find the clutch).

Similarly, the fewer the dimensions along which objects differ, the harder it is to establish discriminative stimulus control over our behavior. For example, it is not too easy to discriminate a good golf ball (S^D) from a bad one (S^Δ). The two golf balls are similar in so many dimensions and differ in only a few, subtle dimensions, like roundness, resiliency, and hardness of cover.

So to establish that discrimination, you might start with a good golf ball (S^D) and one that's not good (S^Δ). But to make the discrimination easier, you'd color the loser (S^Δ) green so that the student could easily discriminate between the good one (S^D) and the bad one (S^Δ), though on an irrelevant stimulus dimension. Then you'd gradually fade out the difference between the S^D and the S^Δ, fading the green to white. Eventually the only difference between the good and the bad golf ball would be roundness, resiliency, or hardness of cover. And that relevant stimulus dimension would be the only basis for the discrimination. Presumably the student would still be properly discriminating between the two balls, even though they were now the same color and the discrimination was much more difficult. The procedure you used is called **fading.**

---
[3]This section is based on Whaley, D., & Welt, K. (1967). Uses of ancillary cues and fading techniques in name discrimination training in retardates. *Michigan Mental Health Research, 1,* 29–30.

Definition: Concept
Fading procedure
  ○ At first, the S^Δ and the S^D differ along at least two stimulus dimensions.
  ○ The difference between the S^Δ and the S^D along all but one dimension is reduced until there is no difference along the reduced dimensions.
  ○ Then the S^Δ and the S^D differ along only one dimension.

QUESTIONS

1. *Stimulus dimension*—define it and give an example.
2. *Fading*—define it and give an example.

Compare and Contrast
STIMULUS CLASS VS. STIMULUS DIMENSION VS. RESPONSE DIMENSION

Recall: A *stimulus class (concept)* is a set of stimuli all of which have some common property. *Stimulus dimensions* are the characteristics of a stimulus or stimulus class.

Question

What are red triangles—a class or a dimension?

Our Answer

A stimulus class—a set of stimuli all of which have the common properties of red on the color dimension and triangularity on the shape dimension. Green circles are another stimulus class. They differ from the class of red triangles along both the color and the shape dimensions.

Question

What is the intensity of a light—a class or dimension?

Our Answer

Intensity of light is a stimulus dimension—a characteristic of the light stimulus. Such characteristics constitute the differences among stimulus classes—a set of stimuli all of which have some common property. For example, along the stimulus dimension of light intensity, we might have bright lights and dim lights. All bright lights form one stimulus class because they have the common property of being bright. And all dim lights form another stimulus class, with the common property of being dim.

Question

What is red—a stimulus class or a stimulus dimension?

Our answer

Neither. Red is a value on the color dimension, so it can't be a dimension itself. Red is a property of a stimulus or stimulus class. The classes of red apples and green apples differ in that they have different values on the dimension of color. However, we could have a class consisting of all red objects and another consisting of all green objects. But simply the color *red* is neither a class nor a dimension. Red is an **abstraction.** What about 2 inches? That also is a value on the length dimension; it is neither a stimulus class nor a stimulus dimension by itself.

Question

What is force of a lever press, from the rat's view—a stimulus class or stimulus dimension?

Our Answer

We've got another "neither" here. From the rat's view, the force of its lever press is a **response dimension**—a physical property of a response. If the red apple is, shall we say, "mature," you needn't use much force when you bite into it. Responses and response classes differ from each other along response dimensions, just as stimulus classes do along stimulus dimensions. Now that's normally true, but one student did suggest a type of exception. Suppose Newton had been sitting under a cherry tree instead of an apple tree. Then a cherry might have struck him with light force, rather than an apple with moderate force (with your luck, Sir Isaac, please stay away from palm trees). So we could say that the two stimuli, being hit by a cherry versus an apple, differed in force. Therefore, on rare occasions we might consider force to be a stimulus dimension— basically when we're talking about the force of something being done to you rather than force you exert when you respond. But usually we behavior analysts are talking about the response dimension when we use the word *force*.

QUESTION

1. Be able to discriminate between examples of stimulus class, stimulus dimension, and response dimension.

Example of Errorless Discrimination
Behavioral School Psychology
TEACHING READING[4]

Mae used the fading technique with Jimmy: First she and her staff showed Jimmy a card with the letters of his name on a white background; they also showed the name of another resident, Susan, on a card with the same style and color of lettering but on a black background.

They told Jimmy, "Pick up the card with your name." Then they reinforced the correct response with a raisin. Once Jimmy picked up the correct card on 40 trials, they removed his name from the white card and put it on one that was slightly less white, one that approached a light gray. Now the difference was still apparent. When he did 40 trials without any error, they changed the shade of the card to a slightly darker shade. They introduced a new shade each time Jimmy achieved 40 correct trials. In that way they faded the shades 11 times, until the card with the name Jimmy was the same black shade as the card with the name Susan.

Fading initially involved making the two cards as dissimilar as possible along one dimension, the shade of the background. The other dimension in which the two cards differed was the lettering. The differences in lettering remained constant while the staff varied the darkness of the background. The results? At first, Jimmy's response came under the control of two very different stimuli—the shades of the two backgrounds. Then they decreased the differences in those two shades so slowly that Jimmy made no errors. Such a fading technique establishes a discrimination with no errors—an **errorless discrimination,** in which the subject makes the correct response without a single error in a discrimination-training procedure.

> *Definition: Concept*
> **Errorless discrimination procedure**
> ○ The use of a fading procedure
> ○ to establish a discrimination,
> ○ with no errors during the training.

---

[4]Based on a case study by Donald L. Whaley with a girl from an institution for the developmentally disabled.

Reinforcement-Based Discrimination

QUESTION

1. *Errorless discrimination training*—define it and diagram an example.

Compare and Contrast
SHAPING, FADING, AND REINFORCER REDUCTION

People often confuse fading with shaping, as well as with a procedure we'll call **reinforcer reduction.** First, let's review shaping: Before using shaping, we decide on a goal—the terminal behavior. We select a response resembling the terminal behavior, we reinforce it, and then we reinforce successive approximations to the terminal behavior. We move our criterion for reinforcement closer and closer to the terminal behavior until the subject ultimately exhibits the terminal behavior. The type of response we reinforce changes as the frequency of that response increases. The response we initially reinforce may resemble the terminal behavior in only a superficial way. We soon discard and exchange this response for one that more directly resembles the terminal behavior.

At first glance, a fading procedure may appear similar to a shaping procedure because in both cases things change gradually. But, unlike shaping, the gradual change in a fading procedure involves the stimulus and not the response. Thus, in shaping, the response itself changes because of differential reinforcement. But, in fading, the response stays the same; what changes is the values of the stimuli.

A similar type of gradual change may entail the replacement of one type of reinforcer for another. Here's a common example: We might first reinforce a response with a primary reinforcer, such as

food or ice cream. Then we gradually replace the food with praise or other social reinforcers. A less common, but feasible, situation could involve the reduction in the reinforcer. A rat may first receive three pellets during reinforcement, but later only one pellet for reinforcement could maintain the same response. We can use the concept *reinforcer reduction* to refer to all these variables—schedule, amount, and type of reinforcer reduction. A gradual reinforcer reduction may be an important part of a behavior modification plan.

In the chart we compare these techniques of gradual change—shaping, reinforcer reduction, and stimulus fading.

Each of these three procedures is conceptually independent and can occur without affecting the other two. In practice, we may find it useful, or necessary, to use two or even all three procedures to get the desired behavioral result.

Techniques of Gradual Change		
Procedure	Area of Application	Purpose
Shaping	Response differentiation	To bring about a response not made by the organism
Reinforcer Reduction	Type and amount of reinforcer	To maintain responses already made or to establish a particular pattern of responses*
Fading	Stimulus discrimination	To bring the response under the control of stimuli that didn't exert control initially

*We might also use reinforcer reduction to transfer control from the added performance-management contingency to some built-in, natural contingency.

QUESTIONS

1. Give an example of each of the following techniques:
   ○ shaping
   ○ fading
   ○ reinforcer reduction
2. What are the differences between these three procedures?
3. What are the similarities?

INTERMEDIATE ENRICHMENT

In the Skinner Box
Experimental Analysis
STIMULUS-GENERALIZATION GRADIENTS[5]

Stimulus generalization is more or less the opposite of stimulus discrimination. On the one hand, we say two stimuli exert stimulus control to the extent that the individual responds **differently** in the presence of the two. For example, a pigeon might peck the key in the presence of the S^D and not in the presence of the $S\Delta$. This is *stimulus discrimination.*

On the other hand, we say the stimulus control by one stimulus generalizes to another stimulus to the extent that the individual responds in the *same* way in the presence of the two stimuli. For example, suppose a pigeon has had considerable training with an S^D but little training with an $S\Delta$. Then the bird might respond at almost as high a rate in the presence of the $S\Delta$ as in the presence of the S^D. This is *stimulus generalization*. The control of the S^D has generalized to the $S\Delta$.

Guttman and Kalish showed a similar sort of stimulus generalization in their classic experiment.

Training with Intermittent Reinforcement

During the training phase, these experimenters reinforced the key pecks of a pigeon in the presence of a training stimulus—a yellow-green light (a light with a 550 mµ wavelength). They used an intermittent reinforcement procedure in which they reinforced only an occasional response in the presence of the yellow-green light (a variable-interval schedule of reinforcement). Most of the key pecks didn't get reinforced.

Training Procedure: Intermittent Reinforcement

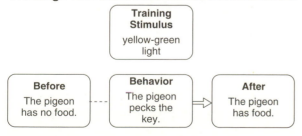

[5]Guttman, N., & Kalish, H. I. (1956). Discriminability and stimulus generalization. *Journal of Experimental Psychology,* **51,** 79–88.

Note that we're not calling the training stimulus an S^D. Why? Because there was no $S\Delta$, and we need an $S\Delta$ in order to have an S^D. Remember?

Testing in Extinction

Once the pigeon responded reliably in the presence of that yellow-green light, Guttman and Kalish tested for stimulus generalization using an extinction procedure with a set of test stimuli (a variety of novel light colors) in addition to the training stimulus (the original training color) This means that during testing no key pecks produced reinforcement. The experimenters presented their 11 different colors, blue to red, in a random sequence.

Testing Procedure: Extinction

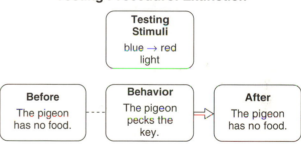

You should understand that color (hue) is a natural stimulus dimension (the physical dimension is the wavelength of the light). And the colors are naturally arranged in a sequence. You can see that stimulus dimension by looking at a rainbow or looking at white light through a prism, which will give you a rainbow effect and arrange the colors side by side according to their wavelengths. For example, you will see that orange is closer to yellow-green than red is.

It is important to note that the testing procedure involved extinction—no reinforcement in the presence of any of the stimuli, either the training stimulus or the test stimuli. Why'd they do it that way? Why didn't they continue reinforcing the response in the presence of the training stimulus and extinguish in the presence of the test stimuli? To reduce the effects of discrimination training. They wanted to measure the amount of "natural" stimulus generalization without the biasing or sharpening effects of stimulus-discrimination training.

An alternative testing procedure might have been to intermittently reinforce all responding—the responding in the presence of the training stimuli as well as that in the presence of the test stimuli. But again, that training effect might bias the results too much and show too much stimulus generalization.

By the way, note that key pecking was not reinforced in the presence of the 10 testing colors while it was being reinforced in the presence of the original yellow-green training stimulus (in fact, the testing colors were not even presented during the training procedure; only the yellow-green training color was presented then). Therefore, we're still reluctant to call the yellow-green training stimulus an S^D or the 10 testing stimuli S^Δs.[6]

Results

What do you think happened? The pigeons made progressively fewer responses as the colors were more and more dissimilar from the yellow-green training color. They responded most in the presence of the original yellow-green light, less with the yellow light, still less with an orange light, and least with a red light. Similarly, the response rate decreased as the colors went in the other direction from the original yellow-green, to green, to blue-green, and finally to blue (Figure 13.1).

The Guttman-Kalish experiment is typical of experiments on stimulus generalization: We reinforce a response in the presence of one stimulus. Then we measure the responding when we change some property of that stimulus. The greater the responding with the changed stimulus, we say the greater the stimulus generalization.

A stimulus-generalization experiment usually produces a ***stimulus-generalization gradient.*** Such gradients show that as some property of the stimulus becomes increasingly different from the discriminative stimulus used during reinforcement, the response rate decreases. In other words, the more dissimilar two stimuli are, the less the stimulus generalization and the better the discrimination. (***Gradient*** refers to the extent that something changes, such as the *grade* of a road might become steep. A ***stimulus-generalization gradient*** refers to the extent that response rate changes when a test stimulus changes from the training stimulus.)

Definition: Concept
Stimulus-generalization gradient
  ○ A gradient of responding showing
  ○ a decrease of stimulus control
  ○ as the test stimulus
  ○ becomes less similar to the training stimulus.

The pigeons' rate of responding decreased as the test stimuli became less similar to the yellow-green training stimulus. The test stimuli exerted less stimulus control.

QUESTIONS

1. For the pigeon experiment that shows stimulus generalization:
   a. Diagram the training procedure.
   b. Diagram the testing procedure.
   c. Draw a graph of the results.
   Danger: Study this section extra carefully, because students often mess up their answers to this question on the quiz.
2. *Stimulus-generalization gradient*—define it and give an example.

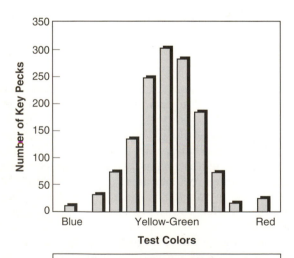

A pigeon's key pecks were reinforced in the presence of a yellow-green light and then tested in the presence of yellow-green and other colors.

Figure 13.1   Stimulus-Generalization Gradient

---

[6]But don't be shocked if your instructor prefers a slightly different analysis.

Compare and Contrast
AMOUNT OF GENERALIZATION VS. AMOUNT OF DISCRIMINATION

Look at the original gradient in Figure 13.2. It's the same one we showed for the original Guttman and Kalish experiment in the previous graph; but this

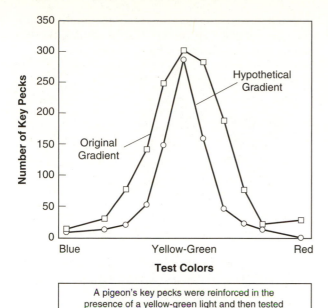

A pigeon's key pecks were reinforced in the presence of a yellow-green light and then tested in the presence of yellow-green and other colors.

Figure 13.2 Stimulus-Generalization Gradient

time we used little squares for the data points and connected them with lines. In other words, this is a line graph rather than a bar graph. In addition, we added a hypothetical stimulus-generalization gradient—one we just made up.

1. Compared to the original gradient, does this hypothetical gradient show more or less stimulus generalization from the yellow-green training stimulus to the other test stimuli?
   a. more stimulus generalization
   b. less stimulus generalization

2. Compared to the original stimulus-generalization gradient, does this hypothetical stimulus-generalization gradient show more or less stimulus discrimination between the yellow-green training stimulus and the other test stimuli?
   a. more stimulus discrimination
   b. less stimulus discrimination

If you have less stimulus generalization between a training stimulus and a test stimulus, you have more stimulus discrimination; in other words you have more stimulus control. **Amount of stimulus generalization is the opposite of the amount of stimulus discrimination (stimulus control).**

The hypothetical gradient shows more discrimination and less generalization.

3. On the previous graph, draw a gradient that shows less discrimination and thereby more generalization.

Your stimulus-generalization gradient should be flatter.

Suppose we used a training procedure based on discrimination training instead of the training procedure Guttman and Kalish used (they exposed the pigeons to only the yellow-green light during training). In other words, we would alternate the yellow-green light with the other colors, reinforcing key pecks in the presence of yellow-green and extinguishing in the presence of the other colors.

4. The yellow-green light would be an
   a. S^D
   b. S^Δ

5. The other colors would be
   a. S^Ds
   b. S^Δs

6. If we did use such a discrimination-training procedure, which gradient would we probably get? One like
   a. the hypothetical gradient we drew on the graph that showed more stimulus control?
   b. the flatter hypothetical gradient you just drew on the graph that showed less stimulus control?

QUESTION

1. Be able to answer the preceding questions.

THE BEGINNINGS OF HEAVY-DUTY INTELLECTUALITY

We've looked at concept training and conceptual stimulus control. Now let's step back a minute and think about what we're doing. We're moving into something that looks a little like heavy-duty intellectuality. Much more subtle, much more sophisticated than light on, push lever, water; light off, push lever, no water.

Conceptual stimulus control is a big intellectual deal. In this course, we cover about 165 concepts. And being able to write the definition when presented with a behavioral term is a big deal but pretty much on the same level as light on, push lever, water. However, being able to identify novel examples of each of the 165 concepts is a really big intellectual deal, way beyond light, lever, water. In fact, if you can correctly label examples of simple and complex human behavior with each of the 165 concepts, we're talking big-time PhD behavior-analyst material (i.e., big intellectual deal).

And, now we're going to look at matching to sample; we're going to move into more heavy-duty intellectuality. We're going to push the envelope a bit further.

MATCHING TO SAMPLE

The Pigeon

Polly Pigeon pecks a response key, a plastic disk with a green light showing through it (the sample key).

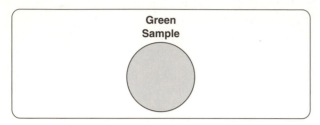

Then two other response keys light up (the comparison keys), a green one on the right of the sample key and a red one on the left.

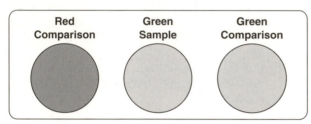

Polly pecks the green comparison key (the one that matches the sample key), and she gets access to a grain trough for 3 seconds (the reinforcer). Sometimes the sample key is green; sometimes it's red. Sometimes the green comparison key is on the right and the red one on the left; sometimes they're reversed. Whenever Polly pecks the comparison that matches the sample, the response is reinforced; pecking the nonmatching comparison key is extinguished. Polly is **matching to sample.**

Definition: Concept
Matching to sample
  ○ selecting a comparison stimulus
  ○ corresponding to a sample stimulus.

The Autistic Child

Jimmy touches the running shoe (sample stimulus) lying on the table between him and Sue.

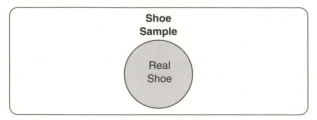

Then Sue puts on the table an identical running shoe and a cup (comparison stimuli), one on each side of the sample-stimulus shoe.

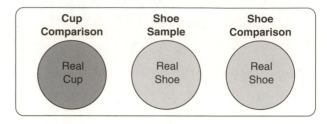

Jimmy touches the comparison-stimulus shoe (he matches to sample), and Sue turns on 3 seconds of Smashing Pumpkins (the reinforcer) for his correct matching to sample. Half the time, the cup is the sample stimulus. And also half the time, the positions of the comparison stimuli are switched.

As each set of stimuli come to control Jimmy's matching to sample, other stimuli are added, such as a doll and a spoon. Then Jimmy and Sue move on to pictures of the objects as the sample stimuli, keeping the real three-dimensional objects as the comparison stimuli. They also move on to stimulus-class matching; for example, the sample stimulus is the running shoe and the matching comparison stimulus is a dress shoe (both types of shoe are in the same stimulus class—shoes). Cool, huh?

And they move on to puzzles. First the sample stimulus is the cutout in the board in the shape of Bunny, and Jimmy picks up the cutout Bunny from the set of four comparison-stimulus animals. He then turns Bunny (comparison stimulus) until it really matches the cutout in the board (sample stimulus); and he puts Bunny home. Yes, we're still in the matching-to-sample business.

Step by step, Jimmy is acquiring the skills that may someday allow him to be a student in a regular-education classroom. And one of those steps is an even more complex, more subtle form of matching to sample. Now Jimmy puts puzzle pieces in a rectangular frame with no internal guides, eight pieces, each 3 to 4 inches in width, with random, wavy cuts that form a simple picture when he properly fits them all into the frame.

Nothing's automatic, nothing's easy; but step by step, Jimmy is making big progress.

The Regular-Education Preschooler

The four colored blocks lay in a row: red, green, yellow, and blue (they combine to form the sample stimulus). Rachel has four other colored blocks that she arranges in the same red-green-yellow-blue sequence (she is now constructing the comparison stimulus). She has just matched to sample, and she has just completed one item on an IQ test for pre-verbal, preschool children.

The College Student

The red stripes form a complex, geometric pattern on the white background, with one part missing (this complex, geometric pattern is the sample stimulus). Four comparison stimuli lie below the sample stimulus; these four stimuli are different geometric forms. Sue touches the comparison stimulus that would complete the complex pattern in the sample stimulus. She has just matched to sample, and she has just completed one item on an IQ test for verbal adults.

The mysterious IQ test is nothing more than a sample of learned skills ranging from simple to complex.

The Pigeon (Advanced Course)

Polly Pigeon pecks the greenlighted sample key.

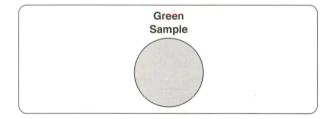

Then the comparison keys light up, one with the word *green* and the other with the word *red*.

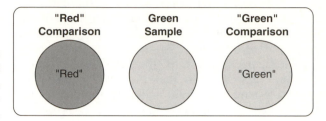

Now Polly's doing **symbolic matching to sample**—*matching to sample in which the relation between the sample and comparison stimuli are arbitrary.* For Polly, the relation is arbitrary because we could just as well have reinforced her matching the words *squig* and *squag* with the green and red lights. We don't want to say Polly's reading, but it sure looks like it, doesn't it? Ain't Polly cool?! (When the sample and comparison stimuli are physically identical, as in our earlier examples, it is sometimes called **identity matching.**)

QUESTIONS

1. *Matching to sample*—define it and illustrate it:
   a. in the Skinner box
   b. with an autistic child
   c. in an IQ test.

ADVANCED ENRICHMENT[7]

STIMULUS EQUIVALENCE—PUTTING THE NAME WITH THE FACES[8]

A few illegal beers, no seat belt, a fast pickup truck, a missed curve, and sudden impact with an unyielding oak tree caused extensive, diffuse brain damage in 19-year-old Al. And now, after 11 years in a traditional brain-injury rehab program, Al still couldn't identify the therapists he saw daily. This is a common outcome of some brain injuries—the inability to do certain kinds of symbolic matching to sample, the inability to match spoken and written words (comparison stimuli) to their corresponding objects, people, or events (sample stimuli). However, like many others with such brain injuries, Al could do some other sorts of symbolic matching; he could match the therapists' written names (comparison

---

[7]This is the first time we've slipped in an *Advanced Enrichment* section, but the topic has become so important that we had to include it; and the concepts are so complex, that we would be guilty of false advertising if we claimed it was only of intermediate difficulty. However, we've done our best to make it as clear as possible; so if you can find a clearer explanation anywhere else in the known universe, let us know and we'll plagiarize it for our next edition.

[8]Based on Cowley, B. J., Green, G., and Braunling-McMorrow, D. (1992). Using stimulus equivalence procedures to teach name-face matching to adults with brain injuries. *Journal of Ap-*

plied Behavior Analysis, 25, 461–475. This was Brian Cowley's master's thesis in Behavior Analysis and Therapy at Southern Illinois University at Carbondale, a major center for behavior analysis. Incidentally, Gina Green is one of the most prominent researcher/practitioners in the field of autism and was a president of ABA.

stimuli) when Dawn spoke their names (sample stimuli); and he could also match (say) their spoken name when Dawn pointed to a written name (sample stimulus); in other words, he could still read.

After 11 years of traditional therapy, Al still needed to look at a written schedule to determine the name of the therapist he was to work with next—the speech therapist, the occupational therapist, the rehabilitation therapist. His inability to do people-name symbolic matching limited his independence. He couldn't function like a normal person.

Symbolic Matching to Sample

Now it was time to implement some behavioral training. Dawn said, "Mark" (sample stimulus), and Al pointed to a color photo of Mark (comparison stimulus on the left). Dawn said, "That's right" (the presumed learned reinforcer).

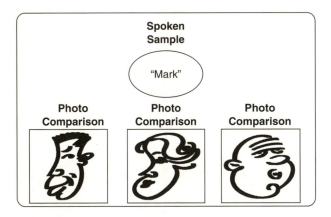

Then she started a new trial by saying, "Bev." But this time Al pointed again to Mark's photo instead of Bev's (comparison photo in the center, in case you couldn't tell), so Dawn said, "Try again." When Al pointed to Bev's photo, Dawn said, "That's right," and went on to the next trial.

For the next month, Dawn and Al did matching to sample with Dawn speaking the names of Al's three therapists and Al attempting to point to the appropriate photo. It took them 2,160 trials before Al became essentially perfect at matching the photos to the spoken names. Now that's a lot of trials; however with this sort of intensive, behavioral training, they made more progress in 1 month than the traditional therapists had made in 11 years. Very few traditional professionals seem to appreciate the importance of such intensive training.

Symmetry

But that's not the whole story. Before Al was trained to point to the photo when Dawn said the name:

> (Spoken name) → (Photo)

Al had also not been able to say the name when Dawn pointed to the photo:

> (Photo) ⇸ (Spoken name)

But now, after the training of spoken name to photo, Al could say the name when Dawn pointed to the photo:

> (Photo) → (Spoken name)[9]

This is novel stimulus control. And that's a big deal; perhaps it saved Al and Dawn an extra month's intensive training.

You might be tempted to say, "Of course, if Al knows this is Mark's photo, then he *knows* that '*Mark*' is the name of the guy in the photo." But it ain't necessarily so. Not with Polly Pigeon, and not with Jimmy before he had true verbal behavior (language). For example, you could do symbolic matching to sample with either Polly or preverbal Jimmy, where they would be given a color green and they would peck or touch the arbitrary symbol, the word *green*.

> (Green) → (Written "green")

---

[9]When we talk about matching to sample, either identity matching or symbolic matching, we're talking about matching a comparison **stimulus** to a sample stimulus, not a comparison **response** to a sample stimulus. To be more precise, we might say Al is matching the auditory stimuli arising from his saying the name (comparison stimulus) to the auditory stimuli arising from Dawn's saying the name (sample stimulus). And the same will apply even when we will later talk about Al's saying the name covertly; here the comparison stimuli are whatever the stimuli are that arise when Al "hears" himself "speaking" covertly, "talking to himself" covertly. Of course, Al's response of generating the comparison stimulus by actually speaking the auditory name is much more complex than his response of selecting the comparison stimulus by merely pointing to the written name.

But given the word *green,* they would not then be able to peck or touch the color green.[10]

(Written "green") $\not\rightarrow$ (Green)

That's the trouble with using commonsense, mentalistic words such as *know,* as in, "Of course, if Al *knows* this is Mark's photo, then he *knows* that 'Mark' is the name of the guy in the photo." Using such commonsense, mentalistic words causes us to get too sloppy in our analysis. Taking it back to the Skinner box, with Polly's symbolic matching to sample, brings us back to reality, strips us of our hidden assumptions, and helps us tighten it up.

Al has achieved what's called *symmetry,* which means that because Al is trained to pick the photo when he hears the name, he can also say the name when he sees the photo.

Symmetry

Training: (Spoken name) $\rightarrow$ (Photo)
Results: (Photo) $\rightarrow$ (Spoken name)

In other words, the stimulus control exerted by the name and the photo is *symmetrical*—it works either way. By *symmetry* we mean that if A $\Rightarrow$ B, then B = A (e.g., if 1 + 2 = 3; then 3 = 1 + 2), as you remember from your first algebra course.

Theory

So how did brain-injured Al do this, when neither Polly nor preverbal Jimmy could achieve symmetry with symbolic matching to sample? We don't know for sure, but here's our theory: Dawn said, "Mark"; and Al said, "Mark," also—

(Spoken "Mark") $\rightarrow$ (Spoken "Mark")

—though perhaps covertly, under his breath, when he touched Mark's photo.

(Mark's photo) $\rightarrow$ (Covertly spoken "Mark")

And then Dawn said, "That's right," reinforcing both Al's touching Mark's photo and his covertly saying, "Mark." So when Dawn pointed to Mark's photo and asked, "Who's this," it was easy for Al to increase the intensity of the covert, under-his-breath "Mark" to an out-loud "Mark," a response that had been reinforced throughout the preceding 2,160 training trials.

(Mark's photo) $\rightarrow$ (Overtly spoken "Mark")

But neither Polly nor Jimmy could say, "green"; so they were out of luck when it came to their test of symmetrical stimulus control.

Transitivity

And there's a more amazing result than the symmetrical stimulus control. Remember that even before training, Al could match the written names to Dawn's spoken names.

(Spoken name) $\rightarrow$ (Written name)

And after 2,160 trials, he'd could match the photos to names Dawn spoke;

(Spoken name) $\rightarrow$ (Photo)

and, because of symmetrical stimulus control, he could also say the name when Dawn pointed to a photo.

(Photo) $\rightarrow$ (Spoken name)

Now here it comes: After those 2,160 training trials, it turns out Al could also match the written names to the photos; in other words, when Dawn touched Mark's photo, Al would touch Mark's written name;

(Photo) $\rightarrow$ (Written name)

and he would do this even though he'd never had symbolic matching-to-sample training involving both the photos and the written names in the same procedure. This also is novel stimulus control; by *novel stimulus control* we mean a "correct" response to a stimulus when that response to that stimulus had not been reinforced previously; in this case, neither the stimulus nor the response were novel, but this response to that stimulus was novel; so we've got novel stimulus control. And again, neither Polly nor Jimmy could achieve this. Only verbal Al could.

So Al also has achieved what's called *transitivity*, which means that because Al is trained to pick the photo when he hears the name and because he can also pick the written name when he hears the name, now he can pick the written name when he sees the photo and vice versa. In other words, the stimulus control exerted by the written name and the photo has a *transitive* relationship. By *transitivity* we mean that if A = B, and B = C, then A = C; and if A > B, and B > C, then A > C, and so on. More first-year algebra.

Transitivity

> Training[11]: (Spoken name) → (Written name)
> Training: (Spoken name) → (Photo)
> Results: (Photo) → (Written name)

Theory

How? More speculative theory: When Al sees Mark's photo, he says, "Mark," either overtly or covertly, as he'd learned from the training.

> (Photo) → (Spoken name)

And he was already able to match the written names to Dawn's spoken names.

> (Dawn speaks name) → (Written name)

So now he just matches the written names to his own speaking of the names.

> (Al speaks name) → (Written name)

And we've got what's called a *behavioral chain:*

> S^D (Photo) → Response (Al speaks name) → S^D (Sound of name) → Response (Al touches written name)

Al touches the correct written name when Dawn points to one of the therapists' photos, even though he was never explicitly trained to do so.

Reflexivity

Just for the record, there's one more term that goes with *symmetry* and *transitivity;* that's **reflexivity.**

Reflexivity refers to the results of simple, nonsymbolic matching to sample, like Polly's matching red with red or Jimmy's matching a shoe with a shoe. Similarly, even before Dawn's training, Al could match written words with identical written words, and photos with identical photos. In other words, his behavior was already under reflexive stimulus control. By reflexivity, we mean if A = A—again, from your first algebra course. Yes, boys and girls, all those years of rigorous math training is finally paying off!

Practical Implications

If Al's behavior could not come under symmetrical and transitive stimulus control, it might have taken him many months, instead of just one, to master the various combinations of matching between the spoken names, the written names, and the photos. And the time saving gets even greater, for example, when you're teaching reading, using a larger set of words and stimuli.

There was another practical result of the present intervention: Al's training with Dawn transferred to his daily life at the rehab center. He could now name the therapists themselves, not just their pictures. This meant, for example, that when he wanted to talk to his physical therapist, he could find her and identify her. Al now had much greater independence in his daily life.[12]

---

[11]Really a result of training Al must have had before Dawn started working with him.

[12]It is beyond our purpose and available space to go into the more complex, though perhaps more practical, applications of stimulus-equivalence training, but they exist: In regular preschool education, researchers have used stimulus equivalence to teach reading, writing, and arithmetic.

Stimulus Equivalence

Most behavior analysts say a set of arbitrary, symbolic stimuli has formed an **equivalence class** if all stimuli in that set are reflexive, symmetrical, and transitive with each other (e.g., Mark's written and spoken name and his photo). Equivalence classes result from **stimulus-equivalence training,** the sort of symbolic matching to sample Al did. Stimulus-equivalence training is especially useful when you don't have to do symbolic-matching training with all combinations of the stimuli to produce an equivalence class, but instead some of the reflexive, symmetrical, and transitive stimulus-control relations emerge when just a few of the combinations are explicitly trained, as was the case with Al. Those stimulus-control relations that emerge without being explicitly trained are called *emergent relations*.

Equivalence Class vs. Stimulus Class

A *stimulus class (concept)* is a set of stimuli all of which have some common physical property. (For example, red apples is a concept that has such common physical properties as color, size, shape, and taste, though no two red apples are identical). But an equivalence class is a set of arbitrary symbolic stimuli that need not have common physical properties. (For example, the spoken and written stimuli *"Mark" and Mark* share no common physical properties with the photo of Mark; instead, they are arbitrary, symbolic stimuli.) An equivalence class is an arbitrary class, a class that is formed only as a result of symbolic, matching to sample, stimulus-equivalence training. Now philosophers may come down on us for this, but a stimulus class is inherently a class, regardless of whether we do concept training. The only reason we do concept training is to get our behavior under the control of the already preexisting concept. But an equivalence class does not exist until we've done some equivalence training to make the stimuli within it function equivalently for the person who's been trained. Heavy.

QUESTIONS

1. Describe an intervention using stimulus-equivalence training to help a brain-injured man be

Al's Equivalence Class

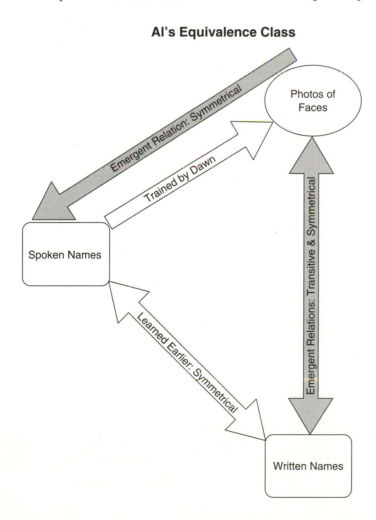

able to match faces to written and spoken names and vice versa.

a. What was the equivalence class in this intervention?

b. What were the emergent relations in this intervention?

c. What were the transitive relations?

d. What was an emergent symmetrical relation?

e. Just for the record, what was one of the reflexive relations?

f. What were the two practical results of this stimulus-equivalence training?

14 Imitation

Example of Imitation
Behavioral Special Education
ESTABLISHING IMITATION IN A MENTALLY-HANDICAPPED CHILD[1]

Marilla was a profoundly mentally handicapped 12-year-old girl who lived at the Firecrest School in Seattle. Marilla would only make an occasional grunting sound. She responded to only a few simple vocal commands, such as, *Come here* and *Sit down.* She didn't begin to walk until she was 7 years old. She was 12 before she could dress and feed herself and before she was toilet-trained. She had reasonable hand-eye coordination and could make simple responses, such as turning a knob or opening a door.

Once, when Dr. Donald Baer visited the Firecrest School, a staff member pointed out Marilla to him. "Dr. Baer, we've done everything we can for this little girl, but I'm afraid that it isn't much. She's pathetic. She seems too dumb to learn anything. I wonder if your reinforcement techniques could help her."

He and two grad students, Robert Peterson and James Sherman, tried to help Marilla. At first, the behavior analysts spent a few days observing Marilla. For example, they played with her on the ward for several hours. In the course of this play, they repeatedly asked her to imitate simple responses, such as hand clapping and waving. Marilla always failed to imitate, yet they had observed her making some of these responses at other times. They concluded that Marilla could not imitate. They

thought Marilla's lack of imitative skills might account for her painfully slow learning of functional behaviors. Imagine how hard learning would be for a child who couldn't imitate.

Definition: Concept
Imitation
- The form of the behavior of the imitator
- is controlled by
- similar behavior of the model.

Intervention

On the first day of the intervention, one of the grad students worked with Marilla just before her lunch hour. He said, "Do this," and raised his arm. Marilla just stared at him. The behavior analyst repeated this several times, but Marilla made no response. Finally, he *physically prompted* her response: He said, "Do this," raised his arm once more, but this time also took Marilla's hand and raised it for her. Then he fed her a spoonful of her lunch; at the same time, he said, "Good."

Definition: Concept
Physical prompt (physical guidance)
- The trainer physically moves the trainee's body
- in an approximation of the desired response.

After several trials with physical prompts, he began to reduce his assistance gradually: He only partially raised Marilla's arm, requiring her to raise

---

[1]Based on Baer, D. M., Peterson, R. F., & Sherman, J. A. (1967). Development of imitation by reinforcing behavioral similarity to a model. *Journal of the Experimental Analysis of Behavior, 10,* 405–415.

it the rest of the way. And when she did so, he reinforced her response. He reduced his help until Marilla made an unassisted arm-raising response. Then he gave her a bite of food and said, "Good." Occasionally Marilla would raise her arm even when he had not done so. On these occasions he didn't reinforce the response, and it gradually extinguished. Eventually she raised her arm only when he said, "Do this," and raised his arm.

Thus far we have shown a simple discrimination. In the presence of the S^D (the behavior analyst's saying, "Do this," and raising his arm), a response occurred (Marilla raised her arm), and he reinforced that response (presentation of food and praise). In the presence of an S^Δ (the behavior analyst's saying nothing and not raising his arm), he didn't reinforce the response (Marilla's raising her arm).

Imitation Training: Stimulus Discrimination

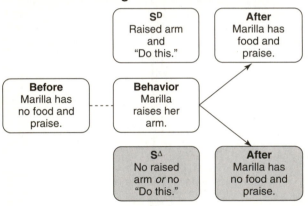

But discrimination training isn't the whole story. There's also response differentiation. Marilla not only had to respond at the right time, but she also had to make the right response. So the behavior analysts reinforced only her arm raises and not, for instance, her nose scratches. They used differential reinforcement of arm raising.

Imitation Training: Differential Reinforcement

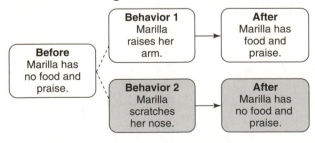

After Marilla's arm raising was under good stimulus control and well differentiated, the behavior analyst used the same discrimination training and response differentiation techniques to establish several other imitative responses. The next one con-

sisted of his tapping a table with his left hand whenever he said, "Do this." When he first introduced a new imitative S^D, some shaping and physical prompting was necessary. But he made less and less use of shaping and physical prompting, as part of the response differentiation procedure, on each successive response. By the time they got to the seventh new response, Marilla had just finished imitating nose tapping. Then he said, "Do this," and for the first time tapped the arm of a chair. Marilla immediately imitated that response by also tapping the arm of the chair. She had made this particular imitative response though he had never reinforced that particular response. Reinforcement of previous imitative responses had **generalized** to this new response.

> *Definition: Concept*
> **Generalized imitation**
> ○ Imitation of the response
> ○ of a model
> ○ without previous reinforcement
> ○ of imitation of that specific response.

Marilla had finally shown **generalized imitation**.[2] The behavior analysts breathed a sigh of relief. They had needed to establish only seven imitative responses before generalized imitation had developed. Now, the rest would be easy going. To continue Marilla's acquisition of generalized imitation, the trainer moved on to the next response. He tapped the table's leg and waited several seconds for Marilla to do the same. Nothing happened. After 10 seconds had elapsed with no response from Marilla, he went through the sequence of responses Marilla had previously learned. Again he reinforced each imitative response he had previously reinforced and eventually got back to the response of tapping the table's leg. But Marilla still wouldn't imitate it. They still had a long way to go. Marilla would need much more training before establishing more general imitative behavior.

They returned to guiding and shaping the response. They had to establish two more imitative responses before observing another instance of

---

[2]The first definition of *imitation* we might call *regular imitation* or *reinforced imitation*, to contrast it with *generalized imitation*. But we're inclined to leave it as just plain old *imitation*, with the understanding that we mean *reinforced imitation*. Also note that we could define *generalized imitation* as, *the behavior of the imitator is under stimulus control of the behavior of the model and matches the behavior of the model, without previous reinforcement.* But that's too long and cumbersome, even for us. So we hope you understand that *imitation of the response of a model* says the same thing.

generalized imitation. Marilla had just imitated the response of extending the left arm. Now the behavior analyst began making a circular motion with that arm for the first time. Marilla immediately imitated this motion. They then went through the sequence of imitative responses Marilla had learned. The behavior analyst reinforced all those responses he had previously reinforced, but he was careful not to reinforce tapping the chair or making the circular motion with her arm. Both of these generalized imitative responses maintained; they didn't extinguish in spite of repeated nonreinforced occurrences intermixed with the reinforced imitative responses.

Then he said, "Do this," and stood up. But, once again, it was necessary to shape the imitative response. In fact, it wasn't until the 23rd new response that a new imitation again occurred without reinforcement. That imitative response consisted of tapping the shoulder. The percentage of new responses that Marilla correctly imitated without reinforcement on the first demonstration gradually increased. After she had imitated about 120 different responses, she imitated all the new responses without reinforcement. Some responses were more interesting than the earlier ones. They consisted of such things as scribbling, placing geometric forms on a form board, crawling under a table, flying a toy airplane, and burping a doll. Though they used reinforcement and shaping for many responses, near the end of the study Marilla required only a few trials before she could perform most of the responses, whereas at the beginning of the study, they had to use much shaping, physical prompting, and reinforcement for each new response. It took an average of over three sessions to establish each of the first 10 new responses, but after establishing 20 responses, each response required an average of less than half a session. This rapid rate of acquisition of new imitative responses remained fairly consistent for the remainder of this phase of their intervention.

Then they attempted to establish more elaborate sequences of imitative responses called **behavioral chains.** Initially, they worked with only two-response chains. (See Chapter 20.) The behavior analyst working with Marilla that day would make two responses such as raising his left arm and then standing up. Then he reinforced Marilla's imitation of the same sequence of two responses. After Marilla mastered the two-response chains, they gradually increased the number of responses in a single chain to as many as seven. Marilla could correctly imitate these long sequences after only 10 hours of reinforcement of the various response chains. At times, some response chains even contained new responses that Marilla had not previously performed.

When Marilla could imitate almost any new motor response, they began working on her verbal behavior. At first, the behavior analyst said, "Ah." He repeated this several times and also tried several other vocal responses interspersed with the usual motor responses. Marilla always imitated the motor responses but never the vocal responses. The training of imitative motor responses didn't seem to generalize to imitative vocal responses. This was true, though Marilla did occasionally make grunting noises.

The behavior analysts would have to shape the vocal response; they would have to reinforce successive approximations of vocalizations. They included vocal responses in a response chain composed mainly of motor responses. The first time they tried this, the behavior analyst said, "Do this," then rose from his chair, walked to the center of the room, turned toward Marilla, said, "Ah," and returned to his seat. Marilla immediately jumped up from her chair, walked to the center of the room, turned toward the behavior analyst, and then made a strange facial expression vaguely resembling the model's when he said, "Ah." But no vocal response was forthcoming. That was all right; the facial expression was a step in the right direction, and they reinforced it. On successive trials, the facial expressions became more and more like the model's, and eventually she began to emit vocal responses. They continued to reinforce responses that more and more closely approximated the model's vocal response, until Marilla was saying, "Ah," like an expert. The chain of motor responses became shorter and shorter. Eventually, the model was able to remain in his seat and say, "Do this," followed by "Ah," and Marilla would imitate the vocal response.

In this way, they shaped imitations of simple sounds, combined them into longer or more complex sounds, and finally combined them into usable words. After 20 hours of imitation training of vocal responses, Marilla was able to imitate such words as "Hi," "Okay," "Marilla," and the names of some objects.

After Marilla's imitative repertoire was considerably larger, they presented her with new people as models to determine whether she would imitate their behavior. She did. She imitated the behavior not only of other males but also of females as well as she had imitated the original models.

Incidentally, Bob Peterson, one of the grad students who worked on this project, continued working with Marilla for his doctoral dissertation. Bob proposed to a faculty committee that he would teach Marilla 20 responses using imitation training and 20 other responses using other procedures; then he would compare the effects of various variables on both of these response classes. One professor, who was not sufficiently familiar with the effectiveness of the principles of reinforcement, objected. Because he had so much trouble teaching normal college students anything, he thought that it would be impractical to take the time necessary to teach a mentally-handicapped child so many new behaviors. Bob replied that, with imitation stimuli and reinforcement, he expected to take only an hour or two. This impressed the skeptical professor. It turned out that Bob's prediction was correct. He showed Marilla what to do, and she did it—just like any bright kid!

Analysis

You may ask what maintained Marilla's imitative behavior. Being the shrewd student of behavior analysis you are, no doubt you suspect that food and social reinforcement are the main factors. A reader with less understanding of the problem than you might say, "That's silly. The whole purpose of this study was to show that you could get generalized imitation without reinforcement." "Of course," you would reply, "But you fail to understand the subtleties of the issue at hand."

In fact, these behavior analysts showed that Marilla could perform **specific** imitative responses without direct reinforcement of those **specific** responses. **But reinforcement of some other imitative responses must occur before the unreinforced imitative responses occur.** They reinforced some imitative responses so that imitative stimulus control could generalize to other unreinforced responses.

QUESTIONS

1. *Physical prompt*—define it and give an example.
2. *Imitation*—define it and give an example. Make the example one that is not an example of generalized imitation.
3. *Generalized imitation*—define it and give an example.
4. To train imitation, we need both a discrimination contingency and a differential reinforcement contingency.
   a. true
   b. false
5. Why?
6. Diagram the contingency for establishing imitation for a child who previously showed no imitative stimulus control.
7. Also describe how you would establish generalized imitation for such a child.

8. To get generalized imitation, we must reinforce some imitative responses.
   a. true
   b. false
9. How would you show that you have achieved generalized imitation?

ADDED VERSUS BUILT-IN CONTINGENCIES FOR IMITATION

In Marilla's case, the behavior analysts added a contingency to reinforce imitation. Let's look at another example of an added contingency and then at a different sort of contingency for imitation.

Imagine a commonplace scene between parents and children: Sid takes a swig of soda from a can. Rod watches; then he takes a swig of soda from the can. Sid pats Rod on the back and praises him (an added reinforcement contingency). This may be the main way imitation is learned; the behavior of the imitator (Rod in this case) is reinforced by someone else (Sid), if it's similar to that of the model (Sid).

Added Reinforcement Contingency for Rod's Imitative Behavior

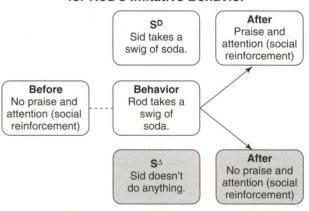

In this case, the model's behavior (Sid's swigging the soda) is an S^D in the presence of which, similar behavior of the imitator (Rod's swigging) is more likely to produce the added reinforcer (Sid's praise and attention).

But a built-in reinforcement contingency is also present—the sweet taste of the soda, when Rod takes a swig. However, for this built-in contingency, Sid's swigging isn't an S^D because there's no S^Δ; in other words, Rod's swigging will produce the sweet reinforcer, whether or not Sid had just swug. In this case Sid's swigging the soda is a prompt, rather than an S^D. The S^D is the *Super-Soda* written on the can (the can itself is the operandum).

Built-in Automatic Reinforcement Contingency for Rod's Imitative Behavior

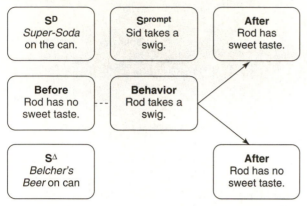

Being under imitative prompt control helps imitators contact automatic, built-in, reinforcement contingencies they would otherwise have missed.

These are two contingencies that cause the learning of imitative behavior—the added reinforcement contingency and the natural reinforcement contingency.

QUESTIONS

1. Give an example of an added contingency for imitation and an automatic, built-in one.

Example
USING EXCESSIVE IMITATION TO ESTABLISH NORMAL LANGUAGE SKILLS[3]

As we walked down the hospital corridor, we heard a high-pitched voice singing:

Go tell Aunt Rhody.
Go tell Aunt Rhody.
Go tell Aunt Rhody
the old gray goose is dead.

When we turned the corner we saw that the singer was a 7-year-old boy. We kept walking, but something bothered us. Where had we seen this kid before? He was 3½ years old the last time we saw him. Oh, yes, this is Dicky, the autistic child. Dr. Todd Risley and Dr. Montrose Wolf saved Dicky's eyesight by shaping the appropriate wearing of glasses. Sure enough, we turned around, and Dicky was still wearing his glasses. We were pleased to note that Dicky was now so well adjusted that he walked down the hall singing happily. We turned

[3]Based on Risley, T., & Wolf, M. (1967). Establishing functional speech in echolalic children. *Behavior Research and Therapy, 5,* 73–88.

around and walked after him. We wanted to chat with him to see how he had been getting along during the last few years. We shouted after him, "Wait a minute, Dicky, we want to talk to you."

Dicky stopped singing but kept walking. He began chanting with gradually increasing vigor. "Wait a minute, Dicky, we want to talk to you. Wait a minute, Dicky, we want to talk to you! Wait a minute, Dicky, we want to talk to you!"

This alarmed us; so we ran up to him and put our hand on his shoulder. "What's the matter, Dicky?"

He stopped walking and began stamping his feet, on the verge of tears. "Want a spanking. Want a spanking! Want a spanking!! Want a spanking!!!"

This really bothered us. We had thought Dicky was in good shape, but we were wrong. Our efforts to console him had no effect; fearing we might be reinforcing this undesirable behavior, we left Dicky.

A few months later, we had a chance to check into Dicky's case. We found that the hospital staff had once again called Todd Risley and Mont Wolf to help Dicky. At first, they observed that Dicky never requested anything, never asked questions, never made comments. Even though he sometimes imitated other people's behavior, he didn't imitate when asked to do so. So they started by trying to get rid of his inappropriate imitation, while maintaining appropriate imitation.

Describing Past Events

As with Marilla, the work with Dicky took place during mealtimes, so they could use food as a reinforcer, in addition to social praise. A ward attendant worked with him. On the first day, she held up a picture of Santa Claus and **verbally prompted,** "This is Santa Claus. Now say 'Santa Claus.'" No response. Then she held up a picture of a cat and said, "This is a cat. Now say 'cat.'" Still no response. After she had presented all five of her pictures, she mixed them in a different order and went through them again. Each time she named the picture and asked Dicky to do the same.

Definition: Concept
Verbal prompt
- A supplemental verbal stimulus
- that raises the probability of a correct response.

Finally, on the third time through the sequence, the attendant showed a picture of the cat and verbally prompted, "This is a cat. Now say 'cat.'" Dicky's response: "This is a cat. Now say 'cat.'" That wasn't exactly what the attendant had hoped for, but it was good enough for a beginning. She immediately said, "Good boy," and gave him a bite of his meal. The reinforcement worked. Dicky began imitating more and more often. After a week of reinforcement, he was imitating practically every verbal prompt and also everything the attendant said during the reinforcement sessions. But she reinforced only those imitative responses that occurred at appropriate times—when she asked for them. And she didn't reinforce imitative responses she had not asked for.

Dicky's verbal responses came under the control of the attendant's spoken words, but the pictures seemed irrelevant. Dicky rarely even bothered to look at them. Instead, he twisted and turned in his seat. To bring Dicky's verbal behavior under the stimulus control of the pictures, the attendant used an **anticipation procedure:** She held the picture for several seconds before giving the verbal prompt. If Dicky correctly named the picture before she presented the prompt, he got a bite of food more quickly than if he waited until after the prompt.

The Imitative Verbal Prompt

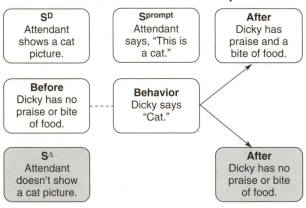

(Notice that, in this diagram, we slid the S^D and S^Δ to the left in order to squeeze in the S^{prompt}.)

Now, you might ask why doesn't Dicky always wait until the attendant gives the prompts, "This is a cat." That prompt reliably controls Dicky's saying, "Cat." So why would showing the picture of the cat come to control Dicky's saying, "Cat"?

Because this is a form of differential reinforcement of answers with short latencies. Because, of course, Dicky will get the praise and food sooner after the attendant shows the picture, if Dicky responds immediately than if he doesn't respond until after the attendant's prompt of "This is a cat."

Differential Reinforcement of Short Latencies

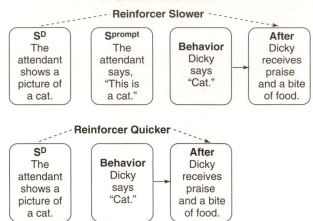

(This diagram of differential reinforcement is almost the same as the diagram of the imitative verbal prompt, just changed slightly to make our point clearer—we hope.)

I'd bet that Dicky's saying "Cat" would not come under the stimulus control of the picture of the cat, if the attendant held off on giving the praise and food for several seconds after she had presented the picture of the cat, just as if he hadn't said "Cat" until after the prompt.

But with the anticipation procedure, Dicky's naming objects gradually came under the control of the pictures without verbal prompts. Within three weeks of reinforcement, Dicky's verbal behavior was under appropriate stimulus control of ten different pictures. The attendant then started showing common household objects and pictures, and Dicky began to name them with increasing ease.

Describing Past Events

Though Dicky's performance was impressive, there's more to verbal behavior than naming pictures and objects. One of the main advantages of verbal behavior is that we can talk about things no longer present. How could we use reinforcement to get Dicky's verbal behavior under the control of stimuli outside of his immediate environment?

To tackle this problem, the attendant would take Dicky outside to play on the swing or sliding board. Then she would bring him back inside and ask, "What did you do outside?" If he didn't respond in a few seconds, she used an imitative verbal prompt for his response by saying, "I was swinging." Then she would reinforce Dicky's imitation of this prompt stimulus (S^{prompt}).

1. Please complete the diagram this contingency. *(But be careful with the S^Δ: it's tricky. Note that the S^D has two necessary components, Dicky's swinging*

AND the attendant's asking. So the absence of EITHER of these components constitutes an S^Δ.)

The Imitative Verbal Prompt

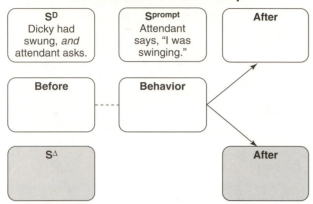

Eventually, Dicky began answering the questions **before** the attendant had presented the imitative verbal prompt; naturally, these quicker answers got reinforced sooner after the attendant's question than those that didn't occur until she had presented the prompt. On trials with these quicker answers, the contingency diagram would be just like the preceding one, except there would be no S^prompt.

This is a form of differential reinforcement of answers with short latencies.

2. Please complete this diagram.

Differential Reinforcement of Short Latencies

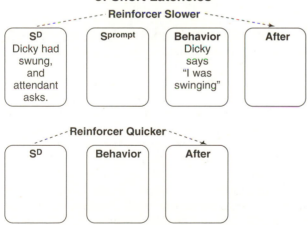

As a result, Dicky gradually answered more and more quickly, until he rarely waited for the prompt and was, thus, answering in a more normal manner.[4]

Dicky also began to answer other questions, such as, "What is your name?" or "Where do you live?" If he didn't answer the question, the attendant would provide a verbal prompt and reinforce the correct imitative response.

After several weeks of training, Dicky's imitation of verbal stimuli increased notably, although much of his behavior was still unusual. He would sometimes imitate the questions before answering them, and he would often reverse his pronouns, for instance, he would ask for a drink by saying, "He wants some water."

When Dicky left the hospital, his parents continued the training (something we now recognize as an important feature of effective training of so-called *autistic* children). After about six months with his parents, Dicky was using pronouns perfectly and was initiating many requests and comments, although he was still making inappropriate imitative responses. He attended a laboratory preschool at the University of Washington for two years. Many of the procedures at this preschool involved the principles of reinforcement. After 2 years there, his verbal skills had developed to the point that he was ready for special education in the public school.

At that point, Dicky's verbal behavior resembled that of a skilled 5-year-old. This means that his rate of language development had been approximately normal since this intense behavior analysis training. After that, the naturally occurring reinforcers for normal verbal behavior appeared to maintain and expand his verbal repertoire.

This is one of a growing number of examples where behavior analysts have used reinforcement techniques over a long period of time with a person having severe learning problems. Dicky is now able to function almost normally. Since this pioneering research, many others, especially Ivar Lovaas and his students, have used similar interventions with great success.

QUESTIONS

1. *Verbal prompt*—define it and give a clear example.
2. Diagram a contingency showing how you can use verbal prompts to take advantage of excessive imitation and establish more normal ver-

---

[4]You are deserving of praise for being such a thoughtful student, if you're puzzled by our using *Dicky's having swung* as part of the S^D, even though, a couple chapters ago, we said the S^D shouldn't proceed the opportunity to respond by more than 60 seconds. In truth, we've taken a little poetic license; what we really have is a rule-governed verbal analog to an S^D. That such analog S^Ds exert stimulus control over Dicky's behavior shows

that he is far advanced in acquiring a normal verbal repertoire.

No doubt you are also deserving of praise for being such a thoughtful student, even if you weren't puzzled by our using *Dicky's having swung* as part of the S^D. It's just that you're waiting for an even more impressive opportunity to demonstrate your thoughtfulness.

bal behavior under more normal stimulus control.

- Do such a diagram for a procedure for establishing control by stimuli that are present

- Do such a diagram for a procedure for establishing control by stimuli or events that are not present

3. In both cases, diagram the procedure for differential reinforcement of short latencies.

BASIC ENRICHMENT

Example of Imitation
THE INVASION OF THE ADVERTISERS FROM OUTER SPACE

"Your Sovereign Mistress of All Creatures in the Universe."

"Yes, my loyal Wizard."

"We have still not dominated one planet."

"We missed one? How can that be?"

"I've been trying, but they're holding out."

"What is the name of this reluctant planet?"

"They call it the planet Earth."

"Oh, yes. I've heard of it."

"With your generous permission, Your Sovereignty, I would like to try a new tactic. I stole it from some of Earth's most brilliant strategists."

"What is it?"

"They call it the domino theory."

"I haven't heard of that."

"If I can weaken and then knock over the strongest nation, the United States, then all the other countries will topple right over."

"But how can you weaken such a powerful country?"

"With an even more powerful drug—if only we can trick them into taking the drug."

"The drug's your lever to topple the first domino?"

"Yes. I have calculated that with this drug we can sap the nation's wealth at well over $50 billion per year."

"That much money could make a big dent in our intergalactic debt!"

"With this drug, they will start slaughtering each other at well over 25,000 per year, especially the ones who are young and strong."

"You make even me shudder."

"I plan to introduce over 95 percent of them to this drug before they graduate from high school."

"Clever."

"Soon over 12 million of them will be addicted."

"You say this is a strong nation? It must be a stupid nation. How will you get them to take this terrible drug? Will it taste good?"

"No. I've tried it. It tastes terrible. We need lots of sugar or something."

"Then they can't be so dumb as to take it."

"It costs money to make money."

"I should have known you were getting to that. How much?" And the Sovereign Mistress reached for her purse.

"$4 million or more."

"To manufacture this drug?"

"No, to pay athletes to consume it on TV. The kids spend more time watching TV than they do going to school."

"And?"

"To fill the magazines and newspapers with ads, especially the college papers."

"And?"

"I will tell them they are not cool if they do not take the drug. College students believe anything."

"You have to be kidding. They can't possibly be that stupid."

"Trust me. It is so easy to program these people. And here is my best trick."

"Yes?"

"To throw them off the track, I will start a rumor that taking the drug results from moral weakness, not the $4 million I spend on advertising each year."

"They won't believe it."

"With all due respect, Your Sovereignty, they will after awhile. Then I'll change the rumor. I'll program them to believe that it's due to an inherited factor X."

"If they fall for that crap, they deserve to be the first domino to topple. What will you call this magic drug that will consume over $50 billion of their income and over 25,000 of their lives every year?"

"I will name it after our planet."

"Alcohol?"

The statistics are real; and it ain't no joke. If I wanted to weaken the United States, I'd say, "Have another Bud. If Mickey Mantle drinks lite beer, why shouldn't you?" Isn't imitation[5] wonderful? Two hundred and fifty million sheep can't be wrong. Baahhh, Baahhh.

INTERMEDIATE ENRICHMENT

HOW DO YOU KNOW IF IT'S REALLY IMITATION?

Remember our definition of **imitation:** *the form of the behavior of the imitator is controlled by similar behavior of the model.* In this definition, the **form of behavior,** usually refers to the topography of the response.[6]

When we say the *form of the behavior of the imitator is controlled by similar behavior of the model,* we mean the behavior of the imitator is similar to the behavior of the model because of experience with a special reinforcement contingency. In this history with the special reinforcement contingency, behavior of the imitator has been reinforced contingent on similarity to the behavior of the model. For example, when the mother says, "Mama," the baby says, "Mama." Then the mother showers the baby with reinforcing, enthusiastic affection. The mother is reinforcing the behavior, at least in part, because of the similarity to her own behavior.

When defining imitation, we do **not** just mean that the behavior of the imitator is similar to the model's behavior. It would not be imitation if the similarity were because both the imitator's behavior and the model's behavior were controlled by the same contingency.

For example, it would not be imitation, if in the presence of a very loud noise, the imitator and the model both put their hands over their ears. The same contingency, escape from the loud noise, would be maintaining both behaviors. The removal of the aversive condition (the loud noise) in this escape contingency wouldn't necessarily depend upon the similarity of their behaviors.

For another example, the movement of automobiles when the light turns green doesn't necessarily mean the drivers are imitating each other. Most likely the green light directly controls the behavior of each of the drivers—at least most of them. (Of course, there still might be an occasional imitator in the crowd, one who goes with the flow, rather than the light.)

So, to be sure you have imitation, you must show that the behavior of the imitator is under the stimulus control of the behavior of the model. In other words, you must show that the similarity of their behaviors is not under the control of some third factor. We say people *imitate* the behavior of a model. when their behavior resembles that of the model and changes in the behavior of the model produce similar changes in the behavior of the imitator.

Theory
GENERALIZED IMITATION

We've presented a **definition** of generalized imitation—imitation of the response of a model without previous reinforcement of the imitation of that specific response. And we've pointed out that generalized imitation occurs only if some other imitative responses are being reinforced. Now we'd like to present a **theory** of generalized imitation—an explanation of why reinforcement of some imitative responses maintains other imitative responses that we are not reinforcing.

You might ask, why do we need more explanation; why do we need a theory of generalized imita-

---

[5]Note that this is a special type of imitation, *delayed imitation,* where the imitative behavior occurs a considerable time after the modeled behavior. In other words, if you do imitate Mickey's beer drinking, there will probably be a considerable delay between the time you see him drink the beer and when you actually drink the beer itself. The process underlying such delayed imitation may be fairly complex: There might be some form of rule-governed analog to imitation, where the next day you say, I think I'll have a Bud, so I can be like a great baseball player. But it also might be real imitation, a type of generalized imitation.

[6]The form of most nonvocal behavior is easy to see (overt). The form of vocal behavior is somewhat covert, but the results of the response can be observed (in other words, we can hear the sound). The observability of a response is generally assumed when imitation occurs. However, there can be imitation where the similarity is the product of the response, rather than the form, as when you imiatively whistle a tune someone just played on a guitar.

tion? Aren't we just talking about simple stimulus generalization? Reinforce the pigeon's pecks on the green key and you'll get generalized pecking on the yellow-green key, right? Stimulus generalization. Reinforce Marilla's imitation of nose tapping and you'll get imitation of chair tapping, right? Stimulus generalization?

Yes and no. You get chair tapping, and you haven't reinforced it, but that doesn't always result from simple stimulus generalization. We can't know for sure with Marilla, but in other studies the behavior analysts have asked the kids which imitative responses would get the added reinforcers and which would not. And the kids knew. They might say, "You give me a bite of food when I tap my nose right after you tap your nose. But you don't give me anything when I tap my chair right after you tap your chair." In other words, **the kids kept on making unreinforced imitative responses, even though they knew that subset of responses wouldn't be reinforced by the behavior analyst.** The kids weren't confused, but they showed generalized imitation anyway. Why? That's the question this theory of generalized imitation addresses. We need a theory to explain why we get generalized imitation, even when the imitator knows the experimenter will provide no added reinforcers contingent on such generalized imitation.

Definition: Theory
The theory of generalized imitation
○ Generalized imitative responses occur
○ because they automatically produce imitative reinforcers.

Definition: Concept
Imitative reinforcers
○ Stimuli arising from the match between
○ the behavior of the imitator
○ and the behavior of the model
○ that function as reinforcers.

Marilla's behavior matches the model's. This correct imitation automatically produces visual and internal stimuli—Marilla's seeing and feeling her behavior matching the model's. These automatic, imitative, reinforcing stimuli reinforce Marilla's imitating new responses that have never been reinforced by the behavior analysts.

However, before we go on with this theory, let's pause for a brief review.

REVIEW

How to Establish Learned Reinforcers

Remember our definition of **learned reinforcer:** *a stimulus, event, or condition that is a reinforcer because it has been paired with another reinforcer.* For example, every time Rudolph the Rat presses the response lever, you dip the water dipper into the water reservoir; and as you bring up the dipper for Rudolph to drink, the metal dipper clicks against the bottom of the Skinner box. And when there's no click, there's no water.

Pairing Procedure

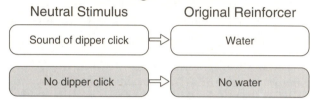

So you're pairing the sound of the dipper click with the water reinforcer. In that way, the click becomes a learned reinforcer.

You can now use the click to shape a new response—for example, chain pulling. You dangle a chain from the roof of the Skinner box, and every time Rudolph approximates pulling the chain, you click the water dipper. However, now you don't lower the dipper all the way into the reservoir, so all Rudolph gets is the click and a dry dipper. But because you pair the click with the water reinforcer at other times, the click keeps its reinforcing value and reinforces Rudolph's successive approximations to chain pulling.

In summary, you paired the click with an existing reinforcer—water. This pairing caused the click to become a learned reinforcer. Then you used the learned reinforcer to reinforce new behavior. Now let's go back to the theory of learned imitation.

How to Establish Learned Imitative Reinforcers

You established a learned reinforcer for Rudolph by pairing the click with water. In the same way, the behavior analysts established a learned imitative reinforcer for Marilla, by pairing the stimuli resulting from imitation with a bite of food and some praise. For Marilla, the stimuli were the sights and the feelings of her muscles (proprioceptive stimuli) that resulted from her seeing and feeling her behavior match the model's.

Pairing Procedure

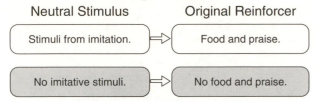

Neutral Stimulus   Original Reinforcer

Remember, that, as we pointed out in Chapter 11, the pairing procedure actually involves two pairings: If we pair a neutral stimulus (stimuli from imitation) with an original reinforcer (food and praise), logically that means that the absence of that stimulus is paired with the absence of that reinforcer. Please keep this in mind when you generate your own examples of the pairing procedure or deal with them on quizzes. But now back to Marilla.

The behavior analysts had to go out of their way to establish the imitative stimuli as learned reinforcers. But these stimuli automatically followed Marilla's imitating the model; the behavior analysts didn't themselves present those stimuli. So once the imitative stimuli had become learned reinforcers, these learned, imitative reinforcers automatically followed each of Marilla's correct imitations. This means that even a novel imitation will automatically produce a learned imitative reinforcer (the stimuli arising from Marilla's seeing and feeling her behavior matching that of the model's).

Remember, that to train imitation, we need both a discrimination contingency and a differential reinforcement contingency. And, also, to maintain generalized imitation, we need both a discrimination contingency and a differential reinforcement contingency:

Generalized Imitation: Discrimination Contingency[7]

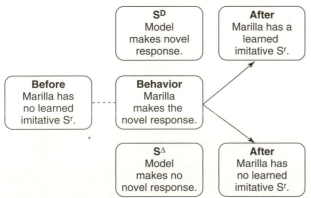

[7]The symbol S^r stands for learned reinforcer. The symbol S^R stands for unlearned reinforcer.

Generalized Imitation: Differential Reinforcement

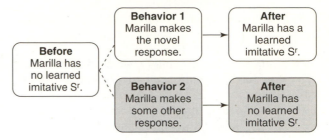

So **the theory of generalized imitation** states that Marilla's generalized imitative responses occur because they automatically produce learned, imitative reinforcers—stimuli arising from the match between her behavior and the model's.[8]

QUESTIONS

1. *Imitative reinforcer*—define it and give an example.
2. Diagram how we establish learned imitative reinforcers.
3. *The theory of generalized imitation*—define it and give an example.
4. For generalized imitation, diagram:
   ○ the discrimination contingency
   ○ the differential reinforcement contingency.
5. Why do we need a theory of generalized imitation?

Verbal Behavior (Language)
IMITATION AS A PREREQUISITE TO LANGUAGE DEVELOPMENT

Rod's first birthday party. The family gathers to watch the birthday boy cram his first piece of chocolate cake into his mouth. Dawn says, "Sid, get the camera."

[8]In everyday life, children imitate models in a variety of situations, under a variety of deprivation conditions, receiving a variety of different reinforcers. When they are water deprived, they might happen to imitate Mommy's drinking; and naturally they get a water reinforcer (not from Mommy, but from the water glass). When they are food deprived, they might happen to imitate Daddy's eating; and this time they would naturally get a food reinforcer. Etc. In that way, the imitative stimuli are paired with a large number of different reinforcers under a large number of different deprivations. This means that the imitative reinforcers can become generalized learned reinforcers, which may account for the fact that imitative reinforcers seem to control so much of our behavior.

"Cama," imitates Rod.

"Got it" says Sid

"Goggit," imitates Rod

"Let's give him the cake," says Dawn cutting a slice.

"Cake!" imitates Rod.

Everybody laughs, and Dawn hugs Rod.

You have already seen that sound is an unlearned reinforcer; and we've suggested that this unlearned reinforcing property of sound may be responsible for babies' initial babbling. And we've said that babies' babbles are gradually shaped into the sounds of their own language. This occurs because the sounds of their own language are learned reinforcers that differentially reinforce the behavior that produces them.

Now get ready for a really difficult distinction. We've just said that babies sound like their parents because the sounds themselves are **simple** learned reinforcers. Now we are going to say that babies also sound like their parents, because they are imitating their parents, because the sounds are **imitative** learned reinforcers. And imitative learned reinforcers involve a little more special training than simple learned reinforcers.

A child's imitation of a parent's vocal behavior can be maintained two ways (*these are the two main causes of imitation mentioned earlier in the chapter*):

○ First, the imitative vocal response produces learned imitative reinforcers just as many other imitative behaviors in the past produced imitative reinforcers.

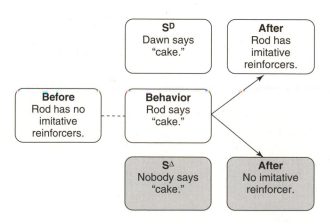

○ Second, the vocal imitative behavior may be reinforced by social or other reinforcers.

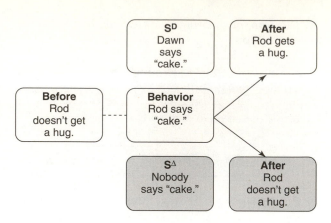

So, as Rod is learning language, his extensive imitative repertoire is essential. We've seen that children who fail to acquire an imitative repertoire have a hard time learning desirable behaviors, in general. Now we see how important an imitative repertoire is to learning verbal behavior, in particular. Without a generalized imitative repertoire, imitative verbal responses are not likely to occur. (If Rod didn't have a generalized imitative repertoire he probably wouldn't have said "cake" when Dawn said "cake"). If imitative responses should happen to occur, they aren't reinforced by imitative reinforcers. Without a generalized imitative repertoire, the match between Rod and Dawns behavior wouldn't be reinforcing.

Where there is an absence of imitative reinforcers, there will be an absence of generalized imitation. The only way for imitative responses to be strengthened in the absence of imitative reinforcers, is for each response to be reinforced by an added contingency. We've seen added reinforcement contingencies can increase imitative behavior (as in the case of Marilla). Unfortunately, parents rarely use intensive added reinforcement contingencies until after nonimitative children have great verbal deficits.

QUESTIONS

1. Why is generalized imitation crucial for language learning?

GENERALIZED IMITATION OF INAPPROPRIATE BEHAVIOR

Three-year-old Rod said, "Good boy" to his teddy bear, a favorite remark of Sid and Dawn's. What's going on here? Has Rod become the youngest behavior modifier in history? No. And Rod's saying, "Good boy" surprised Dawn and Sid. They hadn't taught him to explicitly say that.

It just means generalized imitation is ever present. The imitative reinforcer of the match between Rod's behavior and his parents did the trick.

The real kicker came when Rod surprised his parents by spontaneously imitating Sid's swearing. Therefore, eventually, Dawn and Sid got Rod's generalized imitation under control by creating a **conditional** learned imitative reinforcer. Here's how:

Pairing Procedure

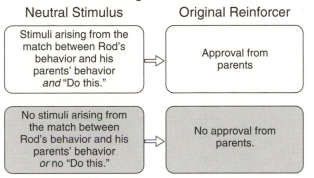

Neutral Stimulus   Original Reinforcer

| Stimuli arising from the match between Rod's behavior and his parents' behavior *and* "Do this." | ⇒ | Approval from parents |

| No stimuli arising from the match between Rod's behavior and his parents' behavior *or* no "Do this." | ⇒ | No approval from parents. |

Notice that, at least initially, this pairing of the matching behavior with an already-established reinforcer (approval) is conditional on (or only occurs when) "Do this" is part of the stimulus. As a result, Rod's imitative reinforcers became less reinforcing when it was not occurring in the presence of, "Do this."

Research Methods
AN ADEQUATE CONTROL CONDITION TO SHOW REINFORCEMENT

Suppose your behavior analysis professor invites you and a friend to his home. Further suppose that your friend hasn't had the enlightening experience of reading this book. During the course of an hour's chat, you observe your teacher's 5-year-old daughter. Like all behavior analysts' children, she is extremely charming and seems to be one of the happiest people you have ever seen (yeah, right). While not being boisterous or unruly, she is amused, entertained, and fully content. You also observe that, like most behavior analysts, your professor takes great pleasure in his child and expresses it by often showering attention, affection, love, and an occasional piece of delicious fruit upon her.

You can't help but notice that the behavior-analyst parent only delivers these reinforcers after the child has made some happy sort of response. Your

naive friend is amazed at the happy home life. But you, knowing your professor is a strong advocate of reinforcement principles, had expected nothing less. You explain to your friend that "happiness is not a warm puppy . . . happiness is a group of reinforced responses." Your professor is intermittently reinforcing his daughter's behavior of behaving happily and having a good time.

Your friend points out that you don't reinforce happiness; happiness just happens. This skeptic asserts that happiness will be more likely to happen in a warm, loving home—just what the behavior analyst is providing. You counter this notion by saying that a warm, loving home is not enough. What is important here is presenting warmth and love immediately after occurrences of happy behavior.

You both agree that warmth and love may be crucial factors. You know they must immediately follow the desired happy responses. Your friend argues that the particular child's behaviors that the father's love and warmth follow are beside the point. Your friend says it doesn't matter when you show warmth and love; it just matters that you show it. How would you go about resolving this disagreement?

Right you are; you would perform an experiment. But just what sort of an experiment would you perform? Someone less skilled than yourself in scientific research might suggest a simple extinction control procedure. In other words, you would stop giving the supposed reinforcers of love, warmth, and so forth, and see if the frequency of happy responses decreased.

As you know, the simple extinction control procedure wouldn't do. If you simply withheld love and warmth, you would predict that happy responses would decrease in frequency, and your friend would make the same prediction. Your friend would say that when you take love and warmth from the house, happiness, of course, goes with them.

As you knew all along, you would need the potential reinforcer present in the situation. But you must make sure it doesn't occur immediately following a happy response. In other words, if the love and warmth are still there, the friend will argue that happiness should remain. On the other hand, because love and warmth no longer immediately follow happy behavior, you will argue that happiness will be on its way out.

What you would have to do is wait until times when the child wasn't being happy. Then you'd shower the kid with love and warmth. You'd do this over a period of several days. Your friend would predict that happiness would remain because the love and warmth remained, even though it was no longer contingent on happiness. But you would predict that the happiness would drop out because the reinforcers of love and warmth were no longer contingent on happy behavior.

Incidentally, at the end of Chapter 7, we presented another adequate control condition—variable-time stimulus presentation, where you present the presumed reinforcer independent of the occurrence of the response. When possible, however, it might be even better to use the procedure of this section, because presenting the reinforcer when the response is not occurring will prevent accidental reinforcement of that response. And it is also a form of punishment by the prevention of a reinforcer, so you might see an even more rapid decrease in the frequency of the response than with variable-time reinforcement.

QUESTIONS

Danger: Study this section extra carefully, because students often screw up the following questions on their quizzes.

1. Why isn't extinction the best control procedure for demonstrating reinforcement?
2. What is?

15

Avoidance

FUNDAMENTALS

Example
Behavioral Medicine
"SIDNEY SLOUCH STANDS STRAIGHT"[1]

The Problem

Juke stood silently in the doorway of Sid's office. Sid did not see him. He sat with his elbows on his desk, his head in his hands. Juke stared at his friend for a couple of minutes before he spoke; then he said gently, "What's happenin', Sid?"

Sid raised his head slowly but didn't look directly at Juke. In spite of his tinted glasses, Juke thought Sid's eyes looked red. "What's happenin', Sid?" Juke repeated.

"Not much."

"You look bummed out, Sid."

"I'm depressed." Sid still didn't look at Juke.

Juke moved into Sid's office, closed the door, and sat down in a tattered, but comfortable stuffed chair in the corner. "So what's bringing you down?" Juke asked.

After a few moments of silence, Sid said, "It's my students. I bust my tail for them, and they don't appreciate it. I thought we were friends. Even my best student, Joe."

"I know you work hard, and I'm sure your students appreciate it too," Juke said.

"They wouldn't talk about me the way they do if they appreciated me."

"What do they say?"

"They call me names."

"Names? What do you mean?" Juke asked.

"I overheard Joe, and Sue, and Max talking. And they were talking about 'the *Slouch*.'" It took a minute before I realized they were talking about me! That's an awful thing to call anyone."

Juke strained to suppress a smile. He thought about when he and Sid had been freshmen at Big State University, 10 years ago. People had called Sid "the Slouch" even then. But maybe they'd never called him that to his face. Of course, they were right. He had the worst posture on campus, and it had gotten worse. At a distance, he looked almost like an old man.

As if he'd read Juke's thoughts, Sid added, "Of course, they're right. My posture isn't perfect. But you'd think they'd have more respect for me than. . . . I wish I could improve my posture, but it's so unnatural to stand straight. Even when I try, I forget to stay straight. And there I am again—the Slouch. You can't change a lifetime's bad habits." Sid stared at his desk.

"What is that, Sid, some new principle of behavior? You can't change a lifetime's bad habits? That's about as dumb as, 'It took you a long time to get into such bad shape, so it'll take you a long time to get back into good shape.' Some kind of simple-minded poetic justice? Good posture is just behavior, and you're a behaviorist. So get it together."

"Don't hassle me!" Sid said.

Juke thought, I deserve that. I forgot one of Dale Carnegie's major general rules: When people have troubles, they value sympathy more than solutions. So Juke backed off, gave Sid a good dose of sympathy, and then returned to his general rule: Don't complain about problems; solve them. Juke gradually talked Sid into taking his problem to his wife, Dawn. Dawn was the practical behavior analyst in the family; Sid was the theoretician.

---
[1]Based on Azrin, N., Rubin, H., O'Brien, F., Ayllon, T., & Roll, D. (1968). Behavioral Engineering: Postural Control By A Portable Operant Apparatus. *Journal of Applied Behavior Analysis, 1,* 99–108.

The Solution

Sid and Dawn sat at their breakfast table, that Saturday morning, searching for a solution. Dawn said, "The first question is: What's the response we want to manage or modify?"

"My slouching, of course."

"I'm not so sure," Dawn said. "For you, slouching may be the absence of a response. When you don't do anything special, you naturally fall into your old slouch."

"OK, then my response is standing straight," Sid said.

"So we've got to come up with a reinforcer for the response."

"Having a Clint Eastwood posture and avoiding people laughing behind my back doesn't seem to do the trick."

"Because no one instance of standing straight makes that much difference. Standing straight for one minute won't turn you into Clint Eastwood, and it won't prevent people from hurting your feelings."

"Well, we can't have someone give me an M&M every time I stand tall."

"No, we need some sort of automatic reinforcement procedure; and it should be with you all the time. Let me check through the back issues of *JABA*."

Dawn leafed through the cumulative index of the behaviorist's bible, the *Journal of Applied Behavior Analysis*. She found the solution in a research report Dr. Nathan Azrin and his colleagues had published when they had been at Anna State Hospital in Anna, Illinois.

With the help of the apparatus technician at Big State U, Dawn and Sid built a harness that Sid strapped around his torso.[2]

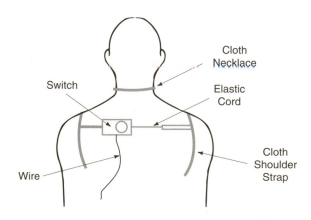

---

[2]This drawing is from N. Azrin, H. Rubin, F. O'Brien, T. Ayllon, & D. Roll. (1968). Behavioral Engineering: Postural control by a portable operant apparatus *Journal of Applied Behavior Analysis, 1*, 102. Copyright 1968 by the Society for the Experimental Analysis of Behavior, Inc. It is reprinted with permission.

The back section consisted of an elastic cord cut in half and then fastened to a snap switch. The snap switch was activated whenever Sid stopped standing or sitting in an erect way. Whenever he stopped maintaining his good posture, his shoulders would round, stretch the elastic cord, and activate the switch. The switch, in turn, activated a moderately loud tone, an aversive condition for most people, at least when they are in a social situation (sort of electronic flatulence). They also arranged a 3-second timer, so that when Sid would stop maintaining his posture, he'd hear the soft sound of the timer clicking on and then, 3 seconds later, the aversive tone.

The Results

So far, the procedure's been working well. Before the behavioral intervention, Sid usually slouched. When he wears the slouch apparatus, he avoids slouching almost all the time. When he removes the apparatus, he still avoids slouching much of the time (Figure 15.1). He hopes that after a while he will be able more or less to stop wearing the apparatus and maintain his good posture. But even if he has to keep wearing it, wearing the behavioral apparatus is much less of a hassle than the rigid back brace that many people use to maintain a good, healthy posture.

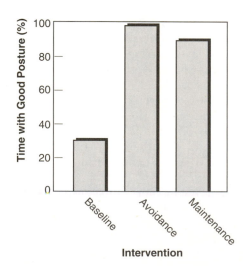

Figure 15.1   Avoidance of an Aversive Tone by Maintenance of Good Posture

Concept
AVOIDANCE CONTINGENCY

Let's take another look at the Slouch—we mean Sid—and the contingencies of the behavioral intervention. We can view the procedure Azrin and his team developed as an **avoidance contingency.** Sid avoided the presentation of the aversive tone by maintaining a good posture—standing and sitting straight.

Furthermore, another stimulus was involved. Remember the click the timer made? That warning stimulus always preceded the aversive tone by 3 seconds. If Sid maintained his erect posture continuously, he would not only avoid the aversive tone but also he would avoid the warning stimulus—the click.

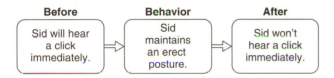

> *Definition: Concept*
> **Avoidance contingency**
> ○ the immediate,
> ○ response-contingent
> ○ **prevention** of
> ○ an aversive condition
> ○ resulting in an **increased** frequency of that response.

Operating behind this contingency is the **avoidance principle:** *A response becomes more frequent in the future if it has immediately prevented an aversive condition in the past.*

Note, by the way, that avoidance contingencies are a type of reinforcement contingency. In other words, avoidance contingencies increase the frequency of the causal response. This is reinforcement by the prevention of the presentation of an aversive condition.

Avoidance contingencies constantly keep us on our toes. I become especially aware of avoidance contingencies when I'm driving on one of those frantic eight-lane highways going into Chicago.

You drive perfectly and defensively or else it's wipe-out city.

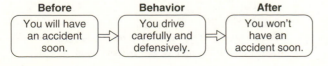

In fact, avoidance contingencies maintain the skilled locomotion of our bodies, as well as of our cars. Walking properly avoids the pain from stumbling, falling, and running into walls and doorways.

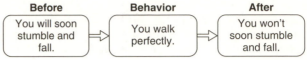

We may not appreciate the crucial role these aversive contingencies play in our lives, perhaps because we so easily avoid those mild aversive outcomes. The avoidance contingencies are so effective in shaping our behavior that by the time we're old enough to discuss them, we're so good at walking we don't even know they're there.

But that might not be true of the novice roller-skater. When you first learned to skate, you were painfully aware of those contingencies—thud! Have you ever hammered nails? Then surely you've come into contact with avoidance contingencies there as your thumb came into contact with your hammer—splat! What about cutting vegetables? Slice. And did you ever use a chain saw, not on vegetables but on logs? Zip.

QUESTIONS

1. *Avoidance contingency*—define it and diagram its use:
   ○ to improve posture
   ○ to maintain good driving
   ○ to maintain good walking.

Example from
Developmental Disabilities
AVOIDANCE OF AN AVERSIVE CONDITION (A MILDLY AVERSIVE OVERCORRECTION)

Jimmy's Eyes[3]

In working with the autistic child, Jimmy, Sue had used differential reinforcement of alternative behavior to reduce his disruptions. For their practicum in Sid's behavior analysis course, Joe and Eve also worked with Jimmy at Mae's school. They were

---

[3]This section is based on Foxx, R. M. (1977). Attention training: The use of overcorrection avoidance to increase the eye contact of autistic and retarded children. *Journal of Applied Behavior Analysis, 10,* 488–499. See also: Harris, S. L. (1975). Teaching language to nonverbal children with emphasis on problems of generalization. *Psychological Bulletin, 82,* 565–580.

doing this so that Jimmy could have more help than Sue alone could provide. But they had made no progress. Mae observed a training session; then she pointed out what might have been a problem.

"When you're having trouble with a training program, you always ask this question: Does the student have the prerequisite skills? Now it turns out that eye contact is a prerequisite for most instructional programs, and I notice that Jimmy looks everywhere but at you two. So you need to work on that first."

And work on it they did, 20 training trials a session, 10 sessions a day: "Look at me, Jimmy. . . . Good, you looked at me." Eve handed Jimmy a small piece of his favorite food, bologna. Eve, Joe, and Jimmy progressed a little, but not much. They got Jimmy making eye contact on 24% of the trials; but after 1,000 trials, they hadn't gotten any further with this refinement of the discrete trial procedure. Back to Mae.

"OK, you've met the ethical standards of behavior analysis. You've tried to use reinforcers. Not only have you used a learned reinforcer—social approval—but you've also used an unlearned reinforcer—Jimmy's favorite food, bologna," Mae said.[4]

"But that wasn't good enough," Eve said.

"Right, the guidelines for the client's rights to effective treatment indicate that Jimmy has a right to effective treatment, even if it involves aversive control. So now you should try aversive control, because probably it will be effective, and you've made a reasonable effort with nonaversive procedures," Mae said. "When he was at Anna State Hospital, Richard Foxx developed an avoidance procedure based on overcorrection."

"Oh, yes," Joe said, "overcorrection requires that the client overcorrects for any problem behavior. We read about this in Chapter 4, on punishment. When Ann trashed the hospital ward, she had to make it even better than it was. But how do we apply overcorrection to Jimmy?"

"Instead of a punishment contingency, you should use an avoidance contingency. Jimmy avoids the mildly aversive overcorrection procedure when he answers your request that he look at you," Mae said. "But if he doesn't look at you, then do what Foxx did. Stand behind Jimmy and tell him to look up, down, or straight ahead. If he doesn't, you use your hands to guide his head. He should hold each of the three positions for 15 seconds. Then go back to your eye contact training procedure." [Note that

this is overcorrection, though it involves physical guidance.]

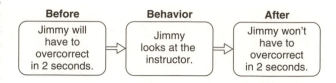

Eve and Joe used Foxx's avoidance procedure and got immediate results: On the first day of the avoidance procedure, Jimmy went from 24% eye contact to 74%. By the 10th day, he was around 97% (Figure 15.2). Now that Jimmy was "attending" to them, Eve and Joe were ready to get down to some serious language training.

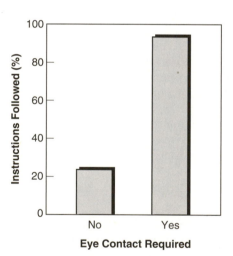

Figure 15.2 Avoidance of Overcorrection Improves Eye Contact Which Improves Following Instructions

QUESTIONS

1. Be able to diagram a behavioral contingency used to get eye contact with an autistic child.
2. What kind of contingency is it?
   a. avoidance of an aversive condition
   b. avoidance of the loss of a reinforcer
   c. escape
   d. punishment

   (To be confident of your answer to such questions, always check the title of the chapter and section.)

---

[4]May, J. G., Risley, T. R., Twardosz, S., Friedman, P., Bijou, S., & Wexler, D. (1975). *Guidelines for the use of behavioral procedures in state programs for retarded persons.* Arlington, TX.: National Association for Retarded Citizens.

EYE CONTACT[5]

Sid's Seminar

Tom: I've got a problem with "Jimmy's Eyes." I don't think eye contact is really needed for attention. I can attend to people without even looking at them, let alone making eye contact.

Max: And I might make eye contact without really attending to what the other person is saying or doing.

Eve: In some cultures, it's a sign of disrespect to make eye contact with the speaker, so people avoid making eye contact.

Sid: I agree; you're all making good points. But suppose you're having trouble bringing someone's behavior under the stimulus control of what you're saying. To put it loosely, suppose you're having trouble getting someone to listen to you. Maybe the person is watching the tube. Wouldn't you think it more likely that what you said would affect the person's behavior if you turned off the tube and waited until he or she looked at you before you started talking?

Joe: Yeah, I don't think the book was talking about a biological or cultural universal—just a rough general rule.

Max: Yes, here it is: **Eye contact general rule:** *If you're having trouble getting a person to listen to you, be sure you have eye contact before you start talking.*

Sid: Yes, eye contact may be neither necessary nor sufficient to get someone to follow your instructions. But it helps, especially when you're working with autistic and developmentally disabled clients and with school children having academic problems. Carolynn Hamlet, Saul Axelrod, and Steven Kuerschner collected some excellent data supporting that general rule.

QUESTION

1. According to the book, if someone (e.g., an autistic student) isn't listening to you, what might you do to get his behavior under the control of your verbal instructions?

---
[5]This section is based on Hamlet, C. H., Axelrod, S., & Kuerschner, S. (1984). Eye contact as an antecedent to compliant behavior. *Journal of Applied Behavior Analysis, 17,* 553–557.

Concept
AVOIDANCE-OF-LOSS CONTINGENCY

Sid's Satiny Satanic Sins

It was July 4th. The noon sun was sizzling—102° Fahrenheit. No traffic. A perfect time for Sid to go for a bike ride. He rode past the local Dangerous Dairy Delights, with its high-cholesterol, high-fat, high-sugar temptations. He was proud of himself for passing up those satiny satanic sins. But on his way back after an hour's hot riding, he couldn't resist. He bought a triple-dipper cone—one dip red raspberry, one white vanilla, and one blueberry—the patriotic July 4th special. He found himself riding home, steering his bike with one hand and trying to balance the monstrous cone with the other, doing his best not to lose the precarious top scoop and licking as fast as he could to get to his ice cream before the sun did.

Sid was balancing and licking as he'd never done before, because avoidance of the loss of a reinforcer (the ice cream) was contingent on this behavior.

The Terrible Trio Meets The Avoidance of Time-Out

Once upon a time, there were three completely off-the-wall kids in the 7th-grade class of Mae's school. The classroom teacher was using a token economy, but that didn't cut it with the terrible trio. So she added a time-out procedure. She used time-out because life in the classroom seemed to be a reinforcer for these kids: They were rarely late for class and almost never missed a day (though the teacher wished they would miss a few).

At first, Mae was going to suggest that the teacher use a traditional punishment procedure based on the time-out. But after looking at the baseline data of the kids' disruptions as part of a functional analysis, she decided not to. These kids came up with so many different ways to disrupt the class that she couldn't specify any limited set of responses to punish with the time-out. So she decided to use an avoidance contingency. Each member of the trio could avoid time-out from the classroom by being on task—by working hard. The teacher would set a kitchen timer to go off every few minutes, after variable periods of time. If a kid was working hard when the bell rang, he got to stay in the classroom. If a kid was staring out the window, whispering, sleeping, out of his seat without permission, clowning, throwing spitballs—anything but working—it was into the hall for 3 minutes. But you can bet she wouldn't put them in the hall as a team; it was strictly one-on-one. This is another example of reinforcement by the avoidance of the loss of a reinforcer.

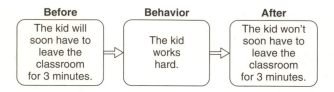

Before	Behavior	After
The kid will soon have to leave the classroom for 3 minutes.	The kid works hard.	The kid won't soon have to leave the classroom for 3 minutes.

Incidentally, only the teacher could see the timer. The kids had no clue; so they couldn't keep one eye on the timer, goof off until right before the bell would ring, and then start working hard (the response that would avoid the time-out). Neither Mae nor the teacher were that dumb.

Definition: Concept
Avoidance-of-loss contingency
○ response-contingent
○ **prevention of loss**
○ of a reinforcer
○ resulting in an **increased** frequency of that response.

Operating beneath this contingency is the **principle of avoidance of loss**—*a response becomes more frequent in the future if it has immediately prevented the loss of a reinforcer in the past.*

Again, note that this is also a type of reinforcement contingency, because it increases the frequency of the causal response. It is reinforcement by avoidance of the loss of a reinforcer.

QUESTION

1. *Avoidance-of-loss contingency*—define it and diagram some examples.

Example from Behavioral School Psychology AVOIDANCE OF REPRIMANDS[6]

It was summertime in Centereach, NY. Eight 1st-, 2nd-, and 3rd-grade students were attending remedial summer school because they had blown it in

[6]Based on Pfiffner, L. J., & O'Leary, S. G. (1987). The efficacy of all-positive management as a function of the prior use of negative consequences. *Journal of Applied Behavior Analysis, 20,* 265–271. Susan O'Leary is on the faculty of the Department of Psychology of the State University of New York at Stony Brook, a most prominent behavior analysis department.

reading or math during the regular school year. Six of them also had behavior problems. The challenge was to keep them on task long enough that they could get some schoolwork done and to keep them from shouting out, hopping out of their seats, daydreaming, fighting—you name it.

The teacher started out using nothing but reinforcement for being on task—praise, bonus work, and public posting of assignments. Better than nothing, no doubt, but not good enough. Then the teacher added more reinforcers—stars, work breaks, puzzles, coloring, reading comic books, running errands, and a host of other super-reinforcers. A little more on task, but not much.

Finally, the teacher looked at the other side of the coin. Besides reinforcing on-task behavior with the presentations of reinforcers, why not add another contingency—one based on aversive conditions? The aversive conditions were brief, specific reprimands—"Joyce, get back in your seat and get to work." "Joyce, don't just sit there, get back to work."

Now here's the question: What's this aversive-control contingency?

a. Punishment of goofing off by presenting reprimands
b. Avoidance of reprimands

Well, in the second edition of *EPB*, we had this example in the punishment chapter. And one of our university students said we were wrong and that the following contingency was wrong.

The Wrong Contingency Diagram

Before	Behavior	After
Joyce receives no reprimand.	Joyce goofs off.	Joyce receives a reprimand.

She said *goofs off* is too large a response class—it also includes doing nothing, and doing nothing isn't behavior. *Doing nothing* fails the dead-man test. Dead men can do nothing. Well, what do you do when the dead man raises his ugly head from the grave? We roll him over. If we thought we had some sort of reinforcement contingency, we've really got some sort of punishment contingency. And if we thought we had some sort of punishment contingency, we've really got some sort of reinforcement contingency—probably avoidance. That means, instead of punishing goofing off (being off-task), we're reinforcing studying. And, as in this case, that reinforcement will usually be in the form of an avoidance contingency.

How can Joyce avoid reprimands? By studying.

The Right Contingency Diagram

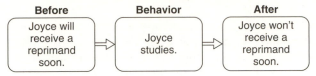

At last, the combination of the two types of contingencies did the trick—reinforcement for on-task behavior and avoidance of brief reprimands (another form of reinforcement, really). The students finally got down to business. And their hard work produced academic payoffs, too. The accuracy of their work improved from about 59% during the reinforcement conditions to 80% when the teacher added the avoidance contingency (Figure 15.3).

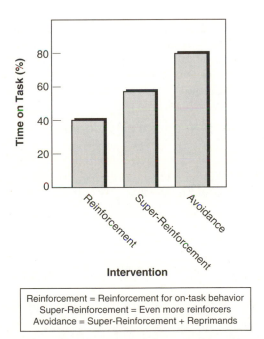

Figure 15.3   Avoidance of Reprimands for Goofing Off in Class

QUESTION

1. Describe the use of an avoidance contingency to ensure students stay on task. Diagram and label the relevant contingencies.

Compare and Contrast
ESCAPE VS. AVOIDANCE

Let's look at two similar reinforcement contingencies—**avoidance (prevention) of an aversive condition** (the one we're studying in this chapter) and **removal of an aversive condition** (our old friend the escape contingency).

With **avoidance,** the response prevents an aversive condition from being received. For example, with Foxx's procedure, Jimmy avoided a mildly aversive overcorrection procedure whenever he looked at Eve or Joe during their instruction program. This greatly increased Jimmy's looking at these two instructors when that avoidance contingency was in effect.

With **escape,** the response causes an aversive condition to be removed. For example, suppose Eve and Joe played a mildly aversive tone each time they asked Jimmy to look at them. And suppose Jimmy could escape the tone by looking at them. This might greatly increase eye contact when that escape contingency was in effect.

In short, the two contingencies are similar—avoidance prevents an aversive condition from being presented, and escape removes an aversive condition that has already been presented.

QUESTION

1. Compare and contrast *escape* versus *avoidance.*

BASIC ENRICHMENT

In the Skinner Box
AVOIDANCE OF AN AVERSIVE CONDITION

These prevention contingencies are tricky, to say the least. To clarify them a bit, let's look at the simplest cases—in the Skinner box. The following four sections deal with four types of avoidance.

Cued Avoidance

A buzzer (warning stimulus) comes on, and 3 seconds later, a mild, but aversive, shock comes on for a few seconds. Then both the buzzer and the shock go off. However, suppose the rat presses the lever within the 3 seconds after the buzzer (warning stimulus) comes on. Then the buzzer will go off, and the rat will have avoided the shock (the shock won't come on). Or suppose the rat waits until the shock comes on and then presses the bar. Then both the shock and the buzzer will go off.

Escape

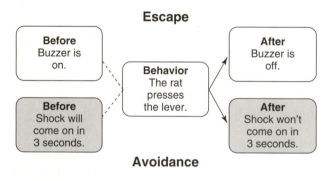

Avoidance

After some training (exposure to these contingencies), the shock-escape contingency controls the behavior. As soon as the shock comes on, the rat presses the lever.

And what happens after even more exposure to the contingencies? The rat starts pressing the lever during the 3 seconds the buzzer is on by itself. When the rat responds during the buzzer, it not only turns off the buzzer but also avoids the shock. We call the buzzer the *warning stimulus* because it occurs before the aversive stimulus. But, at the beginning, the buzzer is a *neutral* stimulus—neutral in the sense that it is neither a reinforcer nor an aversive stimulus. However, after repeated pairing with the aversive stimulus, the buzzer stops being neutral and becomes aversive.

So another way to look at it is that the cued avoidance procedure is really just a tricky way to implement our old buddy the **pairing procedure**—*pairing of a neutral stimulus with a reinforcer or aversive condition*. And the pairing procedure brings into play another old buddy, the ***value-altering principle***—*the pairing procedure converts a neutral stimulus into a learned reinforcer or learned aversive condition.*[7]

Pairing Procedure

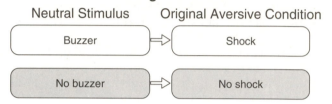

By the way, the escape/avoidance contingency is called *cued* avoidance because of the warning stimulus (e.g., the buzzer), which is supposed to be the cue. However, as we will see later, this is misleading terminology.

Continuous-Response Avoidance

But it didn't work that way for Sid. He also could avoid the click of the timer, as well as the aversive tone. How could he do that? By continuously maintaining good posture.

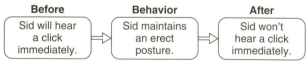

How could we take it to the Skinner box? How could we set up the contingencies for a continuous avoidance response for Rudolph? Well, we might set it up so that as long as Rudolph holds down the lever he will prevent the buzzer from sounding.

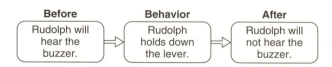

---

[7]Some of us think that it is only the escape contingency that directly controls the behavior. The avoidance contingency simply serves to ensure that the buzzer has had a sufficient history of pairing to become aversive enough that its termination will reinforce the escape response.

Now Sid avoided not only the aversive tone but also the preliminary click by maintaining that posture.

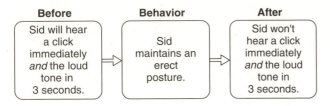

Before	Behavior	After
Sid will hear a click immediately *and* the loud tone in 3 seconds.	Sid maintains an erect posture.	Sid won't hear a click immediately *and* the loud tone in 3 seconds.

It wasn't enough to stand erect briefly and then fall back into his familiar old slouch. Sid had to make a continuous response that avoided the click as long as he kept making that response (i.e., as long as he kept an erect posture).

And we could arrange combination-package contingencies like this to make them analogous to Sid's: Rudolph could avoid the preliminary buzzer as long as he would hold the lever down, but also he would avoid the shock that would otherwise be coming in 3 seconds.

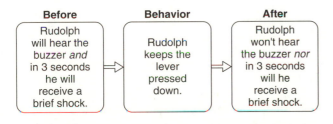

Before	Behavior	After
Rudolph will hear the buzzer *and* in 3 seconds he will receive a brief shock.	Rudolph keeps the lever pressed down.	Rudolph won't hear the buzzer *nor* in 3 seconds will he receive a brief shock.

Note that it isn't essential that continuous-response avoidance involve a package deal like the combination of click and tone or buzzer and shock. Sid's avoiding the click and Rudolph's avoiding the buzzer were also examples of continuous-response avoidance.

Noncued Avoidance

Another variation on the avoidance theme is noncued avoidance. If the rat just sits there and does nothing, a brief shock will come on every 20 seconds (shock-shock interval of 20 seconds), with no warning stimulus. But if the rat presses the bar, it will postpone the shock for 20 seconds (response-shock interval of 20 seconds). So if the rat presses the lever every 19.99999 seconds, it will never get a shock. We could change the contingencies slightly by making the response-shock interval 30 seconds. Then, if the rat presses the lever every 29.99999 seconds, it will never get a shock.

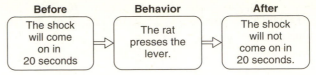

Before	Behavior	After
The shock will come on in 20 seconds	The rat presses the lever.	The shock will not come on in 20 seconds.

Considerable work has been done using this avoidance procedure with monkeys. They soon develop a moderate rate of steady responding that prevents almost all the shocks.

This contingency is **noncued avoidance** because there is no obvious so called "warning stimulus" (e.g., no buzzer).

Avoidance of the Loss of a Reinforcer

We don't know of any actual Skinner box experiments on the avoidance of the loss of a reinforcer, but here's an obvious example: A water-deprived Rudolph the Rat is drinking from a dish of water. But pest that you are, you remove the dish every 20 seconds and keep it out of the Skinner box for 10 seconds. But if Rudolph pulls a chain, you will not pester him for 30 seconds—noncued avoidance of the loss of a reinforcer. If Rudolph pulls the chain every 29.99999 seconds, he will completely avoid the loss of the water.

Avoidance of the Loss of a Reinforcer

Before	Behavior	After
Rudolph will lose the water in 20 seconds.	Rudolph pulls the chain.	Rudolph won't lose the water in 20 seconds.

As we said, we know of no one who's actually done this experiment. It might make a fun research project at the BA, MA, or even PhD level. What do you think? Would it work? If you do it, let us know.

It's easy to confuse avoidance of the loss of a reinforcer with a penalty contingency. Don't. Here's what a comparable penalty contingency would look like:

Penalty (Loss of a Reinforcer)

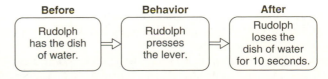

Before	Behavior	After
Rudolph has the dish of water.	Rudolph presses the lever.	Rudolph loses the dish of water for 10 seconds.

In other words, in a penalty contingency, the reinforcer is removed if a specific response occurs.

But in this avoidance contingency, the reinforcer is removed if a specific response doesn't occur. In the case of avoidance, the removal is **not** contingent on the response.

QUESTIONS

1. Diagram cued avoidance in the Skinner box.
2. Diagram either example of the continuous-response avoidance used to maintain erect posture.
3. Diagram either example of continuous-response avoidance in the Skinner box.
4. Diagram noncued avoidance in the Skinner box.

5. Diagram the avoidance of the loss of a reinforcer in the Skinner box.
6. In avoidance of the loss of a reinforcer, is removal contingent on a specific response? Explain your answer.
7. Now this one's not all that straightforward, but what was the terrible trio's avoidance of timeout?
    a. cued avoidance of the loss of a reinforcer
    b. noncued avoidance of the loss of a reinforcer
    c. continuous avoidance of the loss of reinforcer

INTERMEDIATE ENRICHMENT

Compare and Contrast
AVOIDANCE OF AN AVERSIVE CONDITION VS. PUNISHMENT BY THE PRESENTATION OF AN AVERSIVE CONDITION

There's a fine line between reinforcement based on **avoidance** of an aversive condition and punishment based on the **presentation** of an aversive condition. But it may be worth trying to draw that line; so sharpen your pencils.

What we consider to be the crucial response determines how we look at the contingencies. Consider Dawn's perfect-posture contingency. Suppose we think of the response to be slouching. Then the click and tone may punish that response, and we have a punishment contingency (Azrin and his colleagues looked at it that way). Earlier, we considered the perfect posture to be the response. Then we have an avoidance contingency—the perfect posture avoids an aversive condition.

Are these two different ways of saying the same thing—punishment of poor posture versus reinforcement of good posture using an avoidance contingency? Or can we distinguish between two different contingencies? Here's our tentative answer. They're two different deals. Why?

Before we answer that question, let's review an old favorite—the *dead man test: If a dead man can do it, it ain't behavior.*

Dead men slouch. They don't have good posture—at least not before rigor mortis sets in. So slouching doesn't pass the dead-man test.

Here's a less gruesome analysis: Sid slouches when he makes no effort, when he doesn't do any-

thing. So slouching is a nothing, nonbehavior. And what do we do when our proposed behavior fails the dead man test? **Roll over the dead man.** Use the opposite response. What's the opposite of slouching? Having a good posture. And when we roll over the dead man who we thought had a punishment contingency, we always seem to end up with an avoidance contingency. So maintaining a good posture is effortful for Sid. It's a response that avoids the click of the timer.

In sum, if we have to roll over the dead man from a punishment contingency, we always seem to end up with a live man involved in an avoidance contingency. This is so confusing, maybe we should look at another example.

The Amazing Adventures of Behaviorman (Woman)

You and your favorite girlfriend, boyfriend, or spouse are visiting Disney World (Disneyland, for those of you on the West Coast). You've just entered the Haunted Mansion and stepped into the incredible shrinking room. Look up there! What's happening? The ceiling's lowering. It's coming in on us. It's as if you're standing at the bottom of an elevator shaft and the elevator is slowly descending to the basement level. Great fun. It'll stop any minute now, and you'll all have a good laugh.

But the ceiling doesn't stop. It keeps descending. First it's squashing down on the heads of the tallest people. Then all but the shortest kids are bending down. This is carrying a joke too far. People shout, scream, pound on the walls. But the ceiling keeps approaching the floor. Only you stand between your girlfriend, boyfriend, or spouse, a dozen other innocent tourists and the most grisly death imaginable—squashed like bugs in a fun house.

You inconspicuously whip off your outer clothes to reveal a set of striking blue leotards with red initials on a yellow field—*BM,* for Behaviorman (or *BW,* for Behaviorwoman). You get down on one knee, raise your hands above your head (palms up), and push against the ceiling with all your behavioral might. You strain, your muscles ripple, you grunt, you sweat (perspire if you're from the East Coast). Can you stop this ceiling? Can you save these innocent people from one of the most embarrassing deaths known to humankind? And what does your arch foe, the Mad Mentalist, have to do with this?

But, first, a word from our sponsor, *Principles of Behavior.* Ask yourself, as you grunt and strain to hold up the ceiling:

Am I making an active response?

You bet your blue leotards you are.

Is holding up the ceiling the response of interest?

It better be.

Am I avoiding certain death?

Trying.

Is this an avoidance contingency?

Yes, actually cued avoidance, which means a combination of escape and avoidance.

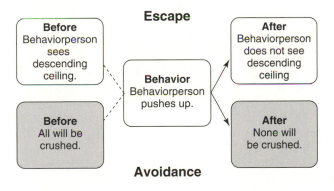

Escape

Before		After
Behaviorperson sees descending ceiling.		Behaviorperson does not see descending ceiling

Behavior
Behaviorperson pushes up.

Before	After
All will be crushed.	None will be crushed.

Avoidance

Would doing nothing, just relaxing, be punished?

Yes, the dead man test would take on new significance.

Careful . . . the ceiling just came down another half inch.

I mean no. No, you can't punish a nothing, a nonresponse.

Good, you just pushed the ceiling up 4 inches.

Punishing a nonresponse (not pushing up on the ceiling) fails the dead-man test. So we roll over the dead man, selecting the opposite of *not pushing,* which is *pushing,* and selecting sort of the opposite of *punishment,* which is *avoidance.*

You see boys and girls, BM (BW) is making an avoidance response. In fact, he (she) must keep passing the dead-man test, or . . . .

The dead-man test is one way to discriminate between avoidance and punishment. Here's a second way that sometimes helps: **Is the so-called *punished* response really a large class, consisting of all other imaginable responses? If, yes, then we've got an avoidance contingency and not a punishment contingency.**

Consider your role as Behaviorperson. Instead of holding up the ceiling, you could pick your nose, scratch your rear end, crack jokes, or take a nap. It doesn't seem too useful to talk about punishing an infinitely large response class. Instead, we should talk about an avoidance contingency that reinforces the smaller response class of holding up the ceiling.

Be sure to tune in next time when Behaviorperson asks: Can we have a contingency based on avoidance of the loss of a reinforcer, or will we get tongue-tied trying to work it out?

QUESTION

1. With a concrete example, compare and contrast avoidance of an aversive condition and punishment by the presentation of an aversive condition.
   - Use the dead-man test.
   - Is the so-called punished response class so infinitely large that it's not useful to think of it as a punishable response class? Explain.

Compare and Contrast
AVOIDANCE OF LOSS OF A REINFORCER VS. PUNISHMENT BY REMOVAL OF A REINFORCER

We've compared reinforcement based on avoidance of the presentation of an aversive condition with punishment by the presentation of an aversive condition—a bit tricky. Well, you ain't seen nothin' yet. Now we're going to compare reinforcement based on **avoidance of the removal** of a reinforcer with our old buddy, punishment by the **removal** of a reinforcer (the penalty contingency).

Let's take another look at Mae's work with the terrible trio. She used avoidance of the loss of a reinforcer. Being on task avoided time-out; it avoided the loss of the reinforcer of being in the classroom.

OK, but could we look at Mae's procedure as punishment by the removal of a reinforcer? What response are we punishing? Not being on task? Dead man! Remember, things get murky when we talk about reinforcing and punishing nonbehavior such as not studying, not being on task. People who keep their eye on the hole and not on the doughnut go hungry.

OK, could we say Mae was punishing throwing spitballs, getting out of the seat, and causing a ruckus? We could, but probably we'd be wrong. Mae didn't put a contingency on throwing spitballs. If she had, it might be something like this: As soon as one of the trio threw a spitball, the offender would be put in time-out. Now we're talkin' penalty contingency.

But the contingency didn't work that way. With Mae's avoidance contingency, the kid might have thrown a dozen spitballs and still not have had to go into time-out. Why not? Because he might have bombarded his buddies and then gotten back to work before the teacher's bell rang, so he would be on task and would thus avoid time-out.

Besides, Dawn specified the response that would avoid time-out. She didn't specify the responses that would receive punishment.

Avoidance of the Loss of a Reinforcer vs. Punishment by the Removal of a Reinforcer		
	Avoidance of the Loss of a Reinforcer	Punishment by the Removal of a Reinforcer
Involves the removal of a reinforcer[8]	Yes	Yes
Removal is contingent on a specific response.	No	Yes
Keeping the reinforcer is contingent on a specific response.	Yes	No
The frequency of the response of interest.	Increases	Decreases

[8]To be more precise, we might say *involves the removal of a reinforcer or the potential for the removal of a reinforcer*. Here's why: Suppose the person always made the avoidance response; then there'd be no actual removal of a reinforcer, but always the potential for its removal if the person ever did fail to respond. Or suppose the person never made the punished response; then, again, there'd be no actual removal of a reinforcer, but always potential for its removal if the person ever did respond.

1. Using two concrete examples (for example, the on-task contingency and the spitball contingency), compare and contrast avoidance of the loss of a reinforcer and punishment by the removal of a reinforcer.
   - Show how each contingency fits the appropriate cells in the preceding table.
   - Use the dead-man test.
   - Is the nonavoidance response class so infinitely large that it's not useful to think of it as a punishable response class? Explain.

Compare and Contrast
WARNING STIMULUS VS. DISCRIMINATIVE STIMULUS

We've been using the term *warning stimulus* throughout this chapter, so maybe it's about time we defined it. We've held off until this point because the context should have made our use clear earlier.

> *Definition: Concept*
> **Warning stimulus**
> - A stimulus that precedes
> - an aversive condition
> - and thus becomes a learned aversive stimulus.

We use the concept when discussing cued avoidance. Remember: A buzzer goes on, and 3 seconds later a shock comes on for a few seconds. If the rat presses the lever within the 3 seconds after the buzzer comes on, the buzzer will go off, and the rat will have avoided the shock (the shock won't come on). The buzzer is the stimulus that occurs preliminary to the presentation of the shock.

Now, traditionally, behavior analysts have analyzed this contingency as if the warning stimulus were a discriminative stimulus. But we think that's not the way to look at it. How would you add a discriminative stimulus to cued avoidance?

First let's review the definition of *discriminative stimulus—a stimulus in the presence of which a response will be reinforced*. What does that mean for cued avoidance? Well, the traditional view is that the warning stimulus (the buzzer) is the stimulus in the presence of which the response (the lever press) will be reinforced (by the termination of the buzzer or the avoidance of the shock).

However, we think it's better to **look at the presence of the warning stimulus as the before con-**

dition. In other words, to say the warning stimulus is the stimulus in the presence of which the escape/avoidance response will be reinforced is like saying no food is the stimulus in the presence of which the food-getting response will be reinforced. You must have the absence of food before getting food is reinforcing, let alone before it is permitted. Similarly, you must have the warning stimulus on before its termination is reinforcing, let alone before it is permitted. But you don't need an S^D before the after condition is reinforcing.

I can tell you're still not convinced. Perhaps it will help to consider what we think *could be* the discriminative stimulus. The discriminative stimulus is a stimulus in the presence of which the escape/avoidance response will be successful, in the presence of which that response will terminate the warning stimulus (the buzzer) and prevent the final aversive stimulus (the shock).

So how might we set up a discriminative stimulus in a Skinner box for this contingency? For example, during S$^\Delta$ (no light), the buzzer comes on for a second or so, and the lever press has no effect. But then the discriminative stimulus or S^D (light) comes on, and the lever press terminates the buzzer and prevents the shock. So now we hope you agree it makes more sense to say the light (not the buzzer) is the stimulus in the presence of which the lever press will be reinforced (by the termination of the buzzer).

Now take a deep breath and check out the following diagram. Don't panic; just take a couple of minutes to figure out what's going on there. It has a lot of logic to it; it makes sense. Once you understand it, you should have no trouble drawing it on your own, without actually memorizing all the details. The logic says it's got to be more or less like this.[9]

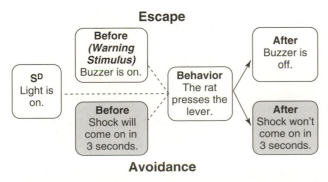

Escape

Avoidance

---

[9]The traditional terminology, *warning stimulus* and *cue*, seem to reflect early confusion in our field by suggesting that the original researchers in avoidance also made the common error of mistaking the before condition for the S^D. And this terminology just makes it all the more difficult for current students to keep it straight. Sorry about that.

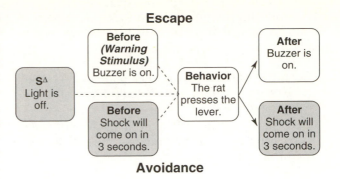

Escape

Avoidance

QUESTIONS

1. *Warning stimulus*—define it and give an example.
2. Be able to diagram the contingency diagram for cued avoidance with an S^D and S$^\Delta$.
3. Describe an escape/avoidance contingency that involves a discriminative stimulus, and explain the difference between the warning stimulus and the discriminative stimulus in that contingency.
4. Where does the warning stimulus go in the contingency diagram?

Research Methods
USING PILOT STUDIES TO HELP YOU GET YOUR ACT TOGETHER BEFORE YOU TAKE IT ON THE ROAD

The avoidance procedure for helping Sid maintain a good posture seemed good in theory, but Dawn and Sid ran into the same problems Azrin's team had met, and they used the same solutions. The problems all involved false alarms—the aversive tone would sound even when Sid was still maintaining a good posture. When Sid looked over his shoulder, his back rounded for that brief time and activated the tone generator. So they added a 3-second timer to the apparatus. This provided a 3-second free period during which Sid would not have to maintain his posture or his straight back.

When Sid reached, his shoulder blades moved and activated the timer. So they placed the straps above his shoulder blades. When he bent forward, this also activated the timer. So they added a tilt switch that prevented the timer from starting when he leaned forward by more than 10 degrees. Now they were ready for business, but only after they had worked hard to improve their original intervention. This illustrates the ***great-new-ideas general rule:*** *New ideas rarely work until you've revised them at least three times.*

And this brief diversion into the development of effective procedures suggests two additional general rules:

- Allow time to recycle (do a pilot study) on any new idea before you actually have to implement it.
- Don't give up when your great new idea doesn't work the first time, or the second time, or the third time.

QUESTION

1. *The general rule for great new ideas—give an example.*

CUED AVOIDANCE AND CONDITIONAL AVERSIVE STIMULI

Jimmy's Eyes

Early in this chapter, we looked at the use of an avoidance contingency to help Jimmy get eye contact with his instructor. At that point, we just diagrammed the avoidance contingency. But because the avoidance contingency was in effect only after the instructor said, "Look at me," we really have a cued-avoidance contingency. But the question is, *What's the warning stimulus?* In other words, *What's the before condition for the escape contingency?*

Our first answer might be to say, *"Look at me," is the before condition,* because Jimmy will be going into overcorrection in 2 seconds after he hears, "Look at me."

Well that's part of the story, but not the whole story. The problem is that *Look at me* isn't quite like the *buzzer on* in the classic Skinner-box escape avoidance. The crucial difference is that the buzzer stays on until the rat escapes it by pressing the lever or until the shock is delivered. But the instructor does **not** say, *Look at meeeeeeeeeeeeeeeee,* until Jimmy looks or until 2 seconds have elapsed and he's gone into overcorrection. Instead the instructor briefly says, *Look at me,* and then Jimmy has 2 seconds of silence before overcorrection. But now, even if Jimmy immediately looks at the instructor, he doesn't escape having just heard *Look at me.* So what does Jimmy actually escape, the instant he looks at the instructor?

This is tricky: I think he escapes a combination of stimuli. I think he escapes the stimuli arising from not looking at the instructor combined with *Look at me* having just been said. Jimmy's not seeing the instructors face combined with just having heard *Look at me* is a compound or conditional stimulus that

gets paired with overcorrection. So we might say Jimmy's not seeing the instructor becomes a learned aversive stimulus, conditional upon having just heard *Look at me.* Only the combination of the two sets of stimuli are paired with overcorrection; neither set by itself gets paired with overcorrection. For example, *Look at me* immediately followed by the sight of the instructor's face isn't paired with overcorrection.

So what we have is a **conditional stimulus:** *Elements of a stimulus have their value or function only when they are combined; otherwise, the individual elements are relatively neutral.* In this case the conditional stimulus we have is a **conditional (combined) aversive stimulus;** the absence of the sight of the instructor's face is aversive, conditional upon (combined with) the instructor's having just said, "Look at me."

We said it was tricky.

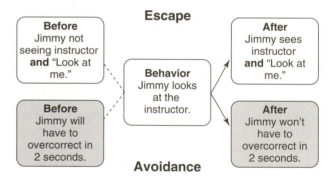

Sidney's Slouch

One of my students pointed out that Sid's stand-straight-and-avoid-the-buzzer contingency was also a cued escape/avoidance contingency, by which Sid escaped a conditional learned-aversive stimulus. Well, 1 hour of diagramming and two Diet Cokes later, I concluded the student was right.

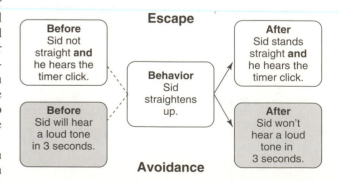

So, my guess is that when Sid first started using the behavioral-posture apparatus, the proprioceptive stimuli arising from not standing straight (slouching) were learned aversive stimuli only because he had just heard the timer click on. They were conditional aversive stimuli. And then the preceding diagram applies. However, if Sid wore the apparatus more or less all the time, then I'd guess the proprioceptive stimuli arising from slouching may have become simple learned-aversive stimuli, and they would have continued to be aversive because of their consistent pairing with the loud tone, even if they had put a silencer on the soft click of the timer.

QUESTION

1. Diagram the escape/avoidance contingency for the eye-contact procedure based on the work of Richard Foxx.

TELEOLOGY

Teleology is the explanation of current events in terms of future events; it's saying the future causes the past. Here's a teleological explanation: *Our ancestors evolved ears and a nose so we, as their descendants, would have something to rest our eyeglasses on.* Most people, these days, consider teleological explanations to be logical errors. It does not seem plausible to us that something that hasn't even happened yet can affect something that is currently happening. For example, the evolution of ears and a nose obviously was not affected by the technological advances that made it possible to improve vision many centuries after that evolution. The invention of glasses did not cause us to evolve ears and a nose.

The reason we mention teleology in this chapter is that some of our more theoretically inclined students have asked if avoidance contingencies are not teleological and therefore illogical. These students raise the question of teleology because we say in the before condition, *the rat **will** get the shock in 20 seconds.*

Avoidance

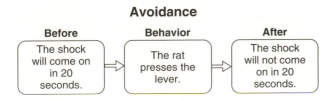

And the way we draw the diagrams, with the arrow going from the before condition to the response, suggests that the before condition causes the response. In other words, it seems like we're saying that the prevention of the shock in the future is causing the current lever press. Right?

Wrong. We're not saying the prevention of the shock in the future is causing the current lever press, in the case of the avoidance contingency. Instead, we're saying that the past instance where the lever presses prevented the shock reinforced the response class of lever pressing and that's why lever pressing increased.

It might help to look at a generic reinforcement contingency to understand the avoidance contingency.

Reinforcement

Before	Behavior	After
No water	The rat presses the lever.	Water

We know that, in the preceding contingency, the first time Rudolph is in the Skinner box he doesn't press the lever even though he is water deprived. But eventually, though shaping or luck, he does press the lever and receives a drop of water. The water reinforces the lever press and his frequency of pressing the lever increases.

Reinforcers increase the behavior they immediately follow. Avoidance of an aversive condition increases the behavior it immediately follows. Neither outcomes affect behavior that is in the past. Both increase behavior in the future. And all the arrow going from the before condition to the response means is that the before condition precedes the response.

QUESTIONS

1. What is *teleology*?
2. And why aren't our avoidance contingency diagrams a teleological explanation?

Experimental Analysis of Behavior
LEARNING WITHOUT AWARENESS CLUELESS AT COLUMBIA: THE CASE OF THE TWITCHING THUMB[10]

Here's one of my all-time favorite experiments. Dr. Ralph Hefferline and two of his grad students at Columbia University worked with a human response so

---

[10]This section based on Hefferline, R. F., Keenan, B., and Harford, R. A. (1958). Escape and avoidance conditioning in human subjects without their observation of the responses. *Science, 130,* 1338–1339.

small that the person making the response was unaware of it. They worked with a tiny thumb twitch.

How could they work with a thumb twitch so small the twitcher was unaware of it? Well, even invisible muscle contractions (e.g., tiny twitches) produce a small but measurable electric voltage (1 to 3 microvolts). So scientists taped small metal disks (electrodes) to the person's left thumb and hand, and wired the disks to an electronic amplifier that amplified the voltage by 1 million so that they could read the voltage on a meter.

They then taped a few extra (nonfunctional) electrodes and wires here and there on the person, to make the thumb wire less conspicuous. The person then sat in a reclining lounge chair, listening to elevator music through earphones. The experimenters worked individually with twelve people, divided into four groups of three people each.

- They told the first group, the completely clueless, that the experiment was about the effects on body tension of noise superimposed on music. The person was just to sit there listening to the music with occasional noise interruptions.
- They told the second group, the semiclueless, that a specific, small, invisible, but unspecified response would briefly turn off the noise. They also said that when the noise was not present, the response would temporarily postpone it.
- They told the third group, the hip, that the effective response was a tiny twitch of the left thumb.
- They told the final group, hip with technology, about the effects of the tiny twitch; but also they put a meter in front of the twitcher during the first half hour of the escape/avoidance phase. This meter was connected to the amplifier and indicated the occurrence of the proper twitches.

During baseline (the first five or ten minutes), the elevator music played with no noise.

During the escape/avoidance phase, the aversive noise came on; and when the noise was **on,** each tiny thumb twitch (1 to 3 microvolts) turned it off for 15 seconds—an escape contingency.

Escape Contingency

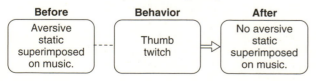

And when the noise was **off,** each tiny thumb twitch postponed it for 15 seconds—an avoidance contingency. So a thumb twitch every 15 seconds would postpone the noise throughout the rest of the escape/avoidance phase.

Avoidance Contingency

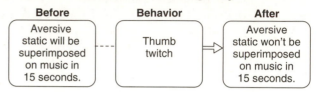

After 1 hour with the escape/avoidance contingency, a 10-minute extinction phase started: the noise came on and stayed on, no matter how much that thumb twitched.

Extinction of the Thumb Twitch

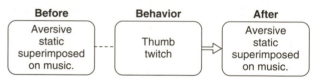

Then they returned to baseline—with no noise, just elevator music.

Results

So, who learned the thumb twitch, and who didn't? Especially, what about the first group, the clueless?

The clueless twitchers did well, greatly increasing the frequency of their effective escape/avoidance thumb twitches, even though they were completely unaware of what was going on.

Skeptical? Are you thinking they may have started out clueless, unaware, but then they figured out what was going on and started thumb twitching so they could escape and avoid the noise? Hefferline was skeptical too, so he asked them. All three still believed they'd had no influence on the noise and were shocked to learn they had been in control. Wow!

But we shouldn't be too surprised that human beings can learn without awareness; Rudolph the rat certainly can. So here's the point: Yes, we can learn without being aware of the contingency or even the response. Outcomes can control our behavior without our awareness.

What about the semiclueless, who knew that some small unknown response would escape and avoid the noise? They did well too, but not in the way you might think. Two gave up searching for the magic response and sank into effective cluelessness. The other guy said he'd figured it out: "I'd act like I was subtly rowing with both hands, wiggle both my ankles, move my jaw to the left, breathe out, and then wait." Yeah, well, whatever.

And the hip, who knew the contingencies and the response? Only one of the three learned the response. The other two kept so busy making large thumb twitches that the small, reinforceable twitches had too little opportunity to occur.

And the hip with technology, the twitch-o-meter?: They did best of all. And during the second half of the escape/avoidance phase, the meter was removed, but they continued with their tiny twitches; having learned them well with the meter, they no longer needed that extra help.

During the extinction phase, when the noise was on continuously, everyone's twitching extinguished. And during the return to baseline with no noise, the twitching was the same low frequency as during the first baseline; and so, fortunately, Hefferline didn't turn the experimental participants out onto the NYC mean streets with dangerously twitching thumbs.

Now, these last three groups were interesting, but let's not lose sight of the first group and the big deal. **THE BIG DEAL IS THAT CONTINGENCIES CAN CONTROL OUR BEHAVIOR, EVEN WHEN WE ARE UNAWARE OF THOSE CONTINGENCIES, THE BEHAVIOR, OR THAT ANY CONTROLLING IS GOING ON,** at least when the outcomes follow the response within a fraction of a second or so. Now, it's a big jump from the Hefferline's tiny twitches, but I'll bet most of us are unaware of most of the contingencies controlling most of our behavior and even unaware of much of the behavior being controlled; but that's another story for another course. Now, it's time to review those Chapter 15 definitions and get ready for tomorrow's quiz, or the quiz you've got in about 15 minutes, depending on how well you've got your act together.

QUESTIONS

1. Describe an experiment that demonstrates learning without awareness.
    a. What species were the subjects?
    b. What was the response?
    c. What were the contingencies?
    d. What were the differences in the procedures for the four groups?
    e. What were the results for the four groups?

16 Punishment by Prevention

FUNDAMENTALS

Concept
PUNISHMENT-BY-PREVENTION-OF-REMOVAL CONTINGENCY

Sid said, "I've got a speck in my eye and it hurts like heck." (An aversive condition, indeed.)

"Hold on. I'll get a cotton swab and see if I can get it out," Dawn said.

With cotton swab in hand, she began her rescue mission. "Now, Sid, you've got to hold still if you want me to get that speck." (*Removal of an aversive stimulus*.) "I can't get it out if you keep batting your eye!" (*Prevention of the removal of an aversive condition*.)

So that prevention contingency may have punished movement. If so, Sid would become a better patient (less movement) with repeated instances of Dawn's rescue efforts to get rid of a painful speck in his eye.

Punishment by Prevention of Removal

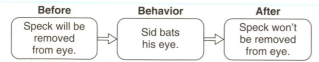

Before	Behavior	After
Speck will be removed from eye.	Sid bats his eye.	Speck won't be removed from eye.

Remember the fable about Androcles and the lion with the thorn in its paw? Everyone made such a big fuss about what a brave man he was to remove the thorn. But what about the lion? Think how cool he was not to keep jerking his paw away each time Androcles tried to remove the thorn. This is the same contingency as with Sid and Dawn—the response of movement would prevent the removal of the aversive thorn.

1. Please complete the following diagram.

Punishment by Prevention of Removal[1]

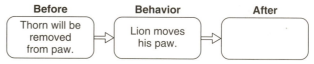

Before	Behavior	After
Thorn will be removed from paw.	Lion moves his paw.	

Neither of these is a planned contingency. The world just works that way. But remember when you had that fight with your big brother? He started twisting your arm behind your back (an aversive condition). You kept shouting, "You ugly bully, let me go!" And he explained the contingency to you, "I won't let you go until you stop calling me an ugly bully"—another example of what might be a punishment contingency—the response (ugly bully) prevents the removal of an aversive condition (your twisted arm).

2. Please diagram the ugly-bully example, with calling your brother *ugly bully* being the behavior.

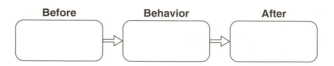

Before	Behavior	After

---

[1]Note that this diagram doesn't say that the lion actually moved his paw. It just says the thorn won't be removed **if** he does move it. In other words, we're just reminding you that a contingency diagram doesn't say the behavior occurred, it just says what will happen *if* the behavior does occur.

276

We know of no examples in which behavior analysts have used such a planned contingency in working with their clients. But our goal is to understand how the world works, for better or for worse. So we should understand all the basic contingencies out there in the real world, even if we don't plan to use them as part of our behavioral technology.

Definition: Concept

Punishment-by-prevention-of-removal contingency
- the immediate,
- response-contingent
- **prevention of removal**
- of an aversive condition
- resulting in a **decreased** frequency of that response.

Operating beneath this contingency is the **principle of punishment by prevention:** A *response occurs less frequently if it has immediately prevented the removal of an aversive condition in the past.* This is *punishment by the prevention of the removal of an aversive condition.*

The following may help you understand this prevention contingency: Suppose the person does nothing and the aversive condition goes away. But if the person makes the punished response, then the aversive condition won't go away. If that's the deal, then you've got punishment by the prevention of removal.

QUESTION

1. *Punishment by prevention contingency*—define it and diagram an example.

Example
JIMMY'S HEAD BANGING[2]

Like many children with autistic behaviors, Jimmy had a bundle of them. He was frequently out of control. The staff often had to restrain him to keep him from seriously injuring himself with his violent fits of

---

[2]Based on Smith, D. M. (November 1984). Managing the aggressive behavior of adults disabled by autism in the community. Paper presented at the meeting of the Association for the Severely Handicapped, Chicago. Figure 16.1 is based on the same article. In the actual case, the client was 18 years old and lived in a group home for autistic clients.

head banging and to keep him from injuring others with his violent aggression. Mae measured his behavior during a pre-intervention baseline session. Jimmy was banging his head 95% of the time.

Then Mae set up a performance-management contingency for her staff. Though Jimmy had only a few phrases in his repertoire, he was able to ask for food, evidently a powerful reinforcer for him. So whenever Jimmy asked for food, the staff gave it to him, **but only if** he was not banging at the time. After 45 days of using this contingency, Mae and her staff reduced Jimmy's banging from 95% of the time to only 7% (Figure 16.1).

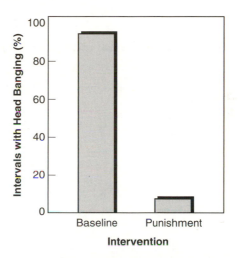

Figure 16.1 Punishment Decreases Head Banging

Concept
PUNISHMENT-BY-PREVENTION-OF-A-REINFORCER CONTINGENCY

Now the question is, what sort of contingency did Mae use to reduce Jimmy's head banging? This one is tricky to analyze, so let's break it down. First of all, whose behavior are we analyzing? People often get confused when more than one person is involved. Usually it's the person whose behavior we're trying to change, and not the performance manager. In this case, it's Jimmy's.

Here's where many students have gotten confused about Jimmy's case: Which of Jimmy's behaviors are we analyzing—his head banging or his asking for food? Usually it's the behavior we're trying to change—Jimmy's head banging.

Punishment by Prevention

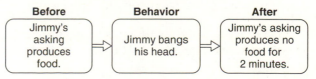

So, as long as Jimmy is cool, he will get food (a reinforcer) when he asks for it. But if he's banging his head, he won't get that food reinforcer when he asks for it. So the response of head banging prevents the presentation of the food reinforcer. And that prevention of a normally occurring reinforcer suppresses or punishes the head banging. In other words, we have a punishment contingency. More specifically, we have **punishment by the prevention of the presentation of a reinforcer** (the food).

Definition: Concept

Punishment-by-prevention-of-a-reinforcer contingency

- response-contingent
- **prevention** of
- a reinforcer
- **resulting in a decreased frequency of that response.**

Operating beneath this contingency is the **principle of punishment by prevention of a reinforcer:** A *response occurs less frequently if it has immediately prevented a reinforcer in the past.*

Many students thought this was an extinction procedure rather than an intricate punishment procedure. Why? Maybe because they were looking at the wrong behavior—asking for food.

Extinction

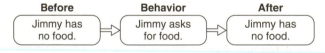

True, the procedure involved the extinction of asking for food, but that's not the behavior Mae was trying to control. However, the contingency designed to reduce head banging was a punishment procedure (see the preceding diagram of punishment by prevention). One way you can tell it wasn't extinction is to note that the before and after conditions aren't the same. In extinction, they are always the same, because, in extinction, the response has no effect.

This type of punishment contingency is so complex we'd better check out another example.

Example
BILL'S FACE SLAPPING[3]

Bill was a profoundly mentally handicapped adolescent who had been living in a state institution for over 10 years. Bill slapped his own face so hard and so often that his cheeks were usually red and bruised. Behavior analyst Henry Corte began a series of 15-minute behavior modification sessions. During these sessions, Henry would give Bill a spoonful of a thick malted milkshake every 15 seconds. But Henry would provide the milkshake only if Bill had not slapped his face during that 15-second interval. If Bill had slapped his face, then Henry would wait 45 seconds before giving him another spoonful.[4]

Actual Prevention of a Reinforcer

So what kind of contingency was Henry using? Punishment by the prevention of the presentation of a reinforcer. Henry punished Bill's slaps by having the slaps prevent the presentation of a spoonful of milkshake—a reinforcer Bill would otherwise get every 15 seconds. How did it work? The slaps decreased rapidly from 20 responses per 15-minute session during baseline to 0 responses during the punishment contingency (Figure 16.2).

QUESTIONS

1. *Punishment-by-prevention-of-reinforcer contingency*
   a. Define it.
   b. Diagram its use to reduce head banging.
   c. Diagram its use to reduce face slapping.

---

[3]Based on Corte, H. E., Wolf, M. M., & Locke, B. J. (1971). A comparison of procedures for eliminating self-injurious behavior of retarded adolescents. *Journal of Applied Behavior Analysis, 4,* 201–213. Figure 16.2 is based on the same article.
[4]I know about 10% of you are going to ask about this, so here it is: Slaps during the first 30 seconds of that 45-second interval had no effect on the presentation of the spoonful of milk shake. But a slap during the last 15 seconds of that interval prevented the presentation of the milk shake and put Bill back into another 45-second cycle. (Sorry for that extra complexity, but you know somebody would have asked if we hadn't mentioned it first.)

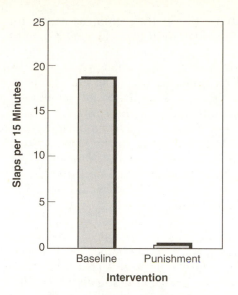

Figure 16.2   Punishment Decreases Face Slapping

Compare and Contrast
PREVENTION OF A REINFORCER VS. REMOVAL OF A REINFORCER

Let's look at two similar punishment contingencies—prevention of the presentation of a reinforcer (the one we're studying right now) and removal of a reinforcer (our old friend the penalty contingency). Note that both punishment contingencies involve decreasing contact with a reinforcer.

For **prevention**, the response prevents a reinforcer from being received. For example, Henry prevented Bill's receiving his normally forthcoming spoonful of milkshake every time he slapped his face. This got rid of Bill's face slapping while that contingency was in effect. For **removal**, the response causes a reinforcer to be removed. For example, suppose Bill were drinking a whole glass of malted milkshake. Then Henry might briefly remove the glass of milkshake Bill was drinking every time Bill slapped his face. This might eliminate his face slapping while that penalty contingency was in effect.

Hypothetical Removal of a Reinforcer

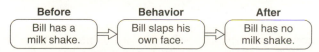

In short, the two punishment contingencies are similar—one prevents a reinforcer from being presented and the other removes a reinforcer that has already been presented.

1. Compare and contrast punishment by the prevention of the presentation of a reinforcer and punishment by the removal of a reinforcer. Do so by diagramming a similar example of each contingency.

Compare and Contrast
THE FOUR BASIC BEHAVIORAL CONTINGENCIES AND THEIR PREVENTION

Let's review the four basic behavioral contingencies we studied in the first few chapters. As you can see from the table, we have two conditions, stimuli, or events; they are reinforcers and aversive conditions. And we have two things we can do with those two conditions; we can present them or remove them, contingent on a response. And whether we present or remove a reinforcer or an aversive condition determines whether we have a reinforcement, punishment, escape, or penalty condition. (Remember that escape is really a special type of reinforcement, and a penalty is really a special type of punishment.)

Contingency Table for the Basic Contingencies		
Stimulus, event, or condition	*Present*	*Remove*
Reinforcer	Reinforcement ⇑	Penalty ⇓
Aversive condition	Punishment ⇓	Escape ⇑

Note: Remember that ⇑ means the response frequency goes up and ⇓ means it goes down.

In this chapter, we've gotten much more complex; we've added prevention to the four basic contingencies. And when we add prevention, we completely reverse the effects of the contingencies. For example, the presentation of a reinforcer increases the frequency of the causal response; that's a reinforcement contingency. But the prevention of the presentation of a reinforcer decreases the frequency of the causal response; that's a punishment contingency. Prevention reverses the effects of the other three contingencies in the same way, as you can see in the next table.

Contingency Table for the Prevention of the Basic Contingencies		
	Prevent the Presentation	**Prevent the Removal**
Reinforcer	Punishment ⇓	Avoidance ⇑
Aversive condition	Avoidance ⇑	Punishment ⇓

QUESTIONS

1. Fill in contingency tables describing the four basic contingencies and their prevention.
   Danger: Quite a few people are blowing their quizzes because they can't do this.
2. Draw diagrams describing the effects of the four basic contingencies and their prevention.
3. Describe the eight contingencies and their effects in sentences as well.

Example
USING PUNISHMENT CONTINGENCIES TO REDUCE A CHILD'S FEAR OF THE DENTIST[5]

"Dawn, Mrs. Green is on the phone," the secretary said.

Mrs. Green? Who's Mrs. Green? Dawn thought, while picking up the phone.

"Dawn, I'm Todd's mother. You helped him a few months ago with his bowel movement problem," Mrs. Green said.

"Oh! Yes!" Dawn smiled, thinking about the Bubblegum Kid. "How is Todd doing?" she asked.

"He's fine with his bowel movements; but now I'm having another problem with him. I thought you could help me again," Mrs. Green said.

"What's the problem?" Dawn asked.

"Todd panics at the dentist's office, and we've scheduled 10 visits. I have to drag him to the office. And when we get there, he pales and shakes all over like a puppy. He screams and hits. And, of course, he never cooperates. Dr. Hook has not been able to do any work with his teeth in four visits."

"When is his next dental visit?" Dawn asked.

"Next Tuesday at 2:00 P.M.," Mrs. Green said.

Dawn showed up at the dentist's office. She wanted to see Todd in action. When Todd entered

[5]Based on Allen, K. D., & Stokes, T. F. (1987). Use of escape and reward in the management of young children during dental treatment. *Journal of Applied Behavior Analysis, 20,* 381–390. The data presented in this section are from this article.

the office, Carol, the dental assistant, told Todd what Dr. Hook would do and what it might feel like. Then Dr. Hook entered. He said, "If you stay quiet I'll give you a prize when we finish." But Todd didn't buy that. He cried, gagged, and moaned 88% of the time—52 minutes of the 60-minute session. He got no treatment and no prize.

Dawn found an ingenious intervention that Keith Allen had done for his doctoral dissertation at West Virginia University, a major center for behavior analysis. She would need the help of Carol, the dental assistant. They would have Todd practice, before seeing Dr. Hook. In the practice, Carol said to Todd, "You can be a big helper by lying still and quiet while we practice working with you. Whenever you're a big helper, we'll stop our work awhile, to give you a rest." Then Carol turned on a drill without a bit and gradually moved it closer to Todd's mouth. Dawn gave Todd "a rest" every 3 seconds, unless he was disruptive. (Each of Todd's disruptions prevented the termination of the aversive sound of that drill until 3 seconds had passed since the disruption. If he had been disruptive every 3 seconds, she would never have turned off the drill. This is a punishment contingency—punishment by the prevention of the removal of an aversive condition.)

When Todd wasn't quiet, Dawn and Carol quit talking to him, avoided eye contact, and turned away slightly, though Carol kept the drill going and kept "working" with him. (So being disruptive was also punished by the removal of attention—a penalty contingency.)

When Todd reliably met the 3-second criterion, Dawn raised it to 10 seconds. Then the first disruption in each 10-second interval was punished by preventing the termination of the drill's aversive sound. When Todd reliably met the 10-second criterion, Dawn raised it to 20 seconds, and finally to 30 seconds.

After Todd had mastered the drilling, they moved on to five other major threats in the dentist's office: dental exploration, water suction, injection (no needle), placement of the rubber dam, and restorative procedures.

Dawn and Carol also added a third punishment contingency: They would periodically give Todd praise and small stickers unless he was disruptive—punishment by the prevention of reinforcers. They placed the stickers on a colored index card containing a picture of a pie sliced into six pieces. They attached the card to the dental light above Todd where he could easily see it. Each time Todd earned enough stickers to fill the card, he got to keep it, a wonderful reinforcer for anyone!

When Todd met the criterion of 30 seconds with no disruptions for each procedure, Dawn and

Carol gave him the 6-minute tests. They did this at the beginning of every visit when he might actually see the dentist. During the test, they used each of the six dental procedures for 1 minute. Todd would pass the test when he managed to be disruptive for no more than 15 seconds per procedure. Then Dr. Hook could come in and start the real dental work. But in two sessions Todd failed to pass the test. So Dawn and Carol went on with more practice and tests with the procedures he'd failed.

Soon Todd was ready for Dr. Hook. Right before real dental work, Todd chose a prize from a set of inexpensive toys. Carol placed the toy on a counter and told Todd he could take the prize home if he was a big helper while Dr. Hook did his work. Again, they gradually raised their criterion: Todd got the prize only if he was 15% less disruptive than the previous visit. Their terminal criterion was disruption no more than 30% of the time—this is what kids normally can do.

It worked. Todd's disruptive behavior decreased from 88% of the time to less than 15% (Figure 16.3). In other words, with the traditional approach, Todd disrupted about 52 minutes per hour; with the behavioral approach, he disrupted less than 6 minutes per hour. Also, Dawn and Carol spent less time in each practice exercise. They went from 45 minutes in the first two sessions to 6 in the fifth. And from visits 6 to 10, Todd needed no practice sessions. Once again, Mrs. Green thought Dawn was the best thing on two feet. And Dr. Hook was so impressed that he let Carol and Dawn test the same procedure with four other children. The procedure worked as well with each of them.

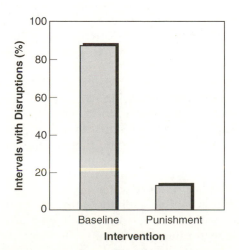

Figure 16.3   Punishment Decreases Dental Disruptions

Analysis

At first, we thought these procedures involved escape and reinforcement contingencies and shaping, so we put this case study in the shaping chapter. But Todd Nadaeu pointed out that these were punishment contingencies. (Todd Nadaeu is not the Todd of our story; he was a student in my graduate seminar on behavior analysis.) So we moved the case study to this punishment chapter. Here's how our conversion went:

What's the escape behavior? What's the behavior being reinforced by the escape contingency?

Being quiet.

Wrong Analysis in Terms of Escape

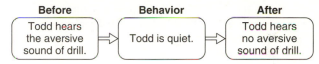

Is being quiet behavior? Does it pass the dead-man test? Could a dead man do it?

Yes, dead men are experts at being quiet. But behavior is anything a dead man can't do, so that means being quiet isn't behavior.

Then how do we find out what behavior we're analyzing?

Roll over the dead man. What's the opposite of being quiet?

Being disruptive?

Yes. And how do we find the proper contingency?

Roll over the dead man's contingency. What's the opposite of reinforcement by escape from an aversive condition?

Punishment by the prevention of the removal of an aversive condition—the aversive sound of the drill.

Punishment by the Prevention of Removal of an Aversive Condition

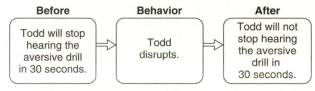

So it's a punishment contingency—punishment of disruptions by the prevention of the removal of an aversive condition. We know it's punishment because it decreases the frequency of disruptions.

And what about the reinforcers of praise and stickers?

They will come every few seconds, as long as Todd doesn't disrupt; so the naive might do the following analysis.

Wrong Analysis in Terms of Reinforcement

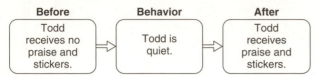

But relying on our good buddy, the dead man, we are not so easily fooled. Again, *being **quiet*** is not behavior. So we roll over the dead man and, again, come up with *disrupting* as the behavior. And we roll over this dead man's contingency and come up with the opposite of reinforcement by presentation of reinforcers—punishment by prevention of the presentation of reinforcers.

Punishment by the Prevention of a Reinforcer

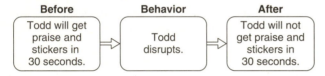

So we have another punishment contingency, but this time it's punishment of disruptions by the prevention of the presentation of reinforcers.

Dawn gradually increased the required duration of no disruptions. Does that make this a shaping procedure?

That's a hard one. For it to be shaping, the duration must be a dimension of the behavior being shaped. And duration would be a dimension of being quiet if being quiet were a behavior. But because it isn't; instead, the behavior of interest is disrupting. And Dawn is not gradually changing the duration of the disruption response; instead, she's just changing the duration of time during which that contingency is in effect. So this isn't shaping.

Here's another way to look at it: Remember, the response of interest is disruption. So if this were shaping, Dawn would gradually increase or (in this case) decrease the duration of Todd's disruption on which the loss of the praise and stickers would be contingent. She might start out punishing only disruptions of 10 seconds' duration and shape shorter and shorter disruptions. She'd shape by gradually decreasing the length of the disruption she would tolerate. Eventually she'd reach the point where a disruption of even a fraction of a second would be punished. But Dawn didn't do that; instead she went right for the terminal behavior, punishing even the briefest of disruptions. So again, Dawn didn't use shaping.

QUESTIONS

1. Describe an intervention to decrease children's disruptions during dental treatment using punishment-by-prevention contingencies. Include:
   a. the response class.
   b. the punishment contingencies.
   c. the results.
   d. Why is the main contingency punishment and not escape?
   e. Why isn't this procedure shaping?

BASIC ENRICHMENT

In the Skinner Box
PUNISHMENT: PREVENTION OF THE REMOVAL OF AN AVERSIVE STIMULUS

We don't know of any experiments on prevention of the removal of an aversive stimulus, but this might do the trick. Put a rat in the Skinner box and reinforce lever pressing with a drop of water for each lever press. Once the rat has acquired lever pressing, turn on a bright light and leave it on as long as the rat keeps pressing the lever. (A bright light is a mildly aversive stimulus for the albino lab rat, which

has no protective pigment in its red eyes.) But if the rat stops pressing the lever for 5 seconds, turn off the light. The lever pressing is preventing the removal of the aversive bright light, and that should work as a punishment contingency to decrease the rate of lever presses, though those presses are producing the reinforcing drops of water.

Why would you reinforce the lever press? So you can be sure you've got a response occurring at a high enough rate that you can demonstrate the effects of the punishment contingency. (Whenever you use a punishment contingency, you need a response to punish, and you need a reinforcement contin-

Reinforcement

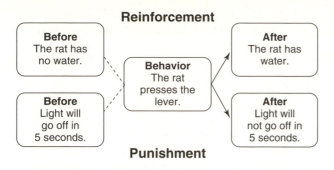

Punishment

gency to get that response to occur.) In a sense the reinforcement contingency and the punishment contingency are competing with each other for control of that response.[6]

QUESTION

1. Diagram the procedure for punishment by prevention of the removal of an aversive condition in the Skinner box.

INTERMEDIATE ENRICHMENT

Controversy:
Compare and Contrast:
PUNISHMENT VS. DRO

Remember Bill, the young man with profound mental impairment? He slapped his face so hard his cheeks were usually red and swollen. Again, let's describe the procedure Henry Corte used to reduce this problem, but this time let's do it from the point of view of reinforcement rather than punishment.

Henry would give Bill a spoonful of a malted milkshake every time 15 seconds passed and Bill had not slapped his face. Traditionally, behavior analysts call this contingency *differential reinforcement of other behavior* (*DRO*). In other words, Henry reinforced all behavior other than face slapping—Henry differentially reinforced non–face-slapping behavior.

You might look at it this way: Consider a 15-second interval with no face slapping. Other behaviors will occur during that 15-second interval. And when Bill gets the spoonful of malt at the end of that interval, the malt will reinforce those other behaviors, especially those behaviors that occurred near the end of the interval (right before the malt).

Differential Reinforcement of Behavior Other Than Face Slapping

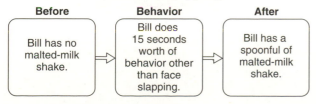

Earlier, we described this as a punishment by the prevention of the presentation of a reinforcer—

Bill's slapping prevented the presentation of the reinforcing milkshake. So here's a review of the diagram of that same procedure viewed as a punishment contingency.

Punishment of Face Slapping by the Prevention of the Presentation of the Malt Reinforcer

So this is the question: Are we equally correct in viewing this contingency as either punishment by the prevention of the presentation of a reinforcer or as reinforcement of other behavior—and it doesn't matter which way? We think that's not correct; we think it does matter how you view the contingency.

Remember that we advocate keeping your eye on the doughnut and not on the hole. Keep your eye on the behavior and not on the nonbehavior—not the nonslapping. It's not really that Henry wanted to increase other behavior with this contingency. What he wanted to do was reduce Bill's slapping. We think people may lose sight of the objective when they

---

[6]As in Chapter 4, we've reviewed the examples of punishment in the fundamentals section of this chapter to see if we could add to their contingency diagrams the reinforcement contingency that was maintaining their behavior. Also, as in Chapter 4, none of those examples had involved a functional analysis to discover the reinforcement contingency; and we were reluctant to speculate about what that reinforcement contingency might be.

talk about reinforcing nonbehavior or other behavior. Here, the objective was to reduce the frequency of a particular response, slapping; and it was that response on which the contingency was based. In short, we think the terminology *differential reinforcement of other behavior (DRO)* misleads people; but many behavior analysts don't—in fact, your professor may not, and you may not; so here's the definition: **differential reinforcement of other behavior (DRO)**—*a reinforcer is presented after a fixed interval of time if the response of interest has not occurred during that interval. (The interval is usually timed from the last reinforcer or the last response of interest, whichever occurred last.)*

We give you the definition of DRO because it's so popular; but we don't really think you should use it except when needed for communication.

QUESTIONS

1. *Differential reinforcement of other behavior*—give an example (include the contingency diagram of your example).
2. Argue for an analysis in terms of punishment by the prevention of the presentation of a reinforcer as opposed to differential reinforcement of other behavior (DRO).

17 Ratio Schedules

Example
THE DIVERS OF NASSAU

The Nassau dock was crowded with tourists of assorted sizes, shapes, ages, and dispositions, their cameras slung about their necks like gawky identification tags. Here and there, tourists perspired beneath sunglasses, their skin already turning pink under the Bahamian sun. The cruise boats were in from Miami: the *Bahama Star,* the *Miami,* the *Ariadne,* and the *Wayward.* The port bustled with enterprise.

In the harbor, the water was a clear blue. Groups of Bahamian boys stood in a cluster by the wharf. They had planned in advance to stay there. No tourist could land on Bahamian soil without first allowing them an opportunity to solicit tribute.

"Hey, Mon, throw in de coin and watch me bring him up."

An occasional tourist tossed a quarter into the cool waters of the harbor. Almost before the coin had passed the tourist's fingertips, the boys were thrashing about in the water, anxiously watching like cats awaiting a winged sardine. Then in a frantic swirl, they disappeared beneath the water in pursuit of the coin gliding on its way through 15 feet of water to the bottom. One by one the divers rose to the surface. Invariably, one would hold the coin high above his head for all to see, the coin glittering in the sun, as its new owner smiled triumphantly.

Fascinated, I watched the Bahamian youngsters for the better part of that afternoon. I noticed one boy in particular. He was smaller than the others and not as adept in underwater recovery. His large brown eyes had reddened from long contact with the saltwater. Twenty, perhaps thirty times, I saw him disappear beneath the water and come to the surface catching his breath, empty-handed. He was growing tired. Finally, when I was all but ready to offer him money if he would not dive again, a tourist threw another coin in the water. I did not see him dive this time. Could he be resting, clinging to a piling beneath the wharf? No, there he was, rising to the surface, his right hand high above his head, a quarter held tightly between his small fingers. He showed his achievement to all, and with renewed vitality he jumped from the water up to the wharf. When a tourist threw the next coin, he was the first to break the water.

Concept
SCHEDULES OF REINFORCEMENT

The behavior of the young Bahamian shows a feature sometimes seen in everyday life: Success does not always follow every attempt. By success, we mean reinforcement. Taking this into account, behavior analysts have suggested *intermittent reinforcement* for instances where reinforcement occurs but not after each response; and they use *continuous reinforcement (CRF)* for instances where reinforcement does occur after each response. For example, when Lisa laughs at every single joke Bob makes, she is reinforcing joke telling on a **continuous reinforcement** schedule.

Definition: Concept
Intermittent reinforcement
  ◦ A reinforcer follows the response
  ◦ only once in a while.[1]
Definition: Concept
Continuous reinforcement (CRF)
  ◦ A reinforcer follows each response.

Continuous reinforcement is more explicit than **intermittent reinforcement.** In other words, knowing that intermittent reinforcement is in effect, we must then ask how often a response produces reinforcement and under what conditions. ***Schedule of reinforcement*** refers to the specific way reinforcement occurs.

Definition: Concept
Schedule of reinforcement
  ◦ The way reinforcement occurs
  ◦ because of the number of responses,
  ◦ time between responses,
  ◦ and stimulus conditions.

Continuous reinforcement is usually best for shaping or maintaining difficult behavior. Recall Andrew from Chapter 8. After Andrew's 19 years of silence, the behavior analyst helped Andrew to speak again. She began by reinforcing Andrew's lip movements and continued reinforcing each behavior that more closely approximated normal speech. She reinforced vague vocal sounds, then vocal sounds that resembled a word, and finally speech. The behavior analyst used a continuous reinforcement schedule; in other words, she reinforced each response that met the criterion for reinforcement of that phase of the shaping procedure. If she had used intermittent reinforcement, shaping Andrew's speech would have been difficult or impossible.

QUESTIONS

1. Intermittent *reinforcement*—define it. Then describe how it applies to the behavior of diving for coins.

[1]One of my students pointed out that I should include *immediate* and *response-contingent* in this and a whole host of subsequent definitions; so I started to do so, but things got too messy—the definitions got too complex. Here's a more technically correct definition of **intermittent reinforcement**: *The immediate, response-contingent, presentation of a reinforcer, in which the reinforcer is presented only once in a while.* You should assume that *immediate* and *response-contingent* are implied wherever relevant in our definitions of contingencies and schedules of reinforcement.

2. Continuous *reinforcement*—define it and give an everyday example.
3. Schedule of *reinforcement*—define it.
4. What type of schedule of reinforcement is best for shaping behavior? Give an example.

Concept
Experimental Analysis of Behavior
FIXED-RATIO REINFORCEMENT

Behavior analysts have extensively studied schedules of intermittent reinforcement in the Skinner box. One of the most common is the **fixed-ratio schedule;** for example, Rudolph must press the lever a fixed number of times for each reinforcer.

Definition: Concept
Fixed-ratio (FR) schedule of reinforcement
  ◦ A reinforcer follows
  ◦ a fixed number of responses.

With fairly large ratios, say 100 responses per reinforcer, it's easy to see a consistent pattern of responding—a high rate of responding until the reinforcer is delivered followed by a pause before responding starts again.

Definition: Principle
Fixed-ratio responding
  ◦ After a response is reinforced,
  ◦ no responding occurs for a period of time,
  ◦ then responding occurs at a high, steady rate
  ◦ until the next reinforcer is delivered.

In Figure 17.1, the horizontal line (*x*-axis, or abscissa) indicates the passage of time; each vertical line indicates a response; and at the end of each ratio of eight responses a reinforcer is delivered (indicated by the star). After each reinforcer, the line is flat, indicating no response occurs for a while. *Postreinforcement pause* is the name of this pause after the consumption of the reinforcer and before the next ratio of responses begins. In reality, a fixed ratio of only eight responses might not produce such a noticeable postreinforcement pause, at least in a well-trained rat.

The postreinforcement pause is another characteristic of fixed-ratio-maintained behavior. The length of the pause is proportional to the size of the

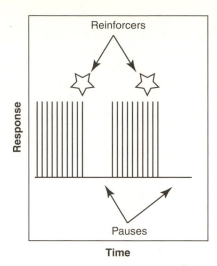

Figure 17.1   Noncumulative Graph

ratio. If the ratio is large, the pause will be long, if the ratio is small, the pause will be short. In extremely small fixed-ratio schedules, the postreinforcement pause may be so small that you cannot see it.

If you wish to establish a high ratio requirement, you need to do so gradually, raising the ratio from 2 to 4 to 6 responses and on up to higher ratios only after a number of reinforcers have been delivered at each ratio value. Otherwise responding will extinguish. So we have the *general rule for establishing intermittently reinforced behavior–First use continuous reinforcement and gradually increase the intermittency of reinforcement as responding stabilizes at a high rate.*

The higher the ratio, the more important it is to introduce it gradually through lower initial ratios. If we made the ratio too high too quickly, then the response would extinguish. Extinction due to this procedural error is known as *straining the ratio.*

By gradually increasing the requirement, we can reduce to a minimum the number of reinforcers needed to maintain behavior. Eventually, we can maintain an amazingly high ratio with few reinforcers. Dr. Findley[2] gradually brought a pigeon to respond reliably on a FR 20,000; after 20,000 pecks the pigeon got several grams of grain. Even though this is more grain than pigeons often get in reinforcement procedures, it does not detract from the pigeon's spending almost all day pecking as fast as it could before getting the reinforcer.

But how could a pigeon count to 20,000? If this is your question, you are suffering from a common misunderstanding about fixed-ratio schedules. Counting is not a requirement for performance of a fixed-ratio schedule. Reinforcement will occur after the pigeon made the required number of responses, regardless of whether the pigeon counted or not. The effectiveness of the fixed-ratio schedule in no way depends on counting. The bird just pecks away until the reinforcer is delivered.

Because students are sometimes confused about the requirements for an FR schedule, let's lay it out. Assume Rudolph's lever pressing was reinforced on an FR 120. That means that when he pressed the lever once, he'd get no water; the second time—none; on up to the 119th time—none. But that 120th lever press would produce that reinforcing drop of water. Then Rudolph would have to start all over again. And again, his first response would produce nothing, and so on up through his 119th lever press. But the 120th would again produce the reinforcer. What the first 119 responses did was move Rudolph closer to the reinforced 120th response. Now humans and nonhumans alike usually pause after each reinforcer, especially on a large FR. But the FR schedule doesn't require that they do; they might fly through the ratios like a bat out of hell, pausing only long enough to pick up their hard-earned reinforcers. Or they might mosey along at a rate so slow it would put the experimenter to sleep. In any case, as soon as they make their fixed number of responses, they get their reinforcer and are ready to start another ratio.

QUESTIONS

1. *Fixed-ratio schedule of reinforcement*—define it and give an example.
2. *Postreinforcement pause*—give an example.
3. What is the relationship between the length of a pause and the size of the ratio in a fixed-ratio schedule of reinforcement?
4. How would you build up to a high ratio requirement?
5. What do behavior analysts mean by straining the ratio?
6. For a pigeon to respond on a fixed-ratio 20,000 schedule of reinforcement, does the pigeon have to be able to count the responses? Explain.
7. Warning: Here's one students often miss: Be able to explain the requirements for performance on an FR schedule. For example, must the organism responding on that schedule be able to count?

---

[2]Based on Findley, J. (1971). Personal communication.

Concept
Experimental Analysis of Behavior
THE CUMULATIVE GRAPH

Another way of plotting the data is in a *cumulative graph* or *cumulative record* (Figure 17.2). Behavior analysts often use this type of graph when studying schedules of reinforcement. Here's a cumulative record of Rudolph's performance on an FR 120.

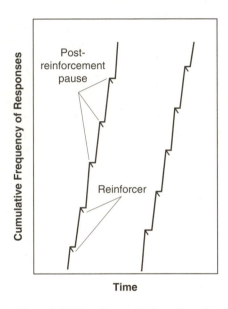

Figure 17.2   Cumulative Graph

We labeled the vertical axis (ordinate) *cumulative frequency of responses,* as opposed to a noncumulative graph in which we labeled the ordinate simply *responses.* The labeling of the horizontal axis (abscissa) for both figures are identical.

In the cumulative record, you can see that Rudolph made the first response and kept pressing as rapidly as he could until he had completed the ratio requirement and gotten his reinforcer. You also can see the postreinforcement pause, where the slope of the line is 0 or horizontal, indicating no responding for a little while before Rudolph starts responding again. Behavior analysts use both noncumulative and cumulative graphs in describing behavior and behavioral change.

QUESTIONS

1. Be able to draw both a cumulative and a non-cumulative frequency graph.

Concept
VARIABLE-RATIO SCHEDULE OF REINFORCEMENT

Now let's look at another ratio schedule—a *variable-ratio (VR) schedule of reinforcement*. We call the pattern of behavior it generates *variable-ratio responding*.

Definition: Concept
Variable-ratio (VR) schedule of reinforcement
- A reinforcer follows
- after a variable number of responses.

Definition: Principle
Variable-ratio responding
- Variable-ratio schedules produce
- a high rate of responding,
- with almost no postreinforcement pausing.

As CRF and FR are abbreviations for their respective schedules of reinforcement, VR stands for a variable-ratio schedule of reinforcement. We designate a specific VR schedule by numerals following the notation. Let us discuss such a specific schedule, a VR 50. If you have suspected that 50 stands for number of responses, you are correct. But rather than standing for a set or fixed number of responses, as in an FR 50, 50 in variable-ratio designates the *average* number of responses required for the reinforcer.

I've had trouble coming up with clean, everyday examples of variable-ratio schedules. But some other behavior analysts answered my Internet plea for suggestions (they should not be held responsible for the literary license I took with their examples).

- Steve Stud hits on the beautiful babes during happy hour at Planet Follywood. His cool line is "Hey, babe, what's your sign?" Believe it or not, that sometimes gets reinforced. Probably a very large variable-ratio schedule of reinforcement. Right? Unfortunately, it's also punished on a very small variable-ratio schedule.[3]
- Under the guise of a budding interest in cultural anthropology, Pubescent Paul skims through his parents' back issues of *National Geographic Magazine* in quest for the occasional bare-breasted maiden in her native habi-

---
[3]A tip of the hat to Lester Wright, WMU behavior therapist, for this clearly fictional example.

tat. Turning pages is reinforced on maybe a VR 350.[4]

○ Uncle Dickie: I can tell my poorly trained dog to sit, and sometimes it takes my saying the "sit" command several times before I get the reinforcing sight of the "dog sitting." And sometimes he will sit on my first command. Putting aside the obvious lack of effective performance-management contingencies for the dog, I believe a variable-ratio schedule controls my behavior of saying "sit."[5]

○ Every now and then the teacher notices that Brutal Bob is picking on the other kids; but many times Bob sneaks in a pinch or a hit without the teacher's catching him. When Bob is caught, he gets 5 minutes of time-out. Presumably this would be VR punishment. We suspect there may be more cases of VR punishment than VR punishment in the everyday world.

○ Paul Potatoe's TV wasn't working correctly. Every now and then, the picture would start rolling, to Paul's irritation. However, if he hit the set, it would stop rolling and the picture would be less irritating (unless Barney was on). Sometimes the rolling would stop after one or two hits, but sometimes Paul would have to hit it several times. (This is really an example of VR escape.)

○ And then there's the classic sick social cycle where the parents occasionally escape the child's whining and pestering by reinforcing meeting the child's request or by providing some sort of distracting reinforcer. This is a variable-ratio schedule of reinforcing for whining and pestering. As we will see in Chapter 18, such intermittent reinforcement makes the behavior more resistant to extinction—harder to get rid of.

What about the young Bahamian coin diver? Most likely, what was his schedule of reinforcement?

a. continuous

b. fixed ratio

c. variable ratio

The way the world pays off for one attempt and fails to pay off for another has produced the old saying "If at first you don't succeed, try, try again." On the variable-ratio schedule of reinforcement, we

can only assume that the more often we attempt, the more often the response will produce a reinforcer.

By the way, *intermittent reinforcement* is a generic term that includes not only fixed- and variable-ratio schedules but also, as we will soon see, other schedules such as fixed- and variable-interval schedules. So do not make the mistake of thinking that intermittent means only one type of schedule, such as variable ratio, for example.

QUESTIONS

1. Define the following concepts:
   ○ variable-ratio schedule of reinforcement
   ○ variable-ratio responding
2. Explain how variable-ratio schedules maintain the door-to-door salesperson's behavior.
3. What will happen if reinforcement no longer becomes available in a ratio schedule of reinforcement? Give an example.
4. Recall the divers of Nassau. What was their reinforcement schedule?
   a. continuous reinforcement
   b. fixed-ratio
   c. variable ratio

Example
RATIO SCHEDULES OF ESCAPE AND PENALTY

Yasako is a pharmacy student at the University of Victoria. Every Saturday afternoon she meets with her chemistry study group in her apartment on the fourth floor of Coral Reef Apartments. Irritable Mr. Bill lives on the third floor, right below Yasako.

Yasako vacuums her apartment on Saturday mornings, before meeting with her group. Soon after she turns on her vacuum cleaner, Mr. Bill starts hitting his ceiling with a broomstick. At the same time, he starts the most vile swearing and shouts threats that he's going to kill her.

After 12 hits, Mr. Bill's violence has frightened Yasako so much that she turns off the vacuum cleaner; and shortly after that Mr. Bill quiets down. But after a few minutes, Yasako again begins worrying that her apartment will be dirty when her friends arrive, so she turns on her vacuum cleaner and starts cleaning again. But soon Mr. Bill is at it again, too. She and Mr. Bill alternate back and forth like that, his pounding a few times, followed by her turning off the noisy vacuum cleaner, followed by her turning it back on a few minutes later, around and around until she gets her apartment clean.

But it's Mr. Bill's behavior we're interested in this time. What's reinforcing his pounding on the

---

[4]A hat tip to Sayaka Endo, Ohio State University, special ed grad student, who will blush to see what I've done with her innocent example.

[5]Hat tip to Dan Sikora, WMU OBM alumnus, who not only demonstrates a nice VR example but also shows that these examples don't have to involve sex to be interesting.

ceiling? Yasako's turning off the noisy vacuum cleaner. What kind of reinforcement is this? Reinforcement by the removal of an aversive condition (negative reinforcement). This is an escape contingency. Now suppose he pounded 12 times before Yasako turned off the vacuum cleaner the first time. Then 10 times, then 14, then 6, 16, and finally 14 again. What kind of schedule is this? A variable-ratio schedule of reinforcement by the removal of an aversive condition. The average number of Mr. Bill's responses was 12, so we have a VR 12.

Now let's look at another case. Nasty Ned often disrupts his third-grade class with bullying. Only about one out of three times, on the average, Teacher Tom notices this. On those occasions he puts Ned in time-out for 5 minutes. What sort of contingency do we have here? "For whom?" you

ask. Good question. In social settings, it's important to stay straight on whose behavior we're analyzing. Ned's behavior. Then assuming time-out is less reinforcing than being in the classroom, we've got a penalty contingency. And what kind of a schedule? A variable-ratio penalty schedule with a mean of three (VR 3).

QUESTIONS

1. *Variable-ratio schedule of reinforcement by the removal of an aversive condition*—give an example.
2. *Variable-ratio schedule of punishment*—give an example.

BASIC ENRICHMENT

Example
RATIO SCHEDULES OF REINFORCEMENT AND PUNISHMENT IN EVERYDAY LIFE

Sid's Seminar

Joe: I'm concerned; I spent 2 hours trying to come up with everyday examples, and I couldn't. I don't think there are many.

Max: Well, the behavior analyst in a lab can program fixed-ratio schedules with no trouble.

Joe: Yes, but nature doesn't often program this type of schedule of reinforcement or punishment.

Eve: Also, we don't often see fixed-ratio scheduling of the reinforcers we get from our society, from other people. For instance, professors don't give us grades on a fixed-ratio schedule.

Sid: You're making good points. I also think fixed-ratio schedules of reinforcement and punishment don't have much direct relevance to the reinforcement schedules in our normal world. But the study of fixed-ratio behavior may give us insight into the effects of similar schedules.

Joe: I couldn't find a single example.

Sid: Well, what about variable-ratio schedules? They seem to occur more often in everyday life, like the case of the door-to-door salesperson.

Max: Yes, and the slot machines in Las Vegas: the response is putting quarters in the slot machine

and pulling the handle. And that gets reinforced after a variable number of quarter-pull responses.

Joe: I think this ratio schedules stuff is all lab hype that has little to do with anyone's everyday life.

Max: That's pretty strong, Joe.

Joe: I'll make a prediction. I predict that almost all the original, everyday examples of ratio schedules you guys came up with aren't. I'll bet they involve stimulus control, like watches and calendars. And I'll bet they also include learned reinforcers that you're not taking into account, and maybe also aversive control you're not accounting for.

Max: What about the slot-machine example? Isn't that pure variable ratio?

Joe: No way!

First of all, it's loaded with learned reinforcers, in addition to the silver dollars.

Max: Like what?

Joe: Like those fruits that appear in the window, one after another—a cherry, another cherry, and then, darn, a lemon. "Well, I almost won." Those two cherries in a row were a big learned reinforcer.

Second is the variable amount of the reinforcer you get at the end of the *so-called variable ratio*. In other words, sometimes you get only one silver dollar, sometimes it's 10, sometimes it's 18, and so on. None of that's like the ratios behavior analysts study in the Skinner box.

Third is *that the size of the ratio is* **much smaller than is typical in the Skinner box of the professional research lab**—like a variable ratio with a mean of 100 responses, a VR 100? You'd never see that in a casino. The customers would revolt if a machine sometimes went 100 or more times without paying off anything.

Sid: You've got some interesting points there, Joe. In fact, slot machines do pay back about 95 dollars out of every 100 the customers put in them.

Tom: It's too bad the behavior analysts, with all their schedules of reinforcement, aren't in charge of gambling. All the casinos would go broke, and we wouldn't have to worry about legalized gambling.

Eve: You know, the behavior analysts may be missing something else when they compare gambling to their typical variable-ratio schedules. They may be missing the excitement. I've been to Reno, and it really is exciting. I think part of it is the near misses. Like maybe the two cherries Joe mentioned are more than just learned reinforcers. It's like almost winning somehow gets you especially excited. So I'd like to add a **fourth factor: The emotional reaction is itself reinforcing.**

Sid: A nice analysis, Eve. Let me summarize the ways typical gambling differs from typical research schedules of variable-ratio reinforcement:

  o There are many other learned reinforcers interspersed throughout the variable ratio of gambling.
  o The amount of the financial reinforcer often varies from ratio to ratio in gambling.
  o The size of the gambling ratio is usually much smaller than that in the professional Skinner box.

These factors combine to produce emotional reinforcers in the gambling ratios that may be absent from the variable-ratio schedule of the Skinner box.

So you can see that the typical casino has added many reinforcers to an easy task. This makes life in the casino much more reinforcing than life in the Skinner box. Could that be why more people spend more of their lives in Las Vegas than in Skinner boxes? If experimental behavior analysts ran Las Vegas, it would close down in 6 months out of boredom.

Compare and Contrast **The Skinner Box and Gambling**		
	Typical Skinner-box variable ratio schedule	*Typical gambling schedule*
Many interspersed learned reinforcers	No	Yes
Amount of reinforcer varies from ratio to ratio	No	Yes
Small ratio	No	Yes
Emotional reinforcers	No	Yes

Our observation is that most of our contingencies of everyday life involve more or less continuous reinforcement and continuous punishment, with maybe an occasional reinforcer or aversive condition missed. They don't seem to be as intermittent as we might at first think. For example, if you bite into a red apple, it will almost always taste good. If you touch a hot stove, it will almost always feel bad. If you sit down in a chair, it will almost always be there to hold you. Once in a while our world gets screwy and someone pulls the chair out from under us, but not too often.

QUESTION

1. Give four differences between typical gambling contingencies and the usual variable-ratio schedules of the Skinner box in the professional research laboratory, not necessarily an introductory student lab. Warning: This one may be crucial for getting your *A* today.

INTERMEDIATE ENRICHMENT

DISCRETE-TRIAL PROCEDURES VS. FREE-OPERANT PROCEDURES

Most Skinner-box research involves **free operant** responding, where the animal is "free" to respond at various frequencies (e.g., 1 lever press per minute to 100 lever presses per minute). In fact, if the subject can make more than one correct response before the reinforcer, it is probably a free-operant procedure. There may not be an S^D, but even if there is, the animal can usually make many responses during each time the S^D is on. And the responses can be reinforced either continuously or intermittently. In other words, in a free-operant procedure, there is no S^Δ after each response; so there is no intertrial interval between each response and the next S^D.

Discrete-Trial Procedure

The light is on in the Skinner box; Rudolph presses the lever. Click. Rudolph has a drop of water and the light goes off. Rudolph presses the lever again. Nothing. Then, after a few seconds, the light comes on again; and Rudolph's pressing is once again reinforced with water.[6] This is an example of a **discrete-trial procedure**—*there is an S^D, a single response, and an outcome, followed by an S^Δ (intertrial interval); then the next trial starts.* When that single response occurs, the S^D ends and the subject immediately receives a reinforcer or goes into S^Δ We can't measure Rudolph's rate of pressing, but we can measure the latency of Rudolph's presses.

In the Classroom

Now lets look at discrete-trial and free-operant procedures in the classroom. Here, Mae and crew are using both in their work with Jimmy, the little boy with the big label, autism.

Discrete-Trial Procedure

Sue sits at a small table facing Jimmy. She puts several objects on the table.

First trial

S^D:[7] Sue says, "Jimmy, point to the horse."

---

[6]This example of a discrete trial procedure is fairly contrived—it would rarely, if ever, actually be done in a Skinner Box.

[7]Remember, S^D—a stimulus in the presence of which a response will be reinforced or punished. It may help to review the concept of a discriminative stimulus in Chapter 12.

Response: Jimmy points to the horse.
Outcome: Sue says, "Good boy, Jimmy." (a learned reinforcer for Jimmy)
S^Δ (Intertrial interval): Sue says nothing.

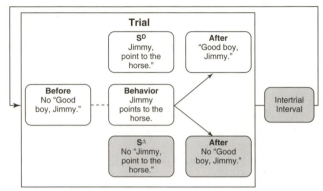

Second Trial

S^D: Sue says, "Jimmy, point to the cup."
Response: Jimmy points to the cup,
Outcome: Sue says, "Good boy, Jimmy."
S^Δ (Intertrial Interval): The basic features of this discrete trial procedure in the classroom are the same as those in the Skinner Box. *There is an S^D, a single response, and an outcome, followed by an $^\Delta$ (intertrial interval); then the next trial starts.* Again, there is an S^D (maybe the same one as before, maybe a new one), a single response, and an outcome, followed by an intertrial interval. Then Sue starts the next discrete trial:

Third Trial

S^D: She says, "Jimmy, point to the shoe."
Response: But this time, he points to the car.
Outcome: So Sue goes into what's called a *correction procedure;* she says, "No, this is the shoe," as she points to the shoe. Then she says, "Jimmy point to the shoe." This time Jimmy points to the shoe. "Good boy, Jimmy." And the correction procedure ends. (We can think of that entire correction procedure as the outcome for the third discrete trial.)
S^Δ (Intertrial Interval): Behavioral approaches to working with children labeled *autistic* make much use of discrete-trial procedures. This training has proven so effective, that parents of such children often ask their school districts to provide discrete-trial training for their children. As a result, the demand for trained behavior analysts has greatly increased.

Free-Operant Procedure

Now lets look at a different type of training procedure. . . .

S^D: Sue and Jimmy at the snack table.
Response 1: Jimmy says, "Juice, please."
Outcome: Sue gives him a sip of juice."
Response 2: Jimmy says, "Juice, please."
Outcome: Again, Sue gives him a sip of juice."
S^Δ **(intertrial interval):** Sue and Jimmy leave the snack table.)

Notice that basic features of this free-operant procedure in the classroom are the same as those in the Skinner Box. *There may or may not be an S^D; then there can be several responses, with the responses being reinforced either continuously or intermittently.* In a free-operant procedure in the classroom, there is no S^Δ after each outcome, and there is no intertrial interval between each outcome and the next S^D.

In the juice example, Jimmy's responses were reinforced continuously. In the next example, his responses are reinforced intermittently. Notice that there is still no S^Δ or intertrial interval in the procedure:

Jimmy and Sue are sitting on the floor in the structured-play area.

Response 1: Jimmy picks up one toy and puts it back in the storage box.
Response 2: Then another.
Response 3: And another, etc.
Outcome: Once all the toys are in the box, Sue says, "Thanks Jimmy, good boy; now what do you want to play with?"

In this case, I don't think there's an S^D, at least not for each, individual response; our operandum test suggests that each toy is an operandum (like Rudolph's lever), rather than an S^D.

In the classroom, just as in the Skinner Box, trials which are separated by intertrial intervals distinguish discrete-trial procedures from free-operant procedures.

Hybrid Discrete-Trial/Free-Operant Procedure

Though understanding the distinction between a free-operant procedure and a discrete trial procedure can be helpful when talking with behavior analysts, it was difficult to come up with a classroom free-operant example.[8] We really had to strain to

---

[8]We don't want to suggest, however, that free-operant responding doesn't exist. Take the very simple example of eating an apple. Each response of biting into the apple is reinforced by the sweet taste of the apple. There is no S^D, no S^Δ, and no intertrial interval. Free-operants surround us every day. It's just hard to use them in the classroom.

come up with such an example without failing our sleaze test (*sleaze test—is the example unnaturally strained or distorted from reality just to illustrate the concept at hand?*). Whenever we have to strain that much to come up with an example, it suggests to us that perhaps there just aren't that many examples in that context. This, in turn, prompts us to take an honest look at what really is going on.

Here's a more typical free-operant example in the classroom:

Jimmy and Sue are sitting on the floor in the structured-play area.

Response 1: Jimmy picks up a piece of the puzzle and puts it in the puzzle form.
Response 2: Jimmy picks up a second piece of the puzzle and puts it in the puzzle form.
Response 3: Jimmy picks up a third and final piece of the puzzle and puts it in the puzzle form.
Outcome: Jimmy now has the completed picture of his much beloved Barney. And Sue says, "Good work, Jimmy."

Now what's so typical about this example is that it's really a **hybrid, discrete-trial/free-operant procedure**—*each free-operant response, itself, consists of a discrete trial.*

Free-Operant—Putting Together the Entire Puzzle

SD: None. The puzzle is an operandum.
Response: Jimmy puts the puzzle together.
Outcome: The puzzle looks like Barney.
S^Δ: None.

When looking at the behavior of completing the puzzle, it is clear that there is a series of discrete-trial components.

First Discrete-trial Component—Putting Each Piece into the Puzzle

S^D: The puzzle form has a particular configuration, and the piece in Jimmy's hand has a particular configuration.
Response: Jimmy puts his piece in the matching hole in the puzzle.
Outcome: The piece fits (and during initial training he also got praise from Sue). Now we are in an S^Δ condition for that piece, but not for the entire puzzle.
S^Δ **(Intertrial interval):** The S^D is for that piece.

This is an example of a discrete trial, because each piece Jimmy puts in the puzzle is an S^D for the next response. It is also an example of free-operant, because Jimmy is free to place each puzzle piece as fast as he "wants," and a measure of his behavior would be a rate measure (e.g., 8 pieces per minute.) It would be discrete trial, completely (not a hybrid), if Sue handed Jimmy each piece of the puzzle, because then measuring Jimmy's behavior would produce a latency measure (e.g., time from Jimmy's receiving a piece until he placed it in the puzzle) or an accuracy measure (80% of the pieces correctly placed), not a rate measure. Remember, you can get rate measures in free-operant and latency or and percentage-correct measures in discrete trial.

Compare and Contrast: Discrete Trial vs. Free Operant Procedures		
	Discrete Trial	**Free Operant**
Is there an S^D and an S^Δ	Yes	Sometimes
Is there an inter-trial interval	Yes	Usually not
The measure is	Latency or Accuracy	Rate

As the compare-and-contrast table shows, discrete trial and free operant procedures differ along three main dimensions. However, measurement is the crucial dimension (in other words, latency or accuracy vs. rate).

QUESTIONS

1. What's an example of
   a. a free-operant procedure in the Skinner box?
   b. a discrete-trial procedure in the Skinner box?
   c. a discrete-trial procedure in the classroom?
   d. a free-operant procedure in the classroom?
   e. hybrid discrete-trial/free-operant procedure in the classroom?

18

Time-Dependent Schedules

FUNDAMENTALS

Now we'll consider ***time-dependent schedules of reinforcement.*** In these schedules, the opportunity for reinforcement occurs as a function of time.

Concept
Experimental Analysis of Behavior
FIXED-INTERVAL SCHEDULES OF REINFORCEMENT

First, we'll look at the ***fixed-interval (FI) schedule of reinforcement:*** In this schedule, reinforcement becomes available after a fixed interval of time since the last opportunity for reinforcement. But the delivery of the reinforcer is contingent on the response. For example, with a FI 2' schedule, reinforcement becomes available after 2 minutes have passed since the last opportunity for reinforcement. On such a schedule, the first response occurring after the interval has timed out produces reinforcement.

Definition: Concept

Fixed-interval (FI) schedule of reinforcement

- A reinforcer is contingent on
- the first response,
- *after* a fixed interval of time,
- since the last opportunity for reinforcement.

Ferster and Skinner studied fixed-interval schedules of reinforcement with pigeons in the Skinner box. Figure 18.1 is what a cumulative response record would look like for a pecking response of a pigeon reinforced with grain on a fixed-interval schedule. Just after reinforcement, a long period of time goes by without the bird's making any response whatsoever. After some time, it makes a few responses. Then the pigeon responds more rapidly as time goes by until, at the end of the interval, it responds at an extremely high rate. This particular pattern of responding is typical of fixed-interval schedule of reinforcement. ***Fixed-interval scallop*** is the name of the shape this record takes.

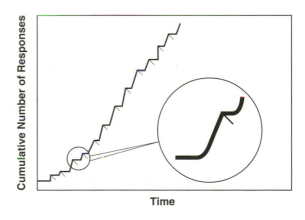

Figure 18.1   Fixed-Interval 2-Minute Schedule

Definition: Principle

Fixed-interval scallop

- A fixed-interval schedule often produces a scallop—
- a gradual increase in the rate of responding,
- with responding occurring at a high rate
- just before reinforcement is available.
- No responding occurs for some time after reinforcement.

By *scallop,* we don't mean something you eat at the Red Lobster. We mean a *curve,* as in the wavy patterns on an ornamental border. A series of fixed-interval scallops looks something like that ornamental border. A circle is drawn around one of the fixed-interval scallops and then expanded to give you a closer look at the scalloped pattern, the pattern that's typical during the first weeks of an animal's fixed interval training.[1]

QUESTIONS

1. Define and give a Skinner-box example of a fixed-interval schedule of reinforcement.

2. Be sure you understand the difference between the concept of fixed-interval **schedule** and the principle of fixed-interval **behavior** (i.e., **scallop**). *At quiz time, people get confused on the quiz with this one.*

ARE EVERYDAY EXAMPLES OF FIXED-INTERVAL SCHEDULES AS SCARCE AS HEN'S TEETH?

Joe's Term Paper

Students of behavior analysis often give what, at first glance, seem to be everyday examples of fixed-interval schedules of reinforcement. But a closer analysis of the contingencies reveals that they are not. Let's examine one of those deceptive examples.

Sid has assigned a term paper for his seminar. Let's look at Joe's behavior of working on that term paper. Sid assigned the paper the first day of class, so Joe has 15 weeks to complete the project—to meet the deadline. Figure 18.2 is a cumulative record of Joe's work under this schedule. We plotted weeks on the abscissa and the cumulative number of the hours he worked on the ordinate.

The first week after Sid announced the assignment, Joe spent no time preparing the paper. We placed a zero at the comparable point on the graph.

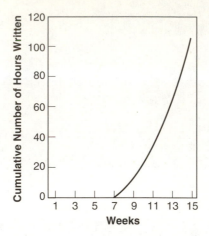

Figure 18.2   A False Fixed-Interval Scallop of Joe's Paper Writing

The same is true of the second, third, fourth, fifth, sixth, and seventh weeks—Joe spent no time on the paper. Finally, in the eighth week, he spent 5 hours trying to select an appropriate topic. In that week, Joe searched for a topic, talked to several people, even to an instructor, and did some reading. In the next week, his efforts increased only slightly, and slightly more on the following week. Then still more, and more again the following week, and once more on the week after that. He spent the final week in a frenzy of long hours in the library and worrying about the paper.

You can see that the cumulative record of the hourly work seems to take the form of the fixed-interval scallop we discussed earlier. In the beginning, Joe didn't work at all. Then small but increasing amounts of work followed in the next weeks until the end of the interval, when, with the deadline approaching, Joe pulled all-nighters, trying to meet the requirement.[2]

An Analysis of the Term-Paper Schedule

Do you think Joe was working under a fixed-interval schedule of reinforcement? Think it through and try to answer this question before you read the next paragraph.

We think not. The requirements of the true fixed-interval schedule and the schedule of term-paper deadlines differ greatly.

---

[1]In every class, at least one student always asks how you time the interval. There are two ways you can do it, and both produce the same results. Suppose you're doing a 10-minute fixed-interval schedule. Ten minutes have elapsed, and now you're waiting for Rudolph to respond so you can give him his reinforcer. Suppose he waits 2 more minutes before he responds and gets his reinforcer. Do you start timing the next 10-minute interval from the delivery of that reinforcer? Or do you start timing it from when the reinforcer would was available and would have been delivered if Rudolph had responded on time? It doesn't matter, because Rudolph will usually respond on time; he'll be responding at such a high rate by the time the reinforcer becomes available that he'll get it within a second or two after the 10-minute interval anyway. So either way of scheduling the next fixed interval will work just fine.

[2]We don't really have good data on students' patterns of procrastinating in writing large papers. Most behavior analysts assume that the procrastination would resemble a fixed-interval scallop, but it may be that students tend to procrastinate until panic really sets in and then go full-tilt boogie, full speed forward, day after day or week after week until the paper's done; in that case, there would be no scallop, just a flat line of no responding and then a straight diagonal line of maximal responding.

1. **Does early responding affect anything?** On a fixed-interval schedule, what effect does responding before reinforcement have? In other words, what's the effect of the bird's pecking the key before the fixed interval has elapsed? None. In the Skinner box, the pigeon can sit on its duff until the interval has elapsed and then make a single key peck. That's all it takes to produce the bird feed.

But on a term-paper schedule, what effect does responding have when responding occurs prior to the availability of reinforcement? In other words, what's the effect of working on the paper before the paper's due date has arrived? Enormous. In the university, you can't normally sit on your duff until the due date and then make a single response. Instead, you've got to start to work well in advance of the due date. In fact, this feature of the term-paper schedule is more like a ratio schedule than an interval schedule. Joe has to make at least some minimum number of paper-writing responses to get a passing grade, let alone the A he's shooting for.

2. **In everyday life, you often get more if you work harder.** On a fixed-interval schedule, what effect does increasing the number of key pecks have on the amount of the reinforcer? None. But on a term-paper schedule? Normally, the more you work on the paper, the better your grade—the bigger the reinforcer.

3. **What are the relevant response classes?** Everyday examples often involve more than one response class, and we often get confused about which response class is most like the key peck of the Skinner box. Here a response that usually occurs after the due date is more analogous to the key peck. What? Not writing the paper; that should occur before the deadline. Now think about it. What is it? Handing the paper in to the teacher. That response that occurs closest to the reinforcer—the grade. Handing in the paper is most like the key peck.

So what happens if you turn the paper in before the deadline? The response counts; it will still produce the reinforcer, the grade. Normally you don't have to wait until the deadline to turn in your paper early. Of course, your professor might have a heart attack if you did turn it in ahead of time (but you can't count on that reinforcer).[3]

And what happens to early key pecks on the interval schedule? As we've said so often, nothing.

4. **Everyday life often involves calendars and clocks.** What response functions most like the key

peck? Turning in the paper. So maybe we'd get a fixed-interval scallop if we plotted a cumulative record of Joe's turning in the paper. In other words, would he first try to turn it in early in the interval, and then turn it in with increasing frequency as the due date approached, until he finally turned it in for the last time, just after the due date? Of course not! Not even Joe would do that.

Why not? Why no scallop? Because Joe has a calendar and a clock. He won't turn it in until the interval has elapsed, not until the calendar shows the right date and the clock shows the right hour.

How would you change the interval schedule in the Skinner box to be most like this? Think! You'd give the pigeon Joe's calendar and clock. To make it simple, let's just give the bird a clock—a simple device, just a big second hand that sweeps into the black area when the interval has elapsed. What do we call the stimulus configuration when the hand is in the black? A discriminative stimulus (S^D). In the presence of that time on the clock, a key peck will produce the grain (and also start the clock running again). What do we call the configuration when the hand is in the white? An S^Δ. Grain isn't available then.

What kind of schedule of reinforcement would we have if we supplemented the fixed-interval schedule with our simple clock and "taught the bird to tell time" (brought the key peck response under the stimulus control of the clock)? We'd have a simple discrimination schedule (sometimes called a *multiple schedule*)—extinction in S^Δ and continuous reinforcement in S^D (except each S^D would end as soon as the bird responded and got its reinforcer).

How do you think the bird would come to respond under this simple discrimination schedule? It would not peck the key until the clock said the interval had elapsed—until it was time to—until the S^D. That's just like Joe; he wouldn't hand in his paper until his calendar and clock said it was time to. The bird then pecks the key and gets the food. Joe then turns in his paper and gets—a thank-you, if he's lucky.

5. **Everyday life often involves deadlines.** The fixed interval elapses, and the pigeon's reinforcer is now available. The next key peck will produce food. What happens if the pigeon waits a few minutes before pecking? Nothing special; it'll still get the food.

The last day of class arrives, and it's time for Joe to turn in his paper. What happens if he waits a few weeks? He will have lost his chance to have Sid grade his paper. He'll get zero for his efforts. In other words, Sid and the university administration have put a deadline on the term-paper schedule. But

---

[3]Just a cheap joke, based on the mythic student-teacher antagonism. Of course your professor's heart attack wouldn't be a reinforcer for you, would it?

the typical fixed-interval schedule doesn't have a deadline.

6. **Everyday life often involves reinforcers that are too delayed to reinforce the causal response.** How soon does the pigeon get its food after it pecks the key? Immediately. How soon does Joe get the grade after he writes and turns in his paper? A few days later, if Sid's on the ball. But that delay's too great to reinforce Joe's writing and turning in his paper. A complex set of contingencies controlled Joe's writing his paper, more complex than the simple reinforcement of his writing by the grade he will ultimately receive. We'll talk more about these complex contingencies in later chapters.

7. **Summary of the term-paper schedules.** Sometimes a table's worth a thousand words. Let's see if this is one of those times.

Contrasting the Fixed-Interval and the Term-Paper Schedules		
Feature	**Fixed-interval**	**Term-paper**
Does early responding affect anything?	No	Yes
Do you get more if you work harder?[4]	No	Yes
Is the relevant response class clear?	Yes	No
Are there calendars and clocks?	No	Yes
Is there a deadline?	No	Yes
Is the reinforcer too delayed?	No	Yes

Other Nonexamples

The TV Schedule

OK, maybe the term-paper schedule isn't a good example of a fixed-interval schedule. But what about watching *Saturday Night Live* (*SNL*) every Saturday night at 11:30 P.M.? Isn't that a 7-day fixed-interval schedule?

---

[4]By *get more,* we mean, for example, more food or a better grade. By *work more,* we mean, for example, peck the key or press the lever more often or spend more hours writing the paper or write a longer paper.

Let's diagram it.

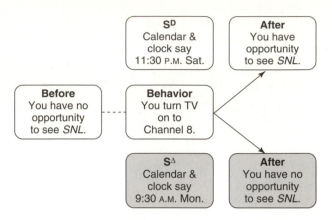

The Saturday Night Live schedule also fails to ring the bell. There are two problems:

Problem 1. You have a calendar and a clock. But Rudolph has none. If you didn't, you might respond much like Rudolph; starting about Thursday morning you'd be flipping on the TV every few minutes, responding more and more quickly as time passed, until by 11:30 P.M. Saturday night, the remote control would be smokin'. Fortunately for you and your remote control, your flipping on the TV is under good stimulus control. So tuning into your favorite TV show is not an example of a fixed-interval schedule of intermittent reinforcement.

Problem 2. You have a deadline, and Rudolph doesn't, at least not on a simple fixed-interval schedule. If you don't flip on the TV by the deadline of Saturday at 11:30 P.M. you will miss some or all of the reinforcer, SNL. Rudolph doesn't have a deadline, once his fixed interval has elapsed, he can take his own sweet time to press the lever, because the reinforcer will still be waiting for him.

Actually, your TV contingency is avoidance of the loss of the opportunity to receive a reinforcer, the complete SNL.

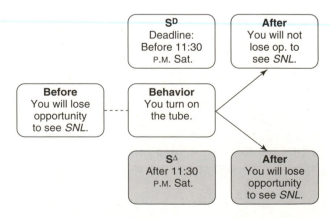

Glancing at your watch is something else; that might be more like Rudolph's fixed-interval schedule, but still not perfect, because what you see when you glance at your watch will sort of act as an S^D or S^Δ for the next glance; and also, you're still working on an avoidance schedule.

The Paycheck Schedule

Ready for another try? What about going to pick up your paycheck at the end of every two weeks? Surely that must be a fixed interval of two weeks? Diagram time again. But this time, it's your turn.

1. Please diagram the paycheck contingency.

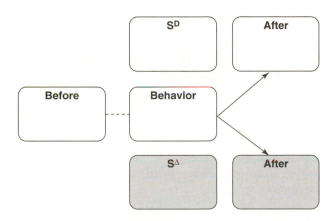

2. This diagram shows that going for the biweekly paycheck is
   a. reinforced on a biweekly fixed-interval schedule of reinforcement.
   b. under stimulus control and reinforced every time the S^D is present.
   c. under stimulus control and reinforced on a biweekly fixed-interval schedule of reinforcement.

3. If going for the paycheck were **really** reinforced on a fixed-interval schedule, we'd expect to see that behavior
   a. spread across the month on a fixed-interval scallop, which **is** what happens.
   b. spread across the month on a fixed-interval scallop, which **is not** what happens.
   c. occur just once, when the check is due, which **is** what happens.
   d. occur just once, when the check is due, which **is not** what happens.

Examples

But all is not lost. Here's an example a student gave: You're watching a *Seinfeld* rerun, the one you still hadn't completely memorized. The commercials come on; so you switch to *Jerry Springer*. But you

keep switching back to *Seinfeld* with increasing frequency as the commercial interval wears on. After an agonizing eternity, one of your flips is reinforced by the sight of Seinfeld. This is a pretty good example of an interval schedule; if the commercial breaks are the same duration, then we've got a fixed interval. It also has something like a limited hold on it, in that the longer it takes you to get back to the *Seinfeld* channel, the more of the reinforcer you will miss (we explain *limited hold* later in the chapter).

Even though the *Seinfeld* example is pretty good, we maintain that it is extremely difficult to find examples of pure schedules in everyday life. So, in the future when you hear someone talking about a real-life example of an interval schedule, be critical. Remember those examples are the exception, not the rule.

QUESTIONS

1. Describe a term-paper schedule of reinforcement and contrast it with a fixed-interval schedule.
   Warning: To get this one right, you must know and understand the preceding 6 differences and be able to construct and fill in the preceding table correctly.
2. Diagram the avoidance contingency for turning on the TV to watch a weekly TV show and give the two reasons why it is or isn't a good example of a fixed-interval schedule.
3. Diagram the contingency of going for your biweekly paycheck and explain why it is or isn't a good example of a fixed-interval schedule.

Example
SUPERSTITION IN THE PIGEON[5]

Dr. Skinner placed a pigeon in his famous Skinner box. The box was just large enough to allow a pigeon a half-dozen paces in any direction. The box contained the usual birdseed feeder, but the response key was disconnected. Soon after Skinner placed the bird in the box, he started a repeating timer set for a 15-second interval. At the end of each interval, the feeder came up for a few seconds and remained within the pigeon's reach, allowing the bird time to eat some grain. Note that the feeder came up at the end of each 15-second interval, regardless of what the bird was doing. In other words, the operation of the hopper was independent of the bird's behavior

---

[5]Based on Skinner, B. F. (1948). Superstition in the pigeon. *Journal of Experimental Psychology, 38,* 168–172.

and would have occurred even if the box were empty.

Skinner placed the first bird in the box. Immediately, the bird began to strut about, exploring first this corner, then that, scratching on the floor, pecking here and then there. After 15 seconds, the hopper came up for the first time. Just prior to this, the pigeon made an abrupt counterclockwise turn. The presentation of the food just happened to reinforce the counterclockwise turn. At the end of that reinforcer, the pigeon once again strutted about the box. But soon the bird began to make counterclockwise turns. The bird had made two, perhaps three, counterclockwise turns when the 15-second interval again expired and the food reinforcer was delivered.

From that time on, the bird showed a regular, stereotyped pattern of behavior—rapid and persistent counterclockwise turning motions. The pigeon stopped turning only when the reinforcer was presented; at that time, the bird went immediately for the grain. If visitors had seen the bird during this final stage, they would have suggested that the bird was disoriented, silly, or drunk.

Similarly, the same procedure in another bird established a head-tossing response that looked much like that of a bull tossing an imaginary matador on his horns. After a few instances of coincidental reinforcement of this behavior, the behavior occurred with precision and regularity whenever Skinner placed the pigeon in the box. Other pigeons developed a pendulum motion with their heads, swinging them to and fro as if keeping time to an unknown and unheard melody.

Concept
Experimental Analysis of Behavior
**FIXED-TIME SCHEDULES
AND SUPERSTITIOUS BEHAVIOR**

Dr. Skinner used a **fixed-time schedule of reinforcement.** In this schedule, a reinforcer is delivered after the passage of a fixed period of time, regardless of the behavior of the organism. In other words, the reinforcer will be delivered at the end of a specific period of time, whether or not the organism responds. Skinner programmed the delivery of grain every 15 seconds, independently of the pigeon's response.

Definition: Concept
Fixed-time schedule of reinforcer delivery
○ A reinforcer is delivered
○ after the passage of a fixed period of time,
○ independently of the response.

We saw what would happen if we dispensed reinforcement independently of behavior on a fixed-time schedule. This schedule is one way to produce **superstitious behavior.** Because of the delivery of reinforcers depending only on the passage of time, pigeons developed whirling, head bobbing, and other weird behavior patterns.

The fixed-time schedule does not require a response for the reinforcer to occur, but the fixed-interval schedule does. On the fixed-interval schedule, a response must occur after the interval elapses, before the reinforcer is delivered.

Definition: Concept
Superstitious behavior
○ Behaving as if the response causes
○ some specific outcome,
○ when it really does not.

The pigeon behaved (whirled and bobbed) as if that response sequence caused some specific following event (the delivery of the food reinforcer), when it really didn't.

Like the pigeon's superstitious behavior, coincidental or accidental reinforcement may account for some superstitious human behavior. For instance, baseball players often develop superstitious behavior. A successful hit accidentally reinforces behaviors that immediately preceded the hit. The result could be that the batter would consistently tap the ground with her bat two times right before the pitcher pitches. But such behavior does **not** produce a successful hit; it's just the result of accidental reinforcement.

QUESTIONS

1. A *fixed-time schedule of* reinforcer delivery—define it.
2. Describe Dr. Skinner's experiment demonstrating the effects of a fixed-time schedule of reinforcer delivery. Specify:
   ○ a response class
   ○ the schedule of reinforcement
   ○ the reinforcer
   ○ the results
   ○ the name for the general type of behavior this schedule can produce
   ○ any other interesting features of the intervention
3. *Superstitious behavior*—define it.
4. Give a human example that illustrates the role of accidental reinforcement.

5. Analyze the example in terms of accidental re-inforcement.

Concept
VARIABLE-INTERVAL SCHEDULES OF REINFORCEMENT

Behavior analysts have studied the effects of many time-dependent schedules of reinforcement. The *variable-interval (VI) schedule of reinforcement* is another such schedule. In this schedule, reinforcement becomes available after a variable interval of time since the last opportunity for reinforcement. The delivery of the reinforcer is contingent on the response. Reinforcement becomes available after the passage of variable intervals of time. The specific values of the schedule come after the VI abbreviation. For instance, a VI 2′ schedule is one in which reinforcement becomes available after an average of 2 minutes.

Definition: Concept
Variable-interval (VI) schedule of reinforcement
○ A reinforcer is contingent on
○ the first response
○ *after* a variable interval of time
○ since the last opportunity for reinforcement.

Note that reinforcement becomes available after the passage of an average interval of time. On a VI schedule, reinforcement may become available, say, after 5 minutes; but the subject does not actually get the reinforcer until making the proper response. Although time alone will bring about the opportunity for reinforcement, the subject must respond thereafter. But making the appropriate response before the end of the interval will not yield reinforcement. It takes both a time interval and the appropriate response after the passage of that time interval. Only under these two conditions will reinforcement follow.

Let's sum up the features of a variable-interval schedule like this:

○ The opportunity for reinforcement comes as a direct function of the passage of time. Thus, we can call the VI schedule a time-dependent schedule.
○ The lengths of the intervals between opportunities are varied, hence the term *variable interval.*

○ Although the opportunity for reinforcement occurs as a function of time alone, the subject must make the response after the interval is over for reinforcement to occur. Time alone will never bring about the reinforcer.

What kind of behavior do variable-interval schedules generate? Figure 18.3 is what a cumulative response record would look like for a pecking response of a pigeon reinforced with grain.

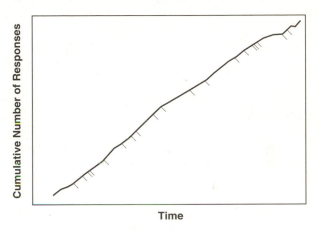

Figure 18.3   Variable-Interval 2-Minute Schedule

The bird was working on a variable-interval 2-minute (VI 2′) schedule. (A VI 2′ schedule means that the opportunity of reinforcement came about on an average of every 2 minutes.) Once the opportunity became available, the pigeon had to peck the key to get the reinforcer. You can see in the slope of the cumulative record that the pigeon was pecking regularly but not with a speed that you might expect from the ratio schedules you studied earlier. Generally, the smaller the average interval between opportunities for reinforcement, the higher the rate will be. Thus, if there were 2 or 3 hours' wait between opportunities, we would expect a low rate of responding, perhaps as low as one peck every 10 or 15 minutes. If, on the other hand, the opportunity for reinforcement occurs often, the rate of response may be high.

You also can see in the cumulative record that reinforcement doesn't occur regularly. Sometimes the bird made many responses from one reinforcement to the next, and other times it made only a small number of responses. The number of responses is a function of the variable interval between reinforcements. But the most important aspect of the variable-interval schedule is that it generates consistent response rates. Notice that at few points in the cumulative record did the pigeon fail to respond. There are virtually no flat areas. The slope of the record tends to be even and uniform throughout.

The variable-interval schedule brings about a steady though not especially fast worker. There are no real postreinforcement pauses; other than the time the bird takes to consume the grain, the pigeon doesn't stop; it eats and gets back to its rather leisurely working pace.

Classic Schedules of Intermittent Reinforcement		
	Fixed	*Variable*
Ratio	Fixed-ratio	Variable-ratio
Interval	Fixed-interval	Variable-interval

Definition: Principle
Variable-interval responding
  ◦ Variable-interval schedules produce
  ◦ a moderate rate of responding,
  ◦ with almost no postreinforcement pausing.

QUESTIONS

1. *Variable-interval schedule of reinforcement*—define it and give an example.
2. Be sure you understand the difference between the concept of variable-interval **schedule** and the principle of variable-interval **behavior.** *At quiz time, people get confused on the quiz with this one.*
3. Describe the procedure and behavioral results of a variable-interval 2-minute schedule of reinforcement (VI 2').
4. List three characteristics of variable-interval schedules.
5. ***Students often blow this one:*** On a variable-interval schedule of reinforcement, must a response occur before the reinforcer is delivered?
6. Relatively speaking, describe the response rate with a variable-interval schedule if
  ◦ the time intervals are small.
  ◦ the time intervals are big.

Concept
EXTINCTION AND SCHEDULES OF REINFORCEMENT

We've said responses can produce reinforcers in two ways:

  ◦ Continuous reinforcement: Every response produces a reinforcer.
  ◦ Intermittent reinforcement: Only some responses produce a reinforcer. Furthermore, we've considered four classic intermittent schedules:

We can make a general statement about these classic schedules of intermittent reinforcement: **Intermittent reinforcement makes the response more resistant to extinction than does continuous reinforcement.** Remember that the extinction procedure consists of no longer reinforcing a response previously reinforced. So the rate of that response decreases. And if we stop reinforcement long enough, the response will stop.

When we stop reinforcement for responses maintained on a continuous reinforcement schedule, the behavior extinguishes rapidly. When we stop reinforcement for responses maintained on an intermittent schedule of reinforcement, extinction takes longer. The subject continues to respond for a longer period of time, although we have withheld reinforcement completely. Thus, we say intermittent reinforcement produces greater ***resistance to extinction.***

Definition: Concept
Resistance to extinction
  ◦ The number of responses or
  ◦ the amount of time
  ◦ before a response extinguishes.

Definition: Principle
Resistance to extinction and intermittent reinforcement
  ◦ Intermittent reinforcement
  ◦ makes the response
  ◦ more resistant to extinction
  ◦ than does continuous reinforcement.

Some intermittent schedules of reinforcement generate behavior that resists extinction more than others. The more an intermittent schedule differs from continuous reinforcement, the more the behavior resists extinction. For example, a fixed ratio of 10,000 will cause the response to resist extinction a heck of a lot more than will a fixed ratio of 10. But all intermittent schedules generate behavior that resists extinction more than does the continuous reinforcement schedule. So if we want to prevent the response from collapsing at the first sign of non-reinforcement, we should use intermittent reinforcement.[6]

QUESTIONS

1. The concept of *resistance to extinction*—define it and give an example.
2. The principle of *resistance to extinction*—define it and give an example.

Compare and Contrast
INTERVAL SCHEDULES VS. TIME SCHEDULES OF REINFORCEMENT

One of the main reasons for presenting the fixed-time schedule is so we can contrast it with the fixed-interval schedule. Why would we go to all the trouble to do that? Because students often make the mistake of talking about a fixed-interval schedule as if it were a fixed-time schedule, as if the reinforcer would be delivered regardless of whether the organism responds.

Students often say something like this: "On a fixed-interval schedule of reinforcement, the pigeon pecks the key at an increasing rate. And then after the fixed interval has elapsed, the bird receives the reinforcer." No. After the fixed interval has elapsed, **the next response** produces the reinforcer. (Of course, the responses prior to the end of the interval have no effect.)

Don't make that mistake. Instead, always remember, with the interval schedules, the passage of time brings about the **opportunity** for reinforcement; but time alone is not enough for the actual delivery of the reinforcer. The organism has to make a response for reinforcement to occur. This second re-

------

[6]Yes, you can maintain behavior on a ratio as extreme as 10,000 key pecks per reinforcement. When I taught at Denison University, I had Polly Pigeon on a simultaneous discrimination schedule where she worked all day pecking the S^D key. Immediately after Polly had knocked off her 10,000th correct discriminative response, I'd generously give her several minutes' access to grain, rather than the typical 3 seconds' access. Of course, I started out with short ratios and only gradually increased their size, to avoid ratio strain. My students sometimes accuse me of using a similar schedule in my courses. Maybe they're suffering from ratio strain. Maybe I don't increase the assignment sizes slowly enough. Or maybe they aren't satisfied with several minutes' access to pigeon food.

quirement ensures that the delivery of reinforcement is contingent on a specific behavior.

So fixed-time schedules of reinforcer delivery and fixed-interval schedules of reinforcement are comparable in this way: They both involve the passing of a fixed period of time before the reinforcer is delivered. They contrast in this way: The interval schedule requires a response after the time period has passed; the time schedule does not.

Interval vs. Time Schedules		
	Fixed interval	*Fixed time*
Involves time	Yes	Yes
Requires a response	Yes	No

QUESTION

1. Compare and contrast a fixed-time schedule of reinforcer delivery and a fixed-interval schedule of reinforcement. **Students have blown this one in the past.**

Compare and Contrast
REINFORCER VS. REINFORCEMENT: A REVIEW

Remember the definition of **reinforcer**—any stimulus, event, or condition whose **presentation** immediately follows a response and **increases** the frequency of that response. And contrast that definition with the definition of **reinforcement**—response-contingent, immediate **presentation** of a reinforcer resulting in an **increased** frequency of that response.

So what are the following?

1. A specific pellet of food for a deprived rat?
   a. reinforcer
   b. reinforcement
2. The immediate delivery of a pellet contingent on a deprived rat's lever press with a resulting increased rate of pressing?
   a. reinforcer
   b. reinforcement
3. A quarter for a deprived professor?
   a. reinforcer
   b. reinforcement

4. The immediate delivery of a quarter contingent on a deprived prof's pleading for a raise, with a resulting increased rate of pleading?
   a. reinforcer
   b. reinforcement

1. *Important quiz hint:* Know the difference between reinforcer and reinforcement so well that you don't mess it up, even in the heat of a quiz, now or ever.

BASIC ENRICHMENT

Compare and Contrast
RATIO AND INTERVAL SCHEDULES OF REINFORCEMENT

When Does the Reinforcer Occur?

Remember, in ratio schedules, the reinforcer follows a specific number of responses. If the schedule is a fixed ratio, the reinforcer follows a fixed number of responses. And, after an initial postreinforcement pause, responding occurs at a high, steady rate until the next reinforcer is delivered.

But if the schedule is a variable ratio, reinforcement follows a variable number of responses. In the variable-ratio schedule, responding occurs at a high rate with almost no postreinforcement pause.

In interval schedules, the reinforcer follows the first response at the end of a time interval. If the schedule is a fixed interval, responding does not occur immediately after reinforcement but increases in frequency as the interval advances. By the end of the interval, responding is rapid. We call such a pattern of behavior the fixed-interval scallop. If the schedule is a variable interval, the reinforcer follows the first response after a variable time interval. In variable-interval schedules, responding occurs at a consistent rate with almost no postreinforcement pause.

What's the Relation Between Rate of Responding and Rate of Reinforcement?

1. With ratio schedules, the faster you respond, the more reinforcers you will get per hour.
   a. true
   b. false
2. With interval schedules, the faster you respond, the more reinforcers you will get per hour.
   a. true
   b. false

In theory, you could earn an unlimited number of reinforcers per hour on a ratio schedule if you could respond fast enough; on an interval schedule, you have to respond faster than the shortest interval, but responding faster doesn't help. For example, on a fixed-interval, 1-minute schedule, you can't earn more than 60 reinforcers per hour, even if you're faster than Superman.

But don't think that Rudolph "knows" he will get more reinforcers per hour if he responds faster on a ratio schedule. In fact, if he's been on a fixed-interval schedule long enough, maybe a couple of months, he'll respond as fast there as he would on a comparable ratio schedule; in other words, he'll respond much faster than he would need to get his maximum number of reinforcers. Don't expect rats to be any more rational than human beings.

QUESTION

Warning: Please take these questions more seriously than those students in the past who didn't and thereby blew their A.
1. Be able to construct and understand the following table. In other words, specify the differences between ratio, interval, and time schedules of reinforcement in terms of
   ○ availability of reinforcement
   ○ resulting behavior
2. Understand the relation between the rate of responding and the rate of reinforcers for ratio and interval schedules.
3. Be able to identify the cumulative records for each of the four basic schedules of reinforcement in the following table.

Figure 18.4 is a stylized version of the cumulative records of the four basic schedules of reinforcement: fixed ratio, variable ratio, fixed interval, and variable interval. The cumulative number of responses goes up the vertical axis (the *y*-axis, or ordinate). Time goes along the horizontal axis

Comparing and Contrasting Ratio and Variable Schedules of Reinforcement		
Schedule	**Reinforcer follows**	**Behavior**
RATIO	A number of responses	
Fixed ratio	A fixed number of responses	After a response is reinforced, no responding occurs for a period of time. Then responding occurs at a high, steady rate until the next reinforcer is delivered.
Variable ratio	A variable number of responses	Responding occurs at a high rate, with almost no postreinforcement pause.
INTERVAL	The first response after a time interval	
Fixed interval	The first response after a fixed-time interval	No response occurs immediately after reinforcement. Then the rate of responding increases slowly as the interval advances, until the final quarter of the interval where responding occurs at a high rate (fixed-interval scallop).
Variable interval	The first response after a variable-time interval.	A consistent and steady rate of responding occurs, with almost no postreinforcement pause.
TIME	A time period whether or not there is a response	
Fixed time	A fixed-time period whether or not there is a response	Typically there will be no behavior, unless it is superstitious behavior resulting from the accidental reinforcement of the response of interest.
Variable time	A variable-time period whether or not there is a response	Behavior is even less likely here than with a fixed-time schedule.

(*x*-axis, or abscissa). The diagonal pips indicate the delivery of reinforcers. The steeper (more vertical) the cumulative records, the higher the response rate. Flat horizontal lines indicate the passage of time with no responding. The ratio schedules show the highest rates of responding, and the fixed schedules show the most pausing after reinforcement.

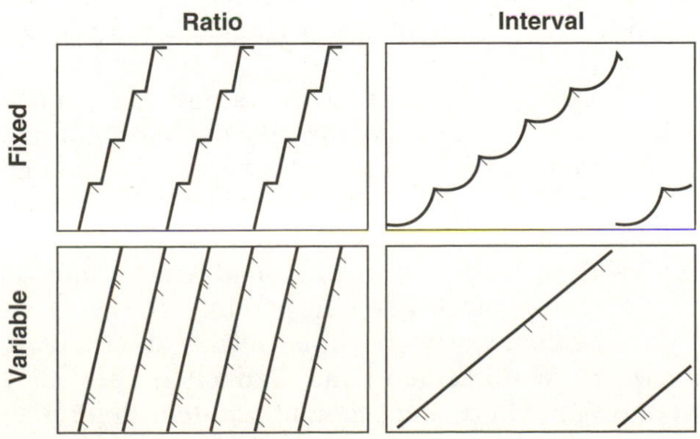

QUESTION

1. Be able to draw and to recognize the cumulative records for each of the four basic schedules of reinforcement.
2. And, oh yes, I almost forgot; be able to fill in the preceding big compare-and-contrast table.

INTERVAL AND TIME SCHEDULES OF PENALTY

Max is thinking, "Gee, this interval schedule business makes sense. Yes! It's an economical procedure. In continuous reinforcement, we reinforce a response every time it happens. In the ratio schedule of reinforcement, we count each response and reinforce one after a given number of responses. But the interval schedule of reinforcement is where it's at. We just set the timer to beep, let's say every 15 minutes, and we glance at our subject with an M&M in hand. We reinforce the first response and wait for the next beep.

"But why do we talk only about schedules of reinforcement? What about the other basic

Figure 18.4   Basic Schedules of Reinforcement

contingencies? What about punishment and penalty? Can't we have interval schedules of punishment and penalty?"

Max jumped out of his chair and rushed to his dusty library. He liked the looks of his library, crowded, full of books. He'd been feeding it since primary school. He had everything—his behavior analysis books, his old *Skeptical Inquirer* collection, old newspaper articles, some old editions of Whitman's poetry. He searched for interval schedules of punishment and penalty in the behavioral literature, but found nothing.

"I've got it! For my practicum project, I'm going to use interval schedules of penalty to get rid of Ted's unbearable behavior." So the next morning there Max was, in Mae's school dealing with his eighth graders. "Ah! Ted, We'll do it this time. I'm going to help you get rid of your pushing, paper-throwing, running around, blurting-out friends in my math practicum class."

As always, Max started the class with his lecture. "Today we are going to review fractions. . . ." At the end of the class, Max filled the blackboard with fractions, from top to bottom and right to left. It was time for the students to practice addition, subtraction, multiplication, and division of fractions. "For the next hour I want you to do this assignment. Please work by yourself. If you have any questions, raise your hand and I'll help you."

Max could see Ted starting to fidget. But this time Max went to Ted's desk and placed 12 colored tokens on it.

Ted looked puzzled. "What is this?" he asked.

Max said "Every token is worth 5 minutes of your lunch break. Any time you stand up from your desk or bother any of your classmates, I'll take one away. Then for each token I take, you will have to stay 5 minutes more during the break to complete your assignment." Ted smiled ironically—no problem.

Max went to his desk and put his micro-tape recorder in his shirt pocket and plugged an earphone in his right ear. (The night before, he had recorded a beep every 5 minutes on this tape.) Max sat down at his desk and began to prepare his next class lecture. Sometimes a student asked a question about the assignment.

Beep. He looked at Ted, who was flying paper airplanes. Max went immediately to Ted's desk and took a token away, without saying a word. He practiced this procedure for the whole hour and removed a total of six tokens. This was the best Ted had behaved in Max's class since the semester started.

The bell rang. The students ran away, Ted one of them. "Wait a minute." Max took Ted by his arm. "You lost six tokens, now you will have to work 30 minutes more."

After three classes of this procedure, Ted became an obedient student. He finished his assignments in class and had full lunch breaks. And Max got an A in our hypothetical story about his practicum project.

QUESTION

1. Give an example of a fixed-interval schedule of penalty.

WHY DOES INTERMITTENT REINFORCEMENT INCREASE RESISTANCE TO EXTINCTION?

The *principle of resistance to extinction* states: *Intermittent reinforcement makes behavior more resistant to extinction than does continuous reinforcement.* That's right, but why? Why do the Skinner-box rats appear to work harder rather than less hard when we pay them off for the hard work with less frequent reinforcement? At first glance, that makes no sense.

Do you want the impossibly complex but more accurate answer or the easy answer? The easy one? OK.

It's **easy** for the rats to "tell the difference" between **continuous reinforcement** and extinction. Why? Because during continuous reinforcement, all the responses produce reinforcers; and during extinction, none of them do. In other words, it's easy for the rats to "tell the difference" between frequent reinforcement and no reinforcement.

But, it's **hard** for the rats to "tell the difference" between **intermittent reinforcement** and extinction. Why? Because during intermittent reinforcement, only an occasional response produces a reinforcer; and during extinction, none of them do. In other words, it's hard for the rats to "tell the difference" between only an occasional reinforcement and no reinforcement.

So, because the extinction is much like intermittent reinforcement for the rats, the ones that had intermittent reinforcement keep on responding much as they had during intermittent reinforcement. And because extinction is so different from continuous reinforcement, the rats that had had continuous reinforcement quickly stop responding.

In other words, the rats quickly discriminate between reinforcement and extinction, but they greatly generalize between intermittent reinforcement and extinction. In still other words, stimulus generalization explains why intermittent reinforcement makes behavior more resistant to extinction than does continuous reinforcement.[7]

QUESTION

1. Why does intermittent reinforcement make behavior more resistant to extinction than does continuous reinforcement?

Example of Limited Hold
from Donald Whaley's Land of Fantasy
THE PIT

The prisoners said the large crystals were magic. They called them *Los ojos de la bruja*—the eyes of the witch. But what was the magic of the crystals? Manuel, like his companions, had wondered at first. Then one day, one of their number, Vicente, bore the heat of the sun as long as he could and then dropped his iron hammer. He hurled himself with no more effort than a small grunt into a cluster of the crystal spires 30 feet below. The crystals turned to rubies with his blood. For the first time since he had been in prison at La Cruz, his face was cool and peaceful. They all understood the magic then.

In the following months, Manuel saw the crystals bloom like crimson flowers, glassy and cool, over and over again. His companions dwindled in number, one by one. At night, Manuel dreamed in his fitful sleep. He saw the crystals as wonderful, giant icicles that could cool the innermost part of a man.

Each day, Manuel found himself moving inch by inch toward the top of the pit. He had reached the end. A long fall was his salvation; a broken leg or crippling wound wouldn't help. He was working at the top of the pit, on the day it came about. The sun burned down, and his hammer rang against the rock, each blow sending fragments spattering his chest and forearms. He felt the strength short-circuit from his body at each contact with the rocks. Soon it would be done; his legs would buckle and he would fall backward, over and down, to the cool crystal spires that patiently awaited him. He made one last contact with the rocks, dropped his hammer, and pulled himself erect, looking for perhaps the first time up to the observation platform where the guards stood vigil. It would only be a minute until

the guard would see him without his hammer and raise the black leather whip above his head with a curse and a bellow. He glanced beyond the guard platform, across the road into the living quarters inhabited by the commandant.

The two-story building was built mainly of crystalline rock with traces of mortar here and there. On top was a tower rising some 20 feet. At the top of the tower was a window covered by heavy curtains. Manuel saw a breeze toy with the curtains, making them flap silently. How long since he had felt a breeze? He could not remember. At that instant, a large gust of wind blew the curtain aside, and then he saw her. Her black hair glistened in the sun. She wasn't facing the window; she had turned her head to the side. Though he couldn't see her eyes from that distance, he knew they were dark and lovely. Her profile revealed precise features. The wind died and the curtain returned to its original position. He continued to stare at the window, watching the breeze nip at the curtain. God, please let it gust again. He found an almost forgotten emotion of hope and caring. Then he felt the whip tearing at his neck. The guard bore down on him; a snarl filled his browned face. In the storm of lashes, Manuel retrieved the hammer and returned to his work, glancing up at the window after each blow. The breeze continued to play with the curtain.

He saw her again three times on that first day. He was disappointed when the long rays of the sunset made the bowels of the pit black and they had to return to the hut where they would rest for the night. The day had gone fast. He had worked tirelessly, almost unaware of the heat and the exhaustion in his bones, his eyes darting like starved animals toward the window. He didn't know when the next gust of wind would come, and he didn't want to miss an opportunity.

The prisoners told stories of a daughter whom the commandant kept secluded from the depressing reality of prison life. The commandant's wife had died, leaving him to care for his daughter. After some years the daughter, a beautiful creature, had fallen victim to that bleak heaven-forsaken grotto in the arid plain. She had become mad in a way common in that harsh land. Now, the story went, she spent her hours secluded in the tower. That night Manuel didn't dream of the crystals; instead, he dreamed of a dark-eyed beauty who laughed and called his name.

The days and months flew by as he worked relentlessly at the crest of the pit. The guards had become suspicious of his renewed vigor and watched him more carefully than before. But Manuel paid no attention to them or to anything but the window. Some days the breezes were kind; but other days, they were stingy and sadistic. He never knew; but he

---

[7]In *EPB 3.0*, I had a much more detailed, more technically correct, and less mentalistic explanation, but I think few students understood it. So I've somewhat reluctantly fallen back on this more simplistic, superficial, mentalistic explanation, much to the students' relief, I'm sure. However, for those intellectuals among you, check out the original version at the POB web site *www.dickmalott.com*

always had the chance of seeing his lady. If only she would turn in his direction, then he could at least pretend she was looking at him. Manuel persisted, his hammer striking hard, a pause and a glance to the window, another stroke with the hammer. Always in the evening he felt a pang of sorrow but also a hope for a day of gusty breezes tomorrow.

Then one morning, perhaps a year after he had discovered his lady, Manuel awoke to find the sun already high in the sky. The guard hadn't come. The prisoners peered out the opening gouged from between loose stones. No guards were there. A group of them pounded on the door with stones, breaking open the rotted plank that latched it. Cautiously, they stepped out, picking up their hammers, defensively. It was as though death had descended into the pit. Manuel was the first to reach the top. For the first time in three years he found himself running. He went directly to the tower that held his lady. Inside, wooden lockers and tables were scattered about the room. Collections of odds and ends and personal belongings were thrown pell-mell on the floor. He spurred up a long, narrow stairway leading to the tower. He burst in through the door into her room. It was hardly a room at all. Several trunks were off to one side. On the shelves, sat dusty volumes of books and broken objects. He looked toward the window and saw the nourishment his soul had feasted on throughout the past year.

His lady was old. Her skin was cracked; a wide scar ran down her right cheek. The hair he had adored in the sunlight was coarse and hard, packed and matted with lacquer. Manuel knelt before the mannequin. Had he endured, dreamed, and hoped for this fake? The iron hammer he still held in his right hand would speak his despair to this dummy, a dressmaker's model of wire and plaster. He raised the hammer, hesitated for an instant, and then lowered it slowly. His lady wasn't all he had expected; true. She had led him on. Also true. Manuel wiped away the dust from her cheek and gently kissed the woman to whom he owed his life. Outside he could hear the prisoners greeting bands of liberators.

Analysis

Manuel had to be alert to take advantage of the reinforcement opportunities. Perhaps the breeze would blow the curtains for only an instant. If Manuel weren't watching carefully, he might miss the chance. We call this feature a *limited hold*—*the opportunity to produce the reinforcer is available for a limited time.*

A variable-interval schedule with a limited hold places a more stringent demand on the behavior than does the simple variable-interval schedule.

Because reinforcement is available for a limited time, a response must occur during the limited-hold period. So, with a short limited hold, the responses must occur at a high rate if the responses are going to produce all the reinforcers that become available.

Consider Manuel's plight. Suppose a gust of wind occurred once an hour, on the average. Furthermore, suppose the gusts usually lasted a minute. How often would Manuel have to glance up to the tower, if he were to collect the maximum number of daily glimpses of his love? Once an hour? No way. Once every minute, though he'd average only one glimpse per hour! If he didn't glance up once each minute, the curtain might blow aside and then close again, with his love remaining unnoticed. Remember that in the variable-interval schedule, the reinforcement will follow the response after a variable interval of time. So the opportunity for reinforcement for Manuel could have occurred 2 minutes in a row and then 1 hour and 15 minutes later, if he were glancing at the window when the opportunity arrived.

But it could be worse; suppose the gusts usually lasted only 10 seconds. Then how often would Manuel need to glance to the tower? Once every 10 seconds! That's 360 glances per hour, 3,600 glances per 10-hour day—and he'd get only ten visual hits per day for all that work. Poor Manuel's neck would soon get as tired as his sledgehammer-wielding arms.

QUESTION

1. Give a fantasy example of a variable-interval schedule with a limited hold.

Advanced Enrichment Section.
Compare and Contrast
DEADLINES VS. LIMITED HOLDS

We all hate them, but I think deadlines are what keeps our civilized world working. Aversive though they are, deadlines are our friends. Without deadlines, we'd procrastinate our lives away. **A deadline is the time *before which* we should make a response or a set of responses or complete a task.** If we blow off the deadline, we won't get something good, such as a high grade on our homework or acceptance into grad school. Or we won't avoid something bad, such as having our phone disconnected.

In the real world, we have many deadlines. In the Skinner box, we have an occasional limited hold. The limited hold is similar to a deadline, but not quite. **A limited hold is a time period *during which* the response will produce the after condition; re-**

sponding either before or after the limited hold will have no effect. For example, consider a 10-minute fixed interval with a 1-minute limited hold. The limited hold lasts from the 10th minute to the 11th minute. Responding early or late will be of no avail. The first response during that limited window of opportunity will produce the reinforcer for that interval.

In the real world, we often have to make a large number of responses, such as many strokes on the computer keyboard so that our term paper will be finished and ready by the end-of-the-semester deadline. A Skinner-box analog to this deadline would be a fixed-ratio schedule with a deadline; for example, Rudolph must press the lever 100 times within 5 minutes for the reinforcer to be delivered. If he only gets in 99 responses before the deadline, that 100th response will go unreinforced. But this is just a rough analog to the sort of deadline tasks you and I normally face; so don't take it too literally. Our deadlines involve clocks, calendars, and the fact that we have language and our behavior can be governed by rules describing the deadline contingency (as we will see in the last few chapters). Rudolph ain't into none of that.

An S^D can be associated with either a deadline or a limited hold. A clock or calendar that indicates that we've not passed the deadline is an S^D. If we had an S^D that came on during the 1-minute limited hold, a well-trained Rudolph would not respond during the prior, 10-minute fixed interval, because the absence of the S^D would be an S^Δ.

QUESTION

1. Compare and contrast the limited hold and the deadline.

Concurrent Contingencies

FUNDAMENTALS

Example
Behavioral Clinical Psychology
PLAY VS. SELF-STIMULATION[1]

Mae and her team of behavior analysis students from the university continued working with Jimmy, the autistic child, to help him become a more normal human being. Jimmy could stay for hours in a room full of toys, ignoring them all; he would sit gazing with a fixed, glassy-eyed look, or grimacing by drawing the corners of his mouth out and down (revealing his upper set of teeth), or waving his hand with his fingers outstretched in front of his eyes, or spinning his personal top, or vigorously and repetitively rubbing his eyes, nose, mouth, ears, hair, or holding nonedible objects in his mouth, or rocking back and forth and side to side, or rolling his tongue, or clicking his teeth, or audibly swishing saliva in his mouth, or repetitively knocking his knees together, or tensing his whole body and shaking, or contorting his legs, or. . . . Jimmy was a living catalog of pathological self-stimulatory responses (responses whose reinforcers consist of the sensory stimulation they produce). Jimmy was a heartbreaking sight.

But Jimmy's awful appearance was only a small part of his tragedy. If Jimmy was like other autistic children, his high frequency of self-stimulation meant his prognosis was bad—probably he'd be autistic or psychotic the rest of his life. On the other hand, if Mae and her team could reduce his self-stimulation, he might have a chance to acquire a more functional repertoire.

So the team set up an intensive intervention at the Rosa Parks Academy. Under Mae's supervision, Sue and Max first used food to shape appropriate play. They used a coloring book and toys that allowed Jimmy to fit geometric forms in their proper slots. After Jimmy had acquired a minimal play repertoire, they recorded his baseline of self-stimulation and appropriate play during 44 five-minute sessions. Jimmy self-stimulated 100% of the time and concurrently played approximately 13% of the time.[2]

Then they added a punishment contingency, and it was a rough one. Each time Jimmy self-stimulated, they would sharply say, "No!" and briskly slap or briefly hold the part of Jimmy's body involved in the self-stimulation. This punishment contingency[3] was supposed to be aversive for Jimmy, and it definitely was for Max. He flinched each time he had to slap Jimmy's hand. Jimmy had such a high frequency of pathological self-stimulation that it was a full-time job for both Max and Sue to keep track of his behavior and punish the inappropriate responses. Sue worked with Jimmy's self-stimulation from the waist down and Max worked from the waist up.

What were the results? Over 50 five-minute sessions, Jimmy's self-stimulation dropped to a low of 13%, and his appropriate play increased to over 85% (Figure 19.1). In this one small area, at least, Jimmy was beginning to look and act like a normal child. Of course, they still had a long way to go.

---

[1]Based on Koegel, R. L., Firestone, P. B., Kramme, K. W., & Dunlap, G. (1974). Increasing spontaneous play by suppressing self-stimulation in autistic children. *Journal of Applied Behavior Analysis, 7,* 521–528. The graph is based on the same article.

[2]Note that because these two classes of behavior were concurrent (they occurred at the same time), we don't add 100% and 13% to get 113%.

[3]Note that this case is based on a 1974 article. Nowadays, using aversive control procedures of this sort is rare; in fact, at the Croyden Avenue School, where my students work with children with autistic behaviors and values, they do not even use the word, "No" to decrease inappropriate or dysfunctional behavior.

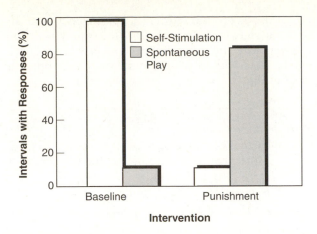

Figure 19.1   Increasing an Autistic Child's Play by Punishing Self-Stimulation

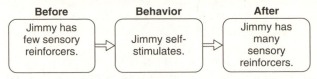

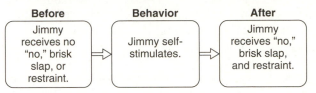

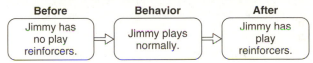

Analysis

Jimmy had two reinforcement contingencies concurrently in effect for two response classes that were somewhat compatible—some forms of self-stimulation and normal play.

In other words, he concurrently self-stimulated 33% of the time that he was playing normally. But in some other sense self-stimulation was largely incompatible with normal play; when they punished self-stimulation, that class of responses, of course, became much less frequent, and at the same time, the normal play became more frequent.

We might look at it like this: Jimmy and some other autistic children don't really differ too much from normal children in terms of the reinforcers for normal play. When Jimmy had a chance to play normally, he did; the built-in reinforcement contingencies in normal play were effective. But, unfortunately, Jimmy's problem was that he didn't have much of a chance to play normally. Why not? Because his self-stimulation competed too well with his normal play. His self-stimulation didn't give his normal play much of a chance.

So the built-in sensory reinforcers for self-stimulation were too effective in reinforcing self-stimulation. And the built-in reinforcement contingencies in normal play weren't effective enough in reinforcing normal play. It was only when they added a third concurrent contingency—the punishment of self-stimulation—that self-stimulation was suppressed enough to give the reinforcers for normal play a chance.

Natural contingency: a contingency typically available prior to performance management. It is not designed to manage performance. It is usually built-in or automatic, not added.

Performance-management contingency: a contingency explicitly used to manage performance when the natural contingencies are ineffective or when they move performance in the wrong direction.

Note: Don't confuse natural contingencies with unlearned reinforcers. For instance, when Jimmy is disruptive, his parents pay attention to him and unintentionally reinforce his disruptive behavior. Their attention is a learned reinforcer, though the contingency is a natural contingency, as it existed prior to performance management and was not designed to manage Jimmy's performance. So both learned and unlearned reinforcers and aversive conditions may be found in both natural and performance-management contingencies.

QUESTION

1. Diagram the three contingencies involved in a behavioral intervention using punishment of self-stimulation to increase normal play.

Concept
CONCURRENT CONTINGENCIES

Concurrent means *at the same time*. So two things that are concurrent exist *at the same time*. That means that **concurrent behavioral contingencies** are available at the same time. Notice I say *available*:

they're sitting there waiting for you. But they may not be operating at the moment. For example, two contingencies are concurrently waiting for you if you jump out of the second-story window of your classroom building: First, there's the thrill of the rapid descent—a reinforcer, at least for bungie jumpers; then there's the pain of broken bones, an aversive condition for all but the most terminally weird. But that concurrent pair of contingencies lies dormant unless you actually jump. Just because behavior is specified in a contingency doesn't mean the behavior is actually happening. And that applies to concurrent contingencies, too.

Remember Grace? She sometimes had an attack of the Gilles de la Tourette syndrome when she was in stressful situations, as when her family got rowdy.[4] Two different escape contingencies were concurrently available there. First, Grace could escape by making the pathological responses involved in displaying her Gilles de la Tourette syndrome.

Inappropriate Escape Contingency

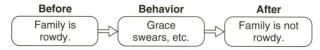

Or at the suggestion of Dr. Goldiamond and Dr. Glass, she could escape more appropriately. She could simply ask her family to quiet down, giving her medical condition as the reason for her request.

Appropriate Escape Contingency

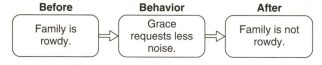

So the pathological escape contingency involved the Gilles de la Tourette syndrome responses followed by the termination of the aversive commotion. And the concurrently available, healthy, escape contingency involved a proper request followed by the termination of the aversive commotion. Again, understand that two contingencies are concurrent if they are **available** at the same time; they need not be actually operating at the same time. In other words, these two contingencies are concurrently available, even though Grace is not both swearing and requesting at the same time.

---

[4]Based on Goldiamond, I. (1984). Training parent trainers and ethicists in nonlinear analysis of behavior. In R. Dangel & R. Polster. Parent training foundations of research and practice. New York: Guilford Press.

Also keep in mind that a contingency is an if-then statement. **If** Grace swears, the family will stop being rowdy; but that doesn't mean that she will swear. **If** you jump off the building, you'll break a leg; but that doesn't mean you have to jump.

> *Definition: Concept*
> **Concurrent contingencies**
> ○ More than one contingency of reinforcement or punishment
> ○ is available at the same time.

Goldiamond also reported the case of Ralph, the smoking accountant. For Ralph, the pathological escape contingency involved smoking a cigarette that allowed him a brief escape from his aversive paperwork. The concurrent, healthy contingency involved the responses of exercising or having a cup of tea that allowed him a brief escape from the aversive paperwork. For both Grace and Ralph, we have two different escape contingencies, each involving a different escape response producing the termination of the same aversive condition.

Concurrent contingencies also controlled Jimmy's behavior: During baseline, sensory stimulation was contingent on self-stimulation; and, concurrently, other stimulation, including sensory stimulation, was contingent on normal play. During intervention, Sue and Max added another concurrent contingency—aversive stimulation contingent on self-stimulation.

Four Types of Concurrent Contingencies

Note that our definition of *concurrent contingencies* suggests four types of concurrent contingencies:

1. Contingencies may be available concurrently for two physically **compatible responses**. The teacher may be reinforcing a Eric's reading by giving him a little attention, and relief from a runny nose may be reinforcing his sniffing—two normally compatible responses because he can both read and sniff at the same time.

Compatible Behaviors

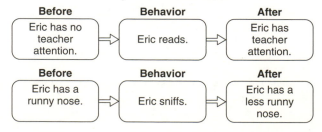

2. **Compatible contingencies** may be available concurrently for a **single response**. The teacher may reinforce Eric's reading by paying attention to him, and the interesting material might also reinforce his reading—two compatible contingencies with a single response. These contingencies are compatible in that they both cause the response frequency to increase. Of course we could also have two compatible contingencies that were both punishment contingencies and both cause the response frequency to decrease.

Compatible Contingencies

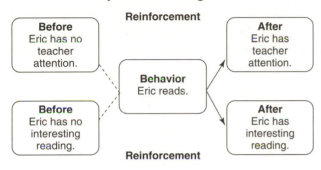

3. **Incompatible contingencies** may be available concurrently for a **single response**. The teacher may reinforce Eric's reading, but a neighbor may throw a spit ball every time Eric picks up the book—two incompatible contingencies with a single response. These contingencies are incompatible in that one causes the response frequency to increase, while the other causes it to decrease.

Incompatible Contingencies

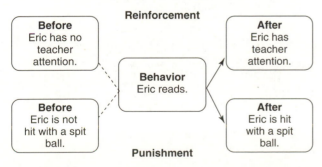

4. Contingencies may be available concurrently for two physically **incompatible responses**. The teacher may reinforce Eric's reading, and a

neighbor may reinforce his whispering—two incompatible responses.[5]

Incompatible Behaviors

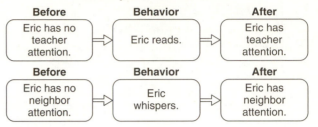

QUESTION

1. *Concurrent contingency*—define it and briefly give three examples.
2. Recall the article by Koegel et al. "Increasing spontaneous play by suppressing self-stimulation in autistic children" (i.e., Mae's punishment of self-stimulation). Is this an example of concurrent contingencies?
   a. yes
   b. no

   Hint: Always look at the titles of the chapter and sections you're reading and relate them to what you're reading.

3. Our definition of *concurrent contingencies* suggests four types of concurrent contingencies. What are they, and how would you diagram examples of them?

Example
Verbal Behavior
CONCURRENT CONTINGENCIES AND THE FACTORS THAT INTERFERE WITH LANGUAGE LEARNING[6]

When Jimmy first came to the Rosa Parks Academy, he had no verbal skills, and he had been labeled *autistic*, without direct evidence of organic problems.

---

[5] When two compatible or incompatible contingencies are concurrently available for the **same** response, they are technically called **conjoint** contingencies, rather than concurrent contingencies. But, for our purposes, it may make sense simply to call all contingencies that are available at the same time (i.e., concurrently) concurrent contingencies, and not deal with the terminological distinction between conjoint and concurrent contingencies. For a thoughtful, authoritative treatment of behavioral terminology, see Catania, A. C. (1998). *Learning* (4th ed.). Upper Saddle River, NJ: Prentice Hall.

[6] This section is based on an impressive, almost revolutionary, theoretical analysis of language learning by Drash, P. W., & Tudor, R. M. (1993). A functional analysis of verbal delay in preschool children: Implications for prevention and total recovery. *The Analysis of Verbal Behavior, 11*, 19–29.

He couldn't tact, mand, and so on. He hadn't learned these verbal skills because the reinforcement contingencies were inadequate.

Concurrent Reinforcement Contingencies for Alternatives to Verbal Behavior[7]

Contingencies for verbal behavior are the most obvious when it's first learned. Parents help to build a child's verbal repertoire by reinforcing many verbal responses. But you've seen that more than one contingency of reinforcement or punishment can be in effect at the same time. Sometimes the contingencies that come to control behavior actually interfere with learning verbal behavior. In general, three categories of concurrent contingencies interfere with language learning, as you will now see.

When contingencies reinforce alternative behaviors to verbal behavior, the alternative behaviors are strengthened. These nonverbal behaviors compete directly with verbal behavior. The contingencies that would reinforce verbal behavior may be available at the same time as the competing concurrent reinforcement contingencies, but the verbal-behavior contingencies lose out.

Disruptive Behavior as an Alternative to Verbal Behavior

Flashback to 18-month-old Jimmy: Jimmy toddles around the kitchen making happy baby sounds. He hasn't eaten yet today, and he's hungry. He begins to whimper. Jimmy's mother, Liza, picks him up and cuddles him. Jimmy cries. Liza puts him down and gives him his favorite toy. Jimmy begins to stomp his feet. Desperate, Liza, asks Jimmy what he wants. Jimmy throws himself on the floor and pounds his fists. Finally, Liza gives him a bottle. Jimmy stops crying and drinks the milk. The opportunity for an approximation to a verbal request (a mand) to be reinforced, is lost. Jimmy's disruptive crying is reinforced instead.

In Jimmy's case, the concurrent contingencies for the appropriate mand of saying "milk" and the inappropriate disruptive behavior are in effect at the same time. The disruptive behavior is reinforced, though, so that is the behavior that increases.

When contingencies support disruptive behaviors, these behaviors prevent the occurrence of reinforced verbal behaviors.

---

[7]For purposes of illustrating these factors, we've packed them all into one fictional case study with Jimmy, though they might or might not all be operative in any real-life situation.

Reinforcement Contingency for Vocal Verbal Mand

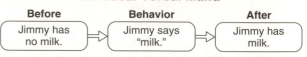

Reinforcement Contingency for Disruptive Behavior

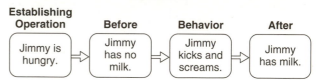

We can see how the reinforcement contingency for disruptive behavior maintains the incompatible response. But let's briefly digress to ask what maintains Liza's behavior of giving Jimmy milk when he tantrums? That's right—escape from Jimmy's aversive crying.

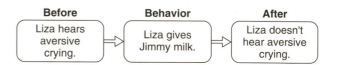

Liza is the victim in the sick social cycle.

The Sick Social Cycle (Victim's Escape Model)

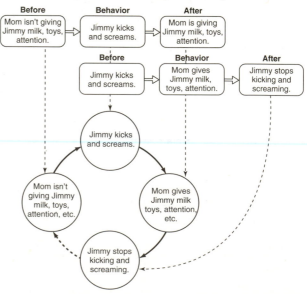

Now, back to our main point: You've seen how disruptive behavior can be established as an alternative to verbal behavior. The disruptive behavior actually serves the same function as verbal behavior.

But nondisruptive behavior can also serve as an alternative to verbal behavior.

Nondisruptive Behavior as an Alternative to Verbal Behavior

Jimmy looked at a ball sitting on the shelf. Liza immediately gave it to him. Later, the ball rolled under the sofa. Jimmy stared after it, and Jimmy's brother Jason got the ball and rolled it back to him. Liza smiled at her two sons. "Jason, you are such a good brother," Liza said. Jason smiled.

Staring, pointing, and gesturing can function as nonverbal alternatives to verbal mands. When parents and family members reinforce nonverbal alternatives, the frequency of those alternatives increases. Unfortunately, they are incompatible with verbal mands.[8]

So, why did Liza reinforce Jimmy's nonverbal alternatives to mands? Perhaps two reasons. First, it's aversive for most parents to think their infant has an unmet need. Second, she also avoided any tantruming that might have occurred if Jimmy didn't get what he wanted.

Liza's Escape Contingency

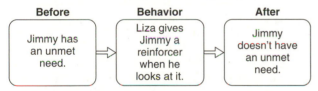

Liza's Avoidance Contingency

Parents also tend to reinforce any behavior of other family members that results in a happy child, just as Liza praised Jason for retrieving the ball when Jimmy looked at it.

---

[8]Many behavior analysts consider pointing and gesturing to be forms of verbal behavior, nonvocal mands. However, I think this debases the concepts of verbal behavior and language. I think it's best to consider such behavior as nonverbal alternatives to mands, just as we think Rudolph's lever presses are not verbal behavior, not language, not mands, and not requests that the experimenter give him a drop of water; instead Rudolph's lever press is simple behavior reinforced by the receipt of water, just as Jimmy's pointing to the cup of water is just simple behavior reinforced by the receipt of water.

Reinforcement for Other Family Members

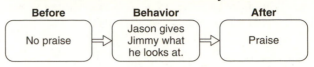

Note: We are *not* saying Liza is a bad mother. Liza is an excellent mother, as demonstrated by the success with which she raised Jason. But somehow, perhaps because of some little incident, or a series of inconspicuous little incidents, Jimmy's behavior and values drifted into the wrong.

Suppression of Verbal Behavior by Punishment

Liza has a headache. Jimmy tries to get her attention. He says, "Muh, Muh, Muh" (his approximation to "Mama"). Jimmy's verbal response could be reinforced by Liza picking him up.

Instead Liza yells at Jimmy, "What is it?!"

Jimmy quiets. His verbal behavior has been punished. Sometimes adults accidentally punish children's verbal behavior instead of reinforcing it. This doesn't mean that the parents are "bad parents." Think of some of the loud, chatty two-year-olds you know. Under some circumstances, their chatter can be very aversive. Parents may not intend to punish verbal behavior; they may simply react to aversive stimuli with aggression.

Punishment for Jimmy's Verbal Behavior

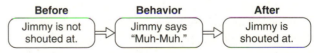

Liza's Escape Contingency

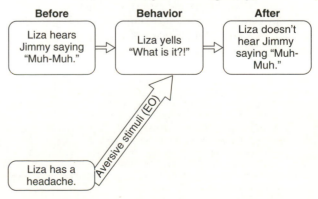

Punishment contingencies that suppress verbal behavior may be in effect at the same time as reinforcement contingencies that support verbal behavior. (Now, we're not saying this will be a problem if a child's verbal behavior is only punished once in a while, but if mama had a chronic headache, then the infant might be in serious trouble in terms of learning verbal behavior.) Concurrent contingencies are everywhere, in real life, there may be more concurrent contingencies than simple, isolated contingencies. And, as you can see, the concept of concurrent contingencies is very useful in helping us solve the mystery of why Jimmy and many other children fail to learn to talk.

TWO MORE FACTORS THAT INTERFERE WITH LANGUAGE LEARNING[9]

Two more factors interfere with language learning. They both have to do with the absence of learn units (learning opportunities). A **learn unit** is (1) an occasion for a response, (2) the response, and (3) an outcome of that response (essentially, a contingency).[10] Though the absence of learn units doesn't specifically involve concurrent contingencies, learn units are essential to all learning and therefore deserve consideration when dealing with language learning. There are at least two reasons for the absence of learn units; as we will now see, no one may be around to reinforce verbal behavior, or those who are around may not require verbal behavior.

No One is Around to Reinforce Verbal Behavior

Liza puts 1-year-old Jimmy in his playpen and turns on the Barney TV show. "Thank goodness for the annoying purple dinosaur! How would I have time to fix dinner if I didn't have that TV?" She leaves the room.

Jimmy spots his stuffed purple dinosaur, a big reinforcer. But does he attempt to mand (ask) for the dinosaur? Probably not. That behavior isn't reinforced when he's alone. And if he spends most of his time alone in the playpen, he's not going to have

enough learn units (reinforced opportunities) to talk.

Even if Jimmy does happen to say some approximation to "Barney" when Liza isn't in the room, saying *Barney* won't be reinforced; so it will extinguish.

Probably, 1 hour of TV-induced extinction of mands, even 1 hour per day, would have little negative impact on a child's learning to mand. But if the child spends most of the day isolated from adult interaction, few learn units will take place.[11]

When Parents Don't Require Any Behavior

When a child appears to be learning at a slow pace, parents may be convinced that their child has a physical or neurological disability even though none exists. Therefore, they may not require their children to produce *any* specific behavior in order to receive reinforcers. The child then gets fewer learn units. The fewer learn units a child has, the more "delayed" he will appear to be. So, when parents lower their requirements of their children's behavior because their children seem to be delayed, they actually perpetuate the problem.

Also, consider parents of children with illnesses or physical disabilities that have no direct effect on a child's verbal behavior (talking). Such parents may not require their children to talk because these parents fear causing further physical problems. For example, the parents of an asthmatic child may not ask their child to produce verbal behavior because they fear the "stress" might produce an asthma attack.

Punishment of Parents' Requiring Their Children to Make Verbal Responses

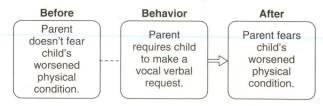

Before	Behavior	After
Parent doesn't fear child's worsened physical condition.	Parent requires child to make a vocal verbal request.	Parent fears child's worsened physical condition.

Probably, the previous factors often work in combination: children don't spend enough time with attentive parents; and even when parents are around, they don't require and then reinforce verbal responses. Whatever the specific situation, the result

---

[9]This section is also based on the impressive theoretical analysis of language learning by Drash and Tudor we referred to earlier.

[10]From our perspective, a *learn unit* is essentially a behavioral contingency, but we find it a handy way of talking about contingencies in instructional settings. *Learn unit* was coined by Doug Greer. (Greer, R. D., & McDonough, S. H. [1999]. Is the learn unit a fundamental measure of pedagogy? *The Behavior Analyst*, *21*, 5–16.)

[11]The brilliant social critic, Chris Rock has some insightful comments about the necessity of learn units for language acquisition, though not in those terms.

is the same for the child: fewer learn units, less learning, and less or no verbal behavior (language).

BIOLOGICAL PROBLEMS THAT INTERFERE WITH LANGUAGE LEARNING

Sometimes a child's physical problems can influence the behavioral contingencies that affect language learning. This may sound like the medical model myth, but it's not. You've learned that baby babble sounds like language of the parents, because the parental sounds are learned reinforcers. And you've learned that children imitate the vocal verbal behavior of their parents, again because the parental sounds are learned reinforcers. But hearing loss hinders learning vocal verbal behavior, because parental sound is less likely to become a leaned reinforcer. Of course, children with a hearing loss can still learn language, but often their language learning is delayed because they don't receive the special training they need early enough.

Although there are many impressive exceptions, most often, both professionals and parents make the circular-logical error of inferring a biological cause for a behavioral problem, even though there is no biological evidence for that biological cause. The error of reification. They blame it on the brain and then no longer feel responsible for finding the behavioral contingencies that most likely caused the problem and no longer feel responsible for finding the behavioral training contingencies needed to eliminate or at least reduce the language problems.

QUESTIONS

1. How might hearing impairment affect a child's language learning?
2. Explain how some people commit the error of reification when looking for a cause for behavioral problems.

DINING OUT WITH CHILDREN— A DANGEROUS ACTIVITY, AT BEST, OR THE INVASION OF THE ANKLE-BITERS[12]

"Mae, I can't stand it anymore. Those two ankle biters are driving me up the wall," Juke said. "It sounded easy when my sister asked if I'd mind tak-

[12]Based on Bauman, K. E., Reiss, M. L., Rogers, R. W., & Bailey, J. S. (1983). Dining out with children: Effectiveness of a parent advice package on pre-meal inappropriate behavior. *Journal of Applied Behavior Analysis, 16*, 55–68. The associated graph is based on the same article.

ing care of her two boys for 10 days, while she and her husband went to San Francisco for their second honeymoon. But those two brats have been here only 2 days, and already I want to ask my sister to cancel her honeymoon. I don't know who's worse, Rob or Roy—the 3-year-old or the 5-year-old."

"What happened to the coolest man in town, the man who can solve anyone's problems?" Mae asked.

"Mae, I don't need someone else to bug me. I need someone to help me or at least give me some advice," Juke said.

"OK, why don't you and I and the two boys go out to dinner tonight," Mae said.

"That'll be just great, and you can watch Rob and Roy destroy the restaurant," Juke answered.

That night the foursome went to one of Juke's favorite restaurants, La Maison de Paris, and his prediction came true. The two boys were all over the place, standing on their chairs, running, hitting, kicking, crying, whining, demanding, humming, singing, hitting each other with their spoons, and interrupting Juke and Mae who were trying to have a serious conversation about what to do with the boys. All that occurred during the brief 20 minutes they waited for the waiter to serve the food. True, the boys did quiet down a bit when the food arrived, though both kids whined and said they wanted a Big Mac and not "that thing" (Chateaubriand).

As they were driving home, Juke said, "From now on, I'm going to keep them locked in the guest bedroom and toss them a couple cold frankfurters every day!"

"Juke, that's not funny. Besides, I think we can solve the problem. I've read Ken Bauman's doctoral dissertation that he did down at Florida State University. I think he's got the solution."

Analysis and Intervention

Mae and Juke did borrow the intervention Ken Bauman and the FSU team had developed and tested. We can look at this intervention largely as an effort to manage various concurrent contingencies.

First, let's consider the disruptive behaviors—running, hitting, and so forth. These acts don't occur out of the blue. They resulted from the boys' behavioral histories, from the past contingencies of reinforcement. Some of those contingencies involved the reinforcing attention of the parents (sometimes it's more reinforcing to be nagged at than to be completely ignored). Then there was the reinforcing reaction of the other brother (for example, Rob's crying when Roy hit him). And there was the reinforcing sensory stimulation that results from acts like singing, pounding, jumping, and running.

So all these contingencies were concurrently acting. First the reinforcing sensory feedback from Roy's pounding on the table won out and controlled that pounding. Then the stimulation from his pounding lost its reinforcing novelty, and the reinforcement contingency involving Rob's crying took over. The result was that Roy started pounding on Rob instead of the table. On and on, from one concurrent contingency to another, and from one disruptive behavior to another.

Inappropriate Natural Contingencies

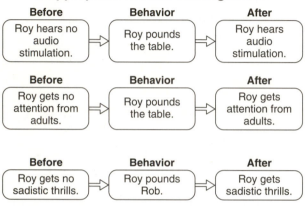

These contingencies are *inappropriate* in that they reinforce inappropriate, disruptive behavior. To combat these inappropriate, disruptive contingencies, Juke added some concurrent performance-management contingencies of his own. He told the boys, in detail, how they were to behave or, more to the point, how they were not to behave: no running, no hitting, and so forth. In other words, he gave them the rules of gentlemanly conduct. Now those rules implied that some new punishment contingencies were concurrently in effect. Juke's disapproval was contingent on their misbehavior. (At least Juke hoped his disapproval would be more aversive than his sister's had been.)

He also said, "I'll be real proud of you guys if you act like little gentlemen." This implied what Juke hoped would be a concurrent punishment contingency based on the loss of his pride in them (a presumed reinforcer), if they misbehaved.

Then he got rid of a few contingencies. He sat them next to the wall. (This prevented their running around the restaurant and thus prevented contact with the associated reinforcement contingency.) He also sat them on separate sides of the table. (This was a mildly successful effort to prevent contact with the reinforcement contingency involving fighting.) And he removed their silverware until the dinner arrived. (This prevented contact with the reinforcement contingencies that supported silverware banging and throwing.)

During the wait for the meal, he gave each of them a favorite cracker when they were being gentlemanly, or, more to the point, when they weren't disrupting.

Concurrent Performance-Management Contingency

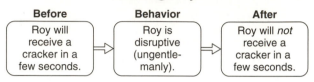

1. What kind of contingency was this concurrent performance-management contingency?

   a. reinforcement

   b. penalty

   c. avoidance of the loss of a reinforcer

   d. punishment by the prevention of the presentation of a reinforcer

Also during the premeal wait, Juke gave them each a couple of small toys to play with—another concurrent contingency. He *hoped* they would be less likely to be disruptive if they were engaged with a toy.

Concurrent Performance-Management Contingency

This Roy-toy contingency is an example of an attempt at differential reinforcement of incompatible behavior.

Results

Always the scientist, Mae had recorded baseline data on the boys' behavior during the premeal interval of their first dinner. Then she recorded their behavior during the premeal interval of the next dinner; this was when Juke had started Bauman's intervention. Both boys showed such great improvement (Figure 19.2) that Juke was almost ready to marry Mae and start raising some kids of their own—almost, but not quite.

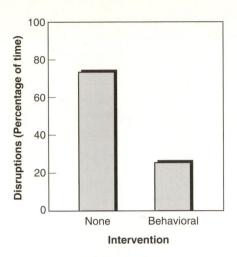

Figure 19.2   Children's Disruptions While Waiting for Dinner

QUESTION

1. Diagram a behavioral intervention to decrease a child's disruptive behavior while waiting for dinner. Include
   a. a few inappropriate natural contingencies
   b. two concurrent performance-management contingencies.

Example
Behavioral Child and Family Counseling
SHOPPING WITH CHILDREN— A DANGEROUS ACTIVITY, AT BEST[13]

Bauman's behavioral intervention package so impressed Juke that he couldn't resist trying another behavioral intervention package when he ran into similar problems on his shopping trips with Rob and Roy. (Rusty Clark and a team from the University of Kansas and the Johnny Cake Child Study Center developed this intervention.)

On their first trips, the boys were all over the store, handling everything that wasn't moving and some things that were, almost constantly asking the buy-me question, and roughhousing. So Juke told them they'd each get 50 cents to buy something at the end of the trip if they were cool. And he defined cool in terms of staying nearby and avoiding the list of uncool moves we just mentioned. And each time they messed up, he'd tell them they'd just lost a nickel off their 50 cents.

In other words, Juke used a special punishment or penalty contingency (punishment by the prevention of the presentation of a reinforcer). Whenever a boy misbehaved, Juke told him he wouldn't get a nickel he'd otherwise have gotten. So there you've got a pair of concurrent contingencies: One is a reinforcement contingency based on the built-in and social reinforcers for misbehavior. The other is a penalty or punishment contingency based on being told he wouldn't get one of his nickels.[14]

Inappropriate Natural Contingency

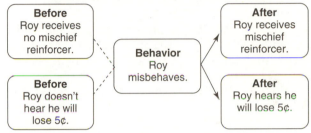

Performance-Management Contingency

But Juke did more. He also kept up a running conversation with the two boys about what they were doing in the store. For example, he'd ask them where they thought they could find what he was looking for, often after he'd gotten them within sight of the object. They'd discuss the price and quality of the item. They'd talk about what they were going to do with the object. Also they'd discuss interesting merchandise as they passed along. At the end, he'd ask them where the toy or candy department was, and they'd cash in on the remains of their 50 cents. Of course, he kept up a high rate of approval for their taking part in the discussion.

Here, Juke was adding another set of reinforcement contingencies to the salad of concurrent contingencies. This contingency would succeed in reducing disruption to the extent that talking to Juke about the shopping trip was incompatible with disruptive behavior. Those reinforcement contingencies involved the reinforcers that are naturally built into an interesting conversation, as well as Juke's frequent approval.

---

[13]Based on Clark, H. B., Greene, B. F., Macrae, J. W., Mcnees, M. P., Davis, J. L., & Risley, T. R. (1977). A parent advice package for family shopping trips: Development and evaluation. *Journal of Applied Behavior Analysis, 10,* 605–624. The graph of data is based on the same article.

[14]As you will see in a later chapter, this is really an analog to punishment by the prevention of the presentation of a reinforcer. Why? Because it violates the 60-second rule. The nickel would have been presented more than 60 seconds after the punished response. Don't worry too much about this now. We'll deal with it later. However, from another view this contingency does pass the 60-second test because, within 60 seconds, Juke would tell the misbehaving boy of his future nickel loss.

Concurrent Performance-Management Contingency

This Uncle-Juke's-approval contingency is an attempt at differential reinforcement of incompatible behavior.

Note that these conversations served two functions: They reinforced behavior that was more or less incompatible with disruptions, and they served to educate the boys about proper consumer behavior and the world of shopping malls.

Did Rusty Clark's intervention package work? Of course. The boy's disruptive behavior and comments immediately fell from 79% to 14% (Figure 19.3). Mae commented that with Rusty's behavioral intervention the boys were now better behaved than Juke normally was when they went shopping. Juke made no comment.

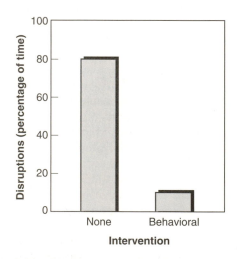

Figure 19.3   Using Reinforcement and Punishment to Reduce Children's Disruptions While Shopping

How did the boys feel about this? In other words, how was the social validation? The boys liked it. And why not? They each lost no more than 10 or 15 cents. Also, Juke wasn't on their case as much as he had been before. During baseline, he'd nagged, shouted, reprimanded, and coerced them 43% of the time. But during his behavioral intervention, he bugged them only 9% of the time. That's not all; his frequency of educational comments rose from 25% to 91% of the time (Figure 19.4).

How'd Juke feel about it? What were his social validation data? He said it was more work than be-

fore but well worth it. Besides, it cost him an average of 65 cents per boy less on each trip. Saving money wasn't Uncle Juke's goal, but still. . . .

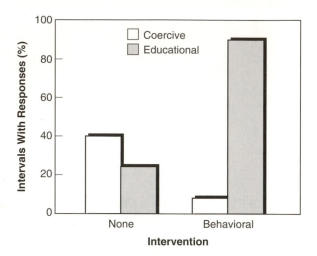

Figure 19.4   Reducing Coercive Comments and Increasing Educational Comments

QUESTION

1. Diagram the natural and performance-management contingencies in a behavioral intervention to decrease a child's disruptive behavior while shopping.

Example of Concurrent Contingencies Behavioral School Psychology
EARL, THE HYPERACTIVE BOY[15]

Earl's parents and grandparents had beaten him so cruelly that, by the time he was 1 year old, he had a fractured skull and a damaged brain. Loving foster parents adopted Earl when he was 3. But it may have been too late; Earl couldn't adjust to the normal demands of the world. By the age of 9, he was still in the second grade and always in trouble. He spent almost no time studying; instead, he talked, looked around the room or stared out the window, tapped, squirmed, fiddled, and wandered about. He played with his classmates by pushing them, pinching them, hitting them, and throwing himself into their midst—disrupting their work and play. He'd even shove his desk around the classroom, ramming into everything that couldn't move fast enough to es-

[15]Based on Patterson, G. R. (1965). An application of conditioning techniques to the control of a hyperactive child. In L.P. Ullman & L. Krasner (Eds.). *Case studies in behavior modification* (pp. 370–375). New York: Holt, Rinehart & Winston.

cape. And because he was 2 years older than his classmates, he was big enough to bully them all.

Inappropriate Natural Contingencies

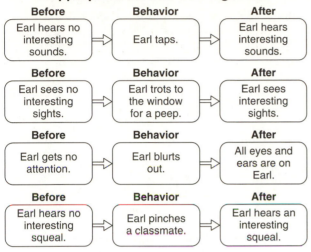

So all sorts of natural classroom contingencies maintained all sorts of disruptive behavior.

The school administrators called in Dr. Gerald Patterson from the Psychology Clinic of the University of Oregon. Gerry Patterson knew the following general rule: The **action rule**: *To change behavior, use action, not words.*

In fact, he helped discover it. He knew traditional ways don't work. He knew it wouldn't help just to bring the child into his office for a little psychotherapy in the form of a few chats. Instead, Gerry went to where the problem was—the classroom. These were times for action, not words. It was time for the M&Ms.[16] Gerry put a small box on Earl's desk. The box contained a light bulb and an electromechanical event counter, a device that looks like an odometer in a car. Gerry told Earl he could earn candies and pennies by paying attention to his schoolwork. Here was the rule: At the end of each 10-second period, if Earl had paid attention to his work for the whole time, the light would flash and the counter would click another count. Then, at the end of each session, Earl would get as many M&Ms

---

[16]Of course, sometimes a few words can be as effective as a lot of action—for example, when someone shouts, "Fire!" And sometimes we behavior modifiers use action when a few words would obviously be the intervention of choice. But most often, in traditional talk psychotherapy, for example, people make the mistake of trying to get rid of problem behaviors simply by discussing them when action is called for—when a change in the contingencies of reinforcement and punishment is called for.

or pennies as the counter had counted—in other words, one reinforcer for every 10 seconds of work. Each daily session lasted from 5 to 30 minutes, so Earl could end the day a wealthy or a full 9-year-old, and better educated, too.

Concurrent Performance-Management Contingency

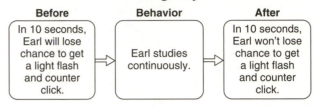

The flash and click had become learned reinforcers because of the verbal analog pairing procedure with the delayed presentation of the M&Ms and pennies—Gerry had verbally paired them by telling Earl about the end-of-session exchange.

1. What kind of contingency was this concurrent performance-management contingency?
   a. reinforcement
   b. penalty
   c. avoidance of the loss of a reinforcer
   d. punishment by the prevention of the presentation of a reinforcer

By the way, this is an example of **continuous-response** avoidance. Earl had to keep studying continuously to avoid the loss of the reinforcers, just as Sid, in Chapter 15, had to maintain an erect posture continuously to avoid the sound of the aversive click.

And what about the other kids? Wouldn't they get jealous of Earl's special privileges? Our experience suggests not. They understand, as well as we do, that a kid like Earl needs special help. They seemed happy to see Earl get that help, especially if that kept him off their backs. But Gerry Patterson took no chances; he brought the classmates into the game, too. He told them they would get a share of Earl's new wealth, and the less they bugged him, the more of that wealth he'd have to share. One result of this teamwork was that at the end of each session Earl's classmates would break into applause when the teacher announced Earl's daily score. And they often walked by his desk to check his score and send some social approval his way, no doubt reinforcing his studying.

Before the intervention, Earl had been spending 25% of his time disrupting the class; but by the end of Gerry's help, Earl was down to less than 5%—about average for the normal kid. In fact, during one 2-hour session, he was the most studious student in the class. He was also less unruly and destructive on the playground, actually playing with the others, rather than tormenting them. Within 4 months, Earl had friends visiting him at home for the first time in his life. And he was making progress in his remedial reading program.

This study impresses us. It shows how you can get almost any behavior under control if you do what it takes. The problem is, most people don't do what it takes. Most people settle for pinning a label on a kid so they can write him off. The label they pinned on Earl was "hyperactive," which, roughly translated, means "a person who horses around so much they're a pain in the rear." Fortunately some behavior analysts like Gerry are so dedicated to helping people they do go to the extreme of delivering a reinforcer every 10 seconds, if it takes that to save a kid.

QUESTION

1. Using the concept of concurrent contingencies for physically incompatible responses, describe a behavioral approach to decrease hyperactivity.
   a. Diagram one of the inappropriate natural contingencies.
   b. Diagram the concurrent performance-management avoidance contingency. (Hint: remember that the outcome is not avoidance of the loss of M&M's and pennies; it's something more immediate.)

Concept
DIFFERENTIAL REINFORCEMENT OF INCOMPATIBLE BEHAVIOR

Analysis

Let's look again at "hyperactive" Earl. Reinforcement contingencies were concurrently available for two physically incompatible response classes. The first class of responses was the disruptive responses; commotion and attention reinforced those responses. The second class of responses was studying; social approval, the flash of light, and click of the counter reinforced those responses. (The actual candy and coins probably came too late to reinforce that class of responses; the same with the applause after the teacher announced Earl's daily score.)

The procedure Gerry Patterson used is called **differential reinforcement of incompatible behavior (DRI).**

To decrease Earl's disruptive behavior, Gerry used avoidance of the loss of a reinforcer to reinforce a behavior physically incompatible with disruptive behavior—he reinforced continuous studying. The two classes of behavior were physically incompatible in that it was more or less impossible for Earl to study continuously and disrupt at the same time. Gerry reinforced continuous studying with a contingency involving avoidance of the loss of a reinforcer. This contingency was more reinforcing than the contingencies reinforcing disruption. So, as the duration of the incompatible behavior (studying) increased, the frequency of the undesirable behavior decreased.

Definition: Concept
Differential reinforcement of incompatible behavior (DRI)
- Reinforcement is contingent on a behavior that is
- incompatible with another behavior.

Notice that Gerry didn't select just any old incompatible behavior. He selected incompatible behavior of value. So not only did he decrease Earl's disrupting; he also increased Earl's studying. Gerry got a two-fer-one.

By the way, we also can look at some other concurrent contingency interventions as involving differential reinforcement of incompatible behavior. For example, Jimmy's self-stimulation was generally physically incompatible with his normal play. So the natural, built-in reinforcement contingencies for his self-stimulation were differentially reinforcing behavior incompatible with his normal play. In other words, differential reinforcement of incompatible behavior does not always require that a performance-management contingency of a professional behavior analyst be involved; sometimes the everyday environment differentially reinforces behavior (self-stimulation) incompatible with other behavior (normal playing).

QUESTION

1. *Differential reinforcement of incompatible behavior—*
   a. Define it.
   b. Diagram the performance-management contingency and one inappropriate contingency

showing its use to decrease disruptive behavior (hyperactivity).

Compare and Contrast
DIFFERENTIAL REINFORCEMENT OF INCOMPATIBLE BEHAVIOR VS. DIFFERENTIAL REINFORCEMENT OF ALTERNATIVE BEHAVIOR

Inappropriate Natural Contingency

Gerry didn't do a functional analysis to determine the reinforcers maintaining Earl's disruptive behavior; so, in the diagrams of the preceding section, we filled in the gap with a few plausible guesses such as auditory, visual, and social reinforcers. But let's consider another possibility: Suppose all that disruptive behavior was maintained by teacher attention—that is, every time Earl disrupted, the teacher scolded him. No doubt the teacher would have assumed that the scolding was aversive and that scolding disruption was a punishment contingency, but often any form of attention in the classroom seems to be the reinforcer maintaining the disruptive behavior.

Performance-Management Contingency

Now let's look at a hypothetical alternative (not what Gerry actually did). Suppose the teacher had paid a little attention to Earl with a pat on the shoulder or a "good boy" whenever he studied for 10 seconds. The teacher would be using more or less the same reinforcer—attention—that had reinforced Earl's disruptions, except now the attention would be reinforcing a more appropriate, alternative behavior—studying. This is a special form of differential reinforcement of incompatible behavior called *differential reinforcement of alternative behavior (DRA)—the replacement of an inappropriate response with a specific appropriate response that produces the same reinforcing outcome* (Chapter 3).

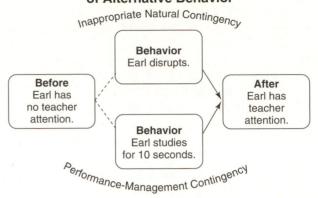

Differential Reinforcement of Alternative Behavior

Studying is incompatible with disrupting, just as was shown in the previous section, except now it produces the same reinforcer as we assumed disruption received. Differential reinforcement of alternative behavior will work best if we are actually extinguishing the inappropriate behavior at the same time—in this case, if the teacher stops paying attention to Earl's disruptions. Of course, then we would no longer have concurrent contingencies.

So DRA and DRI are comparable in that they may both involve concurrent contingencies for physically incompatible responses. They contrast in that DRA is a special type of DRI, in which the reinforcer for the incompatible responses is the same; normally, in DRI, the reinforcers for the incompatible responses are different.

(Remember: Gerry actually used the DRI avoidance contingency we diagrammed in an earlier section, not this DRA reinforcement contingency we diagrammed in this section.)

QUESTION

1. Use a pair of similar examples to compare and contrast DRA and DRI.

BASIC ENRICHMENT

Controversy
SYMPTOM SUBSTITUTION

Sid's Seminar

Tom: You behavior analysts have one big problem: You always treat the symptom; you don't treat the underlying mental illness. You always treat

the sign of the problem, not the underlying problem itself.

Joe: The old medical model. Here we go again.

Tom: You can call it the medical model if you want, but your superficial behavioral approach often fails. You treat only the symptom, not the underlying mental illness. And sure enough, another symptom crops up. The new symptom of the mental illness takes the place of the old one you've gotten rid of.

Sid: Interesting issue. But I also think you're talking from the point of view of the medical model. How did we define it?

Max: The medical model is a view of human behavior that the behavior is a mere symptom of an underlying psychological condition.

Joe: The amazing Max—word for word from Chapter 1—and he didn't even peek at his book.

Eve: When behavior is a problem, the medical model suggests that the underlying condition is an illness or a disease. The problem behavior is just a symptom that reflects the underlying mental illness.

Tom: Right. And you should treat the disease, not the symptom. You shouldn't just get rid of a particular problem behavior. If you do, the disease will substitute another one in its place. It's like treating a sick person's temperature and thinking you've cured the person.

Definition: Erroneous Principle

Symptom substitution

○ Problem behaviors are symptoms of an underlying mental illness.
○ So if you get rid of one problem behavior ("symptom"),
○ another will take its place,
○ until you get rid of the underlying mental illness.

Sid: I think there are two questions here:

○ Does it ever happen that when you get rid of one problem behavior, another takes its place?
○ And if so, what does that say about the behavioral approach to psychology?

Tom: It does happen, and that says the behavioral approach is too superficial.

Joe: What's bringing on this latest attack of myopic mentalism?

Tom: I'll tell you what. Max and Sue have been doing their practicum with Dr. Mae Robinson. And they've been working with an autistic kid, Jimmy, who's into self-stimulation. They finally got rid of one form of self-stimulation, and now Jimmy just substituted another one.

Sid: A good example of the problem.

Tom: A perfect example. As soon as they suppressed one form of self-stimulation, another

form substituted for it. The behavioral approach neglected the underlying mental illness.

Sue: I think just the opposite. I think a behavioral interpretation of those results makes more sense. I like the interpretation in terms of concurrent schedules of reinforcement for competing behaviors. Sensory stimuli reinforce behavior. So we suppress one behavior that produces one sensory reinforcer. And that leaves the field open for another, less powerful sensory reinforcer to reinforce another behavior.

Joe: Like, if one movie is full, you go to your second-choice movie. But you wouldn't call it symptom substitution. And you wouldn't suggest it reflects an underlying mental illness.

Sue: The same thing applies to self-stimulation. It isn't a symptom of an underlying illness. It's just the behavior that normally occurs when no other stronger contingencies concurrently reinforce competing behavior.

Max: Besides, they did manage to suppress all the various self-stimulatory behaviors, with their accompanying sensory reinforcers. And then another concurrent reinforcement contingency took over, the contingency supporting what we consider normal, healthy play. First you added a concurrent punishment contingency to the natural contingency reinforcing his ear hitting.[17]

Inappropriate Natural Contingency

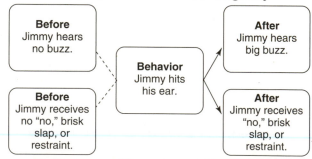

Performance-Management Contingency

Max: And Jimmy stopped hitting his ear. Then you added the concurrent punishment contingency to the natural contingency reinforcing eye pressing.

---

[17]These contingencies are just slightly different ways of diagramming the comparable one for Jimmy early in this chapter.

Inappropriate Natural Contingency

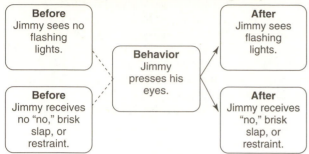

Performance-Management Contingency

Max: And Jimmy stopped pressing his eyes. Then the appropriate natural reinforcement contingencies for normal play could take over.

Appropriate Natural Contingency

Max: The results were that Jimmy started playing normally.

Sue: So why do mentalists make such a big deal out of symptom substitution?

Sid: I think mentalists are not so much concerned with the practical issue of the success of any particular behavioral intervention. Instead, I think they're concerned with a theoretical issue. They're trying to disprove behaviorism. They're offering symptom substitution as proof that behavior is caused by some underlying mental condition and not the environmental contingencies of reinforcement and punishment—the bread and butter of behavior analysis.

Tom: Are you saying symptom substitution doesn't exist?

Sid: Yes, "symptom substitution" does not exist. I agree that if you get rid of one problem, another one sometimes makes an appearance. But most behavior analysts would think it's a mistake to call that symptom substitution. We think the occurrence of the new behavior does not prove that the two behaviors are symptoms of anything, especially an underlying mental illness. They're just behaviors under the control of concurrent contingencies of reinforcement and punishment. I think that's the most straightforward analysis.

Joe: In other words, though the authors of our book are including symptom substitution as a technical concept, they're not suggesting it is a behavioral concept, nor is it an explanation they support. It's an erroneous concept.

Max: Let me add a postscript to this debate. You guys are always making fun of me because I read ahead in the book. But at least I also read the current chapter, and it's not clear to me that any of you have. Remember the section called "Play versus Self-Stimulation"? It points out that when we got rid of Jimmy's dysfunctional self-stimulation, he increased his frequency of "normal" play. Now surely you wouldn't call that symptom substitution!

Eve: Let me add a postscript, too. We should keep in mind that two contingencies may be concurrently present, though one contingency is not making contact with the behavior at the moment because the behavior isn't occurring. That also means that contingency is not visible at that moment. For example, Jimmy's play contingencies were present, though he wasn't playing. If he had started playing, their presence would have just been more apparent, that's all.

Sid: But as the authors said in Chapter 1, "This doesn't mean behavioral problems don't sometimes result from underlying biological problems—for example, brain injury or Down's syndrome." But we don't want to be like those traditional psychologists who misuse the medical model by inventing underlying mental illness as causes of observable problem behavior.

One of my students pointed out that functional assessment deals very well with the problem of symptom substitution. Using functional assessment, the behavior analyst can get a good idea of the reinforcement contingency maintaining the dysfunctional behavior. That contingency is often an escape contingency where the dysfunctional behavior (e.g., a tantrum or aggression) escapes an aversively demanding task, like some discrete-trial-training tasks; or else it's a social-reinforcement contingency, where the dysfunctional behavior gets attention from others.

And rather than using a punishment contingency to suppress the dysfunctional behavior, as was done with Jimmy, nowadays, behavior analysts are more likely to extinguish the dysfunctional behavior and differentially reinforce more appropriate alternative behavior. For example, they would establish a more appropriate response that would allow the child to escape the aversively difficult task; and they would probably also modify the task so that it produced a higher frequency of reinforcement for on-task behavior.

Two Views of One Behavior Automatically Replacing Another

Questions	Mentalistic Medical Model	Behavior Analysis
Does one problem behavior replace another?	Always	Sometimes
Does appropriate behavior replace problem behavior?	No comment	Sometimes
What causes behavior replacement?	An underlying mental illness	Concurrent contingencies of reinforcement
What's the implication?	Behavior analysis is too superficial	Keep working until you've dealt with each of the concurrent contingencies

In Jimmy's case, presumably a functional assessment would show that the dysfunctional behavior was automatically reinforced by stimuli it produced. So the behavior analysts might extinguish the self-stimulating behavior (blocking the initiation of that behavior, by preventing Jimmy from completing the movements that would produce the stimulation). At the same time, they might differentially reinforce incompatible behaviors with reinforcers that would be more powerful than the self-stimulation.

QUESTIONS

1. *Symptom substitution*—define it and give a presumed example.
2. What is a behavioral analysis of this example, in terms of concurrent contingencies? Diagram the contingencies.
3. What theoretical implications does the behavioral analysis have for the debate between the mentalistic medical model and a behavioral approach?
   Hint: Student, know thy tables.

INTERMEDIATE ENRICHMENT

Example
CONCURRENT CONTINGENCIES: ASLEEP AT THE KEYBOARD

Twelve A.M. For the last 5 hours Sid had been at his computer—doing what? Writing his dissertation? No, that's what he was supposed to do. Instead, he was having a computer orgy, a computer pig-out, an activity he found to be a bigger reinforcer than almost anything else, telecommunicating on the BBB, the Behavior Bulletin Board.

At that moment, he was chatting via computer-typed messages with 15 other behavior analyst computer degenerates from as far north as Victoria, British Columbia, as far South as Caracas, Venezuela, and as far east as Tokyo, Japan. They were debating whether sleeping was behavior and whether the principle of reinforcement applied to it.

Sid's chin gradually sunk to his chest. Then his head jerked at the sound of a beep from his computer. He opened his eyes and looked at the computer screen. The little finger on his left hand had written "zzzzzzzzzzzzzz." Beneath his message was a message from a friend at Ohio State University that read, "Sid, your 'zzzzz's' in response to my message are in poor taste."

"Just kidding," he typed back, lying through his fingers. Eyes closed. Chin moved slowly down. Then a quick shake of the head and the eyes opened. Sid loved these debates with his buddies, and he didn't want to miss a thing. But now the messages were flying across his screen so fast he couldn't have kept up even if he'd been fully awake. Still he hung in.

2:20 A.M. And still struggling.
2:21 A.M. Down for the count, slouched in his chair.
2:31 A.M. The computer vainly emitted a warning beep and then disconnected automatically after 10 minutes of no responses from Sid. Otherwise, his phone bill would have cost more than his IBM clone did.
7:10 A.M. A kiss on the lips, a hand through the hair, and a voice in the ear: "Poor Sid, you must have worked all night on your dissertation. Here you are asleep at your computer. But you've got an 8:00 A.M. appointment."

8:06 A.M. Sid rushed into the psych building, Skinner Hall.

Analysis

Question

What's the difference between closing your eyes (a step toward going to sleep) when writing a dissertation and closing your eyes when chatting with the gang?

Answer

Two hours. When he was chatting, Sid made his final go-to-sleep eye-close response at 2:21; but when he was writing his dissertation, he made that response at 12:21. Why?

Well, we can look at these episodes as concurrent contingencies of reinforcement for physically incompatible responses or as incompatible contingencies on the same response.

Concurrent Contingencies of Reinforcement for Physically Incompatible Responses

In writing the dissertation, several concurrent contingencies might have been available. As Sid progressed in his writing, the reinforcers of intellectual stimulation and success might have reinforced this writing. Also, as he progressed, a slight reduction in the fear of failing to graduate might have reinforced his writing. But at the same time, the intellectual effort involved might have punished that writing.

Also, at the same time, escape from the aversiveness of being sleepy reinforced his closing his eyes. And, try as he might, Sid could not both sleep and write at the same time. So by the time the clock in the lower-right-hand corner of his computer screen read 12:21 A.M., sleep had won the night—a triumph for reinforcement of an incompatible response by escape from the increasingly aversive condition of sleepiness.

The contingency (or set of contingencies) that reinforced Sid's computer chatting with his friends was more powerful than those that had supported writing. So chatting held out a little longer than writing had against the the escape contingency that reinforced his closing his eyes.

Incompatible Behaviors

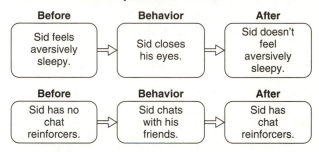

Incompatible Concurrent Contingencies for the Same Response

Now let's consider a different and equally valid way of looking at Sid's reality. Instead of looking at the incompatible writing behavior, we look at the effect the loss of the writing reinforcers will have on Sid's eye closing.

And looking at the penalty contingency for going to sleep while chatting we have the loss of the chat reinforcers.

Incompatible Contingencies

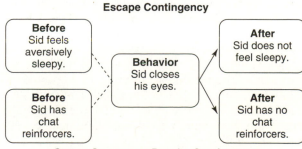

Incompatible Behaviors

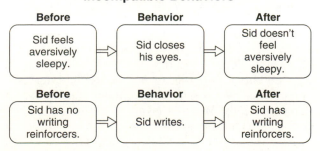

With international computer chatting, the chatting maintained longer—a limited triumph for a more favorable balance of concurrent escape and penalty contingencies that affected working at the computer. The social, intellectual, and other reinforcers contingent on the computer chat may have been especially powerful; and the intellectual effort of chatting may have been fairly mild. So it wasn't until the digits on the screen flashed 2:21 A.M. that sleep won the night. Yes, the escape contingencies for going to sleep always triumph in the end.

Incidentally, in the earlier chapters on punishment, penalty, and punishment by prevention, we pointed out that there was often a reinforcement contingency maintaining the behavior that was being punished. These combinations of punishment and reinforcement contingencies would also be examples of incompatible concurrent contingencies for the same response.

QUESTION

1. In terms of concurrent contingencies of reinforcement and escape for physically incompatible responses, diagram the problem of staying awake when you're working vs. when you're playing (e.g., chatting with friends vs. doing academic writing).
2. Do the same thing in terms of incompatible concurrent escape and penalty contingencies.

Research Methods
INTERVENTION (TREATMENT) PACKAGE

Basic Science

Much of basic science consists of analysis. In fact, our approach to the study of behavior is even called behavior analysis. What does *analysis* mean? An examination of the parts to find their essential features. In science, *analysis* often means an examination of the various variables to determine (find out) which are the independent variables (which factors cause the results we're getting). As we've seen, experimental analysis involves careful experimental designs in which we hold all potential independent variables constant to measure the extent a single independent variable affects our dependent variables. If we try to vary more than one independent variable at the same time, we risk confounding one variable with another.

Behavioral Engineering

However, remember Juke and Mae's use of Ken Bauman's intervention to reduce the hassle of dining out with kids? Neither they nor Ken Bauman did any analysis to determine the crucial independent variables. Instead, they threw in everything but the kitchen Cuisinart to get the two nephews to behave. They varied at least seven independent variables at the same time: (1) Juke gave them the rules of gentlemanly conduct. (2) He said, "I'll be real proud of you guys if you act like little gentlemen." (3) He sat them next to the wall. (4) He sat them on separate sides of the table. (5) He removed their silverware until the dinner arrived. (6) During the wait for the meal, he gave each of them a favorite cracker when they were being gentlemanly. (7) He gave them each a few small toys to play with.

Does this mean Juke and Mae and Ken are poor scientists? No. They weren't trying to do science. They weren't trying to determine which of their various independent variables kept the kids from climbing the walls. They didn't have time for that sort of analysis (it wasn't economical). Juke and Mae were *engineering*. They were trying to engineer (achieve) a specific result—cool kids. To do this they changed several independent variables at once. In other words, they used what behavior analysts often call a *treatment package* (we prefer intervention package, to avoid implying the medical model).

Usually when we're doing behavioral engineering in applied settings, we're hired to achieve specific results, not to do scientific analyses. To do a detailed, scientific analysis of the independent variables might cost too much in terms of time and money. In those cases it's often more economical simply to use an intervention package.

However, sometimes, it might be more economical to evaluate the effects of each individual independent variable, rather than to combine them all in one intervention package. For example, **we might want to evaluate the individual effects of some independent variables if their use was expensive and we anticipate repeated future use.** Suppose, in addition to the seven independent variables we've already listed in Bauman's intervention package, an eighth independent variable involved a computerized monitoring and feedback system that cost $200 per hour to use. You can be darned sure it would be economically wise to evaluate that component independently. But sitting the two kids on the opposite sides of the table doesn't cost that much.

Of course, whether or not we use an intervention package, we still have to evaluate our intervention empirically. We still have to determine if we've gotten the results we want.

TECHNOLOGY DEVELOPMENT

What about Bauman and his crew? Were they doing basic science or engineering? Probably something in between. They were *developing technology*. They were developing and empirically demonstrating behavioral technology effective in achieving desired results. Their goal was not to do a behavioral analysis of each individual independent variable involved in that technology. Again, we might want to evaluate only the individual effects of some independent variables if their use was expensive and we anticipated repeated future use.

Definition: Concept

Intervention (treatment) package

- The addition or change of several independent variables
- at the same time
- to achieve a desired result,
- without testing the effect of each variable.

When Should We Use Intervention Packages?	
Basic Science	Never or rarely; we don't want to risk confounding our independent variables.
Technology Development	Sometimes we just evaluate an intervention package, when the components may not be worth analyzing individually. But, if some components are expensive and will be used repeatedly, then we need to evaluate them individually.
Engineering	Usually we use an intervention package because we just need to get good results and can't afford to evaluate each component, unless some of those components are expensive and will be used repeatedly.

QUESTIONS

1. *Intervention (treatment) package*—define it and give an example.
2. Discuss the use of intervention packages from the point of view of
   a. basic science
   b. technology development
   c. engineering
   d. the economics of intervening.

3. For which of the following is an intervention (treatment) package usually **least** appropriate?
   a. basic science
   b. technology development
   c. engineering
4. If some components of an intervention were expensive and you would be using them repeatedly, then you should combine them as a treatment package rather than testing each component independently.
   a. true
   b. false

In the Skinner Box
Experimental Analysis of Behavior
CONCURRENT CONTINGENCIES AND THE MATCHING LAW

Basic researchers often use concurrent schedules of reinforcement to study various preferences. They usually use two concurrent variable-interval schedules of reinforcement for physically incompatible responses (for example, a 1-minute variable interval for the pigeon's pecking the left key and another 1-minute variable interval for the pigeon's pecking the right key).

Most often, researchers have used the same reinforcer (some particular mixture of "birdseed") for both schedules. With such concurrent schedules of variable-interval reinforcement, these researchers have studied a number of factors affecting preference for pecking, say, the left key over the right key. For example, they might adjust the variable-interval schedule so that the rate of reinforcement is more frequent on the left key. Or they might increase the amount of reinforcer, or the delay from the key peck to the actual delivery of the reinforcer. Sometimes they will even pair a small, immediate reinforcer in one schedule with a delayed, but larger, reinforcer in the other schedule.

But these researchers haven't always used the same reinforcers for both schedules; they've also used concurrent variable-interval schedules to study the preference for different types of reinforcers. For example, using pigeons, Dr. Harold Miller compared the quality of three different reinforcers—wheat, hemp, and buckwheat.[18]

Why are so many experimenters interested in this sort of research? Because this research seems to be helping behavior analysis become a precise,

---

[18]Miller, H. L. (1976). Matching-based hedonic scaling in the pigeon. *Journal of the Experimental Analysis of Behavior, 26,* 335–347.

quantitative science, in which scientists can use mathematical equations to describe the behavior of nonhumans and humans.

Perhaps the most common equation used to describe these data is Dr. Richard Herrnstein's *matching law*.[19] One version of Herrnstein's matching law says that the relative frequency of responding on two concurrent schedules of reinforcement equals (matches) the relative frequency of reinforcers on those two schedules.[20]

$$\frac{\text{\# left-key pecks}}{\text{\# total key pecks}} = \frac{\text{\# left-key reinforcers}}{\text{\# total reinforcers}}$$

or % of left-key pecks = % of reinforcers.

Suppose, during a 1-hour experimental session, left-key pecks produced 60 reinforcers (VI 60″) and right-key pecks produced 30 reinforcers (VI 120″). Then the percentage of left-key reinforcers would be

$$\frac{60}{60 + 30} = 66\%$$

and that means 66% of the total key pecks would be left-key pecks.

So if 66% of the value is obtained for pecking the left key, then the bird will make 66% of its pecks on that key. (When we talk about value, we mean such aspects of the reinforcer as its rate, amount, delay, and quality.

```
Definition: Principle
Matching law
  ○ The relative frequency of responding
  ○ on two concurrent schedules of reinforce-
    ment
  ○ equals the relative value of reinforcement
  ○ on those two schedules.[21]
```

This matching law does two things: It allows scientists to describe precisely data produced by a single set of concurrent contingencies; and it allows them to predict behavior under novel sets of concurrent contingencies. For example, with his pigeons, Miller did this experiment: First he ran one pair of concurrent schedules where **wheat** was the reinforcer for pecking one key and **buckwheat** was the reinforcer for the other. He ran his pigeons on these schedules until they produced stable rates of responding to both keys. Then he changed the procedure by running a different pair of concurrent schedules; here he kept **buckwheat** as one of the reinforcers but replaced wheat with **hemp** for the other. Again, he ran his pigeons on this new arrangement until their responding "preferences between the two keys" stabilized. Finally, he brought back the **wheat** reinforcer from the first contingency and kept the **hemp** reinforcer from the second contingency. And on the basis of their preference for **wheat** vs. **buckwheat** and their preference for **hemp** vs. **buckwheat,** he could use the matching law to precisely predict their preference for **wheat** vs. **hemp.** Not a bad trick.

Here's another impressive trick. Herrnstein even figured out how to use his matching law to make precise, quantitative predictions of responding when he used only a single schedule.[22] In other words, the equation he originally developed for concurrent schedules turned out to work for single schedules as well! (But that's a complex story; check out the reference if you want more details.)[23]

QUESTION

1. State the matching law and describe a situation to which it can be applied.

[19]Herrnstein, R. J. (1961). Relative and absolute strength of response as a function of frequency of reinforcement. *Journal of the Experimental Analysis of Behavior, 4,* 267–272.

[20]Baum, W. M., & Rachlin, H. C. (1969). Choice as time allocation. *Journal of the Experimental Analysis of Behavior, 12,* 861–874.

[21]For information about the theories and related research behind the matching law, see Mazur J. E. (1998). *Learning and Behavior* (4th ed.). Upper Saddle River, NJ: Prentice Hall.

[22]Herrnstein, R. J. (1970). On the law of effect. *Journal of the Experimental Analysis of Behavior, 13,* 243–266.

[23]In Chapter 5, we introduced the law of effect—the effects of our actions determine whether we will repeat them. The matching law is a special case of the law of effect where the effect of one contingency is influenced by concurrent competing contingencies.

20 Behavioral Chains and Rate Contingencies

FUNDAMENTALS

BEHAVIORAL CHAINS

Example
Behavioral Medicine
NANCY, A CHILD
WITH CEREBRAL PALSY[1]

Nancy was a 5-year-old charmer, with long, blonde hair and blue eyes. She was wearing a blue dress edged with white lace at the collar, wrists, and hem, white tights, and black patent-leather shoes. She was the sort of child who made you wish you had your camera as she ran across the neat, green lawn, laughing and blowing bubbles in the air. She was the sort of child whom you'd hope to find standing next to a white picket fence lined with tulips, a white country cottage in the background, the sun of a balmy May afternoon brightening the scene.

But she had never run across any lawn, and she had never stood next to any white picket fence. In fact, in her 5 years of life, she had never run or even stood. And somehow her cute-as-a-button blue-and-white outfit wasn't right. Everything was slightly out of kilter, and her white leotards were dirty.

Nancy had cerebral palsy, and her physician said she would never walk, in spite of her surgery. But he had recommended that Dr. Dawn Baker look at the child, just in case behavior analysis had

[1]Based on O'Neil, S. (1972). The application and methodological implications of behavior modification in nursing research. In M. Batey (Ed.). *Communicating nursing research: The many sources of nursing knowledge.* Boulder, CO: WICHE.

something to offer her. So Dawn did look at Nancy. And she saw the legs frail from lack of use, hidden in the dirty white leotards. She saw Nancy as the child scooted across the floor when her mother called her to come and meet the psychologist. Dawn hid her sadness at this sight with a smile and a caress of Nancy's cheek. And Dawn desperately hoped behavior analysis did have something to offer the child.

Intervention

Remember when Sid started working with Bobbie? The first thing he did was a task analysis—an analysis of the components of masculine behavior. And the first thing Dawn did was a task analysis—an analysis of the components of walking. First, Nancy had to rise to her knees. Then she had to rise to her feet. And finally she had to walk with a crutch. These were the main components of the chain of behaviors Nancy would have to perform.

We call such a sequence of responses a *behavioral chain* (some call it a **stimulus-response chain**). Nancy starts by sitting on the floor, and that position is an S^D in the presence of which making the response of rising to her knees will be reinforced by success. Being on her knees is an S^D in the presence of which making the response of rising to her feet will be reinforced by success. And finally standing is an S^D in the presence of which making the response of walking with a crutch will be reinforced.

Although a baseline evaluation showed that Nancy had never stood or walked, she did rise to her knees from time to time. So Dawn began her shaping procedure by reinforcing Nancy's rising to her

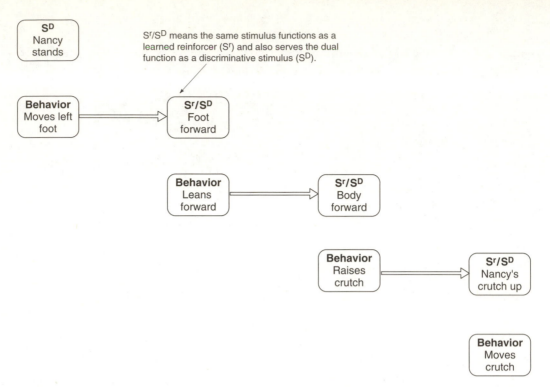

knees. On all such occasions, Dawn gave Nancy lavish praise, an occasional spoonful of ice cream, or a chance to play marbles for a few minutes.

After Nancy was reliably rising to her knees, Dawn gave her the ice-cream reinforcer only when she pulled herself to her feet while holding onto a cabinet. Then Dawn raised the criterion again: Nancy had to rise to her knees, pull herself to her feet, and then walk a few steps holding onto the cabinet, before she got the ice cream.

Next, Dawn replaced the cabinet with a harness that she held to give Nancy support while she walked. Gradually, Dawn reduced the support she gave Nancy and at the same time she required her to walk farther and farther before getting the ice-cream reinforcer.

At one point, Nancy was walking while only holding onto Dawn's index finger. Then it was a 12-inch stick with Nancy on one end and Dawn on the other. Next, two wooden handles connected by a spring. Then Nancy was walking with a crutch that Dawn helped to move. Eventually Nancy earned her ice cream and marbles by walking across the room with no help from Dawn.

Now the little girl who would never walk was walking!

But that wasn't enough. Dawn had to reduce the added reinforcers. First, she stopped using the ice cream and marbles. Then she reduced the frequency of her praise. Finally, the normal reinforcers that reinforce our walking were maintaining Nancy's walking—the reinforcers that normally result from getting where we want to go. But because walking

took so much more effort for Nancy than for us, Dawn asked her parents to give some social reinforcement now and then.

Also, Nancy's parents had to extinguish completely Nancy's well-established response of scooting across the floor; they had to make sure she got the normal physical and social reinforcers she was going for only if she walked toward them, not if she scooted. In other words, they had to make sure that they and the environment differentially reinforced walking and not scooting.

How long did it take Dawn to train the behavioral chain of Nancy's rising to her knees, then to her feet, and to walk with a crutch? One week? Two weeks? No, 60 weeks with four 30-minute sessions per week—a total of 240 sessions. Of course, if Dawn were to do it again, she'd be able to reduce the time; but it would always be a big deal. It was hard work, but if Dawn and the others who developed these techniques hadn't done the hard work, Nancy would never have been able to walk.

If you are going to accomplish much of significance, you have to be passionate. You have to be passionate about improving the well being of humanity, you have to be passionate about helping people, you have to be passionate about saving the world with behavior analysis. You have to be passionately dedicated and have an almost unreasonable amount of faith in behavior analysis, if you're going to work with a little girl like Nancy for 60 weeks so that she can walk and lead a life with greater happiness and dignity. Slackers need not apply.

QUESTION

1. Diagram a behavioral intervention to teach a child with cerebral palsy to walk.

Concept
BEHAVIORAL CHAINS

So far, we've seen one behavioral chain—Nancy's rising to her knees, then to her feet, and finally walking. We could analyze her walking into a more detailed chain, as Dawn, in fact, had to do. Walking is so easy and natural for us, we ignore that it's really a complex behavioral chain, especially if you add a crutch. Here we go: left foot forward, lean forward, raise crutch, move crutch forward, put crutch down, right foot forward, straighten up, right foot down— and then you start the whole behavioral chain again, each separate response putting you in a new position that acts as an S^D for the next response.

Our life is full of behavioral chains: The sight of mashed potatoes on our plate is followed by our picking up the fork (operandum). The fork in our hand allows us to put it into the potatoes. The fork in the potatoes is an S^D for raising the fork. The raised, potato-laden fork is an S^D for putting the fork in our mouth, and so on. We close our mouth,

pull the fork out, chew the potatoes, swallow them, and get our fork ready for the next round—each response producing a stimulus and followed by the next response.

> *Definition Concept*
> **Behavioral chain**
> ○ A sequence of stimuli and responses.
> ○ Each response produces a change in the environment that
> ○ acts as a discriminative stimulus
> ○ or operandum
> ○ for the next response.

Traditionally, we think of a response within a chain as producing an outcome that is a reinforcer for that response and an S^D for the next response. But what about the standard Skinner-box behavioral chain? Rudolph touches a dot on the wall with his nose. The outcome of that response is a chain is lowered into the Skinner box. Rudolph pulls the chain. The outcome of the chain pull is that a light is turned on and Rudolph presses the lever. The outcome is a drop of water. Now, at first glance, we might think that the chain being lowered into the Skinner box is an S^D, but it isn't. The chain is an operandum like

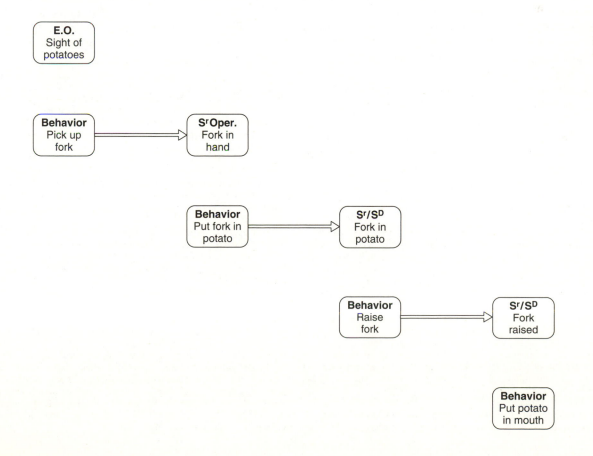

the lever in the Skinner box. The chain isn't the opportunity for a response to be reinforced (the S^D); it's the opportunity for the response to be made (the operandum); Rudolph can't pull the chain if it ain't there.[2]

In the same way, the fork in our hand may be more of an operandum, like Rudolph's lever, than an S^D. We must have the fork in our hand before we can put it in the potatoes.

QUESTION

1. Behavioral *chain*—define it and diagram a dining-table example.

Principle
DUAL-FUNCTIONING CHAINED STIMULI

As we mentioned, a traditional and useful analysis of behavioral chains is that the stimulus resulting from one response actually serves two functions: It acts as an S^D for the next response, and it acts as a learned reinforcer for the response that produced it. (Of course, the reinforcer at the end of the final link in the chain will often be an unlearned reinforcer and may not serve as an S^D.)

Let's look at our potato-eating example again; this time we'll emphasize the ***dual functioning*** of the stimuli:

○ The sight of the potatoes is a stimulus in the presence of which we pick up our fork.[3]

○ The sight and feel of the fork in hand reinforced picking it up (if you'd tried to pick up the fork and it kept slipping from your hand, trying to pick it up wouldn't be reinforced).

○ But at the same time, the sight and feel of the fork in hand also functions as an S^D in the presence of which moving your hand near the potatoes will be reinforced (moving an empty hand near the potatoes either won't be reinforced or will be a little messier than you might like—we're talking soupy mashed potatoes here, not crisp French fries).

○ The sight and feel of the fork in the potatoes reinforced moving the fork toward the potatoes (if someone kept pulling the potatoes away from you as you approached them, we'd be talking extinction city, not to mention frustration city).

○ At the same time, the forked potatoes is an S^D for raising them to your mouth.

So dining is an example of the concept that the same stimulus in a behavioral chain can function at the same time both as a learned reinforcer and as an S^D. It functions as a learned reinforcer (S^r) for the response that produces it and as an S^D for the next response in the chain.

Definition Principle
Dual-functioning chained stimuli
○ A stimulus in a behavioral chain
○ reinforces the response that precedes it.
○ That stimulus also acts as an S^D or operandum for the response that follows it.[4]

---

provides: *An **establishing operation** is an environmental event, operation, or stimulus condition that affects an organism by momentarily altering (a) the reinforcing effectiveness of other events and (b) the frequency of occurrence of the type of behavior that had been consequated by those other events.* (Michael, J. [1993]. Establishing operations. *The Behavior Analyst, 16,* 191–206.) So what does that have to do with sight of potatoes? The sight of the potatoes is a stimulus that increases the reinforcing effectiveness of having the fork in your hand. In the absence of the sight of the potatoes or some other delicious forkable, having the fork in your hand won't be a reinforcer. QED

Having said all that, of course there is an S^D for picking up the fork, and that's the sight of the fork itself. The sight of the fork is an S^D for the behavior of reaching out and grasping. In the presence of the sight of the fork, reaching out and grasping has a consequence of having the fork in the hand. The S^D does not make the fork in hand reinforcing.

[4]For two reasons, we've stated a separate principle of dual-functioning chained stimuli, rather than place this notion within the definition of the behavioral chain. First, it is logically possible to have a behavioral chain without those stimuli's functioning both as S^Ds or operanda and as reinforcers (for example, all but the last stimulus might function as S^Ds; and the last stimulus might be the reinforcer that keeps the whole chain going with no support from learned reinforcers embedded in the chain). And second, a separate treatment of this notion of duality of function might reduce the confusion students often experience when reading about behavioral chaining.

---

[2]A tip of the hat to Brad Frieswyk for suggesting the inclusion of *operandum* in our definition of *behavioral chain*. He raised this issue in our graduate seminar on the principles of behavior in August 1993.

[3]The analysis of the role of the sight of the potatoes is so complex that we're burying it in this footnote. In *EPB 3.0*, we said the sight of the potatoes was an S^D, in the presence of which picking up the fork would be reinforced. But a student in one of my seminars pointed out that this was too superficial. What's the reinforcer for picking up the fork? As we show in the diagram, the reinforcer is having the fork in your hand. Does that mean if you can't see the potatoes (S^Δ) and you pick up the fork, you won't have it in your hand. Of course not. So, because there's no S^Δ, there's also no S^D.

Then what is the sight of the potatoes, if not an S^D? It's an establishing operation! But to appreciate this we need to look at the more detailed definition of establishing operation that Michael

Your hand on the key in the ignition of your car is an S^D for turning that key. The running of your car's engine reinforces turning the key and also acts as an S^D for putting the car in gear. So your car's starting illustrates the principle of **dual-functioning chained stimuli.**

QUESTION

1. The principle of dual-functioning chained *stimuli*—define it and give an example.

Concept
FORWARD CHAINING

The most obvious way to establish a chain is through *forward chaining.* Dawn did that with Nancy. She started with the first link in the chain—Nancy's ris-

ing to her knees—and established that link. Then she added the next—Nancy's rising to her feet. And finally she added the terminal link—Nancy's walking. Establishing that chain went forward from the initial link to the terminal link. (Check out the following diagram.)

Kurt Mahoney, Keith Wagenen, and Lee Meyerson also used forward chaining in toilet training both normal and mentally handicapped children. First they reinforced the initial response in the behavioral chain: When the child walked to the toilet, the trainer would give her a bite to eat and would clap his hands and say, "Good girl!"—an added reinforcement contingency. Then the trainer added the next link, lowering the pants, which also produced those added reinforcers. After the child had acquired the first two links, the trainer added sitting on or facing the toilet (as appropriate). Then eliminating and, finally, pulling up the pants. This was

Forward Chaining

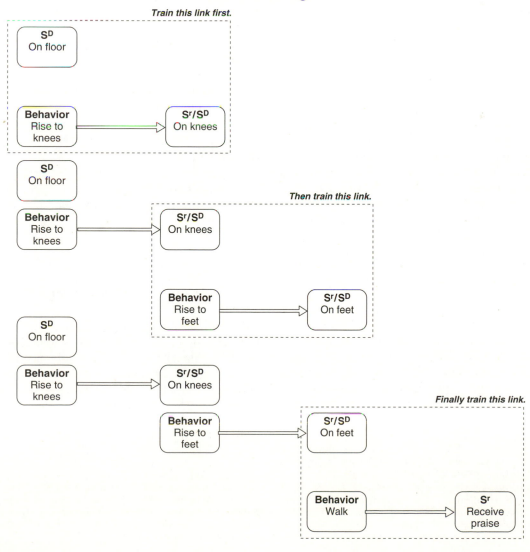

forward chaining because the trainer started with the initial link (walking to the toilet) and progressed link by link to the terminal link (pulling up the pants).[5]

Of course the trainers and parents eventually stopped using the added reinforcement contingencies involving food and praise. Then the chain was on its own. The stimuli resulting from each of the successive responses in the chain served as the reinforcer for the preceding response and the S^D for the next, thus illustrating the principle of dual-functioning chained stimuli. For example, the sight of the toilet reinforced approaching it and acted as an S^D for pulling down the pants. By the way, this behavioral approach to toilet training produced excellent results for both normal and mentally handicapped children.

Definition: Concept
Forward chaining
  ○ The establishment of the first link in a behavioral chain,
  ○ with the addition of successive links,
  ○ until the final link is acquired.

Philip Wilson and his colleagues used forward chaining to help profoundly mentally handicapped clients acquire a repertoire of family-style dining. Their task analysis indicated three major sequences in the chain, with several links of the behavioral chain in each major sequence. For example, the premeal sequence included going to the preparation table, picking up a spoon and a fork, and so on. The meal sequence included grasping the serving bowl with both hands, picking it up, and placing it in the neighbor's hands or within 6 inches of the neighbor's plate. The postmeal sequence included standing up, picking up the plate, and carrying the plate to the preparation table. In total, the chains contained 30 links.[6]

They used forward chaining in this way: They started with the first link in the premeal chain: going to the preparation table. When the client had mastered one link, the trainer added the next one—for example, picking up the spoon and fork.

The trainer used various levels of prompts. The strongest prompt was physical guidance. The next level consisted of a model demonstrating the link in the chain (picking up the spoon and fork). The next level consisted of verbal instructions ("John, pick up the spoon and fork"). Ultimately, the prompts were faded out so that the stimuli arising from the preceding response in the chain functioned as an effective S^D for the next response (the sight of the preparation table that resulted from going to it was an S^D for picking up the spoon and fork). However, when Philip and his colleagues were first establishing the chain, the natural or built-in results of the responses functioned neither as sufficient reinforcers nor as S^Ds. That's why they first had to use the prompts and added reinforcement contingencies.

Praise and small snacks served to reinforce the performance of the various links, as the clients acquired the total behavioral chain. A major sequence of links required an average of thirty 6-minute sessions. So we could expect that it would take about 9 hours of training for a profoundly mentally handicapped client to acquire a repertoire of family-style dining—much work, but worth it, at least in the opinion of the direct-care staff who were responsible for these clients. This is in keeping with the considerable effort being made to help mentally handicapped people live as close to normal as possible.

QUESTION

1. *Forward chaining*—define it and diagram its use to teach walking to a child with cerebral palsy.

Concept
TOTAL-TASK PRESENTATION[7]

Don Horner and Ingo Keilitz used a variation of forward chaining called ***total-task presentation*** to help mentally handicapped adolescents acquire toothbrushing skills. First they did a task analysis of the behavioral chain of tooth-brushing, breaking the chain into 15 components. The chain went from picking up and holding the toothbrush, through wetting the toothbrush, removing the cap from the

---

[5]Based on Mahoney, K., Van Wagenen, K., & Meyerson, L. (1971). Toilet training of normal and retarded children. *Journal of Applied Behavior Analysis, 4,* 173–181.

[6]Based on Wilson, P. G., Reid, D. H., Phillips, J. F., & Burgio, L. D. (1984). Normalization of institutional mealtimes for profoundly retarded persons: Effects and noneffects of teaching family-style dining. *Journal of Applied Behavior Analysis, 17,* 189–201.

[7]Based on Horner, R. D., & Keilitz, I. (1975). Training mentally retarded adolescents to brush their teeth. *Journal of Applied Behavior Analysis, 8,* 301–309; Cooper, J. O., Heron, T. E., & Heward, W. L. (1987). *Applied Behavior Analysis* (pp. 353–353). Columbus, OH: Merrill.

toothpaste tube, to brushing the various surfaces of the teeth, and finally to putting away the equipment.

Unlike the method of forward chaining, with total-task presentation, the learner performed each of the 15 links of the chain before starting over again. In other words, the learner didn't master one link before proceeding to the next. Instead, this procedure was used: The trainer would tell the student to do the response in one of the links. If that didn't work, the trainer would model that response and give verbal instructions. If even that didn't work, the trainer would use physical guidance along with instructions. Then they'd move on to the next link in the tooth-brushing chain. The trainer praised the client each time he or she completed the response in a link of the chain (for example, removed the cap from the tube).

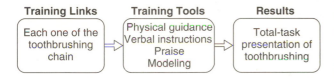

Suppose they start through the behavioral chain and they reach the point where the client must unscrew the cap from the toothpaste tube. Suppose the client isn't able to do this; so the trainer takes the client's hands and guides him through the process of unscrewing the cap until it is completely unscrewed. Then they move on to the next step— putting the toothpaste on the brush. Notice that the client still hasn't mastered the response of unscrewing the cap. He will still need some, though less, guidance the next time they go through the total chain.

Definition: Concept
Total-task presentation
○ The simultaneous training of
○ all links in a behavioral chain.

The clients all acquired the tooth-brushing repertoire, usually within 30 daily sessions. (They went through the behavioral chain once a day.)[8]

---

[8]How does a behavior analyst, teacher, skills trainer determine whether to use total task presentation or some form of behavioral chaining? The lower the skills of the client and the longer the chain, the more likely we'd be to use chaining.

QUESTION

1. *Total-task presentation*—define it and give two examples. Describe:
   ○ the response classes
   ○ the reinforcement contingencies
   ○ the presumed reinforcers
   ○ the results
   ○ any other interesting features of the intervention.

Concept
BACKWARD CHAINING

Backward chaining is the third major way of establishing behavioral chains. Instead of starting by establishing the first link of the chain, then the second, and so on, backward chaining goes in the opposite direction. You establish the last link first, then the next to the last, and so on.

For example, Beth Sulzer-Azaroff and Roy Mayer recommend backward chaining for students having trouble acquiring arithmetic skills. You could use backward chaining in teaching a child to multiply two-digit numbers. First, you do a task analysis of the process of multiplying two numbers. Each response and the resulting number you write down is a link in the chain. For example, you multiply two digits and write down the result or you add two digits and write down the result. You can see this best by looking at a nearly completed problem:[9]

$$
\begin{array}{r}
42 \\
\times\ 23 \\
\hline
126 \\
+\ 840 \\
\hline
??? \\
\end{array}
$$

Here, the final links in the chain are adding 126 + 840 and then writing down 966. Hopefully, students would already have those links in their repertoire by the time they got to multiplication. Then you move backward to the next set of links:

$$
\begin{array}{r}
31 \\
\times\ 24 \\
\hline
124 \\
+\ ??? \\
\hline
??? \\
\end{array}
$$

After the students have successfully gone through a number of problems involving these last two links in the chain, they're ready for problems in-

---

[9]Based on Sulzer-Azaroff, B., & Mayer, G. R. (1986). *Achieving educational excellence* (pp. 244–245). New York: Holt, Rinehart & Winston.

volving the whole behavioral chain, starting with the first link:

$$
\begin{array}{r}
67 \\
\times\ 89 \\
\hline
??? \\
+\ ??? \\
\hline
???
\end{array}
$$

You can see how students could independently acquire the complex behavioral chain of multiplication, using backward chaining. All they'd need would be a few instructions and a few sheets of multiplication problems, the first sheet with problems that are almost completed, the next sheet with less complete problems, until they reach the final sheet, which has nothing but the initial series of multiplication problems.

```
Definition: Concept
Backward chaining
 ○ The establishment of the final link in a be-
   havioral chain,
 ○ with the addition of preceding links
 ○ until the first link is acquired.
```

Example of Backward Chaining
GETTING DRESSED

We don't spend much time thinking about such everyday tasks as how to get dressed unless we must help someone who has not learned how. Suppose you have to teach a mentally handicapped man how to dress himself. What normally seemed so simple and matter-of-fact is now difficult and complex. The act of putting on a pair of trousers now becomes a major undertaking that we can best analyze in terms of a behavioral chain. And we can help the man acquire that repertoire using backward chaining.[10]

In using backward chaining, we would start with the final link and work backwards. This means we would put the trousers on the man and pull them almost all the way up. We might even place his hands on the top of his pants and then provide him with the discriminative stimulus, "Pull up your trousers." We should reinforce this response with either a learned reinforcer, such as praise, or an

---

[10]Based on Breland, M. (1965). Foundation of teaching by positive reinforcement (pp. 127–141); and Caldwell, C. (1965). Teaching in the cottage setting (pp. 159–163). Both in G. J. Bensberg (Ed.). *Teaching the mentally retarded,* Atlanta: Southern Regional Education Board.

unlearned reinforcer, such as candy. This simple response in itself might even require some shaping. We are then ready for the next component in the chain. This consists of leaving the trousers down near the knees and providing the discriminative stimulus, "Pull up your trousers." The next component of the chain may consist of pulling the trousers from just above the ankles, and then going through the standard procedure. Eventually, we can simply place the trousers in front of the man and give the instructions, "Put on your trousers."

Example of Backward Chaining
EATING WITH A SPOON

When Jimmy came to the Rosa Parks Academy he could not feed himself or even grasp or hold a spoon. Here's how Max used backward chaining to help Jimmy learn to eat with a spoon. He started by filling the spoon with applesauce (a highly reinforcing food for Jimmy), placed the spoon in Jimmy's hand, and raised Jimmy's hand to Jimmy's mouth.

After several trials with that physical guidance, Max removed his hand and required Jimmy to complete the rest of the chain by placing the food in his mouth. When this response was established, Max released Jimmy's hand farther away from his mouth. After a few more trials, Max needed only to help Jimmy fill the spoon, and Jimmy soon mastered this final component.

We can establish many behavioral chains of this sort, those that mentally handicapped and autistic people often lack. We would often do this using backward chaining and patience. Efforts from dedicated behavior analysts help such people go through life with more dignity than would otherwise be possible. We can also use backward chaining in training normal children, especially in basic self-care skills.

QUESTION

1. *Backward chaining*—define it and give two examples. Describe
   ○ the response classes
   ○ the reinforcement contingencies
   ○ the presumed reinforcers
   ○ the results
   ○ any other interesting features of the intervention.

RATE CONTINGENCIES

Concept
Behavioral Clinical
DIFFERENTIAL REINFORCEMENT OF LOW RATE[11]

Max soon found that he and Jimmy Lewis weren't out of the woods yet, as far as eating with a spoon was concerned. Once Jimmy had mastered the spoon, he gobbled his food so fast he would finish his meals in 1 to 3 minutes, where it would take most people 15 to 20 minutes. So he made a complete mess of everything, including himself. Jimmy's style of eating was so disgusting, it was still impossible for his parents to take him to eat in restaurants. Also, his rapid eating caused him to vomit after about 15% of his meals.

First, Max searched through *Behavior Modification,* an important journal in our field. There he found an article by Dr. Judith Favell and her colleagues at Western Carolina Center, an institution for mentally handicapped people. Starting with the intervention Judy and her team had designed for a 14-year-old mentally handicapped girl, Max once again analyzed Jimmy's eating as a behavioral chain. This chain involved Jimmy's taking a spoonful of food, moving it toward his mouth, putting it in his mouth, chewing the food, and finally swallowing it.

Often we can either eliminate a chain or control its rate by dealing with the first links. In other words, if we can stop or slow down the first links, then the following links must also be stopped or slowed down. Now Max didn't want to eliminate this chain, but he did want to reduce its rate. So he decided to reduce the rate of the first links in Jimmy's eating chain. He would reduce Jimmy's rate of picking up a spoonful of food and moving it toward his mouth. To do this, Max would use a contingency called *differential reinforcement of low rate* **(DRL).**

What's the reinforcer for Jimmy's moving the food toward his mouth? The reinforcer is probably the opportunity to put the food in his mouth. Therefore Max made that opportunity contingent on a low rate of responding—a low rate of moving the food toward his mouth. That doesn't mean Jimmy had to move his hand slowly. It means he had to wait at least 2 seconds since his last bite before he attempted his next bite. What if Jimmy didn't wait? Max would move Jimmy's spoon hand back to the table and thus prevent the reinforcement of that response. (Recall that Max assumed the reinforcer was the opportunity to put the spoonful of food in his mouth.)

Definition: Concept
Differential reinforcement of low rate (DRL)
- Reinforcement
- for each response following the preceding response
- by at least some minimum delay.

So Max differentially extinguished rapid eating (Jimmy's putting a spoonful of food in his mouth within less than 2 seconds since the last spoonful), and he differentially reinforced a lower rate of eating (Jimmy's putting a spoonful of food in his mouth after at least two seconds had elapsed since the last spoonful). As Jimmy began to slow down, Max gradually increased his requirement from at least 2 seconds between bites to at least 5 seconds.

Reinforcement

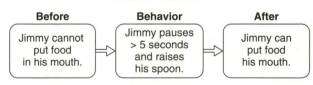

Extinction

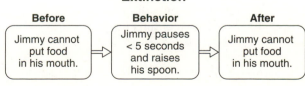

---
[11]This section is based, in a somewhat simplified way, on Favell, J. E., McGimseuy, J. F., & Jones, M. L. (1980). Rapid eating in the retarded: Reduction by nonaversive procedures. *Behavior Modification, 4,* 481–492. Figure 20.1 is based on the same article. (Incidentally, Judy Favell was president of ABA in 1993.)

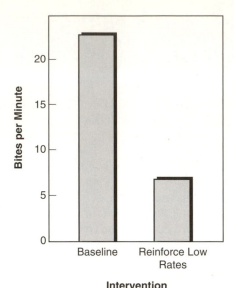

Figure 20.1   Reducing High Rates:
Differential Reinforcement
of Low Rates

It worked: Jimmy's rate of eating decreased from about 22 to about 7 spoonfuls per minute (Figure 20.1).

Furthermore, Herman and Sally Lewis were able to maintain Jimmy's proper eating. Once in a while, they'd praise his slow eating and occasionally prevent (extinguish) his rapid eating. In other words, they intermittently used differential reinforcement of low rate. And that's not all: Jimmy stopped vomiting after his meals, and he stopped being a messy eater. This allowed his parents to take him occasionally to a restaurant for dinner—a treat for the whole family.

QUESTION

1. *Differential reinforcement of low rate*—define it and describe its use to decrease the excessive rate of eating. Specify
   - the response classes
   - the reinforcement contingencies
   - the extinction contingency
   - the presumed reinforcer
   - the results
   - any other interesting features of the intervention.

Concept
Behavioral School Psychology
DIFFERENTIAL PUNISHMENT
OF HIGH RATE[12]

Seven-year-old Satoru was a pain in the rear for Sue and for his classmates. It seemed as if he was always causing a fuss: running in the classroom, rolling on the floor, sliding under desks, standing on chairs and desks, jumping off chairs and desks, sliding furniture, pounding on his desk, hitting, shoving, throwing things, destroying things, and yelling. Not the kind of kid you'd like to have in your classroom. Earlier this semester, Sue had used extinction to get rid of Eric's temper tantrums, but such a variety of reinforcers seemed to maintain Satoru's disruptions that she was having trouble implementing an extinction procedure. So she started browsing through a major behavioral journal, *Behavior Therapy,* and ran across an intriguing procedure that Dr. Samuel Deitz and his colleagues at Georgia State University had developed. Here's how she implemented their procedure.

Sue gave Satoru a piece of paper to keep on his desk. Then every time 2 minutes passed with no more than one disruption, she put a star on the page and complimented Satoru on being such a good boy. At the beginning of each day she reminded him that the stars were worth extra time with her on the playground (each star was worth an extra minute). On the other hand, if Satoru made a second disruption before the 2 minutes had passed, Sue immediately reset the timer and started timing a new 2-minute interval. This meant that if Satoru continued to disrupt more than once every 2 minutes, he'd never get any stars and no outside play. But if he never disrupted more than once in each 2-minute interval, he'd earn one star every 2 minutes.

After 30 minutes, he'd have earned 15 stars. Fifteen stars would entitle him to go outside and play for 15 minutes when recess came.

During baseline, Satoru did an average of 1.3 disruptions every 2 minutes (you can see why he was such a pain); but since this was an average, in some 2-minute intervals he disrupted less than once per interval. So the procedure did take effect, and soon Satoru's disruptions had decreased to an aver-

---

[12]This section is loosely based on Deitz, S. M., Slack, D. J., Schwarzmueller, E. B., Wilander, A. P., Weatherly, T. J., & Hilliard, G. (1978). Reducing inappropriate behavior in special classrooms by reinforcing average interresponse times: Interval DRL. *Behavior Therapy, 9,* 37–46. Sam Deitz and his team at Georgia State University have pioneered creative uses of reinforcers to reduce behavior.

age of 0.3 disruption every 2 minutes. Then Sue raised her criterion to no more than one disruption every 3 minutes. At the same time, she allowed each star to buy Satoru 1.5 minutes on the playground. Then Satoru's disruptions decreased even further to an average of only 0.08 disruption every 2 minutes. Sue was delighted with the new Satoru. His disruptions were so rare that they didn't really interfere with the normal academic activities of her classroom.

Analysis in Terms of the Differential Reinforcement of Low Rates

This contingency is tricky to analyze. Many behavior analysts look at it as differential reinforcement of low rate. In other words, Sue was reinforcing a low rate of disruption (for example, less than one disruption every 2 minutes). But we prefer to analyze it another way:

Remember to keep your eye on the doughnut and not on the hole. Remember to keep your eye on the behavior on which the outcome is contingent and not on nonbehavior. What's the behavior of interest? Disruptions. Is presentation of the outcome (a star) contingent on disruptions? Of course not. Then we're not reinforcing disruptions, not even disruptions at a low rate.

Here's another way to look at it: Remember the dead-man test. Sorry to be so morbid, but this variation is the "dead-student test." Suppose, heaven forbid, young Satoru were unusually quiet; and Sue failed to notice that he was—how shall we put it—no longer with us. What would happen? She'd keep putting stars on the late Satoru's paper. Would she be reinforcing anything? No way. This test shows there was no behavior to reinforce. She surely wouldn't have been reinforcing a low rate of disruptions.

Here's still another way to look at it: With differential reinforcement of low rate, the response of interest must occur before a reinforcer is delivered. Jimmy had to move the spoonful of food toward his mouth (the response of interest) before he could put the food in his mouth (the reinforcer). Max merely required him to do this at a lower rate than he had been. But if Jimmy had "not been with us" he surely wouldn't have gotten any more food in his mouth, no matter how unobservant Max was. With the live Jimmy, we have differential reinforcement of low rate because Jimmy must make the response of interest for a reinforcer to be delivered; however, he must do it at a low rate.

What would happen if Sue really had differentially reinforced Satoru's responding at a low rate? That would mean she'd require him to disrupt before she'd give him a star. The low rate part would mean that also she'd require that the disruption follow the previous disruption by at least 2 minutes. But, of course, she didn't want that; she wanted him to stop disrupting completely, if possible.

One final comment: Don't be confused by Sue's adding stars to the classroom procedure. She added them only so she'd have something to take away (or to refuse to give at as high a rate then). The mere fact of her adding reinforcers to the environment doesn't make this a reinforcement procedure. (See the results in Figure 20.2.)

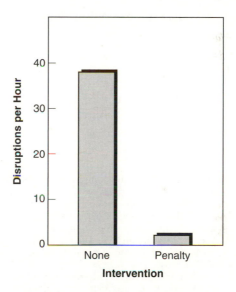

Figure 20.2   Reducing High Rates: Punishment by the Prevention of the Presentation of a Reinforcer

Analysis in Terms of the Differential Punishment of High Rates

So what do we prefer to call Sue's procedure? *The differential punishment of high rate.* In this case it's punishment by the prevention of a reinforcer. Why? If Satoru does nothing, he'll get a star every 2 minutes—the normal frequency of reinforcer delivery. A response (disruption) is penalized when it occurs because that response prevents the delivery of the reinforcer (star). That means it's punishment by the prevention of the presentation of a reinforcer. But Sue penalizes the response only if it occurs at too high a rate (more than once every 2 minutes). That means the procedure differentially penalizes high rates.[13,14]

Before	Behavior	After
Satoru will receive a star and praise in < 2 minutes.	Satoru disrupts twice in 2 minutes.	Satoru won't receive a star and praise in < 2 minutes.

Definition: Concept

Differential punishment of high rates

- The presentation of an aversive condition
- or the loss or prevention of a reinforcer occurs[15]
- for each response that follows the preceding response
- by less than some minimum delay.

QUESTION

1. *Differential punishment of high rate*—define it and diagram its use to decrease classroom disruptions.

---

[13]Occasionally students ask about our example of differential reinforcement of low rate—letting Jimmy have food only when he's paused for 5 seconds before raising his spoon. They ask: Isn't this really a differential punishment contingency—punishment by the prevention of the presentation of a reinforcer—that is, punishing high rates of eating by preventing the automatic presentation of food in Jimmy's mouth? For example, *(Jimmy will have food in his mouth)* → *(Jimmy eats too fast)* → *(Jimmy will not have food in his mouth)*?

Well, that's a tough question; I've spent more time trying to think this through than I'd care to admit. It's a bit of coin toss, but I'd be more inclined to call it differential punishment by prevention if we'd put the food in Jimmy's mouth even if he did nothing, but if he were too hasty with his spoon, we'd stop putting food in his mouth. However, in the case of our differential-reinforcement-of-low-rate example, it's not that Jimmy will be getting free food and then loses that opportunity; instead, the properly paced response is reinforced with the food going into his mouth; Jimmy must make the proper response before the food goes into his mouth. So I'm still inclined to consider our example to be differential reinforcement of low rate. In fact DRL is really reinforcing low rates and extinguishing high rates.

[14]In this contingency, the after condition is delayed by more than 60 seconds, so it's not a simple direct-acting contingency of the sort we've studied so far; instead, it's an analog contingency like those we will introduce in Chapter 22. Probably the only reason it works is that Satoru has language and his disruptions can be suppressed by the statement of a rule describing this analog contingency.

[15]Usually differential punishment of high rates is punishment by the prevention of the presentation of a reinforcer, and not penalizing or punishment by the presentation of an aversive condition. So when we talk about *differential punishment of high rates* we really mean *differential punishment of high rates by the prevention of the presentation of a reinforcer,* but we'd be out of breath by the time we finished, so we'll stick with the shorter, though less precise, terminology. OK?

Compare and Contrast

WAYS TO REDUCE UNDESIRABLE BEHAVIOR[16]

We've just looked at the final procedure for reducing behavior, so now we might compare their pros and cons. Behavior analysts often find punishment to be the most effective method available for reducing the frequency of serious problem behaviors. Like the rest of the world, however, they would rather not use punishment if they can find a more pleasant alternative. So they constantly search for other procedures to decrease the frequency of inappropriate behavior and increase the frequency of appropriate behavior. In this chapter, we've presented the last of our rate-reduction procedures. So here would be a good place to look at a list of the various rate-reduction procedures, along with some of their pros and cons. (Don't be discouraged by each method's having cons as well as pros. Some cons aren't too important; and the benefits of using a procedure will often outweigh those cons.)

The Punishment Contingency

Nowadays, we usually use punishment as a last resort. We try to find the **least restrictive alternative** to reducing the frequency of the inappropriate behavior. And if less restrictive reduction procedures have failed, the client's **right to effective treatment** dictates that we consider punishment procedures. Often when we use punishment procedures or extinction procedures to get rid of undesirable behavior, we also add reinforcement procedures to increase desirable behaviors.

Pros

Punishment's advantages are that it is usually effective, and its effects are often almost immediate and often last for a long period of time. In addition, it is often easy to implement. Punishment is especially useful when a built-in contingency of reinforcement is maintaining the inappropriate behavior so that the behavior analyst has difficulty breaking the contingency to implement extinction.

---

[16]Based on: Carr, E. G., & Lovaas, O. I. (1983). Contingent electric shock as a treatment for severe behavior problems. In S. Axelrod & J. Apsche (Eds.). *The effects of punishment on human behavior* (pp. 221–245). New York: Academic Press; Cooper, J. O., Heron, T. E., & Heward, W. L. (1987). *Applied behavior analysis* (pp. 378–464). Columbus, OH: Merrill; Durand, V. M. (1987). "Look homeward angel": A call to return to our (functional) roots. *The Behavior Analyst, 10,* 299–302; Homer, A. L., & Peterson, L. (1980). Differential reinforcement of other behavior: A preferred response elimination procedure. *Behavior Therapy, 11,* 449–471.

Cons

As Dr. Mark Durand has pointed out, some argue: "We have [no] right to inflict pain and suffering on another person, without their permission, independent of anticipated outcomes." But, as we've mentioned before, advocates of the right to effective treatment argue otherwise. They might suggest that the "pain and suffering" appropriate punishment procedures "inflict" are often much less than the "pain and suffering" surgical procedures "inflict." Put another way, which is more aversive, thousands of dollars worth of medical bills because of lack of effective treatment or a little mist in the face?

One problem with punishment is that its effects may not be permanent. In other words, after you've stopped using the punishment contingency, the inappropriate behavior may eventually recover. But that's true of reinforcement, too: Once you've stopped the reinforcement contingency, the adaptive behavior may extinguish. So, in a sense, these critics of punishment are being inconsistent, to the extent that they don't apply the same criticism to reinforcement.

Mark Durand carries that criticism further, however. He argues that when you use punishment, you're not dealing with the cause of the inappropriate behavior. The cause is the reinforcement contingency maintaining that behavior. He suggests that you haven't really dealt with the problem until you've gotten rid of that cause—that reinforcement contingency, or until you've established a more powerful reinforcement contingency for competing adaptive behavior. The defenders of punishment argue that they can't always get control over the relevant reinforcement contingencies, at least not in a practical sense.

Another problem with the use of punishment is that it requires much supervision to make sure it isn't abused. For example, suppose a defenseless client is aversive. A staff member might then use a punishment procedure more as a form of aggression than as a planned performance-management procedure. So you must closely monitor the use of punishment. Also, clients might imitate the behavior of their teachers, trainers, parents, or other performance managers. And if those performance managers use punishment, then the clients might also. That might not be desirable.

In addition, punishment involves an aversive condition, and the aversive condition may act as an establishing operation that increases the reinforcing value of aggression. So when you use punishment you may get an increase in aggression. In fact, sometimes the use of punishment in behavior modification produces aggression, and sometimes it doesn't. But it's surely one to consider.

Still another potential problem is that the entire setting where punishment occurs and the person delivering the punishment may become aversive. Then the client may attempt to avoid or escape from that setting and the person's presence. Again, sometimes such escape and avoidance behavior occurs, and sometimes it doesn't.

Remember overcorrection? In that punishment procedure, the contingent aversive condition is the requirement that the client must go to the trouble of more than correcting any problems the undesirable behavior produced (for example, after a client trashes a room, she has to go to the effort of putting the room in better shape than it was before). Sometimes this procedure requires much time and effort from highly trained staff, especially if the client resists overcorrecting the problem he or she has created.

Another problem with overcorrection and other punishment procedures may sometimes be that what you think is an aversive condition isn't. For example, sometimes the data suggest that the physical contact involved in overcorrection may actually reinforce the response you're trying to suppress.

The Penalty Contingency

Remember that the penalty contingency is a form of punishment based on the withdrawal of a reinforcer contingent on the occurrence of the undesirable behavior. And time-out is a special form of the penalty contingency where you lose access to a reinforcer for a period of time (for example, Dawn's requiring Sam to sit in a chair facing the wall when he was disruptive).

Pros

It is often easy to use a time-out (for example, you just ask the child to leave the room, and the child does). Most teachers and parents do not find time-out as aversive as punishment based on the presentation of an aversive condition. So they're more likely to use it. Also, time-out is reliably effective and quick.

Cons

When the client is as large and strong as the performance manager, cooperation can sometimes be a problem.

Also, if time-out from your current environment is going to be aversive, then that current environment must be reinforcing. Otherwise time-out from a boring environment won't punish the undesirable behavior. And even worse, the current environment might involve doing a difficult task; in that case, time-out would actually reinforce the undesirable behavior (such as tantruming).

There has been some objection to the use of time-out, and a couple of cases went to court. In both instances, however, the court ruled in favor of cautious, professional use of time-out.

Punishment by the Prevention of the Presentation of Reinforcers (Differential Reinforcement of Other Behavior)

With punishment by the prevention of the presentation of reinforcers, a response prevents the fairly immediate presentation of a reinforcer. For example, based on work by Marcia Smith, we described Mae's use of this procedure to reduce Jimmy's head banging by preventing the presentation of requested food if Jimmy had recently banged his head. Behavior analysts most often call this procedure differential reinforcement of other behavior. But we argue that it makes more sense to us to consider this a punishment procedure rather than a reinforcement procedure.

Pros

Regardless of whether it is a punishment or a reinforcement procedure, some people will find it more acceptable because it does not involve an aversive stimulus, such as physically painful stimulation.

This seems to be a fairly effective technique for reducing undesirable responses, especially when you initially require the client to refrain from that response only for short intervals and then gradually lengthen the intervals.

Cons

First, even skilled professionals sometimes have trouble reducing behavior using this procedure. Second, many performance managers still combine it with other punishment contingencies to achieve the greatest effects. And third, for success, this procedure requires considerable time from highly trained staff.

Differential Punishment of High Rate

Pros

Like other penalty procedures involving the loss of reinforcers, punishment of high rates is probably more socially acceptable than punishment procedures involving the presentation of aversive stimuli. And much data show effectiveness.[17]

Cons

With differential reinforcement of low rate, we don't want to completely get rid of the behavior we're concerned about. We just want to reduce its frequency. But all the uses of differential punishment and penalizing of high rate seem to involve behavior that ideally should be completely gotten rid of. So it's not clear why we shouldn't prefer its closest competitor—the simple penalty contingency.

In other words, we don't see why anyone would ever differentially punish or penalize only high-rate instances of an undesirable behavior when we can punish or penalize all instances of an undesirable behavior. For example, why shouldn't Sue have just used a simple penalty procedure to get rid of Satoru's classroom disruptions? It would have been easier because she wouldn't have needed to use a timer. Instead, she could have given Satoru 15 stars and removed one every time he disrupted class. Besides, the simple penalty procedure might have been more effective because it would have produced a penalty for each disruption, not just some (as was true with the differential punishment procedure). So we do **not** recommend differential punishment or penalizing of high rate.

Extinction

Pros

Sometimes what's called an ecological approach, a change in the client's environment, can be understood as extinction. This is a common practice—for example, when the teacher separates two unruly students, or when the teacher moves a child who is constantly staring out the window to a seat away from the window. How is this extinction? The two unruly students might be reinforcing each other's disruptive behavior. When they are separated, they could still be unruly, but that behavior would receive less reinforcement. For the child staring out the window, staring away from the assignment could still occur, but it would receive less reinforcement if there were no interesting things to stare at outside the window. So here's the advantage of extinction, especially within the context of an ecological approach: It requires no special effort of the teacher. The teacher doesn't have to watch the behavior closely so as to

---

[17]To use the technical concept *social validity,* we would say this procedure has more social validity—the goals, procedures, and results of the intervention are socially acceptable to the client, the behavior analyst, and society.

immediately deliver a reinforcer for desirable behavior or a punisher for undesirable behavior.

Cons

Often it is not clear what the reinforcer is for a particular undesirable behavior. In addition, extinction is sometimes hard to get yourself to do. For example, it's hard to ignore a tantruming person, whether that person is a child or an adult. And staff members often find it too aversive to watch passively as a child continues to do self-injurious behavior during extinction. Furthermore, this self-injurious behavior may be too physically harmful to the child. (That may be why so many children *and* adults become expert tantrum throwers.) Another problem with extinction is that it's sometimes hard to get control over the reinforcer maintaining the undesirable behavior. This can be a problem when the reinforcer is built into the behavior—when the reinforcer is automatic—for example, nose picking. This also can be a problem when the reinforcer is being provided by other people—for example, a juvenile delinquent's peers.

There's a special problem with extinction based on the ecological approach. This procedure is also a discrimination training procedure. The separation of two children is an S^Δ for their disrupting the class, but their getting back together is an S^D for disruption. In a sense, you've merely swept the problem behavior under the carpet; you haven't altered the children's repertoires in a way that will decrease their disruptions when they are around peers who reinforce that undesirable behavior.

Finally, self-injurious behavior often increases in frequency (a burst of responding) during the first part of extinction. And this can put the client at serious physical risk.

Differential Reinforcement of Low Rate

Notice that when we use differential reinforcement of low rate, it's not the behavior itself that's undesirable; it's the rate of the behavior we're trying to reduce.

Pros

If you want the response to occur but just not at such a high rate, then differential reinforcement of low rate may be the intervention of choice. This might involve problems where the behavior produces reinforcers that are so powerful that they cause the rate to be unacceptably high—for example, eating, raising your hand in class, asking questions, or just talking.

Cons

It may not be the treatment of choice if you would like to get rid of the response completely. Why? Because a true differential reinforcement contingency requires that the response occur at least sometimes in order to produce reinforcers. So almost any of the other procedures probably would be more effective at completely eliminating an undesirable response.

Differential Reinforcement of Incompatible Behavior

Recall Chapter 19's discussion of the procedure of differential reinforcement of incompatible behavior. In differential reinforcement of incompatible behavior (DRI), reinforcement is provided for one behavior incompatible with another behavior. Dr. Gerry Patterson used this procedure to reduce Earl's hyperactive behavior in the classroom. As with Earl, we normally reinforce a desirable behavior that's incompatible with an undesirable behavior we want to get rid of.

Here's the question: Can we replace aversive control with differential reinforcement of incompatible behavior? The advocates of this procedure talk about not reinforcing just any arbitrary incompatible behavior. Instead, they search for functional incompatible behaviors, behaviors that will be of value to the individual and the social system where the individual lives. Also, these behaviors should produce built-in, intrinsically reinforcing consequences that are powerful enough to maintain the incompatible behavior once that behavior has become well established.

In a sense, this is the rationale behind the procedure: If a person has nothing to do, that person probably will indulge in all sorts of inappropriate behavior, ranging from obnoxious or harmful self-stimulation to destroying the environment. Your grandmother knew this when she said, "Idle hands are the devil's workshop."

Pros

Most people are more likely to accept a procedure based on reinforcement than one based on punishment. In addition, if you carefully chose the alternative behavior, then the natural environment should eventually maintain that behavior without your continued help.

Cons

You must have a reinforcer available for the incompatible behavior that is more reinforcing than the one controlling the undesirable behavior. This may not always be possible. In actual practice, performance managers often seem to reinforce incompatible behaviors that will effectively compete with the undesirable behavior, but only as long as the performance manager maintains some added reinforcement contingencies. This may just show how hard it is to find built-in reinforcement contingencies for the incompatible behaviors that are more powerful than the reinforcers for the undesirable behaviors. And finally, performance managers often use some form of a punishment procedure to supplement the differential reinforcement of incompatible behavior. This suggests that they are often not confident that the differential-reinforcement procedure will be effective enough without a punishment boost.

Differential Reinforcement of Alternative Behavior

In Chapter 3, Mae and Susan used a procedure developed by Carr and Durand to reduce the violent, disruptive escape behavior of an autistic boy. They used differential reinforcement of alternative behavior—the replacement of an inappropriate response with a specific appropriate response that produces the same reinforcing outcome (i.e., either the removal or reduction of an aversive condition or the presentation of a reinforcing condition).

Pros

As an advocate of this procedure, Dr. Mark Durand argues that the various types of punishment contingencies only temporarily suppress the undesirable behavior but don't address the causes of that behavior. To achieve lasting results with behaviors maintained by the presentation of reinforcers, you must either get rid of the reinforcer (extinction), do an establishing operation that reduces the motivational level, more effectively reinforce some incompatible behavior, or provide the client with a more acceptable way of getting the same reinforcer (differential reinforcement of alternative behavior).

Cons

One temporary problem may be that behavior analysts have not yet used or studied this procedure enough to generate an easy-to-follow set of guidelines that will produce reliable results. So at least at present, the user may need to do a fairly elaborate analysis of the current contingencies to determine just what are the reinforcement contingencies for the inappropriate response and to determine how to substitute a more appropriate response in that contingency.

The Establishing Operation

Mark Durand also recommends the redesigning of situations in which inappropriate escape behaviors occur. For example, a training program may be too difficult for the client. Thus, participation in the program may be too aversive, so the client is doing inappropriate escape behavior. Instead of differentially reinforcing a more appropriate escape alternative, it would often be better to redesign the training program so the client has more success, and thus would find it less aversive, and would therefore less frequently perform any sort of escape behavior.

Along the same lines, the current, appropriate environment (for example, the classroom) may be much less reinforcing than an inappropriate environment (for example, the playground). So being allowed to leave the classroom early to go to the playground might reinforce disruptive behavior. Then it would often be better to redesign the classroom activities so they contain more frequent and more effective reinforcers.

Why do we classify these interventions as establishing operations? Remember: An *establishing operation is a procedure that affects learning and performance with respect to a particular reinforcer or aversive condition.* So decreasing the aversiveness of the training program will decrease the performance of the escape response, and increasing the reinforcers in the classroom will decrease the performance of going into the playground. In a sense, we might call these interventions disestablishing operations.

Decreasing the Effectiveness of the Reinforcer

Satiation. Anticipate the reinforcer and provide it before the person makes the inappropriate response maintained by that reinforcer. Reduce the value of a learned behavioral consequence by not pairing it with other reinforcers.

Decreasing the Effectiveness of the Aversive Condition

Recall that food deprivation establishes food as a reinforcer. And reducing aversiveness decreases the reinforcing value of the nonaversive condition.

Withholding or Reducing the Aversive Condition (Analog to Satiation). A child is working on a hard lesson, making many mistakes and getting few

reinforcers—a frustrating, aversive experience. Frustrating events, in particular, and aversive events, in general, act as establishing operations that increase the reinforcing value of aggression.

So you can decrease the automatic reinforcing value of aggression by making the lessons easier, less frustrating, less aversive, and more reinforcing. Not only will you get less aggression, but also you'll get more learning.

Making a lesson less frustrating and thus less aversive makes aggression less reinforcing. Aggression will also be less effectively reinforced as an escape response.

Also, making sure the client gets enough sleep is an establishing operation that decreases the aversiveness of learned aversive situations and also frustrating situations. This in turn makes it less reinforcing to aggress or escape.

Pros

One of the biggest advantages of this approach is that it results in an overall improvement in the quality of life of the clients and the effectiveness of the training or educational programs they are participating in, in addition to decreasing the frequency of inappropriate behavior. And, as with all alternatives to punishment, probably it will be more acceptable to all the participants.

Cons

Probably the most serious problem with this approach is that it may be too big a task to achieve or it may take too long to achieve it. For example, as authors, we've put hundreds and hundreds of hours into making this book you're reading right now as intrinsically reinforcing and as unaversive as possible. And students tell us we've done a good job. But we've never been able to make it so reinforcing that most students would read it rather than watch TV, unless their teachers have added extra contingencies involving exams on the chapters.

It may turn out that behavior analysts working with autistic and mentally handicapped populations will have similar problems. So we recommend the following strategy: To reduce immediately inappropriate escape behavior, you may need to use some procedure like the differential reinforcement of alternative behavior. But you should always take escape behavior of any kind, either inappropriate or appropriate, to indicate that life for the client isn't what it should be. And that means you should be working to make life or the training program less aversive and more reinforcing.

Summary of Procedures to Reduce Undesirable Behavior

To get the big picture, lets look at the various procedures we've considered for reducing the frequency of undesirable behavior.

1. Punishment
   - The punishment contingency
   - The penalty contingency
   - Punishment by the prevention of the presentation of reinforcers (differential reinforcement of other behavior)
   - Differential punishment of high rates
2. Extinction
3. Reinforcement
   - Differential reinforcement of low rates
   - Differential reinforcement of incompatible behavior
   - Differential reinforcement of alternative behavior
4. The establishing operation

The pros and cons are summarized in the table on p. 348.

QUESTIONS

1. What are nine procedures for reducing the frequency of undesirable behavior? (See the summary table.)
2. Give one pro and one con for each procedure. (See the summary table.)
3. Cite an example of the use of each procedure.

Ways to Reduce Undesirable Behavior		
Procedure	*Pros*	*Cons*
Punishment	Effective Immediate Can combat built-in outcomes	People object Temporary effects[18] Doesn't address cause of problem Requires much supervision May produce aggression Aversiveness may generalize May be time consuming Presumed aversive condition may be a reinforcer
Penalty	More socially acceptable than punishment Often easy to use Reliable Quick	Cooperation can be a problem Must have reinforcing environment Some object
Punishment by Prevention (DRO)	More socially acceptable Effective	Hard to do Requires skilled staff Effortful and time consuming
Differential Punishment of High Rates	More socially acceptable Effective	Won't completely eliminate problem behaviors Other procedures better
Extinction	More socially acceptable Effective Not effortful	Hard to find and control the reinforcer Hard to ignore problem behaviors May come under stimulus control May have extinction bursts
Differential Reinforcement of Low Rates	More socially acceptable Won't completely eliminate response	Won't completely eliminate response
Differential Reinforcement of Incompatible Behavior	More socially acceptable Natural environment may maintain it	Need a powerful alternative reinforcer May be only moderately effective
Differential Reinforcement of Alternative Behavior	More socially acceptable Addresses the cause of the problem	Hard to apply
The Establishing Operation	More socially acceptable Improves quality of life of participant Addresses the cause of the problem	May be difficult to do May not be completely effective

---

[18]People raise the objection of the temporary effect most often with regard to punishment contingencies; but, of course, the effects of all contingencies are temporary if they are removed and some other contingency doesn't take it's place; so this objection really applies to all our options.

BASIC ENRICHMENT

In the Skinner Box
BACKWARD CHAINING

Here's the behavioral chain we want Rudolph the Rat to perform. First he pulls a chain hanging from the ceiling, which turns on a light; then he presses the lever, which causes the dipper to dip down and bring up a drop of water, making a slight click, as it returns; then he drinks the water; and you turn the light off, ready for a new trial. We usually use backward chaining when we establish behavioral chains in nonverbal animals. How would you do that here?

If this were Rudolph's first time in the Skinner box, you'd start with dipper training. That means you'd establish the click of the dipper as an S^D for approaching the dipper. Easy. Whenever Rudolph is moving around (not just hovering over the dipper), you'd dip the dipper into the water and bring it up with an audible click. The click is an S^D, because approaching the dipper is reinforced by the drop of water after a click but not at other times (silence is the S^Δ).

Once you've dipper-trained Rudolph, move one step backward in the behavioral chain. You'd reinforce lever pressing with the light on (S^D). And you'd extinguish lever pressing when the light's off (S^Δ). Presumably the dipper-click would have a dual function; it would now function as a reinforcer for pressing the lever, as well as an S^D for approaching the dipper.

Then you'd move another link back in the chain. You'd reinforce chain pulling, using the onset of the light as the reinforcer. So now the light would be showing dual functionality, functioning as a reinforcer for chain pulling, as well as an S^D for lever pressing.

Once you've finished with Rudolph's training, he should be able to run through several of those behavioral chains each minute. And you'll have found the whole experience almost as reinforcing as Rudolph did.

Note that there's no S^D for the chain-pull response. Light off is the before condition and light on is the after condition. Whenever the light's off, pulling the chain will turn it back on. Remember that to have an S^D we must also have an S^Δ. We'd have an S^D if the only time the chain pull turned the light on was when there was a buzzer buzzing. Then the buzzer would be the S^D and the absence of the buzzer would be the S. Remember that test. Without an S^Δ you don't have an S^D.

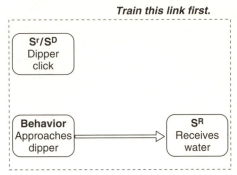

Backward Chaining[19]

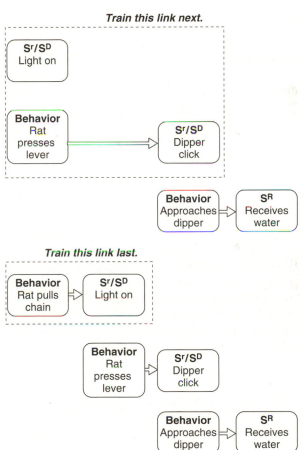

---

[19]**By the Way #1: Excessive Backward Chaining.** Behavior analysts first developed the procedure of backward chaining in the Skinner box. And you can see why; if you click the water dipper after each new component that you add in forward chaining, then the rat would develop the little sequence, or chain, of doing the first link and then going to the water dipper; and you'd have to extinguish that sequence or chain before adding another link (e.g., chain pull → dipper click → approach dipper → water; then inserting the link of pressing the lever before approaching the dipper gets a little tricky). But we might not have so many problems with forward chaining when the learner gets the reinforcer without having to interrupt the sequence by running over to the water dipper. For example, we might be able to train a child to put on his trousers using forward chaining and simply say *"Good boy"* after the completion of each link of the chain, adding a new link as the child mastered the earlier links. We applied behavior analysts, working with verbal human beings, may have been too literal in our adoption of the specific technique of backward

chaining from the animal laboratory. But often with animals and nonverbal human beings, backward chaining might still be useful.

By the Way #2: Arbitrary Sequences. We usually think of a behavioral chain as consisting of the one-and-only way of getting from the first link to the last; for example, you have to put your feet in your trousers before you can pull them up to your waist; and you should pull them up to your waist, before you zip and button them. But suppose you're training people to set the dinner table; whether they put down the fork before or after they put down the spoon is arbitrary, though it might be good to establish a chain where one always occurs before the other, especially if you're training a fairly handicapped person. Another way to put this is that in most chains we discuss, each response is a prerequisite for the next one; but that's not the case when the sequence is arbitrary.

Dual-Functioning Chained Stimuli

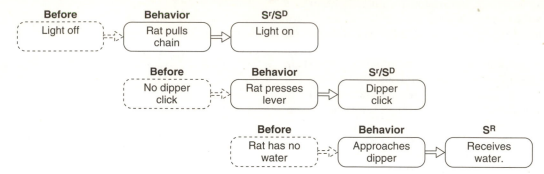

QUESTION

1. Diagram the use of backward chaining in the Skinner box.

In the Skinner Box
DUAL-FUNCTIONING CHAINED STIMULI

Let's take another look at Rudolph's behavioral chain, this time in terms of the dual-functioning stimuli. It's just a series of connected contingency diagrams of the sort we've been using all semester. Here the *after condition* is a dual-functioning stimulus; it functions both as the S^r for the preceding response in that diagram and the S^D for the next response in the diagram below it.

In the case of the chain-pull response, don't make the mistake of confusing the before condition (light off) with the S^D (there is none, and light off is **not** the S^D for the chain pull).

QUESTION

1. Diagram dual-functioning chained stimuli in the Skinner box.

NONCHAINED BEHAVIOR SEQUENCES

Usually, behavior analysts deal with behavioral sequences as behavioral chains (a series of links in which each response produces the stimulus or operandum for the next response). But some behavioral sequences don't seem to work that way. Consider typing the word *the:* Typing *the* may start as a chain and then as the typist gets more skilled the sequence becomes too fast to be a chain. Not enough time for the neural impulse to get from the proprioceptive receptors to the muscle effectors. By the time you get the proprioceptive stimuli from typing the *t,*

it is to late for the stimuli from having typed the *t* to act as an S^D for typing the *h.* A skilled typist types the letters too fast for us to describe that behavioral sequence as a behavioral chain; it takes too long for the neurons to fire to produce the *t,* and after that to fire to produce the *h,* and after that to fire to produce the *e;* that cumulated time may be longer than it takes for a skilled typist to type the single word *the.*

So I think we can best describe that process as follows: The word *the* is an S^D for the three separate typing responses, typing *t, h,* and *e.* But it's an S^D for typing *t* with a short latency (very quickly), typing *h* with an intermediate latency (not as quickly), and typing *e* with a longer latency (even more slowly). Therefore, at the sight or sound or thought of the word *the,* the skilled typist starts typing all three letters at the same time, but with slightly different latencies. Of course, we intermediate-level typists sometimes mess up the latencies with a resulting *teh.*[20]

QUESTION

1. Give an example of a nonchained behavioral sequence.

In the Skinner Box
DIFFERENTIAL REINFORCEMENT OF LOW RATE

After he's been deprived of water for a few hours, you put Rudolph back in the Skinner box. You bag the chaining procedure and just leave the light (S^D)

---

[20]The latency, or reaction-time, argument may no longer be as tenable as it once seemed; but for a more detailed, though more cognitive, argument in support of nonchained behavioral sequences (traditionally called *motor programs*), see Mazur, J. E. *Learning and Behavior* (4th ed.) (pp 329–333). Upper Saddle River, NJ: Prentice Hall. Also see Catania, A. C. *Learning* (4th ed.) (pp. 124–126). Upper Saddle River, NJ: Prentice Hall.

on all the time. This would normally mean each of Rudolph's lever presses would be reinforced with a drop of water. But you know we haven't come this far in the book to do anything that simple. No, instead we're going to differentially reinforce a low rate of lever pressing. We'll require that Rudolph pause for at least 10 seconds (for example) before we reinforce the next response.

What does that mean? He presses the lever and gets a drop of water (the first one comes easy). Then 3 seconds later he presses the lever again. Sorry, too soon. Two seconds and another press. Sorry. One second? No. Five? No. Twelve seconds? Yes! He had waited 12 seconds since the last press, so we reinforce that response. Why? Because 12 seconds is greater than 10 seconds, and we require that Rudolph wait at least 10 seconds since the last press before he presses again. Otherwise, no reinforcer.

Then he waits only 5 seconds before the next response and again, no reinforcer. In the following diagram, each vertical line (|) indicates the passage of 1 second.

$$R \rightarrow S^R \; ||| \; R \; || \; R \; | \; R \; |||| \; R \; ||||||||||| \; R \rightarrow S^R \; ||||| \; R, \text{ etc.}$$

After this last reinforcer, Rudolph rushes back to the lever and presses again, but he'd waited only 2 seconds since the last press. So no deal. Then 5 seconds. Nothing. Eleven seconds. Bingo. Let the good times roll. One more drop of water for Rudolph.

You can think of this as a differential-reinforcement procedure much like the differential reinforcement of force, topography, or any other response dimension. Here we're differentially reinforcing a low rate. So we find that responses that occur immediately after the last response gradually extinguish. And because they're reinforced, responses that involve a pause of at least 10 seconds become more and more frequent. After a few sessions, Rudolph will be pausing 10 seconds or more for about half his responses. He'll still get ahead of himself about half the time, but most of his premature responses will involve pauses fairly close to 10 seconds; they might be 8 or 9 seconds—near misses.

What does all this have to do with the rate of responding? Suppose that during continuous reinforcement, Rudolph paused an average of 2 seconds between each lever press (about the time needed to go to the dipper, drink his drop of water, and return to the lever). What would his rate of lever pressing be? Two seconds for each press. Sixty seconds in a minute. How many presses per minute? Sixty seconds divided by 2 seconds per response equals 30 responses per minute. He makes an average 30 responses per minute, so average rate is 30 responses per minute.

What happens with differential reinforcement of low rate? Let's say he slowed down to an average pause of 12 seconds (on the average, he paused longer than he needed). How many presses per minute? Sixty seconds divided by 12 seconds per response equals 5 responses per minute—his average rate. So you can see that with differential reinforcement of low rate, the average rate (for example, 5 per minute) will be much lower than under continuous reinforcement (for example, 30 per minute).

How does this relate to Jimmy and his food gobbling? Rudolph pressed the bar and then had to wait at least 10 seconds before pressing the bar again in order for a drop of water to be delivered. Jimmy moved the spoon to his mouth and then had to wait at least 5 seconds before moving the spoon to his mouth again in order to have the opportunity to actually place the spoon in his mouth. Differential reinforcement of low rate in both cases.

Differential reinforcement of low rate is a hard contingency to understand. What you should do is ask your professor to demonstrate it for you. The best way to do it is for him or her to be the rat and you be the water dipper. Then you reinforce only those lever presses where the pause since the preceding one has been at least 10 seconds. Give it a shot; it's fun **and** educational.

QUESTION

1. *Differential reinforcement of low rate*—describe its use in the Skinner box.

EXCESSIVE EATING SPEED

Why do you suppose so many mentally handicapped people have the problem of excessively rapid eating? Is there something wrong with their brain that causes them to eat so fast? We think not. We suspect rapid eating is the natural way. Animals don't have good table manners. They go for it. Food tastes good. The good taste is a reinforcer. The more bites you get in a minute, the more taste reinforcers you get in a minute.

We believe our normal, polite, paced eating results from much training from our parents. I suspect my parents frequently said, "Dick, slow down. Don't gobble your food. If you eat like that, we're going to let you eat with the hogs." (We think most parents more often use punishment rather than reinforcement contingencies in establishing table manners.) Incidentally, my parents were not completely successful in reducing my rate of eating. They left the rest of the task to my friends; so feel free to give me corrective feedback should the occasion arise.

Then why do so many mentally handicapped people fail to acquire the repertoire of slower-paced eating? Probably for the same reasons they fail to acquire many other functionally and socially acceptable repertoires. For example, the poor language skills of many mentally handicapped children would make it almost impossible for most parents to teach them good table manners. A weak imitative repertoire also might interfere. In general, we're suggesting that mentally handicapped people who fail to acquire proper styles of eating do so because they don't come in contact with the same contingencies of punishment and reinforcement as we do.

QUESTION

1. Why do so many mentally handicapped people have poor table manners?

Compare and Contrast
In the Skinner Box
DRL VS. FI

What's the difference between differential reinforcement of low rate (DRL) and a fixed-interval schedule of reinforcement (FI)? Well the best way to answer heavy metaphysical questions like that is how? Take it back to the Skinner box! Right. (In the following table we're not really describing how Rudolph would actually behave; he's just behaving in ways that will make it easiest for you to see the difference between DRL and FI.)

QUESTION

1. Study the following table very carefully so that you can explain the differences between DRL and FI on a quiz or exam.

DRL 60″ vs. FI 60″		
What Rudolph Does	**What You (the experimenters) Do**	
	DRL 60″—a reinforcer is contingent on each response's following the preceding response by at least 60 seconds.	**FI 60″**—a reinforcer is contingent on the first response after 60 seconds since the last reinforcement.
Rudolph enters the Skinner box and presses the lever. After 65 seconds, he presses again.	**DRL 60″.** You reinforce the second response (whether or not you reinforce this first response isn't crucial).	**FI 60″.** You reinforce the second response (whether or not you reinforce this first response isn't crucial).
Now Rudolph starts pressing the lever every 10 seconds and does so for 5 minutes.	**DRL 60″.** You give Rudolph no more reinforcers for the entire 5 minutes. Why not? Because he never paused for at least 60 seconds; and on DRL 60 seconds, the reinforcer is contingent on each response's following the preceding response by at least 60 seconds; and Rudolph never paused for more than 10 seconds. It's as if Rudolph resets the clock every time he responds.	**FI 60″.** You reinforce the first response that occurs 60 seconds after each preceding reinforcer; so over a 5-minute period you'll reinforce five responses, one a minute. The response before each minute elapses has no effect. Rudolph can respond as fast as possible or as slowly as possible to a minimum of once every 60 seconds, and his rate of responding will have no effect on his rate of reinforcement.
Now Rudolph presses the lever every 60 seconds and does so for 5 minutes.	**DRL 60″.** You reinforce each of those responses, because Rudolph waited the required 60 seconds between responses. He gets five reinforcers during those 5 minutes.	**FI 60″.** Here you also reinforce each response. And Rudolph again gets five reinforcers during those 5 minutes.

21 Respondent Conditioning

FUNDAMENTALS

Example
BATMAN[1]

At three in the morning, Moses awoke to the sound of his 6-year-old son screaming and Spot barking. He ran to Sammy's room. The little boy was crouched by the side of his bed, screaming and crying. Spot's barking moved closer and closer to Sammy's window. The outside door rattled. Next the bathroom door rattled. Then a shadow fell across the bedroom doorway.

Moses said to Sammy, "Calm down, Son."

Then he went to the doorway. "Is anybody there?" he asked, knowing someone was there.

Police sirens whined toward the house. Three police cars, their flashing red lights creating an eerie Halloween effect, screeched to a halt in the driveway.

A neighbor in the driveway, Mr. Russo, cried, "In the house! In the house!"

Moses turned the lights on. The entrance door was open. Four armed policemen ran into the house. Then Moses saw the intruder, standing paralyzed at the end of the hallway with their stereo in his hands.

"Surrender and nothing will happen to you," the first policeman shouted.

They handcuffed the thief and pushed him into the wired-off back seat of the nearest police car.

The danger was over, thanks to Russo, their neighbor. He had called the police when the thief had tried to enter his own home.

The episode soon ended, but the results lingered on. Ever since, Sammy was frightened at night. He didn't want to go to bed, and when he did, it was only because Moses insisted. Sammy wanted the lights on and asked Moses to sleep in his room with him. The boy would do everything possible to stay awake. Often he played Batman until he got on Moses's nerves. They both ended up being awake a good part of the night.

Moses was a widower and raised Sammy with no extra help. His leather factory demanded most of his time. He normally arrived at work at 6:30 A.M., to supervise the end of the night shift before the first day shift arrived. But now the late nights with his terrified son caused him to be late. And Sammy began to bring home bad grades, though he had always been a top student. So Moses went to Dawn for professional help.

Dawn asked Moses to record each night that Sammy was frightened. She also asked Moses to give Sammy a flashlight. But he could only use it briefly when he was frightened and could not keep it on all night.

Ten days later, Moses brought Sammy to see Dawn.

During the first interview, Dawn found that 6-year-old Sammy loved Batman. He read all the Batman comic books, didn't miss a TV program, watched Batman videotapes and movies over and over, and played with his Batmobile and his Batman puzzles. He loved to wear his Batman cape and mask around the house, trying to impose justice on the world. He reserved a bed in his room for his imaginary friend, Robin. And he called Mr. Russo, the neighbor next door, the Joker. She made use of this bit of info.

Dawn: Sammy, close your eyes. Imagine you're watching TV with your Dad. See, there you are

---

[1]Based on Jackson, H. J., & King, N. J. (1981). The emotive imaginary treatment of a child's trauma-induced phobia. *Behavior Therapy and Experimental Psychiatry*, 12, 325–328.

with your pajamas on. And the Batman program has just finished. Your dad tells you it's time for bed, and just then Batman appears out of nowhere and sits down next to you. Think about it as best as you can. Can you see Batman sitting next to you?

Sammy: Yes.

Dawn: Can you tell me what Batman is wearing? What color are his clothes?

Sammy: He's got black and blue clothes and boots and a gun.

Dawn: Oh! You can see him with a gun?

Sammy: Yes, he needs it for the Joker.

Dawn: That's terrific, Sammy. Imagine that Batman tells you he needs you on his missions to catch robbers and other villains and he's appointed you as his special agent. However, he wants you to get your sleep in your bedroom and he will call on you when he needs you. You're lucky to have been chosen to help him.

Sammy: Yes.

Dawn: Now Dad puts you in your bed and leaves both the lights on and the three blinds up. Batman is also there looking as strong as he always does. Think about it as clearly as you can. Can you see?

Sammy: Yes, I can see Daddy and Batman in my room and all the lights are on.

Dawn: Well, if you're scared, raise your finger.

Dawn repeated this fantasy, but each time she presented a situation that was increasingly aversive—one blind down, two down, three down; one light off, two off; Moses talking, then leaving the room; Spot barking in the distance, then next to the window; the outside door rattling, then the bathroom door; shadows falling across the window, and then across the room.

Sammy lifted his finger if he felt afraid. When he raised his finger, Dawn asked if he could see Batman with him, what he was doing, the color of his clothes and so on.

Dawn followed this technique for four sessions. In the first three sessions, she covered increasingly aversive situations. And she reviewed all of those situations in the fourth session.

Moses recorded each day that Sammy was frightened. During baseline, the 10 days prior to Dawn's intervention with Sammy, the boy was frightened every night. But during Dawn's behavioral intervention, the number of nights Sammy was frightened gradually decreased. Between days 36 and 60, Sammy was only frightened on 3 nights. After that, they recorded no more problems for the

3 months that Dawn followed up on the case. Batman's buddy had found peace at last.

QUESTION

1. Describe an intervention for eliminating the fear of darkness.
   a. Describe the anxiety-generating situation.
   b. List specific components of the anxiety situation, in increasing anxiety-generating sequence.
   c. How would you use fantasies to get rid of fear of darkness?

Concept
PHOBIAS

Sammy's problem is common among children his age; it is often described as a darkness phobia (fear of darkness). Traditionally, we say the term **phobia** refers to a long-lasting, intense, irrational fear.[2]

This fear is produced by what once were neutral stimuli. Those neutral stimuli have acquired aversive properties because they've been associated with other stimuli that already produce fear.

Young children who develop early illness and require a doctor's attention cry or exhibit other emotional behaviors when the doctor approaches them. For these children, seeing the doctor and experiencing aversive events such as getting a hypodermic injection occur at the same time, so the doctor's presence produces fear responses. It is not surprising that these fear responses often generalize to other individuals, particularly to people wearing white coats or, in some instances, to people in general.

We want to emphasize the irrational aspect of the phobia because the situation that the individual

---

[2]But that may be a misleading way to describe the problem because it suggests there is a *thing* called phobia and there is a *thing* called fear. The truth may be simpler, though more difficult to describe: The warning stimulus is a learned aversive stimulus. Escape responses are reinforced by the termination of that learned, aversive stimulus. That warning stimulus may also produce physiological, emotional, conditioned responses, and other emotional responses such as Sammy's screaming and crying, but not always, at least not at a measurable level. So, when we say Sammy fears darkness, we mean nothing more than that darkness is a learned aversive stimulus and perhaps a CS for Sammy. *Phobia* has no special, fundamental, psychological importance; it just means that the person who uses the word thinks it's irrational for someone to find that stimulus aversive, because it will not be paired with other aversive stimuli in the future.

reacts to normally could do that person no harm. People with phobias often consult clinical psychologists. The reactions to the fear-provoking situations are real and we can observe them directly. They often involve avoidance and escape responses. Sometimes the escape or avoidance responses are extreme and in themselves may cause harm to the client or to those around the client. Even if an overt, dramatic escape or avoidance response does not occur, the client may react emotionally, by grimacing, becoming rigid, turning pale, or raising the heart rate or blood pressure, for example.

Often, when the phobic client comes to the therapist's office, the client doesn't know or remember what events resulted in the phobia. Some traditional therapists spend session after session trying to uncover the initiating circumstances. But awareness of the conditions that initiated the phobia doesn't seem to reduce the fearful reaction.

QUESTION

1. *Phobia*—give an example.

IVAN PAVLOV

Does the name Pavlov ring a bell? Dr. Ivan Pavlov was already a world-famous physiologist when he discovered respondent conditioning. In his research on glands and the endocrine system, he surgically implanted tubes into dogs' glands to measure their secretion. So he had to keep the dogs restrained in a harness for a long time. This meant his assistant, Roskolnikov, had to feed the dogs while they were restrained. Usually when he presented food to these dogs, they would salivate and drool. You might observe this in your own pet doggy, Fang, at feeding time. But after some time, Pavlov and his assistants noticed a strange thing: The dogs would salivate whenever Roskolnikov entered the room, even with no food in hand. They salivated as if Roskolnikov himself were the lunch he brought.

From his studies, Pavlov knew that salivation was a reflexive response that occurred regularly in all food-deprived animals when they saw food. In terms of what Pavlov knew about physiology, he couldn't figure out why his dogs salivated only at the sight of Roskolnikov and not at the sight of Dimitri, Rasputin, or Pavlov, himself.

That observation led Pavlov down the experimental trail to respondent conditioning. He placed a dog in restraint as before. He gave the dog meat powder; as with other types of food, meat powder immediately produced salivation. Upon presentation of the powder, he now rang a bell. Over a long series of trials, Pavlov consistently paired the ring with the presentation of the meat powder.

On all trials, the pairing of the bell and the meat powder produced salivation. After the initial pairings, Pavlov ran a series of trials where he omitted the meat powder and presented the bell alone. As you might suspect, the ringing of the bell produced salivation just as had the appearance of the assistant. Pavlov reasoned that salivating when the bell rang resulted from his previous pairings of the meat powder and the bell. The salivation response to the bell was then conditional upon previous circumstances.

This historical experiment determined the development of psychology for many years. Even today, psychologists do experiments following Pavlov's ideas.

QUESTIONS

1. Who was Ivan Pavlov?
2. What was the great discovery of Pavlov and his colleagues?

Concept
RESPONDENT CONDITIONING

Pavlov developed some terms to describe his conditioning procedures. He called the food or meat powder that always produced salivation the **unconditioned stimulus (US).** Meat powder produced salivation without prior conditioning. Pavlov called this salivation response elicited by the meat powder the **unconditioned response (UR),** and the ringing of the bell the **conditioned stimulus (CS).** The conditioned stimulus would produce salivation only if he had previously paired it with the presentation of meat powder. He called salivation in the presence of the bell alone the **conditioned response (CR).** We use the term *conditioning* to describe the procedure of pairing the conditioned stimulus with the unconditioned stimulus.[3]

---

[3]Originally, conditioned stimulus meant a conditional stimulus, one that could only elicit the response conditional only on (dependent on) its having been paired with another stimulus (usually the unconditioned stimulus). Incidentally, in the diagrams for the conditioning procedure, there's a dashed arrow, rather than a solid one between the stimulus to be conditioned and the following stimulus. It's dashed to indicate that the stimulus to be conditioned precedes but does not cause or produce the following stimulus.

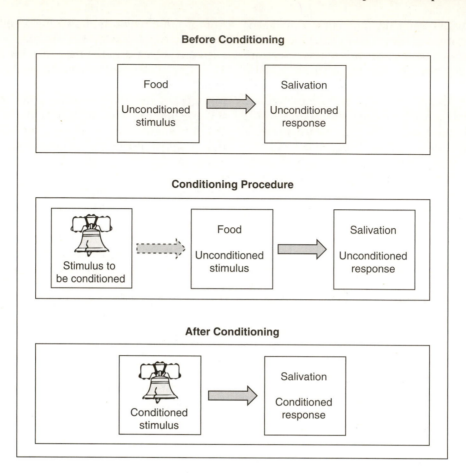

Definition: Concepts

Unconditioned stimulus (US)
- A stimulus that produces the unconditioned response
- without previous pairing with another stimulus.

Unconditioned response (UR)
- An unlearned response
- elicited by the presentation
- of an unconditioned stimulus.

Conditioned stimulus (CS)
- A stimulus that acquires its eliciting properties
- through previous pairing with another stimulus.

Conditioned response (CR)
- A learned response
- elicited by the presentation
- of a conditioned stimulus.

QUESTION

1. Define the following concepts:
   a. unconditioned stimulus
   b. unconditioned response
   c. conditioned stimulus
   d. conditioned response

FEAR AND FOOTBALL

Saturday morning, Big State U's alumni day and an alumni football game, with Gentleman Juke out of retirement to play quarterback. First quarter. The crowd roars, or at least Mae, Dawn, and Sid roar, as Juke sees the monster end rushing toward him. Splat, he's on his back, crushed by the fat brute; he feels the pain, his stomach churns, his heart races, his adrenaline flows. He pushes the brute off himself with mighty force, barely restraining his fist from going for the guy's paunch, and settles for a loud oath.

Second quarter. Juke sees the monster end rushing toward him. His stomach churns, his heart races, his adrenaline flows. He dodges to the right, back, to the right again, and then rushes forward, across the goal line, almost as agile and fast as when he used to be part of the BSU eleven.

The **activation syndrome** is a set of smooth-muscle physiological responses that control the stomach, heart, glands, and so on. It is an uncondi-tioned response elicited by painful stimuli, and it en-hances our strength and speed, often making it pos-sible for us more reliably and more quickly to **escape** those painful stimuli. (Juke escapes the weight of the brute.)

However, the activation syndrome can also be-come a conditioned response elicited by a condi-tioned stimulus (previously paired with painful stim-uli). It again enhances our strength and speed, often making it possible for us more reliably and more quickly to **avoid** those painful stimuli. (Juke avoids the Brute in the second quarter.)

When conditioned stimuli elicit the activation syndrome, we call the activation syndrome an **emo-tional response**.

Tying It All Together

The respondent conditioning process that causes the sight of food to elicit the dog's salivation is the same respondent conditioning process that causes dark-ness to elicit Sammy's activation syndrome (here we label the activation-syndrome emotional response as *fear*). In Sammy's case, the darkness had been paired with loud noises and flashing lights. And it's the same respondent-conditioning process that causes the sight of the rushing monster end to elicit Juke's activation-syndrome emotional response, which we might call fear or anger.

In summary, most psychologists think we ac-quire emotional responses through respondent or Pavlovian conditioning. The consistent pairing of activation-syndrome-producing stimuli with neutral stimuli may bring about the conditioned fear re-sponses to these other stimuli. Sometimes a single pairing can establish an event or object as a condi-tioned aversive stimulus, as with Sammy's fear of darkness.

Compare and Contrast
RESPONDENT AND OPERANT CONDITIONING

The respondent-conditioning procedure differs from the procedures we discussed in the previous chap-ters. In regard to the other procedures, we always spoke of the consequences of behavior. Responses that produced reinforcers or removed aversive con-ditions increased in frequency. Responses that pro-duced aversive conditions or removed reinforcers decreased in frequency. In all instances, the main concern was with the consequences of responses. For instance, in an experimental chamber, the rat

presses the lever and thus operates the mechanism that produces food pellets. Similarly, a bear emits climbing responses that bring him closer to apples in a tree. Learning that involves responses maintained directly by the consequences that produce them is what we call **operant conditioning.** (Operant condi-tioning is what we've been studying in this book up until the current chapter.)

In **respondent conditioning,** reinforcement (as we've defined it) doesn't play a role. The only re-quirement for respondent conditioning is the pre-sentation of the unconditioned stimulus and the con-ditioned stimulus together over several trials. After such pairings, the conditioned stimulus produces the conditioned response. The conditioned response is similar in many respects to the unconditioned re-sponse, even though these responses are elicited by different stimuli.[4]

Respondent vs. Operant Pairing

It's important to note that *the results of respondent pairing differ from the results of operant pairing.* Re-spondent pairings develop conditioned eliciting stimuli (CS), while operant pairings develop learned reinforcers. And respondent conditioned eliciting stimuli aren't the same thing as learned operant re-inforcers.

First, the similarities:

○ Let's start with the obvious—respondent pair-ing and operant pairing both involve pairing. And in both cases, a neutral stimulus is pre-sented immediately before a functioning stim-ulus. In respondent conditioning, a bell might be paired with meat powder; and in operant conditioning, a dipper click might be paired with water. (Of course we could use a bell and meat powder in operant conditioning and vise versa.)

○ Also in both respondent and operant pairing, the neutral stimulus acquires the function of the paired stimulus. (The bell acquires the function of the meat powder and the click ac-quires the function of the water.)

Next the differences:

○ In respondent conditioning, the neutral stimu-lus (the bell) becomes a conditioned stimulus; that is, it acquires more or less the same elicit-

---

[4]Many writers call the unconditioned stimulus a reinforcer; however, we prefer to use separate terms in order to clearly dis-tinguish between the two different procedures of operant and re-spondent conditioning.

ing function as the unconditioned stimulus (the bell elicits the salivation).

- In operant conditioning, the neutral stimulus becomes a learned reinforcer or a learned aversive condition; that is, it acquires more or less the same reinforcing or aversive value as the unlearned reinforcer or unlearned aversive condition. So, after the water and dipper click pairing, the click can reinforce the lever press.

Definition: Concepts
Respondent conditioning
- A neutral stimulus
- acquires the eliciting properties
- of an unconditioned stimulus
- through pairing the unconditioned stimulus
- with a neutral stimulus.

Operant conditioning
- Reinforcing consequences
- immediately following the response
- increase its future frequency; and
- aversive consequences
- immediately following the response
- decrease its future frequency.

Traditionally, psychologists have distinguished between respondent and operant conditioning on a procedural and a behavioral level. Some of the main differences are the following:

- With the operant-conditioning procedure, we present a consequence following the response. Generally, we are not concerned with what stimulus caused the initial response. In operant conditioning, we must wait for the response to occur before we can condition it. (In other words, Rudolph must press the lever before the contingent presentation of a drop of water can increase the frequency of his future lever presses).

- In respondent conditioning, the unconditioned stimulus immediately produces the unconditioned response. In Pavlov's study, once he introduced the meat powder, salivation immediately occurred. Thus, we can bring about the unconditioned response whenever we wish. We have only to pair the conditioned stimulus with the unconditioned stimulus. In other words, the bell produces salivation when it is presented. The bell need not be presented contingently after the response for that bell to produce a salivation response.

- Traditionally, psychologists have said we can respondently condition responses involving the autonomic nervous system and smooth muscles (those controlling our gastrointestinal tract and our blood vessels); but, they said, we can't operantly condition them. Some responses that we can respondently condition are heartbeat, glandular secretions, and pupil contraction and dilation. But it turns out that the psychologists were wrong; we can sometimes operantly condition smooth-muscle and glandular responses. So that traditional distinction doesn't always hold.

- And traditionally, psychologists have said we can operantly condition skeletal-muscle responses, like those of the limbs; but, they said, we can't respondently condition them. Some gross-muscle responses we can operantly condition are running, walking, grasping objects, and writing. And, again, it turns out that the psychologists were wrong; we can sometimes respondently condition gross-muscle responses, such as the leg-contraction response when our foot is shocked or the knee-jerk response when the physician taps our patellar tendon to test our reflexes. Therefore, that traditional distinction doesn't always hold.

- Traditionally, psychologists have said that responses involving our autonomic nervous system and smooth muscles are "involuntary." They said we can condition "involuntary" behavior only with respondent conditioning. And traditionally, they've said skeletal-muscle responses are "voluntary." So they also said we can condition "voluntary" behavior only with operant conditioning. But a distinction between involuntary and voluntary may not be too valid, clear, or useful. Roughly, what *voluntary* means is that if someone asks you to make a particular response, you can, whereas if you can't make the requested response, then that response *might* be involuntary. For example, if someone asked you to slow down your heart rate, it used to be thought that you couldn't; so we would have called heart rate an involuntary response.

- Another distinction is that responses that are conditionable only by respondent procedures are not under voluntary control, whereas the individual can regulate responses that can be operantly conditioned. But, over the years it has become apparent that there are exceptions to these restrictions. Sometimes it is possible to respondently condition skeletal-muscle responses, such as the "startle" response. (Such responses may themselves be unconditioned respondent responses.) And we also operantly condition responses involving smooth muscles and glands.

Traditional Distinctions Between Respondent and Operant Conditioning		
Feature	**Respondent conditioning**	**Operant conditioning**
Procedure	Neutral stimulus and unconditioned stimulus precede response	Reinforcing or punishing consequence follows response
Response occurrence	Response to stimulus need not occur before conditioning	Response must occur to be conditioned
Parts of organism involved	Generally, glands and smooth muscles	Generally, striped muscles
Response control	Generally, "involuntary"	Generally, "voluntary"

In this section, we've looked at traditional distinctions between operant and respondent conditioning. These are the distinctions you find in most traditional textbooks. They all make some sense, but none really do the trick. We think a more important distinction is a procedural distinction based on the difference between the CS and the S^D; we'll discuss this distinction in a later section.

QUESTIONS

1. Define the following concepts:
   a. respondent conditioning
   b. operant conditioning.
2. List three traditional differences between respondent and operant conditioning as indicated in the preceding table.

Example
CONDITIONING A PHOBIA

John B. Watson and Rosalie Rayner conditioned a phobic reaction in an 11-month-old infant. The infant was Albert, the son of one of the nurses on the staff. Albert was a robust infant in all respects, and for this reason the experimenters chose him for the study. Unlike many infants his age, Albert didn't spend a great deal of time crying; he was a happy baby. They thought for a long time before undertaking this study because, after all, phobias might cause Albert real difficulty and discomfort. But they decided he wouldn't be at risk. (They did this experiment in 1920. If it had been done today, the procedure would have been reviewed by a human subjects welfare board and probably rejected. We considered taking this study out of this edition of the text because we question its ethics. But we decided to leave it in. The study is a classic, although of questionable ethics, and is very informative and illustrative. Perhaps, it should not have been done, but it was. So here it is.)[5]

Watson and Rayner found that loud noises startled and frightened Albert. For instance, the sound of striking a resonant piece of metal with a hammer frightened him. After two or three successive strikes, Albert would exhibit fear responses, including crying. But Albert didn't seem upset by any other aspects of his environment. On various occasions Watson and Rayner showed him animals and objects when he wasn't crying: a white rat, a rabbit, a dog, a monkey, toys, and a burning newspaper. Albert typically tried to reach or approach these objects. They decided to try to establish a phobic response to a white rat.

They started by taking a rat from a basket and showing it to Albert. He began to reach for the rat with his left hand. And when his hand almost touched the rat, they struck a metal bar. Albert jumped in an agitated manner and fell forward, burying his face in the mattress. But he didn't cry. Albert then tried to touch the rat with his right hand. And when he was about to touch it, they again struck the bar. Albert jumped suddenly, fell forward, and whimpered.

A week later, they showed him the rat, this time without the loud sound. Albert stared at it but didn't reach for it. Then they moved the rat closer. And when the rat nosed Albert's left hand, he withdrew his hand. He started to reach for the rat's head with the forefinger of his left hand, but withdrew it abruptly before contact.

Then Watson and Rayner tested Albert's reaction to colored blocks. He picked them up, dropped them, and pounded them. In the remainder of the tests they gave him the blocks often to quiet him and to evaluate his general emotional state. They always removed the blocks when the process of conditioning was under way.

Then, for three times in a row, Watson and Rayner presented the rat and the loud sound

[5]Based on Watson, J. B., & Rayner, R. (1920). Conditioned emotional reaction. *Journal of Experimental Psychology, 3*, 1–4.

simultaneously. The first time, Albert started to touch the rat but fell over to the right side. In the two following trials, he fell to the right side and rested upon his hands. He turned his head away from the rat but didn't cry. Then they presented the rat alone. Albert puckered his face, whimpered, and withdrew his body sharply to the left. The next time they presented the rat and the sound jointly. Albert startled violently and cried, but didn't fall over.

Watson and Rayner then presented the rat alone. Albert began to cry, and almost instantly turned sharply to the left, fell over on his left side, raised himself on all fours and began to crawl away rapidly.

We can see that after several pairings the rat alone brought about avoidance behavior and crying. Whereas, before, the rat had been, at worst, neutral, now it had apparently become a fear-eliciting object.

Five days after Watson and Rayner established this response, they conducted a further series of tests with Albert. Initially, they presented the rat to him and he cried and turned away, almost managing to crawl off the table. Later, they presented colored blocks to him. He accepted the blocks, smiling and making gurgling sounds. Next they reintroduced the rat, and again Albert scurried away from it on all fours as quickly as he could. It was obvious that the rat still produced Albert's avoidance responses; but the blocks produced playing responses.

To see if this avoidance generalized to other animate objects, the experimenters presented a rabbit. Albert leaned as far away from the animal as possible, whimpered, then burst into tears. When they placed the rabbit in contact with him, he buried his face in the mattress and crawled away, crying as he went. Next, they presented a dog. The dog didn't produce as pronounced a reaction as the rabbit did. When they placed a fur coat on either side of the dog, Albert quickly turned and moved away from the object.

Albert cried, turned from, and moved away from all objects that resembled the white rat. Also, it seemed as though the more similar the objects were to the furry white rat, the more pronounced and violent were Albert's responses. His responses to the rabbit were extreme, but responses to cotton were much less pronounced. Early in this book, we called this phenomenon stimulus generalization—responding similarly to similar stimuli.

Watson and Rayner thought they had established a phobia that would last for Albert's lifetime if they didn't intervene to get rid of the phobia. An intervention might have involved gradually changing Albert's experiences with furry objects until they were always pleasant. In this way, they might have eliminated the phobia they had experimentally established. Unfortunately, they never had the chance to finish this phase of the experiment because Albert's mother removed him from the hospital after they started the last series of experimental procedures.

Let's review: The striking of the iron bar behind Albert produced a fear response. This type of response to loud noises is common in all infants and perhaps is reflexive, unlearned behavior. Thus, because the sound from striking the metal bar unconditionally produced an unlearned fear response, we'll call that sound the unconditioned stimulus. We could also define the fear responses that resulted when Watson and Rayner struck the metal bar as the unconditioned response because they were a natural reaction to the noise; the white rat functioned as the conditioned stimulus as Watson and Rayner repeatedly paired it with the unconditioned stimulus, the loud noise. After several pairings, the white rat alone produced the fear response. The fear response to the white rat is the conditioned response. This procedure is the same Pavlov used in conditioning the salivation response.

QUESTION

1. Give an example of conditioning a phobia. Include the
   a. unconditioned stimulus (US)
   b. unconditioned response (UR)
   c. conditioned stimulus (CS)
   d. conditioned response (CR)
   e. procedure.

Example
I'M A WOMAN TRAPPED IN A MAN'S BODY—PART IV[6]

Remember Bobbie Brown, the young transgender man who hated his male body? Bobbie had thought surgery was the only solution to his unhappiness. Working with Sid and Dawn, Bobbie was becoming much happier with being a man. By learning to act like a typical man, he had escaped from one part of the torment he suffered. Bobbie had learned to sit, walk, and talk like a typical man; he had even learned to think like a typical man.

But Bobbie still wasn't a typical man. Even though he could maintain extended sexual fantasies about women, they didn't elicit any sexual response. In addition, he felt sexually attracted to other men; for instance, he had erections at the sight of men about five times a day.

---

[6]Based on Barlow, D. H., Reynolds, E. J., Agras, W. S., & Miss, J. (1973). Gender identity change in a transsexual. *Archives of General Psychiatry, 28,* 569–576.

Sid asked Bobbie, "Now, are you sure you want to keep working toward becoming a typical male? It might be easier to ask Dawn to help you accept the way you are."

"No, Mr. Fields. Like I said, I didn't come this far not to go the whole way."

Sid and Dawn needed to use respondent conditioning to help Bobbie achieve sexual arousal to heterosexual stimuli. They used a mechanical strain gauge to measure changes in Bobbie's penile circumference when he looked at slides of nude females. The results? Sexual arousal was nonexistent. Pictures of nude females acted as neutral stimuli for Bobbie. Pictures of nude males, however, caused Bobbie to have approximately 40% of a full erection.

Then Sid and Dawn showed a nude female slide right before each nude male slide. And Bobbie started having sexual arousal with the female pictures.

Now, when Sid and Dawn tested Bobbie's sexual arousal with new nude female pictures, he found that Bobbie averaged 40% of a full erection. But when they stopped pairing male and female pictures, this heterosexual arousal decreased. So he used the pairing procedure again, and again heterosexual arousal increased. Bobbie began to find women sexually attractive, and he began to have sexual fantasies about women 5 to 15 times a day.

But Bobbie continued experiencing strong transgender arousal. He averaged over 40% of a full erection when he saw nude male pictures, and he reported approximately 8 instances of sexual attraction to males and male fantasies a day.

"Bobbie, you now have two sources of sexual arousal, men and women. You sure you don't want to quit while you're ahead of the troops?"

"I told you I want to become a typical man, for better or worse," Bobbie laughed, but with a slight lump in his throat.

So Sid and Dawn were not off the hook yet; they had to help Bobbie get rid of his sexual arousal to male visual stimuli. He asked Bobbie to imagine a transgender fantasy. Then, when Bobbie reported a clear image, he got an electric shock in his forearm until he signaled that the fantasy had ceased.

Sid and Dawn paired sexual fantasies of nude males (established conditioned eliciting stimulus) with electric shock (unconditioned respondent elicit-

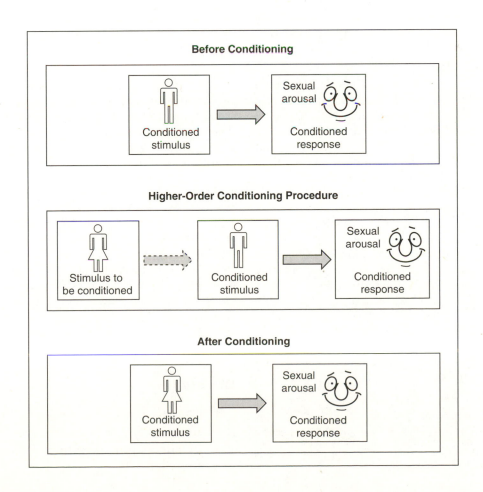

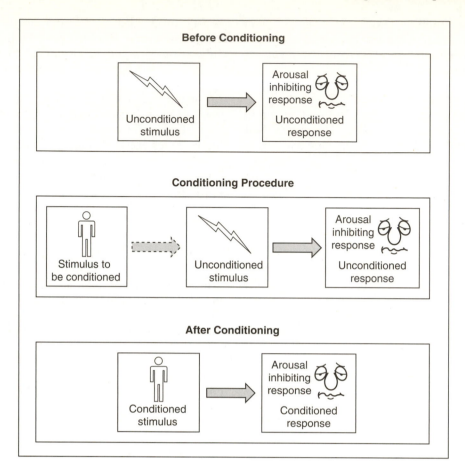

ing stimulus). They were using a respondent conditioning procedure to establish sexual male fantasies as a conditioned eliciting stimulus that elicited responses that would inhibit sexual arousal.[7]

This intervention went on for about 20 sessions over a period of 2 months. Bobbie's transgender arousal gradually decreased. Sexual arousal to males averaged between 0 and 5% and reported fantasies dropped to approximately 3 per day. Female arousal continued to rise and finally reached a level of 60%.

Bobbie's parents were happy. They said he behaved like a man at home and no longer showed isolate or depressive behaviors. He began full-time high school classes for the fall term and felt comfortable and relaxed in most social settings. For the first time in his life, he wanted to date and have sexual relations with females. And he also looked more masculine; he had gained over 15 pounds and had grown 1½ inches during the 8 months of Sid and Dawn's intervention.

In follow-ups, they no longer continued formal treatment, but they saw Bobbie about once a week for a month, then once a month for 5 months. These sessions were mainly supportive. Sid advised Bobbie on how to behave in various social situations. After those months of follow-ups, Bobbie's heterosexual arousal averaged 65% of a full erection and transgender arousal averaged 15%. Bobbie told Sid and Dawn that, for the first time he had had an orgasm and ejaculation as a result of masturbating while imagining sexual intercourse with a woman.

Sid and Dawn continued seeing Bobbie every 3 months. And after 1 year, Bobbie had acquired a steady girlfriend with whom he engaged in light petting. He continued to become more confident and talkative. He also changed his name from Bobbie to Bob.

QUESTIONS

1. Describe a procedure to increase heterosexual arousal to female pictures.
2. Describe a procedure to decrease transgender arousal to male pictures.

---

[7]Alternatively, we could interpret this second part of Sid and Dawn's intervention as an operant-conditioning punishment procedure in which the response was transgender fantasizing and the consequence was the electric shock.

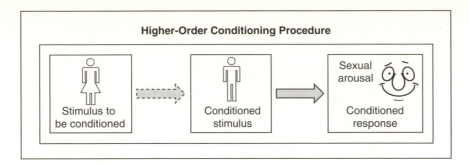

Higher-Order Conditioning Procedure

Stimulus to be conditioned → Conditioned stimulus → Sexual arousal / Conditioned response

Concept
HIGHER-ORDER RESPONDENT CONDITIONING

Bobbie's intervention is one of the most impressive examples of applied behavior analysis in our field. It involved changing what most people call "personality." For us, *personality* means the consistent way we behave or respond in a wide variety of settings. Sid and Dawn were able to help Bobbie change his way of talking, moving, thinking, and feeling. But all this wouldn't have been possible without a lot of effort from the whole team, especially Bobbie. Bobbie's intervention was intensive; it took 8 months of daily intervention and more than a year of follow-up.

So far, we have seen examples of respondent conditioning where the conditioned stimulus resulted from pairing an unconditioned stimulus (e.g., food or an aversive noise) with a neutral stimulus (e.g., a specific person or a rat). In Bobbie's case, however, we saw how a conditioned stimulus could result from pairing an effective **conditioned** stimulus (not an **un**conditoned stimulus) with a neutral stimulus. Nude pictures of males had acquired conditioned eliciting properties for Bobbie (we say the male pictures were **conditioned** stimuli because we think they probably didn't elicit an arousal response from Bobbie until he had had some experience with such images).

They paired nude female pictures (neutral stimuli) with the nude male pictures (conditioned stimuli). This pairing of a neutral stimulus with a conditioned stimulus is called ***higher-order conditioning.***

Definition: Concept
Higher-order conditioning
- Establishing a conditioned stimulus
- by pairing a neutral stimulus
- with an already established conditioned stimulus.

QUESTION

1. *Higher-order conditioning*—define it and give an example.

Compare and Contrast
RESPONDENT EXTINCTION AND OPERANT EXTINCTION

Remember what happened the first time Sid stopped pairing the female pictures with the male pictures?

The female pictures stopped eliciting sexual arousal.

Definition: Concept
Respondent extinction
- Present the conditioned stimulus
- without pairing it
- with the unconditioned stimulus,
- or with an already established conditioned stimulus,
- and the conditioned stimulus will lose its eliciting power.

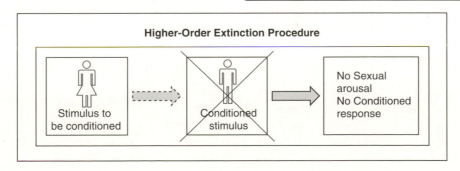

Higher-Order Extinction Procedure

Stimulus to be conditioned → Conditioned stimulus → No Sexual arousal / No Conditioned response

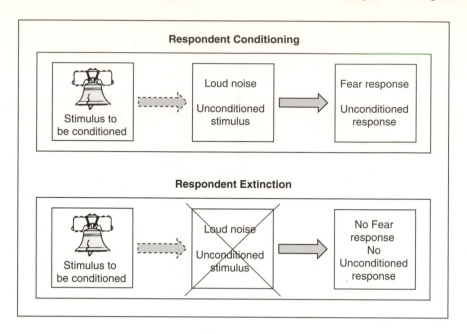

When the conditioned stimulus is repeatedly presented without the stimulus that gave the conditioned stimulus it's eliciting function, the conditioned stimulus will lose that eliciting function. This is **respondent** extinction.

In **respondent extinction,** we present the conditioned stimulus without pairing it with the unconditioned stimulus. Or, in the case of higher-order conditioning, we no longer pair the new conditioned stimulus with the already established CS.

As a result of respondent extinction the CS stops eliciting the conditioned response. (Remember the conditioned response is usually more or less the same as the unconditioned response, except that it was elicited by the conditioned stimulus.).

In Chapter 6, we learned about **operant** extinction. Be careful not to confuse **respondent** extinction with **operant** extinction. In respondent extinction, we no longer pair the conditioned stimulus with the unconditioned stimulus. No response is necessary for this procedure to have an extinguishing effect.

Remember, in operant extinction, we no longer give the **contingent** behavioral outcome. In operant extinction, we no longer follow the response with a contingent reinforcer or with the contingent termination of an aversive stimulus The previously reinforced response *must* occur for the absence of the contingent reinforcer to have an extinguishing effect.

Polka Problems

Whenever Dawn's grandmother plays her favorite album, *The Six Fat Dutchmen Play All-Time Polka Favorites*, little Rod starts to cry. Bowing to Rod's exquisite musical taste, she always rushes to turn off the offending music.

And Dawn wonders, is Rod's crying a respondent reflex in which this low-rent polka music automatically elicits crying because it was paired with an unconditioned stimulus, like pain? Or is it an example of an escape contingency in which Rod's crying in immediately reinforced by the removal of the aversive-sounding music? In other words, is the music a respondent eliciting stimulus or an operant aversive stimulus?

Here's what the operant escape contingency looks like:

Operant Escape Conditioning

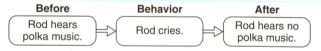

Dawn thinks that maybe she shouldn't let Rod be the musical dictator of the household. So she tries to extinguish his crying.

1. Please fill in the extinction diagram.

Extinction of Escape Behavior

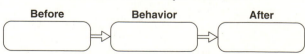

Comparison and Contrast Respondent Extinction			
Procedures	Operation	Is responding necessary for extinction to occur?	Results (After extinction)
Respondent Extinction	Stop pairing the CS with the US	No	CS eventually stops eliciting the CR
Operant Extinction	Stop presenting the reinforcer or removing the aversive condition contingent on the response	Yes, or the lack of a contingency won't have any effect	Response rate sometimes increases at first, then it decreases until it reaches its operant level

2. Which is it, respondent or operant extinction (hint—the fact that there is a response in this diagram should give it away)?

   a. respondent extinction

   b. operant extinction

3. If Rod's crying **fails** to extinguish, Dawn should suspect that the crying is

   a. respondent behavior, and the music is a respondent eliciting stimulus

   b. operant behavior, and the music is an aversive before condition

QUESTIONS

1. Discuss the similarities and differences between respondent and operant extinction, in terms of:

   a. the procedure

   b. the operation

   c. the results.

   Friendly warning: It may be hard to get a good grade on this quiz without being able to answer this question.

2. Illustrate how you could use operant extinction to determine if a stimulus is a respondent eliciting stimulus or an operant before condition.

Example
PHIL'S PHOBIA[8]

"You'll like the zoo," Mr. Jones told his son, Phil. "We can see elephants and monkeys, too. We'll have a great time, so let's have no nonsense, OK?"

"Okay," Phil said.

_____
[8]Based on Lazarus, A. A. (1960). The elimination of children's phobias by deconditioning. (pp. 114–122). In H. J. Eysenck (Ed.). *Behavior therapy and the neurosis*. London: Pergamon.

All the while Phil was getting dressed to go to the zoo, he was strangely quiet. Phil's mother asked him if he felt well. Phil said he did, but later, just as they were ready to go to the car, he disappeared into the bathroom. The rest of the family waited in the car for him. Fifteen minutes passed.

"This is ridiculous," Mr. Jones said.

Five minutes later Mr. Jones got out of the car and said, "I'll straighten that kid out!"

When Mr. Jones entered the house, Phil was standing outside the door of the bathroom. As the father approached him, the boy lowered his head and looked sheepish.

"I've had enough," the father said as he grabbed Phil's hand. He half pulled Phil toward the car. When they were within about 30 feet, Phil ceased moving his feet and legs. Mr. Jones dragged the child into the car and slammed the door.

"Now, Phil, I . . ." Mr. Jones stopped short. Phil had turned white. Beads of perspiration ran down his cheeks, and his eyes looked funny and glazed. Just then he let out a wail of anguish that the neighbors could hear a block away. His small body shook and trembled.

Mr. Jones took Phil back to the house and then returned to the car where the rest of the family waited.

"Well, we'll go to the zoo another time," Mr. Jones said. They all got out of the car and walked slowly back to the house.

Ever since he was 8 years old, Phil had been afraid of cars. Two years earlier he had been in a car accident. His fear was real and caused him and his parents constant distress. When Dr. Lazarus met Phil, it took him only a few minutes to diagnose his problem as a car phobia, a type of phobia that occasionally occurs among children. Dr. Lazarus knew that Phil had learned his fear of cars; so he could also get rid of it.

During the first session, Lazarus talked to Phil and got to know him. He found that Phil was fond of chocolate. During the next session, Lazarus began to treat Phil's phobia. While talking with him, Lazarus would steer the conversation onto the subject of trains, airplanes, buses, and other vehicles. Discussing motor vehicles seems a long way from actually riding in one, but even the confrontations with this stimulus initially elicited mild fear responses in Phil. But Lazarus was sensitive to Phil's reactions and monitored them closely. Whenever Phil showed fear, he didn't comfort the child or try to talk him out of his fear. But as soon as Phil volunteered a positive comment about the subject, he would offer a piece of his favorite chocolate. By the third session, Phil was talking freely and at great length about all types of moving vehicles. He showed no signs of fear. Lazarus thought Phil was ready for the next phase of his treatment.

"Let's play a game today," Lazarus said. He pulled an object out of his pocket. It was a toy car. Immediately Phil stepped back a few steps and looked at Lazarus as if questioning his friendship. Before he said anything else, Lazarus popped a small piece of chocolate in Phil's mouth. Then he took another car and proceeded to play a game in which he sent the two toy cars crashing into one another head-on. Phil turned white and perspiration formed on his forehead. But Lazarus didn't seem to notice Phil or his fearful state; he remained engrossed in his play, time and time again acting out versions of accidents between the toy cars. Soon Phil began to recover some of his color and moved slightly toward Lazarus. At this point, Lazarus lost momentary interest in his absorbing game, popped a piece of chocolate into Phil's mouth, and talked to the child. Then he turned back to his game.

As Phil moved closer to Lazarus and the accident-prone cars, he got more and more of his favorite chocolate and more and more of Lazarus's attention. After each accident game in which Phil evidenced no fear, he got a chocolate. Soon Phil was touching the toy cars with no apparent fear. Later Lazarus and Phil spent hours playing the accident game with the toy cars. The game was interspersed with chocolate breaks, and Phil greatly enjoyed himself.

Eventually, Lazarus and Phil played games outside. Lazarus parked a car nearby. They spent hours sitting in it, discussing the accident in which Phil had been involved. As long as Phil entered into this conversation freely and showed no fear, he got pieces of chocolate and lots of attention from his friend. After awhile, the two began to take short imaginary rides. One day Lazarus searched through his pockets pretending to look for a piece of chocolate. "We're all out of candy, Phil. Sorry," he said.

"Let's go get some more." While telling this to Phil he turned on the ignition and started the car, watching Phil closely as he did. There were no signs of fear. The store was only a block away, but he was in no hurry to get there. Once they did reach the store, they bought a good supply of chocolate, got back into the car, and began to drive around town. They laughed and acted like tourists. Phil chewed his chocolate and watched the sights as he discovered the pleasures of travel.

When they returned to Phil's house, Mr. Jones was waiting in the drive. Phil jumped out of the car and ran to his Dad, and began to talk about his wonderful trip. Phil left Lazarus and his father alone and went inside to tell his adventures to his mother. "I guess we're due to go on an outing," Phil's father said.

"Sounds like a good idea. I hear the zoo is good to visit this time of the year," Lazarus smiled.

You might wonder why such phobias last so long. Why don't they extinguish? The problem is that the phobic person avoids the phobic situation. So the phobia never has a chance to extinguish. For Phil to lose his phobia more naturally, he would have to take many trips in the car; but he avoided that. So, without behavioral intervention, a person might maintain an irrational phobia forever.

QUESTION

1. Describe a procedure to get rid of a car phobia.

Operant Treatment of Phobias[9]

Automobiles had become aversive stimuli for Phil. They exerted two different stimulus functions:

- First, they acted as aversive stimuli or establishing operations supporting operant escape and avoidance behavior. So, in the presence of a car or car-related stimuli, Phil emitted avoidance or escape responses, such as walking away. These responses might also have been reinforced by the attention of people around him.
- Second, cars or car-related stimuli acted as conditioned eliciting stimuli. Remember, Phil

---

[9]For an extensive review of behavioral techniques in the treatment of children's phobias, consult Ollendick, T. H. (1979). Fear reduction techniques with children. *Progress in Behavior Modification*, 8, 127–168.

sweat and shook all over in the presence of a car.

As we can see, phobias can involve the interaction of operant and respondent conditioning.

Lazarus used operant conditioning techniques to eliminate Phil's phobia. He used chocolate candy and attention as reinforcers and differentially reinforced approaching the car. His procedure looked almost like shaping, where he reinforced responses that more and more closely approximated the most fear-eliciting response, riding in a car. However, remember that shaping produces new responses, responses that didn't previously exist at a high rate in the subject's repertoire. And this was definitely not the case with Phil. He was able to play with toy cars and ride in a car. He had made these responses before; they were already part of his repertoire. So it would be more appropriate to talk about differential reinforcement rather than shaping when we describe Lazarus's procedure.

Leitenberg has used the general term *reinforced practice* to describe the use of reinforcement by the presentation of reinforcers to increase approaching aversive and fear-evoking stimuli in the treatment of phobias. But we might say this procedure also involves respondent extinction—the repeated presentation of the conditioned fear-evoking stimulus (car) without pairing with an unconditioned stimulus (the accident). The result was that the car lost its power to elicit the conditioned fear reaction.[10]

QUESTIONS

1. Give an example showing how phobias could evolve from operant and respondent conditioning.
2. Describe the use of operant conditioning techniques to get rid of a car phobia.

Concept
SYSTEMATIC DESENSITIZATION

Systematic desensitization is perhaps the most widely used intervention with phobias. It was first developed by Wolpe in 1958. Unlike reinforced

_____
[10]Leitenberg, H. (1976). Behavioral approaches to treatment of neuroses (pp. 124–167). In H. Leitenberg (Ed.). *Handbook of behavior modification and behavior therapy.* Englewood Cliffs, NJ: Prentice Hall.

practice, in systematic desensitization it is assumed that anxiety must not occur for successful elimination of phobic behavior. In systematic desensitization, we train the client to relax completely. Then we present stimuli in a hierarchy from the least to the most fear-producing ones. The client must be completely relaxed so that the fear is inhibited at each step in the hierarchy.

Definition: Concept
Systematic desensitization
○ Combining relaxation with
○ a hierarchy of fear-producing stimuli,
○ arranged from the least to the most frightening.

Systematic desensitization could be done *in vivo* or with imagination. In *in vivo* **desensitization,** the client uses relaxation skills to face real-life, fear-producing situations. But systematic desensitization can be done in the therapist's office without bringing the client's behavior into direct contact with the real fear-eliciting environment. Instead of actually experiencing stimulus situations closer to those that produce the phobic reaction, the client merely imagines such situations while relaxing in the office.

The therapist using systematic desensitization prefers semihypnotic relaxation induced through instructions. Once the client is deeply relaxed, the therapist asks her or him to imagine various environmental situations or stimuli that normally produce a mild phobic reaction. If the client can imagine these situations and yet remain relaxed, the therapist asks the client to imagine another situation that more closely approaches the one the client claims elicits severe phobic responses. Eventually, the therapist asks the client to imagine the situation that seems to elicit the greatest fear responses. The client will be rid of the phobia if he or she can imagine this situation and still remain deeply relaxed.

After completing the procedure, the client should be capable of leaving the therapist's office and facing real situations without experiencing phobic reactions. As unlikely as it seems, the client often can do this. Case reports of systematic desensitization indicate that therapists can use this procedure to treat many phobic behaviors successfully. This technique, along with other behavioral techniques, has made phobic responses a relatively simple problem for the therapist to deal with.

Earlier in this chapter, Dawn used a variation of systematic desensitization to get rid of Sammy's fear of darkness. She used an **emotive imagery** intervention. Here's the difference: In systematic desensitization, the therapist uses muscular relaxation as the fear-inhibiting response. In an emotive imagery intervention, the therapist uses imaginative situations that elicit positive, pleasant, potentially reinforcing emotional reactions; these reactions are assumed to inhibit the fearful responses.

QUESTIONS

1. *Systematic desensitization*—define it and give an example.
2. What is the difference between emotive imaginary treatment and systematic desensitization?

BASIC ENRICHMENT

CONDITIONING A PHOBIA

We mentioned in the discussion of the Watson and Rayner experiment that Albert's mother took him from their experiment shortly after the experimenters had conditioned the phobia. Watson and Rayner had intended to eliminate the phobia after they had conditioned it. They had felt obligated to do so. Albert's removal led them to speculate that he would retain the phobia throughout his life. A further suggestion made was that when Albert reached manhood, he might well have forgotten the circumstances under which his phobia first arose and might seek psychoanalytic help, complaining of a dreadful fear of seal skins, fur coats, and all other furry objects. Watson and Rayner speculated how a well-meaning therapist who was uninformed as to the actual origin of the phobia might suggest that Albert's problem was linked to some early love for his mother.

It's true that the clinical treatment of phobias has varied greatly in the past decade. Standard forms of therapy appeal to rational behavior or derive from a theory that has been unsuccessful. Behavior analysts have eliminated phobias with applied behavior-analysis techniques, such as in the case of Sammy and Phil.

(We should add that we doubt if Watson and Rayner were successful in establishing a phobia whose generalized effects lasted much longer than it took for Albert to get home, let alone lasting until he reached manhood. Respondent conditioning is often a transient effect that occurs only when all the conditions are just right. It's so difficult to get that we've never heard of students demonstrating respondent conditioning in an introductory laboratory, but thousands and thousands of students have operantly conditioned the bar presses of thousands and thousands of rats.)

Compare and Contrast
OPERANT AND RESPONDENT ANALYSES OF THE GILLES DE LA TOURETTE SYNDROME

Sid's Seminar

Tom: Remember Grace? We studied her problem in Chapter 3. She had that unusual Gilles de la Tourette syndrome. She would clench her fists, making herself rigid and vibrating back and forth. Her lips would twist to the left, and with difficulty, she would then say *the* word. Remember that she could not control this behavior.[11]

Max: How could we forget?

Tom: Goldiamond and Glass thought Grace's attacks were operant behavior, reinforced by escape from an aversive condition. But I don't think so. I think her attacks were respondent behavior elicited by the aversive condition that preceded them. They were reflexive, just like the dog's leg-flexion reflex when its foot touched an electrified grid. For instance, the commotion of her relatives was a respondent eliciting stimulus. It elicited her display of the Gilles de la Tourette syndrome—a respondent.

Sid: That makes sense, and I understand why you think as you do. In our culture, we think of fast behavior as reflexive; and involuntary behavior also seems reflexive to us. The old psychology textbooks even described respondent behavior as involuntary and spontaneous, and they described operant behavior as voluntary and deliberate.

---

[11]Based on Goldiamond, I. (1984). Training parent trainers and ethicists in nonlinear analysis of behavior. In R. Dangel & R. Polster (Eds), *Parent training foundations of research and practice* (pp. 504–546). New York: Guilford Press.

Tom: So what's wrong with that? It seems like Grace's immediate, knee-jerk-like, involuntary attacks must be respondent reflexes.

Sid: Behavior analysts are just beginning to understand the power of contingencies of reinforcement. We're just beginning to understand how so-called "natural" responses are often learned operants under the control of contingencies of reinforcement.

Tom: So how can we find out whether a behavior is an elicited respondent or a reinforced operant?

Sid: Here's one feature of Grace's behavior that might give you a hint. If the response is actually a complex sequence of responses, as language is, then we've probably got operant behavior. And if the response varies from culture to culture, then we're almost sure to be dealing with learned operant behavior—behavior controlled by its behavioral consequences—the contingencies of reinforcement.

Tom: I don't see what that has to do with Grace's attacks.

Sid: Remember the word she always said at the end of each attack? *The* word?

Tom: Yes.

Sid: Well, no doubt, that word is a learned, culturally based operant. If she came from a French culture, that word would refer to the sea animal, the seal. But coming from the United States the word means something else. Anyhow, no one has ever shown how a respondent eliciting stimulus can elicit a complex operant response like speaking a word.

Tom: That all seems too inferential to me, almost theoretical. I need more concrete proof to convince me that a reinforcement contingency controlled those attacks. And I don't think that's something you can prove one way or the other.

Max: There is a way; its called *extinction*. Look at what happens after the response. If Grace's attack were operant responses maintained by their consequences, then you need to prevent those consequences. If you do that, the response should extinguish.

Sue: So suppose her attacks no longer allowed her to escape aversive situations. Suppose she had to stay and finish her dinner when they had guests. If her attacks were escape responses, then they should extinguish. But if her attacks were unconditioned responses elicited by an unconditioned eliciting stimulus (perhaps stress), then they should continue to occur.

QUESTION

1. Compare and contrast operant and respondent analyses of the Gilles de la Tourette syndrome.

Respondent Conditioning and the Body's Regulatory Systems
SID KICKS THE SUGAR MONKEY

Sid stepped on the scale, dreading what he was about to see. He peeked at the red numbers in the digital readout. That couldn't be right! He picked up his left foot. The numbers flickered for a minute and then settled back to the same total.

"Dawn, something's wrong with this scale," Sid said. "It says I've gained 15 pounds in the past two months; that can't be right."

"Sid, your clothes have looked a little tight lately; maybe the scale is right," Dawn said.

"Impossible. I eat a low-fat diet and I exercise. Nothing has changed in my fitness routine. How could I have gained 15 pounds in 2 months?"

"Nothing has changed?" asked Dawn. "It seems to me you've been drinking a lot more Coke lately."

"When?"

"Like when you're staying up all night working on your dissertation. You know Sid, one glass of Coke has 100 calories."

"But I need a caffeine fix to stay awake."

"Well, then, have your drug if you must, but at least switch to Diet Coke," said Dawn. "Then you won't be drinking so much sugar."

Sid was about to argue when he caught a glimpse of the scale again. Instead, he went to the store and bought a 24-pack of Diet Coke.

. . . Later that night . . . .

"Sid, you look exhausted," Dawn said.

"Yeah, I can't keep my eyes open; I've been sitting here working on the same paragraph for the last half hour. Maybe there's less caffeine in these Diet Cokes."

Dawn remembered a study she had read in grad school. Sid was right; his lack of energy was due to his switch to Diet Cokes. But it was not because they contained less caffeine. And yes, boys and girls, it all had to do with (our sponsor for this week's episode) **respondent conditioning.** It wasn't the lack of caffeine; it was the respondent-connection deal.

When Sid drinks the sugar, that sugar in his gut is an unconditioned stimulus (US) that elicits a release of insulin by the pancreas. And the sweet taste of the sugar reliably precedes this US. So that sweet taste becomes a conditioned stimulus (CS) that also elicits the pancreas's release of insulin.

What happens when a Coke junkie like Sid switches from consistently drinking the sugar-laden Classic Coke to the sugar-free Diet Coke? The sweet taste of the Diet Coke continues to elicit the release of insulin. So? So, this released insulin was ordinarily used up in the process of digesting the

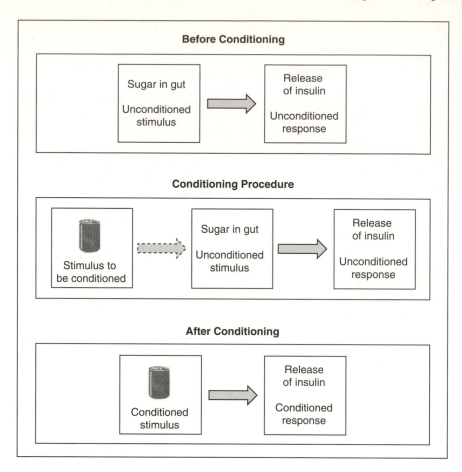

sugar. But when there is no sugar to digest, the increased insulin causes the blood-sugar level to drop. And the drop in blood-sugar level causes the person to feel weak or groggy. All because of respondent conditioning.

To sum up this complex analysis: Why did Sid feel groggy? Because of respondent conditioning, the sugar-free sweet taste causes the pancreas to elicit insulin. And the released insulin brings you down because there's no extra sugar in your blood to use up the insulin during its digestion. In other words, sugar-free insulin elicitation overloads your system and brings you down.

Dawn explained to Sid that the sweet taste of the Diet Coke would soon lose its eliciting power because of respondent extinction; as long as Sid stayed with Diet Coke and the sweet taste of Coke was no longer paired with sugar in his gut, that sweet taste would soon stop eliciting the release of insulin; and, therefore, there would be no excess insulin to bring him down.

QUESTIONS

1. Be able to describe the conditioned insulin phenomenon and diagram the respondent processes.

2. How can respondent extinction get rid of the problem?

*Example of Respondent Conditioning
in Behavioral Medicine*
RESPONDENT CONDITIONING OF THE IMMUNE SYSTEM

Respondent conditioning can also affect the workings of the body's immune system. A classic study shows it best. In a single conditioning trial, rats were given water sweetened with saccharin-flavored water (CS) and then an injection of *cyclophosphamide* (US). This drug suppresses the defensive activity of the immune system; so the UR to the drug was the decrease in activity of the immune system.

Then, a few days later, all the rats were injected with a small quantity of foreign cells (which the immune system would normally fight). Then one half of the rats (the experimental group) received saccharin-flavored water to drink, and the other half of the rats (the control group) received regular water to drink. For the experimental group, the saccharin-flavored water functioned as a CS and elicited the decrease in activity of the immune sys-

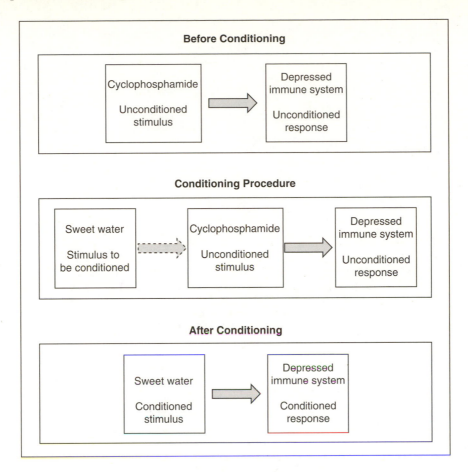

Before Conditioning

Cyclophosphamide

Unconditioned stimulus

→

Depressed immune system

Unconditioned response

Conditioning Procedure

Sweet water

Stimulus to be conditioned

⇢

Cyclophosphamide

Unconditioned stimulus

→

Depressed immune system

Unconditioned response

After Conditioning

Sweet water

Conditioned stimulus

→

Depressed immune system

Conditioned response

tem (CR). Therefore, the immune system of the experimental group was not as able to fight off the invasion of the foreign bodies as was that of the control group that had drunk only plain water, which had *not* functioned as a CS to elicit the decreased immune-system activity.

QUESTION

1. Be able to diagram respondent conditioning of the immune system.

INTERMEDIATE ENRICHMENT

STIMULUS GENERALIZATION IN RESPONDENT CONDITIONING

Suppose that to condition salivation in a dog, a low-pitched bell is paired with meat powder. Thereafter, the low-pitched bell will elicit salivation. However there is some stimulus generalization between the low-pitched bell and other bells. So if a high-pitched bell is presented, it may elicit salivation as well, though not as much. After a neutral stimulus becomes a conditioned stimulus through respondent conditioning, any change in the CS from what it was

during conditioning will result in a smaller conditioned response.

QUESTION

1. Give an example of stimulus generalization in respondent conditioning. Compound conditioned stimuli: overshadowing and Blocking Two neutral stimuli (for example, a bell and a light) can be paired with an unconditioned stimulus (for example, food) at the same time

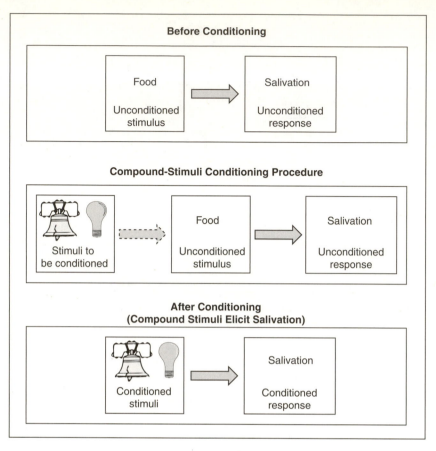

Before Conditioning

Food

Unconditioned
stimulus

→

Salivation

Unconditioned
response

Compound-Stimuli Conditioning Procedure

Stimuli to
be conditioned

Food

Unconditioned
stimulus

Salivation

Unconditioned
response

After Conditioning
(Compound Stimuli Elicit Salivation)

Conditioned
stimuli

→

Salivation

Conditioned
response

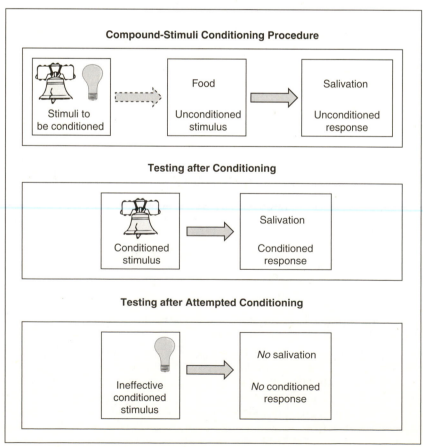

Compound-Stimuli Conditioning Procedure

Stimuli to
be conditioned

Food

Unconditioned
stimulus

Salivation

Unconditioned
response

Testing after Conditioning

Conditioned
stimulus

→

Salivation

Conditioned
response

Testing after Attempted Conditioning

Ineffective
conditioned
stimulus

→

No salivation

No conditioned
response

to make a compound conditioned stimulus that elicits a conditioned response.

When two stimuli form a compound conditioned stimulus, the results of presenting each stimulus individually are unpredictable. Often, one of the stimuli elicits the conditioned response and the other stimuli elicits no response. When this happens, the stimulus that elicits the CR is said to have **overshadowed** the other stimulus.

Though the light and the bell were conditioned together, only the bell elicits salivation. The light elicits nothing.

Here's one reason a component of a compound stimulus might not elicit the conditioned response: The species might be inherently more sensitive to one stimulus than another. (For example, rats are usually more sensitive to sound than to light because of their poor vision; and that could explain why, for rats, the bell overshadows the light.)

But there's another way we might get this same overshadowing: Suppose we first pair the bell with the meat powder so that it becomes a CS that elicits the salivation CR. Then suppose we create a compound stimulus by presenting the bell and the light together. And we pair this compound bell-light stimulus with the meat powder so that the compound light-bell stimulus becomes a CS that elicits the salivation CR (as in the preceding diagram). And then suppose we test the bell and light separately. We would probably find that the bell continues to elicit the salivation, whereas the light never acquired that CS eliciting function. Again, the bell overshadowed the light. When a stimulus fails to become effective as a CS because it's presented with some other already effective CS, we say that the stimulus with the prior history of conditioning **blocked** the conditioning of the new stimulus. *Blocking* is a special kind of overshadowing. In this section, we've just seen the role of compound stimuli in overshadowing and blocking. In the next, we will see the role of compound stimuli in sudden death.

Behavioral Pharmacology
WHY DRUG ADDICTS OD[12]

One night, instead of remaining in his living room, Famous Entertainer enters the privacy of his bathroom to shoot up heroin. The next morning's Metropolis Gazette shows black-and white-photo of Famous Entertainer sprawled on bathroom floor.

If you shoot up heavy drugs often enough, there's a good chance you'll die of an overdose, and you don't have to be a famous entertainer to do so. It turns out that overdose victims have often just injected the drug in a novel environment. But why are heavy drugs and novel environments such a fatal combination?

Some drugs (opiates, amphetamines, and cocaine) can function as a US for a very unusual UR. The UR counteracts the effects of the drug. The drug not only gets you high but also produces an unconditioned response that counteracts that high; so you need a bigger dose to get off on it.

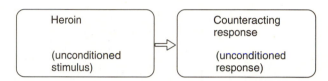

Can you see it coming? We've got a US that produces a UR. Now all we need is a CS—maybe a compound stimulus, such as the prick of the needle combined with the sight of the living room. Then, after a few pairings, this compound CS also starts eliciting the counteracting effect (CR).

So now the CS produces the CR; and that combines with the UR to produce an even bigger counteraction to the main drug effect, the high. Therefore, the addict must shoot up with even bigger doses of heroin.

But what happens when he goes to the bathroom to shoot up? The compound stimulus of the living room and the needle prick is no longer there to elicit its share of the counteracting effect (the needle prick by itself won't do the trick; it has only a CS function when combined with the stimuli from the living room).

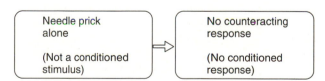

The addict takes his usual large dose, but without the protective counteracting CR. So he dies of an overdose.[13]

---

[12]This analysis was made by Siegel, S., Hinson. R. E., Krank, M. D., & MceCully, J. (1992). Heroin "overdose" death; The contribution of drug-associated environmental cues. *Science*, 316, 436–437.

[13]Our analysis of the drug study is a little more complex than the traditional analysis of this study. We doubt that the familiar environment (e.g., the living room) becomes a CS on it's own. If this were the case, the environment would elicit the CR every time the addict entered it, and then the CR would extinguish because it usually wasn't paired with the US. Instead it seems more plausible that the environment is paired with stimuli produced when actually taking the drug (such as the needle prick), and the combined stimuli become a compound stimulus. Note, however, that this is not a case of overshadowing; it's not the case that either the living room or the needle prick would elicit the counteracting CR, as would need to be the case for overshadowing to be the explanation.

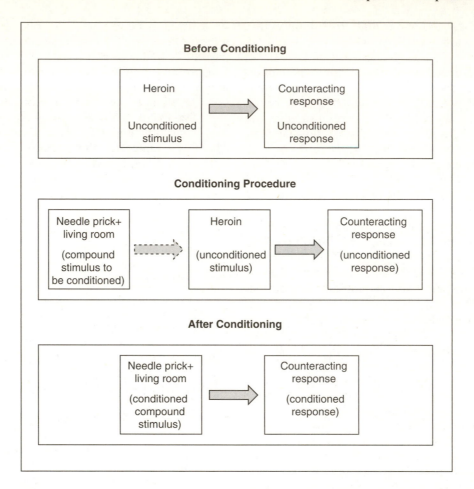

Before Conditioning

Heroin

Unconditioned stimulus → Counteracting response

Unconditioned response

Conditioning Procedure

Needle prick+ living room

(compound stimulus to be conditioned) ⇢ Heroin

(unconditioned stimulus) → Counteracting response

(unconditioned response)

After Conditioning

Needle prick+ living room

(conditioned compound stimulus) → Counteracting response

(conditioned response)

Compare and Contrast
CONDITIONED STIMULUS VS. DISCRIMINATIVE STIMULUS

Both students and professionals often confuse respondent and operant conditioning in two ways. First, they often confuse the operant pairing procedure that turns a neutral stimulus in to learned reinforcer with the respondent pairing procedure that turns a neutral stimulus into a CS. We addressed that confusion earlier in this chapter.

Second, they often confuse the S^D with the CS. We will now address that confusion.[14]

Here's a tricky question: What stimulus function did the white rat exert for Albert's behavior? Did it act as a CS (respondent function) or as an S^D (operant function)? If you are an observer who didn't know what Watson and Rayner had done with

Albert, you wouldn't know whether the white rat was a CS or an S^D. Why? Because both the CS and the S^D always "cause" the response; and you could see that the white rat always "caused" Albert's crying. But you wouldn't know whether the white rat caused the crying because the rat was functioning as a CS or an S^D. You'd have to know the nature of the original pairing.

The way to understand stimulus functions is to look at the history of conditioning. The CS *elicits* the response because in the past it has been paired with an unconditioned stimulus. The S^D *evokes* the response because in the presence of that stimulus that response was previously reinforced. (Notice that, by tradition, we use *elicit* to specify the function of the US and CS; we can use *evoke* to specify the function of a S^D, as well as of a CS, or a US.) For an S^D to acquire its ability to evoke a response, a contingent relationship between a response and an outcome **must** occur in the presence of that potential S^D. For instance, if every time Albert cries in the presence of a white rat, we reinforce his crying by hugging him, we could operantly condition his crying, in the presence of the rat. Then the presence of the rat would act as an S^D rather than a CS.

The CS elicits the response because in the past it has been paired with an unconditioned eliciting

---

[14]Traditionally most students and professionals err by calling learned reinforcers *conditioned stimuli* and by calling S^Ds *CSs,* in other words, by mistaking operant processes for respondent processes. Our experience is that students who learn the operant processes well, as they usually do in reading the first 20 chapters of this book, are much less inclined to make that error. Furthermore, they don't seem to often mistake respondent processes for operant processes.

stimulus. Remember, this is respondent conditioning; an outcome need not be contingent on the behavior for the S^D to acquire its eliciting properties. For instance, if a loud noise elicits crying from Albert then presenting the white rat immediately before the loud bang will make the white rat a CS that also elicits crying.[15]

Some psychologists say another way to judge stimulus functions is by looking at the type of response. They would say, if the response involves smooth muscles and glands, we are probably talking about a CS. And if the response involves skeletal muscles, we are probably talking about an S^D. Although this is generally the case, it's a mistake to assume this before knowing the history of conditioning.

Remember that you can respondently condition motor responses and operantly condition emotional responses. For instance, if every time Albert cries in the presence of a white rat we reinforce his crying by hugging him, we could operantly condition his crying. Then the presence of the rat acts as an S^D rather than a CS.

In addition, many responses involve a combination of smooth muscles, glands, and skeletal muscles—for example, vomiting and crying. So, just by looking at the type of responses, we could not easily infer the history of conditioning involved; and, therefore, we could not easily determine if the evoking stimulus is an S^D or CS.

Let's apply the S^D/CS test to the following example.

1. On hearing his master opening a can of dog food, Spot runs into the kitchen. What is the sound of the can opening and the over all process?

---

[15]By tradition, we use *the term elicit* to specify the function of the unconditioned and conditioned stimulus; we can use *evoke* to specify the function of an S^D, as well as of a conditioned stimulus, or an unconditioned stimulus. We authors of this book no longer make a big deal out of the "proper" use of *elicit* and *evoke*, restricting *elicit* to the action of the CS and *evoke* to the action of the S^D because the dictionary and common use say both terms mean the same thing. And it doesn't seem to help students discriminate between respondent and operant conditioning when the professor says the difference between the CS and the S^D is that one *elicits* and the other *evokes*, and the students are having trouble seeing the difference between these two "key" words, let alone between respondent and operant conditioning. Both words mean *to cause or produce a response*. But, throughout this chapter, we will tend to use the two terms in their traditional behavioral ways, as if it made a difference; this will make it easy for those professors who prefer the more classical approach to continue emphasizing the verbal distinction.

Note: We say a stimulus elicits a response: The bell elicits salivation. We don't say an organism elicits a response. We don't say the dog elicits salivation. And we don't say that a response elicits a stimulus. We don't say salivation elicits a bell. (More importantly we don't say that lever pressing elicits water.)

a. S^D (operant conditioning)
b. CS (respondent conditioning)
Is there a plausible US → UR relation?

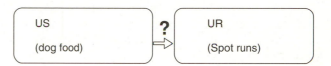

Is it plausible that food is a CS that elicits the conditioned response of running? Of course not; Spot doesn't run every time he has food in his mouth. So then it's not plausible that pairing the dog food with the sound of the can opening would cause the can opening to elicit running.

Is there a plausible $S^D \rightarrow R \rightarrow S^R$ contingency? You bet:

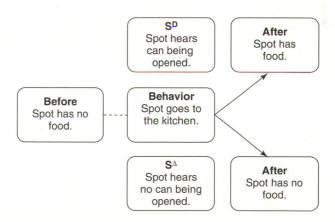

Inferring Spot's behavioral history, it is quite plausible that the sound of the can being opened was a stimulus in the presence of which running to the kitchen was reinforced with dog food (at least intermittently). So it seems much more plausible that the can-opening sound is an S^D and not a US—that we've got operant conditioning, not respondent conditioning.

2. What about this one? You hold the food up, say *OK*, and Spot jumps toward the food. So, what's *OK*?

a. S^D (operant conditioning)

b. CS (respondent conditioning)

(Keep in mind that, for *OK* to be a CS for jumping, the sight of the food must be either a CS or US for jumping. So do you really think that every time you put food in Spot's bowl he starts jumping? Give me a break, Pavlov.)

3. And this one? You drop the food on the floor and Spot bends down toward it.

a. S^D (operant conditioning)

b. CS (respondent conditioning)

As we said in an earlier section, we think this issue of the difference between the CS and the S^D is the crucial distinction between respondent and operant conditioning.

You've seen the two common confusions that students and professionals make when distinguishing between operant and respondent conditioning and the explanations that clarify these confusions. To ensure that you, dear student, never make these mistakes, let's summarize.

First, they often confuse the operant pairing procedure that turns a neutral stimulus in to learned reinforcer with the respondent pairing procedure that turns a neutral stimulus into a CS. We've shown that the two pairing procedures have different outcomes. In respondent conditioning, the neutral stimulus becomes a conditioned stimulus; that is, it acquires more or less the same eliciting function as the unconditioned stimulus. In operant conditioning, the neutral stimulus becomes a learned reinforcer or a learned aversive condition; that is, it acquires more or less the same reinforcing functions as the unlearned reinforcer or aversive condition.

Second, they often confuse the S^D with the CS. To determine whether a stimulus is functioning as an S^D or as a CD, it is necessary to look at the history of conditioning of the stimulus. The history of conditioning tells us the function of that stimulus. The S^D *evokes* the response, because in the presence of that stimulus that response was previously reinforced. The CS *elicits* the response because in the past it has been paired with a US.

QUESTIONS

1. Describe the similarities and differences between the conditioned stimulus and the S^D.

2. Explain why is it risky to infer the history of conditioning by looking at the response.

3. To determine the function of a stimulus—describe this general rule and give an example.

22

Analogs to Reinforcement and Avoidance Part I

Example[1] Behavioral Medicine
MARY, THE STARVING LADY[2]

Mary was dying of starvation. She was 37 years old, 5 feet 4 inches tall, and weighed only 47 pounds.

At the age of 11, Mary weighed 120 pounds, a chubby little girl. She stayed at about 120 pounds until she married at the age of 18. Her physician warned her that she was sexually underdeveloped and that her marriage might "make this worse or might make it better." The United States was in the middle of World War II, so housing was scarce in California, where her new husband was in the military. They had to live in a small, crowded apartment that had no kitchen, and they ate in cheap restau-rants. Mary had trouble with the sexual side of married life, and she was so homesick that she often made the long trip from California to Virginia to visit her family. After the first few months of her marriage, she started eating less and less and began losing weight at an alarming rate. A physician told Mary she should return home to live with her family if she lost any more weight; and she did.

Mary kept losing weight even after she had returned home. Because of her eating problem, she probably got more attention than she had before her marriage. No one pays much attention if we eat normally; we get smothered with attention when we refuse to eat. Friends and relatives will talk to us when we eat poorly, trying to coax us to eat more. Attention reinforces much behavior in this world, for better and for worse. Perhaps this attention played a role in Mary's poor eating.

In any case, she had dropped from 120 to 47 pounds by the time she was 37 years old. If Mary did not gain weight, she would starve to death. Her physicians could find no medical causes, so they called in some behavior analysts to try a new type of intervention—social reinforcement for eating.

They put Mary in a hospital room containing only the bare essentials, and they kept social contact at a minimum. Mary was in such bad shape she could not even move from her bed without aid. A helper had to serve her three daily meals; so, during each meal, she had a companion—the helper. But the companion would talk to her only after she had at

---

least eaten a bite. The behavior analysts hoped this conversation would reinforce her eating.

At first, her companion would chat briefly with Mary whenever Mary lifted her fork toward her mouth; otherwise, the companion remained silent. Mary got to the point where she often reached for bites of food. Then her companion required her to raise the food to her mouth before giving the reinforcer of a few seconds of conversation. Once again, reinforcement worked and Mary frequently moved the fork to her mouth. Then her companion required Mary to chew some food before she got the reinforcing conversation. Still later, the companion reinforced only the response of swallowing the food.

Also, the behavior analysts allowed Mary to listen to a radio or phonograph or to watch television after she had finished her meal. But if she didn't finish her meal, she didn't get this reinforcer. At first, they required her to eat only a bite or two of food; but eventually they required her to eat everything on her plate before she got the entertainment. Later, they added other reinforcers: If Mary ate all the food on her plate, she could choose the food she wanted for her next meal, could invite another patient to eat with her during that next meal, or could eat in the dining room with the other patients. Then they gradually introduced other contingent social reinforcers—walking around the hospital grounds with a companion and receiving visits from her family and friends. Receiving mail and having her hair shampooed and set also were used as reinforcers.

Bit by bit and bite by bite, Mary gained weight. After three months of treatment, Mary had gained 14 pounds—about a pound a week. Imagine the hard work and patience this required of everyone— the behavior analysts, the companion, the family, and most of all Mary—but it paid off.

When Mary returned home, the behavior analysts asked her family to continue reinforcing her eating with social reinforcers such as praise and attention when she ate and to ignore her when she did not eat at mealtimes. At the end of a year of intervention in her parents' home, she weighed 88 pounds (Figure 22.1) and lived a relatively normal and useful social and professional life.

Analysis

We think there's more to the analysis than meets the eye. It took me 21 years to see it. We think this is not just reinforcement by the presentation of reinforcers. At least, that's not the main point.

Why wasn't the intervention just simple reinforcement? To answer this, let's first review our definition: **Reinforcement by the presentation of reinforcers**—*a response becomes more frequent in the*

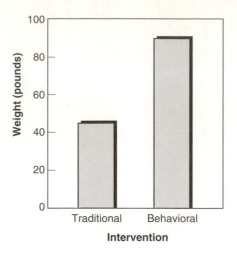

Figure 22.1   Using Reinforcers to Help an Anorexic Woman

future if a reinforcer or an increase in a reinforcer has immediately followed it in the past. The behavior analysts' intervention probably involved some simple reinforcement contingencies—for example, the companion's conversation immediately followed each eating response.

Direct-Acting Contingency

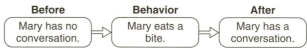

But what about the other presumed reinforcers—choice of food, dining companion, location for the next meal, walks, visits, mail, and the hair treatment? Immediately after Mary ate her meal, her companion announced that Mary had a choice of food, companions, and so forth. So if the presumed reinforcers were actual reinforcers, that announcement and Mary's making the choice also could have reinforced Mary's most recent eating. But the actual food, companions, and so forth that she got the next day were too delayed to reinforce her correct eating.

Our First Approximation

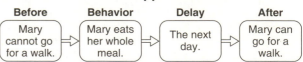

They may have involved something else. Let's look at one more case study before we suggest what that something else might be.

QUESTIONS

1. Describe and analyze the intervention for Mary's anorexia. What part of the intervention seems to be based on simple reinforcement and what part seems to involve reinforcers that are too delayed to be useful in simple reinforcement?
2. What were the results of the intervention?

Example
Behavioral Medicine
BUBBLEGUM AND BOWEL MOVEMENTS—PART II[3]

Remember Todd? The last time Dawn had worked with Todd was to cool him out at the dentist's office in an earlier chapter. But before that, he'd been the bubblegum kid. Todd had had trouble with bowel movements. His mother had reinforced his bowel movements by giving him a piece of bubblegum immediately after each bowel movement (in an earlier chapter).

Direct-Acting Contingency

Before	Behavior	After
Todd has no bubblegum.	Todd has a bowel movement.	Todd receives bubblegum.

But, as Sid pointed out, that reinforcement procedure would be awkward to maintain forever.

So after her early success with Todd using immediate bubblegum to reinforce his bowel movements, and after her later success with him in the dentist's office, Dawn thought it was time to make the bowel-movement intervention more practical. Therefore, she asked Todd's mother to tell Todd they would use a new rule. He could still have bubble gum from time to time, no longer contingent on the bowel movement, but now, if he had a bowel movement any time before dinner, he could have dessert after dinner. It worked. Two years later, Todd was having bowel movements six times per week—not bad for a kid who had been having a bowel movement only once a week.

Analysis

Once again, let's look at our definition of **reinforcement by the presentation of reinforcers**—*a response becomes more frequent in the future if a re-*

---

[3]Based on Tomlinson, J. R. (1970). Bowel retention. *Behavior Therapy and Experimental Psychiatry, 1*, 83–85.

inforcer or an increase in a reinforcer has immediately followed it in the past. Now let's apply that definition to Dawn's final intervention with Todd:

- First, what was the response? The bowel movement (contraction of the colon and the relaxation of the sphincter muscle).
- Was that set of responses more likely to occur? Yes, it was more likely to occur than before Dawn started her first intervention.
- The reinforcer? The dessert. Was it really a reinforcer? It was at least enough of a reinforcer to reinforce Todd's eating it. So that gives us hope that it might be enough of a reinforcer to support the bowel movements.
- Finally, did the reinforcer immediately follow the bowel movement? No! Todd's bowel movements had to occur before dinner; for instance, he might have had a bowel movement in the morning, but he still wouldn't get the reinforcer until after dinner.

Our First Approximation

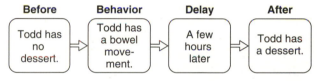

Before	Behavior	Delay	After
Todd has no dessert.	Todd has a bowel movement.	A few hours later	Todd has a dessert.

Just as for Mary, that's the problem: The reinforcer was not immediate. The delay between the bowel movement and the dessert was too great for the dessert to reinforce the bowel movement. Yet the bowel movements maintained.

> **The reinforcer must IMMEDIATELY follow the response to reinforce that response.**

Seems strange. When you think about it, this whole reinforcement business seems fishy. In about 2 minutes, you can think of a half dozen other exceptions, cases where the reinforcer occurred a long time after the response, and yet the reinforcer seemed involved in causing the response. Go ahead, give it a shot. Close your eyes for 2 minutes and see how many exceptions you can think of, cases of delayed reinforcers—for instance, like enrolling in college and getting a college degree years later.

Are the 2 minutes up yet? Remember, don't open your eyes until the time's up. So how many did you get? Like buying groceries this morning so you'll have something for dinner tonight. Like getting tickets in advance so you'll get seats at the concert of Bobby Behavior and the Behaviorettes. Like setting your alarm the night before. Like almost everything you do in your life.[4]

If the dessert intervention wasn't reinforcement, what was it? **Rule control.** The **rule** was: If you have a bowel movement today, you can get a dessert after dinner. Here's why we think the dessert intervention was rule control: Suppose Todd's mother had given him a dinner dessert every day he had had a bowel movement. But suppose she had failed to tell him about the relation between his bowel movements and the desserts; in other words, suppose she had failed to tell him the rule. Would those dinner desserts have reinforced and thereby maintained the regular occurrence of his bowel movements? No, the desserts were too delayed. Todd needed the rule describing the contingency, if his bowel movements were to maintain. The rule controlled the bowel movements. (Of course, the rule would have lost its control if it had proven false and his mother hadn't given Todd his just desserts.)

Here are some relevant, new concepts. But first recall an old friend: **behavioral contingency**—*the occasion for a response (S^D), the response, and the outcome of the response.*

> *Definition: Concepts*
> **Rule**
> - A description of a behavioral contingency.
> **Rule control**
> - The statement of a rule
> - controls the response
> - described in that rule.
> **Rule-governed behavior**
> - Behavior under the control of a rule.
> **Contingency control**
> - Direct control of behavior
> - by a contingency,
> - without the involvement of rules.

The rule describing the dessert contingency specified the occasion (any time before dinner), the

response (a bowel movement), and the outcome (dinner dessert). The rule did control the behavior, so the bowel movement was **rule-governed behavior**. Because Todd needed the rule, the bowel movement was not **contingency-governed behavior** (*contingency-shaped behavior*), during this second intervention.

The same analysis applies to Mary. For example, the rule describing the meal-choice contingency specified the occasion (when food remained on her plate), the response (eating), and the outcome (choice of the menu for the next meal). The rule did control Mary's eating, so her eating was rule-governed. And because Mary needed the rule for the contingency to contol her behavior, the eating was not contingency governed, at least not as far as the meal-choice contingency was concerned.

QUESTION

1. For each of the following concepts: define it and give an example.
   a. rule
   b. rule control
   c. rule-governed behavior
   d. contingency control
   e. contingency-governed behavior (contingency-shaped behavior).

WHEN REINFORCEMENT WON'T WORK: THE PROBLEM OF IMMEDIATE VS. DELAYED REINFORCERS

As we've said, the data indicate that a reinforcer must immediately follow a response for it to reinforce that response, and we've already said as much in our definition of *reinforcement contingency—the **immediate**, response-contingent presentation of a reinforcer resulting in an increased frequency of that response.* But this is such a big deal we'd like to say it a hundred more times. Why? Because even professionals mess up this one.

They're apt to say something like, "Jones campaigned actively and got elected president. So her election must have reinforced her campaigning." What's wrong with this statement? The officials announced the election results too long after her election campaigning, especially the earlier part that she started months before the election. If the reinforcer follows the response by more than a few seconds, it will not reinforce that response. The election results followed the campaigning activities by more than a few seconds. So the election results couldn't have reinforced her campaigning. So any increased frequency of Jones's campaigning in future elections will not have resulted from the direct reinforcement of her winning the election.

---

[4]In these informal examples, we don't suggest that a future outcome can cause a current event. We don't suggest that something that hasn't even happened yet can cause something that is happening now. Having seats at a concert that hasn't occurred can't cause your reserving seats now. With unreliable rock stars like Bobby Behavior, the concert might be canceled. So you would have reserved your seats, even though there turned out to be no concert for you to have seats. The concert was a nothing, but your behavior of reserving the seats earlier was a something. And a nothing can't cause a something. To be logical and safe, we need to make sure the cause has occurred before or at least by the time of the effect (the result). Otherwise, we're making the error of **teleology**—*the doctrine that the future, as well as the past, can influence the present.*

True, often delayed reinforcers do influence or control our actions. Todd's dinner desserts show this. So do compliments: You put on a brand-new sweater in the morning; in the afternoon several friends compliment you on it. Not a bad reinforcer, but too delayed to reinforce putting on the sweater. In other words, you'll put on the sweater more frequently, but not because the compliments reinforced that action. Something else is going on.

Rather than the delayed reinforcers themselves, statements about the possibility of those delayed reinforcers are what more directly influence or control our actions. The promise of reinforcers can control our actions, even before our receipt of those delayed reinforcers: "When you go for your job interview today, remember, smile, look the interviewer in the eye, and wipe the sweat off your palms before you shake hands. Follow my advice and within a few days, you'll be getting a job offer from the main office."

These cases of delayed reinforcers and promises of delayed reinforcers involve more than the simple procedures of reinforcement. We're talking about rule control. The behavior occurs not just because of the contingency but because someone has stated the rule. The person who states the rule might be the person doing the behaving, or it might be someone who has stated the rule to that person.

QUESTION

1. Give an example where behavior is controlled by the promise of the reinforcer rather than the delivery.

THE DEADLINE

OK, that was the easy part of this chapter. Now we take off the training wheels. As I mentioned earlier, it took me 21 years between the first and second edition of this book to realize there was a problem with our analysis of some of the studies: We analyzed them as if they involved simple, Skinner-box-type contingencies, when they really involved delayed outcomes that required rule control. And it has taken another 10 years (between the second and the fifth editions) to discover and address an equally complex problem:

Originally, I had thought the delayed-outcome contingencies were indirect-acting analogs to reinforcement contingencies. But now we realize life is more complex. Most of these indirect-acting contingencies involve deadlines, a fact I had failed to notice when we wrote the second edition.

Mary's Walk Contingency

An example from earlier in this chapter involves an overlooked deadline:

Our Erroneous First Approximation

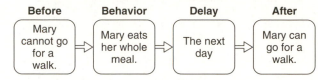

We've left out a crucial component—the deadline. Mary was not free to finish her meal anytime she wanted. She had to eat her whole meal before the mealtime was over. She could not dawdle and procrastinate forever. So the end of the mealtime was the deadline by which time she had to eat her whole meal, if she were to get to go for a walk, the next day.

But I still wasn't out of the woods. It took me another few years to figure out what is the function of the deadline. Now we realize the deadline is an S^D: Before the deadline, eating her whole meal will pay off; but after the deadline (S^Δ), eating her whole meal won't pay off (she won't even have the opportunity).

And still, we can't quite see the light at the end of the woods. We were shocked to realize that putting a deadline into the contingency changes it from a discriminated analog of a reinforcement contingency to a discriminated analog of an avoidance contingency. In other words, if Mary doesn't eat her whole meal by the end of the mealtime, she will lose the opportunity to go for the walk the next day.

So, now we present the latest, most complex version of Mary's contingency as follows:

Our Final Word:
Analog to Discriminated Avoidance

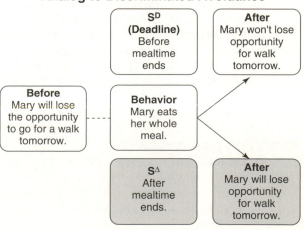

Todd's Dessert Contingency

The same analysis applies to Todd's dessert contingency:

Our Erroneous First Approximation

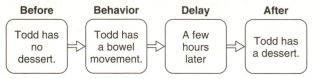

Again, we left out the crucial deadline. Todd had to have his bowel movement before dinnertime (the deadline).

**Our Final Word:
Analog to Discriminated Avoidance**

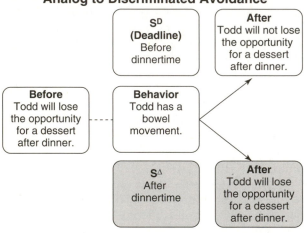

We realize it's a little strained to say *Todd has the opportunity for a dessert* in the before condition when he has not yet had his bowel movement that will earn him his dessert. It might feel more comfortable to say *Todd loses the opportunity to earn a dessert* in the before condition. But then we'd have to say *Todd will not lose the opportunity to earn his dessert* in the after condition. And that seems even more strained because, by the after condition, he has already made that dessert-earning response (the bowel movement). So our preferred wording may not be completely comfortable, but let's try to live with it. (Of course, the same considerations apply to the wording in Mary's contingency.) Here's one more example; we hope this one will seem less strained and will, therefore, give you a better feel of what we're trying to get at with our preferred wording.

Tom's Fort Lauderdale Spring-Break Contingency

If Tom leaves home in time to catch the plane to Fort Lauderdale, he will be able to spend a week in drunken revelry.

Analog to Discriminated Avoidance

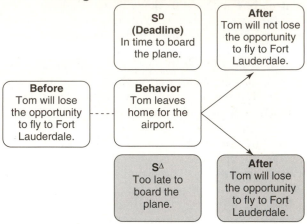

Here, it may seem more intuitively correct to say *Tom will lose the opportunity to fly to Fort Lauderdale, if he misses his plane.* And that's essentially the same wording as in Todd and Mary's contingencies.

QUESTIONS

1. Be able to give an example where an apparent delayed analog to reinforcement is really a delayed analog to discriminated avoidance. Include a discussion of the role of the deadline.

2. Be able to diagram your example.

SOME IMPORTANT DISTINCTIONS

We've casually used the terms *direct-acting* and *indirect-acting contingencies*; now let's get formal.

Definition: Concept
Direct-acting contingency
- A contingency for which
- the outcome of the response
- reinforces or punishes that response.

Here are some contingencies that are probably direct acting: The rat presses the bar and immediately gets a drop of water. You turn the handle on the drinking fountain and immediately get water. The pigeon pecks the key and immediately gets 3 seconds' access to food. You put a coin in the candy machine and immediately get a candy bar. You tell a joke and everyone immediately groans. And so on—you know the story by now; this is what you've been studying throughout this course.

Direct-acting contingencies involve outcomes that follow the response by less than approximately 60 seconds. And indirect-acting contingencies have outcomes that follow the response by more than 60 seconds.

Definition: Concept

Indirect-acting contingency

- A contingency that controls the response,
- but not because the outcome
- reinforces or punishes that response.

If a contingency is indirect acting, what is controlling the behavior more directly? The statement of a rule describing that contingency. Wherever you have an effective indirect-acting contingency, you have rule-governed behavior.

Here are some contingencies that, if they control your behavior, are probably indirect acting: If you apply to college before the deadline, you will avoid the loss of the opportunity to enter college **three months later** (at least if all goes well). If you file your income-tax return and pay your taxes by April 15, you will avoid having to pay a penalty **two months** later. If you study for your exam tonight, you will avoid really blowing it **tomorrow** (at least if all goes well). In all cases, the response may have caused the outcome (the outcome may be contingent on the response). But in all cases, the outcome was too delayed to reinforce the response that produced it. So if the contingencies do control future behavior, they must do so indirectly, not through direct reinforcement of the causal response but rather through rules describing those contingencies.

By the way, though a contingency may be indirect acting, it would not be correct to say *the response is indirectly reinforced*. If behavior occurs, it's because it's reinforced and reinforced directly. There's no such thing as "indirect reinforcement." (In Chapter 23, we suggest some possible reinforcement contingencies that reinforce the behavior in indirect-acting contingencies.)

Definition: Concept

Ineffective contingency

- A contingency that does not control behavior.

Here are some contingencies that are probably ineffective, at least much of the time: The rat presses the bar and an hour later gets a drop of water. Every time you smile, an hour later someone you love gives you a kiss, without telling you why.

You have lactose intolerance, so you become mildly ill the next day after drinking a glass of milk. Many people have suffered this problem all their lives without knowing why and without the contingency controlling their behavior. We're sure the water will be ineffective for the rat. And we'd wager a modest sum that the smile-kiss and milk-illness contingencies would be ineffective for human beings if they can't state the rule describing the contingencies.

Ineffective Contingency
If You Don't Know the Rule

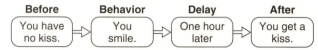

Before	Behavior	Delay	After
You have no kiss.	You smile.	One hour later	You get a kiss.

Note: Two kinds of contingencies are not direct acting. One kind is indirect-acting and, therefore, effective; the other is not effective. If the response immediately produces a food reinforcer, the contingency is probably direct acting. If the response produces a delayed food reinforcer, **the contingency is not direct acting**. For the pigeon pecking the key, the contingency with the delay will be ineffective. For your putting a turkey in the microwave, the contingency probably will be effective (if you're not a vegetarian); but it will be indirect acting, because even with the microwave, the delay of the reinforcer will be too great to reinforce putting the turkey in the microwave.

The following diagram shows the relation between these types of contingencies:

Contingency Tree

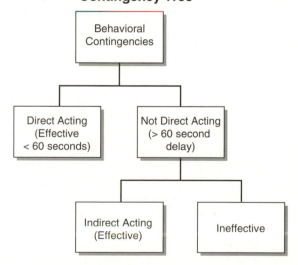

So, we have the general category of behavioral contingencies. And that's divided into two types—contingencies that are direct-acting and effective (because the outcome is delayed by less than 60 seconds) and contingencies that are not direct acting (because the outcome is delayed by more than 60 seconds). But those contingencies that are not direct acting are also divided into two types—effective contingencies that are indirect acting (rule governed) and ineffective contingencies (possibly no rule).

Note that all direct-acting contingencies are effective contingencies, but not all effective contingencies are direct acting; indirect-acting contingencies are also effective. So effective contingencies can be either direct acting or indirect acting.

QUESTIONS

1. Define and give an example of each of the following concepts:
   a. *direct-acting contingency*
   b. *indirect-acting contingency*
   c. *ineffective contingency*
2. Construct the contingency tree.

Concept
THE RULE-GOVERNED ANALOG TO DIRECT-ACTING BEHAVIORAL CONTINGENCIES

Throughout this book, we have discussed several basic behavioral procedures, procedures that involve direct-acting contingencies—for example, the procedure of reinforcement by the presentation of reinforcers. But those procedures also have analogs that involve contingencies that are not direct acting. Therefore, such contingencies will not reinforce or punish a response when the outcome is too delayed.

By the way, here's what we mean by *analog*: Two procedures are analogous when they are alike in some ways and not in other important ways. For example, suppose a response occurs; then immediately afterward, a reinforcer follows, and that response increases in frequency as a result; that's reinforcement.

Now here's an analog; it's like reinforcement in some ways but not in others: A response occurs, and one day later a reinforcer follows; and that response increases in frequency as a result; that's not reinforcement, even though the response increased in frequency. Both the procedure and the results of this analog look much like reinforcement, but not quite—the one-day delay between the response and the reinforcer is too great for this to be reinforcement. Something else must be going on. We say more about what that something else is, in Chapter 23.

True, a contingency that is not direct acting can't reinforce a response; yet a rule describing such a contingency might control the relevant response,

especially if it's an analog to discriminated avoidance, for instance, Mary's walking contingency or Todd's dessert contingency.

It is no accident that, in both cases, the contingency managers gave the clients rules describing the contingencies (e.g., *if you have a bowel movement before dinner, you can have dessert after dinner*). Without the descriptive rules, the contingencies would have failed to control the clients' behaviors. These contingencies look like direct-acting contingencies, but they're not; we call them ***rule-governed analogs to behavioral contingencies***.

Definition: Concept
Rule-governed analog to a behavioral contingency
  ○ An increase in the frequency of a response
  ○ because of a rule describing the contingency.

Perhaps the majority of research in applied behavior analysis uses procedures based on rule-governed analogs to direct-acting contingencies rather than procedures based on direct-acting contingencies themselves. This is especially true when dealing with people who have reasonable language skills. Furthermore, the researchers are often using rule-governed analogs, although they may describe their research as if they were using direct-acting contingencies.

Even when the rule is what controls the behavior, however, the analog contingency might influence the extent to which the rule controls the behavior. For example, suppose a classmate whispered the following rule in your ear: "All you have to do to get a good grade on the quizzes is to memorize the section headings for each chapter." And suppose, in spite of your better judgment, you follow that rule; all you do is memorize the headings. Sure enough, you get an *A* on the test. Then there's a good chance you'll follow that rule for the next test as well. But suppose, instead, when you follow that rule, you end tying the whisperer for the lowest grade in the class. You probably won't follow that rule again.

The study/grade contingency is only an analog to a reinforcement contingency. The grades are too delayed to reinforce your studying. So the contingency is only indirect acting (needs rule support), not direct acting (directly reinforcing). But, as we've just seen, it can indirectly control your behavior by influencing the control the rule exerts over your actions. When an outcome confirms or contradicts a rule, it increases or decreases the frequency with which we'll follow that rule.

QUESTION

1. *Rule-governed analog to reinforcement by the presentation of a reinforcer*—state it, give an example, and explain how your example fits the definition.

2. Give an example showing how such an analog can indirectly control behavior.

Example
Behavioral Counseling
WANDERING WAYNE MEETS THE TV CONTINGENCY[5]

Wayne was a 9-year-old pain in his mother's neck. (The relationship may have been mutual.) Wayne's mother would stand on the back porch and call him to come home for meals, etc. But he wouldn't show. Then she'd search the neighborhood for him. When she found Wayne, she'd be so upset that she'd start shouting at him. Then she'd feel so guilty that she'd never spank him or even threaten to. In addition to this hassle, meals would get cold and Wayne's mother would miss appointments and phone calls because of the time she spent searching for her prodigal son.

She brought Wayne to the Human Development Clinic where I was doing a practicum as a graduate student at Florida State University. I took on Wayne under Dr. Todd Risley's supervision.

We asked his mother to use special data sheets to keep accurate records of Wayne's responses. And we contacted her daily the first week in an effort to ensure that she kept good records. The procedure consisted of the following: Each day she would call Wayne a maximum of four different times (28 calls a week), always from the porch. If he showed up within 10 minutes, she'd write a plus on the data sheet; otherwise, she'd write a minus and start her search for him, as she always had. She followed this procedure daily for the 4 consecutive weeks of baseline before we began the behavioral intervention. Wayne answered, on the average, only 9 of the 28 calls a week during these first 4 weeks.

During the next 4 weeks (the intervention), Wayne's mother used the same procedures, except now for each plus mark, Wayne could watch TV for 5 minutes. But if he arrived after 10 minutes, he earned no TV time. Because his mother thought meals were especially important, Wayne got to watch TV 15 minutes whenever he arrived on time

for meals. Wayne could save his viewing time and use it in a block during the prime evening programs. Of course she told Wayne the rule describing this contingency.

It worked. Throughout intervention, Wayne promptly answered an average of 27 of the 28 weekly calls (Figure 22.2). Perhaps as important as the change in Wayne's behavior was the change in his mother's interactions with him. After treatment, she enjoyed being with Wayne much more. We suspect Wayne felt the same way about being with his mother.

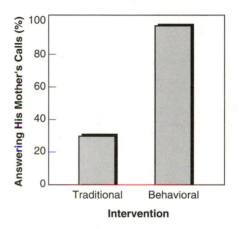

Figure 22.2 A Rule-Governed Analog to Reinforcement for a Boy's Answering His Mother's Calls

Analysis

We've got another rule-governed analog to avoidance of the loss of the opportunity for a reinforcer. Of course, being away from home is not normally aversive for Wayne. But it is aversive when Mom calls him to dinner. Now we have a **conditional** aversive stimulus, conditional upon Mom's call. It's aver-

Analog to Discriminated Avoidance

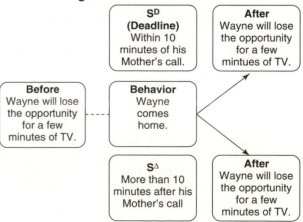

[5]Based on Whaley, D. L., & Risley, T. (1966). The use of television viewing opportunity in the control of problem behavior. Unpublished manuscript. The accompanying graph is based on the same article.

sive because Mom has told him a rule—in essence, *if you're away from home 10 minutes after I call you, you will lose the opportunity to watch the tube.* That's sort of a rule-governed pairing procedure that creates a learned aversive condition—being away from home after Mom's call. So hustling home escapes that aversive condition. And at the same time, Wayne's homeward hustle avoids the loss of the opportunity to watch TV for a few minutes.

QUESTIONS

1. Describe the traditional and the behavioral parenting techniques involved with Wayne.
2. Diagram and label the contingency Wayne's mother used during the behavioral intervention.

BASIC ENRICHMENT

APPLIED BEHAVIOR ANALYSIS WITH VERBAL AND NONVERBAL CLIENTS

Many of the applications dealing with direct-acting contingencies have involved human beings who have had such difficulty learning functional behavior they've been labeled *mentally handicapped,* whereas many of those dealing with analog contingencies will involve human beings who have acquired more functional repertoires—in other words, you and me. This is because, in these particular studies, many of those people labeled *mentally handicapped* did not have the language skills needed for their behavior to come under the control of rules. However, the rest of us do have normal language skills; and when possible, it's usually easier to give a rule than to set up and maintain a direct-acting contingency without the use of rules.

RULES, INSTRUCTIONS, REQUESTS, AND INCOMPLETE RULES

Recall our definition of *rule*: a description of a behavioral contingency (the occasion, the response, and the outcome). Here's an example: If every day you study an hour or two for this course, probably you'll ace it. What's the occasion? Every day. The response? Spending an hour or two studying for this course. The likely outcome? Getting that *A*.

Now technically speaking, a rule is a factual description of a contingency. The giver of the pure rule says, in essence, "I don't give a darn whether you ever study and whether you fail the course. I'm just telling you the contingency. Just the facts, ma'am."

What about this one? *Every day, you should study an hour or two for this course so you'll ace it.* That's a rule plus. It's a rule plus the instruction that

you should follow the rule (a mand). All instructions seem to involve rules.

And this? *I'd appreciate it if every day you'd study an hour or two for this course so you can get an A.* This is a rule plus a request that you follow the rule (a mand).

Often a rule plus is also a rule minus—a rule minus one or two of the components. *Study behavior analysis a couple of hours every day.* We've got the occasion and the response but not the outcome. We imply the outcome—that you'll do well.

And *Be quiet!* The minimal rule—just the response. Here we imply the occasion (right now!) and the outcome (or you're really gonna get it!). We call these **incomplete rules**. Sometimes incomplete rules cause no special problem; their context makes them clear, and they control behavior much as the complete version would. But at other times, in elementary-school classrooms, for example, stating and backing up the full rule works better.

QUESTIONS

1. Give an example of a statement of a rule, a related instructional statement, and a related statement of a request.
2. Give an example of a complete rule and an incomplete rule.

ANOREXIA NERVOSA

The official name for Mary's problem is *anorexia nervosa,* but don't let the fancy label fool you. Physicians, psychiatrists, and psychologists love to put labels on people and problems. But labeling a person or the problem is not the same as knowing the cause or the cure for the problem. All *anorexia nervosa* means is that the person doesn't eat much and the physicians have not found a medical cause for the problem. The whole thing can be logically circular if you're not careful: Why doesn't Mary eat? Because she's anorexic. How do you know she's anorexic? Because she doesn't eat. That's like saying Mary doesn't eat because she doesn't eat.

QUESTION

1. What does *anorexia nervosa* mean?

RULES DESCRIBING DIRECT-ACTING CONTINGENCIES

What happens when a person can state the rule describing a direct-acting contingency? We can't be sure. It's hard to know whether the contingency, the rule, or both control the behavior. Consider Todd's bubblegum contingency (the one Dawn used before she started the dessert contingency). Todd's mother did tell him the rule: "Any time (occasion) you have a bowel movement (response), you will immediately get a piece of bubblegum (outcome)." And whenever he asked for an unearned bubblegum, she reminded him of the rule. But he might not have needed the rule. Probably the immediate receipt of the bubblegum would have reinforced and main-

tained the bowel movements without the rule. We don't know for sure.

But suppose Todd had rushed into the bathroom and had a bowel movement right after his mother first told him the bubblegum rule. What then? It doesn't seem likely he would have felt such an exceptionally forceful call from nature just at that moment. So we can be fairly sure the rule was governing his behavior.

QUESTIONS

1. Using the bubblegum contingency, give an example of the difficulty of interpreting the effects of rules describing direct-acting contingencies. Show how it's hard to tell whether the rule or the direct-acting contingency or both are controlling behavior. And explain the problem.
2. Using the bubblegum contingency, give an example where we might be able to infer control by a rule describing that contingency—a direct-acting contingency. Explain why.
3. To do well on the quizzes, you may have to keep in mind that rules can describe direct-acting contingencies as well as indirect-acting contingencies. This is easy to forget because we are mainly concerned with rules describing indirect-acting contingencies.

ADVANCED ENRICHMENT

Theory
DO WE NEED THE CONCEPT OF RULE-GOVERNED BEHAVIOR TO ACCOUNT FOR CONTROL BY DELAYED OUTCOMES?

As you will see in the following sections, the question of the importance of rule control is still a hotly debated theoretical issue. At this point, we don't have enough solid scientific data on the subject to get universal agreement among behavior analysts.

Behavioral Chains

Sid's Seminar

Tom: Remember the principle of the outcome gradient from Chapter 2 where they said reinforcement delays of 60 seconds weren't effective?

Sid: Yes, that's not what they said, but close.
Tom: Well, that's wrong. Even much longer delays have enormous effects. The question is: *How are the reinforcers able to have effects where there are such great delays? Is something besides simple reinforcement operating?*
Sid: The book says it's rule control.
Tom: Rule-governed behavior is just one possible answer. What about behavioral chains as another?
Max: How so?
Tom: OK, Mr. Fields assigned a term paper at the beginning of this semester. We have to turn it in at the end of the semester, when we'll get the reinforcer—I hope—of a good grade. Now, Max, I know you started working on your paper during the first week; and you've been working a bit every week since then. But the reinforcer for all

that work will be delayed by a matter of weeks—until the end of the semester. That's more than 60 seconds.

Max: What does that have to do with behavioral chaining?

Tom: Each week you make some paper-writing responses, and that produces some more library references or outlines or pages written. And those products are stimuli that reinforce your paper writing and act as S^Ds for the next paper-writing responses. Eventually you end with the terminal reinforcer, the good grade at the end of the behavioral chain.

Eve: Now, I'm not sure I understand, Tom. Is this just like the behavioral chain we did with our rat in the Skinner box?

Tom: You understand more than you realize, Eve, 'cause it's exactly like that—the good old rat in the Skinner box.

Eve: Does this mean I could put Rudolph in the Skinner box? He would pull the chain. I'd turn on the light—a reinforcer for the chain pull and an S^D for the next response, the bar press. Then I could take him out of the box for a whole day. Put him back in the next day. And then he'd press the lever. I'd click the water dipper—a reinforcer for the lever press and an S^D for the next response—approaching the water dipper. Then I could take him out of the box again, before he got the water, for a whole day. Put him back in the next day and let him drink his drop of water. And does this mean he would learn that behavioral chain?

Tom: Well, ah, I . . . .

Joe: Of course, that's not right; and Eve knows it. Thomas, Thomas, you've got to be careful. Eve acts innocent, but she's just setting you up to show how illogical you are.

Tom: What do you mean?

Joe: She's just showing you what's wrong with your behavioral chain analysis of delayed reinforcement when that delay extends over several days.

Tom: I don't get it.

Joe: Eve's question is rhetorical.

Tom: What's a rhetorical question?

Joe: It's a question to which she already knows the answer. A question she's asking just to make a point.

Tom: So what's her point?

Joe: Her point is that there's no way you and Rudolph the Red-Nosed Rat could establish a behavioral chain that extends over several days.

Tom: Why not?

Joe: Because the delays between each component are too great. For example, you'd never establish

a dipper click as a reinforcer, with a 24-hour delay between the click and the water.

Tom: OK, but what does this have to do with Max's writing the term paper?

Joe: I think Rudolph's behavioral chain has nothing to do with Max's writing. I think his writing is rule governed. He states the rule to himself every day and that sets the occasion for him to work on his paper.

Stimulus Control

Tom: I still don't think we need the concept of rule control. Max's stating the rule to himself is just simple stimulus control. His statement of the rule is an S^D in the presence of which his paper writing will be reinforced with a good grade.

Eve: Now I'm not sure I understand this time either, Tom. Is this just like the stimulus-discrimination experiment we did with our rat in the Skinner box?

Tom: Of course it is, Evie.

Joe: Thomas, Thomas, you'll never learn, will you?

Eve: Does this mean I could put Rudolph in the Skinner box and this would happen? I'd turn on the light—an S^D for the bar press. He'd press the bar. Then I could take him out of the box for a whole day. Put him back in the next day and let him drink his drop of water. And does this mean the light would come to exert stimulus control?

Tom: If this is another rhetorical question, I don't get it.

Joe: Her point is that the delay of the reinforcement is too great to reinforce Rudolph's lever press—even you must admit that, so the delay would be too great for the light to exert stimulus control. And if you don't believe me, why don't you do your senior research project trying to establish stimulus control with Rudolph using a 24-hour delayed reinforcer; the rest of us will have our PhDs before you make any progress with that one.

Max: Come on, Joe, get off his case.

Joe: Sorry, Tom. Anyhow, the delay wouldn't work with Rudolph, so you can't just appeal to simple stimulus control to account for Max's amazing feat of working every week on his term paper. I still haven't started mine. Oops, I forgot you were here, Mr. Fields. Max's amazing feat is an example of rule control, not simple stimulus control. But I'll have to admit I don't understand exactly how rule control works.

Tom: Well, I'm glad to hear you'll admit something.

Max: We get into the workings of rule control in Chapter 24.

Joe: We know, Max, you've been reading ahead again.

Learned Reinforcers

Tom: I still don't think we need the concept of rule control. What about Todd's mother telling him he could have a dessert at dinner if he had a successful bowel movement any previous time during the day. It worked, but it wasn't rule control. It was still just plain old reinforcement.

Eve: I don't understand this time either, Tom. Isn't the reinforcer too delayed to reinforce the bowel movement?

Tom: Of course it is, Evie. The reinforcer that does the reinforcing of the bowel movement is not the dessert; it's the feel and maybe the sight of the successful bowel movement. Those stimuli became learned reinforcers because they were paired with the dessert. Every time, after a bowel movement, he got a dessert. That pairing turned the feel and sight into a learned reinforcer.

Joe: Tom, you are a dubious dude.

Eve: Then what about this? I put Rudolph in the Skinner box. I click the water dipper. I take him out of the box for an hour. Then I put him back in and let him drink his drop of water. Does this mean the delayed pairing of the click and the water would turn the click into a learned reinforcer?

Tom: If this is another rhetorical question, I don't get this one either.

Joe: Her point is that the delay between the click and the water is too great to establish the click as a learned reinforcer. The pairing of the neutral stimulus and the reinforcer must be immediate for the neutral stimulus to become a learned reinforcer.

Sue: And that means the delay between the stimuli from Todd's bowel movement and the dessert is too great for those "neutral" stimuli to become learned reinforcers.

Joe: So you can't just appeal to simple learned reinforcement to account for Todd's maintaining his bowel movements. You still need the concept of rule-governed behavior.

The Correlation-Based Law of Effect

Not all behavior analysts agree that the delayed delivery of reinforcers prevents reinforcement from occurring. Some believe the **correlation-based law of effect** can account for delayed reinforcement. This law states that both verbal human beings and nonverbal animals increase their rate of responding when that increased rate raises the overall rate of reinforcement. In other words, the rate of reinforcement is *correlated* with the rate of responding; the harder you work, the more you get. And according to this correlation-based law of effect, the rein-

forcers don't have to follow the response immediately; the rates of reinforcement and work just have to be correlated.

But the research supporting the correlation-based law of effect deals with correlations averaged over a period of a few minutes or an hour or so at most. In other words, if you respond faster, you'll get reinforcers at a higher rate within the next few minutes or at least within the next hour. However, we're often concerned with responding now and getting reinforcers 6 months from now. So what would it mean, even if the correlation-based law of effect does win the laboratory controversy (though no theory has clearly won at this point)? What would it mean if we find that reinforcers in the laboratory need not be delivered as immediately as we had thought? It doesn't mean too much for the sort of everyday situations we've been discussing. Few advocates of the correlation-based law of effect would argue that their law could account for the control exerted by reinforcers delayed as much as 6 months; and that's often the sort of delays we're discussing.

Knowledge of the Contingency

Some other behavior analysts take a commonsense approach. They say delayed reinforcement will occur if you understand the relation between your action and the delayed reinforcer. The understanding in some usually unspecified way allows for the reinforcement by delayed outcomes. A few behavior analysts have been more specific; they have argued that knowledge of the causal relation between the response and the reinforcer focuses the reinforcing effect of that reinforcer on that particular response. In other words, they have argued that being able to state the correct rule describing the contingency prevents the reinforcer from reinforcing all the competing responses that occur between the causal response and the delayed reinforcer.

But others would argue that the ability of knowledge to prevent reinforcement from occurring has not been proven. And before we invent new principles of behavior, we should be sure the old principles won't do the trick. (We will discuss the relevance of the old principles in Chapter 26.)

QUESTIONS

1. What are the arguments for and against an analysis of rule control in terms of
   a. simple behavioral chains?
   b. simple stimulus control?
   c. learned reinforcers?

2. What is the correlation-based, law-of-effect argument that delayed reinforcement actually reinforces the response on which the reinforcers were contingent?

3. What is the knowledge-of-the-contingencies argument that delayed reinforcement actually reinforces the response on which the reinforcers were contingent?
   a. What do you think of the various arguments that we can get delayed reinforcement?
   b. What's your position on the arguments for and against an analysis of rule control in terms of simple behavioral chains?

HARD SELL FOR THE SKEPTICAL

Show us someone who's studied behavior analysis for more than 5 minutes before picking up this book, and we'll show you someone who's skeptical of our challenges to the simplistic use of the principle of reinforcement, someone who wonders about all this new-fangled, rule-governed behavior stuff. We mainly address this section to such readers. (Most readers who are getting the word for the first time are probably relieved to know there may be more to life than the simple principle of reinforcement.)

OK, the difference between contingency control and rule control is the difference between your pet dog and your little brother. Try this experiment. For your dog, select some response that has a low operant level, a response it makes about once a week. (Remember, the *operant level* is the rate of responding before intervention.) Do the same for your brother. Like maybe when Fido (the dog, not the brother, right?) brings you your slippers; that may have a low operant level. And like when little brother says, "Thank you"—a low operant level. Each time the dog brings the slippers, give it one of its favorite dog biscuits—but not right away; give the biscuit to Fido the next day. Do the same with little brother for his "thank you," except your mother might get uptight if you used dog biscuits, so use the little devil's favorite, tooth-rotting dessert—those chocolate cakes with white stuff inside.

Experiment for a year, carefully recording the frequency of the two responses. Mail us your results. We predict the frequency of slipper carrying and "thank you" will not increase. We also predict that you wouldn't want to bet otherwise. A 1-day delay is too great for reinforcement to occur. These particular dog-biscuit and dessert contingencies are *ineffective contingencies*—they don't control behavior.

We said the difference between contingency control and rule control is the difference between your dog and your brother. But, instead, they're giving us the same results. That scientifically proves there's a bit of the dog in your brother.

So let's go to the final phase of the experiment. Tell your little brother the rule; tell him every meaningful "thank you," on the right occasions, will produce the opportunity to play your Nintendo for 15 minutes, the next day. If you insist, you can tell Fido his rule also.

Are you ready for our next big predictions? First, we predict your little brother will say "thank you" so frequently he'll become a nuisance. And second, we predict you'll still have to get your slippers six out of seven days a week; Fido will let you down. Actually, we're so confident, you don't even need to mail us your data.

All this is to suggest two kinds of effective behavioral contingencies: One kind will control actions without language—giving Fido a dog biscuit immediately after his bringing your slippers. The other kind *may* control actions, but only if we bring language into the picture—the delayed reinforcer to your brother—but only if you state the rule describing the contingency. As we said before, we call these two types of contingencies *direct-acting contingencies* (immediate dog biscuit) and **indirect-acting contingencies** (a discriminated analog to the avoidance of the loss of the opportunity to get a dessert one day later). In other words, immediate reinforcers (and also aversive conditions) that generate contingency control are involved in direct-acting contingencies.

Direct-Acting Contingency

Rules describing delayed outcomes are involved in indirect-acting contingencies.

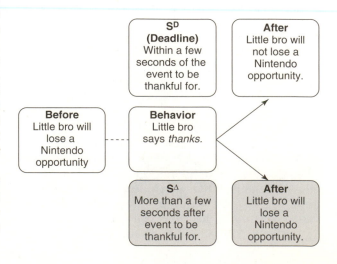

And of course there's a deadline causing this to be an analog to avoidance of the loss of the opportunity to get a reinforcer, rather than an analog to simple reinforcement. Little bro can't wait until the end of the day and then say, "Oh, by the way, there are several acts of kindness which you performed for me today; and I would now like to take time out of my busy schedule to thank you for them." That won't get it.

(Note that skeptics may consider our experiment to be only suggestive, not a final proof of the importance of language and rule control. Your little brother and Fido differ in more ways than language. And one of those other differences might account for the difference in the results with these two subjects. For example, someone who really resists the notion of rule control might suggest the crucial difference is not language but that Fido walks on all fours and your little brother doesn't. But remember, the indirect-acting contingency didn't work for your brother until we used language to tell him the rule describing that contingency.)

QUESTION

1. Present an argument for the necessity of analyzing some sorts of behavior in terms of rule-governed behavior.

THE IMPORTANCE OF DEADLINES

It's 6:25 P.M., October 20th. Sid drives his car at high speed through a residential neighborhood, risking life and limb of himself and any hapless soul on the street at that time. Cold sweat soaks his shirt. He slams on the brakes, grabs a file folder, hops out of the car, and leaving the door ajar, dashes into the Fed Ex office. The sign on the door says, *Office hours: 8:30 A.M. to 6:30 P.M., Monday through Friday.*

"Am I too late?" he asks.

"Just under the wire," she replies, with a condescending smile.

"I need overnight delivery. Got to get this symposium proposal to the Association for Behavior Analysis tomorrow, or we won't be able to present our papers at ABA's conference."

Another condescending smile. Yes, she thinks, we should change our name to *Procrastinator's Express.*

It's the end of the day; she's tired; she's irritable; why not go for a little aggression reinforcer, to cheer her up? "If you had finished your proposal a few days earlier, you could have mailed it through regular mail, saved yourself some money, and not had to drive into our parking lot at 50 miles an hour."

Sid rubs his eye.

"I suppose they didn't tell you about the deadline until yesterday," she says, actually supposing no such thing, just probing a little harder for that aggression reinforcer.

Sid rubs his eye again and says, "No, I knew a little before that."

She wouldn't let up. "Oh, really, when?"

"A few months," Sid mumbles, as he fills out the mailing label.

The grand inquisitor rests her case, satisfied with her own moral superiority over this pathetic procrastinator. Besides, she needs to close the office as soon as possible in order to get home, where she and her husband have to dispose of the accumulation of 2 months of household neglect; her mother-in-law will be visiting them the next morning, and nothing pleases that woman more than finding a little dust on her daughter-in-law's windowsills.

Analysis

Fiction was first. Now the facts behind the fiction: Consider ABA's 1999 conference.[6] The submissions start trickling in at a rate of one or two every day or so (you can't even see them on the graph). The rate of submissions doesn't start getting serious until 3 days before the deadline. Figure 22.3 shows the number of submissions as a function of date. This is one of those pictures worth a thousand words.

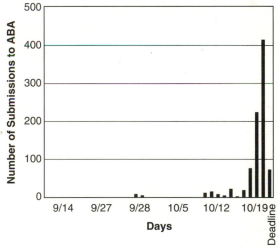

Figure 22.3   Procrastinating Professionals

Does this mean the majority of ABA members, including the most famous people in behavior analysis, are all pathetic procrastinators? Well, yes,

[6]Dams, P. (1998) The ABA program book: A process analysis. *The ABA Newsletter,* 21(3) 2–3.

but no more so than any one else, or at least not much more so.

Then why do so many people procrastinate so much? And what causes them to get it together at the last minute? Let's tackle the second question first.

Why Do Deadlines Control Our Behavior?

Question: What causes people to get it together by the last minute?

Answer: The deadline. The deadline or, at least the description of the deadline, is an S^D.

Analog to Discriminated Avoidance

Explanation: In the presence of the S^D, Sid's response of turning in his proposal will avoid the loss of the opportunity to present a paper at ABA, 7 months later. But, if he turns in his proposal after the deadline, turning in the proposal won't avoid the loss of that cherished opportunity. He would have missed the bus.

Suppose there were no deadline; then we could submit our proposals anytime we wanted. If we had to submit the proposals by the day of the conference, that's when we'd do it. But that's still a deadline.

Suppose we could wait until even after the conference. I think most proposals would never get submitted.

Why Do We Procrastinate?

Question: Why do so many of us procrastinate?

Answer: Because we don't break out into a cold-sweat panic until we can hear that deadline clock ticking.

Explanation: Here's what I think is happening. As Sid and his fellow behavior analysts get closer to the deadline, the risk that they won't get their proposals written in time increases. We each have our own risk tolerance, but sooner or later the risk of

blowing the deadline gets so high, and thus so aversive, that eventually we start writing our proposals.

Now, a few people panic weeks before the deadline; and a few people don't panic soon enough to make the deadline. But by the time most people have gotten fairly close—but not too close, like within four days of deadline—their panic has become so aversive that they start to write their proposals. And that writing slightly reduces the aversive panic.

Another way to put it is that the approaching deadline is more aversive if we're not taking action than if we are (a conditional aversive stimulus). So Sid and the rest of us escape the extreme aversiveness of the approaching deadline combined with our inaction; we start to act and thus enter the somewhat less aversive condition of the deadline's approach while we're taking action. The approach of the deadline is still aversive, but less so; and that slight reduction in aversiveness is good enough to reinforce our escape response. (Rudolph would press the lever that reduced the intensity of the shock even if it didn't turn the shock completely off.)

But what about the 60-second test? This outcome follows the response by more than 60 seconds; so prevention of the loss that will happen 7 months after meeting the deadline is clearly too far removed to reinforce that response. Try that with Rudolph; try getting him to press the lever that prevents the occurrence of a shock 7 months later. No way.

The fact that our writing the proposal immediately reduces the aversiveness of inaction gets around the 60-second criterion. Without 950 behaviorists experiencing the deadline-proximity panic, there would be no ABA convention.

Direct-Acting Escape

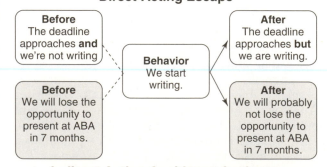

Indirect-Acting Avoidance Analogue

INDIRECT-ACTING AVOIDANCE ANALOGUE

In summary, people procrastinate (put things off until the last moment) because they don't start to panic until they're near the last moment (the deadline). And they do get things done at the last moment because they escape their aversive fear of blowing the deadline by doing the thing they were putting off.

QUESTIONS

1. Why do so many people procrastinate so much?

2. And what causes them to get it together only at the last minute? Diagram and explain the relevant escape and avoidance contingencies.

3. Why do we need deadlines to control our behavior?

4. Give an example that shows how people procrastinate up to the deadline.

23

Analogs to Reinforcement and Avoidance Part II

FUNDAMENTALS

Example
Behavioral Sports Psychology
THE OFFENSIVE BACKFIELD ON A POP WARNER FOOTBALL TEAM: A CASE OF FEEDBACK AND PRAISE[1]

Juke hadn't heard from Red since they'd played football together at BSU. So he was pleased to accept Red's invitation for dinner that Sunday. But Juke had learned that whenever long-lost friends call, a request for a favor usually follows. Sure enough, after they'd finished dinner and reviewed their four years of college glory, Red said, "Juke, I know you're busy, but I also know you like kids. I wonder if you could see your way clear to giving me a hand."

"Sure, Red, what's up."

"I got this Pop Warner football team I've been coaching—you know, 9- and 10-year-old kids. Been working with 'em a couple seasons."

"I heard about that. Glad you're givin' a little back to the kids, Red."

"Yeah, well I love the kids; but, jeez, these kids sure don't know how to play football. They're the worst team in the league. Everyone's down on 'em. Their folks are p.o.'ed. The kids feel like losers, and they are. The whole mess is depressing. I don't want to do another season, but . . . you know."

"Yeah, I do know; you're gonna coach 'em anyhow. Well, remember what Coach Cochran never said."

"Huh?"

"It's not whether you win or lose, it's . . ."

"Cut it out, man. They lose, and they play a lousy game."

"Here's the way I see it, Red. Football's just like business and industry. It's the product versus the process. Many folks think if you pay people off for a good product, the process will take care of itself. But I think that's often wrong. I think more often it's just the opposite."

"What do ya' mean, Juke?"

"I mean you've got to look at the process—you've got to look at what it takes to succeed, to win the game, to produce the good product. You've got to look at what the producer has to do to produce a class product. You've got to give 'em feedback on how well they're doing what needs to be done. And you've got to pay 'em off when they do a good job on those component behaviors. You can't wait until they've finally produced a major product or won a game."

"Juke, you always were big on philosophy. Tell me what to do to win the game."

---

[1]Based on Komaki, J., & Barnett, F. T. (1977). A behavioral approach to coaching football: Improving the play execution of the offensive backfield on a youth football team. *Journal of Applied Behavior Analysis, 10,* 657–664. The graphs are based on the same article.

"First, you've got to forget about winning the game. Maybe forever and at least for now. You've got to care about each of those kids—each one of 'em."

"I do."

"And your caring must lead to action. Care without action doesn't get it."

"Come on, Juke; stop preachin'. Tell me what to do."

"You've got to break the game into behavioral components—the plays."

"I do that already."

"Of course, but then you've got to break the plays into their components. And you've got to give each kid feedback and praise for each component of each play."

"Whenever the kids gain yardage or score a point, I congratulate 'em."

"Great. But I'm talkin' each component of each play."

"Sounds like many details."

"That's my point. Take care of the details, and the big picture will take care of itself. Take care of the process, and the product will take care of itself."

Juke may have been overselling the process at the expense of the product. However, after he had gotten Red working more with the details, he planned to get him to reexamine the long-range results. The next time around, he wanted Red to look at the long-range benefits for the kids, more than the winning of a few games. Except for an occasional Sunday afternoon's reminiscences over dinner with an old teammate, the glory of the game was soon lost. What lived on were the kids and the repertoires Red would help them acquire.

Juke and Red spent many Sunday afternoons and many dinners doing the task analysis—more work and more details than even Juke had imagined. But more fun too. They worked on three plays: the option play, the power sweep, and the off-tackle counterplay. They analyzed each of the three plays into five behavioral components. For example, in the option play, they had the quarterback-center exchange and the quarterback-right halfback fake among others, and they specified the detailed behavior sequence in each component. For example, in the fake, they wrote, "With the ball in his hands, the quarterback moves quickly down the line as the right halfback goes toward the middle of the line. The quarterback fakes a hand-off to the right halfback—that is, places the ball in the right halfback's hands. As the right halfback bends over and runs low appearing to have the ball, the quarterback pulls the ball back and continues going down the line."

Just as practice season began, Juke and Red completed the task analysis and prepared a checklist for each of the three plays' components. Red explained each component and gave its rationale. He modeled the proper movements, and he walked the backs through the plays. During the scrimmage sessions throughout the season, the players would run over to Red after each play, and Red would give them feedback by showing them how he had scored each of the five components of that play and explaining why. He pointed out not only what they had done wrong but also what they had done right on that play. He gave them lavish praise for each correct component. At the first practice session after each game, Red gave the players feedback, explanations, and, where appropriate, praise for the correct performance of each component of each play of that game.

The results? Each player played better; and each measure of performance of the backfield as a unit improved—the percentage of perfect play components and perfect plays increased, the percentage of lousy plays decreased, and the percentage of perfect quarterback decisions and quarterback blocks increased (Figures 23.1, 23.2, and 23.3). Each boy was winning, and the team was winning. Red became a sharper observer of the details of the kids' performance, and so did the kids themselves.

At the end of the season Red said to Juke: "You know what I like best out of all the benefits of your behavioral intervention? That I've stopped getting on their case all the time and started using praise. The kids are happier and I'm happier. Everyone works harder, everyone plays better, and everyone has more fun."

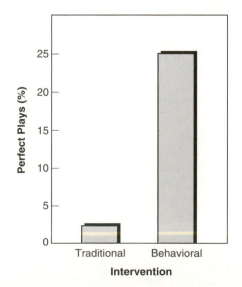

Figure 23.1   Rule-Governed Analogs to Reinforcement, Feedback, and Perfect Plays by a Boys' Football Team

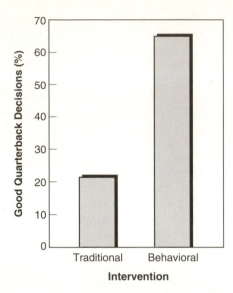

Figure 23.2   Rule-Governed Analogs to Reinforcement, Feedback, and Good Quarterback Decisions to Pitch or Keep for a Boys' Football Team

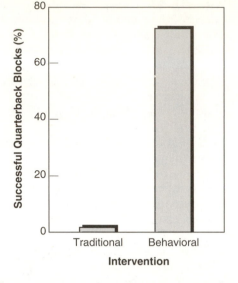

Figure 23.3   A Rule-Governed Analog to Reinforcement Combined with Feedback to Improve a Boys' Football Team

---

Definition: Review. General Rule
Process vs. product
  ○ Give feedback and reinforcers for the details of the process,
  ○ not just the product (outcome).

Rember that you only need to add feedback and reinforcers for the process, when you can't get quality products of sufficient quantity, though you've provided feedback and reinforcers contingent on those products.

Definition: Concept Review
Task analysis
  ○ An analysis of complex behavior
  ○ and sequences of behavior
  ○ into component responses.

Definition: Concept
Feedback
  ○ Nonverbal stimuli or
  ○ verbal statements
  ○ contingent on past behavior
  ○ that can guide future behavior.

Many behavior analysts look at feedback as if its function were to reinforce or punish the relevant behavior. We agree it may serve that function, but we also believe that function is incidental. When we say feedback *guides* behavior, we are saying that its stimulus control function is its defining feature. So we suggest that to function as an S^D for future behavior, feedback should occur as close as possible to that future behavior. And, contrary to the common view, we believe it need not immediately follow the preceding response, as it should if feedback were functioning to reinforce or punish that response.

This means we don't think feedback is a fundamental concept. We could talk about it simply as an S^D. But *feedback* **is a special type of S^D (or analog to an S^D), one relevant to the class of behavior that produces it.** So it is convenient to have a special name for that type of S^D (or S^D analog), and that name is *feedback*.[2]

---

[2]By S^D analog, we mean a stimulus that functions like an S^D but is really a rule-governed analog to an S^D. In other words, the stimulus may precede the response by more than 60 seconds; so it probably wouldn't work with Rudolph, the rat, in the Skinner box. And feedback often precedes the next opportunity to respond by minutes, hours, days, etc. And the only way it would control the behavior to which it was relevant is if the person would repeat the feedback right before making the next response. That's why it may be important to give feedback immediately before the next opportunity to respond, rather than immediately after the last response, contrary to popular dogma.

QUESTION

1. Define and give an example of the following:
   a. task analysis
   b. the process vs. product general rule
   c. feedback.

Analysis

What are we talking about here, reinforcement or its rule-governed analog? Here's one way to think about it: Could the contingencies have controlled the behavior of a nonverbal animal? If they could have, then we may be dealing with a direct-acting contingency—simple reinforcement. If not, then we must be dealing with an indirect-acting contingency—a rule-governed analog to reinforcement.

So could Red's contingencies have controlled a nonverbal animal? If we were really clever, we might be able to train a chimpanzee to do a simple five-component play. At the end of each play, the chimp could trot over to the coach, and the coach could reinforce the whole sequence with a banana. (Actually, we doubt if any of us are clever enough or patient enough to train a chimp to do as complex a play as these boys did if we reinforce only at the end of the sequence—especially when the chimp is first acquiring the repertoire.)

But reinforcing the whole sequence misses the point of feedback based on the task analysis. Red didn't reinforce the whole chain of behavioral components that are the play. He didn't just say, "Good work boys." He said, "Good work, on the second component—the fake component—but you were slow on the center exchange." (Try that on Bonzo and see what your graphs look like!)

So we think the boys' behavior was under the control of rules like "Do the fake the same way next time and you'll have it right" and "Speed up the center exchange and you'll have a good play." What about the postgame feedback Red gave his team at the next session after each game? We don't see how any simple direct-acting contingency of reinforcement could operate there. The feedback occurred several days after the actual behavior.

It's hard work to be crisp, alert, and do a complex, difficult play well. The player might prefer to dog it a bit. But if he doesn't play his best, he'll lose the opportunity for Red's positive feedback (a strong reinforce for all the boys). So he does the hard work of executing the play well, because that will avoid the loss of the opportunity to receive Red's reinforcer a few days later at the next practice.

Now you might say, fine, then what we've got is an analog to reinforcement. But we don't think so. There's a deadline—the start of the play. And, if the

player doesn't play well at that time, he's forever lost the opportunity for Red's reinforcer for that play. So he's avoiding the loss of that opportunity.

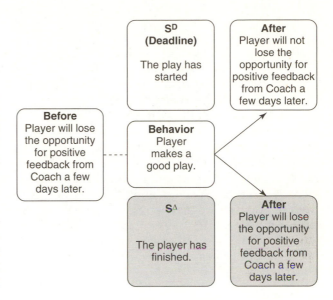

But Red's feedback is a double-edged sword. If the player fails to make a good play, he'll receive Red's corrective feedback. Now that doesn't mean Red's going to beat up on the kid, but it's aversive to hear that you screwed up, no matter how tactfully that feedback is put; and Red isn't a master of tact. So, we've got another analog avoidance contingency—an analog to avoidance of an aversive condition.

1. Please diagram this analog avoidance contingency:

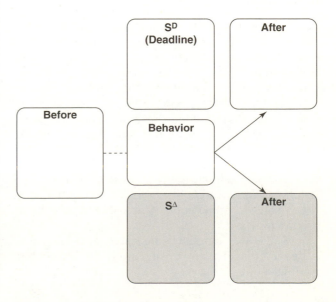

QUESTION

1. Please diagram and explain the role of delayed feedback in a behavior-analytic coaching procedure.

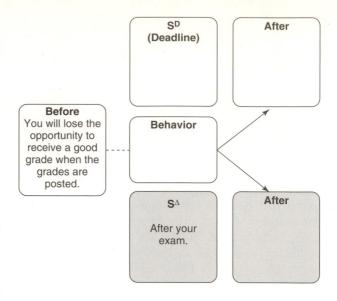

Example
Education
PUBLIC POSTING AND THE POST-EXAM CRUNCH

Many behavior analysts use public posting of client's accomplishments to help manage the client's behavior. It does help. Public posting consists of putting a record of the person's accomplishments on a wall chart or graph where that person and perhaps others can see it.

Question

Suppose, for example, your professor posts your exam grades in the hall outside the classroom after every exam. That's an example of public posting. Is it also an example of a reinforcement procedure for studying? What do you think? And why?

Our Answer

Public posting may reinforce something, but it won't reinforce studying. Why not? Even if your instructor is more conscientious than you have any right to expect, he or she probably will not get your grade posted before the day after the exam. That's too long a delay for the grade to reinforce studying. That delay is too long, even if you were studying up to the time for the exam (which you probably were). In other words, the reinforcer will not reinforce the response if the delay between the response and the reinforcer lasts more than 60 seconds. We used to think public posting was an example of a rule-governed analog to reinforcement by the presentation of a reinforcer for studying. But, as is so often the case, there was a hidden deadline: you must finish studying before the exam. If it were a simple analog to reinforcement, then you could study any time you wanted and also, subsequently, take the exam anytime you wanted; but life rarely works that way. So your studying avoids the loss of the opportunity to receive a good grade and avoids the receipt of a bad grade (hopefully).

1. Please diagram the preceding indirect-acting contingency involving studying and public posting.

Was public posting a reinforcement procedure for anything? You bet—for looking at the posted grades. If you don't believe us, just stand in front of the grade sheet when the students return to class the day after the exam. The opportunity to see their grades is such a powerful reinforcer that the horde of students descending on the posted grades may trample you if you don't get out of the way. In other words, the reinforcer (sight of the grade) reinforces what occurred just before the sight. The sight of the grades may even reinforce putting an elbow in your neighbor's ribs so you can get a better look.

(Incidentally, before you publicly post people's names, you may want to check out any public relations or even legal problems that could arise. Probably it'll work as well to use some anonymous code.)

Example
Behavioral Medicine
ANOREXIA NERVOSA[3]

Touyz and colleagues compared two contingencies for helping anorexic patients gain weight. Here is how one excellent textbook describes those contingencies: "In the former [program], patients were reinforced for each pound of weight they gained using a contingent, individualized schedule of reinforcement. In the latter [program], patients could have unrestricted (i.e., noncontingent) access to rein-

---

[3]Based on Touyz, S. W., Beumont, F. J. V., Glarin, D., Phillips, T., & Cowie, I. (1984). A comparison of lenient and strict operant conditioning programs in refeeding patients with anorexia nervosa. *British Journal of Psychiatry, 144,* 517–520.

forcers if they gained a minimum of three pounds a week."

Question

What is wrong with this description?

Our Answer

First, we reinforce behavior, not patients. So what behavior did the behavior analysts reinforce? Eating? No. Why not? Because the reinforcers were too delayed. The patients didn't just gorge on a large quantity of food, hop on the scale, and then pick up their reinforcer, especially during the second procedure where the reinforcer depended on the weight gain at the end of the week. This is a good example of where talking about reinforcing people rather than reinforcing behavior can lead to a superficial and inaccurate analyses of the contingencies.

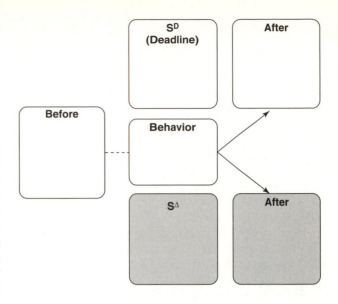

OK, enough quibbling. What happened to the anorexic patients? They gained weight. The rule-governed analog to avoidance of the loss of the opportunity to receive a reinforcer worked well. Here, the rule describing a large reinforcer contingent on eating enough to achieve a large weight gain worked as well as the rule describing a smaller reinforcer contingent on eating enough to achieve a smaller weight gain.

Example
Behavioral Community Psychology
COMMUNITY APPLICATIONS

Behavior analysts have begun working with problems of concern to the whole community. They've even begun trying to modify the behavior of all the members of entire communities. Here are some examples:

Billy Goat Gruff and the Bay Bridge: Carpools[4]

McCalden and Davis studied the following contingency: Carpoolers could enter special uncongested lanes on the San Francisco–Oakland Bay Bridge. The results? Carpooling increased, and traffic flowed more smoothly.

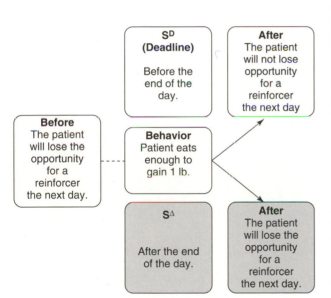

The other rule said, *Every week that you have eaten enough to gain 3 pounds, you will get unrestricted access to reinforcers.*

1. What's the implicit deadline for this other rule?
2. What's the contingency?
   a. Reinforcement
   b. Analog to reinforcement
   c. Analog to avoidance of the loss of the opportunity to receive a reinforcer.
3. Please diagram the contingency.

---

[4]Based on McCalden, M., & Davis, C. (1972). Report on priority lane experiment on the San Francisco–Oakland Bay Bridge. Sacramento, CA: State Department of Public Works. Cited in Wilson, G. T., & O'Leary, K. D. (1980). *Principles of Behavior Therapy,* Englewood Cliffs, NJ: Prentice Hall.

Question

Is this reinforcement for ganging together in a single car?

Our Answer

At first glance, it looks as if this might be a reinforcement contingency. A group of you are riding together in a car. While you're doing that, you get a reinforcer: a free lane. Maybe that did reinforce riding together in the car, but we've got to look at more details of the behavior. The initial behavior for carpooling requires advance planning. You've got to recruit the riders and arrange for a time and place to meet. That probably occurs at least the night before the reinforcer. So the reinforcer comes too late to reinforce the planning. Therefore, at second glance, it looks as if this might be an analog to a reinforcement contingency. But at third glance, we see some hidden deadlines. That means we're not talking about a simple reinforcement procedure.

We think people told themselves rules like, *I'd better get this pool organized tonight* (deadline) *so we can get the special privilege tomorrow.* And this rule governed their behavior. In other words, we're talking rule-governed analog to avoidance of the loss of the opportunity for a reinforcer (driving in the special uncongested lanes). (Their following the rule paid off, and that payoff will affect their future following of that rule. But the payoff was too delayed to **reinforce** the rule following. This is true in all our examples. More on this in Chapter 24.)

1. Please diagram the avoidance analog for organizing the carpool.

Smokey the Bear Fights Litter[5]

We have a real problem with resources: If we don't use 'em up, we trash 'em up. In 1971, the National Forest Service spent $22 million cleaning up after slobs.

Behavior analysts to the rescue again. Clarke, Burgess, and Hendee offered kids the chance to earn reinforcers like a Smokey the Bear patch for gathering trash and putting it in 30-gallon plastic bags. It worked. On one Saturday, kids from seven camping families filled 26 bags with about 750 pounds of litter. That was so much trash it completely filled the trunk and back seat of the car belonging to one of the behavior analysts. As of 1977, 26 national park services had adopted this behavioral system. If you're not part of the solution, you're part of the pollution.

1. What is the preceding contingency? Keeping in mind that, realistically, the behavior analysts probably didn't get the Smokey patches to the kids within 60 seconds after they'd brought in a bag of litter. Also, keep in mind that there must have been a deadline, like before the behavior analysts left the park.
2. Please diagram that contingency.

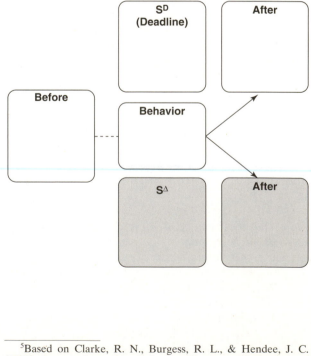

---
[5]Based on Clarke, R. N., Burgess, R. L., & Hendee, J. C. (1972). An experimental analysis of antilitter procedures. *Journal of Applied Behavior Analysis, 5,* 1–7.

The reinforcers (the Smokey the Bear patches) were too delayed to reinforce the cleanup behavior, though the promise of the reinforcers got the behavior to occur. We think the instructions functioned as rules that controlled the children's behavior of cleaning the campgrounds. You guessed it: a rule-governed analog to avoidance of the loss of the opportunity to receive a reinforcer.

Helping Parents be Good Parents: Child Dental Care[6]

Fifty-one out of 180 kids had dental problems in a little, country grade school in a poor school district in Florida (the mean [average] income of the kids' families was $5,000 in the 1970s). The school sent notes to one group of parents telling the parents about their children's dental problems and recommending that they see a dentist, possibly at the free dental clinic. Twenty-three percent of the parents followed this good advice. With another group of parents, the school sent the notes plus the promise of a $5 reinforcer for visiting a dentist. Sixty-seven percent of these parents followed the advice.

Question

Reinforcement?

Our Answer

No way. The promise of the $5 reinforcer acted as a rule that controlled taking the children to the dentist. Originally, we thought this was a rule-governed analog to reinforcement by the presentation of a reinforcer.

Question

Is this a rule-governed analog to reinforcement?

Our Answer

Probably not, because we think there's a deadline lurking below the surface of this example also. But this deadline is even more subtle, because it was not imposed by the behavior analysts. Remember these families were very poor, living close to the edge. So, no doubt, they we're facing many crises with built-in deadlines, like if we don't go to the dentist's by Fri-

day, we won't get the $5 to help us make it through this weekend. That could be a serious deadline.

Why do we persist so doggedly in our search for deadlines? Because we think that, without deadliness, this sort of analog contingency leads to infinite procrastination. And 67% of these parents did not procrastinate indefinitely. (We'll discuss this more in Chapter 24.)

1. So what kind of contingency is this?
2. Please diagram the contingency.

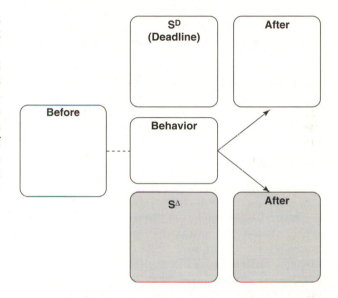

QUESTIONS

1. For each of the following areas, give an example of research showing the successful use of a rule-governed analog to avoidance of the loss of the opportunity to receive a reinforcer. Explain how your examples are best understood in terms of this contingency.
   a. education
   b. medicine
   c. carpooling
   d. litter control
   e. dental care.
   (Warning: You've probably got to be able to do this to do well on your quiz.)

---

[6]Reiss, M. L., Piotrowski, W. D., & Bailey, J. S. (1976). Behavioral community psychology: Encouraging low-income parents to seek dental care for their children. *Journal of Applied Behavior Analysis, 9,* 387–396.

Example
SHOOTING BASKETS

Here's what some other authors said, but this is **not** our view; instead, we're going to try to figure out what they got wrong:

Allowance must be made for the fact that a re-inforcer tends to condition [reinforce] the response that immediately preceded it. For example, suppose a youngster had, 10 minutes earlier, been practicing shooting baskets by herself, and now is sitting on the grass watching a hummingbird among some flowers. If at that point the physical education instructor says, "Good for you, Susie, you were practicing by yourself," this may cause the youngster to sit on the grass and watch hummingbirds more often, but it is not likely to have much effect on her practicing shooting baskets. This example serves to emphasize the importance of immediate reinforcement for appropriate behavior.

Question

What do you think about the analysis those authors did?

Our Answer

We think their analysis is wrong. We think their example shows the importance of not letting your basic behavioral concepts get in the way of your common sense, even if you're a pair of outstanding behavior analysts, as the authors of that example are. Allowance must be made for the fact that people aren't completely stupid. True, "a reinforcer tends to condition [reinforce] the response that immediately preceded it." And Susie might tend to sit on the grass more frequently in the future, because that's where she gets the compliments from her instructor. But that's not the whole story.

For example, suppose that 20 minutes earlier, the phys. ed. instructor had been using the procedure of reinforcement to get her students to practice shooting baskets. Now, the instructor is sitting on the grass watching a hummingbird among some flowers. If at that point the school principal says,

"Good for you, Jennifer, you were using behavior modification by yourself. Here's a $100 bonus." Will this cause the instructor to sit on the grass and watch hummingbirds more often? Be real. The instructor will be off the grass and into class in 10 milliseconds. The principal has just implied a rule: Use b. mod. with your squad, and you may earn a wad. This example serves to emphasize the importance of rules in controlling appropriate behavior, even when those rules oppose the effects of immediate reinforcement by the presentation of a reinforcer. In these two examples, both rules would win out. Both the instructor and the student would get off the grass and get on the task, in spite of the possible reinforcement for doing otherwise. We've got rule-governed analogs to reinforcement by the presentation of a reinforcer.

People make two kinds of errors in dealing with rule-governed analogs: Most often they act as if a rule-governed analog to reinforcement were itself reinforcement. Less often they make the error of acting as if a rule-governed analog to reinforcement would not work; they overlook rule-governed behavior. The first analysis, of Susie shooting baskets, involves this latter error—acting as if a rule-governed analog to reinforcement would not work.

QUESTIONS

1. What two common errors do behavior analysts make concerning rule-governed analogs?
2. Give an example of each type and explain why they are errors.

   Hint: In answering these two questions, be able to explain why the delayed praise for shooting baskets will increase shooting baskets and won't just reinforce sitting on the grass.

   Warning: Students who don't really understand these issues often do poorly on the quiz.

BASIC ENRICHMENT

IF PREACHIN' WAS TEACHIN'

> **IF PREACHIN' WAS TEACHIN'**
> **WE'D BE SMARTER THAN WE ARE.**
> **BUT WE AIN'T;**
> **SO IT AIN'T, BY FAR.**

The set of examples of community applications impressed us, for a couple of reasons, one positive and one negative. First the positive: Behavior analysis is such an action-oriented approach. You got a problem. OK, let's don't talk about it. Let's get crackin'. Let's do something. Let's fix it.

The world needs action. And we're pleased to be part of this action-oriented approach. We're impressed with the imaginative ways those behavior analysts used a behavioral approach to start pecking away at some of the world's problems. That gets at what this movement is all about. And we think behavior analysis is a movement—a concerned and practical one. Behavior analysts are not just a bunch of thumb-twiddling academicians. But don't get us wrong; you must think before you leap. However, you still have to leap, if you're going to get to the other side of the gorge.

The negative part: the preachin' ain't teachin' part. All these behavior analysts start off their articles by showing that telling people what to do doesn't do the trick. You can preach 'til the cows come home about the harmful effects of the consumption of nonrenewable resources, the harmful effects of pollution, the value of carpooling; but usually the preaching has no effect, at least no lasting effect.

And yet, as Hayes and Cone said, "Curiously, information in the form of massive educational campaigns seems to be the main strategy adopted by governmental agencies and power companies to control the consumption of energy." Or as Clark, Burgess, and Hendee said, "Knowledge of formal sanctions and the existence of highway litter control signs and litter barrels had no impact on littering. . . . [And] anti-litter propaganda, posted messages, and plentiful garbage cans . . . proved largely ineffective . . . in movie theaters. . . ." Or Seaver and Patterson on reducing energy consumption said, "the thrust of the policy [of the federal government] has been to inform consumers about the importance of saving energy and methods for achieving savings. . . . A study by Heberling . . . of the electricity consumption of apartment dwellers indicated that the informational campaign of the federal government had no effect on the electricity consumed. Further, it showed that a letter sent directly to apartment dwellers from a group advocating conservation had no effect on consumption." Or Reiss, Piotrowski, and Bailey said, "Efforts to prevent and control dental disease usually take the form of dental-health education programs that saturate our private, public, and parochial school systems, . . . mass-media campaigns. . . . More often than not, improved dental-health practices . . . resulting from these programs are the exception rather than the rule. . . ."

Preachin' ain't teachin'—or at least it ain't a very effective behavior management procedure. It seems as if we behavior analysts have a better handle on this issue than any other group. We know what the big trick is. The big trick is to give people reinforcers when they change their behavior. Then they do it. Otherwise, they don't change. And often we don't even have to give the reinforcers right away. We don't even have to reinforce the behavior of concern with those reinforcers for them to have their effect. The reinforcers can be involved with rule-governed behavior.

The irony: We behavior analysts know preachin' ain't teachin'. And we behavior analysts know you need to provide incentives, like reinforcers. But what do we behavior analysts do when we try to change the behavior of the government and business officials responsible for encouraging community-conscious behavior in we the people? Preach, of course. So our next step is to figure out how we can provide effective incentives for our leaders. If we want to influence behavior, we need access to the reinforcers that maintain that behavior.

Here's a secret, so don't tell anyone, 'cause it'll put 'em up tight. Our motto is:

QUESTION

1. Give three of our examples of how information was not enough to get people to act in their best interests and the best interests of the community.

INTERMEDIATE ENRICHMENT

Process vs. Product
MONDAY-MORNING QUARTERBACKING THE POP WARNER FOOTBALL TEAM

Football season was over, at least for the Pop Warner league. Juke sat in Sid's study. They had been buddies since their freshman year in Professor Harper's Psych 101. He and Sid and Mae had all competed for the highest *A* in that course; but Dawn got it. Now Juke was telling his friend about the triumph he, Red, the team, and behavioral coaching had had over old-fashioned coaching.

Sid tilted back his desk chair, put his feet on his desk, and closed his eyes for a few seconds. Then he said, "I always get nervous when you start talking about putting contingencies on the process rather than the product—when you start talking about providing reinforcers for the behavior that leads to the accomplishment rather than the accomplishment itself. I always think of my high school principal. He was really into process. He told us we had to come to school looking like serious students if we were going to get anywhere. We couldn't even get in the front door of Bronx Central if we didn't meet his dress and hair codes. I always think of that old son of a gun and his dress codes when you talk about putting contingencies on the process."

"Yeah, I know what you mean. It's risky business. You really have to do a careful task analysis to be sure you're putting the contingencies on the right behaviors."

Sid continued, "You have to watch out for your personal biases and your cultural prejudices when you start telling people how to do the process, rather than just making the reinforcers contingent on the final product, the outcome. And you have to make sure people aren't just looking busy but not really increasing the quantity or quality of their product. Also it's hard work for the performance manager."

"Yes, you should put contingencies on the process (the detailed responses) only when you have to, when you can't get the product or accomplishment you want. And I find that's most of the time, both in sports and in business and industry. You almost always get better results if you deal with the process as well as the product."

"The only problem with that is, my high school principal lost sight of the product—how much we ac-

tually learned and what we learned. He spent all his time on dress codes and hall conduct. *And it's too easy for us to get lost at the nuts-and-bolts level, to get sucked into the details to the point where we lose sight of the goals.*"

"That's true," Juke replied. "You need to analyze the whole system, not just the component behaviors of the individual members. You need to keep your eye on the product as well as the process."

In summary, here are some of the issues involved in putting contingencies on process rather than just the product:

○ First do a careful task analysis.
○ Be prepared to spend more effort monitoring performance.
○ Guard against your personal biases and cultural prejudices.
○ Discriminate between people's merely looking busy and their actually being productive.

But if you address those issues properly, you can often have a big impact on product.

QUESTION

1. When should you put contingencies on behavior leading to the accomplishment and not just on the accomplishment?
2. List the four issues to address when putting contingencies on the process in addition to the product.

Research Methods
MULTIPLE BASELINE

Juke knew Sid still wasn't off his case yet, not Sid, the professional critic and skeptic. Sid's skill as a thoughtful critic was one reason Juke had kept in touch with him over the years. If Juke could get an analysis past Sid, it was tight. It was almost like coming back to grad school for a refresher course every time he got together with Sid.

Again, Sid closed his eyes for a few seconds and then asked, "Why are you so sure your behavioral intervention is what got Red's backfield clicking so well? Maybe they would have gotten better just with more traditional coaching. Maybe behavioral coaching just looked good because the kids were a year older than they had been during the previous season. You did say they had all played the year before?"

"You're right. I didn't do a controlled, scientific experiment. I was just doing behavioral technology, just applying the results of someone else's research."

"Then someone else had done the experiment."

Juke knew Sid was always skeptical when he said "someone" or "they" and didn't give the actual names of the scholars who supported his points. This time he'd checked his references before he came. "Sure, Komaki and Barnett, 1977, *Journal of Applied Behavior Analysis.* They ran a multiple baseline across the three plays. No improvement in any play until they put the behavioral coaching on that particular procedure. Clean data."

The problem is, how can you be sure your behavioral intervention has an effect? How can you be sure the performance wouldn't have improved even if you hadn't shown up with your behavioral bag of tricks? As we've seen, you measure performance for a few days or weeks before you intervene. And if you see a big change in the performance after you intervene, you can be fairly certain the change resulted from your intervention. But maybe it was a coincidence. Maybe the weather changed at the same time you intervened, and maybe the weather, rather than your intervention, caused the change. But the longer the baseline and intervention phases, and the bigger the differences between the performances in the two phases, the more confident you are that your intervention was a winner. Nothing's 100%, but you can get close.

Here's one way you can get closer to being 100% sure your intervention affects the performance you're measuring: Repeat the intervention or the experiment. Suppose Juke carried out the same behavioral coaching procedures with several different teams. And suppose he collected baseline data each time before intervening. And suppose he intervened at different times throughout the season. And finally, suppose each team improved when he started the behavioral coaching. Such data would impress even Sid. We say you *replicate* an intervention or experiment each time you repeat it. The more replications, the more convincing the data.

In this hypothetical case, Juke would have been replicating across groups. In the real case, Komaki and Barnett replicated across behaviors—actually, across plays. They ran a baseline of 23 practice and game sessions before intervening on the option play, then another 10 sessions before intervening on the power sweep, and finally 10 more sessions before intervening on the off-tackle counterplay. In each case the performance showed no consistent improvement until the intervention for that particular performance. So we become truer believers in the value of behavioral coaching with each successful replication across plays in this multiple-baseline experimental design.

As we mentioned earlier, the steadier the data within a phase, the more confident we are that the changes between phases are real. Komaki and Barnett had some variability in their data. But it was mainly in the baseline, and it's mainly toward the low end; the backfield zeroed out several times during baseline, but not once during the behavioral intervention. So this time the variability may even add to our confidence. This is because the variability (the low percentages during baseline) is in the opposite direction of the raised percentages during intervention.

Behavior analysts have been able to show many cause-effect relations (functional relations) using various experimental designs. And one of the most powerful of these designs is the **multiple-baseline** experimental design. The experimental design is the way we arrange such things as the change in the values of our independent variables (for example, when we start presenting reinforcers). We say we have a multiple-baseline design because we have a new baseline with each replication. Also, with a multiple-baseline design, we start each new intervention at a different time; that way we can be fairly sure that any change in our dependent variable resulted from our change in the independent variable (the intervention). In other words, with the multiple baseline, we can reduce the odds that the change in our dependent variable resulted from some coincidental change in some other cause, some factor we hadn't thought of, like a change in humidity or temperature.

Definition: Concept

Multiple-baseline design

- An experimental design
- in which the replications involve baselines
- of differing durations and
- interventions of differing starting times.

Juke's hypothetical experiment involved a multiple baseline across groups. Komaki and Barnett's real experiment involved a multiple baseline across behaviors (the three different plays).

QUESTION

1. *Multiple-baseline design*—define it.
   a. Why is it useful?

b. Give an example of a multiple baseline across groups.

c. And one across behaviors.

Analysis
"INNER" FOOTBALL: REINFORCEMENT OF COVERT BEHAVIOR VS. RULE-GOVERNED BEHAVIOR

For a third time, Sid leaned back, closed his eyes, and just sat there. Juke knew he wasn't off the hook yet. "What do you think are the behavioral concepts involved in your new coaching methods?" Sid asked.

"Mainly, we've got an indirect-acting contingency—the rule-governed analog to avoidance of the loss of the opportunity to receive a reinforcer," Juke replied.

"I wonder. I wonder if direct-acting reinforcement of covert behavior also isn't floating around there, though you don't know it."

"How so?" Juke asked.

"Maybe when Red gives the team feedback about a behavioral component of a play, maybe the guys are imagining the play, visualizing it, as they had actually done it. Red says, 'Now, about that last quarterback block'; and the quarterback visualizes the block. 'You did it just right,' and Red's praise reinforces the quarterback's imagined behavior of blocking."

"Interesting analysis," Juke said. "Red's praise probably did reinforce the quarterback's visualizing his block. But that's not the same as reinforcing the actual behavior of blocking. If your reinforcement of covert behavior worked too well, we could end with our whole team standing around visualizing plays, while the other team beats their socks off."

"Very funny," Sid said. "But I suppose you're right. We can be fairly sure of only one thing: Red's praise reinforced the team's visualizing—at least if they were visualizing at the time of the praise. We can't assume that the response of visualizing the play transfers to the responses of doing the real-life play. And yet it seems like visualizing helps."

"Yeah, visualizing the components might help the guys develop more precise rules describing what they should do. Then they say the rules to themselves, when they run through the sequence of components back in the scrimmage," Juke said. Like 'I've got to bend over more when I fake carrying the ball.' With enough practice involving direct-acting contingencies of reinforcement and punishment, those direct-acting contingencies may come to control the proper performance of the sequence and the rule control may drop out." [Note: Rules can describe direct-acting contingencies in addition to indirect-acting ones.][7]

When you read *covert*, you may think of the covert operations of one political party trying to steal the campaign plans of another political party. But, as we use *covert*, it simply means "private," "inside the person." So, by **covert behavior,** we mean private behavior happening inside the person, behavior like thinking, visualizing, imagining, dreaming, imaging. By reinforcement of covert behavior, we mean the *reinforcement of private, internal behaviors,* like thinking and visualizing. Now the actual reinforcers could be external, as when Red compliments the players about a play while they're visualizing the play.

Definition: Concept
Covert behavior
- Private behavior (not visible to the outside observer).

What do you think would happen if Red had praised the players for their excellent play while they were daydreaming about a TV show they had seen the night before? Our guess is that two things would happen: First, the praise would have reinforced their daydreaming, though he had not meant it to; and second, he would have changed their rule-governed behavior a bit, though not through simple reinforcement. They would now be more likely to state and follow a rule telling themselves to do the play the same way the next time.

The reinforcer in reinforcement of covert behavior also could be internal or private, such as when someone chuckles about something amusing. We assume the intrinsic or built-in reinforcement contingency of the humor reinforced that thinking.

Reinforcement works with covert behavior just as with overt behavior.

The opposite of covert is *overt.* Overt events are public or external, visible to others. Thinking the amusing thought is covert. Chuckling out loud is overt.

---

[7]Another possibility is that the visualizing had little to do with it. Maybe the verbal feedback was specific enough that the players would just repeat the feedback-generated rule when it came time to play again, and any imaging that occurred was just icing on the cake.

QUESTIONS

1. *Covert behavior*—define it and give an example.
2. *Reinforcement of covert behavior*—give an example.
3. What are the possible roles reinforcement of covert behavior might play in behavioral coaching, and what, if any, are the limitations on those roles?

Analysis
THE SHIFT FROM RULE CONTROL TO CONTINGENCY CONTROL

Sid smiled, "I can sit here, right now and picture the quarterback saying the rules to himself as he goes through a play. 'Ah, what was that rule the coach gave us? Oh, yes.' And Wham! A monster end nails the poor kid."

"For sure. Once you're in the game, everything's got to be automatic. You don't have time to say rules. That's why our players practice their tails off. They keep going through the plays until their moves become more automatic. Until they're playing by feel. Until the feel of doing it right reinforces their behavior. Until direct-acting contingencies of reinforcement and punishment control their behavior."

The football player's transition from rule control to contingency control is typical. Often we start out with a complex sequence of responses under the control of a rule. But as we repeat that sequence, the responses come under the control of the direct-acting contingencies. For example, in the good old days, they had what is called a *manual transmission.* With your left foot, you pushed in a pedal attached to what is called the *clutch.* And you gradually pushed down on the accelerator. Then at just the right time you shifted gears. Tricky indeed. First, the novice driver would learn the rule describing that sequence of responses. Then as he or she learned to drive with a manual transmission, the behavior came under the control of the feel of shifting the gears properly. The driver no longer even remembered the original rule.

In your Spanish lessons, you say the rule about putting the adjective after the noun instead of before it as you compose a sentence. But after a summer in Mexico, you no longer say the rule. Your speaking and writing Spanish sentences is now more under the control of the direct-acting contingencies—the sound of it. Your Spanish is now more intuitive, as well as more fluent.

This use of *intuition* fits with our definition from Chapter 13: **intuition (intuitive control)**—

control by a concept or set of contingencies the person does not define or describe. It's the same as contingency control. What we're saying is that when people talk about using their intuition, they mean essentially that their behavior is under contingency control. We've found the phrase *intuitive control* useful: It allows us to get away from reifying or creating an explanatory fiction such as *intuition;* and yet the phrase allows us to talk about these intuitive phenomena in a useful and careful way.

Definition: Principle
Shifting from rule control to contingency control

○ With repetition of the response,
○ control often shifts from control by the rule describing a direct-acting contingency
○ to control by the direct-acting contingency itself.

Note that when we talk about shifting from rule control to contingency control, we're talking about direct-acting contingencies, where the outcome occurs less than 60 seconds after the response. But if the rule describes an indirect-acting contingency, we wouldn't expect such a shift. For example, consider your studying hard so you'll get a good grade at the end of the semester. That's pretty clearly rule-controlled. And, unfortunately, because it involves a delayed outcome, you will always need to be restating the rule to yourself. Studying now so you can get a good grade at the end of the semester will never become automatic; it will never shift from rule control to contingency control like playing football, driving a car, and speaking a foreign language. Similarly, the hard work of writing this book will never shift from rule control to contingency control. Although, we've done several editions of this book, sitting down and starting to write has never become automatic; it's always rule governed. Studying and writing are controlled by indirect acting contingencies with delayed outcomes; so the control will never shift to automatic, direct-acting contingencies—unfortunately.

QUESTION

1. The principle of *shifting from rule control to contingency control*—state it, give three examples (e.g., football, driving, and Spanish), and explain how your examples fit the principle.

REINFORCEABLE RESPONSE UNIT

Suppose Rudolph pulls the chain, which immediately turns on a light; then he immediately goes to the lever, immediately presses the lever, immediately hears the dipper click, immediately bends down, immediately licks the dipper, and immediately gets a drop of water. That's a behavioral chain. And the drop of water either directly or indirectly reinforces that entire sequence of responses. Because there is no pause greater than 60 seconds between any link in the chain, the drop of water reinforces the entire behavioral chain and not just the terminal link, the lick of the dipper; all the links in the chain will occur more frequently and in the right sequence as a result of that reinforcement. In other words, that entire behavioral chain acts like a single response, a single, reinforceable response unit.

But suppose, the sequence had gone like this: Rudolph pulls the chain which 3 minutes later turns on a light; then 3 minutes later he goes to the lever, and 3 minutes later presses the lever, and 3 minutes later hears the dipper click, and 3 minutes later etc., etc. And because of the 3-minute pauses, the drop of water would not reinforce that entire sequence of responses, even though it might reinforce the dipper lick. Because there are pauses greater than 1 minute in the response sequence, that sequence isn't a reinforceable response unit.

A *reinforceable response unit* is a response or sequence of responses with no disruptions greater than 60 seconds within that response or sequence of responses. An immediate reinforcer at the end of the sequence will reinforce the entire sequence, either directly or indirectly.

However, the reinforceable response unit, itself, may be considerably longer than 60, if it contains no 60-second gaps. For instance, at St. Cloud University, Jerry Mertens' had a response-chaining apparatus that covered the floor of a large lab. It would take the rat 5 minutes to complete the chain. But the reinforcer at the end of the behavioral chain reinforced the entire response unit, because the well-trained chain contained no 60-second gaps.

Once a visiting PhD behavior analyst offered the following example of reinforcement: You go to college for 4 years and get a bachelor's degree.

Question

What's wrong with that example?

Our Answer

A couple things. First of all, receipt of the degree, no doubt, follows the final response by more than 60 seconds. And going to college for 4 years is certainly not a reinforceable response unit. Even the most gung-ho student would have zoned out for longer than 60 seconds a few times during those 4 years.

Throughout this book, we've conscientiously tried to make sure most of our examples involved reinforceable response units. But now that we're dealing with rule-governed analog contingencies, it is often more convenient to deal also with rule-governed analogs to reinforceable response units. A *rule-governed analog to a reinforceable response unit* is a response unit with 60-second gaps.

The reason we deal with analog response units now is that, when people describe analog contingencies, they usually state rules referring to analog response units. For example, if the patients ate enough to gain one pound, they'd get a reinforcer, but surely they paused for more than 60 seconds during their consumption of the necessary 3500 calories.

And, as another example, all but the most desperate of the students studying enough to get a good grade on an exam would surely have to take a few 60-second breaks, even if they did take the book with them when they went to the john.

But not all analog contingencies involve analog response units. For example the football play hopefully contained no 60 second gaps, even though it would be more than 60 seconds until they got Coach Red's feedback.

QUESTIONS

1. What's a reinforceable response unit?
2. Give an example.
3. What's an analog to a reinforceable response unit?
4. Give an example.

WHY ANALOGS TO AVOIDANCE ARE NOT DIRECT-ACTING CONTINGENCIES

Thoughtful students often wonder if analogs to avoidance contingencies aren't really direct-acting avoidance contingencies. For example, let's reconsider the carpooling contingency diagram on the next page.

Thoughtful students will say this: *Immediately after the driver arranged the carpool the night before, she would know she'd avoided the loss of the opportunity to drive in the fast, uncontested lane the next day; so that must be a direct-acting contingency.*

Our answer is, *Weeeelllllll. . . . Well, we need to look even deeper.* We've really got two contingencies here, one that's indirect acting and one that's direct acting. The indirect-acting contingency is the analog avoidance contingency we just diagrammed. And the direct acting contingency is more-or-less

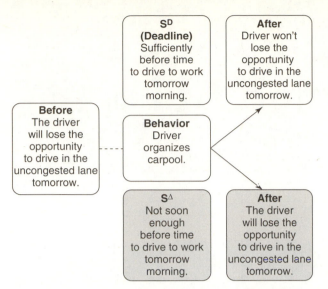

the knowldege-of-success contingency the thoughtful student just suggested.

We use *fear* because it is simple and makes intuitive sense and because the man, Skinner, himself, used that term. But many methodological behaviorists start tugging at their collars when we use that terms. So here's a more precise, or at least more detailed, way to talk about it.

Direct-Acting Escape Contingency

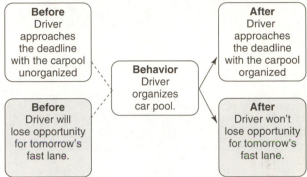

Indirect-Acting Avoidance Contingency

Direct-Acting Escape Contingency

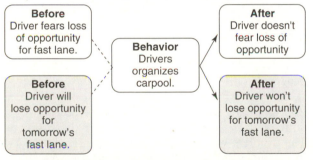

Indirect-Acting Avoidance Contingency

So, yes, as soon as she organizes the carpool, the driver does escape her fear of losing the fast-lane opportunity. And, so, yes, that is a direct-acting contingency. And, as we'll see in Chapter 24, that contingency is crucial. But that's not the contingency we were originally talking about; we were talking about the avoidance contingency. And because the outcome is delayed until tomorrow, it is really a rule-governed, indirect-acting, analog to an avoidance contingency—an analog to avoidance of the loss of the opportunity to receive a reinforcer (the opportunity to drive in the fast lane).

In this escape contingency, the before condition is a conditional aversive stimulus (remember the definition from Chapter 11, **conditional stimulus**—*elements of a stimulus have their value or function only when they are combined; otherwise, the individual elements are relatively neutral.*) The two elements in this conditional aversive stimulus are the approaching deadline and the unorganized carpool. The approaching deadline is aversive, only when combined with the unorganized carpool. When the driver organizes the carpool, then the approaching deadline is no longer aversive. So by organizing the carpool, the driver has escaped that conditional aversive condition. Cool (I hope).

QUESTIONS

1. Please explain why rule-governed, indirect-acting avoidance contingencies, really involve delayed outcomes. Diagram an example.
2. Describe the relevant direct-acting escape contingency. Diagram an example.
3. Describe the concept of the conditional stimulus and it's relevance to your example.

24

A Theory of Rule-Governed Behavior

FUNDAMENTALS

Example
University Teaching
DR. SIDNEY J. FIELDS[1]

Once again, the alert observer would notice a tear trickle down Juke's cheek. Mae noticed. Juke was more moved seeing Sid walk across the stage to receive his PhD diploma than when he got his MA diploma or when Mae got her PhD diploma.

The Problem

As BSU's most promising doctoral student in psychology, Sid had finished his course work in record time, with straight *As*. He also had collected all the data for his doctoral dissertation. The only things left were to write a report of his dissertation and have his oral defense. So the faculty of the Psych Department had unanimously voted to offer Sid a position as assistant professor. Of course, he'd finish his writing and have the oral defense of his dissertation during the summer, before he started teaching that fall.

But Sid didn't get his dissertation written that summer. In fact, he barely got started. And once the fall semester began, Sid hardly had time to look at

his dissertation. No problem, he'd finish it during the next summer's break. But by the end of that next summer's break, the dissertation still remained uncompleted. The department chair warned Sid that if he didn't graduate by the next April, his contract as an assistant professor wouldn't be renewed. Sid felt like he was rapidly falling from the role of the department's favored son to the department's embarrassment. But he still wasn't making any progress.

What was the problem? Writing the dissertation was hard work, the hardest work Sid had ever done. But he *could* do it; that wasn't the problem. The problem was that he *didn't* do it. He did everything but write. He did more literature reviews in the library. He learned how to use new computer programs to improve his writing and make it go faster. He created a database of all his references. He cleaned the house—almost daily. He started a vegetable garden. But he didn't write. He meant to, and he definitely would—the next day, just after he got the house really clean. But the next day he planted the garden instead. And so on, with only an occasional lapse into the hard work of writing. Procrastination after procrastination until the summer was over.

The Solution

Two months after the department chair had warned Sid that he was in danger of losing his job, Sid still hadn't written more than a few pages. So he went to his buddy, Juke, for help.

Juke: What you need is a behavioral research supervisory system.

---

[1]Sid Fields is a fictional character. Resemblance to any people living or who wish they were dead is purely a result of the ineffective contingencies in the lives of so many ABDs (All But Dissertation). The data reported for Sid are a fictionalized composite of the typical case. The graphed data are real. This section is based on: Dillon, M. J., & Malott, R. W. (1981). Supervising masters theses and doctoral dissertations. *Teaching of Psychology, 8,* 195–202; and Garcia, M. E., Malott, R. W., & Brethower, D. (1988). A system of thesis and dissertation supervision: Helping graduate students succeed. *Teaching of Psychology, 15,* 186–191. (The relevant data in the current chapter are from this article.)

Sid: I don't know what that means, but it has all my favorite words.

Juke: It's the same sort of performance management system I use in most of the consulting I do with business and industry. It's a form of performance contracting in which the contracts are designed especially for doing thesis and dissertation research.

Sid: In performance contracting or behavioral contracting, I write down a list of tasks I'm going to do and give them to my contractor.

Performance Management Rule #1
Put it in writing.

Sid: So do you have time to be my contractor—my performance manager?

Juke: I have neither the time nor the inclination to be your performance manager. But I don't know anyone else who could manage a hard case like you, so I'm it. You owe me one. I'll do it, but only if you're willing to put your rear end on the line. I've had it with trying to manage people's performance when we don't have effective behavioral contingencies we can add. In the behavioral research supervisory system, students usually have either grades, credit, or money contingent on completing their contracts. What's your choice?

Sid: I really need to get this done. I'm desperate; so let's make two outcomes contingent on my completing each contract. I've signed for dissertation credit; so how about having some of that turn into no credit if I blow off too much of my contract. Also, I'm willing to have some money riding on my performance. I'll deposit $50 with you, and you deduct some every time I screw up.

Juke: Let me make it heavier than that. Write ten checks for $5 each, and make them out to the American Nazi Party. Then down in the memo section of each check write this: "Although I'm Jewish, I admire your work so much I wish to make this contribution." I'll mail one of those checks every time you screw up. Heh, heh.

Sid: Come on, Juke, give me a break.

Juke: No, man. I want to turn the heat on. I want you to know that each time you blow off a task, you're supporting the thing you hate most—the American Nazi Party.

Sid: I think you're going too far. But if I have got to do it to satisfy your taste for sadism, I'll do it.

Juke: Should I sweeten the pot by giving you back one of those checks each time you meet your contract?

Sid: No, making regular progress toward my graduation is sweet enough for me. I'm willing to live with indirect-acting contingencies that are based on analogs to avoidance of the loss of the dissertation credit and the loss of dollars.

Performance Management Rule #2
Have effective behavioral consequences.

Juke: OK, now we need to meet once a week, so you can show me your permanent products, evidence you've done everything you agreed to. And at the same time, you should show me your performance contract for the next week—a list of tasks you're going to do and the time you're going to put in.

Sid: Do really need to meet once a week? That's sort of a nuisance, isn't it?

Juke: Yeah, we really do. The weekly monitoring date is a deadline. That way you can't procrastinate more than a week on doing that week's tasks. The weekly deadline is our best procrastination preventer.

Performance Management Rule #3
Performance not monitored once a week turns to Jello.[2]

Sid and Juke prepared the contract on p. 412 for the first week (note that a performance contract is essentially a set of rules, and the performance it specifies is rule-governed behavior).

Juke: Here are the performance-management contingencies we probably should use: Any time you fail to do any item of your contract, I send out one of your checks. The second time, within a single semester when your cumulative percentage of points earned falls below 90%, two of your credits for your dissertation turn to no credit, and you'll have to sign up again for those credits. (By the

---

[2]Actually Jell-O isn't the word we were thinking of, but this is a family book.

Behavioral Research Supervisory System Performance Contract					
Contractee: Sid **Performance Manager: Juke**					
Tasks	**Proof**	**Hours**		**Points**	
		Do	**Done**	**Pos.**	**Earn**
Write 8 hours on introduction.	4 new pages	8		8	
Meet with Dr. Harper to review writing progress (every two weeks).	notes from meeting	1		1	
Analyze data.	2 graphs	2		2	
Graph points earned (cumulative and noncumulative).	updated graphs	0.1		1	
Prepare contract for next week (before meeting with Juke).	contract	0.2		1	
Meet with Juke.	obvious	1		1	
Totals		12.3		14	

way, would you add to your contract for next week to get Dr. Harper's agreement on that credit-loss business?)

Performance Management Rule #4

Specify the contingencies clearly.

Sid: For example, I must analyze my data before my next performance-management meeting with you. And if I don't, I will lose the opportunity to earn 2 points; so my cumulative percentage of points earned lowers, and I move a little closer to losing 2 credit hours.

Juke: Yes, we've got avoidance of the loss of the opportunity to earn a reinforcer (the two points).

Sid: Actually a rule-governed analog to avoidance of loss, because the loss of points would occur at the weekly meeting, probably more than 60 seconds after I analyzed the data—at least, I hope more than 60 seconds.

Juke: Exactly. And your avoidance response will successfully prevent the loss of the opportunity to earn the 2 points, as long as it occurs during the S^D (before the meeting for that week).

And, now, it's about time we formally define the concept of this all-powerful performance contract:

Definition: Concept
Performance contract (behavioral contract or contingency contract)
 ◦ A written rule statement describing
 ◦ the desired or undesired behavior,
 ◦ the occasion when the behavior should or should not occur, and
 ◦ the added outcome for that behavior.

The Results

It wasn't easy. Even with his performance contract, Sid still had to fight that procrastination devil; and he was already working more than full

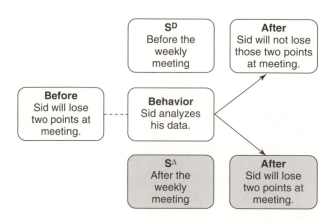

time with his teaching job. During the rest of the academic year, he lost a total of $40 and 2 academic credits. And his cumulative average of points earned (roughly the same as tasks completed) was 88%. He averaged about 13 hours per week working on his dissertation; and during the 3 weeks before he had to turn his dissertation into the graduate college, he averaged 35 hours per week. But he got it done: He passed the oral defense over his dissertation, he got his teaching contract renewed, and he got his dissertation accepted for publication. He is now Dr. Sidney J. Fields, Ph.D., a man who is no slouch in the field of behavior analysis.

Figure 24.1 shows that a behavioral research supervisory system can really help students.[3]

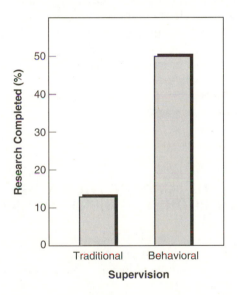

Figure 24.1   Completion of Projects, Theses, and Dissertations

QUESTIONS

1. Describe the use of the behavioral research supervisory system. List and illustrate the four rules of performance management.

2. *Performance contract*—define it and give an example (it need not include more than one behavior).

---

[3]These data are from Garcia et al. (1988). They represent the percentage of projects, theses, and dissertations completed during the Garcia study; of course, more were completed after the end of the study.

Theory
HOW DO RULES GOVERN OUR BEHAVIOR?

In Chapters 22 and 23, we presented the slightly theoretical, and thus slightly controversial, notion that many contingencies of interest to behavior analysts are not direct-acting contingencies of reinforcement and punishment—a contradiction of the assumption behavior analysts had formerly made. And in this chapter we present the slightly more theoretical, and thus even more controversial, set of notions about *how* rules control our behavior.

Before we return to Dr. Sidney J. Fields and the behavioral research supervisory system, we'll start this theoretical analysis by reviewing a few of the important issues we've covered thus far in this book:

First, the environment exerts two major types of psychological control over our behavior—**operant control** (control by the immediate consequences of our actions) and **respondent control** (control by the immediately preceding eliciting stimuli). Most of the behavior we've dealt with has been controlled by its immediate consequences.

Second, we may not have actually said it, but by default, we've implied that that's all there is; there ain't no more. However, many people find that implication aversive. Also, this narrow-mindedness doesn't make much sense (as we suggested in Chapter 22), especially when you consider all the people working toward long-term goals with no obvious immediate reinforcers, no performance managers popping M&Ms in their mouths every few seconds—all the cases where **indirect-acting contingencies** control our behavior.

Third, in Chapter 22, we also suggested that **rule control** could explain the influence of indirect-acting contingencies—contingencies where the outcomes are too delayed to reinforce or punish the causal behavior. Does this mean we're abandoning our narrow-minded position that all our behavior is controlled either by immediate operant or respondent processes? Does that mean we think there's more to life than the ringing of bells, the immediate delivery of a bite of food or a friendly smile, the immediate cessation of electric shock?

No, we still think that's all there is, but the bell ringing and the food gobbling and the shock flinching can get much more subtle than we used to realize. We don't think we're being narrow-minded; instead, we're being strict and rigorous; we're not letting ourselves cop out to easy but superficial and false answers to these crucial issues of behavior analysis. We think that with the simple concepts presented in the first part of the book, behavior analysts can understand essentially all of human psychology with its wonderful richness, depth, and complexity.

Yes, we still have some serious explaining to do. Rule control may explain the influence of indirect-acting contingencies, but now we have to move on to the fourth major issue—a new issue: What explains rule control? Well, hold on, because here's where we get really theoretical—and controversial.

Theory
RULE STATEMENTS AS ESTABLISHING OPERATIONS

Remember, as behavior analysts use the term, a *rule* is a description of a behavioral contingency. Most behavior analysts believe these rules function as reinforcement-based or punishment-based S^Ds. That is, they believe rules are stimuli in the presence of which the specified response will be reinforced or punished. However, we think that should also mean the absence of the rule is a reinforcement-based or punishment-based S^Δ—a stimulus in the presence of which the response will be less likely to be reinforced or punished. But we're not so sure rules usually work that way.

For example, the delicious taste of a fruit smoothie will be as likely to reinforce your drinking it, whether or not someone has given you a rule about how much you'd enjoy drinking it. And the pain of an electric shock will be as likely to punish your putting your fingers across the two terminals of your car's battery, regardless of whether or not someone has warned you of the danger. Yet someone might give you rules saying you'll like drinking the smoothie and you won't like touching the batteries. And probably those rules would govern your behavior, though they don't seem to us to be S^Ds. Now maybe we're being too restrictive in our use of S^D, but the following theoretical interpretation makes more sense to us.

The rule statement is an *establishing operation* that establishes noncompliance with the rule as an aversive condition. For example, you state the following rule to yourself: If I don't start reading this chapter, I'm not going to be ready for the quiz. After you've stated that rule, your goofing off produces an aversive condition. (Some would call that aversive condition "fear," or "guilt," or "anxiety," or "nervousness.") So stating the rule and not working is like turning on the shock in an escape experiment. And working on your assignment is the escape response. Perhaps just starting to work reduces the aversiveness a bit; and finishing the assignment may allow you to escape completely from this self-generated aversive condition. Is it this way with you?

In conclusion, we still have a direct-acting contingency controlling our rule-governed behavior,

even when the rule describes an indirect-acting contingency. For example, the poor grade on the quiz or even the poor performance during the quiz would be too delayed from the behavior of studying to be part of a direct-acting contingency controlling that studying. The delayed grade could influence only indirectly. But we think all operant control requires direct-acting contingencies; so we've theorized that the direct-acting contingency is the escape contingency based on the learned aversive condition that results from your stating the rule. The direct-acting contingency is the reduction in the aversiveness associated with noncompliance with the rule.

QUESTIONS

1. What's the conventional interpretation of the role of rule statements?
2. What is the authors' objection?
   a. State their theory.
   b. Give an example illustrating their theoretical analysis.

   Warning: Students often get a lower quiz grade because they miss this one.

Theory
THE MYTH OF THE CAUSE OF POOR SELF-MANAGEMENT

Years ago, I made what I then considered my first major contribution to psychology. It was the publication of the following insight: The problem of self-management is that our behavior is controlled by immediate outcomes and not by delayed outcomes. So we fail to do what's in our long-run best interest. (Then I reread one of Skinner's books and found he had said the same thing before me. Probably I had gotten the idea from him and then forgotten the source.)

In more recent years, I made what I now consider to be my first major contribution to psychology. It was the publication of the following insight: The problem of self-management is not that delayed outcomes fail to control our behavior. Poor control by delayed outcomes is not why we fail to do what's in our long-run best interest. (Then I reread Skinner's *Contingencies of Reinforcement* and found he had said the same thing before me. Probably I had gotten the idea from him and then forgotten the source. Moral: Read Skinner's books only once; then you won't experience the humiliation of discovering you're not an ivory-towered creator of brilliant insights but just a street dealer of secondhand ideas.)

So now we propose the following as a falsehood, a myth:

Definition: False Principle
The mythical cause of poor self-management
- Poor self-management occurs
- because immediate outcomes control our behavior
- better than delayed outcomes do.

Here's a common version of that myth: Because we can't delay our gratification, we fail to act in our long-run best interest. You've heard it many times, *The problem with your generation is that you can't delay your gratification; you're too much into immediate gratification, not like your parents' and grandparents' generations.* Well, even if the older generations hadn't been dissing the younger generation in that way since Aristotle's time (yes, they really have), we'd still think it's a myth.

We call the preceding a false principle and a myth because we do **not** believe that poor self-management occurs because of the failure of delayed outcomes to control our behavior. True, we don't think delayed reinforcement works. But because of rule-governed behavior, delayed outcomes and rules describing those delayed outcomes can control our behavior. We **do** believe there are other reasons for our poor self-managment, as you shall soon see.

In Chapter 22, we gave several examples of likely control by rules describing delayed outcomes: When your little brother says, "thank you," he will get another piece of cake from you **one day later.** When you mail in a magazine subscription, you will start getting the magazine **after a few weeks.** When you apply to college, you will hear from the admissions department **after a few months.**

In Chapter 23, we gave several more examples of the likely control by rules describing delayed outcomes: When football players make the right plays, they'll receive delayed feedback and praise, **after a few minutes.** When you study and then take an exam, you'll see the results posted, **after a few days.** When Mary, the anorexic woman, ate her meal, she'd have access to reinforcers, **after several hours.** We also looked at what was probably control by rules describing delayed outcomes in many cases of behavioral community psychology (especially in environmental concerns).

All these examples suggest that we can easily get our behavior under the control of rules describing delayed outcomes (as long as those outcomes are probable and sizable). In turn, our lack of difficulty suggests that delayed outcomes are not why we fail

to do what's in our long-run best interest. However, the ease with which delayed outcomes control our behavior does **not** suggest that delayed outcomes reinforce and punish that behavior. It's just that those delayed outcomes can reliably, though indirectly, influence our behavior if we can state rules describing the contingencies in which those outcomes are imbedded.

So what's the behavioral myth of the cause of poor self-management? That our inability to cope with delayed outcomes (delayed gratification) is the major cause of our troubles in self-management. Instead, we think delayed outcomes don't cause us much of a problem. Of course, this is a controversial view (that's why we've put it so near the end of the book). Behaviorists have invested so many years thinking the other way that it's hard to turn around. It's true, most of the devil's delights involve immediate reinforcers:

You are the sugar in my caffeinated tea.
Your nicotine gets the best of me.
And driving fast gives me a rush.
Oh, guilty conscience, why don't you hush.
There is no question.
There is no doubt.
Immediate reinforcers can wipe us out.

Our behavior is always controlled by immediate reinforcers and immediate aversive consequences, for better or worse. And we're always swimming in a sea of concurrent contingencies. But rules stating sizable and probable outcomes can be our life raft, though the outcomes are delayed. Such rules act as the establishing operations we need. They establish the value of the outcomes in effective concurrent contingencies that do battle with the devil's temptations. It'd be fairly easy to slow down to the speed limit when you saw a cop with a radar speed checker, even if the police are set up to let you whiz on by and would be content to send you your summons days later in the mail (they got your license number). Again, immediate contingencies are at the bottom of it all. It's just that rules specifying delayed outcomes can set up those immediate contingencies based on fear, guilt, or whatever you want to call that private hell that keeps us all more or less in line.

In the next section, we present what we consider the behavioral truth about the cause of poor self-management.

QUESTION

1. According to the authors, how important are delayed outcomes in causing problems of self-management?
   a. Please explain.

   Warning: Students often get a lower quiz grade because they miss this one.

   b. Give a couple of examples illustrating your explanation.

Theory
THE SMALL, BUT CUMULATIVE, OUTCOMES

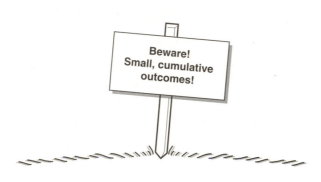

If delayed outcomes aren't what hangs us up, what is? We think the biggest problem is when an immediate outcome for each specific instance of a behavior is too small to reinforce or punish that behavior, though the cumulative impact of many such outcomes may be large. For example, the harmful effects of one spoonful of ice cream are too small to punish the response of eating that spoonful. Those harmful effects only gradually sneak up from behind to bite you on your ever-expanding rear end. Those small, harmful effects are of only cumulative significance.

Doesn't that make sense, when you stop to think about it? Of course, the harmful effects of one spoonful are too small to punish even the tiny sin of eating that spoonful. "Yes," the skeptic replies, "but those harmful effects accumulate—into a significant outcome only after a considerable delay. So you haven't gotten rid of the problem of the delay. I still think the delay is mainly why people eat ice cream in spite of its deadly results."

True, the harmful outcomes of eating ice cream aren't part of a direct-acting contingency that punishes the behavior of eating, and that's for two reasons. One is that the immediate, harmful outcomes are too small. The other is that the sizable harmful outcomes are too delayed. But the question here isn't why the outcomes are not part of a direct-acting punishment contingency.

Question

Why do we have so much trouble following rules that specify those outcomes?

Our Answer

We think people have trouble following rules that specify outcomes that are small and of only cumulative significance. For example, suppose the following hypothetical rule were true: *If you eat one more bite of ice cream, you will gain 50 pounds, your blood pressure will enter the danger zone, your arteries will plug with plaque, and you'll have a mild heart attack. One little bite will definitely cause all these horrible things; however, those horrible things won't happen until exactly one year after that bite. But remember, just one bite will do it.*

I think even the skeptic must agree that most of us would shun that spoonful of ice cream as if it were connected to 220 volts and we were standing in a pool of water, at least if we believed the rule. In other words, the rule specifying the delayed disaster would effectively control our behavior.

But the following rule does a poor job controlling our behavior, even though it is true and most of us believe it: *If you continue eating ice cream and the like you will gradually gain 50 pounds, your blood pressure will gradually rise to the danger zone, your arteries will gradually plug with plaque, and you'll be at serious risk for a fatal heart attack (not just a mild one).* Millions of people know and believe this true rule. But still this rule does a poor job of controlling their behavior. Why? Because one more bite won't hurt. Even one whole quart won't hurt. *Just one more, and then I'll stop.* Sure you will. Those small but relentlessly cumulative outcomes can kill you.

They also can be costly, as you probably know if you have a credit card. I'm not exactly sure how much I've charged to my card this month, but I'm sure it hasn't been too much. So I'll just buy these three new compact discs . . . oh, yes, and this one too, it's on sale. Yes, your debt to MasterCard can grow in a small but cumulative way until you're in deep Jell-O. And what about the cost of those long-distance phone calls to your boyfriend or girlfriend? Small but cumulative.

QUESTIONS

1. Give an example showing how rules describing small but cumulatively significant outcomes often fail to control our behavior.

2. Now change your example rule to show how a similar rule probably would control our behavior if the cumulative outcome were, instead, one single, though delayed, outcome.

3. Define the mythical cause of poor self-management.

Theory
THE IMPROBABLE OUTCOME

But there's more:

If everyone in the United States wore their seat belts, thousands of lives a year would be saved, tens of thousands of injuries would be prevented. By now, most of us know what a lifesaver seat belts are. But fewer than 20% of us regularly buckle up without special coercion.

And if everyone in the United States practiced safe sex, we'd virtually wipe out AIDS. Instead, it's wiping us out.

What does this mass stupidity illustrate? A cultural death wish? No, we think it shows that it's hard to follow rules specifying low-probability outcomes. In other words, the probability is very, very low that you'll be in a serious accident on any specific trip. However, if you were a professional daredevil, or a Hollywood stunt person, or race car or demolition-derby driver, probably you'd buckle up, at least when you were on the job. Why? Because the probability of an aversive outcome is much higher than when you're driving to the supermarket.

Similarly, with AIDS, the probability that that cute boy or girl is a carrier is low. So why bother with a condom? However, if you knew the person had AIDS, you'd practice safe, safe, safe sex. Those low probabilities are killing us.

QUESTION

1. Give an example showing how rules describing improbable outcomes often fail to control our behavior.

Theory
THE TRUTH ABOUT THE CAUSES OF POOR SELF-MANAGEMENT

So here's the way we see it. People can easily follow rules describing indirect-acting contingencies, though the outcomes are delayed, as long as those outcomes are sizable and probable (buy your plane ticket today so you can use it this coming weekend). And, of course, people also can easily follow rules describing direct-acting contingencies (last call for boarding the plane). But people have a heck of a time following rules that specify what we call ineffective contingencies—small but cumulative outcomes (dieting) and improbable (though immediate) outcomes (buckling up).

Definition: Principle
Rules that are easy to follow
○ Describe outcomes that are
○ both sizable
○ and probable.
○ The delay isn't crucial.

Definition: Principle
Rules that are hard to follow
○ Describe outcomes that are either
○ too small (though often of cumulative significance)
○ or too improbable.
○ The delay isn't crucial.

We distinguish between basic and higher-order principles of behavior analysis. ***Basic principles*** include the principles of reinforcement, punishment, and stimulus control. We cannot explain these principles with other still more basic principles of behavior analysis. ***Higher-order principles*** include these principles stating the conditions that make rules hard and easy to follow. We think eventually someone will be able to explain them with the more basic principles such as the principles of reinforcement and punishment. Sometimes we don't know if a principle is basic or higher order. Herrnstein's probability matching law is another example of a principle whose status as fundamental or higher order is not clear to everyone.

We also should note that these two principles concerning hard and easy rules are new kids on the block and not nearly as well established or accepted as are, for example, the law of effect or most of the other principles in this book. But we thought they were so important that you should know about them.

To summarize the last few sections, let's look at the diagram showing the relations among two types of rules and the three types of contingencies:

**Contingency Tree with
Outcome Properties**

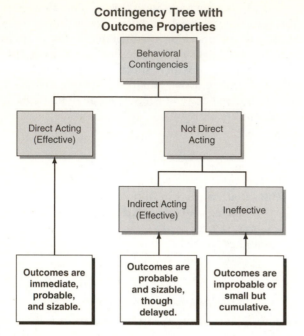

So, we have two types of rules—**easy to follow** and **hard to follow.** Rules that are easy to follow describe two types of contingencies—direct acting and indirect acting. For a contingency to be direct acting, the outcome must be all three—immediate, probable, and sizable. (For example, in the Skinner box, the drop of water won't appreciably reinforce the lever press if it follows the response by too great a delay or with too low a probability or if it's too small. We've said that a reinforcer delayed by more than 60 seconds won't normally reinforce a response. Less data are available on the probability of a reinforcer, but we would guess that if the probability were as low as 1 in 100,000 it would be way below the value needed to detect reinforcement.)

For a contingency to be indirect acting, the outcome must be delayed, probable, and sizable. (If the outcome weren't delayed, the contingency would be direct acting.) Rules that are hard to follow describe ineffective contingencies. For a contingency to be ineffective (for verbal human beings), the outcome must be either improbable or small, regardless of whether it's immediate or delayed. And that brings us to the correction of what we now consider a false principle:

Definition: Principle
The real cause of poor self-management
  ○ Poor self-management results from
  ○ poor control by rules describing
  ○ outcomes that are either
  ○ too small (though often of cumulative significance)
  ○ or too improbable.
  ○ The delay isn't crucial.

QUESTIONS

1. *Rules that are easy to follow*—state the principle and give an example.
2. *Rules that are hard to follow*—state the principle and give an example.
3. Draw and explain the contingency tree with outcome properties.
   Warning: May be crucial to getting a good grade on this quiz.
4. Define the real cause of poor self-management.

Theory
WHAT'S WRONG WITH SMALL BUT CUMULATIVELY SIGNIFICANT AND IMPROBABLE OUTCOMES?

As we've seen, a contingency may still be effective, though it is not direct acting. The contingencies lose control of the behavior of verbal, rule-governed human beings only when the outcomes are improbable or small, though of cumulative significance.

Why do improbable and small outcomes often fail to control our behavior? Well, those contingencies fail to control our behavior, even indirectly, because the rules describing the contingencies are hard to follow.

So why are those rules hard to follow? According to our theoretical analysis, it's because those rules don't act as effective establishing operations. In other words, their statement doesn't establish a sufficiently aversive condition. For example, consider this rule describing a low-probability outcome: I should buckle up because if I don't there's one chance in a million I'll be killed. Stating that rule fails to establish noncompliance as a sufficiently aversive condition (a condition of fear, anxiety, whatever you want to call it). Therefore, escape from that condition of noncompliance will not reinforce buckling up, especially when buckling up is mildly effortful and mildly aversive. The same applies to the following rule describing a small but cumulatively significant outcome: I shouldn't eat this heavenly hot fudge sundae because if I do I will gain an unnoticeable amount of fat and be unnoticeably less beautiful and healthy. Stating that rule also fails to establish noncompliance as a sufficiently aversive condition. And therefore, entering that condition of noncompliance will not punish pigging-out, especially when the taste of that sundae is such a powerful reinforcer.

Then why doesn't the statement of rules specifying low probability or small, but cumulative, outcomes establish sufficiently aversive conditions? Sorry, we've answered two of your questions; and that's enough for one section. Besides, we're still trying to figure out the answer to this third one. What's your answer?

Understand that this section is on the cutting edge of behavior analysis, and messing with cutting edges is risky. In other words, this section is even more theoretical and debatable than the previous one; but it's our best shot.

QUESTIONS

1. Why does our behavior tend not to be controlled by contingencies with improbable or small but cumulative outcomes?
2. Present our theoretical analysis of why rules describing such contingencies usually fail to control people's behavior.

Theory
WHY DO WE MISS DEADLINES?

Let's look at another example. We have argued that it is easy to follow rules that specify delayed outcomes, as long as the outcomes are sizable and probable. Yet a few times we ourselves have missed and almost missed planes and trains when the outcome of boarding the plane or train was delayed by an hour or more from the response of preparing to depart (for example, finishing some chores at home, packing, and starting for the airport or train station). Does this contradict what we've been arguing? We think not.

We think starting to prepare for departure involves a rule that can be hard to follow, but not because the outcome of departing is too delayed from the act of starting the preparation. Instead, according to the present theoretical analysis, the rule is hard to follow because it is not clear how much time we'll need to finish our chores, pack, and get to the airport. And being too optimistic, many of us tend to underestimate the time we need to get it all together. So, because we naively think we've still got plenty of time, our failure to comply with the rule, *I've got to get my rear in gear,* doesn't generate a very aversive condition. Therefore, escape from that not very aversive condition doesn't reinforce our actually getting it in gear.

We can always procrastinate just one more minute before starting to pack. Surely we can wait until the end of the Seinfeld rerun. Surely we can tidy up the house just a little bit. The outcome of waiting one more minute is too small and often achieves significance only after too many of those minutes have accumulated. Then it's panic city—"Oh my gosh, we're going to miss the plane!"

So, our theory is that, in general, failure to meet deadlines is a problem of small and cumulative outcomes resulting from the difficulty of estimating the time needed to complete large tasks before delayed deadlines. It is not a problem of delayed outcomes.

Remember this rule: It always takes twice as long as you had planned to perform a task, even when you considered this rule in your planning.

QUESTION

1. Using an example, explain why failure to meet a delayed deadline is a result of small and cumulative outcomes, not a result of delayed outcomes.

Theory
THE SECRET OF PERFORMANCE MANAGEMENT

So what does all this theory say about performance management?

It gives us a brand-new perspective. It gives us a new answer to the question: How do we manage performance? But first:

When do we need performance management?

We need performance management when the natural contingencies do not effectively support the appropriate behavior.

Come on now, don't be a pedantic[4] pain. You know what we mean by *natural* contingencies. We mean the contingencies present in our work, in our home, in our school, in our life—the contingencies that cause all the problems the behavior analyst is called in to fix. In this context, by *natural* we don't mean "correct." The *natural* contingencies are the automatic, built-in (intrinsic), nonprogrammed contingencies, not the added (extrinsic), programmed ones.

And what do we mean by *appropriate behavior*? Behavior that does two things: (1) It in-

---

[4]I thought you might want to add this to your active repertoire of high-class put-downs, even though it may not be on your quiz (you'll thank me later): **pe · dan · tic** adjective. Characterized by a narrow, often ostentatious concern for book learning and formal rules: a pedantic attention to details. And while we're at it: **os · ten · ta · tious** adjective. Characterized by or given to ostentation; pretentious. *The American Heritage® Dictionary of the English Language* (3rd ed.). Copyright © 1992 by Houghton Mifflin Company. Electronic version licensed from INSO Corporation.

creases the individual and the group's long-range contact with beneficial conditions; and (2) it also decreases contact with harmful conditions. (Often, though far from always, *beneficial conditions* means *reinforcers* and *harmful conditions* means *aversive conditions*.)

Nonverbal Clients

> **How do we manage the performance of nonverbal clients?**
>
> **We add or remove the direct-acting contingencies to supplement the ineffective natural contingencies.**

For example, remember Velma and Gerri, the two profoundly retarded women who ground their teeth (bruxism) so much that their teeth were almost completely destroyed? The natural (biological) contingency between tooth grinding and tooth destruction was ineffective. Why? Because the harmful outcomes of tooth grinding were too small to punish that behavior. The harmful outcomes were significant only after they had accumulated.

In Chapter 4, we described the punishment procedure Ronald Blout and his colleagues used. They added a direct-acting punishment contingency—a few seconds of an ice cube on the client's face each time the client ground her teeth. And tooth grinding decreased from about 60% of the time to about 3% of the time.

Ineffective Natural Contingency

Before	Behavior	After
The client has better teeth.	The client grinds her teeth.	The client has slightly worse teeth.

Effective Direct-Acting Performance-Management Contingency

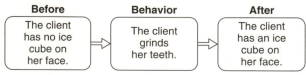

Before	Behavior	After
The client has no ice cube on her face.	The client grinds her teeth.	The client has an ice cube on her face.

Incidentally, to be complete, we really should include an effective natural contingency in this diagram—a contingency that maintains teeth grinding. Your first response might be that teeth grinding is a

respondent, not an operant, so the biting wasn't maintained by a contingency of reinforcement. A hard one to prove either way, but here are a couple of reasons to think it was operant: First, teeth grinding involves skeletal muscles; and skeletal muscles are usually under operant control. Second, teeth grinding is clearly under operant control with the ice-cube punishment contingency. So if teeth grinding is an operant, what is the reinforcer? Maybe the aggression reinforcers for biting. When the two women bit and ground their teeth, that behavior produced built-in stimulation. Perhaps aversive conditions might increase the reinforcing value of such built-in stimulation. That stimulation is what we mean by *aggression reinforcer*.

Theory
VERBAL CLIENTS AND THE INEFFECTIVE NATURAL CONTINGENCY

Blout's intervention shows how we can add an effective direct-acting contingency to an ineffective natural contingency with nonverbal clients. But what about verbal clients? We think the following answer is an important contribution of this theory of rule-governed behavior.

> **How do we manage the performance of verbal clients?**
>
> **Often we add indirect-acting contingencies to the ineffective natural contingencies. In other words, we supplement rules that are hard to follow by adding rules that are easy to follow. (Of course, sometimes we add or remove direct-acting contingencies.)**

Recall the community issues we discussed in Chapter 23. For example, in one study, the majority of parents didn't take their children to the free dental clinic, though the parents knew their children had dental problems. Why not? Perhaps because the rule describing the natural contingency was hard to follow. What was the natural contingency? An analog to escape from an aversive condition? Maybe not. The child's having a dental health problem most likely wasn't too aversive because the problem wasn't obvious—he or she didn't have a painful tooth. If the child had been crying because of a toothache, most parents would have rushed the child to the dentist.

Then what was the natural contingency? We think it was an ineffective analog to avoidance. Here's the hard-to-follow rule that describes it: If you take your kids to the dentist today, they will avoid infinitesimally more dental decay tomorrow. The trip to the dentist won't escape a current aversive condition but would avoid a future infinitesimal increase in aversiveness.

Ineffective Natural Contingency

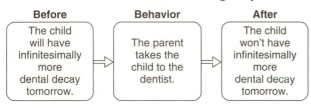

This dental analog to an avoidance contingency works like this: The parent's going to the dentist that day has prevented the tiny increase in the amount of decay that would have come otherwise.

Why does the avoidance contingency control the behavior of the rat, though this particular analog to an avoidance contingency fails to control the behavior of the parents? Maybe because the rat's pressing the lever avoids something sizable—an electric shock that will otherwise come in the next few seconds. But the parent's taking the kid to the dentist today would avoid something that's too small—one day's increase in decay. Even a dentist couldn't detect an extra day's decay.

Perhaps that's why the rule about taking the children to the dentist was hard to follow; its outcome was small and only cumulatively significant. If parents didn't take their children to the dentist today, nothing much would happen—just one more day's tiny contribution to poor dental decay. The parents could always go to the dentist tomorrow, or maybe the next day. In other words, we suspect most parents intended to take their children to the dentist but just never got around to it. We don't mean the cumulative outcome of their procrastination wouldn't be aversive to the parents. They'd find their children's poor dental health aversive, but they wouldn't find one more day's contribution to that poor dental health too aversive.

On the other hand, many people would argue that the dental analog contingency is ineffective because the outcome of serious dental problems is too delayed. But we think the delay is more or less irrelevant for verbal people. To better understand this theoretical analysis, let's look at a prediction: Sup-

pose the $5 rule worked because it reduced procrastination. If so, then here's another rule that should work as well because it also should reduce the procrastination of those poverty-level parents who value their kids' dental health. This rule would impose a deadline: *To receive free dental treatment, you must take your child to the dental clinic today. After today, the free services will end because the government is cutting back its support of social services.*

Effective Performance Management Contingency

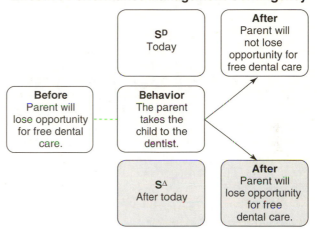

We suspect that's an easy rule to follow, in spite of the delay. We suspect almost all parents who believe the rule would take their kids to the dentist that day. Why? Because the outcome would be sizable (some serious cavities) and probable (definitely have the cavities), even though that outcome would be delayed. In summary, we argue it wasn't the delay; it was the small, though cumulative, nature of the aversive event being avoided that made the rule so hard to follow.[5]

Theory
VERBAL CLIENTS AND EFFECTIVE INDIRECT-ACTING PERFORMANCE-MANAGEMENT CONTINGENCIES

As a behavioral intervention, Maxine Reiss and her colleagues offered parents $5 for taking their kids to the dentist. Then the percentage of parents who helped their kids rose from 23% to 67%.

Does this mean the parents loved the $5 more than their kids? No way. Then why was the $5 rule so much easier to follow? Perhaps because the $5 rule allowed for less procrastination. Recall that the mean (average) income of the families was only

---

[5]A tip of the hat to Yvonne Hueng for helping with the analysis of this hypothetical contingency.

$5,000. So they were living so close to the bone, they may have often been broke. Then that $5 might allow them to get something they wanted or needed right away, like enough food on the dinner table. And if they procrastinated, they'd have to go without dinner for one more day, a powerful procrastination preventer.

In other words, with the rule describing a natural contingency, one more day's procrastination only had a small effect—just one more day of dental decay. But with the performance-management rule, one more day's failure to respond had a large effect—for example, a day without enough to eat.

To be more technically precise: For the natural analog to be an avoidance contingency, the event being avoided (one more day's decay) was too small to be aversive enough to support the avoidance response. (The aversiveness was only cumulatively significant.) For the effective performance-management analog-to-an-avoidance contingency, the event being avoided (loss of an opportunity to buy enough food for the family dinner table) was aversive enough to support the avoidance response (taking the kids to the dentist).

The $5 contingency for poor people may have implied a deadline: You must get to the dentist's office before closing time to avoid the loss of an opportunity to spend $5 on your family's dinner today. This "loss of an opportunity to spend $5 today" is getting complex; so let's discuss it.

In what sense do they have the opportunity to spend $5 today before they've even earned the $5? In the sense that before the dentist's office closes they still have a chance to earn the $5 and then spend it. After the office closes, they no longer have that chance. The opportunity to spend $5 today is a big reinforcer if you're broke. So the contingency is avoidance of the loss of a reinforcer—not the loss of the $5 (they don't have the $5 to lose); instead the contingency involves the loss of the opportunity to spend the $5 today.

By the way, don't think we're being too off the wall by suggesting some poor people in the United States don't have enough money to buy dinner. Many of poverty's children go to bed hungry. But even if hunger weren't the case for many of the families Reiss worked with, they still might not have had enough money to go to the movies that night or buy gas for the car or whatever.

Finally, we need to do an even more speculative theoretical analysis to answer this question: **Why do rules stating or implying deadlines work?** In other words, how can we use the basic principles of behavior to explain the value of the $5 rule and the predicted value of the deadline rule? What are the direct-acting contingencies of reinforcement?

As we said earlier, stating such rules establishes noncompliance as a sufficiently aversive condition that escape from that aversive condition reinforces compliance. In other words, the thought of losing the opportunity to spend the $5 today or missing the needed free dental care would be aversive enough that escape from that thought would reinforce going to the dentist. But the thought of just adding one more day's worth of insignificant dental decay would not be aversive enough.

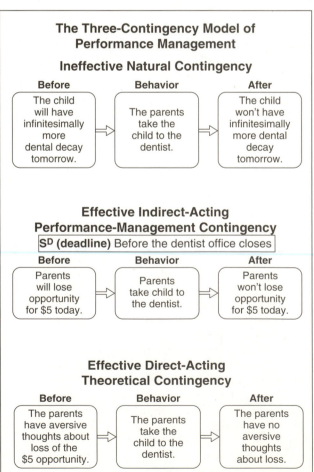

The Three-Contingency Model of Performance Management

Ineffective Natural Contingency

Before	Behavior	After
The child will have infinitesimally more dental decay tomorrow.	The parents take the child to the dentist.	The child won't have infinitesimally more dental decay tomorrow.

Effective Indirect-Acting Performance-Management Contingency

S^D (deadline) Before the dentist office closes

Before	Behavior	After
Parents will lose opportunity for $5 today.	Parents take child to the dentist.	Parents won't lose opportunity for $5 today.

Effective Direct-Acting Theoretical Contingency

Before	Behavior	After
The parents have aversive thoughts about loss of the $5 opportunity.	The parents take the child to the dentist.	The parents have no aversive thoughts about loss.

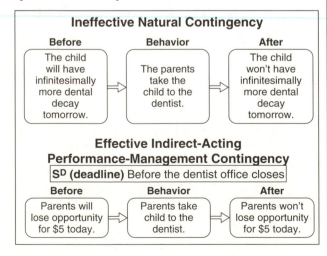

Ineffective Natural Contingency

Before	Behavior	After
The child will have infinitesimally more dental decay tomorrow.	The parents take the child to the dentist.	The child won't have infinitesimally more dental decay tomorrow.

Effective Indirect-Acting Performance-Management Contingency

S^D (deadline) Before the dentist office closes

Before	Behavior	After
Parents will lose opportunity for $5 today.	Parents take child to the dentist.	Parents won't lose opportunity for $5 today.

The parent states the rule, I must get my kid to the dentist today, or I'll lose the chance to spend the $5 today. That rule statement is an **establishing operation.** It establishes noncompliance with the rule as an aversive **before condition** because then noncompliance produces aversive thoughts about the loss of the opportunity to spend the $5 when needed.

Incidentally this analysis is an example of what we call the **three-contingency model of performance management.** We use it to explain the need for performance management and the effectiveness of indirect-acting performance-management contingencies. You don't need the theoretical contingency when the performance-management contingency is direct acting, as in the case of putting the ice cube on face of a tooth-grinding client.

Definition: Model

The three-contingency model of performance management

- The three crucial contingencies are: the ineffective natural contingency,
- the effective, indirect-acting performance-management contingency, and
- the effective, direct-acting theoretical contingency.

Deadlines

Are we contradicting ourselves? We say people miss deadlines, and yet we say deadlines are often crucial to good performance management. No, they often miss delayed deadlines, but fairly immediate deadlines are our saving grace. We stressed immediacy when we presented performance-management rule #3: Performance not monitored once a week turns to Jell-O.

OK, but then are we contradicting ourselves when we say rules must specify fairly immediate deadlines, and yet delayed outcomes aren't a problem? No, the rule *should* specify a fairly immediate deadline, though it can specify a delayed outcome. For example, Sid needs weekly deadlines for the completion of the various tasks that will produce his dissertation. But the rule specified a delayed aversive outcome—having to pay the university for extra dissertation credit for failure to meet the deadlines; and that outcome wouldn't occur until registration for the next semester.

Verbal Clients and Low-Probability Outcomes

We've been talking about the problems with small but cumulative outcomes and the lack of deadlines. What about the problems with low-probability outcomes? What about our national failure to wear seat belts? For example, in North Carolina, seat-belt use rose from an estimated 20 to 49% when buckling up became a state law. However, use rose further to 78% when failure to buckle up became what is called a *primary offense* (that means police could start ticketing motorists who failed to obey the buckle-up rule). The rise in buckling up from 49 to 78% was accompanied by a decline of 12% in fatalities and a decline of 15% in serious injuries.

How might we interpret this? The probability of legal sanctions increased somewhat when buckling up was made a law, and perhaps the probability of legal sanctions (penalties) increased a bit when failure to buckle up became a primary offense (the size of the aversive outcome may also have increased). So now the probability of an aversive outcome for failure to comply seemed high enough to get fairly good compliance and save quite a few lives.

QUESTIONS

1. When do we need performance management? Please explain and give an example.
2. How do we do performance management with nonverbal clients? Please explain and give an example, including a contingency diagram.
3. How do we do performance management with verbal clients? Please explain and give an example, including a contingency diagram.
4. Apply the three-contingency model to the problem of getting parents to take their children to the dentist.
5. Define the three-contingency model of performance management.

Theory
AN ANALYSIS OF PROCRASTINATION

We have two questions to answer:

1. Why did a good student like Sid have so much trouble finishing his dissertation?
2. Why was the research supervisory system so effective in helping him finish his dissertation?

First, why so much trouble? People often make the mistake that if someone doesn't do something it's because that person doesn't care. Sid cared. He'd worked his tail off to get his Ph.D. He loved his job and didn't want to lose it. The problem was procrastination. Sid could always putter about the house and garden for just another hour or so. Not that he was avoiding his dissertation, in fact he enjoyed working on it, once he got started; it's just that he needed to finish weeding the tomato patch. Doing almost anything was less intellectually effortful than working on the dissertation.

Also we've suggested that the typical behavioral myth doesn't apply. It wasn't that graduation was so far down the road; it wasn't that the outcome of his efforts would be too delayed.

The problem was that the progress Sid would make during any given hour of writing his dissertation was small compared to the total progress he needed to make. And the harmful results were insignificant for procrastinating just another hour or so or even another day or so. So his behavior wasn't controlled by the ineffective rule; I need to start writing my dissertation during this hour so I can make a tiny bit of progress toward getting my degree and keeping my job.

That rule described a small outcome of only cumulative significance. So a statement of that rule didn't establish *not writing* as a very aversive condition. Therefore, even when he stated the rule, getting to work wasn't reinforced by the reduction of any heavy guilt, fear, anxiety, aversiveness, or whatever.

This doesn't mean Sid wasn't terribly upset about his problem. It doesn't mean he wasn't afraid he would lose his job. It means that starting to work right now wouldn't reduce that fear much. Why not? Because he really could still start in just a few minutes from now, and he'd be almost as close to finishing as if he'd start right now. What a problem!

Therefore, let us reword our first question: **Why is it that, without help, Sid and thousands of other bright, hardworking grad students just like him will flounder around and never graduate?** Here's our answer:

Stating the rule about immediately starting to write doesn't generate a very aversive condition. In more popular words, the fear or anxiety isn't great enough. So actually starting to write will reduce only a mildly aversive condition or state of fear or anxiety. And that slight reduction in aversiveness isn't enough to reinforce the escape response of starting to write.

By the way, some students have objected that we were violating our own rule about not talking about nonbehavior. 'Tain't so. You should not talk about nonbehavior when you're trying to analyze a response. But nonbehavior can be a stimulus. For example the undertaker should always apply the dead-man test.

QUESTIONS

1. Why do good students often have so much trouble finishing their doctoral dissertations? Show how your answer applies to the actual writing of the dissertation.
2. Don't they really care about graduating? Please explain.
3. Graduation is a delayed outcome. Is that a serious problem? Please explain.

Analysis
University Teaching
THE RESEARCH SUPERVISORY SYSTEM

Now for our second question:

○ **Why does help in the form of the research supervisory system work?**

Because that system provides performance management. And we need performance management when the natural contingencies are ineffective in supporting appropriate behavior. The natural contingencies are often ineffective in supporting writing theses and dissertations or even writing postcards, for that matter.

We often do performance management with verbal clients by adding indirect-acting contingencies to the ineffective natural contingencies. We supplement rules that are hard to follow by adding rules that are easy to follow. Juke adds the rules of the performance contract that are easier to follow. The new rule is: Do all your 12.3 hours of work before your meeting with Juke this Friday at 3:00 P.M., or it'll cost you at least $5 and some embarrassment and put you much closer to losing 2 hours' worth of dissertation credit. That's an outcome that's probable and sizable. So it's an easy-to-follow rule.

Furthermore, there's a limit to how much Sid can procrastinate. At the latest he can procrastinate until around 1:00 A.M. Friday. That would leave him just enough time to get his 12.3 hours of work done and brush his teeth. What this means is that as Sid uses his slack time, not writing becomes more and more aversive (because not writing generates more and more thoughts about losing the money, etc.). Finally his thoughts become so aversive he escapes that aversiveness by getting his rear in gear and his words written. Now he may not have waited until that close to the last minute before he started to work, but let's just say he was at his computer a lot more on Thursday and Friday than he was on Monday and Tuesday.

So here's our theoretical answer to, *Why does help in the form of the research supervisory system work?* **Performance contracting within the research supervisory system produces rules that make it clear when you're dangerously off task; and those clear rules with their probable, sizable outcomes are effective establishing operations that support the reinforcement of getting on-task.**

The **ineffective natural contingency** involved the small, but cumulative, progress toward completing the research (and thus graduating) that resulted from each minute's work (ineffective indirect-acting reinforcement contingency). The **effective performance management contingency** could be indirect acting because it dealt with the behavior of verbal graduate students. This indirect-acting contingency involved the prevention of a definite and sizable, though delayed, loss of points that would move Sid much closer to losing some money and academic credit (effective indirect-acting contingency). The **theoretical, effective direct-acting contingency** involved the definite, sizable, and immediate reduction in the aversiveness established by the statement of rules of the behavioral research supervisory system (effective, direct-acting, escape contingency). Note: **If there had been no deadline, the statement of those rules wouldn't have established noncompliance as such an aversive condition.** The fairly immediate deadline was crucial. We can summarize all this in our three-contingency model

1. Please complete the following diagrams.

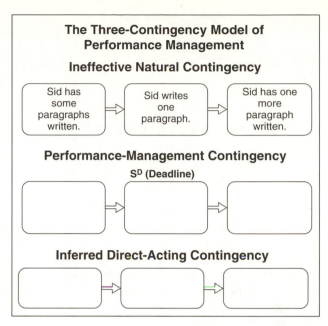

In order to have a reinforceable response unit, we just analyzed writing one paragraph rather than writing the entire dissertation. But mammoth task of writing a dissertation consists of a series of smaller, reinforceable response units, like writing a paragraph. The outcome of having one more paragraph written is not a sufficient reinforcer to maintain paragraph writing in itself. The loss of $5 is. Notice that the deadline for writing the first paragraph isn't really Friday at 3:00 P.M. Friday at 3:00 P.M. is when he will lose the $5. But the deadline for starting the first paragraph is at least 12.3 hours before Friday at 3:00 P.M. In other words, the deadline for the response and the time the reinforcer will be lost need not be the same.

Always remember this: **Performance management contacts designed to increase or maintain behavior should specify outcomes that are**

- **sizable and**
- **probable**
- **though possibly delayed.**

QUESTION

1. Why does help in the form of the behavioral research supervisory system work? Please illustrate each component of your answer with an example.

2. Apply the three-contingency model to dissertation completion.

3. What kind of outcomes should be used in performance management contracts designed to increase or maintain behavior?

INTERMEDIATE ENRICHMENT

Theory
AN INTERACTION BETWEEN THE PROBABILITY AND THE SIGNIFICANCE OF THE OUTCOME

We were in paradise—sitting in our bathing suits on a large rock overlooking a tranquil, crystal-clear lagoon in the Galapagos Islands, off the west coast of South America. Eighty degrees and sunny. Perfect for a swim. Our boat's skipper encouraged us to dive in. But the crystal clear water revealed a school of a half dozen sharks, 3 to 6 feet long. Danger in paradise. The sharks didn't stop our French companions, nor the Equadorian skipper. But they stopped us, though the captain assured us that he'd swum many times with the sharks and had no problems.

No doubt the skipper was right. No doubt the probability of a shark attack was low. But the significance of a shark attack was extremely high. The rule describing the unlikely but highly significant outcome stopped us dead in our tracks, even though the same reinforcement contingency for swimming on that perfect day was in effect for us just as it was for our French and Ecuadorian companions.

Another time, we left our umbrella in our car when we came home from work. The radio said it might rain the next morning (then again, it might not). The probability of getting wet if we didn't get the umbrella was fairly high, but the significance was low. The rule describing the moderately probable, but only mildly significant, outcome had no effect. We went to bed.

No doubt whether or not a rule controls our actions is a function of both the probability and the size of the outcome that rule describes. If the outcome is significant (e.g., a shark attack), the rule may control our behavior, though the probability of that outcome is fairly low. If the outcome is not significant (getting rained on briefly), the rule may not control our behavior, though the probability of the outcome is fairly high.

But most people still have trouble following the buckle-up rule.

Grad student, Yukiko Washio suggested that it's not a question of real probability but of imagined probability. The imagined probability of a shark attack is high after seeing *Jaws*. Not a bad point.

Theory
CAN WE BUILD A WORLD FREE OF AVERSIVE CONTROL?

What do the hippie flower children of the 1960s and most behavior analysts of today have in common? The naive belief that we can build a world free of aversive control.

Why Can't We Build a World Free of Aversive Control?

Our physical world is full of aversive control (for example, punishment contingencies when we touch the hot stove and escape contingencies when we turn on the air conditioner). Of course, we continue to engineer toward a user-friendly, forgiving world—one where we won't accidentally touch the hot stove, one where the automatic thermostat on the air conditioner anticipates our escape response. But, unless we end regressing to the womb, we will always need to deal with an occasional mildly aversive physical reality.

Furthermore, our modern psychological world is full of another, more subtle form of aversive control—the deadline. A *deadline* is a time and date when something bad will happen if you haven't previously made the right responses. The bad thing might be the presentation of an aversive condition: You will wake with frost on your nose if you don't close the windows before you go to bed. Or the bad thing might be the loss of a current or potential reinforcer: Your garden tools will rust if you don't pick them up before the night's dew.

The outcomes involved in these deadlines are often too delayed to reinforce or punish directly the causal behavior. Instead, according to one theory of rule-governed behavior, deadlines set up avoidance contingencies that indirectly control our behavior, causing us to avoid chattering teeth or the loss of clean tools.

These aversive outcomes control our behavior indirectly. People state rules describing the deadline contingencies. For example, I must take my cookies out of the oven in about 15 minutes or they'll burn. Such rule statements establish noncompliance as an aversive condition. Oh, my gosh, the 15 minutes are up. I almost "forgot".[6] And we escape that aversive condition by complying: Excuse me while I take out the cookies.

One more example: class preparation (the student must prepare the next assignment and the teacher must grade the last assignment). You state this rule to yourself: I must be prepared by class time or I'll look bad. As class time approaches, the aversiveness (fear, anxiety, whatever) increases, until beads of cold sweat dot your forehead. At last you've reached your threshold of aversiveness; so you make the escape response—you get off your duff and prepare for class, just at the last moment, of course.

The deadline can involve such indirect-acting aversive conditions as being cold or looking bad. Or it can involve indirect-acting reinforcers like tasty cookies or looking good. In either case, the direct-acting contingency is an aversive escape contingency; you effectively cope with the deadline by immediately escaping from or reducing a learned aversive condition—one associated with failure to comply with the rule that describes the deadline contingency. (Humble social validity of this analysis is provided by the frequent complaints people make about the high pressure [aversiveness] of deadlines.)

Why Can't We Live in a World Based Solely on Reinforcers, with No Aversiveness?

Because our world contains many aversive conditions, such as the painful stimulation of a hot stove. Furthermore, it contains many deadlines that fortunately control our behavior, but only through the escape from learned aversive conditions (the fear or anxiety associated with noncompliance with relevant rules).

But Why Can't We Prepare for Class Simply as a Result of Reinforcement by the Presentation of Reinforcers?

We could, if we were pigeons in a Skinner box, reduced to 80% of our free-feeding weight, with no concurrent schedules maintaining incompatible behavior. We'd prepare for class way before the dead-

line if the experimenter gave us a bite to eat every time we read a page.

OK, but Why Can't We Use Large Enough Learned Generalized Reinforcers to Reinforce Our Preparing for Class without Such Heavy Deprivation?

Suppose you get $10 as soon as you complete each page. Even that may not do the trick. You're still in procrastination city. You don't need the $10 right away; you can always do it later and catch a few zzz's now. Only two things will stop your procrastination: (1) an immediate need for the $10 (you're hungry and can buy food) or (2) escape from the learned aversiveness of approaching a deadline after which you can no longer earn the $10.

Then Why Not Build the Reinforcers into the Task?

Well, we try. The built-in reinforces is one of the main features of this book. We're doing our best to build in as many reinforcers as we can. And most students tell us we do a good job. Still, when do they usually read the book? Right before class, of course. Even literature teachers need the aversive control of deadlines to get their students to read such great authors as Shakespeare, Hemingway, and Updike. So teachers of behavior analysis are in no better position with lesser authors like us. But suppose Hemingway had been able to load his books with irresistible reinforcers; that's still not a general solution, because there just aren't enough Hemingways to go around.

Conclusion

So the physical world has aversive control built into it, and deadlines demand aversive control if compliance is to be achieved. Furthermore, we can't realistically escape from the need for aversive control by using added unlearned reinforcers, added learned reinforcers, or built-in reinforcement contingencies. However, we can try to minimize our contact with aversive events. We can try to make our aversive control as unaversive as possible. Some mild but consistent aversive control is needed. But that doesn't mean we should shout at our kids, our friends, or our employees. It doesn't mean we should pollute our environment with self-indulgent temper tantrums when we don't get our way. It *does* mean we might try to make interactions with us so reinforcing that people will do anything to avoid losing those interactions (though we shouldn't be constantly beating them over the head with the threat of such losses).

---

[6]In terms of behavior analysis, what's going on here? I failed to state the rule. Or my behavior is not under the control of the earlier stated rule. And that's because of the time lapse since the statement. In a sense, if we kept restating the rule, we'd be cool, like repeating the phone number we just looked up in the phone book. The problem is that there's no S^D for stating the rule. Or there's no establishing operation. If there were, we'd be OK. In a sense, the real question is why do I sometimes "remember."

QUESTIONS

1. Why can't we build a world free of aversive control?
   a. What are two types of aversive control provided by our physical world?
   b. What is the role of aversive control with deadlines?

2. Why can't we prepare for class simply as a result of reinforcement by the presentation of reinforcers?

3. Why can't we use large enough learned generalized reinforcers to reinforce our preparing for class without such heavy deprivation?

4. Why not build the reinforcers into the task?

25 Pay for Performance

FUNDAMENTALS

In the preceding chapter, we presented a theoretical analysis of why rules control our behavior. In this brief chapter, we apply that theory to the analysis of several of our favorite performance management interventions.

Example from
Behavioral School Psychology
A FIFTH-GRADE CLASS[1]

Here's a typical remedial fifth-grade class (this one was in New York City): The kids hated to write. (Can you relate to that?) It would take the teacher 10 minutes to get them settled down to work on their writing, and then they'd complain and moan: "It's no fun." "I don't want to write today." "I can't write." And they would escape from the aversive condition of writing as soon as they could.

Effective, Incompatible, Natural Contingency

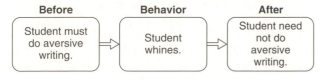

It was that way until Thomas Brigham, Paul Graubard, and Aileen Stans set up a behavioral intervention: The teacher told the students a rule: *I will give you a point for each word you write in your stories, and later you can buy things with your points.* At the end of class, the teacher would count the words and give the children their points. Still later, the students could use their points to buy classroom privileges (their favorite was an arts-and-crafts program).

The results? The mean number of words each student wrote rose from 40 to 95 per session (Figure 25.1). And the time they spent writing went from 10 to 32 minutes per session. What did the kids say about all this? "I like to write." "Can we write today?" "I'm a good writer."

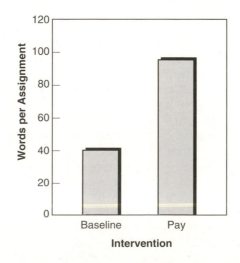

Figure 25.1   Pay for Performance in the Fifth Grade

---

[1]Based on Brigham, T. A., Graubard, P. S., & Stans, A. (1972). Analysis of the effects of sequential reinforcement contingencies on aspects of composition. *Journal of Applied Behavior Analysis, 5,* 421–429. The data are from the same source.

Direct-Acting or Indirect-Acting Contingency?

Is This Intervention an Example of Reinforcement by the Presentation of Tokens?

Traditionally, behavior analysts would say, "Of course." So you can bet your bottom token we'd say, "Probably not." Then what is it? Rule-governed behavior—control by the rule describing the pay-for-performance contingency—control by the rule saying a student would earn one point for each written word he or she wrote.

Why Is This Rule-governed Behavior?

Three factors cause us to suspect we've got control by the rule describing the contingency and not direct control (reinforcement) by the contingency itself:

1. **The teacher stated the rule.** He didn't secretly count the words and then give each student a set of tokens equal to the number of words that student had written. You can imagine that such a procedure would not control writing well, at least not until the student had figured out the rule. Also, you can imagine that the behavior analysts thought the students needed the rule statement or they wouldn't have made it a formal part of their intervention. So the teacher told the students they would get one point for every word written. (When working with people who have gone to the trouble to learn a language, why not use that language? Why reduce them to nonverbal organisms?)

2. **Performance changes as soon as the teacher states the rule and before the student has experienced the reinforcement of the points.** Figure 25.2 shows this more powerful reason to suspect control by the rule describing the contingency and not direct control (reinforcement) by the contingency itself.

    The first 9 sessions are baseline—no points contingent on the words written, no pay for performance. At the beginning of session 10, the teacher gave the students the point-contingency rule. And bang, the average number of words zoomed to 160 for that session—before the students had gotten any points for their words, before the points had a chance to reinforce the writing of the words.

3. **The contingency failed the 60-second test.** If the outcome follows the behavior by more than 60 seconds, then it's too delayed to reinforce or punish the causal behavior. So if that contingency controls behavior, it must be

through rule control. And no doubt, the teacher gave the points more than 60 seconds after the children finished their stories—he couldn't have counted the words for all the children and given the points in 60 seconds. Of course, the 60-second test is our acid test.

Now this 60-second test has two implications:

○ If the contingency fails the 60-second test and yet still controls behavior, then we know it's indirect acting.

○ If it's indirect acting, it must be rule governed.

So the contingency's being indirect-acting is our third reason for knowing the behavior is rule governed and not contingency controlled—not under direct control of the contingency without the involvement of rules.

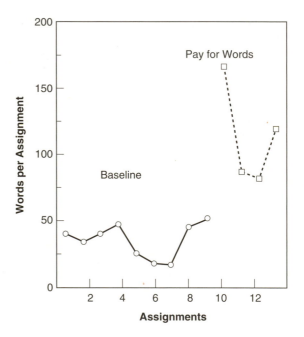

Figure 25.2   Pay for Performance in the Fifth Grade

So we think there's no question but that the point contingency was not a direct-acting contingency of reinforcement. It was an indirect-acting contingency, an analog contingency.

To be more precise, but also more long winded, if the person's behavior is in accord with the rule, the person's knowing the rule only suggests that you may rule control, rather than or in addition to contingency control. But if the outcome is delayed, or the performance changes immediately, then I'd say you've definitely got rule control.

Definition: General Rule

The it-is-probably-rule-control rule
  ○ It is probably rule control, if
  ○ the person knows the rule,
  ○ the outcome is delayed, or
  ○ the performance changes as soon as the person hears the rule.

The Ever-Present Deadline

1. Here's a tricky question: Does the points-for-words contingency involve a deadline?
   a. yes
   b. no

You think not? How about this: The deadline is the end of the writing class. The student will get points only for those words written by the end-of-class deadline. And this deadline business is a big deal; it's important for performance management involving delayed delivery of reinforcers—indirect-acting, analog contingencies. Why? Because of procrastination. Without the deadline, the students would procrastinate; they'd put off writing their words until later, and then later, and then still later because there'd always be time to do that hard work of writing the words, and now there are so many more reinforcing things to do, such as staring out the window or causing a ruckus.

So, after thinking hard about this for the last few years, we've come up with a conclusion that startled us. **Without deadlines, most effective, indirect-acting, performance-management contingencies wouldn't work.** Hard to believe, but just keep it in mind as you examine other performance-management contingencies.

Analog to Reinforcement or Avoidance?

Here's another tricky question:

1. What's the points-for-words contingency? An analog to
   a. reinforcement
   b. avoidance of the loss of a reinforcer

You say *analog to reinforcement*. We used to agree. In the second edition of this book we thought the points-for-words contingency was a straightforward analog to reinforcement. But after thinking about it for about 5 years and examining dozens and dozens of other analog performance-management contingencies during that time, we came to another

conclusion, one that startled us. We have an analog to avoidance of the loss of the opportunity to receive reinforcers (points)—not an analog to reinforcement. And here's why:

We think adding the deadline turns the contingency into an analog to avoidance of the loss of a reinforcer. If this were just an analog to reinforcement, the students could take their own sweet time getting around to writing the words and they'd lose nothing. But with the deadline (the end of the writing class), they've got to hustle to avoid losing the opportunity to earn their maximum amount of points.

Furthermore, we think **this is true of essentially all analog contingencies that increase or maintain performance—they're all analogs to avoidance**. Why? Because they all have deadlines, and the deadlines mean something bad's going to happen if they're not met—either the person's going to lose something (like the opportunity to get the maximum amount of points) or the person is going to receive something aversive (like a scolding).

We think these issues of the deadline and the avoidance contingencies are so important that we're going to state them as principles; but you'd better check with your professor before you have them tattooed onto your shoulder because there's a good chance your professor might not agree that they're important or even correct and might not include them on your next quiz. And your professor's way cool, too.

Definition: Principle

The analog to avoidance principle
  ○ If an indirect-acting contingency
  ○ is to increase or maintain performance,
  ○ it should be an analog to avoidance.

The deadline principle
  ○ If an indirect-acting contingency
  ○ is to increase or maintain performance,
  ○ it should involve a deadline.

Now, you'll often run into apparent exceptions; but when you look a little deeper, they aren't. For example, Mom tells Sis she gets $20 when she mows the lawn. Looks like pure reinforcement—no deadline and, therefore, no avoidance. Well, if there really isn't a deadline, then Sis may procrastinate 'til the snow falls. Or maybe she mows the lawn just in time to get the money to buy that great new top she needs for the party that night. But that's a deadline, though not one imposed by Mom. Or there may be an implicit deadline from Mom. For example, if Sis doesn't get her rear in gear within a reasonable number of minutes, hours, or days, Mom will kick her gearless rear. The problem with these unspoken deadlines is there may be no consensus, and Sis will be surprised and indignant when she sees Mom's boot rapidly approaching her rear. The moral is still this: There really is a deadline if you look closely enough; and if there isn't, there should have been.

The Rule Statement as an Establishing Operation

How Did the Rule Control the Students' Behavior?

The statement of the rule established noncompliance with the rule as an aversive condition. For example, after the teacher stated the rule, a student might think, *if I don't start writing, I'm not going to get many points*—an aversive thought. So the student would then escape that aversive thought (or at least reduce its aversiveness) by starting to write, by starting to produce the words that would earn the points.

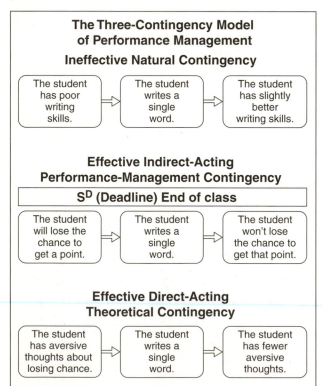

The Three-Contingency Model of Performance Management

Ineffective Natural Contingency

| The student has poor writing skills. | → | The student writes a single word. | → | The student has slightly better writing skills. |

Effective Indirect-Acting Performance-Management Contingency

S^D (Deadline) End of class

| The student will lose the chance to get a point. | → | The student writes a single word. | → | The student won't lose the chance to get that point. |

Effective Direct-Acting Theoretical Contingency

| The student has aversive thoughts about losing chance. | → | The student writes a single word. | → | The student has fewer aversive thoughts. |

The ineffective, natural contingency involved the small but cumulative improvement in writing skill that resulted from writing each word, or sentence, or assignment. The **effective performance-management contingency** could be indirect acting because it dealt with the behavior of verbal human beings. This indirect-acting contingency involved the definite and sizable, though delayed, presentation of a point for each word written. The **theoretical, effec-**

tive direct-acting contingency involved the teacher's rule statement establishing not writing as an aversive condition. This, in turn, allowed the escape response of starting to write to produce a definite, sizable, and immediate reduction in that aversive condition.

Let's look a little deeper into the deadline. The students had 1 hour to finish each writing assignment. If there had been no deadline, the statement of those rules wouldn't have established noncompliance as such an aversive condition. Immediate deadlines make the world go around. (How immediate must a deadline be to make the world go around? The more immediate, the faster the world spins. If you had a deadline for some little task, every 5 minutes, you know you'd be hoppin'. Life would be one continuous Nintendo game.)

QUESTION

1. Describe a behavioral intervention to increase the writing in a remedial fifth-grade class.
   a. Present a diagram of the three types of contingencies.
   b. The *it-is-probably-rule-control rule*—state it and show how it applies to this study.
2. The *analog to avoidance principle*—define it and give an example.
3. The *deadline principle*—define it and give an example.

Example from
Behavioral Social Work
NEIGHBORHOOD YOUTH CORPS AIDES[2]

The Setting

It was the summer of 1970 at Turner House, a community center in the poorest neighborhood of Kansas City. Turner House contained a game room for the local kids.

The Participants

Seven black teenagers from low-income families were Neighborhood Youth Corps trainees in Turner House. They received on-the-job training as recreation aides. This was part of a federal effort to reduce unemployment. (Black teenagers from low-in-

---

[2]Based on Pierce, C. H., & Risley, T. R. (1974). Improving the performance of neighborhood youth corps aides in an urban recreation program. *Journal of Applied Behavior Analysis, 7*, 207–215. The data are from the same source.

come families had an unemployment rate eight times higher than the rest of the labor force.)

The Problem

The recreation center director gave these instructions to the seven aides: "I want you to help the kids, to teach the kids to play different games and to supervise their play." So what happened? The aides spent all their time playing the games themselves, competing with the clients of the center for access to the games, and generally ignoring their jobs. Everyone became angry with the aides.

Specify Performance

What Should You Do First When Performance Is Poor?

Make sure everyone knows what the job is; write and distribute a detailed description of each of the tasks. That's what the director did. For example, here are the task descriptions for the aide who was the snack-bar supervisor: Operate a snack bar in the game room, inventory supplies, maintain a record of receipts of all purchases, and supervise cleanup periods in the snack area. (Incidentally, the aides suggested improvements of the job descriptions and agreed that the assigned tasks were appropriate.)

Give Feedback

What Should You Do Second? Make Sure Everyone Knows How Well They're Doing Their Jobs.

Give them frequent feedback on their performance. That's what the supervisor did. From 10 to 25 times each day he gave each aide two types of feedback: (1) whether they were where they should be and (2) whether they were doing what they should do.

What were the results? Before the more detailed job descriptions and feedback, the aides completed almost no tasks. But after receiving job descriptions and feedback, they completed 50% of their tasks—a small miracle.

Threaten Firing?

But the director wanted a big miracle. Fifty percent didn't impress him as big enough. So he used a common management technique. He threatened to fire the aides if they didn't shape up. The threat worked. Almost everyone improved. But within a few days, almost everyone's performance was back down to the 50% level or lower.

Pay for Performance

You get what you pay for, at least if you're lucky. The director was paying the aides $1.65 per hour (remember, this was 1970) for being at work—pay for attendance. And he was getting good attendance but poor work. So, instead, he started paying $1.65 per hour for each hour of actual work—pay for performance. (The Neighborhood Youth Corps had agreed that he could change the emphasis from "**hours** worked" to "hours **worked**.") The aides would now earn their money in terms of work time rather than clock time.

Definition: Concept[3]
Pay for performance
- ○ Pay is contingent on
- ○ specific achievements.

Therefore, the director paid the aides according to how much of the time they were at their assigned locations and according to the percentage of their tasks they completed. If they were at the right spot doing the right things only half the time, they'd receive pay for a half day's work.

Their performance shot to 100% and stayed there (Figure 25.3). Human performance tends to match the payoff schedule. If the performance isn't appropriate, check out the payoff schedule. **The point isn't how much you pay but what you pay for.**

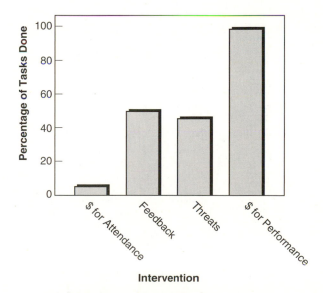

Figure 25.3 Performance of Youth Corps Aides

---

[3]When using pay for performance, the pay is usually money or the equivalent, and the performance is usually agreed-upon by the performer and the payer.

Direct-Acting or Indirect-Acting Contingency?

Is This an Example of Reinforcement by the Presentation of Dollars?

We think it's rule-governed behavior—control by the rule describing the pay-for-performance contingency—control by the rule saying an aide would earn dollars only for doing the work.

Why Is This Probably Rule Control?

Again, let's look at the three main reasons to suspect we've got control by the rule describing the contingency and not direct control (reinforcement) by the contingency itself.

1. **The person knows the rule.** The director stated the rule; he didn't secretly monitor the work and then pay each aide in proportion to the work done. You can imagine that such a procedure might not control the work well, at least not until the aide had figured out the rule. (Tell 'em, when you can.)
2. **The outcome is delayed.** The workers didn't get paid until the end of the week.
3. **The performance changes as soon as the person hears the rule.** They got immediate performance improvement. Figure 25.4 shows the

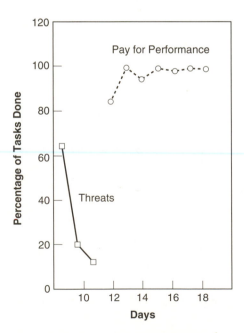

Figure 25.4   Pay for Performance with Youth Corps Aides

more powerful reason to suspect control by the rule describing the contingency and not reinforcement by the contingency itself.

During the three days of threats, the aide's performance rapidly fell down. But his performance immediately shot up as soon as the director told him his pay was now contingent on his performance. His work increased before the contingent pay had any chance to reinforce it. And according to the immediate-change rule, if performance changes as soon as a rule is stated, you've got rule control, not contingency control. So, at least during the first day of pay for performance, we think the work increase was due to an indirect-acting contingency—an analog to avoidance.

4. **The contingency failed the 60-second test.** You know the director didn't pay them within 60 seconds of their doing their work.

The Ever-Present Deadline

Here's our tricky question again:

1. Does the dollars-for-work-done contingency involve a deadline?
   a. yes
   b. no

You're getting wiser now. You know we've got an indirect-acting contingency here. And you know that if an indirect-acting contingency is to increase or maintain performance, it should involve a deadline. What was the deadline? In essence, there was a deadline every few minutes, or at least once an hour; if the aides hadn't gotten a reasonable amount of work done when the director made his periodic visits, they wouldn't get paid for that time.

The Rule Statement as an Establishing Operation

How Did the Rule Control the Aides' Behavior?

The statement of the rule established noncompliance with the rule as an aversive condition. For example, after the director stated the rule, an aide might think, If I don't start working (or don't keep working), I'm going to lose the opportunity to get my full pay—an aversive thought. So the aide would then escape that aversive thought (or at least reduce its aversiveness) by starting or continuing to work.

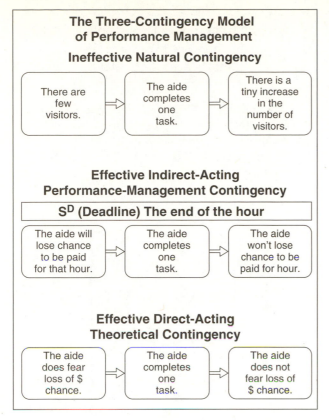

The Three-Contingency Model of Performance Management

Ineffective Natural Contingency

There are few visitors. → The aide completes one task. → There is a tiny increase in the number of visitors.

Effective Indirect-Acting Performance-Management Contingency

S^D **(Deadline) The end of the hour**

The aide will lose chance to be paid for that hour. → The aide completes one task. → The aide won't lose chance to be paid for hour.

Effective Direct-Acting Theoretical Contingency

The aide does fear loss of $ chance. → The aide completes one task. → The aide does not fear loss of $ chance.

As we saw, **effective performance-management contingency** was probably indirect acting because the receipt of the dollars was delayed. But that contingency caused the rule statement to be an effective establishing operation because the dollars were a highly probable and sizable reinforcer—failing to earn them would be aversive.

It's crucial to understand the role of the deadline here. Suppose there had been no deadline; the aides could complete the tasks whenever they wanted, even tomorrow or next week. And suppose the director didn't frequently come around to see if they were on task. What would have happened then? The rule statement wouldn't have established noncompliance as such an aversive condition. Being off task would be no big deal; the aides could always play now and work later. Without deadlines, it's procrastination city.

Notice the after condition in the ineffective natural contingency—a tiny increase in the number of visitors. Now whether or not a large increase in the number of visitors would be a reinforcer for the aides is open to question. The important points about an ineffective natural contingency is that it is ineffective, for whatever reason, and that society would be better off if that contingency were effective. Now it's my observation that workers such as the aides usually want their organization to be suc-

cessful; in this case, the aides would like to see the center serving a large number of kids (sizable organizational effectiveness is a reinforcer for most workers); it's just that the actual natural contingencies do not effectively control their performance to get them to act in ways that will produce that reinforcer.

QUESTION

1. *Pay for performance*—define it and describe its use to increase the work by the Youth Corps aides.
   - Present a diagram of the three types of contingencies.
   - Show how the it-is-probably-rule-control rule applies to this study.
   - Discuss the role of the deadline.

Example from
Behavioral Social Work
JOB TRAINING FOR UNEMPLOYED YOUTH[4]

This is the story of seven junior high school and high school dropouts. These young people averaged 18 years of age. They took part in a vocational/educational training program where they worked toward acquiring the skills they needed to get their high school equivalency diploma (GED); they generally needed their GED to get the jobs they were training for.

> **Let he (she)**
> **who is without**
> **alcohol, nicotine, caffeine,**
> **or a spreading waistline**
> **be the first to cast criticism**
> **at the student whose**
> **act isn't together.**

The program ran three hours per day, five days per week, and the students earned $2.35 per hour

---

[4]Based on Kelly, M. L., & Stokes, T. F. (1982). Contingency contracting with disadvantaged youths: Improving classroom performance. *Journal of Applied Behavior Analysis, 15*, 447–454. The data are from the same source.

(1980 wages) for attending. Without that special incentive built into the program, their attendance no doubt would have been as lousy as the attendance that led to their dropping out of school in the first place.

It's not that they didn't value getting the GED and job skills needed for the jobs they were heading toward. It was just that they could easily rationalize not attending for any given day, because, in fact, no single day mattered that much. But the cumulative deficit of a large number of single missed days wiped out the student.

> **People may not do what it takes to win the prize, but that doesn't mean they don't value that prize.**

So without the special incentive system, missing one day was no big deal. But with the pay-for-attendance program, the students lost the opportunity to earn $7.05 each time they failed to show. A big enough deal. The result: They attended—at least 84% of the time, which may be a world's record for dropouts.

Established folk wisdom says: Though you can lead a horse to water, you can't get it to drink. Established educational wisdom says: Though you can lead a student to the classroom, you can't get him or her to learn. And established wisdom was winning the day. It was goof-off city. The teacher raised a continuous din of reprimands and threats of dismissal. No effect. The students were out of control. The whole class was sliding toward failure of the GED exam.

Then Mary Lou Kelly and Trevor Stokes came on the scene. First, they worked with the state and county officials to make a number of policy changes that would allow them to set up a pay-for-performance program. Then the students had not only to attend class, they also had to perform well in class: They had to complete correctly a mutually agreed-upon number of workbook items to earn their daily $7.05.

Each week the teacher sat down with individual students to write out a performance contract. They negotiated and recorded the required number of workbook items. This gave the student a chance to practice setting and achieving goals. Yet this also allowed the teacher to keep some control.

> **Structured environments often help people attain evasive goals.**

The results? The students quadrupled the number of items they correctly completed each day. The mean during baseline was 15 correct per session. During pay for performance, it was 59 per session (Figure 25.5).

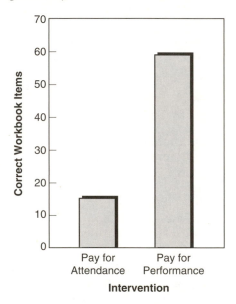

Figure 25.5   Classroom Performance of School Dropouts

Furthermore, the students said they preferred working under the pay-for-performance program rather than the easier pay-for-attendance program. With pay for performance, they and the teacher always knew where they stood, they got less hassling from the teacher, and they felt a greater sense of accomplishment.

Also, five of the seven students received their GED. (One student had left the program to take a full-time job without taking the GED exam, and the other student had passed some subtests on the exam.) All seven ended either employed or in college (Figure 25.6).

Direct-Acting or Indirect-Acting Contingency?

As with the other cases of pay for performance, we think this isn't an example of reinforcement by the presentation of dollars. We think it's a rule-governed analog contingency. Why?

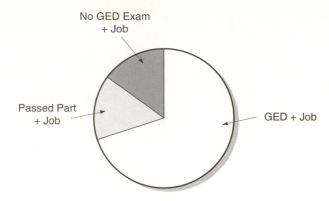

Figure 25.6   Outcome of Pay for Performance

1. **The person knows the rule:** The teacher stated the rule (in the form of the weekly performance contract). He didn't secretly monitor the work and then pay each student in proportion to the number of items they correctly completed.

2. **The outcome is delayed:** The students got paid at the end of the workday.

3. **The performance changes as soon as the person hears the rule:** The performance of one student shows the more powerful reason to suspect control by the rule and not reinforcement by the contingency itself. During the last 4 days of pay for attendance, he got 0 workbook items correct. But he got 83 items correct as soon as the teacher contracted for his pay to be contingent on his performance. His work increased before it had any chance to be reinforced by the contingent pay. And according to the immediate-change rule, this suggests rule control—an analog to reinforcement. (Incidentally, this student's mean performance increased from 35 items correct to 66 items correct when the teacher switched from pay for attendance to pay for performance.)

The Rule Statement as an Establishing Operation

How Did the Rule Control the Students' Behavior?

The statement of the rule established noncompliance as an aversive before condition. After the teacher wrote the performance contract, a student might think, If I don't start working (or don't keep working), I'm not going to earn many dollars—an aversive thought from which the student might escape by working.

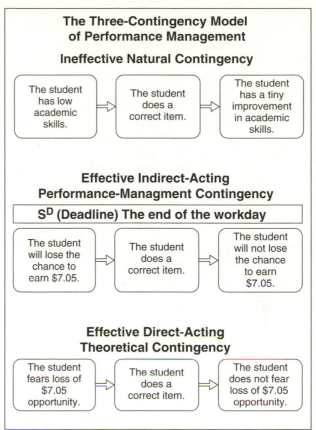

The **performance-management contingency** caused the rule statement to be an effective establishing operation because the dollars were a highly probable and sizable reinforcer—failing to earn them would be aversive.

We think this wouldn't have worked nearly as well without the daily deadline (the students contracted for each daily session of 2½ hours). With no deadline, the students could have procrastinated with no fear of failing to earn their pay and might not have gotten to working nearly as often. This is because the rule statement wouldn't have established noncompliance as such an aversive before condition, nothing worth escaping by getting to work.

QUESTION

1. Describe a behavioral intervention to increase the number of workbook items completed by school dropouts.
   a. Present a diagram of the three types of contingencies.
   b. Show how the it-is-probably-rule-control rule applies to this study.
   c. Discuss the role of the deadline.

Example from
Organizational Behavior Management
YOU CAN BANK ON IT[5]

Here's a brief tale of one of the most impressive per-formance-management projects in the history of be-havior analysis. The principal creators of this tale were a team of two bankers (Hall McAdams, execu-tive vice president, and Wayne Dierks, senior vice president, of Union National Bank of Little Rock, Arkansas) and two behavioral analysts (Dr. William Abernathy and Dr. Kathleen McNally). They gradu-ally built a pay-for-performance system in their bank that can inspire us all. At the time we wrote this, their program had been in place for 16 years—a long time for the young field of applied behavior analysis.

They started with the proof operators. A proof operator typed a number at the bottom of each check the bank was processing, so a computer could read it. How many of these checks would an opera-tor proof per hour? An average of 1,065, which was typical of most banks.

Then the four pioneers in organizational be-havior management moved in. They paid the opera-tors individual bonuses for each check accurately proofed. At last report they were processing an av-erage of 3,500 per hour—the theoretical limit of the proofing machine.

When proof operators would leave that job, the employees asked that they not be replaced be-cause the remaining operators correctly anticipated that they could cover the extra work and thereby in-crease their take home pay. Thus the number of em-ployees in the proofing department was reduced from 12.5 to 6 full-time equivalents, and the over-time per year dropped from 457 to 13 hours. The in-creased interest the bank earned because of faster processing time was $100,000 per year.

Fine for the bank, but what about the employ-ees? Their bonus, incentive pay, grew to 60% of their base pay. But does that produce too much stress? Perhaps not, because the percentage of ab-senteeism was about half what it had been, and the percentage of turnover (quitting) was zero (Figure 25.7). (In most banks, the turnover rate is high.)

At Union National and other banks, pay for performance has produced similar great results for both the bank and the employees when working with tellers, operations managers, and branch man-agers. In fact, 70% of Union National's 700 employ-ees ended up on a pay-for-performance incentive system; that even included the vice presidents.

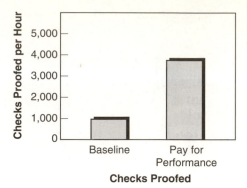

Checks Proofed

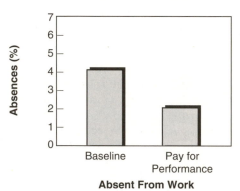

Absent From Work

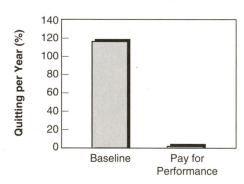

Proof Operators Quitting the Job

Figure 25.7   Operator Results

Benefits of Pay for Performance

- More Productivity
- Higher Quality
- Less Waste
- More Profit
- Fewer Absences
- Less Turnover
- Better Pay
- Happier Employees
- Happier Employers

---

[5]Based on Dierks, W., & McNally, K. (1987). Incentives you can bank on. *Personnel Administrator, 32,* 60–65. The data are from the same source.

Everyone benefited; for example, as with the proofing department, when someone left one of the other departments, the employees often ask that the position not be refilled; they preferred to divide the extra work and profit among themselves.

Don't you wish they had pay for performance where you work?

QUESTION

1. Briefly describe a behavioral intervention with the operators in a bank's proofing department.
   a. Describe the performance management contingency.
   b. Generally describe the results

THE THREE-CONTINGENCY MODEL OF PERFORMANCE MANAGEMENT

Now that you've seen a few examples of the three-contingency model, what is it? It's a way of diagramming behavioral contingencies, when the outcome in the performance-management contingency is too delayed to reinforce or punish the behavior being managed. (You don't need this model for contingencies involving immediate outcomes.)

As you know by now, in this model, the first contingency is the ineffective natural contingency, the one that we wish controlled behavior but doesn't (if it did, a behavior analysts wouldn't need to intervene). And the natural contingency is ineffective because the outcome is either too small, though of cumulative significance or too improbable. And contrary to popular belief, the delay of the outcome is rarely the culprit for verbal clients who can state the rule.

The second contingency is the effective, indirect-acting performance-management contingency. It is effective because the outcome is sizable and probable. And once again, contrary to popular belief, the delay will have little effect on the performance of verbal clients who can state the rule. In cases where we want to increase the frequency of behavior, these indirect-acting contingencies need to involve a deadline; otherwise, we have infinite procrastination. And again, contrary to popular belief and to the consternation of many behavior analysts, the deadline converts what might otherwise be an analog to reinforcement to an analog to avoidance, usually avoidance of the loss of the opportunity to get a reinforcer. (Analogs to punishment don't need deadlines.)

Finally, the third contingency is the inferred, theoretical direct-acting contingency. If the performance-management contingency is an analog to avoidance, then the direct-acting contingency is an escape contingency; and if the performance-management contingency is an analog to punishment or penalty, then the direct-acting contingency is a punishment contingency. Now, we may have emphasized the off-putting inferred, theoretical nature of this contingency more than need be. Instead of talking about *fear* and *aversive thoughts*, we can always talk about conditional before and after conditions. In the case of analogs to avoidance, we can always talk about the approaching deadline combined with the behavior not being done; that's not inferred or theoretical. However, we still need to infer that the approaching deadline is aversive, conditional on the behavior not being done. But this inference does not require a major leap of faith by behavior analysts with a modicum of awareness of the variables impinging on them and their behavior.[6]

---

[6]For more information on the three-contingency model, see: Malott, R. W. (1993, October). The three-contingency model applied to performance management in higher education. *Educational Technology, 33,* 21–28. Malott, R. W. (1998). Performance management and welfare reform: The three-contingency model of performance management applied to welfare reform. *Behavior and Social Issues, 8,* 109–140. Malott, R. W. (1993). A theory of rule-governed behavior and organizational behavior management. *Journal of Organizational Behavior Management, 12,* 45–65.

26 Moral and Legal Control

WE'VE MOVED THIS CHAPTER TO THE WEB. CHECK IT OUT AT WWW.DICKMALOTT.COM.

FUNDAMENTALS[1]

False Parable
THE LEGEND OF BIG BOB'S BOVINE

Once upon a time, two husky teenage members of the Future Farmers of America were arguing about who was the stronger.

Big Bob said, "I'll bet 5 bucks I can lift your young heifer there."

Big Bruce replied, "You can lift Beulah? No, way, Jose. She weighs 1,000 pounds. You've got a bet."

Big Bob lifted, and grunted, and strained, and finally collapsed beside Beulah. After he'd forked out the 5 dollars, he said, "OK, I lost this time. But I'll make you a bet. I'll bet my pickup with the .22 in the rear window against your Beulah. I'll bet that within less than a year I can lift a 1,000-pound steer."

"You're on," Big Bruce replied.

As luck would have it, that very week a 50-pound calf was born on the farm of Big Bob's daddy. And everyday, before going to school, Big Bob would lift that young calf. As the calf grew in weight, Bob grew in strength. But when the calf had reached

400 pounds, Big Bob was having to strain just to get it off the ground (he'd long since stopped above-the-head, one-hand grandstanding).

The calf kept growing; and so did Big Bob's strength. Now Big Bruce had been eyeing Big Bob's progress, and panic set in when he saw Big Bob lift the 900-pound steer. So he fell back on an unfair ploy, "Big Bob," he said, "my daddy says I got to sell Beulah at the 4-H fair tomorrow. So you either lift a 1,000-pound steer today, or all bets are off."

Big Bob hadn't yet gotten to the 1,000-pound mark, but the bank was ready to foreclose on his daddy's farm. If he could win Beulah, he himself could sell her at the 4-H fair, make the next payment on the farm, and keep the bankers away. Then he and his daddy could harvest their crops and completely pay off the loan.

With one hand, Big Bob slung a 100-pound feed sack over the back of the 900-pound steer (if quantitative analyses aren't your thing, let's just say that totals 1,000 pounds). Then, with a false air of confidence, he squatted down, put both of his massive arms beneath the steer's belly and gradually lifted. The steer went higher and higher in the air, centimeter by centimeter. But Big Bob couldn't get his hoofs off the ground. After two minutes of straining, he finally collapsed.

Big Bruce smiled. "Where's the keys to my new truck?"

"Just a moment. You know I get three tries."

And try he did, but with even less success the second time.

After resting for 5 minutes, while Big Bruce sat in the pickup blowing the horn, Big Bob lumbered for one last time over to the side of the steer, which by this time was becoming a bit agitated. Everything depended on this last lift—the pickup, the .22, the farm, his chance to go to BSU on a 4-H scholarship,

---

[1]For theoretical literature supporting and contrasting with the analysis in these next two chapters, see Esch, J. W. (1987). In response to Kohler and Greenwood's "Toward a technology of generalization." The Behavior Analyst, 10, 303–305, Kohler, F. R., & Greenwood, C. R. (1986). Toward a technology of generalization: The identification of natural contingencies of reinforcement. The Behavior Analyst, 9, 19–26; Johnston, J. M. (1979). On the relation between generalization and generality. The Behavior Analyst, 2, 1–6; Kimberly, K. C., & Bickel, W. K. (1988). Toward an explicit analysis of generalization: A stimulus control interpretation. The Behavior Analyst, 11, 115–129; and Stokes, T. F., & Baer, D. M. (1977). An implicit technology of generalization. *Journal of Applied Behavior Analysis, 10,* 349–367. (This article is the classic in the field—the starting point for all other articles and approaches.)

and his beloved Betty Sue, whose father would not let her keep the company of poor trash, which he would be if he didn't lift the 1,000-pound steer on this last lift and thereby avoid losing the farm.

He stood straight, flexed his arms, did three knee bends, put his arms beneath the steer's belly and gradually lifted. The steer went higher and higher in the air, centimeter by centimeter. And it kept going, and going, until all four hoofs were 6 inches off the ground. Big Bob spun around in a 360-degree circle, with the steer in his arms, walked over to the pale Big Bruce and sat the steer in front of him. Big Bob smiled and said, "Let's get in my pickup; I need to get my new heifer."

Skeptical? You should be. This rural myth is made out of what Big Bob often stepped in as he trudged across the cattle pen to pick up the calf. Now let's look at a similar psychological myth.

Controversy
THE MYTH OF PERPETUAL BEHAVIOR AND THE MYTH OF INTERMITTENT REINFORCEMENT

You've heard of the quest for the perpetual-motion machine? You wind it up, start it going, it generates its own energy, and never runs out of fuel. No more inputs required—no more gas, no more electricity, no more turning the crank. (And while the perpetual-motion machine's doing all our work, we can retire to Florida and fritter away our time in the quest for the fountain of perpetual youth.) Everyone wants the perpetual-motion machine, but no perpetual-motion machine exists.

Behaviorists often get sucked into their own similar futile quest. Behaviorists search for the *perpetual-behavior intervention:* **You modify the behavior, the modified behavior maintains itself, and you never have to deliver another behavioral consequence.** That's the myth of perpetual behavior. Once you intervene, the improved behavior runs on forever, with no more inputs required—no more performance management, no more behavioral contracts. Everyone wants the perpetual-behavior intervention. No perpetual-behavior intervention exists—at least not when you need it most.

Everyone wants a quick fix. The preacher wants to preach an hour on Sunday and have the parishioners lead lives of virtue the rest of the week. The psychoanalyst wants to psychoanalyze an hour on Monday and have the patients lead lives of mental health the rest of the week. The teacher wants to lecture an hour on Wednesday and have the students lead lives of intellectual inquiry for ever.

Everyone's naive. There ain't no easy fix.

There ain't no easy solution.

Behaviorists often get too desperate in their quest for the perpetual-behavior intervention. They try to fuel that perpetual maintenance with schedules of intermittent reinforcement—for example, variable-interval and variable-ratio schedules. Why?

Well, first, recall the concept of resistance to extinction—the number of responses or the time before a response extinguishes. And recall the principle of resistance to extinction—intermittent reinforcement makes the response more resistant to extinction than does continuous reinforcement. The illogical reasoning in the quest for the perpetual-behavior intervention goes like this: We use continuous reinforcement to establish some desirable behavior, and then we change the schedule of reinforcement to one with fewer and fewer reinforcers. So the person builds greater and greater resistance to extinction. In time, reinforcement becomes so rare and the resistance to extinction so high that we can stop reinforcement altogether. Then the person will keep on responding forever and ever, without limit. This is what we call the myth of intermittent reinforcement: You can gradually reduce the frequency of reinforcement until the behavior maintains without reinforcement. It's like Big Bob's gradually increasing the weight he was lifting, and gradually increasing his strength, until he could lift almost any weight, without limit. What about the popular notion of unlimited resistance to extinction based on a history of less and less reinforcement? It's made of the same organic barnyard matter as the legend of Big Bob.

Moral: Our bodies are subject to the laws of physics, including the law of gravity. And our behavior is subject to the laws of behavior, including the law of effect. Just as the law of gravity says our bodies will fall if not supported, the law of effect says our behavior will stop if not reinforced. (As a reminder, the law of effect says the effects of our actions determine whether we will repeat them.)

Although there is no perpetual-behavior intervention, we can almost constantly maintain good performance and suppress undesirable performance in two ways. The first part of this chapter is about that. But it's not about trying to become independent of the law of effect.

Definition: Concept
Performance maintenance
  ○ The continuing of performance
  ○ after it was first established.

There's still some confusion, so let me repeat the main point: There is no such thing as unlimited resistance to extinction; so you can't use it to maintain performance indefinately.

QUESTIONS

1. What is the myth of the perpetual-behavior intervention?
2. What is the myth of intermittent reinforcement?
3. How does the law of effect relate to these myths?
4. Performance maintenance—define it.

Example from
Behavioral School Psychology
JUNGLE JIM, THE SOCIAL CLIMBER[2]

Jim spent most of his time at preschool wandering about, bored, sampling first one activity, then another, almost always avoiding physical games, not impressed, not entertained. Once in a while, he'd try to play with the other kids, but in his clumsy way he'd always mess it up, and the teachers would have to come to his rescue.

> **Teacher, beware:**
> **Don't reinforce disruptive behavior**
> **with your attention.**

The teachers wanted Jim to take part in physical activities so he'd have a chance to play constructively with the other kids; they hoped he might learn better social skills through such play. But before they started to intervene with their planned reinforcement procedure, they measured his performance during baseline. They found that 25% of the time, Jim just hung out, simply standing by himself or walking around, and 75% of the time, he did quiet things by himself, like playing in the sandbox.

Then it was time to start their reinforcement procedure. Whenever Jim walked by the monkey bars, the teachers would talk to him, smile, pat him on the shoulder, and bring him things to play with. At other times, they ignored him, busying themselves with other activities. Because of this reinforcement procedure, Jim gradually came to spend more time closer and closer to the monkey bars—somehow life was better in that neighborhood,

though Jim probably had not realized life held more reinforcers near the monkey bars or even that he was now hanging out in this new spot. (Therefore, the direct-acting contingency of the social reinforcement probably controlled Jim's behavior; it was probably not rule governed.)

After a while, Jim began touching the monkey bars and even climbing them briefly. From then on, the teachers reinforced only his climbing; just being in the right neighborhood no longer did the trick. In this way, the teachers used the method of successive approximation to shape Jim's climbing the bars, so that after 9 days of reinforcement, he was climbing the bars 67% of the time. In the process he also became much less of a climbing klutz, perhaps not a young Tarzan, but not bad. (The teachers also started sending a few social reinforcers Jim's way when he played with any of the other active toys, like the ladders, packing boxes, and other frames.)

However, the playground teachers couldn't always be reinforcing Jim's athletic acts, so they slowly increased the number of times Jim climbed on the monkey bars before delivering their reinforcing attention. (In that way, they went from continuous reinforcement to the more cost-effective intermittent schedule, probably ratio reinforcement, though a variable interval schedule might have worked just as well.)

Also, as the days passed, they reduced the size of the reinforcer. Near the end, Jim's athletics got only a brief nod. And at the close of their intervention, Jim got no more attention than did the other kids in the preschool; yet he was spending a third of his time in vigorous activity (before they intervened, he spent less than 1/10th of his time in such activity). And when he came back to the preschool the next fall, Jim spent more than half his outdoor play in vigorous activities, just like any other normal kid (Figure 27.1).

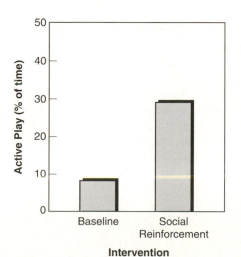

Figure 27.1   Using Social Reinforcement to Shape the Active Play of an Apathetic Child

[2]Based on Johnston, M. K., Kelly, C., Harris, F. R., & Wolf, M. M. (1965). An application of reinforcement principles to the development of motor skills of a young child. Unpublished manuscript.

QUESTIONS

1. Describe a behavioral intervention to increase the active play social interactions of a withdrawn preschool child.
   ◦ What's the behavior?
   ◦ The various reinforcers?
   ◦ The schedule of rerinforcement at first and then later?

Definition: Principle
Behavior trap
- Add a reinforcement contingency
- to increase the rate of behavior.
- Then the behavior will frequently contact
- built-in reinforcement contingencies,
- and those built-in contingencies
- will maintain that behavior.

Concept
SETTING A BEHAVIOR TRAP TO MAINTAIN PERFORMANCE[3]

At first glance it might look as if the teachers were going for the illusive perpetual-behavior intervention based on the myth of intermittent reinforcement. But we think not. As they gradually decreased the frequency and duration of their added social reinforcement, the built-in reinforcement contingencies of the monkey bars were themselves coming to control Jim's playing. So, in the end, Jim didn't need the added reinforcement contingencies; the built-in reinforcement contingencies were enough. This is an example of a **behavior trap.**

Let's look further at behavior trap. Suppose Jim never played on the monkey bars. Then, of course, the reinforcers naturally built into such play could not help him acquire an adequate play repertoire. Or suppose he had sometimes played but with little skill. Then his behavior still might not have contacted those built-in reinforcement contingencies, or at least not often enough to help him acquire that skilled repertoire. Here's what the teachers' social reinforcers did. They caused Jim to monkey around the bars frequently enough for two things to happen: (1) He acquired good climbing skills, and (2) the built-in delights of the activity frequently reinforced and thus finally "trapped" his climbing. So a behavior intervention leads a behavior into a behavior trap. A *behavior trap* is a procedure using a shifting set of reinforcement contingencies that get ahold of behavior and won't let go.

Originally, *behavior (behavioral) trap*[4] referred to the unprogrammed social reinforcers that maintained behavior, once someone had learned that behavior. But the concept has more generality than that. For example, the reinforcers intrinsic in reading maintain that behavior, once a person has learned to read.

Behavior traps are great things, but they ain't always there when you need 'em. So once you get the behavior occurring at a high rate, don't just walk away, assuming a behavior trap will come along to maintain it. Often when it seems natural that there should be one, it won't show up.

QUESTION

1. Behavior trap—define it and give an example.

Example from
Behavioral Medicine
BEHAVIOR TRAPS, EXTENDED PROGRAMS, AND DICKY AT 13[5]

Remember Dicky, the 3-year-old autistic boy from Chapter 8? Wolf, Risley, and Mees saved Dicky's eyesight, using ice cream to differentially reinforce Dicky's putting on his glasses. Happily, Dicky didn't need the added ice cream reinforcer forever. We assume this is because the built-in reinforcement contingency of seeing so much better came to maintain putting on the glasses. In other words, Dicky fell into a behavior trap. The automatic reinforcers of seeing better maintained Dicky's performance: those reinforcers trapped Dicky's putting on his glasses and saved his eyes.

Remember Dicky, the 7-year-old autistic boy from Chapter 14? Risley and Wolf and then Dicky's parents helped Dicky learn to talk normally, using imitation, verbal prompts, and discrimination training. Again, Dicky fell into a behavior trap as the natural reinforcers for speaking came to maintain his performance—his continuing to speak normally.

[3]Based on Baer, D. M., & Wolf, M. M. (1970). The entry into natural communities of reinforcement. In R. Ulrich, T. Stachnik, & J. Mabry (Eds.), *Control of human behavior* (vol. 2, pp. 319–324). Glenview, IL: Scott, Foresman.

[4]We prefer *behavior trap* to the older terminology *behavioral trap* because it emphasizes that it is behavior that's being trapped. (Of course, you could say *behavioral behavior trap,* but please don't!)

[5]Based on Nedelman, D., & Sulzbacher, S. I. (1972). Dicky at thirteen years of age: A long-term success following early application of operant conditioning procedures. In G. Semb (Ed.), *Behavior analysis and education.* Lawrence, KS: University of Kansas, Follow-Through Project.

Because of continued work with Dicky, his overall IQ had risen from being unmeasurable at age 3 to 81 at age 13; and his verbal IQ was 106. Not only that, he had progressed so much that he could start attending regular classes in the public school. Dicky still had some autistic behaviors, like rocking and hand clapping, but he had come a long way. For example, he could carry on long conversations using an advanced vocabulary for his age. With proper behavioral programs, behavior traps, and other support systems, major repertoire changes can be made and maintained.

The last we heard of Dicky he was in his thirties, living in a supervised apartment and doing supervised janitorial work in the state of Washington. Dicky has copies of some of the articles describing the research he participated in.

QUESTION

1. How did behavior traps help Dicky, the autistic boy, continue to wear his glasses and maintain his talking?

Example from
Behavioral Medicine
RECLAIMING A SMALL GIRL FROM AN INSTITUTION FOR THE DEVELOPMENTALLY DISABLED[6]

Sally was a young resident of a center for the developmentally disabled. She could barely walk and could not perform even simple movements with her hands. She couldn't speak a sentence or name objects, but she was able to mimic other people's words. She was so lacking in skills that she couldn't be tested on the so-called intelligence tests.

Because Sally had weak leg muscles and poor coordination, she found no built-in reinforcement contingencies when she tried to ride a bicycle or engage in other physical activities. So Dr. Todd Risley used candy to reinforce her physical activities. He mounted a bicycle on a stationary frame so that the wheels turned when she pushed the pedals. In the first stage, Todd reinforced her sitting on the bike. In a later stage, an automatic candy dispenser delivered a small piece of candy each time she turned the wheels of the bicycle around for five revolutions (fixed ratio 5). After she had perfected this, the requirement gradually increased until she had to turn

the wheels around many times before getting a piece of candy. At the same time, and by small degrees, Todd adjusted the pressure on the back wheel so that it took much more effort to turn the pedals.

After some months of this training, Sally's muscles developed to the point where she spent hours pedaling her bicycle and eating her candy reinforcers. When she gained enough coordination and strength, Todd took the bicycle down from its stationary position; and, through the use of reinforcement, Sally learned to ride it in the driveway. Once Sally could ride her bike freely, she no longer needed the added candy reinforcers; then she rode for hours just like normal children do. Her behavior was trapped by the built-in reinforcement contingencies involving riding.

During this same time, Todd began a lengthy and intensive behavioral program to improve Sally's language skills, her responding to different stimuli, and her naming objects. He also trained her to play games and work puzzles. As an example of these interventions, Todd uttered a word and if Sally repeated it, he quickly gave her a small piece of candy and perhaps a pat on the head while he said, "Good." After months of this procedure, she was able to name objects and finally talk using short sentences.

Following this training, Sally progressed to the point where Todd tested her skills with a standard intelligence test. Her intelligence quotient increased enough to allow her to leave the institution and enter a special class in the public school system. Probably Sally would still be in that institution if Dr. Todd Risley hadn't intervened with these intensive behavioral procedures.

Analysis

Sally's bicycle riding shows performance maintained by the behavior trap. She had neither the behavioral skills nor the physical strength to make contact with the natural, built-in reinforcement contingencies supporting biking. She needed the help of added reinforcement contingencies from Risley's behavioral intervention. But once she had acquired the strength and skills, the natural reinforcers of biking were an effective trap to maintain that behavior.

QUESTIONS

1. Describe a procedure to help a developmentally disabled child acquire the needed strength and skills for bike riding.

2. What role did the behavior trap play?

---

[6]Based on T. Risley (personal communication, 1965).

USE INTERMITTENT CONTINGENCIES TO MAINTAIN PERFORMANCE

In Chapter 15, we discussed the program Linda Pfiffner and Susan O'Leary used to help grade-school students get on task in a remedial classroom. They used concurrent reinforcement with all sorts of goodies and avoidance of reprimands to move the students from being on task 41% of the time to 80%.

Now the question was, could they reduce the frequency of reprimands and yet keep the students on task? When they stopped the reprimands abruptly, time on task fell to 47%. But when they slowly reduced the reprimands to a low level, over a 6-day period, the students stayed on task 87% of the time. This suggests that avoidance of an aversive condition that's only intermittent may do the trick, once you've already got a high rate of avoidance responses.

QUESTIONS

1. Describe a procedure used to maintain the performance of grade-school students in a remedial classroom.
2. What point does this illustrate?

MAINTAIN THE CONTINGENCIES AND YOU'LL MAINTAIN PERFORMANCE

Remember Peter, the developmentally disabled boy who choked, kicked, hit, pulled, and pushed people an average of 63 times each 6-hour schoolday (Chapter 4). Within a couple of days of using contingent exercise as a punishment procedure, Stephen Luce and his colleagues got big results. They had reduced that violent physical aggression to an average of two times a day.

Great, but how can we keep Peter cooled out? Simple: Just keep the exercise contingency in place. That's what they did, and it worked. Twenty-six days later, Peter's physical aggression had dropped to one attack a day.

Perpetual-Performance Contracting

In earlier chapters, we mentioned the concept of performance contract—a written rule statement describing the desired or undesired behavior, the occasion when the behavior should or should not occur, and the added outcome for that behavior. Performance contracting is the most useful tool Maria and I have for keeping our acts together. I've been using

performance contracts for 25 years to break that old procrastinatin' rhythm. Without it, we wouldn't have gotten the first edition of our book written, let alone this edition. We do performance contracting for our work, our diet, our exercise—you name it. We've used all sorts of methods: face-to-face, weekly, or even daily meetings with a performance contractor, a daily telephone meeting with a contractor we never saw (she was called "Conscience" and worked in Dr. Joseph Parson's Conscience International at the University of Victoria), and now daily telecommunication on the Behavioral Bulletin Board on CompuServe Information Service, an international computer network).

Here's my point: Often there's no behavior trap to grab your performance in its gentle grip and keep you going in the right direction. That sure seems true with dieting, exercising, and writing. We enjoy having done them, and we even enjoy doing them. But that's not enough. The unprogrammed contingencies are small and of only cumulative value. So most of us need some sort of contracting to achieve optimum performance. Most of us need rules that are easy to follow, even if they describe contingencies that are not direct acting. We need rules that describe sizable, probable outcomes, even if they are delayed.

Don't feel as if you're a loser if you can't pull off the big ones without help. Even professional writers constantly fight the devil and her temptations. The winners use all sorts of goal-setting, word-counting, and charting techniques to manage their performance.[7] Imagine what they could do with Conscience International.

Maintain the contingencies and you'll maintain the performance. By perpetual-performance contracting, we mean that you'll get the most out of performance contracting if you use it to maintain desirable performance all your life. You don't think of it as a phase you go through. For example, suppose you want to lose weight and then keep it off. You shouldn't go on a diet until you've hit your goal weight and then go back to pig-out city. You need to be on a diet the rest of your life. And we find perpetual-performance contracting is our best way to keep a lifelong diet. The same applies to exercise, writing—all of life's evasive goals.

QUESTIONS

1. Give an example of maintaining a punishment contingency to maintain the suppression of undesirable behavior.

---

[7]Based on Wallace, I., with introduction by Pear, J. J. (1977). Self-control techniques of famous novelists. *Journal of Applied Behavior Analysis, 10,* 515–525.

2. What do you do when there's no behavior trap to maintain performance? Give an example.

THE MAIN POINT

What's the main point of this chapter? The main point is that the only way you can maintain an increased rate of performance is to maintain some sort of supporting contingencies. It doesn't matter whether those supporting contingencies are built-in natural contingencies the client now makes contact with or whether they are added performance-management contingencies a performance manager must always provide. Avoid the traditional error that once you've really modified behavior, the behavior will maintain itself. Not true. BEHAVIOR WILL NOT BE MAINTAINED WITHOUT SUPPORTING CONTINGENCIES.

QUESTION

1. What's the main point of this chapter?

INTERMEDIATE ENRICHMENT

WHAT TO DO AFTER THE PERFORMANCE MANAGER GOES HOME OR AFTER THE DOCTORAL STUDENT FINISHES THE DISSERTATION

It's hard to develop performance management systems that maintain for the years clients often need them. Part of the problem is that behavior analysts are controlled by direct- and indirect-acting contingencies, just like everyone else. Many of the articles published in journals are grad students' dissertations. But by the time the students demonstrate that their interventions work, they're tired of living on peanut-butter-and-jelly sandwiches and want to earn a decent living. So they can't afford to stick around long enough to demonstrate performance maintenance.

However, the problem of developing a maintainable technology is so crucial that some behavioral journals now have the policy of publishing only articles that have at least a 6-month follow-up. This should move our field in the right direction.

One solution might be for the students to train the direct care staff in how to maintain the interventions. Unfortunately, this only works if the contingencies support the direct care staff's behavior of maintaining the intervention. But, the contingencies in the "real world" rarely support maintenance.

28 Transfer

FUNDAMENTALS

Concept
TRANSFER OF TRAINING

"The problem with behavior modification is that the behavior change won't transfer outside the behavior analyst's lab."

"What do you mean, it won't transfer?"

"Well, suppose you work with someone who has a behavior problem in your lab. Let's say your client no longer talks. Suppose you use reinforcement procedures and gradually reestablish talking. Now you have reinforced talking in the lab. But will it transfer out onto the ward? And, even if it does transfer, will it continue to occur, or will the conditions in the ward get rid of talking again?"

I realized she was baiting me; she knew I was a strong advocate of the use of reinforcement principles in behavior modification. On the other hand, I knew she wasn't merely teasing me; she had criticized the use of the principles of behavior in her psychology lectures. I should convince her the principles of behavior would work. Then she might be less likely to say this in her class and mislead her students. Besides, I was a junior member of the psychology department, and this was my first job; I wanted to please and impress her, so I replied, "What you say is complete and utter nonsense and indicates your lack of understanding of the principles of behavior."

I could see by the expression on her face that she was impressed. I continued, "We must be concerned with two things, in transferring behavior change: First, we must make sure the **situation of the intervention is similar to the client's normal environment;** then behavior change will transfer to the normal environment. A good way to deal with this problem is to actually intervene in the patient's normal environment rather than in the lab.

"Second, we must make sure the client's **normal environment maintains the behavior change** we bring about. For example, the client may want to get rid of some undesirable behavior. And we might eliminate such behavior; but then we want to be sure the client's normal environment doesn't reinforce that behavior again. Here is one way to do it: Attention might have reinforced the inappropriate behavior. We could reinforce some other response—one more effective in getting attention but one that also is more socially desirable. Then the client's normal environment might never reinforce the undesirable response again.

"A problem in the maintenance of behavior change occurs when we want to reinforce some missing behavior. Then we must be sure reinforcement procedures operate in the client's normal environment so the behavior won't extinguish.

"One solution is to **reinforce desirable behavior that will be successful in obtaining reinforcers in the client's normal environment.** The client's environment might be effective enough to maintain the behaviors once we reinforce those behaviors but might not be effective enough to reinforce them in the first place. Because of an inappropriate environment, a child might not have learned to talk. But if we shape an adequate repertoire of verbal responses in the lab, then natural reinforcers that maintain most of our verbal behavior might maintain the child's verbal behavior. We call those natural reinforcers a behavior trap."

I paused for dramatic effect and then looked the antagonist straight in the eye. "So you see, we can transfer and maintain behavior change to the client's everyday environment."

I expected her to jump from her seat, run around her desk, pound me heartily on the back, and exclaim, "I apologize, my good man, for not having sooner recognized that you speak the truth." To that I would reply, "Ah, don't apologize. I realize that we new faculty members must prove ourselves." In so doing, I would display my good breeding, humility, and generosity.

But instead the ingrate stared at the desk and merely said, "Hah."

"Well, does what I say make any sense to you?" I asked.

"Yes," she mumbled, and began shuffling through some papers on her desk.

I walked out feeling I had done humankind a good deed. Now she would no longer tell her students that behavior modification was no good because it wouldn't transfer to other stimulus situations.

Several days later I had an experience—the first of several similar experiences—that gave me a valuable lesson. I overheard some of her students discussing a lecture she had just given. They were saying how impressed they were as she argued that behavior modification wasn't of much value because its effects wouldn't transfer. At least it was clear that the effects of my attempts at modifying her behavior had not transferred from her office to her classroom. Later I came to realize that a person's refusal to violently disagree with me simply may mean that person no longer wishes to argue.

This dialogue is not as far-fetched and ivory towered as it might seem, and it's not altogether hypothetical. Similar dialogues occur everyday at clinics, institutions, and public schools. The disagreement revolves around this situation: A behavior analyst, whether a psychologist, nursery school teacher, or other professional, uses behavior modification techniques (extinction, reinforcement, stimulus control) to bring about changes in the behavior of clients, students, or subjects. And the behavior analyst is successful in changing behavior for the well-being of the patient.

The critic admits the initial success in changing behavior. But the critic says that such change is shallow. The behavior analyst has not cured the client's problem. Although the behavior has changed, it won't endure over time, or won't maintain in the client's everyday environment. For the critic, the word cure is important. The critic views behavior problems as diseases; and, of course, what can you do with a disease but cure it? If it's a real cure, the disease wouldn't come creeping back (another problem with the medical model myth).

Those who have used reinforcement principles in changing behavior agree with the critic. And they may reply that the behavior change may not hold up over time and in different environments. But that doesn't mean the original behavior problem was a disease, or that the behavior intervention was a cure.

They modified behavior under a certain set of conditions. The job only begins with changing the behavior. The job ends with maintaining the behavior for longer periods of time in other settings.

Most behavior analysts know the problems involved in transferring behavior change. Generally, they know what to do. They may agree that to increase the probability of maintaining the behavior outside the training setting, they need to expose the client to many of the similar stresses, strains, and stimulus conditions he or she would find outside. If they slowly and gradually introduce aspects of the external environment, the client's behavior would transfer from the training setting to the community more easily. But sometimes these procedures are unrealistic and costly and require too much time. Then behavior analysts either must find a new technique or admit that they don't have the time, money, or control to pull it off. But transfer of behavior modification remains a technical problem, not a fundamental theoretical one.

Definition: Concept

Transfer of training
- Performance established
- at one time
- in one place
- now occurs in a different time and place.

QUESTIONS

1. *Transfer of training*—define it and give an example.
2. What do critics of behavior modification say about the transfer of training and the maintenance of performance?
3. And what might a behavior analyst reply?

REDUCE STIMULUS CONTROL AND INCREASE TRANSFER

We discussed Velma and Gerri in Chapters 4 and 24. These women with profound mental impairment ruined most of their teeth by constantly grinding them (bruxism). Ronald Blount and his colleagues used a mild punishment contingency based on brief contact with an ice cube to reduce their teeth grinding from 62% to 3% of the time.

They also tested for transfer of the effects of this contingency to times during the day when it was not in effect. They found a frequency of 27% during these tests of transfer. Not as good as the 3% when the contingency was in effect, but much better than the 62% during baseline, and it was free—no one was managing their performance then.

The considerable transfer they got might be due to poor stimulus control. The stimulus conditions differed little between the punishment-based discriminative stimulus and the punishment-based S$^\Delta$. Especially for Velma, who was blind and deaf, the main difference was whether she had recently ground her teeth and then felt the ice cube on her face.

The authors said they might have further decreased that stimulus control if they had had frequent, brief periods of training spread throughout the day, rather than the two longer sessions per day.

Let's run this down one more time, because some students find it confusing; and let's also toss in a little refresher course along the way:

1. *Stimulus discrimination (stimulus control)*—
   a. the occurrence of a response more frequently in the presence of one stimulus than in the presence of another, usually as a result of a discrimination-training procedure
   b. the occurrence of a response with close to the same frequency in the presence of one stimulus as in the presence of another, usually as a result of a discrimination-training procedure
2. *Stimulus discrimination* and *stimulus control* are the same thing.
   a. true
   b. false
3. Responding at the same frequency in the presence of the S$^\Delta$ as in the presence of the S^D shows
   a. little stimulus discrimination
   b. much stimulus discrimination.
4. Responding at the same frequency in the presence of the S$^\Delta$ as in the presence of the S^D shows
   a. little stimulus control
   b. much stimulus control.
5. Responding at the same frequency in the presence of the S$^\Delta$ as in the presence of the S^D shows
   a. little stimulus generalization
   b. much stimulus generalization.
6. Stimulus control (stimulus discrimination) is the opposite of stimulus generalization.
   a. true
   b. false
7. Suppose Velma and Gerri grind their teeth at almost the same low frequency when the punishment contingency is *not* in effect as when it is in effect. This is an example of
   a. much stimulus generalization
   b. little stimulus generalization.

8. Suppose Velma and Gerri grind their teeth at almost the same low frequency when the punishment contingency is *not* in effect as when it is in effect. This is an example of
   a. good stimulus control (stimulus discrimination)
   b. poor stimulus control (stimulus discrimination).

QUESTIONS

1. Explain the relation between stimulus control and transfer of training to reduce teeth grinding.
   Warning: Quite a few students blow this one on the quiz. Please be sure you've got it.
2. While you're at it, it wouldn't hurt to be sure you can correctly answer those little multiple-choice review questions, just in case one pops up on your quiz.

Example from
Developmental Disabilities
STREETWISE[1]

Problem

Fact 1: Crossing the street is hazardous to your health. Every year, in the United States, 3,500 people are killed trying to cross the streets.

Fact 2: To help developmentally delayed people live better lives, human services agencies are moving them from institutions (*deinstitutionalization*) to more normal environments (*normalization*). The normal environment is dangerous enough for "normal" people, let alone those with behavior problems.

Solution

For his master's thesis at Western Michigan University, Terry Page, along with Brian Iwata and Nancy Neef, did something to help. Working with five developmentally delayed young men, these behavior analysts developed a program to teach independent street crossing, without taking their students onto the streets.

The students worked with a poster-board model of four city blocks. The model had streets,

[1]Based on Page, T. J., Iwata, B. A., & Neef, N. A. (1976). Teaching pedestrian Skills to retarded persons: Generalization from the classroom to the natural environment. *Journal of Applied Behavior Analysis, 9,* 433–444.

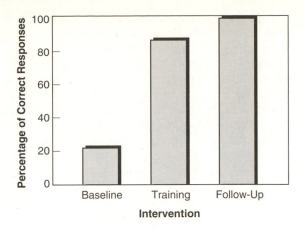

Figure 28.1   Safety of Street Crossing Transfer of Training with a Model

houses, trees, people, cars, stop signs, a traffic light, and a "walk, don't walk" pedestrian light.

Terry and his colleagues did a *task analysis* of the *behavioral chains* involved in safely crossing the street. For example, crossing at a pedestrian light involved: stopping at the intersection, crossing with a latency of less than 5 seconds after the *walk* signal, looking both left and right while in the street, and never stopping until reaching the other side.

Training consisted of the student's moving a small pedestrian doll from one location to another on the model. When the student did all components of the chain right, he received praise. When he made an error, he received imitation training, with a demonstration by the trainer, along with another chance to do it right.

But now comes what we think is the most innovative and most crucial part of this program. The students had to say what the doll was doing. In essence, the students had to state the rule of safe street crossing for each component of the task.

Results

The students learned to move the doll safely in the classroom. But more to the point, they also learned to move themselves safely on the mean streets. They went from 4.3 of 17 possible correct responses during baseline to 15 out of 17 at the end of training and to 17 out of 17 during a follow-up (as long as 35 days after training had stopped; Figure 28.1). How well do you think you would score?

QUESTION

1. Describe a procedure to help developmentally delayed people acquire a repertoire of safe street crossing. What was the:

a. task analysis?
b. training setting?
c. training procedure?
d. training responses?
e. reinforcer?
f. testing setting?
g. testing responses?

Warning: You may have to have the details wired to do well on a quiz over this chapter.

STIMULUS GENERALIZATION IS NOT ENOUGH

Now, what the heck's going on here? Behavior analysts are sweating bullets trying to get training to transfer to novel settings. But Terry and crew got almost perfect transfer with almost no effort.

Many behavior analysts would make the mistake of saying this is stimulus generalization. By *generalization,* they usually mean *stimulus generalization* and *response generalization (response induction).* But that view should make us itch. *Stimulus generalization* more or less means *confusion.* It means *poor stimulus control.* It means *failure to discriminate.* But even though these people had IQ scores around 60, they could tell the difference between a poster-board model sitting on the table in a classroom and four real city blocks with real cars, trees, and so on. And they certainly could tell the difference between moving a small model pedestrian and their own walking across a street. They sure as heck could tell the difference between themselves and the small pedestrian doll they were shoving around the table.

In fact, the physical similarity between the model and the real thing is so small, you'd probably get no stimulus generalization between the two, not even with a pigeon, let alone with a human being.

And what about response generalization? Do you think moving the doll around with your hand is in the same response class as moving yourself around with your two feet? Do you think they're enough alike on any response dimension, such as topography? Do you think they serve the same function (produce the same outcome)? In other words, is getting a doll on the other side of a play street the same thing as getting yourself on the other side of a real street? You should have answered with a long string of *no*'s.

And suppose you're training your average chimpanzee. Suppose you managed to get it to move the doll properly around the model streets. Do you think the doll movements would in any way share the effects of the reinforcement with the chimp's crossing the real streets? Do you think increasing doll safety would increase chimp safety? *No, no.*

We hope you did answer all those questions with a *no way*—no stimulus generalization and no response generalization. Not only could a pigeon or a chimp see the difference between the model and reality, we think they couldn't see the similarity.

QUESTIONS

1. *Stimulus discrimination* and *stimulus control* are the same thing.
   a. true
   b. false

2. Responding at the same frequency in the presence of the S^Δ as in the presence of the S^D shows
   a. little stimulus control
   b. much stimulus control.

3. Responding at the same frequency in the presence of the S^Δ as in the presence of the S^D shows
   a. little stimulus generalization
   b. much stimulus generalization.

4. Stimulus control (stimulus discrimination) is the opposite of stimulus generalization.
   a. true
   b. false

5. The trainees could readily discriminate between all aspects of the training setting with the models and the real world on the streets.
   a. true
   b. false

6. The trainees showed much **stimulus** generalization between all aspects of the training setting with the models and the real world on the streets.
   a. true
   b. false

7. The trainees showed much **response** generalization between all aspects of the training setting with the models and the real world on the streets.
   a. true
   b. false

8. Their transfer of training is a good example of stimulus and response generalization.
   a. true
   b. false

COULD RULE-GOVERNED BEHAVIOR SUPPORT TRANSFER OF TRAINING?

The developmentally delayed students did show terrific transfer; but surely stimulus and response generalization can't be the cause. Then what could be? As we hinted earlier, we think this terrific transfer of training results is an example of rule-governed behavior. The students learned to say the rules while being trained with the model person, car, crossing, and so on. And the student's statements of the rules governed the behavior of their moving the model person. For example, we suspect the model of the street crossing was an S^D for the students to say, "Stop at the crossing." or simply, "Stop."

At this point, we must rely on a complex behavioral history of these young men, though they were classified as developmentally delayed. For example, we think the model and the real crossing were part of the same "stimulus class." Not because of physical similarity but because of an elaborate, language-based behavioral history. In essence, someone had told them the model crossing "stood for" the real crossing.[2] So when they came to the real crossing, it may have evoked the verbal response, "Stop," at the crossing (though not through any simple process of stimulus generalization.) And that implied rule may, in turn, have caused them to stop.

Of course, our analysis is so untested it really belongs in the Enrichment section and not here. But we think the traditional analysis, in terms of generalization, is too misleading. And we had to offer you at least something to chew on until the real thing comes along. And even if we are crossing the right street at the right crossing, we need research on what behavioral history causes this rule-governed transfer of training and why verbal behavior seems so crucial.

QUESTION

1. Describe the role of rule control in the training and transfer of safe street crossing.

Example from
Behavioral School Psychology
MODIFICATION OF A CHILD'S MULTIPLE BEHAVIOR PROBLEMS[3]

Problem

The teacher wanted to kick 5-year-old Karl Shambaugh out of kindergarten—too many bad behaviors. For example, when separated from his mother,

---

[2]We put quotes around *stimulus class* because this is probably some sort of rule-governed **analog** to a stimulus class. But we don't know of any research showing pointing to the behavioral processes underlying the creation of such analog stimulus classes.

[3]Based on Patterson, G. R., & Brodsky, G. A. (1966). A behavior modification program for a child with multiple problem behaviors. *Journal of Child Psychology and Psychiatry, 7,* 277–295.

he began biting, kicking, throwing toys, screaming, and crying. The teacher's legs were a mass of black-and-blue marks; also, several times he had tried to choke her. His mother reported occasional enuresis (bed wetting). His speech was immature, showing several minor articulation defects. He also had problems getting along with adults, and it was hard to get him to dress or feed himself. The mother thought he might be developmentally delayed, but his IQ turned out to be within normal range.

Nonetheless, the mother felt Karl's behavior was so extreme and had persisted so long that it was unlikely to change. She said Karl was strong-headed. She was worried about his behavior when she brought him to school in the mornings. For example, in the week before her first interview, he had held on to her dress with his teeth preventing her from leaving. Perhaps related to this, at the age of 2 years, Karl had stayed in a hospital a few days for a diagnostic study of suspected leukemia. The results had been negative; but after the hospital stay, it was hard to leave him with baby-sitters.

Karl's few interactions with other children mainly involved his pushing, elbowing, pinching, kicking, and once, actually choking one. So, of course, children avoided him most of the time. The teacher would try to comfort and reassure him during his temper tantrums, and she always stayed close at hand to prevent him from seriously injuring another child.

Karl spent nearly all his time tantruming, sulking, or attacking other children. Only once in a while did he engage in peaceful, isolated play. The teacher spent most of her time dealing with Karl, so she found it almost impossible to run her kindergarten. To her regret, she finally had to expel Karl from school. She wasn't able to help him, and Karl took so much of her time she was less effective with the other children; and she feared for the safety of the other kids.

Intervention

Because of Karl's forthcoming expulsion, Mrs. Shambaugh went to the University of Oregon Child Guidance Clinic, where she met Dr. Gerald Patterson. (Remember, we read about Dr. Patterson's work with hyperactive children.) After the first interview at the clinic, Mrs. Shambaugh agreed to bring Karl to Dr. Patterson's lab; but she was skeptical about the success of the venture.

In the Lab

The next day Mrs. Shambaugh brought Karl to the door of the lab, but Karl refused to go inside.

"You see what I mean, Dr. Patterson? It just won't work."

"That's all right." Then Gerald reached over to pick up Karl. Karl started screaming and kicked him in the legs. But Gerald finally managed to pick up the screaming and crying child and carried him into the lab. Karl began to kick the lab equipment as they passed because he was no longer able to kick Gerald.

Gerald took Karl into a cubicle, closed the door, and pinned him to the floor by his ankles. While Karl screamed, bit, and threw objects, Gerald made every effort to prevent Karl from injuring him, and at the same time, sat looking as bored as the circumstances would permit. He looked at Karl and talked to him when he was calm. Gerald told Karl he could leave as soon as he quieted.

During this time, Gerald's colleague, Dr. Brodsky, took Mrs. Shambaugh into an adjoining room where they could observe Karl and Gerald through a one-way glass. Mrs. Shambaugh was horrified. "I knew this wouldn't work. Dr. Patterson is just making things worse. Look, he's holding Karl down on the floor, and that will upset Karl more. Why doesn't he try to reassure Karl and make him feel at home? Maybe I'd better go in and help."

"It'll be all right, Mrs. Shambaugh. You see, whenever Karl throws a temper tantrum, someone pays attention to him. When he is in a classroom and throws a temper tantrum, you stay with him, or the teacher hugs him and reads stories to him. All this attention reinforces Karl's temper tantrums," Dr. Brodsky explained.

"But when the poor child is so frightened and upset, we have to do something to reassure him and let him know we love him."

"Yes, but the problem is that when you do, you reinforce his temper tantrums. This makes it more likely he will have more temper tantrums in the future."

"I think I see what you mean, but it seems so cruel to let Dr. Patterson hold him down on the floor like that. If I went in there for a few minutes, he would stop crying."

"Yes, you're probably right. If you went in right now, I am sure you could get Karl to stop crying. The problem is that if you go in there and stop his crying, your attention will reinforce his crying. He will be more likely to cry again the next time he is in that situation. We're not so concerned with getting him to stop crying this time; what we do want is to get rid of his temper tantrums in future times. You see, when we take care of the immediate problem, we create more of a problem for the future."

"Well, I guess you're right; you're the expert. But it's going to be hard for me to go against my natural inclinations."

"Yes, it'll be hard; but it'll pay off in the long run."

After about 30 minutes, Karl quieted down. At that point, Gerald released him and allowed him to leave the clinic with his mother.

The next day, Mrs. Shambaugh had to drag Karl to the clinic. Once inside, he refused to go with Gerald to the playroom; but Gerald picked him up kicking, screaming, shouting, and crying. In the playroom, Gerald again pinned him to the floor by his ankles. But Karl cried for only 30 seconds this time. As soon as he stopped the tantrum behaviors, he could leave.

Dr. Brodsky explained to Mrs. Shambaugh, "You see how soon Karl stopped crying today. Each day that goes by without reinforcing Karl's crying, he will cry less on the next day."

Dr. Brodsky continued, "Now Gerald is going to show Karl how he should behave when he is at home, at school, and various other places. But he's going to try to do this right here in the lab without actually taking Karl outside. He's going to use some dolls and see if he can get Karl to make the dolls behave properly in these settings. The hope is that teaching Karl how the dolls should behave will affect the way Karl, himself, will behave when he actually gets in those situations." Gerald reinforced Karl's playing responses when those responses involved the doll's behaving properly. The reinforcement increased the frequency of proper playing. Gerald hoped that the responses of having the doll behave properly would transfer to Karl's behavior, so he would behave properly in the real situations that corresponded to the play.

Gerald showed a strange little box to Karl. "This is a 'Karl' box. It has a bell. Whenever this bell goes off, I'm going to drop an M&M in your cup. Now, you see this little boy doll? This is Henry. And this mother doll is Henry's mother. Let's put them next to each other. See? Little Henry is holding onto his mother's hand. Is he afraid?"

No answer.

"Now you see the mother doll lean down and say to Henry, 'It sure is a nice day today, isn't it, Henry?' Now is Henry afraid?"

"No." Immediately the bell rang, and an M&M dropped into Karl's cup.

"Now the mama doll takes little Henry by the hand, and they walk out of their house. Is little Henry afraid?"

"No, why should he be? He's with his mama."

"Little Henry says, 'Where are we going?' and his mother says, 'We're going to the doctor's.' Is little Henry afraid?"

"Yes. He doesn't want to go to the doctor's."

"But does little Henry start to cry, or does he keep walking on with his mother like a brave boy?"

"He doesn't cry. He goes with his mother."

The Karl box rings and an M&M drops into Karl's cup.

"Little Henry's mother lets loose of his hand, and they keep walking to the doctor's office. Is little Henry afraid?"

"No. He's not too afraid." Once more a bell rings and an M&M falls in his cup.

"They finally get to the doctor's office, and Henry's mother goes in. Does Henry go in with her?"

"Yes, he does."

The bell rings; and Gerald puts an M&M into Karl's cup. The M&M quickly disappears into Karl's mouth.

"Is Henry afraid?"

"Yes."

"Does he stay in the room, or does he leave?"

"He stays in the room."

The bell rings, and Karl gets another M&M.

This first session lasted 15 minutes. Karl participated in a series of six doll-play sequences and got 30 M&Ms in each session.

In the Home

After the session in the playroom, the two behavior analysts, Karl, and Mrs. Shambaugh talked for a few minutes. The behavior analysts asked Mrs. Shambaugh to give Karl a reinforcer on those occasions when he didn't act frightened when separated from her, when he was cooperative, and when he acted grown-up. They asked her to bring in notes describing four occasions when she had given those reinforcers. Karl listened to this conversation with some interest.

In the Kindergarten

Meanwhile, Gerald explained to the kindergarten teacher that they could get rid of Karl's problem behaviors, but it would help if they could work on some of his problems while he was at the kindergarten. The teacher looked at her black-and-blue legs, smiled, and agreed. That day, Gerald and the Karl box arrived at the kindergarten. During the recess periods, he told Karl that the bell would ring each time he played with another kid without hurting him. If Karl was within range, Gerald also praised him for appropriate initiations of social interactions. He informed Karl that he would divide the candy he earned among all the children during snack time. Karl earned 70 M&Ms in a 10-minute period; during this time he showed no aversive behaviors.

On the next day, the tantrum behaviors occurred at the clinic. Again, Gerald picked up and carried Karl to the playroom, screaming, kicking, and crying. But today the tantrum stopped as soon as Karl arrived in the playroom. This time, the doll play lasted about 20 minutes. Karl earned 30 M&Ms and a plastic ship.

The remainder of the intervention went like this: Within the next few days, Gerald met Karl's mother. She told of the various behaviors she had reinforced on the preceding days. Gerald had used candy to reinforce friendly interactions of Karl with other children at the kindergarten. He also reinforced appropriate interactions of other children with Karl. Gerald shaped Karl's walking up the stairs of the lab without the use of force. He also gradually removed the presence of the mother when Karl was in the room without crying. Karl became more tolerant when his mother left him at school, and he was cooperative at home. Within a short time, the mother, the teacher, and Karl all agreed that Karl no longer needed the behavior modification program.

Results

The overall results: within 9 days, the total duration of Karl's temper tantrums in the kindergarten decreased from between 30 and 35 minutes to zero (Figure 28.2).

Gerald didn't observe any temper tantrums during occasional follow-ups for the next 3 months.

During the first few days, the percentage of time Karl spent by himself also decreased, from about 35 to 0%, and remained at 0% for the next 3 months. (See the first pair of bars in Figure 28.3.)

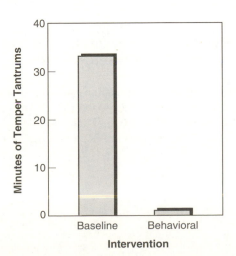

Figure 28.2   Transfer of Training From Lab to Kindergarten: Temper Tantrums

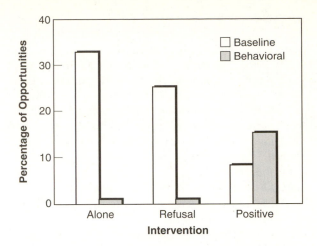

Figure 28.3   Transfer of Training From Lab to Kindergarten: Multiple Behavioral Problems

The percentage of times Karl refused to follow instructions or suggestions from the teacher dropped from about 25% to near 0% and stayed there for the next 3 months. (See the second pair of bars in Figure 28.3.)

The other children had avoided Karl, probably because of his pushing, elbowing, kicking, and pinching. Gerald thought that if he could get rid of that behavior, Karl's classmates might interact with him more often. So he praised appropriate interactions, such as talking, smiling, playing, and touching. The percentage of time Karl initiated positive interactions increased from 8 to 20%, and then decreased to 15%, where it remained for the following 3 months. (See the third pair of bars in Figure 28.3.)

Positive interactions of Karl's classmates also increased from near 0 to 8%, and then decreased to 4% and remained there for the rest of the 3 months. We should point out that Gerald got these data on positive interactions between Karl and his classmates during a 20-minute period before he reinforced such interactions. So these data reflect the transfer from preceding reinforcement periods.

Discussions with both parents and the teacher during the follow-up period indicate that Karl is "a changed boy." The casual observer in the classroom would have no reason to select Karl as showing deviant behavior. His behavior is characterized by less avoidance of social contacts and increased responsiveness to social reinforcers. Although still somewhat impulsive, Karl no longer displays temper tantrums, nor does he isolate himself.

This study shows how the skillful use of behavioral techniques can change a person's entire mode of behaving. Speaking in nontechnical terms, we might say the entire personality, or the whole person, has changed.

Analysis

When we included this case study in the first edition of our book, we didn't know about the concept of rule-governed behavior. So we were puzzled by the results. Now we can understand them more easily.

Recall Gerald Patterson's pinning Karl to the floor while the boy tantrumed. This involved two direct-acting contingencies. One was extinction of a direct-acting reinforcement contingency—the attention Karl normally got for kicking up a fuss. The other was a direct-acting punishment contingency—the aversiveness of being pinned to the floor, contingent on Karl's tantruming.

But that's not all. Gerald also used rule control. He told Karl he could get up when he stopped tantruming. And possibly Karl's behavior was controlled by a rule-governed analog to punishment by the prevention of the removal of an aversive condition rather than by the punishment contingency itself. Why? Because his tantruming may possibly have decreased too quickly to have been caused by the punishment contingency—30 seconds the second day and 0 seconds the third day. (Whenever instructions are involved [a rule], there's a good chance we've got rule control, even if the rule describes a direct-acting contingency. However, that's only a rough general rule because some direct-acting punishment contingencies also produce quick suppression.)

But the most interesting analysis in terms of rule control deals with playing with the dolls. When we wrote the first edition of this book, we couldn't figure out why the training with the dolls would transfer outside the lab. But it's clearer if we think in terms of rule-governed behavior, especially now that we have the benefit of the study on street safety that Page, Iwata, and Neef published 10 years later.

Gerald didn't directly teach the rules to Karl, but almost. Instead, Gerald reinforced Karl's describing the desired response. Now, we would guess that Karl's verbal description of the desired response didn't generalize to his actually making the desired response. Instead, when he got in the real situations (going to kindergarten, for instance), Karl would state the rule to himself, and the rule would govern his behavior. (With 20-some years' hindsight, we'd explicitly teach Karl to say the rules at the right times, like "If I don't cause a fuss, I'll get an M&M.")

But rule control probably played an even bigger role in this transfer from the training setting to the testing setting (the home, in this instance). Recall that Karl listened intently while the behavior analyst gave his mother the rules. In essence, they said, "When Karl doesn't cause problems, give him an M&M." His quick compliance again suggests control by rules rather than control by direct-acting contingencies.

(By the way, in our first edition, we interpreted those contingencies as reinforcement contingencies. But if you look closely at the rules, you'll see they really describe what Karl was supposed **not** to do— for example, not act frightened. So it looks more like an analog to punishment by the prevention of the presentation of a reinforcer. Every time Karl acted up, he prevented his mother giving him an M&M.)

Finally, Gerald told Karl the rule that the whole class would get candy if Karl played with the kids without hurting them. And Karl's earning 70 M&Ms in 10 minutes suggests rule-governed behavior.

So this study may be a good example of the importance of rule control in the transfer of training. It also shows how good behavior can fall into a behavior trap. As Patterson and Brodsky point out, perhaps the behavior analysts' job is to get the client's appropriate behavior to transfer to the natural environment and to ensure that the behavior is such that the environment will then reinforce and maintain it.[4]

QUESTIONS

1. Concerning the intervention to reduce a 5-year olds problems of aggression, what was the
   a. training procedure in the lab?
   b. analog to a punishment contingency?
   c. analog to extinction?
   d. reinforcement contingency?
   e. analog to punishment in the home?
   f. analog to reinforcement in the kindergarten?
2. Analyze the transfer from doll play in the lab to the real activities in the home and school, in terms of rule control.

Example
RULE-GOVERNED BEHAVIOR IN THE CLASSROOM[5]

A cloud hung over Mae Robinson ever since she'd gotten the letter from the board of education. They would close down the Rosa Parks Academy at the end of the year. They valued her work but just didn't

---

[4]One of my students asked if this was really transfer, because they used M&Ms in the transfer settings, the home and kindergarten. Good question. The answer is probably. It might be that, even with the M&Ms, they wouldn't have gotten good performance nearly as quickly in the transfer settings without the prior training in the lab. But they would have needed to do an experiment where they compared performance in the transfer settings with and without the prior training, to be sure.

[5]Based on Guevremont, D. C., Osnes, P. G., & Stokes, T. F. (1988). The functional role of preschoolers' verbalizations in the generalization of self-instructional training. *Journal of Applied Behavior Analysis, 21,* 45–55.

have the money. Sure they value my work, Mae thought. She sat with her head in her hands. No one really cares about these kids or the work we've done.

When she heard footsteps approaching her office, Mae dropped the role of the unappreciated and assumed her role of principal and founder of the Rosa Parks Academy.

Once again, Herman Lewis strode into Mae's office. It had been 6 months since his first visit. Jimmy Lewis had made great progress. Sometimes he had a tantrum, but he'd stopped pulling out his hair and rarely banged his ear with his fists. He could speak in sentences, dress himself, and use the toilet.

"Dr. Robinson, you've done wonders with my son. Louise and I can't thank you enough."

"That's nice of you to say, Herman. But you and Louise and Jimmy did most of the work. A child like Jimmy can't act anywhere near normal unless his parents dedicate much of their lives to helping him. You and Louise have done that. The work we do at the school with an autistic child won't transfer to the home unless the parents keep the program going."

"It's funny, Dr. Robinson, but of all Jimmy's progress, you know what we value most? His becoming a loving and affectionate son. Before, he treated us like pieces of furniture. Now he treats us like people he loves and cares for. I can hardly wait to see what you've done for him by this time next year."

"I'm sorry, Herman. In spite of all your help and your arguing with the school board, there won't be a next year—at least not for the Rosa Parks Academy. We'll be a parking lot."

"Damn! I thought we'd won that battle. What we need are more data about how good your school is."

"Unfortunately, Herman, data don't always convince school boards."

"Well, I know someone who built her life on data—one of my buddies at the club. She's a computer engineer, and she's made a fortune using data-based techniques to evaluate and improve her product line. She also donates some of that fortune to human service and education programs that convince her they're worthwhile. But few have convinced her. She says most human service and education programs are just hot air—a waste of money.

"She knows Jimmy, and his progress impresses her. She also knows you need support. But she remains a scientific skeptic; she's waiting for you to prove that Jimmy can make academic progress. Not only that, she thinks Jimmy needs to be able to work in a more typical special ed classroom, one with one teacher and several children, not just the one-on-one training you've been using. She says she wants a more cost-effective procedure.

"You've got only a few weeks until the bulldozers roll in, but if you can pull it off, I think she'll save your school."

Though she didn't think it would work, Mae put Jimmy in the special ed classroom where Max was doing his behavior analysis practicum. Disaster city: Jimmy only did 1% of his worksheet problems correctly. Mae and her staff were already working full-time with Jimmy. Now they had to work overtime.

Training Jimmy to Self-Instruct

Remember stimulus matching—selecting a comparison stimulus equal to a sample stimulus (Chapter 14)? Jimmy had no problem matching, so now it was time for him to do something more like traditional academic work, something that would impress even the skeptical computer engineer. This time, Mae selected stimulus matching in which the stimuli were common sequences of written letters. Here's an example:

Stimulus-Matching Task	
Sample stimulus	Comparison stimuli
ock	mick
	dock
	luck
	clock
	sick

In each class, Jimmy had a series of problems like that. He was to circle the comparison stimuli whose last letters matched the sample stimulus. But now Mae wanted Jimmy to be able to work on the problems by himself in a class with other children, without a trainer giving him instructions for each move. Mae wanted Jimmy to give instructions to himself.

Mae wanted Jimmy to give himself a series of problem-oriented instructions each time he had to solve a new stimulus-matching problem. Here are the instructions Jimmy was to give himself:

Problem-Oriented Instructions	
Type	Self-instructions
Problem orientation	"What do I have to do first?"
Task statement	"I have to circle the words that have the same letters."
Guiding self-statement	"Not this one, so I won't circle it." or "This one, so I will circle it."
Self-acknowledgement	"Good job."

Remember *covert behavior* (private behavior, not visible to the outside observer) and the opposite concept, *overt behavior* (public behavior, visible to the outside observer)? Talking to yourself versus talking out loud? Mae planned first to train overt self-instructions and then move to covert self-instructions. They would start with overt self-instructions because the proper behavior could be observed and reinforced.

Eve was the trainer. She and Jimmy worked together in a private room next to the group classroom. At first, she used a standard one-on-one training program—modeling, reinforcement, specific feedback, and punishment: She **modeled** self-instructing as she solved the problems. Jimmy **imitated** her. She praised Jimmy's correct self-instructing **(reinforcement)**. When he made a mistake, she gave **specific feedback**, such as "You said the instruction right, but you didn't circle the right answer." If Jimmy made the same mistake again, she removed his pencil and turned her back for 5 seconds of **time-out (punishment)**.

They didn't want the sight of Eve to act as an S^D for Jimmy's self-instruction, so during the last 10 minutes of each session, she stood behind him. And at the end of each session, Eve said to Jimmy, "Use the instructions you learned today to help you on your worksheets in Max's classroom."

The training worked well in the training sessions. Within five 20-minute sessions, Jimmy's matching accuracy rose from 1% to 86%.

Training for Transfer of Training

But that wasn't enough. During these same days of Eve's one-on-one training, Jimmy kept on attending Max's classroom with five other children. There he again worked on the same sort of letter-matching worksheets, but his accuracy remained low (2%) in spite of his good performance in the one-on-one sessions with Eve. No transfer of training. Eve and Max could already hear the bulldozers moving toward the Rosa Parks Academy. So could Mae, but she pretended not to.

"Jimmy's right on schedule," she told her two frantic apprentices. "I'm basing our intervention on the work that David Guevremont, Pamela Osnes, and Trevor Stokes did. We could go faster, but we need some baseline data to convince this mysterious, skeptical computer engineer that we're doing real behavioral engineering here, too.

"For the next few days, Max, I want you to tell Jimmy to say the instructions that Eve taught him out loud while he does his work."

"But suppose Jimmy doesn't say the instructions?" Max asked.

"Good point. Let's also use a rule-governed analog to a punishment procedure. Suppose Jimmy scores less than 75% on a worksheet and also fails to say his instructions. Then say to him, "'You'll have to do another worksheet, because you're not using your instructions enough.'"

The procedure worked. Jimmy's homework accuracy shot to 85% the first day Max asked Jimmy to self-instruct. It averaged 89% over a 12-day period, and it stayed about the same (94%) even after Eve stopped asking Jimmy to self-instruct (a return to baseline).

Training for Covert Self-Instruction

Then, for 3 days, Eve trained Jimmy to use covert self-instruction. She said, "Jimmy, I want you to say the instructions you learned to yourself, while you do your work." For the next 21 days Max told Jimmy to keep saying the instructions to himself, and it seemed to work: Jimmy's accuracy averaged 95% and remained about the same (98%) during the return to baseline, where Max stopped telling Jimmy to self-instruct (Figure 28.4).

Analysis

Mae showed Herman Lewis a graph of Jimmy's excellent data, and Herman showed it to the mysterious, skeptical computer engineer. But the skeptic remained skeptical. She wanted more than a graph; she wanted to observe Jimmy herself. Mae feared that the presence of the extra adults in the classroom would disrupt Jimmy's performance. But she had no choice if she wanted to save her school.

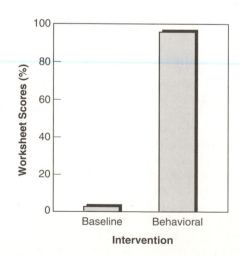

Figure 28.4   Transfer of Training from Lab to Classroom Using Self-Instructions

On the day of the big test, a nervous Mae, a nervous Herman, and a calm but skeptical computer engineer sat in the back of Max's classroom and watched Jimmy work like a champ, raise his hand when he'd completed the assignment, and score 100%. Then the convinced computer engineer wrote a check for $200,000, made it out to the Rosa Parks Academy, smiled, and placed the check in Mae's shaking hand. Mae's mouth was so dry she had to try three times before she could say, "Thank you."

"How did you do it?" the computer engineer asked.

"First, we trained Jimmy to state a series of rules that told him how to do his assignment. And we praised him when he followed those rules," Mae, the behavioral engineer, answered.

"Why didn't you just train Jimmy to do the tasks without bothering with the rules?" the computer engineer asked.

"Two reasons," Mae said. "First, with complex tasks, such as Jimmy's assignments, it seems easier to learn the rules and then prompt ourselves with the rules than to try to learn the tasks without the rules (but we need more data on this). And second, it may be easier to transfer rule stating from the training setting to the normal setting than it is to transfer the behavior the rules describe (but we need more data on this, too)."

Mae went on, "We also trained Jimmy to state the rules and follow them, even when he couldn't see the trainer. And in the group classroom, we gave him another rule, that he should say the problem-solving rules as he was doing his worksheets. We also told him the rule that he had to do an extra worksheet when he did poorly on one he'd just turned in. Finally, we told him the rule that he should say his problem-solving rules to himself, not out loud."

"Dr. Robinson, I like your style," the computer engineer said. "You work just like I do; you take nothing for granted. You nail down each tiny part of the procedure—detailed rules for problem solving, training with the trainer out of sight, instructions to state the rules in the group classroom, a rule for what happens to poor performance, and instructions to state the problem-solving rules to yourself."

"Thank you," Mae said.

"Frankly," the computer engineer went on, "I think most educators and human service workers take too much for granted. They don't worry enough about the details. And they don't get the results. It's a pleasure to see a real scientist in the classroom, Dr. Robinson."

Mae bowed her head slightly, acknowledging the compliment. Her hands finally stopped trembling.

There ain't no easy solution.

QUESTION

1. Describe a procedure for achieving transfer of training from one-on-one training sessions to group classrooms.
   a. Describe each step in the procedure.
   b. Describe the role rules play in each step.
   c. What were the general results?

OVERALL SUMMARY OF MAINTENANCE AND TRANSFER

In our view, many people have been confused about the maintenance of performance and its transfer to novel settings. So let's review these last two chapters, Chapters 27 and 28, as we try to clarify.

The biggest problem results from confusion between *stimulus and response generalization* and what we call *the maintenance and transfer of performance*.[6] *Transfer* is taking place when performance in a test setting shows the effects of a behavioral intervention in a training setting. For example, the training setting might be the classroom, and the test setting might be the home. The behavioral intervention in the training setting might involve reinforcement or punishment contingencies, or it might involve analogs to reinforcement or punishment supported by rule control.

Transfer with Nonverbal Clients

Sometimes we intervene with nonverbal clients (for example, Velma and Gerri, the two women with profound mental impairment who constantly ground their teeth). And sometimes we intervene with verbal clients but in a nonverbal way. (For example, we might socially reinforce a depressed client's positive statements, without pointing out that contingency to the client.)

How do we get transfer of training with these nonverbal clients? We must depend on stimulus and response generalization. The test setting must be at least somewhat physically similar to the training setting, and the test responses also must be at least somewhat physically similar to the training re-

---

[6]We use *transfer* rather than the more common *generalization* in this context to reduce the confusion. For an earlier use of *transfer of training* within this context, see Kazdin, A. E. (1975). *Behavior modification in applied settings* (pp. 212–228). Homewood, IL: Dorsey Press.

sponses, if stimulus-and-response generalization is to occur.

Maintenance with Nonverbal Clients

And how do we get maintenance of performance with these nonverbal cases? We must maintain the contingencies of reinforcement or punishment as we did during the original training. We can do this in either of two ways:

Testing Similar to Training

Suppose the stimuli and responses in testing are so like those in training that complete stimulus discrimination and response differentiation will never occur. Then, once in a while, we can reintroduce the training setting and contingencies. That way we can give an occasional booster shot. In other words, this alternating between testing and training allows the reinforcement or punishment contingencies of training to make occasional contact with the performance and thus maintain it in testing. (This happened with Velma and Gerri.)

Testing Different from Training

Or suppose the stimuli and responses in testing differ greatly from those in training. Then, after a while, complete stimulus discrimination and response differentiation may occur. Then maintenance would stop. We prevent this discrimination or differentiation if, once in a while, reinforcement or punishment contingencies similar to those of training occur in testing. This can happen in either of two ways:

Behavior Trap

Sometimes the test setting will contain a behavior trap with natural contingencies that will automatically reinforce or punish the performance (for example, Jungle Jim and the monkey bars).

Added Contingencies

But life doesn't always work out that simply. So sometimes we may need to add an occasional contingency in the test condition to maintain the performance. (For example, the grade-school students in the remedial classroom needed an occasional reprimand to maintain their performance.)

What all this means is that there's no free lunch. Performance doesn't maintain forever without supporting contingencies.

Transfer with Verbal Clients

Consider transfer of training following nonverbal interventions (for example, with nonverbal clients). This must be simple stimulus and response generalization. In other words, here we get transfer because of a failure of stimulus discrimination and response differentiation. If we had tight stimulus control, we wouldn't get transfer of training.

But, fortunately, that's not so with verbal interventions. Verbal clients can learn rules in training and then use those rules to govern their behavior in testing. They can use those rules in novel testing settings, though they can discriminate perfectly between the training and the testing settings and though they can differentiate perfectly between the training and testing responses (for example, the developmentally delayed men who learned street safety skills).

Maintenance with Verbal Clients

Rule control also may help us maintain our performance in the absence of natural, direct-acting contingencies of reinforcement and punishment. For example, in the general training life provides us, we learn the rule that if we don't pay our taxes we're in deep dung. And in the annual test life provides us, we make the avoidance response (pay our taxes) each time, though Uncle Sam has never thrown us in jail. We have almost no experimental work and little theoretical work on this topic, but it does seem likely that rule control helps us maintain.

The following table gives a summary:

Summary Comparison and Contrast Transfer and Maintenance with Verbal and Nonverbal Clients		
	Nonverbal	*Verbal*[7]
Transfer	Stimulus and response similarity	Rules
Maintenance	Behavior trap or added contingencies	Rules

In looking at this table, understand that *maintenance* means maintenance of the effects of training. It might not always mean maintenance of a high frequency of responding. For example, we might want to maintain the effects of a punishment contingency used in training. In that case we'd want

---

[7]Of course, the procedures for nonverbal clients can also work with verbal clients.

to maintain a low frequency of responding. Also, the nonverbal features can also facilitate transfer and maintenance for verbal clients, but they are less crucial, at least for transfer.

This is so complex let's do one summary of transfer of training with and without language:

Second Summary Comparison and Contrast: Transfer and Maintenance with Verbal and Nonverbal Clients	
Without language	*With language*
You can't have rules.	You can have rules.
So the training and the testing settings must be physically similar, to get transfer of training. training.	So the training and testing settings need not be physically similar, to get transfer of
In other words, you need much stimulus generalization and little stimulus discrimination.	In other words, you don't need much stimulus generalization; you can get transfer, even if you have much stimulus discrimination.
That was the case with nonverbal Gerri and Velma. Because they were deaf and blind, they could not discriminate between training and testing conditions. So they had excellent maintenance and also transfer.	That was the case with the verbal clients receiving the street-crossing training, where the model in the training setting was much different from the real street crossing setting. In spite of the obvious differences, they had excellent transfer. Maintenance wasn't addressed.

QUESTION

1. Compare and contrast transfer and maintenance with nonverbal and verbal clients.
   a. Be able to fill in the summary tables and describe their significance, **even if the labels are in a different order.**
   b. Be able to give an example of each aspect of the table.

INTERMEDIATE ENRICHMENT

Research Methods
INTERVENTION PACKAGES

Doctors Patterson and Brodsky used an intervention package to modify Karl's multiple problem behaviors. An ***intervention package*** is the addition or change of several independent variables at the same time to achieve a desired result, without testing the effect of each variable individually (see Chapter 19).

Their work is a good example of a problem that arises when we do scientific research in an applied setting, such as a clinic. If they had conducted this study only in a lab or in a kindergarten designed

for research, they might have done it differently. They might have tried one single procedure (like doll playing only) and observed its effects; if it didn't work, they might have added some other procedure (like an analog to reinforcement in the classroom). They wouldn't have had to worry about getting impressive results the first time.

But they needed to help Karl as soon as possible; otherwise, he might have had to drop out of kindergarten. They needed to get fast results; that's why they used an intervention package rather than a study testing one aspect of the procedure at a time. A study like this shows that something important is happening with their multiple interventions, but it doesn't pinpoint the important controlling variables. At this point, we don't know the individual importance of the analog contingencies in the lab, the doll-play procedure, the analog contingency in the home, and the analog contingencies in the school.

We know the overall intervention package greatly changed Karl's behavior. So now it would be worthwhile to do a more systematic study with similar children, to determine the exact causal factors.

We should emphasize that this study is important in showing that an intervention package could control Karl's behavior, though the study didn't indicate exactly what variables controlled it. It will be expensive and time-consuming to repeat such a study and to isolate all the factors. But when we initially don't have an opportunity to do the perfect study, we should go ahead and do the best we can for the time being. This is exactly what Patterson and Brodsky did in their valuable exploratory work.

QUESTIONS

1. Why did Patterson and Brodsky use an intervention package rather than a study of one variable at a time to modify Karl's multiple problem behaviors?
2. How could you do a follow-up study to isolate the crucial causal variables?

29 Research Methods

In this chapter, we'll summarize a few of the issues we've dealt with and add a few more. We'll do so as we give you our answers to three questions: Why should we do behavior analysis? How should we do behavior analysis? And how should we evaluate behavior analysis?

WHY SHOULD WE DO BEHAVIOR ANALYSIS?

HOW CAN WE UNDERSTAND THE WORLD?

In this book, we've emphasized the practical side of behavior analysis and science—we've stressed their contributions to improving life in the universe. We've done this for several reasons: That's the goal of most science and technology of behavior analysis; that's the easiest to understand; and that's what students are initially most interested in. In fact, this is our slogan:

> **Save the world with behavior analysis.[1]**

But there's also a theoretical side. There's also the notion that science, including behavior analysis, is of value in its own right. More precisely, there's

---

[1]For the pedantically challenged, we say *working toward the well-being of humanity,* rather than *save the world with behavior analysis.* The sophomorically pedantic say behavior analysis can't save the world, because we don't know enough; and besides, you need biology, physics, political science, etc.; and besides, who's to say what a saved world is? I say, give me a break, have a life; it's just a rough guideline, a political, religious, philosophical slogan, a joke—go with cynical idealism.

the notion that our scientific understanding of people, the world, and the universe is of value regardless of whether it helps us save the world. According to this view, science, including behavior analysis, is like art and music. Even if it doesn't contribute much to saving the world, it makes the world a better place to live in and thus a world more worth saving. Just as we have art for art's sake, so we have scientific knowledge for knowledge's sake.

We also advocate the value of pure knowledge. One of the things we like most about behavior analysis is that it gives us insights and understanding concerning the behavior (the psychological nature) of human beings and of our cousins in the animal kingdom. So we have another slogan:

> **Understand the world**
> **with behavior analysis.**

We should do behavior analysis for two reasons: to save the world and to understand the world.

HOW CAN WE BUILD A BETTER WORLD?

We said the goal of humanity should be the well-being of life in the universe. **The well-being of the universe should also be the goal of behavior analysis,** as it should for every profession. So we should concentrate on designing systems that make people happy, healthy, and productive, that maximize human potential for contributing to the well-being of the universe.

We are behavior-change professionals; we analyze and deal with problems that might affect a person, group, community, ecosystem, or future generations. We ought to understand behavior and what maintains it. We ought to change behaviors that harm the universe. We ought to maintain behaviors that help the universe. We ought to use our profession to build a better world.

We don't have to look too hard to find areas where behavior analysts could make a difference. Just think close to home for a minute: your parents, your spouse, your children, your friends, your boss, your dog, yourself. Can you see anything wrong there? Can you find anything worth improving?

Would you work to improve the quality of life—physical health, psychological well-being? Would you add quality years to people's lives by helping them follow healthy diets and exercise programs? Would you reduce hassles between people—between mothers and daughters, between brothers and sisters, between husbands and wives, between workers and employers, between government and citizens, between colleagues, between friends? (We even have hassles within single people; many of us hassle ourselves more than we do anyone else.) Would you contribute to a better environment by getting rid of water and air pollution? Would you reduce conflicts between countries? Would you prevent starvation, illness, and wars (both nuclear and conventional)? Behavior analysts have developed and tested an effective behavioral change technology; that's what this book is all about. Now it's time to continue with the extension and testing of this technology in these broader areas we've just mentioned. So one way to build a better world is to use behavior analysis as one of the building tools.

QUESTION

1. What are the two main goals or values of science, including behavior analysis?

HOW SHOULD WE DO BEHAVIOR ANALYSIS?

THE LAW OF EFFECT

Why do we behave as we do? Behavior analysis suggests one major answer:

> *Definition: Review Principle*
> **The law of effect**
> ○ The effects of our actions
> ○ determine whether we will repeat them.

In the hands of behavior analysts, this basic principle differentiates behavior analysis from other approaches to psychology. Rather, the causes of behavior are not in the unconscious mind, not in the self, not in cognitions, not in a supernatural power. The causes of behavior are in the environmental contingencies; the immediate effects or outcomes of behavior help determine the future occurrence of that behavior.

REINFORCEMENT

If behavior occurs often, an event, stimulus, or condition has reinforced that behavior. Behavior can be reinforced by the presentation of a reinforcer, by the removal of an aversive condition, or by either the prevention of an aversive condition or the prevention of the removal of a reinforcer. For example, Dina is an avid guitarist. What maintains Dina's guitar playing? The following table presents four contingencies that could maintain this behavior. Her guitar playing (1) causes an audience to enter the room to listen to Dina's melody, (2) reduces her muscle tension and stress, (3) prevents her brother's crying, (4) prevents the audience from leaving the room. (See the first table on p. 461.)

PUNISHMENT

If Dina isn't playing the guitar, why not? Here are four alternatives: (1) The behavior isn't in her repertoire; Dina might not play the guitar because she hasn't learned how or because her guitar playing has been extinguished. (2) There is a physical constraint; she broke her hand. (3) She doesn't have a prerequisite skill; she can't tune the guitar. (4) Something might punish guitar playing.

Guitar playing might be punished by the contingent (1) presentation of an aversive condition, (2) removal of a reinforcer, (3) prevention of the presentation of a reinforcer, (4) prevention of the removal of an aversive condition.

The second table on p. 461 shows the four contingencies that might punish Dina's guitar playing. Her playing might (1) produce untuned aversive sounds, (2) cause the audience to leave the room, (3) prevent her from hearing the beautiful sounds of the birds singing outside the window, (4) prevent an unpleasant visitor from leaving her house.

This third table on p. 465 summarizes all the direct-acting behavioral contingencies we've studied in this book; it's a combination of the previous two tables. Check it out.

The Reinforcement Contingencies

Behavioral relationship	Outcome	Contingency	Description of the contingency
Presentation	**Reinforcer:** attentive audience	Reinforcement	**Presents a reinforcer:** attentive audience enters the room
Removal	**Aversive condition:** tense muscles, stress	Escape	**Removes an aversive condition:** terminates her tension and stress
Prevention of presentation	**Aversive condition:** brother's crying	Avoidance	**Prevents the presentation of an aversive condition:** prevents her brother's crying
Prevention of removal	**Reinforcer:** attentive audience	Avoidance	**Prevents the removal of a reinforcer:** prevents attentive audience from leaving the room

The Punishment Contingencies

Behavioral relationship	Outcome	Contingency	Description of the contingency
Presentation	**Aversive condition:** untuned aversive guitar sound	Punishment	**Presents an aversive condition:** listening to an untuned guitar
Removal	**Reinforcer:** attentive audience	Penalty	**Removes a reinforcer:** attentive audience leaves the room
Prevention of presentation	**Reinforcer:** singing birds	Prevention of reinforcement	**Prevents the presentation of a reinforcer:** can't hear the birds singing
Prevention of removal	**Aversive condition:** unpleasant visitor	Prevention of escape	**Prevents the removal of an aversive condition:** unpleasant visitor stays in the house to listen to her music

The Direct-Acting Behavioral Contingencies

Behavioral relationship	Outcome	Contingency	Description of the contingency	Frequency of behavior
Presentation	Reinforcer	Reinforcement	Presents a reinforcer	Increase
	Aversive condition	Punishment	Presents an aversive condition	Decrease
Removal	Reinforcer	Penalty	Removes a reinforcer	Decrease
	Aversive condition	Escape	Removes an aversive condition	Increase
Prevention of presentation	Reinforcer	Punishment by preventing a reinforcer	Prevents the presentation of a reinforcer	Decrease
	Aversive condition	Avoidance	Prevents the presentation of an aversive condition	Increase
Prevention of removal	Reinforcer	Avoidance of loss of a reinforcer	Prevents the removal of a reinforcer	Increase
	Aversive condition	Punishment by preventing the removal of an aversive condition	Prevents the removal of an aversive condition	Decrease
None		Extinction	Stops the reinforcement contingency	Decrease[2]
		Recovery	Stops the punishment contingency	Increase

[2]Sometimes you will get an initial increase in frequency before the decrease.

DIRECT-ACTING AND INDIRECT-ACTING CONTINGENCIES

Look at the immediate consequences of behavior: direct-acting contingencies of reinforcement and punishment. **Indirect-acting contingencies** are those contingencies involving delayed outcomes. These contingencies do not themselves reinforce or punish the behavior. Only **direct-acting contingencies** reinforce and punish behavior. Direct-acting contingencies involve immediate, sizable, and probable outcomes.

So what controls behavior when the contingency of interest involves delayed, small, or improbable outcomes? Lurking around somewhere there must be a direct-acting contingency controlling behavior. This is where the concept of *rule* comes into play. A rule is a description of a behavioral contingency; we think it acts as an establishing operation. The rule statement establishes noncompliance with the rule as an aversive condition. Compliance with the rule is reinforced by a reduction of an aversive condition. This direct-acting escape contingency is what controls behavior and not the outcome specified in the indirect-acting contingency.

For example, what controls writing your term paper? A stimulus in the environment evokes stating a rule, such as If I don't start preparing my term paper now, I'll fail the course. This statement establishes goofing off as an aversive condition, like fear or anxiety. Can you relate to this aversive condition? Working on your term paper escapes or reduces that aversive condition and therefore reinforces your working. It is this direct-acting escape contingency that reinforces working on your term paper, not the long-term outcome of success in the course.

HOW TO DO A FUNCTIONAL ASSESSMENT

As we mentioned in Chapter 3, behavior analysts nowadays ask what maintains an inappropriate behavior before trying to eliminate it, or what prevents an appropriate behavior before trying to reinforce it. They ask, What function does the problem behavior serve for the client? Perhaps a less purposive way of putting it would be, What is the functional (causal) relation between the behavior and its reinforcing outcomes? We can also ask such similar questions when appropriate behavior doesn't occur often enough; for instance, What is the functional relation between the behavior and its punishing outcome? Another way to put it is, what are the effective natural contingencies maintaining inapprpriate behavior and supressing appropriate behavior? The systematic, empirical search for an answer to such questions, before implementing a behavioral inter-

vention, is called a **functional assessment.**[3,4] (Incidentally, functional assesments may have the drawback of focusing too much attention on effective, natural competing contingencies and away from the possibility that the natural contingencies for appropriate behavior may simply be ineffective, even in the absence of competing contingencies.)

Definition: Review Concept
Functional assessment
  ○ An analysis
  ○ of the contingencies responsible for
  ○ behavioral problems.

Note that you usually do this assessment before the intervention.

The table on p. 467 titled *The Steps of a Functional Assessment* shows how we recommend doing a functional analysis. The answers to the questions in each step provide information about the contingencies responsible for behavioral problems.

This diagram shows the relations among the steps of the function analysis listed in the preceding table.

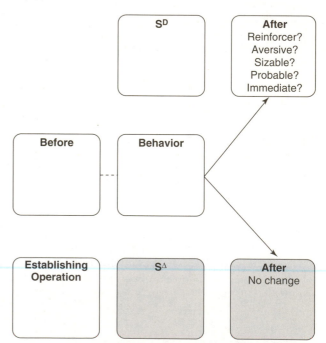

To illustrate the six steps of a functional assessment, we'll use a semi-hypothetical example from our autism practicum in the Pre-primary Impaired

---

[3]Inspired by Durand, V. M. (1987). In response: "Look homeward, angel": A call to return to our (functional) roots. *The Behavior Analyst, 10,* 299—302.

[4]One component of a functional assessment is a ***functional analysis*** in which the behavior analyst puts together a contrived situation to analyze the contingencies responsible for behavioral problems.

The Steps of a Functional Assessment—What to Identify		
1. Behavior	**What is the behavior of interest?**	
	What are some instances?	
	What are some noninstances? (other behaviors that occur instead)	
	How often does the behavior occur during baseline?	
2. Before condition	**What is the before condition?**	
	Is it a reinforcer, aversive condition, or neutral condition? (may be more than one)	
3. After condition	**What is the after condition?**	
	Is it a reinforcer, aversive condition, or neutral condition? (may be more than one)	
	Is the after condition sizable?	
	Is the after condition probable?	
	Is the after condition immediate? (if not, the maintaining contingency isn't direct acting)	
	What is the long-term outcome?	
4. Establishing operation	**What is the establishing operation?**	
5. Discriminative stimulus	**What Is the discriminative stimulus, if there is one?**	
6. Contingency	**If there is a direct-acting contingency, what is it?** (it may help to diagram it)	
	Reinforcement (presentation of a reinforcer)	
	Punishment (presentation of an aversive condition)	
	Penalty (removal of a reinforcer)	
	Escape (removal of an aversive condition)	
	Avoidance (prevention of the presentation of an aversive condition)	
	Punishment by the prevention of the presentation of a reinforcer	
	Avoidance of the removal of a reinforcer	
	Punishment by the prevention of the removal of an aversive condition	
	Or is there no direct-acting contingency (i.e., extinction)?	
	If any, what type of analog contingency exists between the behavior and the after condition? (What type of indirect acting contingency is in effect?)	

Classroom of Kalamazoo's Croyden Avenue School. Because most functional assessments are of the contingencies controlling inappropriate behavior, this example will deal with the disruptive behavior of Jason, a preschool autistic child doing discrete-trial training.

1. **Behavior.** Jason has a wide variety of disruptive behavior (e.g., getting out of his seat, grabbing instructional materials, lying on the floor, taking his clothes off, leaving the study booth). Appropriate behavior consists of doing the discrete-trail training tasks. He has such a high rate of disruptive behavior that the behavior technicians are sometimes reduced to tears; he often spends more time disrupting than doing his learning tasks.

2. **After Condition.** What is the immediate outcome? Usually, there are two: He escapes the discrete trial task, which may be difficult and thus aversive. And the tech chases him, grabs him, and coaxes him to sit down and do his tasks, which may be forms of social reinforcement.

3. **Before Condition.** Jason is doing a difficult tasks and he is not getting nearly as much attention, nor nearly such dynamic attention as when he's disrupting.

4. **Establishing Operation.** What is the establishing operation? For escape contingencies, we don't distinguish between the establishing operation and the before condition, so it's just his doing the difficult tasks, which may be aversive. And for the social reinforcement contingency, we usually don't deal

with the establishing operation for learned reinforcers (e.g., social reinforcers like attention); so we can bypass the establishing operation.

5. **S^D and S^Δ** What are the S^D and S^Δ? We notice that Jason disrupts much more frequently with inexperienced techs than with experienced techs. So, we suspect the inexperienced techs might be the S^D and the experienced techs might be the S^Δ. In other words, whether the relevant contingency is escape from the difficult task or inadvertent social reinforcement, the experienced tech might be better at extinguishing the disruptive behavior, at being an effective S^Δ for disruption.

6. **Contingency.** What contingency maintains the disruptive behavior. As we've said, it might be escape from an aversively difficult task and/or social reinforcement with attention.

Without doing functional assessments, we had typically assumed the disruptive behavior was escape maintained and had not been very sensitive to the possibility of the accidental social reinforcement we might be providing as we attempted to prevent the escape. With the consulting of Pamela Osnes, we've begun functional assessments showing that the disruptive behavior of our various little Jasons is often a result of social reinforcement.

Also as a result of Osnes's consulting, we are attempting to increase the density of social and physical reinforcers our Jasons receive when they are working on their tasks or at least not disrupting. Our goal is to have the children almost swimming in reinforcers, as long as they're cool. And this seems effective, regardless of whether the disruptive behavior is escape maintained or attention maintained. If it's attention maintained, Jason is getting so much attention while he's on task, that it's hardly worth his time to disrupt and go off task. If it's escape maintained, the addition of all those reinforcers while he's doing the aversively difficult tasks, will counteract that aversiveness and reduce the frequency of his disruptive escape behavior.

SHOULD WE DO FUNCTIONAL ASSESSMENT?

Many behaviorists argue we need to analyze behavior to select the intervention. But is this really the case? Why do we have to do this analysis? Couldn't we use a penalty contingency when the undesirable behavior occurs too often, or a reinforcement contingency when the behavior occurs too rarely? Do we need to analyze the contingencies maintaining behavior? Do we need to do a functional assessment?

Doug's mother, Shirley, shouts at him every time he turns up the volume on the TV because then she can't concentrate on her studies. His undesirable behavior maintains at a high frequency in spite of her shouts. Without doing a functional analysis, Shirley uses an analog to a penalty contingency. She follows the rule that for every time Doug turns up the volume on the TV, he'll miss 5 minutes of *The Simpsons,* his favorite TV program. This will probably work. Shirley will get rid of Doug's disruptive behavior. And she wouldn't need to do a functional assessment.

However, we might come up with several intervention options if we did a functional analysis. For example, Doug might have a hearing impairment. So a hearing aid might be all he needs. Or earphones for Doug and earplugs for Shirley might be ideal. Or a simple extinction procedure where Shirley doesn't say anything when Doug raises the volume on the TV might work, if Shirley's shouting is what reinforces Doug's turning up the volume. (It might sound unlikely to most people not familiar with behavior analysis that what at first appears to be an aversive condition [shouting] is really a reinforcer under some conditions.)

A functional analysis might suggest a more humane and equally effective intervention than the analog to the penalty contingency; and it might suggest an intervention more likely to transfer across settings (a hearing aid) or be easier to maintain (stereo earphones) than a penalty contingency (Shirley is likely to let a punishment contingency fall through the cracks as she gets preoccupied with other problems). Generally, functional analyses might suggest interventions more cost-effective, less intrusive, more humane, more transferable, and more maintainable than interventions not planned from such analyses.

So far, we've reviewed our recommendation for the goal of humanity—the well-being of life in the universe. And we've suggested this should be also the goal of behavior analysts. More generally, we said the goals or values of science, including behavior analysis, are to save the world and to understand how the world works. Also, we've studied how to do a functional assessment so that we can design better interventions to help save the world. Now we'll review techniques to determine whether the problems we're tackling are socially significant, whether they will really contribute to the save of the world. In addition, we will review techniques to determine whether our interventions are having any impact at all on the world, or at least on small parts of the world.

QUESTIONS

1. What is the law of effect?
2. Define functional analysis.
3. List the six questions you should ask when doing a functional assessment. Give an example of each question.
4. Should you do a functional assessment before or after designing an intervention? Explain.

HOW SHOULD WE EVALUATE BEHAVIOR ANALYSIS?

Concept
SOCIAL VALIDITY

Social validity tells us whether we have selected what our clients consider socially significant **target behaviors**—those worthy of improving. **Social validity** also tells us whether we have an acceptable intervention, to some extent regardless of its outcome.

Definition: Concepts
Social validity
- The goals,
- procedures, and
- results of an intervention
- are socially acceptable to
- the client,
- the behavior analyst, and
- society.[5]

Target behavior
- The behavior being measured,
- the dependent variable.

Van Houten pointed out that we should use social validity procedures to determine the target behavior, optimal levels of the target behavior, and intervention results.[6] We'll fail if the intervention

[5]Based on Bernstein, G. S. (1989). In response: Social validity and the report of the ABA Task Force on Right to Effective Treatment. *The Behavior Analyst, 12,* 97; and Wolf, M. M. (1978). Social validity: The case for subjective measurement, or how applied behavior analysis is finding its heart. *Journal of Applied Behavior Analysis, 11,* 203–214.
[6]Van Houten, R. (1979). Social validation: The evolution of standards of competency for target behaviors. *Journal of Applied Behavior Analysis, 12,* 581–591.

stops below the lower limit the community expects for competent performance. A behavioral intervention might improve Jim's grades from *E*s to *D*s, but the community might not consider *D*s good enough. Though we, behavior analysts, might feel our intervention had succeeded, social validity might show the contrary.

Two methods commonly used to estimate social validity are social comparison and subjective evaluation of experts. **Social comparison** consists of comparing the performance of clients exposed to the intervention with a comparable or "normal" group. The intervention is successful if the subjects' performance during intervention is like that of the comparison group. Another method, **subjective evaluation of experts,** involves evaluators who have expertise or familiarity with the client.

Definition: Concepts
Social comparison
- A comparison of the performance of clients
- exposed to the intervention
- with an equivalent or "normal" group.

Subjective evaluation of experts
- Experts' evaluation
- of the significance of
- the target behavior and the outcome.

Social comparison and subjective evaluation of experts have limitations.[7] In social comparisons, normative data might have little relevance for the functioning of the client; and subjective evaluation of experts offers no guarantee that the experts' judgments are the best criteria to determine the success of the intervention. Using both methods at the same time may overcome these problems.

A complete social validity will also tell us how acceptable our intervention is. For example, even though Jim may have gotten straight *A*s, we've failed if our intervention required more work from the teachers than they believed appropriate.

QUESTIONS

1. What is social validity?
2. Describe two social validity methods and their limitations.

[7]Kazdin, A. E. (1982). *Single-case research design.* New York: Oxford University Press.

Concept
OBTRUSIVE AND UNOBTRUSIVE OBSERVATION

How can we discover the problem behavior? *Observation* is the answer. But we must avoid contaminating our observations by using obtrusive assessment procedures. Kazdin pointed out that most behavioral assessment procedures are obtrusive, and they affect the results independently of the intervention.[8]

Definition Concept
Obtrusive assessment
  ◦ Measuring performance
  ◦ when the clients or subjects are aware
  ◦ of the ongoing observation.
Unobtrusive assessment
  ◦ Measuring performance
  ◦ when the clients or subjects
  ◦ are not aware
  ◦ of the ongoing observation.

Behaviors assessed under obtrusive and unobtrusive conditions sometimes bear little relation to each other. For instance, observe the behavior of students in a grade-school classroom when the teacher is in front of it with wide-open, intimidating eyes. You'll notice a quiet and dedicated team. However, chaos reigns when the teacher leaves.

You could use unobtrusive direct observations by delegating the observation to a regular participant in the client's environment, observing behavior behind a two-way mirror, videotaping with a hidden camera, and evaluating products of behavior.

Products of behavior are also usually unobtrusive assessment methods. Examples are records of behavior and physical proofs. **Records of behavior** could include number of arrests, attendance lists, or number of times a client was readmitted to the hospital. **Physical proof** is evidence that the behavior has occurred—the result of the behavior. For instance, to study academic behavior, we could review written exercises and essays. To study cigarette smoking, we could count cigarettes left in a client's cigarette pack, after agreeing that cigarettes smoked during the day would come only from that pack. To study dieting, we could weigh the client once a week to see if he had followed the diet.

This example shows the difference between record and product. You might have a performance contract to write two pages every day. At the end of each day you would record your pages written on a graph; and you'd show your cumulative graph once a week to your performance manager. That's a record of behavior. But you might know that you have a bit of the sleaze-ball tendency; you don't trust yourself. So you all commit to showing the actual, dated pages. That's physical proof. But both are products of behavior.

Products of behavior are not direct measures of behavior; they involve the result of the behavior rather the behavior itself. However, we use products of behavior for purpose of convenience or unobtrusive assessment.[9]

Definition: Concept
Products of behavior
  ◦ Record or evidence
  ◦ that the behavior has occurred.

QUESTIONS

1. *Obtrusive assessment procedures*—define them and give an example.
2. *Unobtrusive assessment procedures*—define them and give an example.
3. *Products of behavior*—define them and give an example.

Concept
UNITS OF MEASUREMENT

The basic units of measurement are frequency, duration, and force. A violation of your diet won't make you fat, but a violation once a day, or even once a week, might. Smoking a cigarette won't kill you, but 20 a day for 20 years might. You can survive a hassle with a friend once, but a hassle every time you open your mouth might end the relationship. Throughout this book we have studied many examples that involve measuring frequency—for instance, Todd's frequency of bowel movements per week, Jimmy's percentage of disruptive escape responses in 10-second intervals, Ange's frequency of sneezes, Dawn's frequency of nail biting per day, Bob's frequency of aggressive episodes.

---

[8]Kazdin, A. E. (1979). Unobtrusive measures in behavioral assessment. *Journal of Applied Behavior Analysis, 12,* 713–724.

[9]But if you're going to do an unobtrusive assessment of human behavior, you generally need to get the informed consent of the human beings whose behavior is being assessed, or at least the informed consent of their family or legal guardians. Nowadays, Big Brother must also get approval of the Human Subjects Institutional Review Board before he can go into the Big-Brother-is-watching business.

Duration consists of the length of time the response lasts. We studied a few instances, such as the number of minutes Rod's crying episodes lasted and the number of seconds Bobbie, the transsgender student, maintained a sexual fantasy of a female. **Force** means intensity of response. We studied a few examples: increasing Melanie's voice intensity and the force (in grams) with which Rudolph the Rat pressed a lever.

Definition: Concepts
Duration
  ◦ The time from
  ◦ the beginning
  ◦ to the end
  ◦ of a response.
Force
  ◦ Intensity of response.

QUESTION

1. Define and give an example of each of the following behavior measures:
   a. frequency or rate
   b. duration
   c. force

Example of Measurement
Organizational Behavior Management
SAMUEL DEE'S TOY FACTORY

In this semi-hypothetical case study, Samuel Dee has been CEO for 3 years of PlasToy, Inc., a small plastic toy manufacturing company. Orders had increased during the last few months, and the sales forecast for the rest of the year was higher than ever. Though the sales department celebrated, the production department was not coping. Many shipments were late, and customers were looking for other suppliers who could deliver orders on the due date.

PlasToy had 10 molding presses and three 8-hour shifts. The pressroom was scheduled to work 24 hours a day, 5 days a week. S. Dee wasn't sure what to do. Everyone told him that PlasToy needed more presses, but S. Dee couldn't afford to buy more presses. S. Dee wanted to assess how much his presses were used before deciding what to do. He called the quality control inspectors of each shift and asked them to walk through the pressroom every hour and record whether or not each press was working.

After a week of data collection, S. Dee found that all 10 presses combined were working only 72 hours a day on the average, including three shifts. The daily averages were 12 hours for first shift, 36 for the second, and 24 for the third. But 72 hours were too few, considering that there were 240 possible production hours a day (8 hours per shift × 10 presses × 3 shifts = 240 hours). Seventy-two hours was only 30% of PlasToy's capacity. No, S. Dee thought, this must be an unusual week. So he asked the inspectors to continue collecting data for the next several weeks; but the data consistently showed that presses were running only 30% of the time. And, surprisingly, the second shift ran more press hours than the other two shifts; this made no sense. S. Dee could think of nothing that would make the second shift more productive than the other two shifts.

Suspicious of the data, he checked it out himself. For a few days he came to work during second shift, from 3:00 P.M. to 11:00 P.M. He went to the control office, his preferred place in the plant. He had designed that office in his plant manager's days. From there, he could observe the whole pressroom without being noticed. At the sound of the hourly beep on his watch, he would look through the window and record how many presses were running.

The next day, S. Dee compared records. The second-shift inspector counted 30 hours running time, but S. Dee counted only 20. So he analyzed the two sets of data like this: If for a given hour both agreed the press was running, he wrote **RUN;** if both agreed the press was down, he wrote *Down;* if they disagreed on whether the press was running or not, he wrote Dis. He recorded agreements and disagreements in the table on p. 472.

In the table, you can see that S. Dee and the second-shift inspector agreed Press 1 was running at 3:00 P.M. and Press 2 was down at 8:00 P.M. They disagreed as to whether Press 4 was running or down at 6 P.M. S. Dee found that only 48% of his observations agreed with the second-shift inspector's.

Why was agreement between observation records so low? In reviewing his notes, S. Dee noticed that the second-shift inspector wrote **RUN** when a production worker was getting a press ready to mold. For instance, at 6:00 P.M. the materials handler was cleaning the hopper of Press 2 before filling it up with plastic; the second-shift inspector wrote **RUN** at that time, even though the press was off. S. Dee wrote *Down.* He wrote **RUN** only if the press was producing toys. He also found that on some days the second-shift inspector walked the pressroom every half hour during the first 4 hours, and she would stay in her office the last 4 hours of the

Press	3 P.M.	4 P.M.	5 P.M.	6 P.M.	7 P.M.	8 P.M.	9 P.M.	10 P.M.
1	**RUN**	**RUN**	Dis	Dis	**RUN**	**RUN**	**RUN**	**RUN**
2	Dis	Dis	Dis	Dis	Dis	Down	Down	Down
3	**RUN**	**RUN**	Dis	Dis	Dis	Dis	**RUN**	**RUN**
4	Down	Down	Down	Dis	Dis	Dis	**RUN**	**RUN**
5	Down	Down	Dis	Dis	Down	Dis	Dis	Dis
6	Dis	Dis	Dis	**RUN**	**RUN**	Dis	Dis	Dis
7	Down	Down	Down	Down	Dis	Dis	**RUN**	Dis
8	Dis	Dis	Dis	Dis	Dis	Dis	Dis	Dis
9	Down	Down	Down	Down	Down	Down	Down	Down
10	Dis	Dis	Dis	Dis	**RUN**	Dis	Dis	**RUN**

shift studying for school. But she identified each record as an hourly record. Of course, this would also create disagreements between her observations and S. Dee's.

So S. Dee called the inspectors and explained what "press running" meant. He asked them to write **RUN** only when the press was producing parts, not when someone was working near it, removing a mold, washing the press, or trimming parts molded another day. He also reviewed carefully the observation procedures. Every hourly check must start on the hour, and it should take no more than 10 minutes. He also said that someone else would be recording press running time independently for comparison.

S. Dee trained the maintenance department inspectors to track press-running time, exactly in the same way as the quality control inspectors. Maintenance and quality control inspectors were never to see each other's observation records. Then S. Dee compared records every day by shift, and 99% of the observations agreed; he trusted the data.

He learned that presses were active about 25% of the time, and in general, there were no differences in performance between the three shifts. He also learned that the production department was very inefficient. He was positive that with performance management he could make a significant improvement in production. There would be no need to buy more presses. What a relief!

Concept
INTEROBSERVER AGREEMENT

S. Dee found that their initial measure of press running was not reliable. He found this by using a method called **interobserver agreement.**

> *Definition: Concept*
> **Interobserver agreement**
> ○ Agreement between
> ○ observations of
> ○ two or more independent observers.

Interobserver agreement forces us to define the critical behavior or products of behavior so clearly that two or more observers can get the same observational records independently. The second-shift inspector had a different definition of press running. Of course, her records and S. Dee's differed. But this difference reflected only a poor definition of "press running."

Sometimes, observers are affected by personal biases. For instance, press-running data might be affected by how much the second-shift inspector liked the second-shift supervisor. If she thought a high record would benefit the supervisor, she might have reported higher press-running times than a neutral observer would have.

Reviewing the criteria for recording observations only once is not enough. Observers tend to change their definition of the behavior over time. So variation in the data may be caused by changes in the observer's definition of the observation criterion rather than actual changes of the dependent variable. That's why it's important to review the observation criteria periodically during data collection.

Interobserver agreement also forces us to clarify procedures. For instance, S. Dee had to tell the second-shift inspector that recording was to be done at the beginning of each hour, because it had turned out that the inspector was making her observations at anytime convenient time with in the hour. Also S. Dee was measuring once during each of the 8 hours of the shift, while the inspector was only measuring during the first 4 hours. So, of course, their interobserver agreement was low.

By the way, S. Dee, made sure that he and the supervisor made independent observations, even though they were observing the same thing at the same time. In other words, neither of them could see what the other was writing on their recording forms, otherwise, the supervisor might be tempted, either consciously or unconsciously to kiss up to S. Dee, by always writing down the same thing S. Dee wrote, even though she sometimes disagreed with his observations. Interobserver agreement is meaningless if the observers aren't independent.

To compute the 48% interobserver-agreement ratio, S. Dee used the **point-by-point agreement ratio,** one of the most commonly used methods in applied behavior analysis research to estimate interobserver agreement. This ratio indicates whether or not we can trust observation records. In the table, you can see that S. Dee agreed with the inspector that presses were running 17 hours (add all the RUN records) and presses were down 21 hours (add all the *Down* records). They disagreed on 42 records (add all the *Dis* records). With this information, S. Dee computed the point-by-point ratio by following these steps:

1. He added all the agreements; 17 RUN hours plus 21 Down hours equaled 38 hours.
2. Then he computed all possible instances; he added all 38 agreement records to 42 disagreement and got 80 possible observations for second shift.
3. Finally he computed the point-by-point agreement ratio; he divided 38 total agreement records by 80 possible records and multiplied by 100. This was 47.5% or, to round it up, 48%.

The second-shift inspector and S. Dee's initial observations agreed only 48% of the time. In other words, their observation records were not reliable; he could not trust the data. Normally, behavior analysts consider data reliable only when the agreement is over 80%. Furthermore, you can end this section assured that S. Dee and the supervisor eventually achieved interobserver agreement well above the 80% goal, as a result of his efforts to get agreement on the measurement criteria and the measurement procedures. Getting good interobserver reliability isn't easy, but it is essential, before you intervene; otherwise, you can't evaluate the success of your intervention. And you can also end this section assured, that once he had good objective measures of the press operator's performance, S. Dee was able to reliably measure that performance and implement a pay-for-performance intervention that eliminated most late shipments, increased customer satisfaction, fattened the worker's take-home checks, and removed the necessity of buying expensive new presses, the commonsense solution everyone had originally suggested. Win, win, win.

Objectivity vs. Subjectivity in Technology

In Chapter 2, we introduced the concepts of subjective and objective measurement, arguing that objective measurement is essential for our science to achieve a reliable understanding of the physical and psychological world. But objectivity is also essential for applied technology, such as S. Dee's organizational-behavior-management efforts. If S. Dee had just trusted his subjective opinion of whether or not the presses were being fully utilized, he might have bankrupted the company by unnecessarily buying expensive, new presses. Unfortunately, many CEOs have too much confidence in their own subjective evaluations, with the possibility of disastrous results for their companies; instead, they need to use objective measures with high interobserver agreement, before making important decisions.

QUESTIONS

1. *Interobserver agreement*—define it and give an example.
2. Explain how you would compute an interobserver-agreement ratio using the point-by-point agreement procedure and be able to do the computation, given a set of interobserver data.

HOW SHOULD WE EVALUATE BEHAVIOR ANALYSIS? (RESEARCH DESIGN)

Example
THE SHAMAN AND THE BACKACHE

Vitoria Sousa's husband ran a small grocery store in Santa Cruz das Flores, a Portuguese town of 500 people. Vitoria and her family lived above the store in a two-story Portuguese-colonial building.

Vitoria was 35 but felt like 55. Her weight had increased so much through the years she didn't look like the girl in her wedding picture on her vanity table. At the time of her wedding, she dreamed about how great the future would be. Now she dreamed about how great the past had been. Life hadn't worked out as she had hoped.

A few days after her 35th birthday she had given birth to Orlando, her ninth child. Vitoria hoped Orlando would be the last. She had also had a few miscarriages. Vitoria felt guilty because she hadn't looked forward to the birth of Orlando as she had Carlos, her oldest son. She no longer dreamed about the newborn's future during the 9 months. Pregnancy was just another burden. She just got pregnant and had babies. Her beautiful fantasies became worries: "Can we pay for school, clothes, shoes, the doctor? Will we manage with another child under this roof?"

One day, soon after Orlando was born, Vitoria bent over to pick him up. As she lifted the infant, she let out a horrible scream that brought her husband running up the stairs from the grocery store. He arrived to see her bent double, barely holding Orlando, her mouth twisted, her brow perspiring.

"What's the matter?" he asked.

After a minute, Vitoria muttered, "It's my back. It hurts so much . . . and I can't stand up."

Vitoria's husband took Orlando and then helped Vitoria hobble to the bed.

The next day, Matilde, her sister-in-law came with the news: "Everybody in town is talking about a shaman who has supernatural powers. He's a priest who uses magic to cures any illness. He looks at you and can tell what's wrong. He cures you in one visit. Let's fix your back. It only costs 10 escudos." Matilde continued with a long list of people who had been cured of blindness, cancer, ulcers, unhappiness—you name it. A back pain had to be a cinch!

Matilde and Vitoria drove to Vila do Conde, a 3-hour trip through the mountains. Vitoria was in pain all the way. In spite of Matilde's long, wrinkled page of directions, they got lost more than once. But they knew when they had arrived: A line of waiting people started in the road and ended in a humble house with a wretched garden. Vitoria and Matilde went to the end of the line, waited for hours, and shared experiences. Everybody told the history of their pains and illness. The shaman was their last hope, and all but the most skeptical knew it would work.

Matilde went first; she wanted the shaman to cure her recurring migraines. She returned with a smile from ear to ear. "Your turn," Matilde said.

The room was 15 feet by 15 feet with no windows, no door (just an open entrance), no chairs, and a dirt floor. An altar was against the south wall. It was a large, wooden table holding crude statues of the Virgin Mary, Jesus Christ, and Saint Joseph. The flowers, incense, and lighted candles filling the rest of the table reminded Vitoria of the familiar fragrance of her church in Santa Cruz das Flores. The walls were covered with overlapping posters and religious paintings. The 70-year-old shaman, with torn, dirty clothes, sat on the dirt floor in front of the altar. Vitoria was shaking and still bent with pain.

The shaman asked how she was feeling. "I've had a back pain for the last few days that's killing me; I can't stand it any more," Vitoria said.

The shaman replied, "Don't worry; after today, you'll feel no more pain." He asked her to kneel down and close her eyes.

He touched her forehead and said, "Relax, you will be cured within the week." With his hand still on her forehead, he whispered a prayer. Vitoria felt relaxed and transported. Then the shaman stood up and walked around her continuing with his whispered prayer.

He touched her lower back and asked, "Is the pain here?"

After Vitoria nodded yes, he said, "I can feel your pain."

After more prayer, he said, "Soak in a hot tub when you get home, and do so once a week. Also walk at least 15 minutes every day and you will no longer suffer pain." He paused a minute and added, "It's 10 escudos."

Vitoria was slow in her reaction. She took the money from her purse. The shaman placed it in a 2-liter jar, nearly full of cash—today's fees. Vitoria hobbled out, a smile of confidence on her face.

The shaman was right. Vitoria stopped having pain and became another one of his supporters.

Concept
CASE STUDY

This was quite a deal for Vitoria, as you can imagine if you've ever been bent over with such lower severe back pain that you had to rest your elbows on the edge of the sink when you washed your hands. Vitoria was amazed at the cure. Yet you will never read of this shamanistic spiritual/medical intervention in the *New England Journal of Medicine*. Why not? For many reasons, as you can no doubt see. But even if we did have a careful independent measure of Vitoria's back pain, we still would have troubles with confounding variables.

Definition: Review Concept
Confounded variables
- Two or more possible independent variables have changed at the same time;
- so it is not possible to determine which of those variables caused the changes in the dependent variable.

For example, Vitoria's back pain might have gone away in a few days anyhow. This means the wise man's spiritual intervention is confounded with the normal relaxing of the muscle spasms correlated with the passage of time. So this normal relaxing of the muscles is an independent variable (possible cause) that confounds the spiritual intervention. This confounding makes it impossible to be sure the spiritual cure caused the relief from back pain.

That's the trouble with this sort of preexperimental, anecdotal **case study.** You can never be sure what caused what.

Definition: Concept
Case study
- ○ The evaluation of the results of
- ○ an applied intervention or
- ○ a naturally changing condition
- ○ that involves confounded variables.

A case study is not a poorly designed experiment. Instead, it may be an intervention done to produce particular results. For example, the shaman did not perform his magical intervention to prove that his magic works. Instead, he intervened to remove Victoria's back pain. His intervention combined with the removal of Victoria's back pain becomes a case study when we offer it (perhaps tentatively) as evidence for the power of shamanism.

Similarly, as people in our culture age, they usually get that middle-age midriff. This naturally changing condition does not occur to prove that aging causes weight gain. However, specific instances of this correlation between weight and age becomes a case study when we offer it as evidence of the effect of age on weight. Because it is a simple case study, there is a confounding of variables, for example age may be correlated with, and thus confounded with, other possible causes such as an increase in calorie consumption or a decrease in calorie-burning exercise.

Incidentally, by *cause,* we typically mean the *independent variable;* and by *effect,* we typically mean the *dependent variable.*

The case study is the most primitive within-subject research design. In the case study, the intervention is often introduced before collecting baseline data, making it practically impossible to rule out confounding variables and to test the effects of the independent variable on the dependent variable. For that reason, we consider the case study to be a preexperimental research design. Another way researchers talk about this weakness of the study is to say it can not rule out threats to **internal validity.**

Definition: Concept
Internal validity
- ○ The extent to which a research design
- ○ eliminates confounding variables.

An internally valid study is one in which no more than one independent variable is presented at the same time (not confounded). If you eliminate confounding of independent variables, you are better able to determine what independent variables are responsible for changes in the dependent variable.

Definition: Concept
Research design
- ○ The arrangement of the various conditions of an experiment or intervention
- ○ to reduce the confounding of independent variables.

As we said, the case study is a primitive research design because it does not prevent threats to the internal validity of its research design (confounding of the independent variable), but it can still be of great value. For example, Freud's career was based on his reporting and insightful analyses of clinical case studies. But now it's time to look at more powerful research designs that do a better job of eliminating confounding variables so we can get a clear picture of what's causing what.

Concept
SIMPLE BASELINE DESIGN

Frank was a young man sent to the Psychology Service. He spent many hours slapping his own face, so the staff had restrained him. Fortunately, we collected baseline data on the frequency of the response before intervening.

Definition: Review Concept
Baseline
- ○ The phase of an experiment or intervention
- ○ in which the behavior is measured
- ○ in the absence of an intervention.

During eleven 30-minute observation periods without restraint, Frank's frequency of face slapping dropped from over 600 an hour to nearly zero. And we hadn't done anything! This was just baseline.

Suppose we had given Frank a tranquilizer every day, in the hope that this would get rid of his face slapping. And suppose we had used the drug without getting baseline data first. It would have looked as if the drug had caused the decrease in slapping. Then there would have been a good chance that Frank would have unnecessarily been on that drug for the rest of his life.

The data collected on Frank illustrate an important point in research design: We must collect baseline data before we implement the intervention.

Definition: Concept

Simple baseline design

  ○ An experimental design
  ○ in which the baseline data are collected
  ○ before the intervention.

The **simple baseline design** is better at ruling out confounding variables than is the case study that doesn't involve baseline. Let's look at another example.

Example
THE SNEEZE

Recall Ange from Chapter 4, the 17-year-old who had been sneezing about once every 40 seconds for 6 months until Dr. Kushner implemented a punishment contingency based on mild electric shock. Within 6 hours she had completely stopped sneezing. For the first time in almost 6 months, Ange spent a full night and day without a single sneeze.

The 6 months of sneezing before the punishment contingency was the baseline. That long, stable baseline, combined with the dramatic, abrupt decrease in sneezing immediately after the intervention, strongly suggests that the punishment contingency was the independent variable that changed the frequency of sneezing. Given the length and stability of the baseline data, it seems unlikely that some other crucial independent variable would have accidentally changed at the same time Kushner introduced the shock. For example, it seems unlikely that there was a change in the weather right at the end of that 6 months of baseline that really caused Ange to stop sneezing. That seems like too much of

a coincidence. It seems much more likely that the punishment contingency is what caused Ange to stop sneezing.

But suppose the baseline had been for only a few days; and suppose her frequency of sneezing had varied from once every 10 seconds to once every 12 hours during those few baseline days. Further suppose that the decrease after the shock took several days instead of a few hours to occur; and suppose her frequency of sneezing decreased only to an average of once every 4 hours instead of almost zero. Now it's still possible that the punishment contingency caused that slow and moderate decrease in the frequency of sneezing, but we're less confident. Now we think there was a higher chance that some confounding variable such as a change in the weather or Ange's fatigue might have caused the decrease.

So the simple baseline design works well if we have a long, stable baseline followed by an abrupt and sizable change in the dependent variable when we change the value of our independent variable. Otherwise, we need a more powerful research design to rule out the threats to internal validity that confounding variables cause.

Concept
REVERSAL DESIGN

In Chapter 12, Mae's teachers gave the children toys only when they asked for them using color-noun combinations, for example, green car, red apple.[10] Following this intervention, the frequency of using color-noun combinations increased from 0.4 to 14.2 an hour. But this simple baseline design didn't allow Mae to be completely sure her intervention had increased behavior. Maybe the increase in color-noun combinations would have occurred anyhow. Maybe some confounding variable had really caused the increase in the color-noun frequency. How could Mae find out if her intervention had made the difference?

She asked her teachers to remove the intervention (in other words, to reverse to the original baseline condition). This is called a **reversal design**. During this reversal to the baseline condition, the children got snacks and materials regardless of whether they used a noun alone or a color-noun combination. Mae kept this reversal to baseline conditions going for the next 18 days. And, sure enough, the frequency of using color-noun combinations de-

---

[10]Based on Hart, B. M., & Risley, T. R. (1968). Establishing use of descriptive adjectives in the spontaneous speech of disadvantaged preschool children. *Journal of Applied Behavior Analysis, 1,* 109–120.

creased to 7.4 per hour.[11] Now Mae was more confident that requiring her students to use the color-noun combinations had increased their frequency. In fact, she was confident enough that she didn't keep the baseline going for longer than 18 days to see if the frequency of color-noun combinations would have eventually dropped to the original baseline frequency of 0.4 per hour.

Definition: Concept
Reversal design
- An experimental design
- in which the intervention (experimental) and baseline conditions
- are reversed
- to determine if the dependent variable changes as
- those conditions (independent variable) change.

Behavior analysts often call the reversal design an ***ABA design***. *A* stands for the baseline condition and *B* for the intervention. In an ABA design, a second baseline phase follows the intervention. Usually, if the performances in both baseline conditions are similar and different from the intervention, you can be pretty sure that the intervention is what changed performance. Most likely, you've ruled out any confounding variables. Consecutive ABA replications, like ABABABA, increase the internal validity. The reversal design provides more convincing evidence than the simple baseline design that the intervention is responsible for the change.

But we can't reverse some processes—for example, the training processes. If we implement a training program to teach someone to drive a car, when we stop the training program, the natural reinforcers will maintain the person's driving skills without our continued training. So we couldn't use the reversal design to demonstrate effectiveness of our training program. Also, we wouldn't want to use the reversal design when returning to baseline is too dangerous. For instance, suppose we're working with a dangerously self-abusive child. And suppose the frequency of self-abuse goes to near zero during intervention. We wouldn't want to reverse to the dangerous baseline condition to rule out the threats

that confounding variables pose for our internal validity. We need some other research design.

Concept
MULTIPLE-BASELINE DESIGN

In Chapter 23, Juke helped Red coach his young football team.[12] They worked on three plays: the option play, the power sweep, and the off-tackle counter-play. They task-analyzed the three plays into five behavioral components. For example, in the option play, the components included the quarterback-center exchange and the quarterback-right halfback fake. They specified the detailed behavior sequence in each component.

Juke and Red then prepared a checklist of the behavioral components for each of the three plays. Baseline consisted of the traditional training method: The coach gave verbal description of plays and offered suggestions from the sidelines when the team was on the field. The coach also gave feedback on what the players had done correctly and what they could improve. The intervention consisted of the presentation and explanation of the appropriate task-analysis checklist and frequent contingent feedback and recognition for instances of desired play execution.

Suppose Juke had implemented the intervention package with one team at a time, after collecting baseline data for differing durations for each team. This design is known as the **multiple-baseline design** across groups.

Definition: Review Concept
Multiple-baseline design
- An experimental design
- in which the replications involve
- baselines of different durations
- and interventions of different starting times.

In the multiple-baseline design, the intervention could be implemented across behaviors, settings, and groups or subjects. It's like several reversal designs, where the intervention is implemented

---

[11]Would you be surprised to know that the real researchers on whose work our fiction is based got exactly the same results? See Hart, B. M., & Risley, T. R. (1968). Establishing use of descriptive adjectives in the spontaneous speech of disadvantaged preschool children. *Journal of Applied Behavior Analysis, 1,* 109–120.

[12]Based on Komaki, J., & Barnett, F. T. (1977). A behavioral approach to coaching football: Improving the play execution of the offensive backfield on a youth football team. *Journal of Applied Behavior Analysis, 10,* 657–664.

at different times across different baselines. If performance consistently changes during the intervention, and across baselines, we could be sure it's the intervention that's causing the change.

Example
DRIVER EDUCATION[13]

About 23% of Utah's high-school students fail their driver ed. course; and in Utah that means they can't get their driver's license. That's a bigger deal than just losing the chance to cruise for 'burgers. Not being able to drive is correlated with social isolation, dependence, and poverty. Most students (94%) who failed driver ed. failed the written part of the tests. So four behavior analysts at Utah State University—Bell, Young, Salzberg, and West—developed a behavioral training program to help high-risk high school students pass that part of their test.

The program involved highly structured peer-tutoring sessions of 10 minutes each day. A fellow high school student would ask questions about complex driving maneuvers involving backing, turning, and passing. The peer tutor would also model correct answers using verbal descriptions and diagram drawing. Then he would encourage the student to practice answering the questions with high speed and accuracy (fluency). The peer tutor would also provide immediate feedback and record the student's performance.

Bart was a 16-year-old male with a normal IQ who had already failed driver ed. once and was going down the tubes a second time. Fortunately, he got to take part in the program. In addition to the tutoring, every day his tutor also gave him a 1-minute speed test on each of the three tasks: backing right, turning left, and passing. The tutor collected several days' baseline data before starting the tutoring and continued his tests throughout the training. Figure 29.1 shows some of Bart's results. It's a bit deep, so take a big breath before you dive in.

One of the measures the tutor took was the number of errors per minute Bart made. Look at the first data point in the top graph. See that during day 1, Bart made 80 errors in his speed test on writing about and diagramming how to back right (each wrong letter and each misplaced line was an error). If you follow the graph, you can see that he made at least 40 errors per minute for the first 7 school-days—baseline. Then the 10-minute daily sessions of behaviorally structured peer tutoring started. And

Bart's error rate immediately dropped to 8 per minute and quickly went on down to 0 per minute, with one little flare-up on day 13.

So it looks like behavioral peer tutoring really helped Bart. But you can't be sure. Maybe the improvement was only a coincidence. Maybe his noisy sister had just gone off to college, thus allowing Bart to seriously crack the books for the first time.

Bell and his colleagues controlled for that possibility. Look at the middle graph. These behavior analysts kept the baseline for turning left going for 2 more days before they started the peer tutoring on that problem (peer tutoring for turning left started for the data just to the right of the vertical dashed line). When you compare the two graphs, you can see that the error rate on the turning-left problem didn't go down when the rate went down for the back-right problem. The error rate for turning left didn't go down until the peer tutoring started for that specific problem, day 10.

And it's hard to say the sister's leaving (or whatever) on day 8 caused this abrupt improvement in the turning-left graph on day 10. So the behavior analysts could be fairly confident that the peer tutoring was causing the decreased error rates because they had two different baselines that ended on two different days; and they got abrupt changes in performance each time they introduced peer tutoring the day after baseline. In other words, they successfully used a multiple-baseline experimental design.

But they wanted to be even more confident. Maybe poor Bart's second loud sister had gone off to a different college (or whatever) on day 10; not likely, but maybe just another coincidence. So the bottom graph shows their confidence-building third baseline. This baseline (for the passing problem) didn't end until the 12th day. And sure enough, the error rate dropped from 60 on the last day of baseline with no tutoring to 18 on day 13 when the tutoring intervention started. Now, no one could be so unlucky as to have three noisy big sisters, who just happened to go off to college on the three days the behavior analysts just happened to start each of their three interventions. Not likely. Nor is it likely that some other positive changes happened coincidentally with each of the three interventions. Surely the three improved performances resulted from the three peer-tutoring interventions.

In summary, for each of these multiple baselines, the error rate was higher on every baseline day than for any of the intervention days. And the error rate dropped way down each time the intervention was started. This excellent use of the multiple-baseline design seems pretty much to eliminate the chance that the results were due to a coincidental change in some other factor rather than due to the behavioral tutoring.

---

[13]Based on Bell, K. E., Young, K. R., Salzberg, C. L., & West, R. P. (1991). High school driver education using peer tutors, direct instruction, and precision teaching. *Journal of Applied Behavior Analysis, 24,* 45–51.

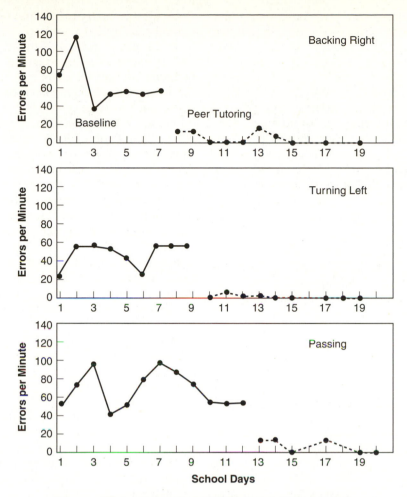

Figure 29.1   Behavioral Tutoring & Driver's Ed.

By the way, Bart passed his driver ed. course, passed his driver's test, got his driver's license, and has driven 25 miles to work every day, with no accidents or traffic tickets for the last 8 months. That's better than what a third of his classmates have done. What about you?

Concept
CHANGING-CRITERION DESIGN

Every day for the last 2 months you've resolved to start exercising—tomorrow. Yet you've never gotten into exercise clothes, visited the gym, attempted to jog, or done any exercise, except for your regular daily activities, like pushing the buttons on the remote control of your TV. But you really do want to get in shape.

When all else fails, people turn to applied behavior analysis for help. So do you. You call Conscience International. With the help of the woman at the other end of the line, you set up a performance

(behavior) contract based on an analog to avoidance of the loss of a reinforcer. In addition to a small charge for your daily phone calls, you deposit $200 with Conscience International for your penalty pool. You will lose $5 every weekday you fail to do some sort of exercise in the university gym and report on it to Conscience.

Because you're so out of shape, you think 10 minutes of exercise a day is good enough for openers. So for each day you don't exercise for 10 consecutive minutes, you lose $5. After a few weeks of consistent performance at around 10 minutes a day, 5 days a week, you up the minimum criterion to 20 minutes a day. Now if you continue to exercise for only 10 minutes, you'll lose $5. Every few weeks, you raise your exercise criterion by 10 minutes until you hit 60 minutes a day. And your performance rises to match whatever criterion is in effect on that day. You fail to hit criterion only three times, and rarely do you exceed it by more than a few minutes.

After 6 months, you start to wonder if the contracting's worth it. There's the daily charge plus the hassle. Maybe the performance contacting wasn't really crucial to your success. Maybe you should kiss Conscience good-bye and continue to exercise on your own.

But you're nervous. You've got a roll going with Conscience International. And you're afraid that if you stop performance contracting and your exercise falls apart, you may need another 5 years before you get your act together enough to give it another shot. You tell your troubles to sympathetic Conscience, and she tells you you've already got a solution. It's called the **changing-criterion design.**

Definition: Concept
Changing-criterion design
  ○ An experimental design
  ○ in which the replications involve
  ○ interventions with criteria of differing values.

The changing-criterion design is a special type of experimental design in which the experimenter repeats the experiment with differing values of the independent variable and measures changes in the dependent variable. If the values of the dependent variable change systematically with the changes in the independent variable, coincidental confounding variables are probably eliminated. Then we have internal validity, and there is probably a causal or functional relation between the independent and the dependent variables. In the case of the changing criterion design, the value of the independent variable that is being changed is the criterion required to meet a behavioral contingency.

And in the case of your performance contract, that criterion being changed is the number of minutes you need to exercise to avoid the $5 loss. Conscience points out that your amount of exercise has varied systematically and abruptly every time you change your criterion. This means that something about the intervention package of your performance contract is crucial. You don't know whether you need all the components—the daily goal, the daily phone call to Conscience, and the daily analog to an avoidance contingency (the potential $5 loss); but you can be confident that at least some of those components are crucial. With your changing-criterion experimental design, you've shown a causal or functional relation between your contracting and your amount of exercise.

Let me add some personal data to these hypothetical data. When writng this section, I was training to run a marathon and was contracting with Conscience to run either 6, 12, or 18 miles each day.

Otherwise, I, too, paid $5. I never ran 18 miles when I could run 12; and I never ran 12 when I could run 6. And I almost never had to pay the $5. This informal changing-criterion design convinced me that my performance in the marathon that spring hung by the fragile thread of my performance contract with Conscience.

All experimental design involve some sort of comparison between two different conditions, between an experimental condition and a control condition or between various experimental conditions. We just saw that the changing-criterion design involves comparisons of performance between differing response requirements (e.g., differing amounts of exercise required to avoid paying a fine, differing forces of a lever press to get the water reinforcer, or differing percentages of completed homework problems, to get an *A*). If the performance tends to match the different criteria, we are safe in concluding that the contingency we're using is controlling behavior. This is an excellent research design, but it is limited to evaluating the effectiveness of behavioral contingencies. The next design is more general.

Concept
ALTERNATING-TREATMENTS DESIGN

Remember David in Chapter 4? He was 21 years old and had lived in an institution for the mentally handicapped for the previous 9 years. He showed a high frequency of stereotyped behaviors, such as weaving his head, staring at his hands, and repeatedly manipulating objects. These stereotyped behaviors prevented him from taking part in vocational placement, and they embarrassed his family.

Jordan, Singh, and Repp (in the research described in Chapter 4) used an **alternating-treatments design** to compare the effectiveness of visual screening, gentle teaching, and baseline conditions. Visual screening consisted of a punishment contingency, in which the trainer covered David's eyes with one hand and held the back of his head with another hand for 5 seconds contingent on the occurrence of a stereotyped behavior. Gentle teaching consisted of using almost no vocal instructions, only gestures and signals. This intervention included a combination of physical guidance, reinforcement of the desirable behavior, and extinction of the undesirable behavior, but no punishment. During baseline, no procedure was in effect.

The experimenters did their research by implementing the three different procedures, in three different 30-minute training sessions, all three on each day of training. In other words, within each day, they alternated between the three experimental conditions—visual screening, gentle teaching, and baseline. Behavior analytic experimenters use such an alternating-treatments design to compare two or more interventions using the same subject.

Definition: Concept
Alternating-treatments design
- An experimental design
- in which the replications involve
- presenting different values of the independent variable
- in an alternating sequence
- under the same general conditions
- or in the same experimental phase,
- while measuring the same dependent variables.

In other words, you go back and forth between two or more specific treatments (values of the independent variable).

To appreciate the value of this experimental design, let's compare it with a couple of others. The experimenters might have used a **between-subjects** or **between-groups design.** They could have used gentle teaching with one client or group of clients, visual screening with a second, and baseline conditions with a third. Then they could have compared the amount of stereotyped self-stimulation among the three clients or groups.

The experimenters couldn't have been sure the differences in self-stimulation were due to their three different experimental conditions (interventions) if they had used three different clients. The problem is that it's too hard to be sure you've really got three equal clients. Maybe the three clients had different rates of self-stimulation to begin with. Or maybe they weren't equally influenceable by the interventions. This raises the possibility that the differences between the results obtained with the three interventions might have been attributed to the differences between the three clients. So it's to hard to rule out the confounding variable of the different clients.

There are a couple of problems with a between-groups design in which you would randomly assign a large group of clients to each of the three interventions and compare their performances. First, it's hard to get large groups of clients with similar behavioral problems. And second, it's easy to lose sight of the details of the effects of the interventions when your data consist of group averages rather than the performance of individual clients.

Another approach would have been to work only with David but to use the three conditions successively, perhaps a week of baseline, a week of gen-

tle teaching, followed by a week of visual screening. But then it's not easy to be sure that the three weeks were comparable. Maybe one week was hotter than the others. Or maybe David would have done less self-stimulation during the third week no matter which condition was in effect. Perhaps his self-stimulation would have decreased as a function of his becoming more familiar with the trainers. In other words, maybe the differences between the three conditions of intervention had nothing to do with the interventions. Such a design would have made it difficult to rule out these and other confounding variables that would have threatened the internal validity of the experiment.

The alternating-treatments design elegantly dealt with all these problems. It ensured that the subjects in the three experimental conditions were alike, by using the same subject—David. And it ensured that the days of exposure to the three conditions were alike, by using all three conditions on the same day (but in a different order each day).

However, the experimenters had to pay a price for using this design. The price was the potential for an **experimental interaction.** Experimental interaction is a risk you always run when you expose an experimental subject to more than one experimental condition. The risk of interaction is that exposure to one condition may have influenced the effects of another condition. For example, the advocates of gentle teaching might argue that gentle teaching would have been much more effective if the experimenters had not also exposed David to the punishment contingency involving visual screening. The risk of this sort of interaction is higher because the experimenters used the same trainers, tasks, and setting with David.

Definition: Concept
Experimental interaction
- One experimental condition
- affects the results of another.

So, here are advantages of the alternating-treatments design:

- The subject is the same during all treatments.
- The conditions of the treatment are essentially the same.
- Single-subject data can be analyzed, rather than averaged data.

And here is a disadvantage of the alternating-treatments design:

◦ Experimental interactions can not be ruled out.

Rarely does a single experiment decide complex theoretical and practical issues such as gentle teaching versus punishment contingencies. We will need many more such careful experiments, conducted by both the advocates of gentle teaching and the advocates of punishment contingencies. But each experiment, with its design strengths and design compromises, moves us closer to an understanding of how the world works and how to help the world work better.

QUESTIONS

1. Define and give an example of the following concepts:
   a. research design
   b. internal validity
   c. experimental interaction
   d. interobserver agreement
2. Define and give an example of the following research designs:
   a. case study
   b. simple baseline
   c. reversal
   d. multiple baseline
   e. changing criterion
   f. alternating treatments
3. Why is the case study a preexperimental design?
4. Give an example of the importance of collecting baseline data. Explain what could happen if we don't.
5. What advantage does the multiple-baseline design have over the reversal design?
6. Give an example of the use of a multiple-baseline design to demonstrate the value of behaviorally based peer tutoring in driver education.
7. What are two advantages and disadvantages of the alternating-treatments design?

GENERALITY OF RESULTS

In this chapter, we've emphasized the importance of doing research that will contribute to the well-being of the universe. And we've pointed out that science in general, and behavior analysis in particular, can contribute in two ways. First, it can contribute as a means toward an end, as a means toward better physical and behavioral health. But science can also contribute as an end in its own right: Knowing how things in the physical, biological, and behavioral worlds work makes it more reinforcing to be alive, just as art, music, and sports do, even if they turn out to be of little utilitarian value.

We've discussed the role of functional analyses in improving the contribution of behavior analysis to universal well-being. And we've discussed the role of research methods in making sure we discover valid cause-effect or functional relationships—internal validity. Finally, let's address the notion of **external validity** or *generality of results*.

External validity means the extent to which the cause-effect relation or functional relation you've shown in your experiment is valid under conditions external to your experiment. External validity means the generality of your results. For example, imagine this:

In the 1930s, a man named Skinner put a small number of simple rats in a small number of simple Skinner boxes, along with a small number of simple behavioral contingencies. He discovered a small number of simple behavioral principles and concepts. No big deal, perhaps. But over the next 70-some years, a few thousand behavior analysts, both scientists and practitioners, discovered that those simple principles and concepts applied to essentially all endeavors of the human and the nonhuman animal. Furthermore, they discovered that the applications of the principles of behavior could improve those endeavors, no matter what those endeavors were. Skinner's results with the rats in his experimental box generalized to mentally handicapped children learning to tie their shoes, to parents trying to coexist peacefully with their children, to doctoral students trying to complete their dissertations, and to corporate presidents trying to make a profit and benefit their employees at the same time. Now that's **external validity.**

Definition: Concept
External validity
◦ The extent to which the conclusions of an experiment
◦ apply to a wide variety of conditions.

QUESTION

1. *External validity*—define it and give an example.

30 Jobs and Grad School

WE'VE MOVED THIS CHAPTER TO THE WEB. CHECK IT OUT AT WWW.DICKMALOTT.COM.

WHERE SHOULD I GO FROM HERE?

WHERE SHOULD I *NOT* GO FROM HERE?

HOW DO I FIND THE RIGHT GRAD PROGRAMS?

WHAT ARE SOME GOOD MA AND PhD PROGRAMS?

WHAT ARE SOME GOOD MA PROGRAMS?

ABA APPROVED PROGRAMS

WHAT ARE SOME GOOD INTERNATIONAL PROGRAMS?

WHAT DEGREE SHOULD I GET—BA, MA, EdS, MSW, OR PhD?
- The BA Degree
- The MA, MSW, and EdS Degrees
- The PhD Degree
- OBM + Autism = Solution to Hard Times
- Clinical Grad School Warning!

MA JOBS

WHERE CAN I FIND A JOB?
- Board Certified Behavior Analyst

HOW DO I GET INTO GRAD SCHOOL?
- What Do I Do About a Low GPA?
- What Do I Do About a Low GRE?
- What Should I Minor In?
- What Experience Should I Get?

THE TIMETABLE
- How Long Can I Procrastinate?

Glossary

Addictive reinforcer A reinforcer for which repeated exposure is an establishing operation.

Aggression reinforcer Stimuli resulting from acts of aggression.

Aggression principle Aversive stimuli and extinction are establishing operations for aggression reinforcers.

Alternating-treatments design An experimental design in which the replications involve presenting different values of the independent variable in an alternating sequence, under the same general conditions or in the same experimental phase, while measuring the same dependent variables.

Analog to avoidance principle If an indirect-acting contingency is to increase or maintain performance, it should be an analog to avoidance.

Aversive condition (negative reinforcer) Any stimulus, event, or condition whose **termination** immediately following a response **increases** the frequency of that response.

Avoidance contingency The immediate, response-contingent **prevention** of an aversive condition resulting in an **increased** frequency of that response.

Avoidance-of-loss contingency The immediate, response-contingent **prevention of loss** of a reinforcer resulting in an **increased** frequency of that response.

Backward chaining The establishment of the final link in a behavioral chain, with the addition of preceding links, until the first link is acquired.

Baseline The phase of an experiment or intervention where the behavior is measured in the absence of an intervention.

Be concrete Always pinpoint specific behaviors when you deal with a behavioral (psychological) problem.

Behavior A muscle, glandular, or electrical activity.

Behavior analysis The study of the operation of the principles of behavior with both human beings and other animals.

Behavior trap Add a reinforcement contingency to increase the rate of behavior. Then the behavior will frequently contact built-in reinforcement contingencies, and those built-in contingencies will maintain that behavior.

Behavioral contingency The occasion for a response (behavior), the response (behavior), and the outcome of the response (behavior).

Behavioral chain A sequence of stimuli and responses. Each response produces a change in the environment that acts as a discriminative stimulus or operandum for the next response.

Case study The evaluation of the results of an applied intervention or a naturally changing condition that involves confounded variables.

Changing-criterion design An experimental design in which the replications involve interventions with criteria of differing values.

Check the presumed reinforcer first Before spending much time trying to reinforce behavior, make sure you have a true reinforcer.

Cognitive structure An entity assumed to cause action, the way the organism sees the world, including the organism's beliefs and expectations. It is material but not behavior.

Cognitive behavior modification An approach that attempts to modify behavior by modifying the cognitive structure.

Concept training Reinforcing or punishing a response in the presence of one stimulus class and extinguishing it or allowing it to recover in the presence of another stimulus class.

Conceptual stimulus control (conceptual control) Responding occurs more often in the presence of one stimulus class and less often in the presence of another stimulus class because of concept training.

Concurrent contingencies More than one contingency of reinforcement or punishment is available at the same time.

Conditional stimulus Elements of a stimulus have their value or function only when they are combined; otherwise, the individual elements are relatively neutral.

Conditioned stimulus (CS) A stimulus that acquires its eliciting properties through previous pairing with another stimulus.

Conditioned response (CR) A learned response elicited by the presentation of a conditioned stimulus.

Confounded variables Two or more possible independent variables have changed at the same time; so it is not possible to determine which of those variables cause the changes in the dependent variable.

Contingency control Direct control of behavior by a contingency, without the involvement of rules.

Continuous reinforcement (CRF) A reinforcer follows each response.

Control condition A condition not containing the presumed crucial value of the independent variable.

Control group   A group of subjects not exposed to the presumed crucial value of the independent variable.

Deadline principle   If an in-acting contingency is to increase or maintain performance, it should involve a deadline.

Dead-man test   If a dead man can do it, it ain't behavior. And, if a dead man can't do it, then it is behavior.

Dependent variable   A measure of the subject's behavior.

Deprivation   Withholding a reinforcer increases relevant learning and performance.

Different before condition test   Does the S^D differ from the before condition?

Differential-punishment procedure   Punishing one set of responses and withholding punishment of another set of responses.

Differential reinforcement of alternative behavior (DRA)   The replacement of an inappropriate response with a specific appropriate response that produces the same reinforcing outcome.

Differential reinforcement of incompatible behavior (DRI)   Reinforcement is contingent on a behavior that is incompatible with another behavior.

Differential reinforcement of low rate (DRL)   Reinforcement for each response following the preceding response by at least some minimum delay.

Differential-reinforcement procedure   Reinforcing one set of responses and withholding reinforcement for another set of responses and extinguishing another set of responses.

Direct-acting contingency   A contingency for which the outcome of the response reinforces or punishes that response.

Discrimination training procedure   Reinforcing or punishing a response in the presence of one stimulus and extinguishing it or allowing it to recover in the presence of another stimulus.

Discriminative stimulus (S^D)   A stimulus in the presence of which a particular response will be reinforced or punished.

The don't-say rule   With nonverbal organisms, don't say *expects, knows, thinks, figures out, in order to* (or *so that he, she, or it could . . .*), *tries to, makes the connection, associates, learns that, imagines, understands.* With any organism, don't say *wants.*

Dual-functioning chained stimuli   A stimulus in a behavioral chain reinforces the response that precedes it. That stimulus also acts as an S^D or operandum for the response that follows it.

Duration   The time from the beginning to the end of a response.

Errorless discrimination procedure   The use of a fading procedure to establish a discrimination, with no errors during the training.

Error of reification   To call a process or activity a thing.

Escape contingency   The immediate, response-contingent removal of an aversive condition resulting in an *increased* frequency of that response.

Establishing operation   A stimulus, event, or condition that affects learning and performance with respect to a particular reinforcer or aversive condition.

Experimental interaction   One experimental condition affects the results of another.

Experimental group   A group of subjects exposed to the presumed crucial value of the independent variable.

External validity   The extent to which the conclusions of an experiment apply to a wide variety of conditions.

Extinction   Stopping the reinforcement or escape contingency for a previously reinforced response causes the response frequency to decrease.

Extinction/recovery test   Is the S^Δ contingency always extinction or recovery?

Fading procedure   At first, the S^Δ and the S^D differ along at least two stimulus dimensions. The difference between the S^Δ and the S^D along all but one dimension is reduced until there is no difference along the reduced dimensions. Then the S^Δ and the S^D differ along only one dimension.

Feedback   Nonverbal stimuli or verbal statements contingent on past behavior that can guide future behavior.

Fixed-interval scallop   A fixed-interval schedule often produces a scallop—a gradual increase in the rate of responding, with responding occurring at a high rate just before reinforcement is available. No responding occurs for some time after reinforcement.

Fixed-interval (FI) schedule of reinforcement   A reinforcer is contingent on the first response *after* a fixed interval of time since the last opportunity for reinforcement.

Fixed-ratio (FR) schedule of reinforcement   A reinforcer follows a fixed number of responses.

Fixed-ratio responding   After a response is reinforced, no responding occurs for a period of time, then responding occurs at a high, steady rate until the next reinforcer is delivered.

Fixed-time schedule of reinforcer delivery   A reinforcer is delivered after the passage of a fixed period of time, independently of the response.

Force   Intensity of response.

Forget forgetting   There's no such thing.

Forgetting procedure   Preventing the opportunity (or occasion) for a response.

Forward chaining   The establishment of the first link in a behavioral chain, with the addition of successive links, until the final link is acquired.

Functional assessment   An analysis of the contingencies responsible for behavioral problems.

Generalized imitation   Imitation of the response of a model without previous reinforcement of imitation of that specific response.

Generalized learned reinforcer (generalized secondary reinforcer or generalized conditioned reinforcer)   A learned reinforcer that is a reinforcer because it was paired with a *variety* of other reinforcers when the organism has been deprived of those other reinforcers.

Goal-directed systems design   First you select the ultimate goal of a system, then you select the various levels of intermediate goals needed to accomplish that ultimate goal, and finally, you select the initial goals needed to accomplish those intermediate goals.

Group research design   The experiment is conducted with at least two groups of subjects. And the data are usually presented in terms of the mean (average) of the performance of all subjects combined for each group.

Higher-order conditioning   Establishing a conditioned stimulus by pairing a neutral stimulus with an already established conditioned stimulus.

Imitation   The behavior of the imitator is under stimulus control of the behavior of the model and matches the behavior of the model.

Imitative reinforcers Stimuli arising from the match between the behavior of the imitator and the behavior of the model that function as reinforcers.

Incidental teaching A teacher requires that a student emit the proper form of a request before reinforcing that request, in the student's regular environment.

Independent variable The variable the experimenter systematically manipulates to influence the dependent variable.

Indirect-acting contingency A contingency that controls the response, but not because the outcome reinforces or punishes that response.

Ineffective contingency A contingency that does not control behavior.

Informed consent Consent to intervene in a way that is experimental or risky. The participant or guardian is informed of the risks and benefits and of the right to stop the intervention.

Initial behavior Behavior that resembles the terminal behavior along some meaningful dimension and occurs with at least a minimal frequency.

Intermediate behaviors Behavior that more closely approximates the terminal behavior.

Intermittent reinforcement A reinforcer follows the response only once in a while.

Internal validity The extent to which a research design eliminates confounding variables.

Interobserver agreement Agreement between observations of two or more independent observers.

Intervention (treatment) package The addition or change of several independent variables at the same time to achieve a desired result, without testing the effect of each variable individually.

It-is-probably-rule-control It is probably rule control, if the person knows the rule, the outcome is delayed, or the performance changes as soon as the person hears the rule.

Latency The time between the signal for a response and the beginning of the response.

Law of effect The effects of our actions determine whether we will repeat them.

Learned aversive condition (secondary or conditioned aversive condition) A stimulus, event, or condition that is an aversive condition because it has been paired with another aversive condition.

Learned reinforcer (secondary or conditioned reinforcer) A stimulus, event, or condition that is a reinforcer because it *has* been paired with another reinforcer.

Legal-rule control Control by rules specifying added analogs to behavioral contingencies and added direct-acting behavioral contingencies based on material outcomes.

Matching law The relative rate of responding on two concurrent schedules of reinforcement equals the relative value of reinforcement on those two schedules.

Matching to sample Selecting a comparison stimulus corresponding to a sample stimulus.

Materialism The doctrine that the physical (material) world is the only reality.

Materialistic mentalism The doctrine that the mind is physical, not spiritual.

Medical model myth An erroneous view of human behavior that behavior is always a mere symptom of an underlying psychological condition.

Mentalism The doctrine that the mind causes behavior to occur.

Methodological behaviorism An approach that restricts the science of psychology to only those independent and dependent variables that two independent people can directly observe.

Mind An entity or collection of entities assumed to cause behavior. It may be either material or nonmaterial, but it is not the behavior itself.

Moral (ethical)-rule control Control by rules specifying added analogs to behavioral contingencies. Such rules specify social, religious, or supernatural outcomes.

Multiple-baseline design An experimental design in which the replications involve baselines of differing durations and interventions of differing starting times.

Mythical cause of poor self-management Poor self-management occurs because immediate outcomes control our behavior better than delayed outcomes do.

Obtrusive assessment Measuring performance when the clients or subjects are aware of the ongoing observation.

Operandum test Does the S^D differ from the operandum?

Operandum (manipulandum) That part of the environment the organism operates (manipulates).

Operant conditioning Reinforcing consequences immediately following the response increase its future frequency; aversive consequences immediately following the response decrease its future frequency.

Operant level The frequency of responding before reinforcement.

Overcorrection A contingency on inappropriate behavior requiring the person to engage in an effortful response that more than corrects the effects of the inappropriate behavior.

Pairing procedure Pairing of a neutral stimulus with a reinforcer or aversive condition.

Parsimony The use of no unnecessary concepts, principles, or assumptions.

Pay for performance Pay is contingent on specific achievements.

Penalty contingency The immediate, response-contingent **removal** of a reinforcer resulting in a **decreased** frequency of that response.

Performance contract (behavioral contract or contingency contract) A written rule statement describing the desired or undesired behavior, the occasion when the behavior should or should not occur, and the added outcome for that behavior.

Performance maintenance The continuing of performance after it was first established.

Physical prompt (physical guidance) The trainer physically moves the trainee's body in an approximation of the desired response.

Premack principle If one activity occurs more often than another, the opportunity to do the most frequent activity will reinforce the less frequent activity.

Procedure of shaping with punishment The differential punishment of all behavior **except** that which more and more closely resembles the terminal behavior.

Procedure of shaping with reinforcement The differential reinforcement of only that behavior that more and more closely resembles the terminal behavior.

Procedure of variable-outcome shaping Shaping that involves an increase in the magnitude of a reinforcer or a decrease in the magnitude of an aversive outcome as performance more and more closely resembles the terminal behavior.

Procedure of fixed-outcome shaping Shaping that involves the delivery of a fixed magnitude of a reinforcer when performance meets the changing criterion, or the delivery of a fixed magnitude of an aversive outcome when performance fails to meet the changing criterion.

Process versus product Sometimes you need to make reinforcers and feedback contingent on the component responses of the process, not just the product (outcome).

Products of behavior Record or evidence that the behavior has occurred.

Prompt A supplemental stimulus that raises the probability of a correct response.

Punishment contingency The immediate, response-contingent **presentation** of an aversive condition resulting in a **decreased** frequency of that response.

Punishment-by-prevention-of-a-reinforcer contingency The immediate, response-contingent **prevention** of a reinforcer resulting in a **decreased** frequency of that response.

Punishment-by-prevention-of-removal contingency The immediate, response-contingent **prevention of removal** of an aversive condition resulting in a **decreased** frequency of that response.

Radical behaviorism An approach that addresses all psychology in terms of the principles of behavior.

Real cause of poor self-management Poor self-management results from poor control by rules describing outcomes that are either too small (though often of cumulative significance) or too improbable. The delay isn't crucial.

Recovery from punishment Stopping the punishment or penalty contingency for a previously punished response causes the response frequency to increase to its rate before the punishment or penalty contingency.

Reinforce behavior Reinforce behavior, not people.

Reinforcement contingency The immediate, response-contingent **presentation** of a reinforcer resulting in an **increased** frequency of that response.

Reinforcer (positive reinforcer) Any stimulus, event, or condition whose **presentation** immediately follows a response and *increases* the frequency of that response.

Outcome gradient The effect of the reinforcement and punishment procedures decreases as the delay between the response and the outcome increases. Reinforcers and aversive conditions delayed more than 60 seconds have little or no reinforcing or punishing effect.

Reliability measurement The comparison of measurements of dependent variables and independent variables obtained by independent observers.

Repertoire A set of skills. What a person or animal can do.

Research design The arrangement of the various conditions of an experiment or intervention to reduce the confounding of independent variables.

Resistance to extinction and intermittent reinforcement Intermittent reinforcement makes the response more resistant to extinction than does continuous reinforcement.

Resistance to extinction The number of responses or the amount of time before a response extinguishes.

Respondent extinction Present the conditioned stimulus without pairing it with the unconditioned stimulus or with an already established conditioned stimulus, and the conditioned stimulus will lose its eliciting power.

Respondent conditioning A neutral stimulus acquires the eliciting properties of an unconditioned stimulus through pairing the unconditioned stimulus with a neutral stimulus.

Response class A set of responses that either (a) are similar on at least one response *dimension,* (b) share the *effects* of reinforcement and punishment, or (c) serve the same *function* (produce the same outcome).

Response dimensions The physical properties of a response.

Response test Is the response the same for both the S^D and the S^Δ?

Response topography The sequence (path of movement), form, or location of components of a response relative to the rest of the body.

Response-cost contingency The immediate, response-contingent removal of a *tangible* reinforcer resulting in a decreased frequency of that response.

Reversal design An experimental design in which we reverse between intervention (experimental) and baseline conditions to determine if the dependent variable changes as those conditions (independent variable) change.

Rule A description of a behavioral contingency.

Rule control (the general rule) Start looking for rule control if behavior is controlled by an outcome that follows the response by more than 60 seconds.

Rule control The statement of a rule controls the response described in that rule.

Rule-governed analog to a behavioral contingency An increase in the frequency of a response because of a rule describing the contingency.

Rule-governed behavior Behavior under the control of a rule.

Rules that are easy to follow Describe outcomes that are both sizable and probable. The delay isn't crucial.

Rules that are hard to follow Describe outcomes that are either too small (though often of cumulative significance) or too improbable. The delay isn't crucial.

Same before condition test Is the before condition the same for both the S^D and the S?

Satiation Consuming a substantial amount of a reinforcer temporarily decreases relevant learning and performance.

Schedule of reinforcement The way reinforcement occurs because of the number of responses, time between responses, and stimulus conditions.

S-delta (S^Δ) A stimulus in the presence of which a particular response will not be reinforced or punished.

S^Δ contingency test Is there also an S^Δ? (If not, then you also don't have an S^D.)

S^D/CS test To determine if a stimulus is an S^D or CS, look at its history of conditioning: look for a plausible US $\rightarrow$ UR relation; and alternatively, look for a plausible $S^D \rightarrow R \rightarrow S^R$ contingency.

Shifting from rule-control to contingency control With repetition of the response, control often shifts from control by the rule describing a direct-acting contingency to control by the direct-acting contingency itself.

Sick social cycle (victim's escape model) In escaping the perpetrator's aversive behavior, the victim unintentionally reinforces that aversive behavior.

Sick social cycle (victim's punishment model) The perpetrator's aversive behavior punishes the victim's appropriate behavior. And the victim's stopping the appropriate behavior unintentionally reinforces that aversive behavior.

Simple baseline design An experimental design in which the baseline data are collected before the intervention.

The simplistic behaviorist error People don't think.

The simplistic biological-determinist error Analogous behaviors are homologous behaviors.

The simplistic cognitivist error Rats think.

Single-subject research design The entire experiment is conducted with a single subject, though it may be replicated with several other subjects.

Social validity The goals, procedures, and results of an intervention are socially acceptable to the client, the behavior analyst, and society.

Social comparison A comparison of the performance of clients exposed to the intervention with an equivalent or "normal" group.

Spiritualism The doctrine that the world is divided into two parts, material and spiritual.

Spiritualistic mentalism The doctrine that the mind is spiritual (nonphysical).

Spontaneous recovery A temporary recovery of the extinguished behavior during the first part of extinction sessions that follow the first session.

Stimulus class A set of stimuli, all of which have some common property.

Stimulus discrimination (stimulus control) A response occurs more frequently in the presence of one stimulus than in the presence of another, usually as a result of a discrimination training procedure.

Stimulus dimensions The physical properties of a stimulus.

Stimulus generalization The behavioral contingencies in the presence of one stimulus affect the frequency of the response in the presence of another stimulus.

Stimulus-generalization gradient A gradient of responding showing a decrease of stimulus control as the test stimulus becomes less similar to the training stimulus.

Subjective evaluation of experts Experts' evaluation of the significance of the target behavior and the outcome.

Superstitious behavior Behaving as if the response causes some specific outcome, when it really does not.

Symptom substitution (erroneous principle) Problem behaviors are symptoms of an underlying mental illness. So if you get rid of one problem behavior ("symptom"), another will take its place until you get rid of the underlying mental illness.

Systematic desensitization Combining relaxation with a hierarchy of fear-producing stimuli, arranged from the least to the most frightening.

Target behavior The behavior being measured, the dependent variable.

Task analysis An analysis of complex behavior and sequences of behavior into component responses.

Terminal behavior Behavior not in the repertoire or not occurring at the desired rate the goal of the intervention.

Theory of generalized imitation Generalized imitative responses occur because they automatically produce imitative reinforcers.

Three-contingency model of performance management The three crucial contingencies are: the ineffective natural contingency, the effective, indirect-acting performance-management contingency, and the effective, direct-acting theoretical contingency.

Time-out contingency The immediate response-contingent removal of *access to* a reinforcer resulting in a *decreased* frequency of that response.

To confound variables To change or allow to change two or more independent variables at the same time so you cannot determine what variables are responsible for the change in the dependent variable.

Token economy A system of generalized learned reinforcers in which the organism that receives those generalized reinforcers can save them and exchange them for a variety of backup reinforcers later.

Toothpaste theory of abnormal behavior Abnormal behavior flows out of sick people like toothpaste squeezed from a tube. The abnormal behavior results from inner pressure.

Total-task presentation The simultaneous training of all links in a behavioral chain.

Transfer of training Performance established at one time in one place now occurs in a different time and place.

Unconditioned response (UR) An unlearned response elicited by the presentation of an unconditioned stimulus.

Unconditioned stimulus (US) A stimulus that produces the unconditioned response without previous pairing with another stimulus.

Unlearned aversive condition A stimulus, event, or condition that is aversive, though not as a result of pairing with other aversive conditions.

Unlearned reinforcer A stimulus, event, or condition that is a reinforcer, though not as a result of pairing with another reinforcer.

Unobtrusive assessment Measuring performance when the clients or subjects are not aware of the ongoing observation.

Value-altering principle The pairing procedure converts a neutral stimulus into a learned reinforcer or learned aversive condition.

Values Learned and unlearned reinforcers and aversive conditions.

Variable-interval responding Variable-interval schedules produce a moderate rate of responding, with almost no postreinforcement pausing.

Variable-interval (VI) schedule of reinforcement A reinforcer is contingent on the first response **after** a variable interval of time since the last opportunity for reinforcement.

Variable-ratio responding Variable-ratio schedules produce a high rate of responding, with almost no postreinforcement pausing.

Variable-ratio (VR) schedule of reinforcement A reinforcer follows after a variable number of responses.

Variable-time stimulus presentation The presentation of a stimulus with variable periods of time between presentations, independent of the occurrence of a response.

Verbal prompt A supplemental verbal stimulus that raises the probability of a correct response.

Warning stimulus A stimulus that precedes an aversive condition and thus becomes a learned aversive stimulus.

Author Index

Subject Index